A Companion to Philosophy of Law
and Legal Theory

Blackwell Companions to Philosophy

This outstanding student reference series offers a comprehensive and authoritative survey of philosophy as a whole. Written by today's leading philosophers, each volume provides lucid and engaging coverage of the key figures, terms, topics, and problems of the field. Taken together, the volumes provide the ideal basis for course use, representing an unparalleled work of reference for students and specialists alike.

Already published in the series:

1. The Blackwell Companion to Philosophy, Second Edition
   Edited by Nicholas Bunnin and Eric Tsui-James

2. A Companion to Ethics
   Edited by Peter Singer

3. A Companion to Aesthetics .
   Edited by David Cooper

4. A Companion to Epistemology
   Edited by Jonathan Dancy and Ernest Sosa

5. A Companion to Contemporary Political Philosophy
   Edited by Robert E. Goodin and Philip Pettit

6. A Companion to Philosophy of Mind
   Edited by Samuel Guttenplan

7. A Companion to Metaphysics
   Edited by Jaegwon Kim and Ernest Sosa

8. A Companion to Philosophy of Law and Legal Theory
   Edited by Dennis Patterson

9. A Companion to Philosophy of Religion
   Edited by Philip L. Quinn and Charles Taliaferro

10. A Companion to the Philosophy of Language
    Edited by Bob Hale and Crispin Wright

11. A Companion to World Philosophies
    Edited by Eliot Deutsch and Ron Bontekoe

12. A Companion to Continental Philosophy
    Edited by Simon Critchley and William Schroeder

13. A Companion to Feminist Philosophy
    Edited by Alison M. Jaggar and Iris Marion Young

14. A Companion to Cognitive Science
    Edited by William Bechtel and George Graham

15. A Companion to Bioethics
    Edited by Helga Kuhse and Peter Singer

16. A Companion to the Philosophers
    Edited by Robert L. Arrington

17. A Companion to Business Ethics
    Edited by Robert E. Frederick

18. A Companion to the Philosophy of Science
    Edited by W. H. Newton-Smith

19. A Companion to Environmental Philosophy
    Edited by Dale Jamieson

20. A Companion to Analytic Philosophy
    Edited by A. P. Martinich and David Sosa

21. A Companion to Genethics
    Edited by Justine Burley and John Harris

22. A Companion to Philosophical Logic
    Edited by Dale Jacquette

23. A Companion to Early Modern Philosophy
    Edited by Steven Nadler

24. A Companion to Philosophy in the Middle Ages
    Edited by Jorge J. E. Gracia and Timothy B. Noone

25. A Companion to African-American Philosophy
    Edited by Tommy L. Lott and John P. Pittman

26. A Companion to Applied Ethics
    Edited by R. G. Frey and Christopher Heath Wellman

27. A Companion to the Philosophy of Education
    Edited by Randall Curren

28. A Companion to African Philosophy
    Edited by Kwasi Wiredu

29. A Companion to Heidegger
    Edited by Hubert L. Dreyfus and Mark A. Wrathall

30. A Companion to Rationalism
    Edited by Alan Nelson

31. A Companion to Ancient Philosophy
    Edited by Mary Louise Gill and Pierre Pellegrin

32. A Companion to Pragmatism
    Edited by John R. Shook and Joseph Margolis

33. A Companion to Nietzsche
    Edited by Keith Ansell Pearson

34. A Companion to Socrates
    Edited by Sara Ahbel-Rappe and Rachanar Kamtekar

35. A Companion to Phenomenology and Existentialism
    Edited by Hubert L Dreyfus and Mark A Wrathall

Blackwell
Companions to
Philosophy

A Companion to Philosophy of Law and Legal Theory

Edited by
DENNIS PATTERSON

Blackwell
Publishing

© 1996, 1999 by Blackwell Publishing Ltd

BLACKWELL PUBLISHING
350 Main Street, Malden, MA 02148-5020, USA
9600 Garsington Road, Oxford OX4 2DQ, UK
550 Swanston Street, Carlton, Victoria 3053, Australia

First published 1996
First published in paperback 1999

7   2005

Library of Congress Cataloging-in-Publication Data

  A companion to philosophy of law and legal theory / [edited by]
  Dennis Patterson.
      p.   cm.—(Blackwell companions to philosophy)
  Includes bibliographical references and index.
  ISBN 1-55786-535-3 (alk. paper) — ISBN 0-631-21329-5 (pbk)
    1. Law—Philosophy. 2. Jurisprudence—United States.
  I. Patterson, Dennis M. (Dennis Michael), 1955– . II. Series.
  KF379.C66   1996
  340′.1—dc20   95–46024
                                                          CIP

ISBN-13: 978-1-55786-535-9 (alk. paper) — ISBN-13: 978-0-631-21329-1 (pbk)

A catalogue record for this title is available from the British Library.

Set in 10½ on 12½ pt Photina
by Graphicraft Typesetters Ltd, Hong Kong
Printed and bound in the United Kingdom
by TJ International, Padstow, Cornwall

The publisher's policy is to use permanent paper from mills that operate a sustainable forestry policy, and which has been manufactured from pulp processed using acid-free and elementary chlorine-free practices. Furthermore, the publisher ensures that the text paper and cover board used have met acceptable environmental accreditation standards.

For further information on
Blackwell Publishing, visit our website:
www.blackwellpublishing.com

Contents

List of contributors   ix

Preface   xii

PART I: AREAS OF LAW

1 **Property law**   3
   JEREMY WALDRON

2 **Contract**   24
   PETER BENSON

3 **Tort law**   57
   STEPHEN R. PERRY

4 **Criminal law**   80
   LEO KATZ

5 **Public international law**   96
   PHILIP BOBBITT

6 **Constitutional law and religion**   113
   PERRY DANE

7 **Constitutional law and interpretation**   126
   PHILIP BOBBITT

8 **Constitutional law and privacy**   139
   ANITA L. ALLEN

9 **Constitutional law and equality**   156
   MAIMON SCHWARZSCHILD

CONTENTS

10 Evidence   172
JOHN JACKSON AND SEAN DORAN

11 Comparative law   184
RICHARD HYLAND

12 Interpretation of statutes   200
WILLIAM N. ESKRIDGE, JR

13 Conflict of laws   209
PERRY DANE

PART II: CONTEMPORARY SCHOOLS

14 Natural law theory   223
BRIAN BIX

15 Legal positivism   241
JULES L. COLEMAN AND BRIAN LEITER

16 Legal realism   261
BRIAN LEITER

17 Critical legal studies   280
GUYORA BINDER

18 Post-realism and legal process   291
NEIL DUXBURY

19 Feminist jurisprudence   302
PATRICIA SMITH

20 Law and economics   311
JON D. HANSON AND MELISSA R. HART

21 Legal formalism   332
ERNEST J. WEINRIB

**22 German legal philosophy and theory in the nineteenth
and twentieth centuries**   343
ALEXANDER SOMEK

23 Marxist theory of law   355
ALAN HUNT

24 Deconstruction   367
J. M. BALKIN

25 Postmodernism   375
DENNIS PATTERSON

26 Legal pragmatism   385
RICHARD WARNER

PART III: LAW AND THE DISCIPLINES

27 Law and anthropology   397
REBECCA REDWOOD FRENCH

28 The sociology of law   406
M. P. BAUMGARTNER

29 Law and theology   421
EDWARD CHASE

30 Law and morality   436
ROGER A. SHINER

31 Law and literature   450
THOMAS MORAWETZ

PART IV: TOPICS

32 The duty to obey the law   465
M. B. E. SMITH

33 Legal enforcement of morality   475
KENT GREENAWALT

34 Indeterminacy   488
LAWRENCE B. SOLUM

35 Precedent   503
LARRY ALEXANDER

36 Punishment and responsibility   514
GEORGE P. FLETCHER

CONTENTS

37 Loyalty   524
GEORGE P. FLETCHER

38 Coherence   533
KEN KRESS

39 The welfare state   553
SANFORD LEVINSON

40 Legal scholarship   562
EDWARD L. RUBIN

41 Authority of law   573
VINCENT A. WELLMAN

42 Analogical reasoning   583
JEFFERSON WHITE

Index   591

Contributors

Larry Alexander is Professor at the University of San Diego School of Law, Alcala Park, San Diego.

Anita L. Allen is Professor of Law and Philosophy at Georgetown University Law Center, Washington, DC.

J. M. Balkin is Lafayette S. Foster Professor at Yale Law School, New Haven, Connecticut.

M. P. Baumgartner is a member of the Department of Sociology at William Paterson College in Wayne, New Jersey.

Peter Benson is an Associate Professor at the Faculty of Law, McGill University, Montreal.

Guyora Binder is Professor at the State University of New York at Buffalo, School of Law.

Brian Bix is an Associate Professor of Law at Quinnipiac School of Law, Connecticut.

Philip Bobbitt is Professor at the School of Law, the University of Texas, at Austin.

Edward Chase is Professor at Rutgers University School of Law, Camden, New Jersey.

Jules L. Coleman is John A. Garver Professor of Jurisprudence at Yale Law School, New Haven, Connecticut.

Perry Dane is Professor at Rutgers University School of Law, Camden, New Jersey.

Sean Doran is Senior Lecturer in Law at Queen's University of Belfast.

Neil Duxbury is Professor in the Faculty of Law at the University of Manchester.

William N. Eskridge, Jr, is Professor at Georgetown University Law Center, Washington, DC.

George P. Fletcher is Cardozo Professor of Jurisprudence at Columbia University School of Law, New York.

Rebecca Redwood French is an Associate Professor of Law at the University of Colorado.

Kent Greenawalt teaches at Columbia University School of Law where he holds the title of University Professor and was previously Cardozo Professor of Jurisprudence.

Jon D. Hanson is an Assistant Professor at Harvard Law School, Cambridge, Massachusetts.

Melissa R. Hart is law clerk Justice Stevens on the United States Supreme Court for the 1996–7 term.

Alan Hunt holds Professorships in the Departments of Law and Sociology at Carleton University in Ottawa.

Richard Hyland is Professor at Rutgers University School of Law, Camden, New Jersey.

John Jackson is Professor of Law at Queen's University of Belfast.

Leo Katz is Professor at the University of Pennsylvania School of Law, Philadelphia.

Ken Kress is Professor at the College of Law, University of Iowa, Iowa City.

Brian Leiter is Assistant Professor of Law and Philosophy at the University of Texas at Austin.

Sanford Levinson is Professor of Law and Government at the University of Texas at Austin.

Thomas Morawetz is Tapping Reeve Professor of Law and Ethics at the University of Connecticut School of Law.

Dennis Patterson is Distinguished Professor, Rutgers University School of Law, Camden, New Jersey.

Stephen R. Perry is an Associate Professor at the Faculty of Law, McGill University, Montreal.

Edward L. Rubin is Professor of Law, University of California, Berkeley.

Maimon Schwarzschild is Professor at the University of San Diego School of Law, Alcala Park, San Diego and a barrister of Lincoln's Inn. London.

Roger Shiner teaches Philosophy and Jurisprudence at the University of Alberta.

M. B. E. Smith is Professor of Philosophy at Smith College in Northampton, Massachusetts.

Patricia Smith is Professor in the Department of Philosophy at the University of Kentucky, Lexington.

Lawrence B. Solum is Professor at Loyola Law School, IIT Chicago Kent, Chicago.

Alexander Somek teaches at the University of Vienna.

Jeremy Waldron is Professor at the University of California at Berkeley.

Richard Warner is Professor of Law at the School of Law, IIT Chicago Kent, Chicago.

Ernest J. Weinrib is Professor of Law and Special Lecturer in Classics at the University of Toronto, and a Fellow of the Royal Society of Canada.

Vincent A. Wellman is Professor at Wayne State University Law School, Detroit, Michigan.

Jefferson White is Professor of Philosophy at the University of Maine, Orono.

Preface

It is the purpose of this preface to introduce a collection of essays on current topics in law and legal theory. Each of the essays that follow is an original contribution to the topic. In the course of this preface I wish to do two things. First, I shall state the overall plan of the work. Second, I would like to speak to the question of the readership of this book.

From the start, it was the goal both of the editor and the publisher to assemble the best writers in contemporary jurisprudence to address live issues in the field in the course of providing an introduction to the concerns of contemporary legal theory. Each of the authors was asked both to survey the topic assigned to them and, where appropriate, to indicate their own view of the questions and issues at stake. In short, it was the purpose of the editor and the publisher to have entries that would be of interest both to beginning students and other professionals.

There are two aspects to the question of readership. First, the book has a decidedly American perspective. This is no doubt due to the fact that the editor and most of the contributors are American legal academics. However, it is the student perspective, driven by the sizeable American law school population, which decided the orientation of many of the essays.

It is almost impossible in the modern American law school to encounter any subject matter that does not carry with it a heavy theoretical orientation. For example, in their first semester of law school, students are virtually barraged with all matter of theoretical perspective. Subjects ranging from philosophy to economics to critical theory are all very much a part of American casebooks and the teaching styles of American law professors. To date, no single volume has met the need of the beginning student to get a handle quickly on the vast and diverse theoretical landscape that is the first-year experience. This volume was conceived in direct response to this situation. It is the editor's hope that first-year students will find this volume a useful and rewarding supplement to their casebooks and other first-year materials.

I wish to thank all of the authors who contributed their time and talents to this volume. Many of the essays in this book are remarkable both in their pedogogical depth and originality of thought and presentation.

Let me thank my editors at Blackwell, Stephan Chambers and Steve Smith, for their patience and continuing support of this project.

D. P.

PART I
AREAS OF LAW

1

Property law

JEREMY WALDRON

Philosophical thought about the law of property covers two types of issue. First there are analytic issues, about the meaning and use of the most important concepts in property law, such as "private property," "ownership," and "thing." The second type of issue is normative or justificatory. The law of property, as we know it, involves individuals having the right to make decisions about the use of resources – the land and the material wealth of a country – without necessarily consulting the interests and wishes of others in society who might be affected. So what in general justifies giving people rights of this kind? And specifically, what principles justify the allocation of particular resources to particular owners? The two sets of issues are of course connected, for the point of sharpening our analytical understanding of concepts like "ownership" is to make clearer what is actually at stake when questions of justification are raised.

Analytical issues

Any attempt to define terms like "private property" and "ownership" runs the risk of either over-simplifying the complexities of property law or of losing any sense of the broader issues in a maze of technical detail. Some jurists have argued, indeed, that these terms are indefinable and largely dispensable (see Grey, 1980). They say that calling someone the "owner" of a resource does not convey any exact information about the rights she (or others) may have in relation to that resource: a corporate owner is not the same as an individual owner; the owner of intellectual property has a different array of rights than the owner of an automobile; and even with regard to one and the same resource, the rights (and duties) of a landlord who owes nothing on his property might be quite different from those of a mortgagor who lives on his own estate.

If one is patient, however, it is possible to build up a reasonably clear conceptual map of the area, which respects both the technician's sensitivity to legal detail and the philosopher's need for a set of well-understood "ideal types" to serve as the focus of justificatory debate (see Waldron, 1986, pp. 26–61).

The objects of property

Let us start with some ontology. The law of property is about *things*, and our relations with one another in respect of the use and control of things. What sorts of things? Material things, certainly, like apples and automobiles; but property has never confined itself to tangible objects. Real estate provides an interesting example. A mobile home is a thing, and so is the plot of land on which it sits. In the eyes of the law, however, the land is not a tangible object. It is tempting to identify the land with the soil and rocks on which the mobile home sits; but take away any amount of soil and rock and the land remains. The land is more like the region of space or the portion of the earth's surface at which the soil, the rock and indeed the mobile home are located. A different kind of intangibility is involved with intellectual property. My Madonna CD is a different material object from your Madonna cassette. But they contain the same songs and the songs themselves – the tunes and the lyrics – may be regarded as things in which there can be property rights just as much as apples and automobiles.

A third sort of intangibility involves the "reification" of legal relations themselves. If Jennifer owes Sarah 50 pounds and Sarah despairs of collecting the debt, she may accept a payment of 30 pounds from Bronwen, a specialist debt-collector, in return for which Bronwen acquires the right to recover the 50 pounds from Jennifer (if she can get it). It seems natural to say that Sarah has sold the debt to Bronwen and that therefore the debt was a thing that Sarah owned and had the right to dispose of even before Bronwen entered the picture. The legal term for this sort of thing is "chose-in-action." (More complex choses-in-action include checks and shares in a company.) Now, it may be helpful for some purposes, to regard choses-in-action as an appropriate subject-matter for property law, but in general they do not raise important issues in the philosophy of property in the way that land, intellectual property, and material chattels do. A composition, a plot of land, and an automobile are things which exist independently of the law and about which the law is required to make certain decisions, settle certain disputes, and so on. By contrast, a chose-in-action exists only because the law has *already* settled certain disputes in a particular way. The philosophical issues raised by a chose-in-action are thus better regarded as issues in the law of contracts or corporate law, not issues in the law of property.

The ontological differences between material chattels, land, and intellectual property can have an important bearing on questions of justification. In some ways there is a stronger case for private property in intellectual objects than for private property in land. An original tune that I have composed is, in a sense, nothing but a product of my will and intellect. Apart from my creativity, the song might never have come into existence, and anyone who complains about the profits I derive from my copyright must concede that she would have been no worse off if I had never composed the tune and thus never acquired a right in it at all. A piece of land, by contrast, is sheer nature rather than human product or invention. Or, if we define it as a region in space, land is simply what is *given* in advance of any individual's activity; it is part of the given framework for human life and action.

4

Other contrasts between intellectual and non-intellectual property seem to work in the opposite direction. There is not the same *necessity* for property restrictions in regard to intellectual objects, if those objects are to be usable, as there is in regard to pieces of land or material objects like chairs. When you are using Blackacre for a cricket match, I cannot use it to play football; and two people can seldom sit on the same chair without catastrophic results. But if I perform or record a tune that another has composed, I am not precluding or interfering with the composer's or anyone else's use of it. Songs are not crowdable like chairs or plots of land, and they do not wear out with use. I *may* be interfering with the songwriter's profiting from her composition. But that begs the question of property – for her profiting is simply her exploitation of the right that her property in the tune would confer, viz. the right to exclude others from using the tune if they will not pay her for the privilege.

Types of property system

As we address the issues of justification posed by property rights in different types of object, it is important to understand the main institutional alternatives to a system of private ownership.

We should begin with the distinction between "property" and "*private* property." The distinction is one of genus and species. The generic concept – property – may be used to refer to *any* system of rules governing people's access to and their use and control of things, whether tangible or intangible, natural or manufactured. Following David Hume, we may say that property rules are needed for any class of things about which there are likely to be conflicts concerning access, use and control, particularly things which are scarce relative to the demands that human desires are likely to place upon them (Hume, [1739] 1888, pp. 484–98). Disagreements about who is to use or control such objects are likely to be serious because resource-use matters to people, to their livelihood as well as their enjoyment. Thus any society with an interest in avoiding violent conflict will need a system of rules for pre-empting disagreements of this kind. The importance of such rules can hardly be over-estimated, for their job is to provide a legal framework for the economy of the society in question. Without them, planning, co-operation, production, and exchange are virtually impossible, or possible only in the fearful and truncated forms that we see in "black markets" where nothing can be counted on. Jurists often cite these necessities as the basis of a case for *private* property, but, so far, all they establish is the need for property rules. As we proceed with our analysis, we must bear in mind that certain human societies have existed for millennia, satisfying the needs and wants of all their members, without private property or anything like it in land or the other major resources of economic life.

"Property," I said, is the generic term. There are three broad species of property arrangement: common property, collective (or state) property, and private property.

In a *common property* arrangement, resources are governed by rules whose point is to make them available for use by all or any members of the society. A tract of common land, for example, may be used by everyone in a community for grazing cattle or gathering food. A public park may be open to all for picnics, sports, or recreation. The aim of any restrictions on use is simply to secure fair access for all and to prevent anyone from using the common resources in a way that would preclude their use or access by others.

Collective property is quite a different idea. In a system of collective property, resources are not left open to all-comers. Rather, the community as a whole determines how resources are to be used; these determinations are made on the basis of the social interest through the society's mechanisms of collective decision making. Now what this amounts to will depend in part on the communal institutions that exist in particular societies. It may involve anything from a leisurely debate among the elders of a tribe to a bureaucratic decision implementing a Soviet-style "Five-Year Plan." (In modern societies, collective property amounts in effect to state property, and is often referred to as socialism.) It depends also on the dominant conception of the social interest – for example, whether this is conceived as an equal interest in the welfare of all, or the greatest happiness of the majority, or the promotion of some future goal like national glory, cultural splendour, or rapid industrialization.

Private property is an alternative to both collective property and common property. In a private property arrangement, rules of property are organized around the idea that contested resources are to be regarded as separate objects each assigned to the decisional authority of some particular individual (or family or firm). The person to whom a given object is assigned by the principles of private property (for example, the person who found it or made it) has control over the object: it is for her to decide what should be done with it. In exercising this authority, she is not understood to be acting as an agent or official of the society. Instead, we say that the resource is *her property*; it *belongs* to her; she is its *owner*; it is as much *hers* as her arms and legs, kidneys, and corneas. In deciding how the thing is to be used, she may act on her own initiative as a private person without giving anyone else an explanation, or she may enter into co-operative arrangements with others, for their benefit or her own profit, just as she likes. What is more, her right to decide as she pleases applies whether or not others are affected by her decision. If Jennifer owns a steel factory, it is *for her* to decide (in her own interest) whether to close it or to keep the plant operating, even though a decision to close may have the gravest impact on her employees and the prosperity of the local community.

Though private property is a system of individual decision-making, it is still a system of social rules in the following sense. The owner is not required to rely on her own strength to vindicate her right to make decisions about the object assigned to her: any attempt by others to thwart or resist her decision will be met with the combined force of the society as a whole. If Jennifer's employees occupy the steel factory to keep it operating despite her wishes, she can call the police and have them evicted; she does not have to do this, or even pay for it, herself.

Sometimes we talk about these alternative types of property arrangement – common, collective, and private property – as though they were alternative ways of organizing whole societies. We say the former Soviet Union was a socialist society because the economically most significant resources were governed by collective property rules, whereas in the United States most economically significant resources are governed by private property rules. In fact, in every modern society there are resources governed by common property rules (for example, streets and parks), resources governed by collective property rules (such as military bases and artillery pieces), and resources governed by private property rules (toothbrushes and bicycles). Even among economically significant resources (agricultural land, minerals, railroads, industrial plant), we find in most countries a mix of private ownership and state ownership, with the balance between the two types of arrangement being a matter of continuing political debate.

In addition, there are variations in the degree of freedom that a private owner has over the resources assigned to her. Obviously, an owner's freedom is limited by background rules of conduct: I may not use my gun to kill another person. But these are not strictly property rules. More to the point are things like zoning restrictions and historic preservation laws which amount, in effect, to the imposition on the private owner of a collective decision about certain aspects of the use of a given resource. The owner of a building in a historic district may be told, for example, that she can use it as a shop, a home, or a hotel, or leave it empty if she likes, but she may not knock it down and replace it with a postmodern skyscraper. Or, in the case of Jennifer's steel factory, the owner may find that she is required by law not to close her plant without giving her employees and the local authorities 90 days' notice. Private ownership, then, is a matter of degree. In the examples just given, we may still want to say that the historic building and the steel factory were private property; but if too many other areas of decision about their use were also controlled by public agencies, we would be more inclined to say that the resources in question were in reality subject to a collective property arrangement (with the "owner" functioning as a steward of society's decisions).

Ownership: a bundle of rights

Let us now focus more closely on private property. Analyzed technically, an individual's right to make decisions about the use of a thing has two elements. First, as we have just seen, it implies the absence of any obligation to use or refrain from using the object in any particular way. The owner may decide as she pleases and she is at liberty to put her decision into effect by occupying, using, modifying, perhaps even consuming or destroying the object. Second, private property implies that other people do not have this liberty: they *do* have an obligation – an obligation to the owner – to refrain from occupying, using, modifying, consuming or destroying the object. They can use it of course with her permission; but what this means is that it is up to the owner to decide whether or not to exclude others from the enjoyment of the object.

The owner may give other people permission to use her property. She may lend her automobile, rent her house, or grant a right of way over her land. The effect of her exercise of these powers is sometimes to create other (relatively limited) property interests in the object, so that the various liberties, rights and powers of

7

ownership are divided up among several people. Thus the law of private property deals with things such as bailments, leases, and easements, as well as ownership itself.

More strikingly, the owner is legally empowered to transfer the whole bundle of her rights in the object she owns (including the power of transfer) to somebody else – as a gift, or by way of sale if she insists on receiving something in return, or as a legacy after death. Once she does this, the transferee is in the position of owner; the transferor no longer has any legally recognized interest in the object. With this power of transfer, the system of private property becomes self-perpetuating (which is not, of course, the same as self-enforcing). After an initial assignment of objects to owners, there is no further need for the community or the state to concern itself with distributive questions. Objects will circulate as the whims and decisions of individual owners and their successive transferees dictate. (The exception is inheritance, which provides a set of default rules in case an owner dies without leaving instructions as to who should take over her property; but even these are usually modelled on the arrangements that testators are normally expected to make.) The result may be that resources are widely distributed or concentrated in a very few hands; some individuals may own a lot, others next to nothing. It is part of the logic of private property that no one has the responsibility to concern themselves with the big picture, so far as the distribution of resources is concerned. Society simply pledges itself to enforce the rights of exclusion that ownership involves, wherever they happen to be. As we shall see, philosophers disagree as to whether this is an advantage or an indictment of the system of private property.

These, then, are the most striking incidents of ownership: the liberty of use, the right to exclude, and the various powers of transfer. Other jurists have listed many more (see especially, Honore, 1961), including constitutional immunities against expropriation (such as that laid down in the Fifth Amendment to the US Constitution), and the owner's liability to have judgments (for example, for debt) executed by forced sale of the object. Obviously the formulation and level of detail in this analysis are in part a matter of taste, and in part a matter of what is taken to be most importantly at issue in any normative debate about the institution.

The need for justification

Justificatory issues arise because the laws and institutions we have are not features of the natural world like gravity, but human creations, set up and sustained by human decisions. We are not stuck with the arrangements we have inherited: acting collectively and politically we can choose to change them if we like, either wholesale or in detail. Normative argument is what takes place when we think together about how to guide and evaluate such choices.

Every social institution requires justification if only because the energy and resources needed to sustain it could be used in some other way. Private property, however, falls into a special class of institutions that require justification not only because there are opportunity costs involved in their operation, but because they operate in a way that seems – on the face of it – morally objectionable. In this regard, private property is like the institution of punishment. We require a justification for punishment not just because the money spent on prisons could be spent on education, but because punishment involves the deliberate infliction of death, pain, or deprivation on human beings. Such actions are indefensible unless they serve some morally compelling point, and we want to be told what that morally compelling point actually is.

Similarly, we look for a justification of private property, because it deprives the community of control over resources which may be important to the well-being of its members, and because it characteristically requires us to throw social force behind the exclusion of many members of our society from each and every use of the resources they need in order to live. I said earlier that one effect of recognizing individual powers of transfer is that resources may gradually come to be distributed in a way that leaves a few with a lot, a lot with a very little, and a considerable number with nothing at all. Private property involves a pledge by society that it will continue to use its moral and physical authority to uphold the rights of owners, even against those who have no employment, no food to eat, no home to go to, no land to stand on from which they are not at any time liable to be evicted. That legal authority and social force are held hostage in this way to an arbitrarily determined distribution of individual control over land and other resources is sufficient to raise a presumption against private property. To call for a justification is a way of asking whether anything can be adduced to rebut that presumption.

It may be thought that the justificatory issue is nowadays moot, with the collapse of "actually existing socialism" in Central and Eastern Europe and the former Soviet Union. What are we seeing there, if not the belated recognition (by the erstwhile proponents of collective ownership) that markets and private property are necessary after all – and private property in businesses, factories, minerals, agricultural land, and the means of production generally, not just the private ownership of apartments, toothbrushes, and the occasional smoky automobile?

With this happening in the heartland of Marxism–Leninism, it is easy to conclude that collective property has been thoroughly discredited, and the problem of justifying *private* property solved by default, as it were. The issue can now be firmly handed over to the philosophers, as something with which practical people need no longer concern themselves. The philosophers will continue to play with it of course – but in the same way that they tease each other with questions about the reality of the external world, or whether the sun will rise tomorrow.

It would be wrong to dismiss the issue in this way. Consider an analogy: suppose that as the result of some worldwide "retributive revolution," all the countries that had abolished capital punishment since the 1940s were to reinstate it. Would that lessen any of the concerns that people in the United States currently have about capital punishment in their society – the weakening of the taboo against killing, the danger of executing the innocent, racial disparities in the administration of the death penalty, the barbarism of popular fascination with its grisly details, and so on? It might make us less sanguine about the prospects for reform, but it would not lessen the need to examine whether this was an institution with which we were entitled to live comfortably, from a moral point of view.

Anyway, the point of discussing the justification of an institution is not only to contemplate its abolition. Often we need to justify in order to understand and in order to operate the institution intelligently. Again, an analogy with punishment might help. In criminal law, we study issues about *mens rea* and strict liability, the distinction between justification, excuse and mitigation, the use (or over-use) of the insanity defense, and the similarities between felony homicide and deliberate murder. It is hard to see how any of that can be done without asking questions about the *point* of the criminal sanction. Without some philosophical account of punishment and individual responsibility, the doctrines and principles of the criminal law are apt to seem like a mysterious language with a formal grammar but no real meaning of its own.

Similarly, in thinking about property, there are a number of issues and debates that make little sense unless debated with an awareness of what the point of rules of property (or specifically rules of *private* property) might be. Some of these issues are technical. The rule against perpetuities, for example, the technicalities of the registration of land titles, the limits on testamentary freedom – all these would be like an arcane and unintelligible code, to be learned at best by rote, unless some attempt were made to connect them with the point of throwing social authority behind individual control or individual disposition of control over resources.

The same is true of less technical, more substantive issues. The Fifth Amendment to the US Constitution requires that private property not be taken for public use without just compensation. It is pretty evident that this right prohibits the government from simply seizing or confiscating someone's land (for use, say, as a firing range or an airport). But think of an example we used earlier: what if the state simply places some restriction on the use of one's land? Sarah is told that she may not erect a postmodern office building on her property, because it will compromise the historical aesthetics of the neighborhood. Does this amount to a taking for which she should be compensated under the Fifth Amendment? Certainly Sarah has suffered a loss (she may have bought the land purely with the intention of developing it). On the other hand, it is fatuous to pretend that there is a taking whenever any restriction is imposed. I may not drive my car at 100 m.p.h., but I am still the owner of the car.

I do not think it is possible to answer this question by staring at the words "property" and "taking." Certainly, it is impossible to address the constitutional issue intelligently (as opposed to learning by rote the answers that successive courts have offered) without some sense of *why* private property is regarded as sufficiently important to be given this sort of constitutional protection. Is it protected because we distrust the capacity of the state and its agencies to make collective decisions about resource use? Or is it protected only because we want to place limits on the burdens that any individual may be expected to bear for the sake of the public good? It may make a considerable difference to our interpretation of the takings clause, as well as other legally enshrined doctrines of property law, what we think are the ultimate purposes and values that private ownership is supposed to serve.

Justificatory theories

We turn now to the theories of justification that have actually been proposed. At this point, jurisprudence reaches out to political philosophy and to the debates about property in which thinkers like Plato and Aristotle, Grotius and Pufendorf, Hobbes and Locke, Hume, Smith, and Rousseau, Hegel and Marx, Bentham and Mill, and Nozick and Rawls have participated.

An institution such as private property requires justification in two regards. First, we need to justify the general idea of having things under the control of private individuals. Second, we must justify the principles by which some come to be the owners of particular resources while others do not. In principle, the same argument can perform both tasks, for some general justifying aims are nothing more than compelling distributive principles writ large. Robert Nozick, for example, justifies private property purely on the ground that certain things belong intrinsically to certain individuals, and that we must set up our social institutions to respect those particular rights, whether or not the institution as a whole serves any broader social ends. "Things come into the world," he writes, "already attached to people having entitlements over them" (Nozick, 1974, p. 160). His most persuasive example is body parts. We do not need a general social justification for the rule that my kidneys belong to me. They just do, and any acceptable theory of property had better respect that fact. But it is doubtful whether this particularist approach can be extended to land or other external objects. The best-known attempt is that of John Locke ([1690] 1988, pp. 285–302); but, as we shall see, even Locke found it necessary to complement his theory of particular entitlements with more general considerations of social utility.

General justifying aims

The most common form of justificatory argument is that people are better off when a given class of resources is governed by a private property regime than by any alternative system. Under private property, it is said, the resources will be more wisely used, or used to satisfy a wider (and perhaps more varied) set of wants than under any alternative system, so that the overall enjoyment that humans derive from a given stock of resources will be increased.

The most persuasive argument of this kind is sometimes referred to as "the tragedy of the commons" (Hardin, 1968). If everyone is entitled to use a given piece of land, then no one has much of an incentive to see that crops are planted or that the land is not over-used. Or if anyone does take on this responsibility, they themselves are likely to bear all the costs of doing so (the costs of planting or the costs of their own self-restraint), while the benefits (if there are any) will accrue to all subsequent users. In many cases there are unlikely to be any benefits, since one individual's planning or restraint will be futile unless the others co-operate. Instead, under common property, each commoner has an incentive to get as much

11

as possible from the land as quickly as possible, since the benefits of doing this are in the short term concentrated and ensured, while the long-term benefits of self-restraint are uncertain and diffused. However, if a piece of hitherto common land is divided into parcels and each parcel is assigned to a particular individual who can control what happens there, then planning and self-restraint will have an opportunity to assert themselves. For now the person who bears the cost of re-straint is in a position to reap all the benefits; so that if people are rational and if restraint (or some other form of forward-looking activity) is in fact cost-effective, there will be an overall increase in the amount of utility derived.

Arguments of this sort are familiar and important, but like all utilitarian argu-ments, they need to be treated with caution. In most private property systems, there are some individuals who own little or nothing, and who are entirely at the mercy of others. So when it is said that "people" are better off under private prop-erty arrangements, we have to ask "Which people? Everyone? The majority? Or just a small class of owners whose prosperity is so great as to offset the consequent immiseration of the others in an aggregative utilitarian calculus?"

John Locke hazarded the suggestion that everyone would be better off. Compar-ing England, whose commons were swiftly being enclosed by private owners, to pre-colonial America, where the natives continued to enjoy universal common access to land, Locke speculated that "a King of a large and fruitful Territory there [that is, in America] feeds, lodges, and is clad worse than a day Labourer in Eng-land" (Locke, [1690] 1988, p. 297). The laborer may not own anything, but his standard of living is higher on account of the employment prospects that are of-fered in a prosperous privatized economy. Alternatively, the more optimistic of the utilitarians cast their justifications in the language of what we would now call "Pareto-improvement." Maybe the privatization of previously common land does not benefit everybody: but it benefits some and it leaves others no worse off than they were before. Now this is hardly a reason for the latter group to support or endorse such a change, but it indicates that they have little ground for complaint. The homelessness and immiseration of the poor, on this account, is not a result of private property; it is simply the natural predicament of mankind from which a few energetic appropriators have managed to extricate themselves.

So far, we have considered the utilitarian case for private property over com-mon property. The case for private property over collective property has more to do with markets than with the need for responsibility and self-restraint in resource use (though it must be said that the environmental record of socialist societies is turning out to have been much, much worse than that of their capitalist competi-tors). The argument for markets is that in a complex society there are innumer-able decisions to be made about the allocation of particular resources to particular production processes. Is a given ton of coal better used to generate electricity which will in turn be used to refine aluminum for manufacturing cooking pots or air-craft, or to produce steel which can be used to build railway trucks, which may in turn be used to transport either cattle feed or bauxite from one place to another? In most economies there are hundreds of thousands of distinct factors of produc-tion, and it has proved impossible for efficient decisions about their allocation to be made by central agencies acting in the name of the community and charged with overseeing the economy as a whole. In actually existing socialist societies, central planning turned out to be a way of ensuring rather than preventing economic paralysis, inefficiency, and waste.

In market economies, by contrast, decisions like these are made on a decentralized basis by thousands of individuals and firms responding to price signals, each seeking to maximize profits from the use of the productive resources under its control. Some have speculated that there could be markets without private property, but this too seems hopeless. Unless individual managers in a market economy are motivated directly by considerations of personal profit in their investment and allocation decisions – or unless they are responsible to others who are motivated on that basis – they cannot be expected to respond efficiently to prices. This sort of motivation can be expected only if the resources in question are *theirs*, so that the loss is theirs when a market signal is missed and the gain is theirs when a profitable allocation is secured.

I said earlier that a utilitarian defense of private property is in trouble unless it can show that everyone is better off under a private property system, or at least that no one is worse off. Now, a society in which all citizens derive significant advantages from the privatization of the economy is perhaps not an impossible ideal. But in every private property system with which we are familiar there is a class of people, often many thousands, who own little or nothing and who are arguably much worse off under that system than they would be under, say, a socialist alternative. A justificatory theory cannot simply ignore their predicament, if only because it is in part their predicament that poses the justificatory issue in the first place. A hard-line utilitarian may insist that the advantages to those who enjoy private ownership simply outweigh the costs to those who suffer. That is, the utilitarian may defend private property using purely aggregative measures of output and prosperity. Philosophically, however, this sort of hard line is quite disreputable (Rawls, 1971, pp. 22–33; Nozick, 1974, pp. 32–3): if we take the individual rather than a notional entity like "the social good" as the focal point of moral justification, then there ought to be something we can say to *each* individual why the institution we are defending is worthy of her support. Otherwise it is not at all clear why *she* should be expected to observe its rules and requirements (except that we have the power and the numbers to compel her to do so).

Maybe the utilitarian argument can be supplemented with an argument about desert in order to show that there is justice in some people's enjoying the fruits of private property while others languish in poverty. Locke took this line too. God gave the world, he said, "to the use of the Industrious and Rational, . . . not to the fancy or covetousness of the quarrelsome and contentious" (Locke, [1690] 1988, p. 291). If private property involves the wiser and more efficient use of resources, it is because someone has exercised virtues of prudence, industry, and self-restraint. People who languish in poverty, on this account, do so largely because of their idleness, profligacy, or want of initiative. Now, theories like this are easily discredited if they purport to justify the actual distribution of wealth under an existing private property economy (Nozick, 1974, pp. 158–9; Hayek, 1976). But

13

there is a more modest position which desert theorists can adopt: namely, that private property alone offers a system in which idleness is not rewarded at the expense of industry, a system in which those who take on the burdens of prudence and productivity can expect to reap some reward for their virtue which distinguishes them from those who did not make any such effort.

One can come at the issue of virtue also from a slightly different direction. Instead of (or as well as) rewarding the owner for the virtue that she displays, we might count it as a point in favor of private property that it offers people the opportunity to acquire and exercise such virtues. Owning property in Hegel's words, helps the individual to "supersede the mere subjectivity of personality" (Hegel, [1821] 1991, p. 73); in plain English, it gives them the opportunity to make concrete the plans and schemes that would otherwise just buzz around inside their heads, and to take responsibility for their intentions as the material they are working on – a home, a canvas, or a car – registers the impact of the decisions they have made (Waldron, 1986, pp. 343–89; cf. Munzer, 1990, pp. 120–47). In the civic republican tradition, the virtue argument was associated with the noble independence and self-sufficiency of the yeoman farmer. Owing nothing to anything besides his own industry, neither so rich as to be able to buy another nor poor enough to be bought, the individual proprietor in a republic of virtue could be relied on to act as a good citizen, using in public affairs the virtues of prudence, independence, resolution, and good husbandry that he necessarily relied on in running his private estate. If most economic resources are owned in common or controlled collectively for everyone's benefit, there is no guarantee that citizens' conditions of life will be such as to promote republican virtue. On the contrary, citizens may behave either as passive beneficiaries of the state or irresponsible participants in a tragedy of the commons. If a generation or two grow up with that character then the integrity of the whole society is in danger. These arguments about virtue are of course quite sensitive to the distribution of property (Waldron, 1986, pp. 323–42). As T. H. Green observed, a person who owns nothing in a capitalist society "might as well, in respect of the ethical purposes which the possession of property should serve, be denied rights of property altogether" (Green, 1941, p. 219).

To complete this overview of the general justifications of private property, we must consider the relation between property and liberty. Societies with private property are often described as free societies. Part of what this means is surely that owners are free to use their property as they please; they are not bound by social or political decisions. (And correlatively, the role of government in economic decision making is minimized.) But that cannot be all that is meant, for – as we saw in our analytical discussion – it would be equally apposite to describe private property as a system of *unfreedom*, since it necessarily involves the social exclusion of people from resources that others own.

Two other things are implied by the libertarian characterization. The first is a point about independence: a person who owns a significant amount of private property – a home, say, and a source of income – has less to fear from the opinion and coercion of others than the citizen of a society in which some other form of property predominates. The former inhabits, in a fairly literal sense, the "private sphere" that liberals have always treasured for individuals – a realm of action in which he need answer to no one but himself. But like the virtue argument, this version of the libertarian case is sensitive to distribution: for those who own nothing in a private property economy would seem to be as unfree – by this argument – as anyone would be in a socialist society.

That last point may be too quick, however, for there are other indirect ways in which private property contributes to freedom. Milton Friedman (1962) argues that political liberty is enhanced in a society where the means of intellectual and political production (printing presses, photocopying machines, computers) are controlled by a number of private individuals, firms, and corporations – even if that number is not very large. In a capitalist society, a dissident has the choice of dealing with several people (other than state officials) if he wants to get his message across, and many of them are prepared to make their media available simply on the basis of money, without regard to the message. In a socialist society, by contrast, those who are politically active either have to persuade state agencies to disseminate their views, or risk underground publication. More generally, Friedman argues, a private property society offers those who own nothing a greater variety of ways in which to earn a living – a larger menu of masters, if you like – than they would be offered in a socialist society. In these ways, private property for some may make a positive contribution to freedom – or at least an enhancement of choice – for everyone.

Particular distributive arguments

Assume now, for the sake of argument, that private property is in general a good institution for a society to have. Whether because it maximizes utility, facilitates markets, cultivates virtue, rewards desert, or provides a congenial environment for the growth of liberty, we think it a good idea for resources to be under the control of individuals who will have to live with the effects of the decisions that they make about them. The question now is which individuals are to have control of which resources. How – that is, by what principles – is this to be determined?

The task of justifying a distribution of private property is an important one. In our analytic discussion, we saw that once a private property system is established, with particular resources assigned to particular individuals, no further distributive intervention is required for the system to operate. Even though needs change, people die and one generation is succeeded by another, the institution of private property can largely run under its own steam, so far as distribution is concerned. But the results may not be attractive. In some cases, the concentration of resources in the hands of a few individuals, firms or families may be so extreme that the authorities will feel compelled to intervene in the name of justice and undertake some large-scale redistribution. This has happened historically in a number of countries – in New Zealand in the second half of the nineteenth century, in Mexico at the turn of the century, and more recently in the Philippines. Countries that undertake land reform are in effect approaching the distributive question

15

anew, attempting to establish an assignment of resources to individuals that is justified in the light of the present requirements of their society.

Even in countries where there is no such reshuffling of entitlements, distributive arguments may still play a part in people's thinking about the way in which property rights should be regulated, and the way in which they fit into the overall structure of social and economic institutions. Most developed countries have progressive income and wealth taxes, and provide income support and basic services to their poorest citizens on the basis of that taxation. These schemes are not usually conceived as ways of redistributing property, but they may nevertheless be informed by a sense of how far the existing system is from a just distribution or of what the basic principles underlying property distribution ought to be.

I emphasize this because there is a well-known argument in "law and economics" purporting to show that questions of initial distribution are uninteresting. Imagine that a wheat field beside a railroad is continually being set on fire by sparks from passing trains. It becomes clear that either wheat can be grown on this land or trains run across it, but not both. A theorem due to Ronald Coase (1960) holds that an efficient outcome may be reached by the wheat grower and the railroad, irrespective of whether the former is initially assigned the right not to have his wheat set on fire. If running trains is more profitable there than wheat growing, the railroad will be in a position to pay the farmer damages for the loss of his crop and still make a profit if the farmer has the right to sue; and if the farmer does not have the right to sue, he will be unable to pay the railroad enough out of his profits to persuade them to stop running their trains and damaging his crops. The same applies, *mutatis mutandis*, if wheat growing turns out to be the more profitable activity: the initial assignment of rights makes no difference. But the Coase Theorem shows only that the distributive question is uninteresting from the point of view of efficiency (and even then only under highly idealized assumptions about transaction costs). Coase and his followers concede that the initial assignment of rights will make a big difference to how much wealth *each party* ends up with in the efficient allocation, and they can hardly deny that this is likely to matter more to the parties themselves than the issue of efficiency. In general, Law and Economics professors have made no attempt to show why we should be preoccupied with efficiency to the exclusion of all else, or why the law should take no interest in what has traditionally been regarded as its *raison d'être* – namely justice.

Among the philosophers who discuss principles for assigning resources to particular private owners, some embrace the inherent arbitrariness of the initial assignment, while others insist that unless the initial assignment is morally justified, the subsequent operation of the property system cannot be. Of the latter group – that is, of those who insist that the initial assignment must be morally justified – some maintain that the initial distribution of private property ought to be the subject of collective decision by the whole society, while others argue that morally respectable entitlements can be established by the unilateral actions of individuals. I shall call these three approaches Humean, Rousseauian, and Lockean after their three most famous proponents.

The Humean approach   On the Humean approach, we start from an assumption that since time immemorial, people have been grabbing and fighting over resources, and that the distribution of *de facto* possession at any given time is likely to be arbitrary, driven by force, cunning, and luck. It is possible that this predatory grabbing and fighting (some aspects of which will be physical, others ideological) will continue back and forth indefinitely. But it is also possible that the situation may settle down into some sort of stable equilibrium in which almost all of those in possession of significant resources find that the marginal costs of further predatory activity are equal to their marginal gains. Under these conditions, something like a "peace dividend" may be available. Maybe everyone can gain, in terms of the diminution of conflict, the stabilizing of social relations, and the prospects for market exchange, by an agreement not to fight any more over possessions.

> I observe, that it will be for my interest to leave another in the possession of his goods, provided he will act in the same manner with regard to me. He is sensible of a like interest in the regulation of his conduct. When this common sense of interest is mutually express'd, and is known to both, it produces a suitable resolution and behaviour. (*Hume, [1739] 1888, p. 490*)

Such a resolution, if it lasts, may amount over time to a ratification of *de facto* holdings as *de jure* property.

The Humean approach – which finds a modern counterpart in the work of James Buchanan (1975) – provides an account of initial distribution which is congenial to the spirit of modern economics. It makes no use of any assumptions about human nature except those used in rational choice theory, and it is – accordingly – quite modest in its moral claims. On the Humean account, the stability of the emergent distribution has nothing to do with its justice or moral respectability. It may be equal or unequal, fair or unfair (by some distributive standard), but the parties will already know that they cannot hope for a much better distribution by pitching their own strength yet again against that of others. We should not concern ourselves, Hume argues, with the distributive features of the possessory regime that emerges from the era of conflict. The aim should be to ratify any distribution that seems salient – that is, any distribution support for which promises to move us away from squabbling about who should own what, and towards the benefits promised by an orderly marketplace.

As an account of the genesis of property, Hume's theory has the advantage over its main rivals of acknowledging that the early eras of human history are eras of conflict largely unregulated by principle and opaque to later moral inquiry. In our thinking about property, Hume does not require us to delve into history to ascertain who did what to whom, and what would have happened if they had not. Once a settled pattern of possession emerges, we simply draw an arbitrary line and say, "Property entitlements start from *here*." The model has important normative consequences for the present as well. Those who are tempted to question or disrupt an existing distribution of property must recognize that far from ushering in a new era of justice, their best efforts are likely to inaugurate an era of conflict in

17

which all bets are off and in which virtually no planning or co-operation is possible. The importance of establishing stable property relations on this account is not that it does justice, but that it provides people with a fixed and mutually acknowledged basis on which the rest of social life can be built.

The weakness of the Humean approach is, of course, the obverse of its strength. As we saw in our discussion of the Coase Theorem, distributive justice matters to the law and it matters to us. We would not be happy with a Humean convention ratifying slavery or cannibalism, but, for all that, Hume shows it may well be a feature of the equilibrium emerging from the age of conflict that some people are in possession of others' bodies. And if this pattern of possession really was stable, all would gain – the slaves as well as their masters – from its ratification as property; but we would still oppose it on grounds of justice. What this shows is that even if Hume is right that the sentiment of justice is built up out of a convention to respect one another's *de facto* possessions, that sentiment once established can take on a life of its own, so that it can subsequently be turned against the distribution that engendered it.

The Rousseauian approach   In the Humean model. the peace dividend is secured by mutual forbearance: I agree to respect what you have managed to hang on to, and you agree to respect what I have managed to hang on to. An alternative is to set up a public authority or state to enforce mutual forbearance. But if the state we set up is powerful enough to enforce a *de facto* distribution, it is probably powerful enough to move resources from one individual to another in accordance with its own ideas about justice (that is, those of its constituents and officials).

Indeed, the power of the state may be matched by a general moral sentiment that the people acting together are entitled to establish a new distribution on the basis of broad principles of justice that reflect each person's status as an equal partner in a society. They may insist for example that the resources of the earth were originally given to everyone, so that no one can rightfully be displaced by any individual's appropriation without his own consent. Or they may insist, along lines suggested by Immanuel Kant, that the unilateral actions of an appropriator cannot create the obligations that private property rights assume, obligations that people simply would not have apart from the appropriation. Only a will that is "omnilateral" can do this, according to Kant – only the "collective general (common) and powerful will" associated with public law-giving (Kant, [1797] 1991, pp. 77 and 84).

This position is associated most closely with the normative theory of Jean-Jacques Rousseau. Even if individuals are in possession of resources when society is set up, Rousseau argues that as an inherent part of the social contract we must alienate our particular possessions to the general will of the community, which alone is capable of determining a distribution that provides a genuine basis of mutual respect (Rousseau, [1762] 1973, pp. 173–81). Of course, such submission seems to us terribly risky. But the risk may not seem so great if we consider that the alternative is certain individuals maintaining dominion over resources and hence power over others in a way that is simply unchecked by moral principle. We must remember too that the Rousseauian model is a highly idealized one. The idea is not that everyone – rich and poor – should simply turn over their possessions to whatever band of robbers or vanguard party parades itself as the government. It is rather that the idea of a legitimate set of property rights is inseparable from the notion of a genuine social union in which people address the issue of resources together as free and equal individuals.

What this actually yields in the way of an assignment of resources to individuals is a matter of the distributive principles that survive the test (actual or hypothetical) of ratification by the general will. In fact, most of those who adopt the Rousseauian approach envisage some sort of rough equality of private property.

But it is here that the model runs into its greatest difficulty. If an *initial* set of holdings is to be assessed on the basis of a distributive principle (say, equality), then *any* set of holdings may be assessed on that basis. After all, there is surely no justification for applying the Rousseauian criteria at t_1 which would not also be a justification for applying it again at any subsequent time t_n. But if we are distributing private property rights at t_1, and if – as one expects, they include powers of transfer, then – as Robert Nozick (1974, pp. 162–4) has argued, any favored distribution is likely to be transformed into a distribution at t_2 *un*favored by the egalitarian principle, as a result of voluntary activities like gift-giving, bequest, market exchange and so on. To maintain a distributive pattern of the sort that Rousseauian principles envisage, "one must either continually interfere to stop people transferring resources as they wish to, or continually (or periodically) interfere to take from some persons resources that others for some reason chose to transfer to them" (Nozick, 1974, p. 163). Quite apart from the insult to freedom, the results of this constant application and reapplication of moral criteria might undermine market processes and, as Hume put it, "reduce society to the most extreme indigence; and instead of preventing want and beggary in a few, render it unavoidable to the whole community" (Hume, [1777] 1902, p. 194).

John Rawls, who may be regarded as a modern exponent of the Rousseauian approach, maintains that the problem can be solved by insisting that the principles of justice ratified by a notional Rousseauian union are to be applied not to individual distributive shares, but to the assessment and choice of institutions which, it is understood, once chosen are to run under their own steam and by their own logic. "A distribution," Rawls writes, "cannot be judged in isolation from the system of which it is the outcome or from what individuals have done in good faith in the light of established expectations" (Rawls, 1971, p. 88). But it remains to be seen whether this highly abstract specification can be converted into a way of thinking about and evaluating the actual operation of concrete property arrangements.

The Lockean approach   In the Rousseauian model, the initial allocation of resources to individual owners is done by society as a whole, on the premise that something which affects everyone requires the consent of all. The Lockean approach rejects this as silly and impracticable: "If such a consent as that was necessary, Man had starved, notwithstanding the Plenty God had given him" (Locke, [1690] 1988, p. 288). We come to consciousness, he argued, in a world evidently supplied with the necessities of life, and there cannot be anything wrong with a person's simply taking possession of some of this and using it. What is more, if a person begins to use some piece of land or other natural resource, there does seem to be something obviously wrong with others' trying to interfere or take it from her, unless somehow her appropriation has gravely prejudiced their subsistence. We do not seem to need any collective or "omnilateral" decision to establish the appropriator's entitlement to some sort of respect for the right that she has established.

In its simplest form the theory of unilateral acquisition presents itself to us as First Occupancy Theory: the first person to occupy a piece of land gets to be its owner or, more generally, the first person to act as though he is the owner of something actually becomes its owner, so far as the morality of his or anyone else's actions are concerned. The traditional argument for this has been that second and subsequent occupants necessarily prejudice the interests of someone who came earlier, whereas the first occupant does not. But that will not do. Even if there is no earlier occupant-appropriator, there may still be others whose interests are affected by the first occupant – namely, those who had previously enjoyed the resource in common but who now find themselves barred by the first occupant's putative entitlement from using or enjoying it at all.

John Locke's theory is widely regarded as the most interesting of the philosophical discussions of property, in large part because it represents an honest attempt to deal with this difficulty. The starting point of Locke's analysis is that God gave the world to men in common, so that the unilateral introduction of private entitlements is acknowledged from the outset to represent something of a moral problem.

How does Locke propose to solve the problem? First, he makes it manageable by emphasizing that when private property was invented there was actually more than enough for everyone to make an appropriation. It was only the invention of money, he said, which led to the introduction of larger individual possessions whereby some came to own a lot and others little or nothing; and he argued – not altogether convincingly – that since money was rooted in human convention, that phase of distribution was governed by justificatory considerations of (what I have called) a Rousseauian kind: "Since Gold and Silver . . . has its value only from the Consent of Men . . . it is plain, that Men have agreed to disproportionate and unequal Possession of the Earth" (Locke, [1690] 1988, pp. 301–2).

The chief significance of this argument is that it represents Locke's awareness of the limits of a theory of unilateral appropriation. A similar awareness is evidenced even in his discussion of the origin of property, where we find his theory of individual appropriation complemented throughout by what I referred to earlier as a General Justificatory Theory. Though Locke insists, as much as any theorist of First Occupancy, that a person who takes resources from the wilderness normally acquires a title to them, he is always at pains to add that this is also a good thing from the social point of view, because it rewards industry and promotes the general welfare. Unilateral appropriation never has to stand nakedly on its own in Locke's theory, as it does in the view of his more recent followers, most notably Robert Nozick (1974).

In the end, though, it is the argument about unilateral appropriation that has captured the philosophical imagination. And it is indispensable to Locke's case – if only because it provides the prototype of the individualized rights that the general arguments support and that consent will later ratify. Locke's contribution is to connect unilateral appropriation with the idea of self-ownership:

> Though the Earth . . . be common to all Men, yet every Man has a Property in his own Person. This no Body has any Right to but himself. The Labour of his Body, and the Work of his Hands, we may say, are properly his. Whatsoever then he removes out of the State that Nature hath provided, and left it in, he hath mixed his Labour with, and joyned to it something that is his own, and thereby makes it his Property. It being by him removed from the common state Nature placed it in, it hath by this labour something annexed to it, that excludes the common right of other Men. (*Locke, [1690] 1988, pp. 287–8*)

That something I have worked on embodies a part of me is a common enough sentiment. Locke connected this sentiment with the sense of self-possession that characterized the emerging liberal individual, in a way that also made a convincing economic as well as moralistic case for unilateral appropriation. Since most of what we value in external things is not given by nature but the result of labour, it is not so strange, as Locke puts it, "that the Property of labour should be able to over-ballance the Community of Land":

> [T]hough the things of Nature are given in common, yet Man (by being Master of himself, and Proprietor of his own Person, and the Actions or Labour of it) has still in himself the great Foundation of Property; and that which made up the great part of what he applyed to the Support or Comfort of his being, when Invention and the Arts had improved the conveniencies of Life, was perfectly his own, and did not belong in common to others. (*Locke, [1690] 1988, pp. 296–9*).

The part of Locke's theory which has aroused perhaps the most skepticism in jurisprudence is not the theory of unilateral acquisition, but something which seems to follow from it – namely, that there can be rights of private property prior to the institution of systems of positive law. Lockean property is established in the state of nature, and even though later inequality is ratified by consent, the consent in question has nothing to do with the social contract or the invention of government. Accordingly, when positive law does come into existence, it finds a set of individual entitlements already in existence, and a bunch of prickly citizens who are willing to fight for the proposition that the task of government is to protect their property rights not to reconstitute or redistribute them. So, conversely, those who believe that government should have more Rousseauian power over property than this often predicate their argument on the claim that property rights are unthinkable without law.

21

In fact, the Lockean view is not disposed of so easily. First of all, Locke's state of nature is not an asocial one, only apolitical. Locke takes the plausible view that all sorts of moral relations can exist in a dense web of social interaction, without the specific support of the state or positive law. But if this is accepted as a general proposition, why would property relations be an exception? People may certainly cultivate land whether there is positive law or not, and the idea that others are incapable without law of forming, or sharing or acting on the view that it is wrong to interfere with, or appropriate the products of another's labour seems very implausible. Similarly, we do not seem to need the aid of legal system to explain the existence of exchange and markets. As far as we can tell, trade between the inhabitants of different regions antedates the existence of determinate legal institutions by several millennia.

What is true is that law makes an immense contribution to a property system, and that in the complex circumstances of modern life, property without law – where the rules rely on nothing more robust than shared moral consciousness – is likely to be riddled with disputes and misunderstandings. But Locke recognized this point. That after all was the purpose of entering the social contract – to provide mechanisms for settling details, enforcing rights, adjudicating disputes that did not exist in the state of nature. But it does not follow from the fact that we need these mechanisms – and that only a legal system can supply them – that our thoughts and sentiments about mine and thine, and property and distributive justice, are purely the product of positive law.

Bibliography

Buchanan, J. 1975: *The Limits of Liberty: between anarchy and Leviathan*. Chicago: University of Chicago Press.

Coase, R. H. 1960: The problem of social cost. *Journal of Law and Economics*, 3, 1–44.

Friedman, M. 1962: *Capitalism and Freedom*. Chicago: University of Chicago Press.

Green. T. H. 1941: *Lectures on the Principles of Political Obligation*. London: Longmans, Green & Co.

Grey, T. C. 1980: The disintegration of property. In J. R. Pennock and J. W. Chapman (eds), *Nomos XXII: Property*, New York: New York University Press.

Hardin, G. 1968: The tragedy of the commons. *Science*, 162, 1,243–8.

Hayek, F. A. 1976: *The Mirage of Social Justice*. London: Routledge & Kegan Paul.

Hegel, G. W. F. [1821] 1991: *Elements of the Philosophy of Right*, ed. A. W. Wood, Cambridge: Cambridge University Press.

Honore, A. M. 1961: Ownership. In A. G. Guest (ed.), *Oxford Essays in Jurisprudence*, Oxford: Oxford University Press.

Hume, D. [1739] 1888: *A Treatise of Human Nature*, ed. L. A. Selby-Bigge, Oxford: Clarendon Press.

—— [1777] 1902: *Enquiries Concerning the Human Understanding and Concerning the Principles of Morals*, ed. L. A. Selby-Bigge, Oxford: Clarendon Press.

Locke, J. [1690] 1988: *Two Treatises of Government*, ed. P. Laslett, Cambridge: Cambridge University Press.

Munzer, S. 1990: *A Theory of Property*. Cambridge: Cambridge University Press.

Nozick, R. 1974: *Anarchy, State and Utopia*. Oxford: Basil Blackwell.

Rawls, J. 1971: *A Theory of Justice*. Oxford: Oxford University Press.

Rousseau, J.-J. [1762] 1973: *The Social Contract and Discourses*, tr. G. D. H. Cole, London: J. M. Dent & Sons.

Ryan. A. 1984: *Property and Political Theory*. Oxford: Basil Blackwell.

Waldron, J. 1986: *The Right to Private Property*. Oxford: Clarendon Press.

2

Contract

PETER BENSON

Introduction

Contemporary contract theory is characterized by the following paradoxical situation. On the one hand, the basic form and concepts of contract doctrine in both common law and civil law jurisdictions are, for the most part, firmly and clearly established as well as widely accepted. This has been so for decades now and, in the case of certain aspects of doctrine, for centuries. The present situation, as James Gordley (1991, p. 1) writes, is that "[w]ith the enactment of the Chinese Civil Code, systems of [contract] laws modelled as the West will govern nearly the entire world . . . The organization of the law and its larger concepts are alike even if particular rules are not." In sharp contrast, the world of contract theory presents itself as a multiplicity of mutually exclusive approaches with their own distinctive contents and presuppositions. While these theories typically purport to provide complete explanations of contract, each of them rejects the others as incomplete and inadequate, although rarely on the criticized theory's own grounds. There does not seem to be at present any shared principle or set of principles to adjudicate among their conflicting claims. For this reason, and despite the pervasive identity of contract doctrine across jurisdictions, many scholars share Gordley's conclusion (1991, pp. 230–1) that today there is no generally recognized theory of contract. Indeed, there is widespread scepticism about the very possibility of finding general principles that can account for the rules of positive law or the conclusions which most people regard as fair. The effort to develop a coherent explanation of contract seems to have reached an impasse.

This paradoxical relation of contemporary contract theory to contract law fixes the fundamental situation which the present essay must address and sets the background against which it will pursue its objectives, which are two-fold: to present the main contemporary theoretical approaches to contract and to suggest the direction that future theorizing should take. For these purposes, I will try to identify and explore the basic presuppositions of each of the principal efforts to provide a coherent and plausible explanation of contract. The range of available approaches will be considered. Above all, I want to see whether a given theory is able to live up to its own demands of completeness and adequacy. Thus, while the analysis will necessarily be critical, it will nonetheless take up and move within the different standpoints of the theories discussed.

Three categories of theories will be considered: the first challenges the traditional understanding of the distinctive character of contract as one relatively autonomous part of private law; the second tries to answer that challenge by arguing that contract's specific character can indeed be explained on the basis of a principle of moral autonomy; and the third holds that one needs a teleological justification that views contract as directed toward the realization of some good, such as virtue or maximum general welfare. These constitute at present the main positive theoretical approaches to contract. Based on the examination of these theories and by way of conclusion, I suggest that the first step toward getting beyond the paradoxical situation of contract theory is the development of a "public conception" of contract. This, I argue, sets the immediate goal for future theorizing about contract.

The challenge to the distinctiveness and the coherence of contract

Fuller

Contemporary theoretical reflection on the common law of contract begins with Fuller and Perdue's 1936 article, "The reliance interest in contract damages." Widely viewed as "the most influential single article in the entire history of modern contract scholarship in the common law world" (Atiyah, 1986, p. 73), this essay has largely shaped the course of discussion since the 1940s. As we will see, much of contemporary contract theory may be situated in relation to it, whether as an effort to develop or to answer its challenge.

The main topic of the article is the seemingly technical issue of the choice of the appropriate measure of damages for breach of contract. Building on the work of others, Fuller (who is universally regarded as the main author of the article and, in particular, of its theoretical discussions) distinguishes three purposes or interests which the law may pursue in awarding contract damages. First, the law may deprive a defaulting promisor of gain obtained at the promisee's expense and award it to the promisee, this to prevent unjust enrichment (the restitution interest). Second, the law may compensate the promisee for loss suffered through detrimental reliance on the promisor – for example, if in reliance on the promise, the promisee has made an expenditure now wasted or has given up an opportunity no longer available. The law's purpose here is to put the promisee in as good a position as he was in before he relied on the promise (the reliance interest). Third, the law may give the promisee the equivalent of what was promised him in order to place him in the position he would have been in had the promise been performed (the expectation interest). As a result of the influence of Fuller's article, the analysis of contract damages in both judicial opinions and scholarly writing is now invariably conceived, and often explicitly so, in the very terms proposed by him.

25

The essay's *theoretical* contribution does not lie, however, in this influential classification of remedial interests or, for that matter, in its important claim that courts, in fact, protect the reliance interest along with the expectation interest in awarding contract damages and that they should openly acknowledge this. It is, rather, Fuller's puzzlement over the rational basis of expectation damages and his effort to make sense of them that give the piece genuine theoretical significance (Fuller and Perdue, 1936, pp. 52–66).

In the face of the (still) prevailing view in law and legal scholarship that a promisee's entitlement to sue for expectation damages is a ruling and a just principle, Fuller contends that "it is as a matter of fact no easy thing to explain" why recovery of the expectancy should be the normal rule of contract damages. He sees in this difficulty the still more fundamental problem of "why a promise which has not been relied on [should] ever be enforced at all."

What, for Fuller, is the basic difficulty with expectation damages? To begin, we must recall that in awarding the promisee expectation damages for the purpose of placing him in the position that he would have been in had the promisor performed, the law purports to be *compensating* the promisee; that is, to be giving the promisee the equivalent in value of something that was initially his but that was lost or interfered with as a result of the breach. In Fuller's view, however, the promisee never in fact "had" the expectancy – it was only promised him. Since he never had it, he could not have lost it. Hence, Fuller concludes, the award of the expectancy "seems on the face of things a queer kind of compensation."

Given this conclusion, Fuller suggests that the expectation interest presents a lesser claim in justice to judicial intervention than do the restitution and reliance interests. Whereas protection of the latter interests entails reparation of actual losses and therefore is compensatory in character, protection of the expectancy gives the promisee something he never had and "brings into being a new situation." In passing from compensation for losses to the satisfaction of expectations disappointed by breach, the law ceases to act restoratively and adopts a more active role. Referring to Aristotle's analysis of justice, Fuller notes that in so doing the law passes from corrective justice to distributive justice.

If we examine Fuller's difficulty with the expectation interest, we see that, necessarily, it rests on the following implicit premise: a promise, even if accepted, does not give the promisee anything; it is only if and when a promise is actually performed that the promisee acquires something. Consequently, breach – or, more generally, any failure to perform – cannot be viewed as depriving the promisee of something that is *already* his. Fuller must hold, then, that by obliging a promisor to pay expectation damages, the law imposes on him a positive duty to benefit the promisee rather than a negative duty not to injure him. This is borne out by his endorsement (1936, p. 56, n. 7) of two continental writers, Durkheim and Tourtoulon. In the passage quoted by Fuller, Durkheim contends that in the case of a purely executory agreement (where the promisor has not yet received remuneration and the promisee has not yet detrimentally relied), a breach does not "take from another what belongs to him"; rather, the defaulting promisor "only refuse[s] to be useful to him." Enforcement of the agreement does not repair an injury. Instead it has "an eminently positive nature." Tourtoulon puts the point this way: "the principle that promise or consent creates an obligation is foreign to the idea of justice." As I shall now explain, this view, if correct, has far-reaching implications for the analysis of contract.

It is a basic and distinctive premiss of private law that individuals can be held accountable only for injuring or otherwise interfering with what rightfully belongs to others. The essential idea is that obligation in private law has the form of being correlative to the right of others to be free from wrongful interference with what is their own, whether the latter is inseparable from their person (their bodies, for example) or is something they may have acquired in accordance with a principle of appropriation (such as the rule of first occupancy). By contrast, an obligation to benefit others, to preserve or improve their condition, or to contribute to the fulfilment of their needs and purposes goes beyond this severely limited idea of responsibility and does not belong to private law. Consistent with this, private law principles of appropriation themselves are on their face indifferent to the needs, purposes, and well-being of the individuals who may wish to claim something as their own. Although these ends are relevant in morality or in public law, they cannot be the basis of a claim of justice in private law.

Private law's limited idea of responsibility is reflected in the common law proposition that there can be liability for misfeasance but not for nonfeasance (Benson, 1995a). Misfeasance is thus a wrong that violates another's right to be free from interference with his or her own, in the sense just indicated. Nonfeasance, by contrast, is wrongful conduct that cannot be construed in this way but that must instead be explained on the basis of a duty to care for the well-being of others. Contrary to what is sometimes said, the difference between misfeasance and nonfeasance is therefore not the same as the distinction between acts and omissions: an act can be nonfeasance (for example, attracting a business competitor's customer) just as an omission can be misfeasance (such as failing to warn another of danger in a situation of justified detrimental reliance).

Put in terms of the distinction between misfeasance and nonfeasance, Fuller's difficulty with expectation damages is that they seem to make the promisor liable for mere nonfeasance. The promisor is compelled to improve the promisee's circumstances, not to repair a loss wrongfully caused. The "normal" measure of contract damages appears anomalous from the standpoint of private law itself. For the same reason, the enforcement of purely executory agreements not relied upon by the promisee is problematic, given that the only basis for enforcement can be protection of the expectation interest. Yet it is precisely the enforceability of such agreements that is regarded as the hallmark of modern contract law. No wonder, then, that Fuller sees the normal rule of contract damages as "throw[ing] its shadow across our whole subject." Nevertheless, because expectation damages are available at law, he deems it necessary to suggest possible reasons for the existence of this rule.

After rejecting a variety of possible justifications for the expectation measure, Fuller (1936, pp. 60–3) proposes what he calls a "juristic" explanation: awarding expectation damages is justified as a means of curing and preventing reliance

27

losses and of facilitating general reliance on business agreements. Fuller himself makes explicit the implications and the limits of the proposed explanation. First and foremost, the expectation *measure* of damages (the value of the promised performance) is no longer justified as a way of protecting the expectation *interest* (which aims to put the promisee in the position he would have been in had the promise been performed). The reliance interest replaces the expectation interest as the main motive or substantive basis of the law in giving contract damages. But if the reliance interest is the basis of contractual liability, why use expectation rather than reliance damages as the proper measure of recovery?

Fuller's answer is as follows. In certain circumstances, he notes, the expectation and reliance measures will be the same. When this is the case, it is possible to view expectation damages as compensatory. For example, where a contract of exchange is effected under perfectly competitive market conditions, the value promised under the agreement can equal the value of an alternative exchange which the promisee did not make in reliance on the promisor. Moreover, even where this situation does not exist, it may sometimes be more difficult to prove or measure reliance losses than expectation losses, making an award of expectation damages easier to administer. These examples show that awarding expectation damages may sometimes be a good surrogate for repairing reliance losses. It must be kept in mind here that this compensatory rationale for expectation damages presupposes that the aim is to protect the reliance interest, not the expectation interest. Therefore, where the contract is not an exchange concluded in a purely competitive economic context and/or where reliance losses can be established with the requisite degree of certainty, the rationale "loses force." Then, as Fuller acknowledges, if a court awards expectation damages, they can no longer be viewed as compensatory but assume a quasi-punitive character.

This last point brings out the inadequacy from a legal point of view of the attempt to explain expectation damages simply as a means of curing and preventing reliance losses. In contemplation of law, contract damages – including expectation damages – are compensatory. Moreover, the mere fact that it may be difficult or even impossible to prove one kind of loss (reliance) does not by itself justify recourse to another measure of damages (expectation). That the latter may be more readily ascertained and administered in certain circumstances is insufficient to legitimate its use by the courts. After all, in tort actions for negligence, difficulty in establishing reliance losses is not normally remedied by recourse to the expectation measure. The action may simply fail. Fuller needs a positive general justification for contract law's recourse to a measure other than reliance, if, as he holds, the aim of the law should be the protection of reliance.

The second part of Fuller's juristic explanation is meant to provide the needed justification. It views an award of expectation damages, not as a surrogate for reliance losses, but as a way of encouraging individuals to make and to act on business agreements in order to facilitate the division of labor, to ensure that goods find their way to the places where they are most needed, and to stimulate economic activity. As Fuller notes, this part of the justification implies an essential correspondence between the legal view and actual conditions of economic life. The bilateral business agreement becomes the paradigm case of informal contracts that are enforceable without proof of actual reliance. A major task of contract theory becomes, therefore, the search for an underlying correspondence between law and economics in the various doctrines and aspects of contract law.

We see clearly here that the search for a compensatory rationale for the normal rule of damages has been abandoned. On Fuller's view, breach of contract now appears more like a threat to social co-operation – a social wrong – rather than a violation of an individual's entitlement to performance. This analysis is entirely unconstrained by the limiting principle of no liability for nonfeasance. The juristic explanation does not attempt to justify the normal rule of contract damages on a basis that is consistent with the distinctive character of private law.

Fuller succinctly summarizes the outcome of his analysis: "We might easily base the *whole* law of contracts on a fundamental premise that *only* those promises which have been relied on will be enforced. As the chief exception to this principle we should have to list the bilateral business agreement. The rationale for this exception could be found in the fact that in such agreements reliance is extremely likely to occur and extremely difficult to prove." Yet, we must emphasize, modern contract law in both common law and civil law jurisdictions continues to treat unrelied-on mutual promises in both commercial and non-commercial contexts as fully enforceable with expectation damages. On Fuller's analysis, the divide between the law and theory seems fundamental.

Atiyah

The challenge which Fuller leaves us with is to show that contractual liability can – and should – be entirely explained on the basis of just the two sources of obligation implied by the restitutionary and reliance interests, namely, the receipt of benefits at another's expense and the inducement of justified detrimental reliance. The work of Patrick Atiyah represents to date the most sustained effort to do this. His scholarship is particularly wide-ranging in its treatment of doctrine, history, and philosophy. For present purposes, however, the heart of his argument may be briefly summarized as follows.

According to Atiyah (1986, pp. 11–18), "the classical view of contract", as he calls it, roots contractual liability in the actual intentions of the parties and attributes to promises the power to generate full-fledged enforceable obligations. Atiyah argues for an alternative conception of contract which holds that persons are liable for what they do rather than for what they intend, and which doubts, and may even deny, that a promise can bind absent the receipt of an actual benefit or the inducement of reliance. His argument consists of two parts, one critical, the other constructive. In the critical part, Atiyah examines the law to see whether, in fact, it supports the claims of the classical view. He also considers a wide range of theoretical accounts of the basis of promissory obligation to see whether the classical view can be sustained as a matter of moral principle.

The classical conception, Atiyah contends, treats the unrelied-on and unpaid-for executory contract, consisting just of mutual promises, as the paradigm of enforceable agreements. One of his objections against this view is that such agreements are, in fact, exceedingly rare. Most enforceable agreements involve the receipt of actual benefits or the inducement of actual reliance either at the moment of formation or very soon thereafter. In addition, Atiyah takes the classical view to be in tension with certain basic aspects of contract doctrine, such as the objective test of formation (by which parties may be bound irrespective of their intentions), the doctrine of consideration (which stipulates the existence of benefit or detriment as a condition of enforceability), or the mitigation requirement (which seems to be explicable only on the basis of the primacy of the reliance interest). Still, Atiyah acknowledges, as Fuller did before, that the law *does* enforce wholly executory, unpaid-for, and unrelied-on mutual promises with expectation damages. Even if we grant that such promises may be statistically infrequent, the fact that they are enforceable as a matter of principle – and, historically speaking, have been treated as such since the emergence of the action in *assumpsit* – is surely an important datum for contract theory. Fuller leaves us with the challenge of trying to explain this well and long established feature of contract law within the bounds of liability for misfeasance only. How does Atiyah approach this question?

Atiyah begins by exploring the basis of promissory liability. He examines an impressive number of the more significant philosophical accounts of promising – including classical utilitarianism and natural law, in addition to contemporary theories. In the end, he finds them all wanting. I will not attempt to discuss or to evaluate his treatment of the various approaches. For present purposes, it is sufficient to note that he measures them all against a single problem. According to Atiyah, every theory of promising must explain how a promisee can be *entitled* to expect the promisor not to change his mind. This, for Atiyah, is perhaps the fundamental question for contract theory (Atiyah, 1981, pp. 127ff). Let us see why.

Atiyah starts from the premise that people regularly do, and normally have the liberty to, change their minds. Not having this freedom to change one's mind can interfere significantly with one's choices, thereby imposing definite and sometimes serious costs on oneself. Why then, Atiyah asks of each theory, should a promisor's first statement of intention (the promise) be accorded priority over his second (change of mind)? Which preference should be accorded priority as an entitlement: the promisor's desire to change his mind or the promisee's desire to have his expectations fulfilled? "There is simply no basis," Atiyah writes, "unless and until the entitlement decision is made, for ascribing any loss or disappointment of expectations suffered by a promisee to the promisor" (Atiyah, 1981). Atiyah contends that *all* theories of promising – whether they are welfare based (such as utilitarian or economic approaches) or autonomy based (such as natural law or contemporary liberal approaches) – are obliged to settle this question on pain of begging the issue. As I have mentioned, he does not find a satisfactory answer in any of the theories canvassed. In his view (1986, pp. 121–79), this is especially true of leading contemporary accounts, such as the economic analysis of contract or Charles Fried's liberal theory. Consequently, they do not explain why a bare, unpaid-for, and unrelied-on promise should by itself give rise to an obligation, whether moral or legal.

If a promise is to be enforceable, Atiyah holds that it must be so in virtue of the reasons for which it was given or because of the consequences which it has had. A promise may be given, for example, to obtain something of value from the promisee or, alternatively, to induce the promisee to change his position to his detriment. These are reasons for promising. As I have already noted, Atiyah holds that contractual obligation should be founded on parties' acts, not their intentions. In his view, conferral of benefit and detrimental reliance are the two main types of acts that can take place in a contractual setting. They are also consequences of promising. Now the actual receipt of a benefit at another's expense and the inducement of detrimental reliance can give rise to obligations in unjust enrichment and in tort respectively, and these obligations do not, of course, presuppose or derive from an obligation to keep one's promises. So, in addition to being reasons for promising, the receipt of benefits and the inducement of reliance represent, as consequences of promising, possible substantive bases of obligation. On Atiyah's view, then, promises are enforceable only when a benefit has been conferred or when reliance has taken place, and the basis for enforcement is in unjust enrichment or in tort respectively. But if this is so, what role is left for the promise itself to play?

Atiyah's answer is that a promise made to obtain a benefit or to induce reliance can play a "formal" role in shaping the legal consequences attaching to these effects (Atiyah, 1981, pp. 184ff). In particular, a promise may function, not as a separate substantive basis of obligation, but as a *conclusive admission* by the promisor that clarifies and sometimes settles a variety of issues pertinent to the existence and the extent of his obligation in unjust enrichment or tort:

> [In the case of benefits rendered to the promisor] the promise is usually evidence that the transaction is an exchange and not a gift [hence at the expense of the promisee], and it is evidence of the fair value of the exchange . . . [In the case of detrimental reliance induced by the promisor] the promise is evidence that the promisor himself thought that the promisee would be justified in acting in reliance on the assertion expressed in or implicit in the promise. (*Atiyah, 1981, p. 193*)

This conception of promises as admissions is the core of the constructive part of Atiyah's theory. He puts it forward as plausible in principle and as more consistent with the law than the classical view. Yet there are important difficulties with this idea, some of which Atiyah himself acknowledges and addresses.

First, we must, of course, explain why a promise is to be treated as a *conclusive* admission. After all, since the promisor may have changed his mind, it is not self-evident why his initial expression of intention should be given precedence by being treated as conclusive.

Second, one must show how the making of a promise in the context of conferred benefits or induced reliance can *alter* the unjust enrichment or tort analysis that

31

already applies in virtue of these facts, when the legal significance of the promise is supposed to be *merely* evidentiary. Let me explain. In circumstances of induced detrimental reliance, the duty of care in tort can often be fully satisfied if the defendant simply notifies the plaintiff of his change of mind even after the plaintiff has relied, so long as the notification does not come too late for the plaintiff to regain his prior position without loss. And further, the measure of damages in a case of breach of that tort duty will be only for the actual detriment caused. By contrast, when contract law enforces the reliance-inducing promise, the promisor is deemed to be in breach of his duty just because he has failed to perform as promised. Notification will not, in general, discharge that duty. And the measure of damages will be for the value of the promise, not just the reliance loss. It is not at all evident how a merely evidentiary conception of the role of promising can account for this difference in legal result.

Third, there is the basic difficulty that the evidentiary conception alone neither accounts for nor explains away the fact that mutual promises can be legally binding from the moment of formation whether or not there has been any actual conferral of benefits and any detrimental reliance. On this legal analysis, the function of promises at the moment of agreement cannot be to provide evidence of factors that relate to the benefit/detrimental reliance analysis simply because, by hypothesis, conferral of benefit and inducement of reliance can be legally irrelevant. The law, at least, seems to attribute to promises something more than the purely evidentiary function that Atiyah proposes.

The effort to ground contractual obligation on detrimental reliance is vulnerable to a further, though related, objection. The law usually distinguishes between reliance that the promisor expressly or implicitly *requested in return for* his promise and reliance that he merely foreseeably induced. In the first case only, the reliance is treated as consideration for the promise, with the legal consequence that the promise becomes contractually enforceable with expectation damages. By contrast, where reliance is merely (foreseeably) induced, the promise can give rise at most to an estoppel governed by principles of tort law: the promise is not as such binding, nor does its breach normally give rise to expectation damages. This dichotomy has important implications for the theory of contract. From the standpoint of legal doctrine, both reliance and promising play roles in contract formation that are qualitatively different from their functions in tort. A theory that purports to provide an account of the law cannot simply assume *ab initio* that there is a single undifferentiated notion of reliance or of promising that underlies contract and tort. To the contrary, it must begin by seeing whether it is possible to identify the specific structure that gives reliance and promising a character that is distinctively contractual. In legal doctrine, I have said, this structure is set by the requirement that the reliance must be requested in return for the promise. In contract theory, it is above all "autonomy-based" approaches that attempt to identify and to justify the specific structure of contract.

The work of three scholars – Joseph Raz, Charles Fried, and Randy Barnett, each of whom invokes a conception of moral autonomy to explain contract law – will now be considered.

32

Three autonomy-based theories

Autonomy theories view contract law as a legal institution that recognizes and respects the power of private individuals to effect changes in their legal relations *inter se*, within certain limits. These theories resist the reduction of contractual and promissory obligation to tort and unjust enrichment. They try to account for both the legal point of view, which continues to hold that mutual promises can be fully enforceable independent of actual enrichment or detrimental reliance, as well as the ordinary intuitive notion that rational persons can bind themselves just by promising, assuming that certain requirements (such as voluntariness) have been satisfied. To meet the challenge of Fuller and Atiyah, however, autonomy theories must also show that their proposed justifications of promissory obligation respect the basic principle of no liability for nonfeasance. In Atiyah's terms, they must make clear the basis of the promisee's entitlement to performance despite the promisor's change of mind.

Raz

The contrast between tort and contract – and between the roles of promising and reliance in each of these – is reflected in a distinction drawn by Joseph Raz between two different conceptions of promising – the "intention" and the "obligation" conceptions of promising (Raz, 1977, 1982). Raz contends that the distinction between these two conceptions of promising is intelligible in principle and that it is the obligation conception which most fully captures our common idea of promising.

The "intention" conception defines promise as the communication of a firm intention to do something when one is aware that it may be relied on by the addressee or when one intends to induce or to encourage such reliance. According to Raz, the intention conception brings into play the estoppel principle: if the addressee has actually relied, the one who has communicated the firm commitment must avoid harming him by disappointing that reliance. There must be actual detrimental reliance for estoppel to apply and for the addressor to be bound. From a legal point of view, the protected interest at stake here is the reliance interest.

By contrast, the "obligation" conception defines promising as the communication of an intention to undertake, by that very communication, an *obligation* to do something (not just an intention to act, as in the intention conception) and to invest the addressee with a right to its performance. A promisor communicates to the promisee the belief that she (the promisor) knows that she will be obligated and that she wishes to be so obligated just by expressing this intention to the promisee. In a given society, there may be a variety of conventional ways of communicating this intention. These conventions help determine what acts can reasonably be taken to express an intention to undertake an obligation and to confer a right. Individuals may avail themselves of these conventions as ready means to channel and to fulfil their desire to bring themselves under an obligation. However, the existence of such conventions is not essential to the making of promises.

33

An intention to undertake an obligation can be communicated even in a society that does not recognize the practice of promising. Moreover, while an intention to bind oneself may be conveyed, given the requisite shared background understandings, by the promisor inviting the promisee to rely, this does not mean that the obligation conception of promising is reducible to the intention conception. An invitation to rely and an intention to undertake an obligation by the very communication of that intention are categorically distinct. The first is, as such, neither necessary nor sufficient to establish the second (Raz, 1972, pp. 98–101).

One way of expressing the basic difference between the two conceptions is that in the case of the obligation conception, promising is a form of what Raz calls a "voluntary" obligation. What makes an obligation voluntary in Raz's sense is not just that the obligation is attached to a voluntary act of some kind. The voluntary character of an obligation tells us something about the reason or justification for the obligation. In the case of a voluntary obligation, part of the reason the obligation is imposed is that the person obligated willed to be, or at least knew she could be, so obligated by her act. The person's awareness is morally relevant in a specific way: it is itself a *positive* reason for imposing the obligation. By contrast, if a person's state of mind (in willing or at least in being aware of the obligation) is not itself to any extent part of the positive justification for the obligation, the obligation is not voluntary, even if it attaches to a person's voluntary acts. For example, I may buy goods in another country with full knowledge that I will have to pay custom duties on them when I return home. The purchase is voluntary and informed. However, my awareness that I will have to pay custom duties is not itself part of the positive reason for my obligation to pay them. The moral significance of my awareness is that but for it, it might be unfair to oblige me to pay: people are entitled as a matter of fairness to know in advance that if they buy goods abroad, they will have to pay duties on their return home. This knowledge fulfils a merely negative justificatory role. It does not provide, even in part, a positive reason for the duties – which, we suppose, will rest on a variety of policy considerations. The positive justification is entirely independent of the agent's awareness of the obligation.

Social life is replete with different forms of voluntary obligations. Promises, where the assumption of the obligation is undertaken in the form of an explicit communication to that effect, are but an extreme case of voluntary obligation at one end of a wide spectrum. Most voluntary obligations are not established with this degree of explicitness. Indeed, it is the mark of a healthy relationship that the number of explicit promises is small.

While all promises communicate an intention to undertake an obligation, they do not necessarily succeed in doing so. Raz holds that promises bind only if we suppose that it is *desirable* to give effect to the promisor's intentions. A promise purports to create a special bond between promisor and promisee, obliging the former to view the latter's claim as having peremptory force and not just as one of the many claims that persons may have, in general, to his respect and aid. The moral bindingness of a promise presupposes that this kind of relationship and the fact that it is voluntarily created and shaped by the choice of the parties are valuable. People have a normative power to bind themselves and invest others with rights because this is a form of life deemed to be intrinsically desirable. This is a moral presupposition of the obligation conception of promising.

According to Raz (1982, pp. 933ff), the purpose of contract law should be – and largely is – to protect both the practice of undertaking voluntary obligations (including promises) and the individuals who rely on this practice. He offers this analysis as an alternative to the view that contract is a hybrid of principles based on tort and restitution (Atiyah's approach) and as well to the idea that its purpose is the enforcement of promises (Charles Fried's theory). On Raz's view, the function of contract law should be supportive and facilitative by recognizing and reinforcing the already existing social practice of undertaking voluntary obligations (including promises). This facilitative function of the law is, however, circumscribed by a "harm principle," which holds that the only legitimate purpose for imposing legal obligations on individuals is to prevent harm. In light of this principle, the goal of contract law should not be the enforcement of voluntary obligations (and promises) by making promisors perform or by putting promisees in the position they would have occupied had there been performance. To take the enforcement of promises as the end of contract law would be, according to Raz, to enforce morality, no different than the legal proscription of pornography. Protecting the practice of promising, by compensating individuals for harms they suffer as a result of relying on broken promises and by ensuring that people do not intentionally or carelessly debase the practice by letting it appear as if they have promised when they have not, *are* legitimate goals. These are individual and institutional harms which the law may seek to discourage or to repair within the bounds of the harm principle.

Raz's conception of individual harm rests primarily on the need to protect the reliance interest and ultimately the practice of promising itself. Thus, according to him, reliance damages should in principle be the standard legal remedy for breach of contract. Expectation damages may, however, be awarded where this is needed to protect the reliance interest. For the prevention of institutional harm, Raz invokes the principle of estoppel. If people were often to allow it to appear (even through carelessness) that they have promised when they have not, the appeal and the utility of promising would be undermined. This would discourage individuals from entering and relying on agreements. In addition, they could be harmed by relying on supposed promises. To prevent this erosion of the practice of promising, the law, in its supportive role, should judge actions in accordance with how they reasonably appear to others. Where it appears that one has promised, one should be stopped from denying that one has promised. In this way, Raz justifies the common law's use of the so-called "objective test" in different areas of contract doctrine, in particular for contract formation. Yet, as he points out, this results in the validation of numerous "promises" that are not, in Raz's sense, voluntary obligations at all.

This result, which, as Raz notes, seems paradoxical, may betray a fundamental tension in his analysis of the foundation of contractual liability. Let me explain.

We have seen that Raz's analysis is based on the idea of promise as a voluntary obligation and on the presupposition of the intrinsic value of relationships that embody this idea. Essential to the notion of voluntary obligation is the positive moral relevance of the actor's actual intention and state of mind: obligation is voluntary if and only if it is actually wanted by the actor – if it is the object of her actual intention. The intrinsic value ascribed to self-wrought relationships depends crucially on the relationship being initially envisaged and wanted in this way. Absent this connection with the actor's actual intention, there is no reason to attribute goodness to the resulting relationship *qua* voluntarily undertaken.

On the basis of this analysis alone, the goal of protecting the practice of promising (as one form of voluntary obligation) can clearly entail recognizing and supporting a *liberty* to promise, if a person so wishes; that is, the making of a promise should not be deemed wrongful and neither persons nor the state should act in a way that treats it as such. But a stronger conclusion is not warranted. In particular, the analysis does not justify binding a promisor to perform what she has now come to regret or never actually wanted. For this cannot be rooted in her actual intentions. Yet unless a theory can show how a person can be so bound irrespective of past intentions, it cannot begin to explain contract law. In Raz's analysis, the promisee's reliance interest and the social utility of a credible practice of promising provide the needed basis for this stronger conclusion. But these reasons, as Raz himself emphasizes, are conceptually and normatively distinct from the idea of a voluntary obligation.

In short, Raz invokes two sets of ideas, both of which are essential to his explanation of contractual liability. Yet they point in different directions. The first, the idea of voluntary obligation does not justify anything more than a mere liberty (in the limited sense just discussed) to make promises. The second, the promisee's reliance interest and the general utility of promising, may justify a stronger conclusion but they do so at the cost of undermining the voluntary character of promises.

This point should be taken one step further. Given Raz's conception of voluntary obligation, the harm principle would seem to require that legal intervention – over and above legal recognition of a mere liberty to promise – be justified on grounds that are entirely distinct from the idea of voluntary obligation. To hold a promisor liable for a presently regretted promise for the reason that this shows respect for her interest in undertaking voluntary obligations is to oblige her to participate in a form of good – one that she does not want in the particular circumstances. This is to enforce morality. By the harm principle, a promisor should not be under a duty to confer the benefit of a special relationship on the promisee, even if the latter may want and expect it in light of the promisor's previous communication.

The harm principle requires, therefore, that considerations other than the idea of voluntary obligation be invoked to ground contractual liability. But while the considerations that Raz proposes – the promisee's reliance and the social utility of promising – may not offend the harm principle, they do not seem to account for the central and distinctive feature of contract. Simply stated, protecting the reliance interest and invoking the estoppel principle to prevent the erosion of promising do not justify a contractual analysis. As Raz acknowledges, both the reliance interest and the estoppel principle belong to tort. They do not require anything more than a conception of promising in which the promise functions as a representation inducing detrimental reliance – that is, an "intention" conception of promising. How there can be contract formation prior to and independent of reliance cannot be explained on their basis. The analysis satisfies the harm principle in a way that fails to preserve the essential character of contract from a legal point of view.

Raz leaves autonomy theorists with the challenge of seeing whether it is possible to account for contract on the basis of a conception of autonomy that need not invoke nonpromissory considerations such as the promisee's reliance. The next theorist to be considered, Charles Fried, has attempted to provide just such an explanation.

Fried

Among contemporary theorists, Charles Fried (1981) has developed the most comprehensive and systematic autonomy-based theory of contractual obligation which, like Raz's, is based on an obligation conception of promising. Fried's central aim is to vindicate the distinctive character of contract and the primacy of the expectation interest. The argument is in two steps.

Fried begins with the premise that in order for promises to be binding on any particular occasion we must first suppose that there is a general convention of promising which provides individuals with a way to commit themselves to future performances, if they so wish. Fried's object at this first stage of the argument (1981, pp. 12–14) is simply to establish that such a convention would be rationally wanted by individuals, given the ordinary needs of daily life. Whether as an expression of generosity or in order to obtain reciprocal benefits, people will want to be able to give each other a secure moral basis for counting on their word. Without the possibility of such commitment, the range and scope of human purposes would be severely limited. Hence, "it is necessary that there be a way . . . to make nonoptional a course of conduct that would otherwise be optional." We need a device that may be invoked to produce this effect. And for this purpose, one who invokes the convention must know that others know that he has undertaken a commitment by doing so, and they in turn must know that he knows that they know this, and so on. A general convention of promising answers this need. It defines a practice that enables individuals to create in others expectations that they will render certain future performances just because they have committed themselves to do so.

However, as Fried emphasizes, the fact that the convention may be useful does not by itself explain why someone who has invoked it, absent detrimental reliance by the promisee, is morally obligated to keep his promise if he later comes to regret it. One may always come to regret a prior decision to commit oneself to a previously neutral course of action – no matter how firm the initial expression of commitment may have been. The convention of promising is just a device for communicating commitment and for creating expectations in others. We need to

37

know why these effects, produced at one moment, rule out a change of mind later. This, we saw, is the fundamental difficulty raised by Atiyah. If changing his mind does not violate some entitlement in the promisee, it is not at all clear why a promisor may not properly do so if he comes to regret his prior decision – unless, of course, we suppose that the promisor is under an antecedent coerceable duty to promote the interests of the promisee. But such a duty, we will shortly see, would be inconsistent with Fried's understanding of the liberal basis of contract, not to say with the private law principle of no liability for nonfeasance.

Fried's answer (1981, pp. 15ff) to this question forms the second stage of his argument. By invoking the convention of promising, the promisor invites the promisee to trust the promisor on moral grounds. Breach of promise abuses that trust and uses the promisee. For Fried, the wrongfulness of the promisor's breach is like the wrongfulness of lying. Both violate what he calls "basic Kantian principles of trust and respect." But what exactly does Fried mean by "trust" in the context of promising?

While Fried does not explain in detail what he means by trust, he does say that by promising, the promisor invites the promisee to believe that the promisor has committed himself to forward the promisee's good from a sense of right and not merely for reasons of prudence. In doing this, the promisor invites the promisee to make himself vulnerable. According to Fried, it is the intentional inducement of vulnerability that gives rise to the obligation to keep the promise. But what exactly is the nature of the promisee's vulnerability? For Fried, it cannot be the fact that the promisee has detrimentally relied on the promise or that he entertains expectations of future benefit as a result of it. In Fried's view, such reactions to the promise are morally justified and imputable to the promisor only if we already hold that the promise is binding. They cannot explain the obligation, but on the contrary, presuppose it. The promisee's vulnerability must therefore consist in something else.

To make clearer Fried's understanding of the promisee's vulnerability, we must go back to certain first principles of liberal theory which he espouses (Fried, 1981, pp. 7–8, 106–11). Liberal theory, he suggests, views individuals as morally independent of one another in the pursuit of their good. This means that persons cannot claim against each other a right to be assisted in the pursuit of their good. They can only claim a right to be left free from wrongful interference with, or injury to, whatever they have managed to acquire. That being said, liberal theory also holds that persons can be under a *general* duty to care for and to advance the means and conditions of human fulfilment, so far as this is compatible with respect for the freedom and equality of everyone. But this duty is not naturally owed to, and therefore cannot be enforced by, any given person in his individual capacity. Consequently, when someone refuses to promote another's good, he does not for that reason necessarily show lack of respect for that person or his good.

By promising, however, the promisor can change all this. The promisor invites the promisee to bring the furtherance of his good within the sphere of the promisor's commitment and responsibility. The promisor distinguishes the promisee from individuals in general by intentionally conveying to the promisee his commitment to take seriously and to promote the promisee's good as an end worthy in its own right – something that the promisor was under no antecedent duty to do. The promisee is now vulnerable as he was not before: the promisor can show moral contempt for the promisee's good – he can treat it as without moral significance in its own right – by choosing not to benefit the promisee in breach of his promise. It is precisely because the promisor need not have promised and because he was under no antecedent duty to further the promisee's good, in particular, that the promisor can inflict this injury on him. The trust which the promisee places in the promisor is just that the promisor will not do this. This, for Fried, is the trust that, necessarily, is invited by a promise and is violated by its breach – irrespective of whether the promisee detrimentally relies on the promise. It is the basis of the obligation to keep a promise.

Having explained promissory obligation in this way, Fried directly deduces from this obligation the promisee's right to exact the promised performance: "if I make a promise to you, I should do as I promise; and if I fail to keep my promise, it is fair that I should be made to hand over the equivalent of the promised performance." On this basis, Fried upholds the centrality of the expectation measure of damages for breach of contract (1981, pp. 17–21). To limit the promisee to the reliance measure as a matter of principle would excuse the promisor from the full obligation he undertook – indeed it would preclude the promisor from incurring the very obligation he chose to assume at the time of promising. Hence Fried views the claim of Fuller and Atiyah, among others, that damages should be so limited in principle as destructive of the very moral basis of contract, which is the duty to keep one's promises.

Yet there are important questions raised by Fried's account of promissory obligation and by his explanation of the promisee's right to damages. First, it does not seem to be the case that necessarily, or even in most circumstances, a breach of promise should reasonably be viewed as an abuse of trust in the sense discussed above. Except in cases where the promisor has promised without any intention of performing or where he has breached simply out of spite or without any significant reason whatever, the conclusion that a given breach constitutes an abuse of trust will be far from evident. We will want to consider a number of factors, such as the promisor's personal motives for breaching, whether he gave appropriate weight to the promisee's interests in reaching his decision to breach, whether he tried his best to perform in the circumstances, whether he was willing to compensate the promisee for reasonable reliance losses, whether he apologized for the breach or sought to justify it in some way, and so on. But the idea of trust does not tell us what is the appropriate weight that should be given to each consideration in relation to the others. In particular, it does not direct how the promisor should weigh the promisee's interests in the balance with his own. Moreover, from Fried's own standpoint, considerations such as a willingness to cover reliance losses should be completely irrelevant. Finally, while the above-mentioned factors may be important when considering whether a given breach constitutes an abuse of trust, most if not all of them are simply ignored by the law in deciding whether a contract has been concluded or whether it has been breached with resulting liability.

PETER BENSON

At this basic level, the idea of trust seems to have implications that are out of sync with the legal point of view.

Even if we view a breach of promise as an abuse of the promisee's trust, there remains a further – and for our purposes, a more serious – difficulty with the theory. Fried presupposes that a breach of promise, working an abuse of trust, necessarily infringes *a right in the promisee that can be coercively enforced.* But this need not be so.

On Kant's view ([1797] 1991, pp. 45–7), for instance, there are fully binding "duties of virtue," breach of which certainly fails to treat humanity (in ourselves or in others) as an end in its own right. But these merely ethical duties do not have correlative rights in others, so that their performance cannot be directly coerced (whether by an award of damages or otherwise). In this respect, they are categorically different from what Kant called "juridical" obligations, which *are* coercible because they are correlative to rights in others. In the same vein, both the natural law writers, such as Grotius ([1625] 1925, pp. 330–1) (whom Fried cites for his promise principle), and the common law regularly distinguish between promises that may be fully binding in morals but which do not as such give the promisee an enforceable right to performance and those promises that do so even in the absence of detrimental reliance by the promisee. These two kinds of promises are distinguished by fundamental qualitative differences in their formation and their basic structures. Fried's account of trust as the basis of contract does not, however, take cognizance of this difference in the kinds of obligations and promises. It does not explain why the obligation to keep a promise is not simply an ethical duty. In short, it is not clear how Fried has shown that the premise "I should do as I promise" – even if correct – leads to the conclusion that "it is *fair* that I should be *made* to hand over the equivalent of the promised performance."

Barnett

The third and last autonomy theory I will discuss – that proposed by Randy Barnett – does not seem on its face to be vulnerable to this objection. Barnett (1986) starts from the general distinction between uncoercible moral obligations and coercible legal obligations and argues for a conception of intention that justifies the conclusion that a promisor may be legally, and not just morally, bound to perform in certain circumstances. According to Barnett, an expression of commitment to do or not do something is categorically insufficient to explain this consequence. It may at most give rise to a moral obligation to keep one's promise, an obligation that cannot, in principle, be coerced. Barnett suggests that, by contrast, the manifestation of an *intention to alienate one's rights to another* provides the essential basis for finding a legal obligation to perform.

Barnett begins from the premise that respect for our freedom of action requires that we have principles to govern the rightful acquisition, use, and transfer of the relatively scarce resources which we want and need. These principles determine our enforceable entitlements to things *vis-à-vis* others. They establish moral boundaries that must be respected by others on pain of coercion; and they mark a domain

40

within which the right-holder is relatively free to do as she wishes with the object of her entitlement – she may use it or transfer it as she wills. Whereas property specifies the principles governing the acquisition of entitlements and tort law concerns their protection and use, contract deals with the valid transfer of entitlements between persons. Thus far, Barnett's view is the same as Fried's. They diverge, however, when Barnett rests contract on a consent to transfer rights rather than on promising.

A valid transfer of entitlements changes the enforceable moral boundaries between the transferor and transferee. The transferor may now be constrained from interfering with the entitlement that was once hers but that, in virtue of the transfer, has become the transferee's. Barnett derives the crucial condition of a valid transfer, namely, consent, from the fact that, prior to the transfer, the entitlement is already vested in someone – the transferor. Therefore, in a rights-respecting system, the only person who can decide to give up the entitlement and transfer it to another is the transferor himself. Absent her consent and without her act, the transfer must be invalid, being a tortious interference with her rights – hence the fundamental requirement of consent. And because entitlements are, by hypothesis, legally enforceable, the intention to transfer them necessarily implies, according to Barnett, an intention to be legally bound. This, he contends, provides the moral basis for legal enforceability that is missing in Fried's account.

According to Barnett, Fried's promise-based and Atiyah's reliance-based theories are both inadequate because each fails to bring out contract's *interrelational* character: the first focusses one-sidedly on the promisor's intent whereas the second seeks exclusively to protect the promisee's reliance. A central aim of Barnett's consent theory is to correct this defect. Does it present contract as interrelational, and if so, how?

The consent requirement as explained above highlights only one side of a transfer, namely the entitlement vested in the transferor and the need for the transferor's decision to alienate it. What role does the transferee play in the formation of contract in keeping with contract's interrelational character?

The principal, indeed the only reference to the transferee at this basic level is found in Barnett's defence of the objective test for contract formation. For Barnett, the test ensures that at the time of transacting the transferee can ascertain whether or not the transferor has indeed parted with her right and has thereby changed the enforceable boundaries between them. Any act or statement by the transferor that falls short of expression that can fulfil this boundary-determining function will not give rise to a contractual obligation. At the same time, anything a transferor says or does will be interpreted from this standpoint, even if the transferor's actual subjective intention is otherwise. Barnett views this test as protecting the rights and liberty interests of the transferee, whose plans and expectations would be seriously restricted if she were not entitled to rely on things as they are presented to her. In sum, the interrelational character of contract is reflected in the fact that it is the *transferor's* consent, *objectively* construed, that can create a relation of right and corresponding duty between the parties.

The analysis of contract as a transfer of rights has a long and distinguished philosophical history (Gordley, 1991). The earliest philosophical discussions go back at least to medieval thinkers, notably Thomas Aquinas and Duns Scotus. The natural law writers – in particular Grotius – and early modern political philosophers – especially Hobbes – developed the idea with great clarity and system. The latest and arguably the fullest philosophical treatment is found in Kant ([1797] 1991, pp. 90–5) and Hegel ([1821] 1952, §§72–81).

Moreover, the significance of this analysis of contract for contemporary contract theory is far reaching. If justified, this approach would provide a complete answer to the challenge raised by Fuller and Atiyah against the compensatory character of the expectation interest. Contract could now be conceived as a mode of acquisition. At formation and, therefore, independent of any detrimental reliance, or passing of benefits, the promisee would acquire an enforceable entitlement to the promisor's performance; the measure of that performance would be its value; and the vindication of that entitlement would be the expectation measure. A promisor in breach could be viewed, not merely as failing to confer a benefit on the promisee, but as interfering with what already belongs to the promisee in virtue of their contract, thereby making enforcement consistent with the idea of misfeasance and an award of expectation damages truly compensatory.

While a transfer theory of contract is arguably the most promising variant of autonomy-based approaches because it goes furthest in elucidating a structure of correlative rights and duties that is specifically contractual, Barnett's account of this idea is incomplete in certain crucial respects.

For example, while Barnett is correct in emphasizing the promisor's consent as a necessary condition of a valid transfer, it is not a sufficient condition. An act by the promisee is also needed. Otherwise there cannot be a transfer, as opposed to a mere abandonment, of rights. This can be seen if we consider the structure of a present (completed) gift or exchange, through which ownership is transferred. If the transferor's alienation of ownership is not joined by the transferee's receipt, title to the thing may remain with the transferor or, alternatively, the thing may become ownerless, but in any case the transferee will not acquire it. Even in the case of gift, the transferee's act must be combined with that of the transferor. This two-act structure is a requirement of any transfer of right from one person to another. It must, therefore, be fully elucidated by a transfer theory of contract. However, in contrast to a transfer of property, the essential feature of contract is that it can be binding – and hence correlative rights and duties can be created – prior to performance; that is, prior to the point at which a promisee takes physical possession of what was promised him. If a transfer theory is to satisfy the principle of no liability for nonfeasance, it must be able to present a contract as giving the promisee possession prior to performance, possession that, therefore, cannot be physical. Explaining how such non-physical but actual possession is possible is one of the most important tasks of a transfer theory.

Until a consent theory in particular and autonomy-based approaches in general fill out the main features of the structure of contract, they will be vulnerable to the charge of indeterminacy. This objection, made recently by Craswell (1989) and Gordley (1991), holds that autonomy theories do not contain within themselves the conceptual resources to answer a variety of important doctrinal issues ranging from the choice of damage rules to the determination of implied terms in cases of contractual "gaps." The claim is that, absent some reference to substantive values other than the parties' bare consent or choice, it is impossible to account for central features and principles of contract law, especially where parties have not provided explicit contractual provisions to settle the issue that requires resolution. Supposing this objection to be correct, the question is which substantive values should be invoked at this basic level. The following section briefly considers three answers.

Three teleological theories

The three theories discussed in this section endorse the preceding objection to autonomy approaches and postulate certain substantive values as the underlying rationale and goal of contract law. Subject to certain qualifications which cannot be elaborated here, all three theories are teleological in approach; that is, they argue that contract law is best understood and justified if it is viewed as directed toward the fulfilment of some good. We have already seen that Raz postulates the goodness of voluntarily created bonds as part of the justification of contractual obligation. In this respect at least, his theory is teleological in character. The three theories I wish to consider now are James Gordley's Aristotelian interpretation of contract, Anthony Kronman's distributive analysis, and the economic approach to contract law.

Gordley

According to Gordley (1991, pp. 234ff), the problem with autonomy theories such as Fried's is that they seek the ultimate source of obligation in human choice alone. But "without giving a reason . . . other than the mere fact that the promisor willed to be bound," we cannot explain why the law enforces certain commitments or choices and not others. To explain the fact that promises are treated differently than other commitments, we must identify some goal or outcome that the former but not the latter enable a promisor to achieve. Building on his interpretation of Aristotle, Thomas Aquinas, and the Spanish natural law school, Gordley proposes that the virtues of liberality and commutative (or corrective) justice constitute the two main ends of contracting. A party's obligations should depend on which virtue he has exercised.

According to Aristotle, liberality is a virtue exercised "in the giving and taking of wealth, and especially in respect of giving . . . [T]he liberal man . . . will give for the sake of the noble and rightly; for he will give to the right people, the right amounts, and at the right time, with all the other qualifications that accompany right giving." Commutative justice, on the other hand, applies to voluntary and involuntary transactions between persons and it requires that each party's holdings be the same in value after the transaction as they were before it. This fulfils "arithmetic equality" (Gordley, 1991, pp. 12–14).

43

Gordley's main thesis is that a commitment should count as a promise and therefore should be enforceable as such only if doing so will instantiate liberality or commutative justice. So, for example, a contract in which one side will receive a grossly inadequate consideration is not and should not be enforced unless that side intended this deprivation as a gift, thereby manifesting the virtue of liberality. Or, to take another example, terms may be deemed natural to a given transaction and may be implied by a court on this basis if they serve the end of that type of transaction, the end being either liberality or commutative justice. In this way, Gordley provides a comprehensive account, not only of the moral basis of contract, but of the full range of doctrinal issues that constitute the main content of modern contract law.

Without attempting to discuss in any detail Gordley's interpretation of the Aristotelian tradition or his application of it to contract law (see, however, Benson, 1992), it is important to note certain difficulties with and implications of his account.

To begin, while Gordley views both liberality and commutative justice as possible ends of contracting, there is for Aristotle (and Aquinas) a basic difference between these two virtues. Whereas liberality is a virtue that has to do primarily with the state of a person's character – his motives and manner – in accomplishing certain acts, commutative justice is realized primarily in transactions – it is an objective requirement that can be quantitatively determined and that must be respected in interaction with others. Although liberality is instantiated in acts that benefit others, its essence consists in an ordering of character internal to the agent. Commutative justice not only orders how one acts toward others: it is essentially defined in terms of relation to another. Liberality and commutative justice are thus categorically different. If this is so, one must wonder whether they can both be ends of contract in the same way and on the same footing.

This question leads to a further point. The fact that liberality is a virtue of character makes it unclear how it can ever provide a moral basis for enforcing a commitment that could otherwise be revoked without injustice. How can a duty of character be coerced consistently with liberal premises or with the principle of liability for misfeasance only? And why does the virtue of liberality necessarily entail that the promisee has a correlative right to the act of liberality? Unless the virtue of liberality can be expressed in the form of a duty with a corresponding and enforceable right, the theory cannot explain the very kind of juridical relation that contract law presupposes. Here, it should be recalled that considerations of character are in themselves generally irrelevant to the legal analysis of contract. *Prima facie*, then, the invocation of virtues other than justice seems to be incompatible with the legal point of view.

According to Gordley, contract is to be understood on the basis of liberality and commutative justice alone. In this respect, he disagrees with Fuller who, we saw, views the expectation interest as part of distributive justice, not commutative (or corrective) justice. Gordley (1981) contends that the function of commutative or corrective justice is to ensure that whatever distribution of holdings exists at any given time is preserved and not disturbed by transactions. On this view, the

44

distribution is taken as given, whether or not it is fair. But treating the distribution in this way seems morally arbitrary. It does not seem plausible to assume that the preservation of *any* distribution, no matter how inequitable, will always be valuable. Therefore, on Gordley's interpretation of commutative justice, one is compelled to evaluate the fairness of the presupposed distribution in deciding whether a particular transaction is morally acceptable or not. Ascertaining the fairness of a distribution is the work of distributive justice. Thus Gordley's view entails that the moral acceptability of a given transaction depends, not just on commutative justice, but also on considerations of distributive justice.

Kronman

The idea that contract principles should – and do – reflect distributive concerns has been defended by Anthony Kronman (1980). Fuller, we saw, already suggested that the expectation interest may have its justificatory basis in distributive justice. Kronman goes further by arguing that "the idea of voluntary agreement . . . cannot be understood except as a distributional concept." If contract rules are to have even minimal moral acceptability, they must be framed so as to achieve a fair division of wealth and power among citizens. Kronman's argument for this view is in three steps.

Kronman accepts the basic premise of autonomy theories that contracts are voluntary agreements. The question is: what makes an agreement voluntary? Unless we are content to say that the only thing required is that the promisor has deliberately chosen to contract – even if his choice was made in response to a threatened coercion or in error – we will have to refer to *circumstances* that may render consent, albeit deliberately given, involuntary. In this first step of the argument, Kronman contends that if we consider the various circumstances which can produce this effect, they may be analyzed as forms of advantage-taking in exchange relationships: in every case the promisee possesses an advantage – superior information or intelligence, a powerful instrument of violence or means of deception, a monopoly over a given resource – and the promisor's claim is that the promisee has used this advantage at his expense. However, every exchange involves advantage-taking of some kind. Indeed, in transactions that are undoubtedly voluntary and mutually beneficial, each party has something that the other wants and this advantage enables each to extract something from the other in return. We therefore need some criterion or principle to distinguish impermissible from permitted forms of advantage-taking.

In the second step, Kronman considers, only to reject, a non-distributive idea of liberty as a possible criterion. This idea of liberty, as stated by Kronman, holds that advantage-taking by one at another's expense should be permitted unless it violates the latter's rights or the rights of a third party. Kronman notes that this liberty principle is both individualistic and egalitarian in nature. Persons are equally recognized as having moral boundaries that must be respected by others, even if more welfare could be produced by violating them.

Kronman rejects the liberty principle as a basis for distinguishing forms of advantage-taking for the following reason. To know whether an individual's liberty has been violated – and thus whether there has been an impermissible advantage-taking – we must first know what his rights are. But the liberty principle itself does not provide this knowledge. It assumes that we have that knowledge independently of the principle itself. To give the liberty principle meaning, we must supplement it with some other principle or theory that specifies our rights in transactional settings.

In the third step, Kronman presents and defends a principle of distributive justice – the principle of Paretianism – as a basis for distinguishing permissible from impermissible forms of advantage-taking. This principle holds that advantage-taking in a transaction is permissible if, but only if, the person taken advantage of will be better off in the long run if this type of advantage-taking is generally allowed than if it is not. For practical reasons, however, Kronman suggests that the principle requires only that the welfare of *most* people who are taken advantage of in a particular way is increased in the long run.

Take the example of a farmer who sells his agricultural land at a gross undervalue to a buyer who, after expert investigation, has detected valuable mineral deposits beneath it. The question is: should the seller be permitted to back out of the deal, given his own ignorance and the buyer's intentional non-disclosure of the deposits? If the buyer is not entitled to reap the fruits of such deliberately acquired information, people like the buyer may be discouraged from investing time and expense in acquiring it, resulting in the production of less or inferior information of this kind. But this could impair the detection and the allocation of land for this type of use, increasing the price that everyone, including people like the farmer, must pay for a variety of products, thereby making them worse off. The Paretian principle directs us to compare two states: the welfare of most people similarly situated to the seller if buyers are not required to disclose and their welfare if buyers must do so. Only if the first is greater than the second will buyers be permitted to take advantage of sellers and withhold the information from them.

According to Kronman, autonomy theorists should accept the Paretian principle because it gives them a theory of rights that, while distributive, enables them to apply the liberty principle consistently with their underlying moral premises of individualism and equality. Unlike utilitarianism, Paretianism takes seriously the separateness of individuals by holding that no one should have to sacrifice his welfare just to promote the greater welfare of others or to advance some collective value. It is egalitarian because no one is permitted to use any advantage whatsoever at the expense of others unless the latter would be even worse off in the long run if such use was prohibited. The mere fact that someone possesses an advantage does not give him any prior claim to its use and benefit. No one has such a right. All assets and advantages are to be viewed as belonging to a common pool with respect to which everyone is to be treated equally. This baseline of equality requires that no one be granted an exclusive right to use something unless this will make those excluded better off than they would be in the absence of that right.

Kronman's argument for contract law as distributive justice is the most carefully developed contemporary account of its kind. Yet it too does not seem to be free from certain basic difficulties (Benson, 1989, pp. 1,119–45) which should be noted here, even if briefly.

First, Kronman's contention that the idea of voluntary agreement is necessarily distributive rests on his claim that the liberty principle is empty and circular. But this claim is not supported by argument. Kronman does not show that there cannot be a *non*-distributive account of rights that would free the liberty principle from both its alleged emptiness and circularity. In fact, non-distributive accounts of rights are developed with great care and rigor by Kant and Hegel, to name but two of the more important philosophical precedents.

Moreover, the Paretian principle and its moral baseline of equality seem to be in tension with certain widely accepted premises of contract law as well as with the transactional framework that is normally presupposed in the adjudication of contract disputes. For example, viewing all assets as part of a common pool in combination with the principle of Paretianism, in effect, obliges individuals to use their assets only in ways that enhance the welfare of others. But contract law does not treat individuals as under an affirmative coerceable duty to promote the well-being of others or even to take their advantage into consideration as a factor in its own right. There is only liability for misfeasance.

Nor is it clear in Kronman's theory that consent has any morally significant role to play. In law, consent seems to count in its own right as an essential condition of contractual validity. The moral import of this requirement is, at the very least, that a person has a right to exclude others from using an asset even if such exclusion diminishes their welfare. The consent requirement seems to hold and to apply in a way that is indifferent to its impact on the advantage of others. On Kronman's view, however, it is not a person's consent but the Paretian principle that settles whether one can have the exclusive use of an asset. Impact on the welfare of others is the decisive moral factor.

Finally, the kind of welfare analysis required by the Paretian principle necessarily goes beyond the immediate interaction between the parties to a given transaction. Whether a contract is valid between two parties does not depend on the nature of their interaction but on how a rule making the contract valid or invalid would affect less advantaged parties in a whole range of subsequent transactions. But it is hard to see how a court could make this determination with the required certainty. Kronman's distributive analysis does not seem to lend itself readily to decision making in the relevant public institutional setting.

The upshot of the preceding remarks is that, contrary to Kronman's claim, there is reason to doubt whether his distributive approach is consistent with the liberty and equality of persons as these values are embodied in the liberty principle. An individual party can be held to a contract that advantages the other party at his own expense simply because this may be in the long-run interests of most similarly situated, disadvantaged parties, as explained above. The crucial point is that this justification does not require or guarantee that any particular disadvantaged party actually benefits in the long term from being taken advantage of. There can simply be an uncompensated-for detriment. And this means that persons will have to sacrifice their welfare just because it is outweighed by the greater welfare of

47

others. This outcome reflects the tension inherent in any distributive approach between, on the one hand, the global and prospective analysis of welfare effects across an indefinite number of future transactions and, on the other hand, the singular and retrospective analysis of advantage-taking in a particular transaction before the court. It also brings Kronman's distributive theory closer to a welfare-maximizing efficiency analysis of contract, to which I now turn.

The economic analysis of contract law

Among contemporary theories of contract law, the economic approach provides the most detailed and comprehensive treatment of the subject. Indeed, it is currently the dominant academic theoretical perspective. Given the aims and scope of this essay, however, I will not try to present or evaluate in detail the many, often highly complex, applications of economic analysis to contract. Instead, my primary aim will be to identify some of the basic presuppositions and the main theoretical implications of this approach, taking it as a distinct and relatively self-sufficient explanation of contract. And even this discussion will have to be brief.

A basic premise of economic analysis is the assumption that if two informed parties have voluntarily transacted they must have judged that they would be better off as a result of transacting, otherwise they would not have done so (Trebilcock, 1993, p. 7). For economic analysis, which equates well-being with the satisfaction of preferences, this presumption of revealed preferences is sufficient to support the conclusion that the well-being of both parties has in fact been improved by the transaction. Economic analysis expresses this conclusion by saying that the transaction is Pareto superior. A transaction is Pareto superior if it makes at least one party better off without making the other worse off, in comparison to their pre-transaction circumstances. This conclusion crucially depends. however, on the fact that neither party has changed his mind and has come to regret the decision to transact. For then there would be two contrary revealed preferences and the welfare inference could not be made. We have already seen how autonomy-based theories deal with this possibility of regret, a possibility that is immanent to contract given the lapse of time between agreement and performance. How does economic analysis respond to it?

Pareto superiority can still be invoked. A transaction which one party has come to regret can nevertheless be Pareto superior, and thus should be enforced, if the other party receives sufficient gains from it to compensate the first and still be better off than if he had not transacted. Supposing that the second party actually compensates the first, thereby making him indifferent as between his pre- and post-transaction circumstances, one party has been made better off without any diminution to the other's well-being, thus satisfying Pareto superiority. In addition, economic analysis can invoke an alternative conception of efficiency, the Kaldor-Hicks criterion. A transaction satisfies this criterion, and therefore should be enforced, if it benefits a party sufficiently so that *hypothetically* he could fully compensate those disadvantaged by the transaction (making them indifferent as between their pre- and post-transaction circumstances) and still retain a net benefit for himself. In contrast to the Pareto criterion, Kaldor-Hicks efficiency does *not* require that the advantaged party *actually* compensate those disadvantaged. Because the better-off party need not actually compensate the disadvantaged party, the Kaldor-Hicks criterion allows one party to suffer an uncompensated detriment simply because this is outweighed by a greater sum of advantage enjoyed by the other.

Matters are not, however, so simple. Take, first, the application of Pareto superiority to a situation of regret. At the time of their agreement, both parties, we suppose, view themselves as better off. In the light of altered circumstances (a third party offers better terms, a party's tastes or priorities change), one of them regrets the transaction and wants to be released from performance. At one time the transaction is Pareto superior; at the other, this may no longer be the case: which moment should be chosen? From a legal point of view, there is no question: absent certain definite excusing circumstances, the fact of regret is normatively irrelevant and the party must still perform. Autonomy theories attempt to explain why one party's regret does not give rise to any rights or immunities against the other. The Pareto criterion, however, cannot decide between these two points in time. Each represents a set of revealed preferences that can be compared with the parties' pre-transaction circumstances. There is nothing in Pareto superiority to give priority to one set over the other. Trebilcock (1993, p. 103) has referred to this indeterminacy as the "Paretian dilemma."

Moreover, even if we select one set of preferences over the other – say, we give priority to the moment of regret – there is still the further question of which of the two criteria to apply. This comes down to the question of whether we should require the better-off party to compensate the one who is disadvantaged by the transaction. Once again, in law, the answer depends on whether the first party has violated any of the other's rights. One must show that the disadvantaged party is entitled to compensation. If not, the mere fact of regret and disadvantage establishes no claims in justice against the better-off party. But the question of whether to compensate or not cannot be settled by either criterion of efficiency (Coleman, 1988, pp. 92–4). Call this the "compensation dilemma."

The Paretian and compensation dilemmas make clear the need for normative principles to supplement the efficiency criteria. Without these principles, we lack reasonable grounds for applying Pareto superiority in a determinate way or for choosing between it and Kaldor-Hicks efficiency. By themselves, efficiency criteria cannot possibly constitute an adequate normative theory for the analysis of contract.

Economic analysis constitutes a normative approach in virtue of the fact that it invokes a supplementary moral principle. In contrast to autonomy theories, it postulates the maximization of a good, whether utility or wealth, as the aim of contract law. It is only because of this teleological element that the economic approach can purport to be a normative theory. And it is only on this basis that it can apply the efficiency criteria without falling into either the Paretian or the compensation dilemmas.

The basic method of economic analysis can be set forth briefly. What interests economic analysis in general is any act (or omission) that might further or hinder the realization of the goal of welfare maximization. From this perspective, "contract" is a totality of acts (and omissions) that may be relevant in this way. These acts may occur at any point along a continuum stretching from before an agreement is concluded to after performance is due. How far back or forward the analysis should go depends in any given case on the balance of benefits and costs of doing so. Moreover, no act or set of acts has, in principle, special significance in comparison to any other. Here also, the importance of an act depends entirely on the (quantitative) extent of its contribution (positive or negative) to the realization of the goal. This contrasts with the legal point of view which as a matter of principle ascribes qualitatively special normative significance to certain categories of acts (for example, those constituting offer and acceptance) and not to others (such as invitations to treat).

More specifically, the economic analysis of contract law is centrally interested in how a legal rule (actual or proposed) influences the acts and omissions of parties insofar as these relate to the goal of maximum net social benefit. It asks: compared to alternative rules, does a particular rule of contract create more effective and efficient incentives for welfare-maximizing behavior? To bring out and to illustrate some of the central features of this inquiry, I will now briefly consider one application of the economic approach, namely, the discussion by Charles Goetz and Robert Scott (1980) of an optimal enforcement scheme for promising. I select the Goetz–Scott analysis because it is theoretically instructive in a number of important respects.

First, the authors set out clearly and explicitly the basic method and premises of normative economic analysis as a teleological theory. Second, they carefully identify a set of welfare interests and transaction-related decisions at the time of contract formation that bear importantly on the goal of welfare maximization. Goetz and Scott emphasize that too often economic analysis has focussed exclusively on parties' behavior at the time of breach or performance, in this way assuming that the promise has already been made. From the economic perspective, however, this limitation is unjustified: "[t]he decision to enforce promises, and the subsequent choice of remedy, does not merely mold the performance behavior of the parties [but] also shapes the nature and amount of promise-making activity." Their central thesis is that the quality and extent of promise-making activity are crucially important to the goal of welfare-maximization. Moreover, the authors explicitly identify the welfare interests and transaction decisions of the parties in light of a basic conceptual distinction between the promise itself and the future transfer that it announces. The promise itself, they emphasize, is just the production of information about expected future behavior. The task is to identify interests and decisions that are associated with this information-imparting function. Third and finally, while the authors' proposed economic analysis leads at the ideal level of principle to conclusions that are at variance with certain well-established parts of contract doctrine (such as the normal rule of expectation damages), they argue that much of current contract doctrine is best explained as the most efficient regime for implementing the conclusions of ideal theory, once the costs and benefits of administration are taken into account. In this way, they try to close the gap between law and theory.

What, concretely, are the kinds of interests and transactional decisions that Goetz and Scott associate with the making of promises?

Taking the promisee first and keeping in mind the specific information-imparting function of promising, the authors argue that the promisee's positive main interest is in "beneficial reliance" and that his principal transactional decision is whether, and how much, to rely on the promise. Suppose, for example, someone promises to give me a sum of money two months hence. I may, in reliance on the promise, revise my consumption habits during the interim two months, say, by spending more money during that period than I would have otherwise done in the knowledge that after two months I will receive the promised sum. By conveying to me information about the future, the promise enables me to adapt my consumption schedule in a way that is different from what I would do if at the end of two months and without any advance notice, the sum of money were simply transferred to me. By deciding to rely on the promise and change my consumption schedule, I am able to achieve a higher intertemporal level of satisfaction compared to the situation in which I receive the wealth without the advance notice provided by the promise. This adaptive gain the authors call "beneficial reliance." In their view, the production of such gains is perhaps the main social rationale for promising. This, of course presupposes that the promise is kept. Where it is not, the promissory information turns out to be misleading and adaptive behavior by the promisee may result in his being made worse off than if he had never relied on the promise in the first place. (In our example, I do not receive the promised money at the end of two months, leaving me with a shortfall necessitating a cutback in consumption that may not be offset by the increased benefit I received by spending more money during the preceding two months.) This diminution in welfare is called "detrimental reliance." The principal decision a promisee must make is whether to rely on the promise in light of the possibility of non-performance and hence of detrimental reliance loss. The promisee must weigh in any given situation his prospective beneficial reliance gain (probability of performance X value of gain) against his prospective detrimental reliance loss (probability of breach X value of loss). If the latter exceeds the former, he should, as a rational person, take self-protective measures, such as limiting his reliance on the promise. But in addition to reducing the risk of detrimental reliance losses, this also entails concomitant reductions in possible gains from beneficial reliance – the main welfare interest to be promoted by the practice of promising.

As for the promisor, his main interest is in the welfare implications for him of "regret contingencies." A good-faith promisor knows *ex ante* that although he intends to perform, certain circumstances may arise in which he may come to regret having made the promise and may want to breach, if this is costless to him. (Costs of breaching include "self-sanctions," such as guilt or empathetic participation in promisee's disappointment, or "external sanctions," whether extra-legal or legal). A regret contingency is thus *any* future circumstances that would motivate the promisor to breach, if this were costless to him. A promisor knows *ex ante* that when a regret contingency occurs, he will have the option of bearing the loss that he will incur by going through with performance or of breaching and accepting the costs associated therewith. A rational promisor will choose the cheaper of these regret losses. This is the promisor's main transactional decision. If prospective performance loss (or, in other words, prospective benefit from non-performance) is greater than the costs of breaching, the promisor can either qualify the scope of the promise (by inserting excusing conditions) or decide simply not to make the promise at all. Either response will lead to reductions in the promisee's beneficial reliance. If the costs of breaching are greater, the promisor may want to take "reassurance" measures that communicate effectively to the promisee (whether in the contract terms or otherwise) that the promisor *will* perform and that the promisee should definitely rely on him, leading to increases in beneficial reliance.

Absent from the promisor's calculus of losses (except in a derivative and limited way), is however, appropriate inclusion of the promisee's detrimental reliance loss if breach occurs and other costs (for example, loss of beneficial reliance gains) that the promisee may sustain by adapting to the possibility of non-performance. But these are real costs which must be taken into account in ascertaining the net social benefit of promissory enforcement. According to Goetz and Scott, the primary function of an optimal enforcement scheme is to ensure that the promisor's costs of promising be adjusted to reflect any external effects on the promisee. The aim is to encourage informed and efficient cost-reducing behavior by both parties. On the basis of a complex and careful analysis of the costs and benefits of promissory activity in the two main cases of non-reciprocal and reciprocal promises (which themselves are distinguished on economic grounds), the authors propose an optimal damage formula. It is meant to encourage promisors to make promises that produce net beneficial reliance, but to do this in a way that does not induce the promisors to take excessive self-protective measures that reduce either the reliability of their promises or the number of promises they actually make.

It is time to take stock of some central features of the Goetz–Scott analysis, viewed as illustrative of the economic approach. To begin, economic analysis is emphatically *prospective*: the question is how future promise-making behavior is influenced by rules of promissory enforcement (Goetz and Scott, 1980, p. 4). This prospective orientation, which we already saw in Kronman's analysis, is implied by the teleological (or goal-directed) character of the economic theory. It contrasts with the retrospective orientation of the legal point of view in settling the rights and duties of parties to a particular past transaction now before a court.

Further, the Goetz–Scott analysis brings out an important question about the completeness and generality of the principles proposed by economic theory. While the authors seek with reason to correct economic analysis' traditional and exclusive focus on performance-breach behavior by extending the analysis to promise-making activity, it is not enough that the principles regulating the different areas of conduct be justified in isolation of each other: they must be combined in one analytical framework. There is but one goal, namely, the maximization of social welfare, and all the principles have the same relation to it. If there is a multiplicity of principles going to the different aspects of transacting behavior, one must show how each principle is optimal when combined with every other. Nothing short of this can satisfy the normative tendency of a teleological theory. This task is particularly urgent for economic theory. Not only is the work of combination hardly begun. The natural tendency of economic analysis is to focus on differences in types of transactional circumstances. Economic studies like Polinsky's (1989, ch. 5), for example, suggest that "in general, there does not exist a breach of contract remedy [whether expectation, reliance, or restitution damages] that is efficient with respect to both the breach decision and the reliance decision." What is efficient for one objective (for example, expectation damages for the breach decision or reliance damages for the reliance decision) is inefficient for the other. Whether expectation or reliance damages should be available cannot be definitely answered as a matter of principle of general application – as we find in legal doctrine – but only as an assessment of policy that depends crucially on the relative (quantitative) importance in efficiency terms of the breach and reliance decisions in each particular case. Until this is actually ascertained, economic theory cannot say which measure of damages is appropriate in any given circumstance. And this determination must precede the effort to combine and generalize.

The last, and, for present purposes, the most important feature that I wish to note is the particular way in which economic analysis conceives the parties' interests. Going one step further than Kronman's Paretian principle which requires that the pursuit of self-interest benefit (most of) the disadvantaged, economic analysis emancipates these interests completely from *any* normative constraint that imposes on the parties requirements of mutual fair-dealing or that sets limits to the extent of their mutual accountability. Interests are defined solely by each party's preferences; parties are viewed as separate rational maximizers of interests. Each person's interests and preferences, without reference to any antecedent normative criterion, are given equal weight *ex ante* in the calculus of maximum *net* social benefit. But this calculus can also allow, and indeed require, the sacrifice of one person's interests if his loss is outweighed by the greater sum of advantage enjoyed by others. Thus, the Goetz–Scott theory gives full standing to the promisor's regret contingency costs whether or not his regret is fair or reasonable *vis-à-vis* the promisee. Similarly, the promisee's beneficial and detrimental reliance interests are accorded full standing whether or not the promisor has done anything to assume responsibility and thus to be held accountable for what is, after all, the promisee's own voluntary decision. The promisee's reliance is "reasonable" only in the sense that it is probabilistically rational.

Here again the contrast with the legal point of view is striking. In attributing to the parties rights and obligations, the law purports to articulate fair and reasonable (as opposed to merely rational) standards of conduct and these requirements categorically constrain the claims that parties may legitimately make against each other. In addition, as I have emphasized, the law invokes a notion of limited mutual accountability that makes the parties liable only for misfeasance, even if a more extensive liability might be productive of greater net social benefit. In itself, the fact that one party may have decided to rely on another's representation – no matter how rational such reliance may be as a "good bet" – does not in legal contemplation give the first any entitlement against the second. Something more – an assumption of responsibility by the second *vis-à-vis* the first – is necessary.

Goetz and Scott (1980, pp. 1,288ff) freely acknowledge the existence of a significant gap between their conclusions and current patterns of contract doctrine.

Whereas they propose, for example, a reliance measure of recovery and argue that gratuitous promises should be enforced where breach results in net detrimental reliance losses, the law gives expectation damages and treats promises unsupported by consideration as contractually unenforceable. As already noted, they attempt to bridge this gap by suggesting that current doctrine may be rationalized as the most efficient practical way of implementing the ideal conclusions reached by economic analysis, once administrative costs are factored in. What I wish to emphasize, however, is that this refinement does not overcome the gaps between law and theory referred to in the preceding paragraphs. Contract law presents itself as a point of view constituted by a set of principles and categories that articulate certain basic normative ideas. These ideas are specific to contract law as one part of private law, in contrast to other domains of the normative, such as public law, morality, or political life. At no point does economic analysis make the legal point of view with its normative ideas the immediate object of its analysis. It does not, for instance, investigate, as Sidgwick (1929, chs 4–8) did for utilitarian theory, whether the principle of limited legal accountability might be justified on efficiency grounds within a value-maximizing framework. Instead, it begins with interests and preferences and its sole normative principle is welfare-maximization. At most, economic analysis applies this framework directly to the bare conclusions of contract doctrine detached from the normative ideas which give them life and meaning from a legal point of view. It hopes to show that these conclusions coincide with what economics requires *from its own standpoint*. Even if economic analysis were to become complete in its own terms, it is doubtful that it could legitimately claim to be a theory of contract law as opposed to an economics of transactions.

Concluding remark

In the present writer's opinion, this gap between law and theory is the single most important characteristic feature of contract theorizing since Fuller. While the gap is arguably most explicit and therefore most visible in economic analysis, I have suggested that it is also present in different ways in every theory discussed, beginning with Fuller's. And as I shall now indicate by way of conclusion, the resolution of this gap must be the first item on the agenda for future theoretical reflection about contract.

All reflection begins with an object given to it. Theoretical reflection about contract *law* presupposes therefore an object given to us that embodies the *legal point of view*. That there is such a point of view, none of the authors discussed and certainly no lawyer will want to deny. The first task of theory, then, is to uncover and to present this point of view. A theory that fails to begin in this way condemns itself to being irrelevant as a theory of law. Accordingly, we must provisionally set aside existing contract theories that are one step removed from this starting point and make a fresh beginning by examining the public legal culture of contract (judicial decisions, authoritative scholarly interpretations, and so forth) to see whether it yields a conception of contract that is at once coherent and initially plausible. More specifically, we look to well-established parts of contract doctrine and try to make explicit the basic normative ideas underlying them. On this basis, we attempt to construct the conception of contract that fits best. Such a conception may be called a public conception of contract because it is rooted in the public legal culture. It provides us with a preliminary shared object for theoretical reflection. It makes explicit the legal point of view.

This modest yet absolutely indispensable first step has yet to be taken by contemporary contract theory. What a public conception of contract might look like is a question that goes well beyond the scope of the present essay. This much, however, should be said about the way to a public conception. If we can derive any general insight from contemporary contract theory, it is that we must reconsider with fresh eyes the basic but unargued-for premise, not only of Fuller's work but also of most theory since then, that a contract does not give the promisee anything that is juridically "his" prior to performance. We must see whether, after all, the basic doctrines and normative ideas of contract law might be best accounted for on the contrary hypothesis. The simple but decisive question for contract theory still awaits a satisfactory answer: can the long and well-established legal view that expectation damages are distinctive of contract and genuinely compensatory be justified in a way that coheres with the main parts of contract doctrine and that draws on the basic normative ideas of contract law, most importantly the contrast between misfeasance and nonfeasance? In virtue of its structure and presuppositions, the idea of contract as a transfer of rights, presented most recently by Barnett and developed more fully in the philosophical tradition to which I referred earlier, seems particularly well-suited to help us formulate a conception of contract that meets these criteria (Benson, 1995b). Whether we can get beyond the present paradoxical situation in which contract theory finds itself, as noted in the introductory paragraph of this essay, will depend in the first instance on our success in constructing a public conception of contract.

The author would like to thank Richard Craswell for helpful discussion of the economic analysis of contract and Gregory Bordan for written comments on the draft.

Bibliography

Atiyah, P. S. 1981: *Promises, Morals, and Law*. Oxford: Clarendon Press.
—— 1986: *Essays on Contract*. Oxford: Clarendon Press.
Barnett, R. E. 1986: A consent theory of contract. *Columbia Law Review*, 86, 269–321.
Benson. P. E. 1989: Abstract right and the possibility of a nondistributive conception of contract: Hegel and contemporary contract theory. *Cardozo Law Journal*, 10, 1,077–198.
—— 1992: The basis of corrective justice and its relation to distributive justice. *Iowa Law Review*, 77, 515–624.
—— 1995: The basis for excluding liability for economic loss in tort law. In D. G. Owen (ed.), *The Philosophical Foundations of Tort Law*, Oxford: Oxford University Press.

—— 1996: The idea of a public basis of justification for contract. *Osgoode Hall Law Journal*, 33.

Coleman, J. 1988: *Markets, Morals and the Law*. Cambridge: Cambridge University Press.

Craswell, R. 1989: Contract, default rules, and the philosophy of promising. *Michigan Law Review*, 88, 489–529.

Fried, C. 1981: *Contract as Promise: a theory of contractual obligation*. Cambridge, Mass.: Harvard University Press.

Fuller, L. L. and Perdue, Jr, W. W. 1936: The reliance interest in contract damages. *Yale Law Journal*, 46, 52–96, 373–420.

Goetz, C. J. and Scott, R. E. 1980: Enforcing promises: an examination of the basis of contract. *Yale Law Journal*, 89, 1,261–322.

Gordley, C. J. 1981: Equality in exchange. *California Law Review*, 69, 1,587–656.

—— 1991: *The Philosophical Origins of Modern Contract Doctrine*. Oxford: Clarendon Press.

Grotius, H. [1625] 1925: *The Law of War and Peace*, tr. F. W. Kelsey, Oxford: Clarendon Press.

Hegel, G. W. F. [1821] 1952: *Hegel's Philosophy of Right*, tr. T. M. Knox, Oxford: Clarendon Press.

Kant, I. [1797] 1991: *The Metaphysics of Morals*, tr. M. Gregor, Cambridge: Cambridge University Press.

Kronman, A. T. 1980: Contract law and distributive justice. *Yale Law Journal*, 89, 472–511.

Polinsky, A. M. 1989: *An Introduction to Law and Economics*. Boston: Little, Brown, 2nd edn.

Raz, J. 1972: Voluntary obligations and normative powers: II. *Aristotelian Society*, Suppl. Vol. 46, 79–101.

—— 1977: Promises and obligations. In P. Hacker and J. Raz (eds), *Law, Morality and Society*, Oxford: Oxford University Press.

—— 1982: Promises in morality and law. *Harvard Law Review*, 95, 916–38.

Sidgwick, H. 1929: *The Elements of Politics*. London: Macmillan & Co.

Trebilcock, M. J. 1993: *The Limits of Freedom of Contract*. Cambridge, Mass.: Harvard University Press.

3

Tort law

STEPHEN R. PERRY

The law of torts imposes legal liability on persons who in certain ways have caused certain kinds of harm to other persons. In the case of some torts – for example nuisance, which is concerned with interference with the use and enjoyment of land – the usual legal remedy that follows a finding of liability is an injunction, that is, an order issued by the court requiring the defendant to stop engaging in the harmful activity (or otherwise to put matters right). But the more common remedy in a torts case, and the one that typifies tort law as a legal regime, is an award of monetary damages. Damages is a backward-looking remedy that is intended to *compensate* the plaintiff for the harm suffered. The idea is to put the plaintiff, to the extent that it is possible to do so with money, in the position that he or she would have been in had the tort not occurred. The heart of tort law, then, is a legal obligation to pay compensation for harm caused, where the obligation is owed by the person who caused the harm directly to the person who suffered it. But not all harms, and not all ways of causing harm, give rise to such an obligation. Tortious liability is a function of both the nature of the defendant's conduct and the nature of the harm to the plaintiff that that conduct caused. When we focus on the defendant's conduct we ask what *standard of liability* should be employed to assess it, and when we focus on the plaintiff's harm we ask whether the harm was *legally cognizable*, or constituted interference with a *protected interest*.

Many different torts are recognized by the common law, and the range of protected interests is very wide. Since it is far from clear that a single principle or theoretical justification could comprehend the law of torts in its entirety, we will here take the course that is tacitly adopted in most discussions of tort theory. We will focus on two protected interests in particular, namely, the interest in life and security of the person (that is, the interest in avoiding personal injury or death), and the interest in preserving the physical integrity of one's tangible property, both real and personal (that is, the interest in avoiding physical damage to or destruction of one's material holdings). This limitation seems justified because these two interests have always, historically speaking, been of central concern to tort law, and intuitively they also appear to be the most important interests that tort law protects. Let me therefore refer to them as "the core protected interests," or "core interests" for short.

Against what sort of conduct should the core interests be protected? *Intention* offers one possible standard of liability. A defendant is said to intend harm if she either desires to bring harm about, or she is substantially certain that harm will ensue as a (possibly undesired) side-effect of her activity. Unintentional harm can thus be defined as harm that the defendant does not desire to bring about, and that she is not substantially certain will occur, that is, harm of which it can be said that there is only a *risk* that it will occur. There are two standards of liability that are potentially applicable to unintentional harm, namely, *negligence* and *strict liability*. The negligence standard requires the defendant to act with "due" or "reasonable" care if her activities might foreseeably harm the plaintiff. What constitutes due or reasonable care we will consider later. But it should be remarked that the negligence standard can be either "subjective" – based on the defendant's own awareness of and ability to avoid imposing risk – or "objective" – based on a hypothetical "reasonable" person's awareness of and ability to avoid imposing risk. As a first approximation, strict liability can be said to hold the defendant liable for all harm (to a core protected interest) that his conduct *caused*.

Contemporary tort law protects the core interests against both intentional and unintentional harm. In the case of intentional harm, protection is provided primarily, although not exclusively, by the various forms of the tort of trespass. In the case of unintentional harm, the basic tort is negligence. The *tort* of negligence applies the objective negligence standard (that is, negligence understood as a particular standard of liability) both to the two core interests and to certain other protected interests as well. But tort law also recognizes a number of exceptions to the hegemony of negligence: under some circumstances it protects the core interests by means of strict liability instead. The most important of these exceptions is the strict standard that has been applied in the United States (but not in most other common law jurisdictions) in products liability actions, that is, actions brought against a product's manufacturer or seller for harms to person or property that were caused by a defect in the product. Another set of exceptions imposes strict liability for harm caused by certain ultra-hazardous activities, or by certain substances or entities that are safe when confined but pose serious dangers if they escape from control. Although there are differences both in conceptualization of legal doctrine and, to a lesser degree, in substance, the law of delict in civil law systems is broadly similar to the common law of torts, as just described.

With this thumbnail sketch of the relevant legal doctrines in mind, we can now proceed to consider the main theoretical justifications that have been offered for the law of torts as it applies to the core interests. There are two main categories of theory that have been put forward. Theories in the first category hold that tort law does and should serve the interests of society as a whole, where among contemporary theorists the interests of society are understood almost exclusively in utilitarian or, more commonly, economic terms. I shall accordingly refer to these as the "economic" theories. Theories in the second category, by contrast, are concerned with the rights persons have in *justice* to be compensated for the harm they have suffered at the hands of others. These theories I shall label "justice-based." In subsequent sections three types of economic theory will be discussed, based on the core ideas of internalization, deterrence, and loss-spreading. We will then consider two types of justice-based theories. These take as their respective starting-points the two forms of justice that were first distinguished by Aristotle, namely, distributive justice and corrective justice.

It bears mention that all economic theories must at some point take account of the costs of administering the tort system (or whatever alternative to the tort system might be adopted). For example, according to conventional wisdom, a standard of strict liability is simpler and therefore cheaper to administer than a negligence standard, but some and perhaps all of these savings might be offset by the greater quantity of litigation that could be expected to take place under strict liability. The minimization of administrative costs is theoretically a straightforward matter, but its practical implementation will often depend on information that could be very difficult to obtain. Accordingly, in order to avoid empirical inquiries that will not contribute to the theoretical understanding of tort law, the issue of administrative costs will, for the most part, not be considered in this essay.

Economic theories: internalization

Internalization theories hold that "externalities" – costs that initially fall on A because the activity of B has caused him harm – should be "internalized": the costs to A should be transferred to B, the causally responsible party. Drawing on the received economic wisdom concerning the treatment of externalities that had first been propounded by the English economist A. C. Pigou in the 1920s, Guido Calabresi argued in an early article that "resource allocation" – his term for internalization – was necessary to prevent the distortion of market prices that would occur if A were forced, in effect, to subsidize B by bearing some of the costs of producing B's goods: "The function of prices is to reflect the actual costs of competing goods" (Calabresi, 1961, p. 502, cf. p. 514). The point of tort law, on this view, is to accomplish internalization by imposing legal liability for harm on *the* actor or enterprise who caused it (Calabresi, 1961, p. 533). Internalization thus supports a standard of strict liability. (Recall our preliminary characterization of strict liability as, very simply, liability for harm caused.) Historically, internalization has figured as one of several theoretical justifications offered for the adoption in the United States of strict products liability (Priest, 1985, pp. 463, 481).

As a justification for tort law generally, and for strict products liability in particular, internalization has largely fallen into disfavor. The reason for this is almost entirely attributable to the work of Ronald Coase. In what has turned out to be one of the most influential articles on the economic analysis of law, Coase argued, first, that internalization was not, considered in its own terms, a coherent notion; and second, that private market transactions would, under certain circumstances, bring about the economically efficient allocation of resources even if governmental agencies such as courts made no attempt to internalize costs (Coase, 1960). Traditional welfare economics had assumed, following Pigou, that the economically desirable result would only be achieved if the government intervened by, say, imposing a tax, or adopting the appropriate liability rule in tort.

59

Consider first Coase's conceptual critique of internalization (a term, it should be noted, that he did not himself use). Coase argued that it made no sense, in typical cases of harmful interaction, to speak of one party as *the* cause of the other's harm. To illustrate, take the example of crop damage that results when a railway's loco-motives emit sparks. The activity of the railway is not properly identified as the unique cause of the crop damage, since that damage would not have occurred without the actions of *both* the railway (in running trains that give off sparks) *and* the farmer (in planting the crops she did, where she did). "If we are to discuss the problem in terms of causation, both parties cause the damage" (Coase, 1960, p. 13). From this it follows that internalization, which was defined earlier as the assignment of costs to *the* activity that caused them, is not a determinate notion. Coase at one point in his article claimed, rather obscurely, that harm is "recipro-cal" in nature, and on the basis of that remark he is sometimes accused of making a conceptual error about causation (Coleman, 1988, p. 80). In fact, however, he was just adopting a standard analysis of causation, according to which an event A is a cause of effect B if A is a necessary condition of B's occurrence (Perry, 1992, pp. 465–6). This is the understanding of causation presupposed by, for example, the traditional "but-for" test in tort law.

This brings us to Coase's second main point, which is that private market trans-actions can often bring about the economically efficient result without govern-ment intervention. Coase argued that the traditional approach of welfare economics, based on cost internalization – in Coase's terms, on the idea that ac-tivities should bear their "social" as well as their "private" costs – asked the wrong economic question. The proper question is not, which of two interacting activities caused the harm that one of them suffered, but rather, how is the total value of the production of both activities to be maximized? Coase further argued that, under certain conditions, the total value of production would be maximized by private bargains. The most important of these conditions are, first, that there be clearly defined and alienable legal entitlements, and second, that the costs of striking a bargain – the so-called transaction costs – be sufficiently low. The claim that value-maximizing bargains will be struck under these conditions has come to be known as the Coase Theorem. (For a more complete statement of the theorem, see Coleman, 1988, pp. 69–76.)

To illustrate, let us revert to our railway/crops example. Assume that there is just one affected farmer, that she is legally entitled to an injunction that would prohibit the railway from emitting sparks, and that spark control is not feasible. Suppose the crops that would be burnt represent a net annual profit of $600 to the farmer, whereas being able to run its trains along that line increases the railway's net profits by $1,000 per year. According to the Coase Theorem, the railway will buy from the farmer her entitlement to an injunction for an amount between $600 and $1,000, since this will make both parties better off. Such a bargain will maximize the total value of production from both activities by giving effect to the optimal solution, namely, trains and burnt crops. Assume next that the figures are reversed. Now no bargain will be struck, since the optimal solution, no trains and unburnt crops, has already been attained: the total value of production cannot be increased. Analogous examples can easily be constructed on the assumption that the railway has a legal right to emit sparks. So long as transaction costs are less than $400, the initial assignment of the legal entitlement will affect the relative wealth of the parties but not the total value of production. Of course, a more sophisticated economic model would allow for variations in the levels of farming and railroading, and would locate the optimal solution at the point where the marginal profit from railroading equals the marginal damage to crops from sparks (Coleman, 1988, p. 70). To put the point another way, the Coasean bargain would set the levels of farming and railroading in such a way that any further farming would be more costly than forgone railroading, and any further railroading would be more costly than forgone farming. But for present purposes we can ignore this complication.

Coase's work led to the effective abandonment of internalization theories of tort law. Calabresi, for example, reshaped his resource-allocation theory into what he came to call a theory of general deterrence, which will be discussed below. Some theorists remain willing to speak of strict liability as a method of cost internalization, but internalization must now be regarded as a result to be justified rather than a justification in its own right. Most such theorists regard the appropriate source of justification as deterrence, and it is to theories of this kind that we now turn.

Economic theories: deterrence

The abandonment of internalization theories, instigated by Coase, shifted attention among economic theorists to the idea that tort law is a mechanism for deterring economically inefficient behavior. One starting-point for this development was the observation that transaction costs are often high enough to prevent value-maximizing private bargains from being struck. Market failure of this type is likely, for example, in situations of possible unintentional harm to a core interest, since it is ordinarily difficult to know in advance the identity of a person with whom you might have an accident. (Here, transaction costs take the form of information costs.) What tort law must do, according to deterrence theorists, is to set liability rules so as to give persons incentives to behave in value-maximizing ways.

In fact, most contemporary deterrence theories do not aim directly at value-maximization but adopt instead the complementary goal of cost-minimization (or *total* cost minimization, as I shall call it). The idea here is *not* to avoid as many accidents as possible, but rather to minimize the sum of accident costs and the costs of preventing accidents (Calabresi, 1970, p. 26). More precisely, the idea is to minimize the sum of *expected accident losses* and the costs of *taking care*. Expected accident loss can be defined as the probability that a given type of accident will occur, multiplied by the magnitude of the loss that would result if the accident did occur ($P \times L$). The cost of taking care can be understood as the cost of taking steps to reduce or eliminate the probability that an accident of the type in question will occur. (In accordance with the usage first initiated by Judge Learned Hand and still widely observed, I shall represent the cost of taking care by "B," which stands for "burden of precautions.") For purposes of the present discussion we shall follow the usual practice of deterrence theorists and make the admittedly unrealistic assumption that the parties to be deterred are risk neutral, which means that so long as the amount of the expected accident loss (PL) remains constant they are indifferent to whether the magnitude of the potential loss (L) is large or small. The usual justification for this assumption is that people who are fully insured will behave as if they are risk neutral (Landes and Posner, 1987, pp. 57–8; but see the more extensive discussion in Shavell, 1987, pp. 206–61).

We begin by considering the negligence standard for unintentional harm. Let us return to our railway/farming example, but this time adding the assumption that transaction costs between the parties are, for whatever reason, too high to permit a Coasean bargain to be struck. Suppose that the expected loss to crops from fires started by locomotives is $1,000, and that the only available method of taking care is for the railway to install a spark arrester that will reduce the expected loss to zero. In other words, taking care is an all-or-nothing matter. From an economic perspective, negligence is understood as the failure to take care when the cost of taking care is less than the expected loss, that is, when $B < PL$. This is the famous Learned Hand formulation of "due" or "reasonable" care in negligence law; it is so called because it was first propounded by Judge Hand in the case of *U.S.* v. *Carroll Towing* (1947), 159 F. 2d 169. Given our assumption that only the railway is in a position to take precautions, liability in our example should be imposed, under a negligence rule, if and only if the railway did not install the spark arrester, the farmer suffers crop damage caused by sparks from the locomotive, and the spark arrester would have cost less than the expected loss of $1,000. This rule will give the railway, as an economically rational actor, an incentive to install the spark arrester when and only when the cost of doing so is less than the expected loss to crops, thereby achieving total cost minimization.

We have assumed that the cost of taking care is an all-or-nothing matter, and that only the railway is in a position to take care. Both assumptions are unrealistic. If we were to drop the first assumption and suppose instead that taking care was a matter of degree, so that, for example, spark-arresting capacity could be purchased incrementally, then the Learned Hand test would have to be applied at the margin rather than to total costs. On this approach, the optimal level of care is reached when the marginal cost of care – that is, the cost of one more increment of spark-arresting capacity – is equal to the reduction in expected crop loss that would result if that increment were in fact purchased (Posner, 1992, pp. 164–5). But while the proper theoretical formulation of the Learned Hand test requires this marginal form, nothing will be lost for present purposes if we continue to make the simplifying assumption that care is an all-or-nothing matter.

Consider, then, our second unrealistic assumption: that only the railway is in a position to take care. Suppose the railway could eliminate the expected crop loss of $1,000 by installing a spark arrester for $700, but the farmer could also completely avoid the expected loss by planting a fire-resistant crop at a net extra cost to her of $500. Clearly, the goal of achieving *optimal* care – that is, the goal of achieving the level of care on the part of the railway, the farmer or both that will bring about total cost minimization – requires that the farmer take care rather than the railway. One way to create the appropriate incentive for the farmer would be to add to the law a defence of contributory negligence. A first approximation of the proper economic understanding of this defence would deny the plaintiff recovery when she was herself negligent in the Learned Hand sense. This would work for the example just given, but not if we reverse the figures and suppose that it would cost the railway $500 to take care, and the farmer $700. Since the farmer would be denied recovery, she would have an incentive to spend $700 to eliminate the expected loss; the railway, on the other hand, would have no incentive to achieve the same result at a cost of $200 less.

This problem is solved, however, if we define due care for both parties as the level of care that results in optimal care being taken – this is, recall, the level of care by either or both parties that achieves total cost minimization – *if* the other party is exercising due care (Posner, 1992, pp. 169–70). (It can be demonstrated that due care thus defined yields a unique equilibrium, that is, a pattern of conduct to which each party will adhere if the other party adheres to it: Shavell, 1987, pp. 10, 37–8). Due care for the railway will then require spending $500, whereas due care for the farmer will be zero; there is no room for the defence of contributory negligence to apply. At common law, contributory negligence was traditionally a complete bar to recovery, and the economic version of the defence just described is also all-or-nothing. Most common law jurisdictions have, however, replaced contributory negligence by what is known in the United States as comparative negligence, which requires that the loss be shared among the parties in proportion to their respective degrees of fault. (In England and the Commonwealth, the term "contributory negligence" has come to be applied to this apportionment approach.) Perhaps surprisingly, the parties will be led to take optimal care under comparative as well as under contributory negligence. The reason for this is that, given our definition of due care, party A will reason under either regime that if party B takes due care then A *alone* will be found negligent if he or she fails to take care, and hence will have to bear the full loss. For this same reason, formal defences of contributory and comparative negligence, in fact, become *superfluous* in a negligence system (Shavell, 1987, pp. 15–16).

Another consequence of adopting this definition of due care is that optimal care will be achieved not just in cases of "alternative care" – cases in which total cost minimization requires one or the other, but not both parties, to take care – but also in cases of "joint care" – cases in which total cost minimization requires both parties to take some care (Posner, 1992, p. 170; Shavell, 1987, pp. 17–18). We can illustrate the notion of joint care if we suppose that the expected crop loss of $1,000 in our example could be completely avoided if the railway were to run its trains slightly more slowly, at a cost of $200, and if the farmer were also to move her crop back a hundred yards, again at a cost of $200. If we suppose that either of these actions would be completely ineffective by itself, optimal care can only be attained by joint action; due care for each of the parties would thus require an expenditure of $200. If the railway spends $200 on care then the entire expected loss of $1,000 will fall on the farmer unless *she* expends the $200 that due care demands of her and vice versa. (As was remarked earlier, this is true even if there is no formal defence of contributory negligence.) The expected loss would thus be avoided at a total cost of $400, which is less than what we assumed would have to be expended by either party acting alone to achieve the same result ($500 for one of them, $700 for the other).

So much for the economic understanding of negligence. What about strict liability? As Coase, in effect, taught us, strict liability cannot coherently be understood as liability simply for losses caused. For this reason, it requires a prior division of the relevant universe of persons into "injurers" and "victims" (Shavell, 1987, p. 5). This is not true for a negligence regime, however, which can simply hold everyone to a well-defined standard of conduct. Moreover, under a negligence regime the residuary loss-bearers – the persons who must bear the losses that it is not cost-effective to avoid – are victims, and the category of victims is determined prior to and independently of the law; its boundaries are set "naturally," simply by the empirical fact of where the loss falls. But under a rule of strict liability the residuary loss-bearers are injurers, and as Coase's work made clear, this is not a natural category; since actions of both parties to a harmful interaction are properly regarded as causes of the harm, "injurers" must be defined by the law. This is fairly straightforward when, as in our railway/farming example, harm is consistently suffered by only one of two interacting activities rather than by both: the farmer is always the victim, and this makes the railway the inevitable candidate for the status of injurer. But the artificial nature of this division must not be forgotten; consider, for example, the difficulty of dividing in advance the universe of drivers into "injurers" and "victims," and hence of applying a standard of strict liability to accidents between automobiles (that is, accidents not involving pedestrians).

A simple rule of strict liability for railways and farmers would impose all losses on the railway, regardless of which party, if either, had been negligent in the Learned Hand sense. Even though it would bear losses even when it had not been negligent, the railway, as a rational economic actor, would still take care when and only when $B < PL$. But a rule of this kind would not achieve optimal care, since it would not give the farmer appropriate incentives to take precautions. To attain optimal care we must add a defence of contributory negligence, which requires the farmer to bear the loss if she does not exercise due care in the sense defined earlier. In the case of strict liability, then, contributory negligence is *not* superfluous. Both strict liability with a contributory negligence defence, and the negligence standard with or without that defence, will, by inducing the parties individually to take due care, lead to the attainment of optimal care (Shavell, 1987, p. 16). This does not mean, however, that the two regimes are economically equivalent. The reason for this is that on the proper marginal understanding of due care and expected loss, the probability of an accident can be lowered *either* by taking more care *or* by engaging in a reduced level of the activity (Shavell, 1987, pp. 23–6, 29–32). Theoretically, a court could incorporate consideration of activity level into a determination of due care, but this would be very difficult; it would mean, for example, ascertaining how much driving would be socially

64

optimal on the part of a defendant driver, and not just whether he had taken the appropriate degree of care in driving on this particular occasion.

Given the practical impossibility of courts directly determining the appropriate degree of activity level, this is something that must be left up to the parties themselves. The difficulty is that tort law can only give someone an incentive to adjust his activity level by requiring him to bear the residuary accident costs – these are, recall, the losses it is not cost-effective to avoid – but victims and injurers cannot *both* be residuary loss-bearers. Since injurers are the residuary loss-bearers under strict liability, they will be induced by this rule not only to exercise due care but also to adopt levels of activity that are socially optimal (that is, utility-maximizing), whereas victims might be led to participate in *their* activities to an excessive, non-optimal degree. Conversely, since victims are the residuary loss-bearers in a negligence regime, they will, under that regime, engage in their activities only to the optimal extent, whereas injurers' levels of activity might well be excessive. Since it is impossible for a single liability rule to achieve optimal activity levels for both injurers and victims, Steven Shavell suggests that the choice between negligence and strict liability depends on whether, in the particular context, it is more important to control injurers' or victims' conduct. He thinks this may help to explain why the activities the law holds to a strict standard tend to be unusually risky or hazardous (Shavell, 1987, pp. 29–32).

It should be noted that there is another economic conception of strict liability, in addition to the "injurer liability" model just considered. This second conception, which was first described by Calabresi (1970, pp. 135–73) and which has been invoked by him particularly in connection with strict products liability, calls for accident losses to be placed on the "cheapest cost-avoider." The cheapest cost-avoider is the party who could take steps to avoid an accident at the lowest cost. In effect, it is the party for whom B in the Learned Hand formula is lowest. (Recall we are assuming that B is to be understood in an all-or-nothing rather than in a marginal sense; it represents the cost of completely avoiding the expected loss.) For purposes of applying the cheapest cost-avoider test, it does not matter whether, for either party, $B < PL$ or $B > PL$; all that matters, at least in theory, is determining for which party B is lower (although, as Gilles, 1992, pp. 1,315–17 makes clear, this will sometimes require a court to ascertain PL anyway). The idea is that the cheapest cost-avoider will make the appropriate cost-benefit analysis privately, and act accordingly. For this reason, Calabresi labelled this approach general or market deterrence. The main drawback of the cheapest cost-avoider test is that while it will lead to an optimal level of care in alternative care cases, it will not always do so in cases of joint care (Shavell, 1987, pp. 17–18). Stephen Gilles has argued, however, that even in joint care cases the test will still *tend* towards optimality (Gilles, 1992, pp. 1,309–13).

We have so far discussed economic deterrence in cases of unintentional harm to one of the core interests. Intentional harm, when it occurs in the context of a conflict between legitimate productive activities, is treated very similarly; the element of "intention" usually rests on some economically irrelevant factor, such as a particularly high probability of loss. But there is, according to Richard Posner, another category of intentional harm that economics views in a different light. At stake are torts that involve an element of coercive, criminally prohibited transfer. (For example, the tort of conversion corresponds to the crime of theft, while battery – trespass to the person – covers, among other kinds of conduct, personal assault, murder and rape.) The sums invested by the injurer and victim in attempting respectively to accomplish and to prevent the coercive transfer represent a social waste of resources; this, according to Posner, "is the economic objection to theft." There is, of course, a benefit to the injurer in obtaining, say, the car that he steals, but this gain is offset by the corresponding loss to the victim. In cases such as these, we should expect to find, according to economic analysis, that the law is more willing to award punitive as opposed to purely compensatory damages. (Posner, 1992, pp. 206–11; cf. Landes and Posner, 1987, pp. 149–89.)

Economic theories of deterrence obviously provide a very powerful model of, and potential justification for, the institution of tort law. But these theories have themselves been subjected to some very powerful criticisms. Some of the objections are directed towards the economic understanding of specific aspects of tort law, while others are directed at deterrence-based economic theories of tort in general. The most common specific criticism targets the economic understanding of the negligence standard. The basic point is well expressed by Epstein: "[A negligence rule patterned on the Hand formula] allows a defendant to trade the benefits that he (or society at large) receives from his own conduct against the costs inflicted upon the plaintiff" (Epstein, 1985, p. 40). In other words, a defendant is permitted to impose what could well be quite high levels of foreseeable risk on other persons, so long as the cost *to him* of taking precautions exceeds the expected loss (PL). But why should someone else be forced to bear these risks, when it is the person whose actions created them who stands to benefit? This criticism applies *a fortiori* to Posner's analysis of "legitimate" intentional torts, where P (and hence the risk) will tend to be high. (A different but related criticism applies to Posner's analysis of "illegitimate" intentional torts. Posner assumes that the gain to a thief, for example, will be offset by the loss to the victim, but this is not necessarily so. The thief might value what he steals more highly than its present owner, in which case a cost–benefit analysis could well favor the coercive transfer.)

Let us turn to the general criticisms of economic deterrence theory. One common objection is that these theories presuppose a generally unattainable level of information on the part of the persons whose behavior the law is supposed to shape, and that if a more realistic degree of knowledge of B, P, and L is assumed, the deterrent effects of tort liability are seen to be muted or non-existent. (See, for example, Sugarman, 1989, pp. 6–9.)

However, the most fundamental general criticism of economic deterrence theory concerns what Jules Coleman calls the "structure" of tort law (Coleman, 1992, pp. 374–85). By this he means the framework of case-by-case adjudication, between an individual victim and an individual injurer who causally contributed to the victim's injury, that typifies an action in tort. Coleman thus identifies two related elements as central to the social practice of tort law: first, the individualized institutional form which requires a person who has suffered a loss – call her A – to make a claim against, and to recover damages from, not the state but rather some discrete person B; and second, the requirement that some act or, occasionally, omission of B's have been a *cause* of A's loss. Ernest Weinrib's formalist theory of tort law also identifies these two elements as central, although Weinrib is willing to go further and label them as *conceptually necessary* features of the practice; any theory of tort law that does not incorporate these elements, integrate them into a single justification, and treat them as essential to the practice will be, according to Weinrib, incoherent (Weinrib, 1989b, pp. 493–7). But "incoherence" is a strong term, and it is by no means obvious that the thoroughly conceptual approach its use presupposes is warranted (Kress, 1993). Coleman's more modest conception of the structure of tort law focusses, as seems appropriate, on the pragmatic dissonance between institutional framework and economic theory.

The difficulty that arises with respect to the structure of tort law is that neither the individualized procedure of tort nor its basic causation requirement seems to be demanded by, or even to make much sense in the light of, economic deterrence theory. Consider first, tort law's individualized, bilateral procedure. There is no fundamental reason why the incentives that will induce people to take due care must be created by the determination of liability in tort actions between particular injurers and particular victims. For example, suppose that victims had to bear their own losses and injurers were required to pay to the state, rather than to the victim, fines equal to harm done or taxes equal to expected loss. As economic theorists concede, not only would injurers and victims both be led to take due care, but both would also choose optimal activity levels; in this respect, at least, a public law solution would in fact be superior to the tort solution (Shavell, 1987, pp. 29–30).

Consider next tort law's causation requirement, which has traditionally meant that the injurer's (negligent) action must have been a necessary condition of the occurrence of the victim's harm: if the harm would not have occurred but for what the injurer did, then causation has been established (the so-called "but-for" test for factual causation). As economic theorists again concede, neither strict liability nor a negligence rule need be restricted to liability for losses that would not have occurred but for, respectively, the injurer's action, or her negligence in acting, in order to induce injurers to take care; the reason is that, so long as liability is imposed in circumstances where care *would* make a difference, it will be rational for injurers to take due care (Shavell, 1987, pp. 105–10). Landes and Posner (1987, pp. 229–30) go further and argue that the traditional notion of factual causation can and should be dispensed with in an economic analysis of torts. Richard Wright agrees, but from the perspective of a critic; the economic approach is, he says, "analytically incompatible" with the factual causation requirement, "the most pervasive and enduring requirement of tort liability over the centuries" (Wright, 1985a, pp. 435–8). The reason for this incompatibility is that the economic approach is forward looking, collective, and policy oriented, whereas the determination of factual causation is backward looking, individualized, and fact based. Some economic theorists have tried to get around this difficulty by redefining causation as a general, probabilistic relation between *classes* of events (for

67

example, Calabresi, 1975, p. 71), but this maneuver seems artificial and ad hoc; certainly it fails to capture the significance that has traditionally been thought to attach to the factual causation requirement (Wright, 1985a; Coleman, 1992, pp. 382–4).

One response available to the economic theorist is to argue that the structure of tort law can be accounted for by considerations of administrative efficiency: tort law, with its individualized procedure and requirement of factual causation, constitutes a system of private enforcement; such a system, the argument runs, is less expensive to administer than a public regulatory regime. But, as Coleman points out, this argument renders the structure of tort law "radically contingent and far too tenuous to explain its centrality to our actual practice" (Coleman, 1992, p. 378). Coleman concludes that the centrality of that structure is better explained, and tort law as a whole is better justified, by a principle of corrective justice. Weinrib and Wright accept this conclusion as well.

Economic theories: loss spreading

The third type of economic theory is comprised of theories that call for losses to be distributed throughout society as thinly and widely as possible. The basic rationale for such loss-spreading is that it will have the effect, because of the diminishing marginal utility of money, of minimizing the overall social impact that a given loss will have (Calabresi, 1970, pp. 39–41). Thus taking $1 from each of 100 persons, all of whom have $100 of wealth, will, in theory at least, result in less overall disutility than taking $100 from just one of those persons; each further dollar taken from the same person represents a greater share of her total remaining wealth, and its loss is accordingly accompanied by more disutility than the loss of the previous dollar. Sometimes the overall social impact of a loss can similarly be decreased not by spreading it, but by taking it from a "deep pocket." Thus total disutility will in theory be reduced, again because of the diminishing marginal utility of money, by shifting a $100 loss from someone worth $100 to someone else worth $1,000. Loss-spreading theories view tort law as a mechanism for spreading losses, or at least for placing them on deep pockets.

The assumption that a person is subject to the diminishing marginal utility of money is equivalent to the assumption that he is risk averse; this means, for example, that he prefers a sure loss of $100 to a 10 percent risk of losing $1,000, even though the expected loss (PL) is the same in each case (Shavell, 1987, pp. 186–7). Risk-averse parties care about the magnitude of potential losses, since the greater the loss, the greater the marginal impact on their well-being. Thus loss-spreading only makes sense as a goal for tort law if we drop the unrealistic assumption of risk neutrality that we made when discussing deterrence theory. (It is worth recalling in this regard that deterrence theorists base their premise of risk neutrality on the assumption that persons have the ability to spread their losses through private insurance.)

It is often said that if loss-spreading were the only goal of tort law, then the most efficient way of achieving it would be to abolish tort and institute a general social compensation scheme (Calabresi, 1970, p. 46). A social compensation scheme, which could be comprehensive or limited in scope, can be defined as a public regime, usually created by legislation, that compensates for (specified kinds of) losses either by drawing on general tax revenues or by requiring compulsory insurance coverage of some kind. But social compensation offers an alternative to, rather than a justification for, tort law, and our concern here must be with loss-spreading theories that purport to take tort law seriously. The law of torts can play a role in loss-spreading mainly by affecting incentives to obtain private insurance (or to self-insure). Private insurance is itself a loss-spreading mechanism, based on voluntary contractual arrangements. Loss (or first-party) insurance provides direct cover against specified forms of loss, while liability (or third-party) insurance provides cover against being held liable in tort to third parties.

Theories of tort law that view tort as a viable instrument for loss-spreading generally advocate some form of *enterprise liability*. Enterprise liability calls for commercial enterprises to be held liable, regardless of fault, for losses caused by their goods or services, because they can then spread those losses to all their customers through the prices they charge (Calabresi, 1970, pp. 53–4). In effect, enterprise liability requires commercial enterprises to insure consumers against losses their products might cause, and hence to build a premium into the prices of those products. Enterprises can provide this insurance either by using those premiums to purchase liability insurance, or, possibly, by self-insuring. The main rationale for enterprise liability is that it will automatically provide insurance cover for consumers, and, in particular, poor consumers, who might not obtain loss insurance for themselves (Priest, 1987, pp. 1,534–9). It has also been argued that adding a premium to the price of a product is a relatively efficient way of providing insurance, since the risks the product creates are automatically aggregated into one large risk pool (Priest, 1987, p. 1,559). The idea underlying enterprise liability that tort law can be used to spread losses was a crucial factor leading to the introduction in the United States of strict products liability, which holds manufacturers strictly liable for losses resulting from the use of their products when these are defective in certain ways (Priest, 1985).

The theory of enterprise liability has, however, encountered some serious criticisms. As in the case of deterrence theory, one objection concerns a lack of congruence with the structure of tort law (Coleman, 1992, p. 375; Weinrib, 1989b, pp. 498–9). Enterprise liability is concerned with the provision of insurance, and there is no intrinsic reason for making insurance coverage conditional on the outcome of case-by-case litigation, or, more specifically, for requiring that the provider of the insurance have caused the loss. At this point a defender of enterprise liability will typically concede that it is probably not the most sensible or efficient method for spreading losses, but will then add that loss-spreading cannot be regarded as the only goal of tort law: enterprise liability, the argument runs, is a defensible compromise solution for achieving a reasonable measure of both loss-spreading and deterrence (Calabresi, 1970, pp. 37, 54, 312). However, given that *neither* loss-spreading *nor* deterrence fits very well with the structure of tort law, it is far from clear that tort offers the most appropriate framework for pursuing both goals together. For one thing, the two goals may conflict: the general thrust of the loss-spreading rationale is to place losses on enterprises, yet every deterrence theory requires that losses at least sometimes be left on victims. It may be that separate institutions – for example, a public regulatory regime for deterrence, and a social compensation scheme for loss-spreading – is the better way to pursue both goals simultaneously. This is, in fact, the route we have chosen for personal injuries that occur in the workplace (industrial safety legislation plus workers' compensation) and, to a more limited extent, on the highway (traffic codes plus no-fault automobile insurance).

Moreover, some deterrence theorists have begun to question whether loss-spreading is a goal that should be pursued by tort law *at all*. George Priest has argued very persuasively that enterprise liability is an extremely poor vehicle for providing insurance, and that in the United States it has at times undermined insurance markets and led to the withdrawal of some lines of third-party coverage. In Priest's view, tort law should concentrate exclusively on the deterrence goal of total cost minimization; loss-spreading is much more efficiently achieved by encouraging possible victims to purchase loss insurance, something that can be done by requiring them to bear residuary losses (Priest, 1987, pp. 1,538, 1,588–90). Priest gives the following six reasons in support of this view. First, while enterprise liability does a relatively good job of aggregating risks into a risk pool, viable market insurance requires not just aggregation of risks but *segregation* into relatively narrow risk pools, in which the range and variance of risks are limited; otherwise, low-risk members will drop out of the pool because their premiums exceed their expected losses, eventually causing the pool to unravel (the phenomenon of adverse selection). But enterprises have very little control over who buys their products, and hence are very restricted in their ability to segregate risks. Second, viable market insurance requires that the risks within risk pools be statistically independent, but the risks pooled by enterprise liability tend to be highly correlated; if a product is subject to a design defect, for example, all consumers who purchase it are subject to essentially the same risk.

Third, by permitting recovery for non-pecuniary damages such as pain and suffering, which do not directly affect income flow, tort law compensates for losses that people would not, and in fact could not, voluntarily insure against; the premiums built into the prices of products therefore exceed what individuals would pay for the same effective level of coverage provided through loss insurance. Fourth, by providing full compensation for losses – indeed, in insurance terms, *more* than full compensation – tort law does not allow for the kinds of mechanisms found in loss insurance, such as deductibles and limited coverage, for dealing with moral hazard. (Moral hazard is the decreased incentive created by insurance itself to avoid incurring a loss, or to mitigate its effects after the fact.) Fifth, the administrative costs of enterprise liability exceed those of loss insurance; the latter, unlike the former, does not require expensive litigation. Finally and perhaps most importantly, the insurance provided by enterprise liability has a regressive distributional effect. All consumers, rich or poor, pay the same premium that has been built into the price of a given product, but tort law awards higher damages to those who have suffered a greater loss of earnings, or who have a greater wage-earning capacity. In effect, the wealthy receive better coverage for the same premium. This contrasts sharply with loss insurance, where more extensive coverage (for example, for damage to a luxury car) requires the payment of higher premiums. This aspect of enterprise liability is somewhat ironic, given that one of its merits is supposed to be the provision of insurance for the poor.

Justice-based theories: distributive justice

This brings us to the second main category of theories that have been advanced to justify tort law, namely, those that are justice based. We begin by considering theories that take distributive justice as their starting-point, where the point of distributive justice is understood to be the just distribution of material resources, and perhaps other goods, throughout society as a whole. On this view, tort law is regarded as a mechanism for rectifying deviations from a pattern of holdings antecedently determined to be just (and also, perhaps, for moving an unjust pattern closer to a just one). If A deliberately or accidentally destroys property belonging to B, then B will have less than he is entitled to under the relevant distributive pattern. The appropriate moral response, on the view under consideration, is to require A to make good the loss B has suffered, thereby restoring the distributive equilibrium. (See references in Benson, 1992, p. 531.)

The distributive approach faces some simple but strong objections. First, a theory of this type cannot hope to justify tort law in its current form: no existing society can plausibly claim to have achieved a truly just distribution of resources, nor do the courts seriously attempt to use tort as a method for correcting distributive imbalances. Second, this approach appears to apply to just one of the two core interests, namely, the interest in preserving tangible property, since we do not ordinarily think that persons' lives and bodies are subject to distributive justice. The most fundamental difficulty, however, is that, because of its structure, tort law is a particularly inappropriate instrument for maintaining a distributive pattern. Assume, for the sake of simplicity, that the required pattern is equality of material resources, that the relevant society consists of four persons, and that each person has ten units of goods. If A causes the destruction of four of B's units, equality will not be restored if, as a rule of strict liability in tort would require, A gives B four of *her* units. Equality can only be restored if B receives one unit from each of the others, thereby constituting a new distribution of nine units each (Alexander, 1987, pp. 6–7). The point here is that the maintenance of a distributive pattern is a global problem, the solution to which requires taking account of the shares of all persons within the relevant group. But tort law is a mechanism for rectification on a *local* scale, between two persons. As a general matter, the local mechanism cannot respond satisfactorily to the global problem. Moreover, this institutional deficiency reflects a deeper difficulty: the reasons for action arising from distributive justice pertain to society as a whole, whereas the assumption

71

of tort law is that the defendant alone has a reason to compensate the plaintiff (Coleman, 1992, pp. 319, 374).

The difficulty just considered concerns the bilateral nature of tort law. But the other aspect of the structure of tort law, namely, the causation requirement, is also problematic for the distributive approach. A patterned conception of distributive justice should no doubt be sensitive to the losses people suffer, but there is no obvious reason why it should be sensitive to the *source* of a loss; the consequences for the victim's well-being, and the effect on the overall pattern, are presumably independent of how the loss came about. Thus, in our example, it does not matter, from the perspective of distributive justice, whether B lost his four units because of something A did (possibly quite inadvertently), or because of a hurricane. The basic tort requirement that recoverable losses have been caused by human agency thus seems to be an entirely arbitrary restriction on any institutional apparatus intended to maintain a distributive pattern. In light of this and the other problems the distributive approach faces, it should come as no surprise that tort theorists who emphasize the importance of distributive justice tend to advocate the abolition of tort law. To replace it they call for social compensation schemes that do not distinguish among possible sources of loss or, preferably in their view, for broad social *welfare* schemes that focus on need in general and not just on loss (Sugarman, 1989, pp. 127–52).

It bears mention that we have been assuming that the relevant conception of distributive justice is, in Robert Nozick's words, *patterned*, which means that it calls for a distribution of resources based on a formula such as "to each according to his need," "to each in equal shares," and so on (Nozick, 1974, pp. 149–60). Our example of equal shares is a particularly simple pattern, but the general point holds in more complex cases as well, such as John Rawls's difference principle (to each in equal shares except as required to maximize the position of the least-advantaged). Nozick's own historically oriented, non-patterned conception of justice in holdings, which he calls the entitlement theory, is not really about distributive justice at all, as that notion has traditionally been understood. The entitlement theory cannot be considered here, except to observe that it is probably best regarded as a conception of property rights complementary to the libertarian argument to be discussed in the following section.

Justice-based theories: corrective justice

The final type of theory for justifying tort law that we consider is premissed on the notion of corrective justice. The basic idea is that tort law should attempt to do justice strictly between the parties, without taking account of larger distributive issues in the community as a whole. Corrective justice purports to impose an obligation to pay compensation on persons who have caused harm in certain ways to others; those who suffer the harm are viewed as having a correlative right, held against their particular injurers and no one else, to recover for their losses. The general form of corrective justice closely parallels the two elements of the structure of tort law that we considered earlier, namely, the bilateral litigational procedure and the requirement of factual causation. Corrective justice thus holds promise as a possible justification for tort law, but if the promise is to be fulfilled the principle must itself be justified and its content made more precise. In fact there exists a wide range of corrective justice-type theories, some defending a standard of strict liability and some a fault-based approach. In the present essay it will be possible to offer only a brief critical survey of the most important of these theories. (For a more detailed discussion of the various theories, see Perry, 1992.)

Before that survey is undertaken, however, two preliminary matters require mention. The first, which cannot be discussed in detail here, concerns the proper understanding of the causation requirement. The most satisfactory analysis of causation in tort law has been presented by Richard Wright, who argues that the but-for test for factual causation that was discussed earlier is really just a special case of the so-called NESS test. According to the latter, an event A is a cause of event B if A is a Necessary Element in a Set of conditions that are jointly Sufficient to produce B. "Necessary" here means that the element is required to complete the set. The but-for test then provides a satisfactory test for causation in the common circumstance in which there is only one set of existing conditions jointly sufficient to produce B. (But for A, an element in the set, B would not have occurred.) If there is more than one such sufficient set, the situation is one of concurrent causation (Wright, 1985b, pp. 1,794–1,803).

The second preliminary matter is this. If a corrective justice-based theory of tort law is not simply to collapse into a distributive theory, the theory's understanding of corrective justice must be independent, at least to some degree, of background conceptions of distributive justice. This does not appear to be a problem for the first of the two core interests protected by tort law, namely, the interest in life and bodily integrity. If, as seems plausible, my physical person belongs inalienably to me and me alone, it is not the sort of good that can be subject to distributive justice in the first place. But the interest in preserving one's tangible property is a more complicated matter, since wealth in the form of material resources is a paradigmatic object of distributive justice. Corrective justice can only be regarded, so far as damage to property is concerned, as a truly independent principle if the legitimacy of the property rights it protects is not determined *solely* by distributive considerations.

A number of different arguments have been made, attempting to show that moral entitlements to tangible property do not depend on distributive justice alone. For example, Jules Coleman argues that legal property rights can be legitimate even when the background pattern of holdings deviates from an ideally just distribution, so long as the deviation is not too great. If an existing system of private property makes a contribution to individual well-being and social stability, then the legal entitlements it generates are, according to Coleman, morally justified and deserving of the protection of corrective justice; moreover, this is true even if those entitlements are vulnerable to redistributive action by the state (Coleman, 1992, pp. 350–4). Peter Benson offers a very different, Kantian answer to the question of how entitlements to property can be justified in non-distributive terms. Benson argues that "[a] person who, through an external manifestation of will, has brought something under his or her present and exclusive control prior to others is, relative to those others, entitled to it in corrective justice" (Benson, 1992, p. 543). Benson further maintains that an entitlement in distributive justice can simultaneously constitute an entitlement in corrective justice if the holder of the entitlement has brought the relevant item under exclusive control.

Let us turn, then, to the principle of corrective justice itself. There are, as has been mentioned, a number of quite disparate views concerning both the justification of this principle and its more specific content. In general, corrective justice requires A to compensate B for loss caused by A's conduct (in a fault-based theory, by A's *faulty* conduct). This suggests two possible starting-points for explicating and justifying corrective justice, namely, A's exercise of agency and B's subsequent loss. Ernest Weinrib's Kantian/Hegelian theory of corrective justice, which presupposes a view of property rights similar to Benson's, begins with the exercise of agency. The person and tangible property of a given individual are said to be embodiments, in the Kantian sense, of that individual's will, and as such cannot be subjected to wrongful interference by the acts of will of another. "Wrongful" here means either intentional or negligent interference. If A's wrongful exercise of agency results in harm to the person or property of B, A has a duty in corrective justice to compensate B, and B has a correlative right to be compensated (Weinrib, 1989a, 1995, pp. 56–144).

The main difficulty with Weinrib's approach is that the core protected interests are not protected *as* interests, that is, as aspects of human well-being, but only as Kantian embodiments of the will. In Weinrib's view, "the significance of particular rights [that is, embodiments of the will] consists solely in their being actualizations of [the capacity for rights] and not in their contribution to the satisfaction of the rights holders' particular interests" (Weinrib, 1989a, p. 1,290). In tort law, however, a loss is compensated precisely because, and to the extent that, it constitutes an interference with a particular interest. It is thus not clear how Weinrib's theory can justify the paradigmatic tort remedy of compensatory damages (Perry, 1992, pp. 478–88). The more appropriate remedy would seem rather to be criminal punishment, which Weinrib in fact regards as an aspect of corrective justice. Recently Weinrib has responded to this objection by distinguishing a "factual" from a "normative" loss, suggesting that the latter occurs "when one's holdings are smaller than they ought to be." Kantian right is then said to see "the factual in light of the normative": if in causing a factual loss to the plaintiff the defendant has breached a duty correlative to the plaintiff's right, he or she "is required to undo the consequences of [the] wrongful act by making good the factual loss" (Weinrib, 1995, pp. 116, 129). Without more, however, this just seems to beg the question.

The second possible starting-point for an account of corrective justice that we distinguished is the victim's loss. Suppose that A intentionally or negligently harms B. A common argument made in support of obligating A to compensate B is that, as between a faulty injurer and an innocent victim, it is morally preferable that the loss be borne by the injurer. (See references in Perry, 1992, pp. 467–70.) This is, in effect, an argument that treats corrective justice as a form of localized *distributive* justice: B's loss is treated as a burden to be distributed between A and B, in accordance with a criterion of relative fault. The main difficulty with this argument is that there is no good reason to suppose that causation has any normative significance for a distributive scheme of this kind, and hence no reason to limit the distributive group to just these two; there is, in other words, no justification for adopting a localized, as opposed to a more general, distributive scheme (Perry, 1992, pp. 470–5). Jules Coleman in effect recognized as much when he advocated the so-called "at-fault pool" as one method for implementing the distributively oriented approach to compensatory justice that he advocated for many years. The at-fault pool calls for the losses from, say, automobile accidents to be distributed among all those found guilty of faulty driving, in proportion to the degree of fault shown by each and regardless of whether he or she actually caused an accident (Coleman, 1974, pp. 484–8).

George Fletcher has, in a well-known article, defended a variation of the localized distributive-justice idea. Fletcher claims that the moral basis of corrective justice is the following, Rawls-inspired principle of equal security: "[W]e all have the right to the maximum amount of security compatible with a like security for everyone else" (Fletcher, 1972, p. 550). As the analogy with Rawls suggests, this is best understood as a principle of distributive justice (distributing the good of security). Someone who imposes on another person a level of risk that this principle would deem excessive comes under an obligation to compensate for any loss that results because "[c]ompensation is a surrogate for the individual's right to the same security as enjoyed by others" (Fletcher, 1972, p. 550). Fletcher thus appeals, in effect, to a subsidiary distributive principle that reassigns losses so as to maintain the expected level of well-being guaranteed by the initial distribution of security. Since Fletcher assumes that a loss can only be reassigned to the particular excessive-risk imposer who happened to cause it, he is implicitly relying on a *localized* conception of distributive justice. But the underlying logic of the distributive argument offers no basis for this restriction. As with the at-fault pool, it seems more sensible and fair, from the perspective of distributive justice, to require a given victim's loss to be shared among *all* persons who engaged in excessively risky behavior, without regard to whether they caused injury (and thus, *a fortiori*, without regard to whether they caused *this* injury).

The discussion so far suggests that a satisfactory theory of corrective justice cannot be solely grounded in either the injurer's exercise of agency or the victim's suffering of a loss. What we evidently require is a moral link between the conduct of the one and the loss suffered by the other. The concept that seems best able to fill this role is that of *responsibility*, or, to be more specific, responsibility for the consequences of one's actions. Borrowing a term from Tony Honoré, we can call this *outcome-responsibility* (Honoré, 1988). We must next ask what the content, scope, and normative implications of this notion are.

One understanding of outcome-responsibility arises from an argument that, because it has figured prominently in libertarian philosophy, I shall refer to as the libertarian argument. The essential idea is that if a person chooses to act in the

75

world, she is both fully entitled to whatever gains she may make and fully responsible for whatever harms she may suffer or cause. The claim about gains is implicit in the standard libertarian thesis that forced redistribution is in general illegitimate. The claim about harm is meant to capture the idea that, because the harms a person causes are properly regarded as costs of her activity, it would be unfair to require someone else to bear them. Both claims are premised on a certain understanding of the moral significance of action. I have a *choice* about whether to become active in the world, and if I choose activity over passivity then all subsequent consequences, both good and bad, are appropriately chalked up to my moral ledger and no one else's. Thus other persons are not entitled to share in whatever gains may accrue to me as a result of my activity, but by the same token I cannot force passive by-standers to absorb any losses my activities may create. Thus outcome-responsibility, on the libertarian understanding, would lead to a standard of strict liability in tort law. The libertarian argument appears to lie at the heart of Richard Epstein's well-known theory of general strict liability (Epstein, 1973, pp. 158–60), although Epstein does not himself clearly distinguish the argument from a number of other, weaker arguments that he also puts forward (Perry, 1988, pp. 148–59).

We might rephrase the core claim of the libertarian argument by saying that agents should be required, for reasons of fairness rather than economic efficiency, to internalize the costs of their activities. As this formulation immediately suggests, however, a basic weakness of the argument is the Coasean point that tort losses are caused not by one actor or activity alone, but rather by the *interaction* of activities. Thus internalization can no more underpin a moral argument for tort liability than it can an economic one: a tort loss cannot be assigned to one party's moral or economic ledger on causal grounds alone (Perry, 1992, pp. 461–7).

The libertarian argument requires us to distinguish between an active injurer and a passive victim, and this is precisely the distinction Coase says cannot be drawn. But the argument also depends on the related idea that a person is capable of choosing to become active or remain passive in the world. *This* idea was rejected over a century ago by Oliver Wendell Holmes, in the course of criticizing what was clearly a version of the libertarian argument. Holmes stated that "[a] man need not, it is true, do this or that act, – the term *act* implies a choice, – but he must act somehow" (Holmes, 1881, p. 95). Since the human condition gives us no choice but to be active in the world, moral responsibility for an outcome cannot, Holmes implied, attach simply because one has acted: "[T]he only possible purpose of introducing [the element that the defendant should have made a choice] is to make the power of avoiding the evil complained of a condition of liability. There is no such power where the evil cannot be foreseen" (Holmes, 1881, p. 95). This proposition was part of Holmes's positive case for the negligence standard in tort law. Implicit in it, however, is an alternative conception of outcome-responsibility, one premised not on the mere fact of causing an outcome, but rather on the fact that the outcome was foreseeable, and hence avoidable. *Avoidability*, then, becomes the touchstone of responsibility for outcomes (Perry, 1992, pp. 503–7).

Suppose *A* engages in an activity that results in foreseeable harm to *B*. Because the harm was foreseeable, A had it within his power to avoid causing it; even if there were no precautions he could have taken to reduce the risk, he could have forgone the activity altogether. He thus had a certain measure of control over the situation, and even though that control was undoubtedly only partial it seems reasonable to ascribe to him a special responsibility for the outcome that, in general, other persons do not have. This avoidability-based conception of responsibility for outcomes – which is the sense that will henceforth be attributed to the term "outcome-responsibility" – is a normative, and hence reason-affecting, notion. Unlike the libertarian conception, however, it does not necessarily carry with it an obligation to compensate; the agent may have reasons only to obtain assistance, apologize, or otherwise express regret. The possibility is at least raised, however, that he should pay full compensation, which means attempting to undo the harmful outcome entirely, to the extent that this is possible to achieve. In the nature of things, the victim will have to bear the loss if no one else has a reason to bear it. The injurer, by virtue of his outcome-responsibility, potentially has such a reason. The question we must then ask is: under what circumstances does that reason arise?

In order to answer this question, note first that if A is outcome-responsible for harm to B, that means that A *could have* acted differently so as to avoid the harm. It does not automatically follow, however, that he *should have* acted differently. It is impossible to act without imposing risk on others, and a risk that was foreseeable may, nonetheless, have been relatively low; there may have been no strong grounds for asserting that the agent ought to have done something different. Consistent with this idea is the fact that, in negligence law, reasonable foreseeability is a necessary but not a sufficient condition of liability. If, however, a risk was not only foreseeable but should have been avoided, it seems appropriate to conclude that outcome-responsibility takes the form of an obligation to compensate. Under what circumstances, then, should foreseeable risks be avoided? The sensible answer seems to be: when they are associated with actions that are either negligent or intended to cause harm – in other words, with actions that are faulty in the usual tort sense (Perry, 1992, pp. 507–12).

A view roughly similar to the one we have been describing seems to be embodied in Jules Coleman's "mixed" conception of corrective justice. According to that conception, a duty to repair a loss is grounded in the injurer's responsibility – that is, "his exercise of the powers of autonomous agency" – but it arises only if the loss was "wrongful." A loss is wrongful, for Coleman, if it results from conduct that is either wrongful in itself or infringes one of the victim's rights (Coleman, 1992, pp. 326, 332, 482). The mixed conception replaces Coleman's earlier annulment theory, which called, quite simply, for wrongful losses to be eliminated or annulled (Coleman, 1988, pp. 184–201). As Coleman now acknowledges, the concern of the annulment theory was really with distributive rather than with corrective justice, since reasons for annulling losses pertained, in effect, to everyone, rather than to individual injurers (Coleman, 1992, pp. 309–11). In order to find a primary moral obligation in injurers, the concept of individual responsibility is required.

Intention, as a standard of liability and a criterion of fault, is, for the most part, relatively straightforward. But defining the precise content of the negligence standard – specifying, in other words, which risks of unintentional harm should not be imposed on others – is a more complex matter. The Learned Hand test seems unsatisfactory in this regard, for the reasons considered earlier in connection with deterrence theory. Other suggestions concerning which risks should be characterized as unacceptable, for the purposes of corrective justice and tort law, include the following: non-reciprocal risks, meaning risks imposed by the defendant on the plaintiff that exceed those imposed by the plaintiff on the defendant (Fletcher, 1972, p. 546); risks that exceed a background level existing within a given community or activity (Fletcher, 1972, p. 549); risks that a reasonable person would recognize as substantial (Perry, 1988, pp. 169–71); and risks that arise because the agent has failed to conform with certain community conventions (Coleman, 1992, pp. 357–60). Each of these suggestions has some initial plausibility, but the determination of which among them, if any, is correct is by no means a simple one.

While this issue cannot be further considered here, it seems appropriate to conclude with the following observation. Even if the pure Learned Hand test is not an appropriate formulation of the negligence standard, it might, nonetheless, be the case that considerations of economic efficiency properly figure, either directly or indirectly, in the determination of what constitutes due care. Perhaps the central role of corrective justice is to define the form of responsibility that injurers owe to victims, namely, outcome-responsibility. If that is so, then it may be that the precise standard of conduct that should be taken to constitute "fault," contravention of which will trigger an obligation to compensate one's victim, should be defined, at least in part or as a matter of default, by reference to economic considerations. If this admittedly speculative suggestion turned out to be correct, then tort law would in an important sense be, to use Jules Coleman's provocative phrase, "a mixture of markets and morals" (Coleman, 1992, p. 428).

Bibliography

Alexander, L. A. 1987: Causation and corrective justice: does tort law make sense?. *Law and Philosophy*, 6, 1–23.

Benson, P. 1992: The basis of corrective justice and its relation to distributive justice. *Iowa Law Review*, 77, 515–624.

Calabresi, G. 1961: Some thoughts on risk distribution and the law of torts. *Yale Law Journal*, 70, 499–553.

—— 1970: *The Costs of Accidents*. New Haven: Yale University Press.

—— 1975: Concerning cause and the law of torts. *University of Chicago Law Review*, 43, 69–108.

Coase, R. H. 1960: The problem of social cost. *Journal of Law and Economics*, 3, 1–44.

Coleman, J. L. 1974: On the moral argument for the fault system. *Journal of Philosophy*, 71, 473–90.

—— 1988: *Markets, Morals and the Law*. Cambridge: Cambridge University Press.

—— 1992: *Risks and Wrongs*. Cambridge: Cambridge University Press.

Epstein, R. 1973: A theory of strict liability. *Journal of Legal Studies*, 2, 151–204.

—— 1985: *Takings: private property and the power of eminent domain*. Cambridge, Mass.: Harvard University Press.

Fletcher, G. P. 1972: Fairness and utility in tort theory. *Harvard Law Review*, 85, 537–73.

Gilles, S. G. 1992: Negligence, strict liability, and the cheapest cost-avoider. *Virginia Law Review*, 78, 1,291–375.

Holmes, O. W. 1881: *The Common Law*. Boston: Little, Brown.

Honoré, T. 1988: Responsibility and luck. *Law Quarterly Review*, 104, 530–53.

Kress, K. 1993: Coherence and formalism. *Harvard Journal of Law & Public Policy*, 16, 639–82.

Landes, W. M. and Posner, R. A. 1987: *The Economic Structure of Tort Law*. Cambridge, Mass.: Harvard University Press.

Nozick, R. 1974: *Anarchy, State, and Utopia*. New York: Basic Books.

Perry, S. R. 1988: The impossibility of general strict liability. *Canadian Journal of Law and Jurisprudence*, 1, 147–71.

—— 1992: The moral foundations of tort law. *Iowa Law Review*, 77, 449–514.

Posner, R. A. 1992: *Economic Analysis of Law*. Boston: Little, Brown, 4th edn.

Priest, G. L. 1985: The invention of enterprise liability: a critical history of the intellectual foundations of modern tort law. *Journal of Legal Studies*, 14, 461–527.

—— 1987: The current insurance crisis and modern tort law. *Yale Law Journal*, 96, 1,521–90.

Shavell, S. 1987: *Economic Analysis of Tort Law*. Cambridge, Mass.: Harvard University Press.

Sugarman, S. D. 1989: *Doing Away with Personal Injury Law*. New York: Quorum Books.

Weinrib, E. J. 1989a: Right and advantage in private law. *Cardozo Law Review*, 10, 1,283–1,309.

—— 1989b: Understanding tort law. *Valparaiso University Law Review*, 23, 485–526.

—— 1995: *The Idea of Private Law*. Cambridge, Mass.: Harvard University Press.

Wright, R. W. 1985a: Actual causation vs. probabilistic linkage: the bane of economic analysis. *Journal of Legal Studies*, 14, 435–56.

—— 1985b: Causation in tort law. *California Law Review*, 73, 1,735–828.

4

Criminal law

LEO KATZ

"Philosophy of criminal law" may have a remote, impractical air about it, but in fact just answering relatively commonplace legal questions quickly propels one into the thicket of it. Imagine the legislature were thinking about a radical new law sharply increasing the penalty for drunk driving from its currently modest levels (consisting chiefly of the suspension of one's driving license) to something as draconian as life imprisonment. The law may sound a bit harsh, its sponsors acknowledge, but they point out that at the cost of ruining the lives of a few drunk drivers we would be saving the lives of legions of potential drunk-driving victims. And let us suppose further that the law's sponsors actually have the statistics to back up this claim. Would such a law be a good, or even an acceptable idea?

If one believes, as a number of criminal codes explicitly say, that the purpose of the criminal law is to deter and rehabilitate, then one might well say yes to this question. But do those codes, in fact, correctly state the purposes of criminal law? Most of us will react with decided unease to the prospect of meting out such draconian punishment for something like drunk driving. It just seems all out of proportion to the blameworthiness of the defendant's conduct. However salutary the consequences of such a law from a utilitarian point of view, it seems unfair. It seems in excess of what some deep-seated sense of just deserts calls for. It offends against some vague but strong sense of what kind of punishment fits what kind of crime, what kind of retribution is due what kind of misdeed. If one believes that it is this sense of proportionality that ought to determine how severely something like drunk driving can be punished, one is really embracing a rationale of punishment quite different from the fairly utilitarian aims of deterrence and rehabilitation, one is endorsing retributivism, the pursuit of retribution: proportionate punishment, one's just desert for its own, quite non-utilitarian sake.

Although retributivism tends to conform more closely to people's intuitions about punishment than utilitarianism, it is not without difficulties, and resolving those difficulties has been the subject of much debate. The most important challenge to retributivism has been its alleged vagueness: everyone may agree that five years in prison is unjustly harsh desert for shoplifting, or that a five dollar fine is unjustly lenient desert for rape, but beyond such clear cases our intuitions seem to fail us. Is two years, five years, or ten years the proper sanction for a rape? How about a bank robbery? Or accepting a bribe? Our sense of just deserts here seems to desert us. Which then makes us wonder: Is retributivism really a meaningful enough concept to be a suitable rationale for punishment?

But we shouldn't be too quick to give up on retributivism. Some startling empirical studies have shown that our judgments about just deserts are actually a lot more precise than at first appears. These studies had their beginnings in a landmark book by Thomas Sellin and Marvin Wolfgang called *The Measurement of Delinquency* (Sellin and Wolfgang, 1964). Sellin, Wolfgang, and those who came after them confronted ordinary citizens with vivid descriptions of a range of offenses and furnished them with a variety of means of expressing their feelings about the gravity of an infraction. Aside from doing the obvious – having the subjects rate the offenses on a numerical scale – they furnished them with various mechanical means to better give vent to their feelings: they had subjects squeeze a power gauge (also known as a dynamometer), and they had them adjust the brightness of lights and the loudness of sounds – the assignment in each case being to squeeze, adjust, and otherwise manipulate the equipment with an intensity of effort that seemed subjectively commensurate with the crime's seriousness. On the basis of those recorded intensities, they would assign a severity rating to that crime.

The experimenters then asked subjects to contemplate prison sentences of varying lengths and again to express their feelings about the seriousness of the punishment by squeezing gauges and adjusting lights and sounds. The experimenters then assigned each sentence a severity rating. When the dust had settled, a remarkable finding emerged. Generally speaking, the sentence which the criminal justice system metes out for an offense turned out to carry the same severity rating as the offense itself. All of this strongly suggests that underlying our punishment practices is a fairly refined sense of just deserts (Gescheider et al., 1982).

Retributivism is thus able to deflect the charge of vagueness. But there are other serious challenges which retributivism has a much harder time answering. Here are three of the more serious ones. Consider the case of a perfectly sane individual who commits a perfectly ordinary crime, and who goes perfectly mad *after* he has been caught. The general rule is that if he goes mad, that puts the criminal process on hold: if he has not yet been tried, he cannot be tried, and if he has been tried and sentenced already, he cannot be punished, indeed if he has been sentenced to die he cannot be executed, *until and unless he recovers*. (He can be put in an asylum, but that's different from punishment.) This rule is a fairly well-entrenched feature of our criminal justice system, and more importantly, one that comports well with our intuitions about what justice calls for. But it is a rule that is very difficult to square with retributivism: it is hard to see how any insanity that befalls a criminal after he has committed his crime diminishes the punishment that is his just deserts. (For an especially clear statement of this, see Duff, 1987.)

Retributivism faces another, perhaps even more intriguing difficulty. Imagine the following. A man robs a bank in New York City. He is wearing no disguise, his image is accurately caught on the bank's cameras, wanted-posters of him are quickly put up, and a man closely resembling the poster is soon arrested. At around the same time, another man commits premeditated murder in Los Angeles. As it happens, he too does so in full view of a camera, wanted-posters of him too are quickly produced and disseminated, and again an arrest of someone closely resembling him is soon made. But then a difficulty surfaces. Don't laugh, but the two men are identical twins. So despite the wonderfully clear-cut photographic evidence, the prosecutors are in a quandary. They know that one of the two committed the murder and one committed the bank robbery but since neither is talking they can't figure out who did what.

Imagine now further that the two cases are tried jointly before a judge, who arrives at the following solomonic solution: he declares both defendants guilty of bank robbery and imposes a commensurate sentence. He notes that since we know beyond a reasonable doubt that each of them is guilty of an offense *at least* as serious as bank robbery, though one of them of course is guilty of something far more serious yet, each at the very least deserves the bank robbery sentence. But the judgment will almost certainly be reversed on appeal. Any appellate court following the common understanding of the proof-beyond-a-reasonable-doubt requirement will insist that the crime of which the defendant is convicted (in this case bank robbery) be proved beyond a reasonable doubt. This has not been done. Therefore the verdict cannot stand. Yet from a retributivist point of view that is very hard to explain, since under the judge's verdict no defendant would be receiving a harsher sentence than he deserved.

Does this problem just seem too crazy to be taken seriously? It isn't. What I have given you is a highly stylized version of a very real, almost commonplace phenomenon: judges and juries not infrequently find themselves in the position where they know that the defendant has committed at least one of several crimes, but cannot tell which. The defendant is in possession of some stolen goods, which it is clear he obtained in one of several forbidden ways, by committing either (1) robbery, (2) larceny, (3) blackmail, (4) fraud, or (5) the purchase of stolen goods. Unless the court knows which of these he did beyond a reasonable doubt, it will have a hard time justifying a conviction. Another interesting, not all that uncommon illustration of the same phenomenon is this: X is charged with murder. His friend Y gives heavily self-incriminating testimony, leaving the jury with the strong impression that X couldn't have committed the murder, because he, Y, did it! The problem is that although Y's self-incriminating remarks are good enough to create reasonable doubt about X's guilt, they will usually not be good enough to prove his own, Y's guilt beyond a reasonable doubt. We are now in a position where we are totally certain that Y is guilty of one of two crimes: he either committed perjury when he gave his self-incriminating testimony or he actually committed the murder. We simply cannot prove beyond a reasonable doubt which of the two he is guilty of, and we thus have to let him go.

Finally, there is a third objection to retributivism – the one that may yet persuade you that the draconian drunk-driving law with which I started this inquiry may be acceptable after all. The legal scholar Larry Alexander asks us to imagine the case of a man who "receives a call from a burglar who says, 'I've been spying on you and know you're going out tonight. I plan to burglarize your house in order to steal your valuables. But I want you to know that I have a very bad heart, and if you hide your valuables, I might well suffer a heart attack by expending a lot of energy and suffering anxiety in looking for them. So please leave them in plain sight; for I am definitely going to enter your house and look for them until I find them or drop dead.' The listener hangs up the phone, takes his valuables, hides them on the very top shelf of his closet, and leaves. He returns home and finds the burglar, dead from a heart attack, on the floor" (Alexander, 1980, pp. 75–6). What the owner of the valuables has done seems perfectly all right, and yet, isn't death rather excessive retribution for a non-violent burglary? But if it is acceptable to protect valuables by putting them beyond an ailing thief's easy reach, why isn't it also acceptable to protect one's property with an electric fence (accompanied by a conspicuous warning), a vicious dog, a crocodile, a spring-gun – or a law that provides for draconian measures for even minor non-violent burglaries? And if this can be done with burglaries, why not drunk driving?

I don't mean to provide an answer to the drunk-driving puzzle. Indeed I don't have a slam-dunk answer. My purpose in raising it was merely to show that even considering a relatively humdrum, fairly practical issue of criminal law quickly makes a philosopher of even the most pragmatic decision maker.

Figuring out the overall purpose of punishment has been just one of the preoccupations of the philosophy of criminal law. Another preoccupation has been the explanation of what is commonly referred to as the General Part of the criminal law. At the core of criminal law doctrines lie a series of concepts that make their appearance in connection with nearly every crime for which we might seek to hold someone liable. They are concepts like *act, omission, intent, recklessness, causation, complicity, attempt, necessity, duress,* and *self-defense.* That's because in connection with any offense – be it murder, rape, theft, treason, tax evasion, or insider trading – it will matter whether the offense was committed intentionally or recklessly, whether the harm in question was precipitated by an act or an omission, whether it can really be said to have been caused by the defendant, whether the defendant was the perpetrator of the crime or a mere accomplice, whether he merely attempted it or whether he actually succeeded, and whether he acted under special pressures such as self-defense, necessity, or duress. Making these determinations raises numerous philosophically vexing questions. Not infrequently, the most narrow-sounding doctrinal issue, posed by the pedestrian facts of some every-day case, will turn out to be the miniature version of one of the deepest of moral conundrums, as I hope to show you with the three examples that follow.

My first example involves a thorny problem of causation. A man who happens to be afflicted with a frequently fatal, sexually transmitted disease, something like AIDS, and who knows that he is afflicted with this disease, nonetheless has intercourse with a woman without first warning her. He infects her, though luckily she never comes down with a full-fledged version of the disease. In addition, however, to infecting her, he also impregnates her. *The child that comes of this union also carries the fatal disease and dies within a year of its birth.* The question for the court is a simple and basic one: is the defendant guilty of homicide, specifically, has he committed involuntary manslaughter, or perhaps even murder?

On the one hand, one is inclined to say that of course his reckless act of inter-course fairly directly led to the child's death, and therefore, yes, he is guilty of manslaughter and given the extreme recklessness of his behavior, maybe even murder. On the other hand, there is the fact that the child is not really worse off on account of his father's recklessness: it isn't as though, but for his father's reck-lessness, the child would be flourishing. But for the father's recklessness, the child would never have been conceived in the first place! Given that, can one really find him guilty of homicide?

Which of these two possible ways of looking at the matter is right? Whichever view we choose turns out to have some oddball implications. If we say that he is guilty of murder, it seems we might then have to convict all parents who know that they carry a genetic disease that will eventually lead to their offspring's death. Worse yet, it seems we might be led to convict an obstetrician who prevents an endangered fetus from being spontaneously aborted, if it is then born with a fatal ailment that leads to its death a few years later. That's because both the parent with the genetic disease and the helpful obstetrician took actions which they knew had a high probability of leading to the death of the person in whose birth they had such a crucial part. Indeed if we press the logic of this view further, are we not driven to conclude that every mother is a murderer by virtue of the fact that she knowingly causes the death of every creature she causes to be born?

Unfortunately, if we take the alternative view, that the man with the infectious disease did not kill the baby, we are driven to some equally troublesome conclu-sions. Think of a woman who takes a perfectly legal recreational drug late in her pregnancy which she knows will precipitate the death of her baby soon after its birth. We tend to think she should be found guilty of something. Now suppose she argues that if she had realized that she would not be permitted access to that drug late in her pregnancy she would never have gone through with the pregnancy. If we exonerate the AIDS-infected father on the ground that but for his recklessness the child would never have been born in the first place, don't we have to exoner-ate that mother as well on the grounds that but for her recklessness her child would never have been born either? But for being able to take that drug, the mother would not have carried her child to term.

Lurking behind this somewhat specialized case is nothing less than the more general question that has come to preoccupy a number of philosophers, whether it is ever possible for one generation to complain about the actions of an earlier generation. That's because in a fundamental sense, all of us bear a very similar relationship to most mishaps that befall our children as the AIDS-infected father bears to his offspring. Suppose our generation decides to binge on energy, and that as a result five generations from now there is next to none left for our descendants. Do they have a right to complain? In a sense, they certainly do: our bingeing on energy causes their misery. On the other hand, is it really true that if we hadn't binged, they would now live more splendidly? No, it is not true. It is not true because of an easily overlooked fact, to which some moral philosophers have very insistently drawn attention. If we today had pursued a different, less spendthrift energy policy, a lot of other things would be different as well. Different people would marry or mate with different people and would conceive children at different times. Some children would then be born that otherwise wouldn't have been. To be sure, in the first generation after us only a few such children would be born. But these children would mate with others and in the second generation there would be more children yet who would not have been born otherwise. And five generations down the pike an entirely different population would exist than would exist if a different energy policy had been pursued. What this means is that a future generation will never be in a position to claim that it would be better off if we had not binged on oil. Someone would be better off, but not they. They would not have been conceived. That is, here as in the AIDS hypothetical, the very act which renders the lives of the future generation bad ones also causes them to come into existence. Therefore, here as in the AIDS hypothetical, the complainers *can* say that their ancestors' actions led to their plight. But they *cannot* say that but for those actions they would be better off. They would not be around.

So which is the appropriate perspective? Can future generations complain about past generations or not? Philosophers are all over the map on this. Thomas Schwartz who first focussed on this problem said they can't complain (Schwartz, 1978). Derek Parfit who has examined the problem in more detail since then says they can complain, and has devised a brilliant hypothetical to prove his point (Parfit, 1987). Imagine, he says, two drugs both dispensed by the government. There is a disease which, if it afflicts women, causes their children to be born with some prominent congenital defect, say, a missing limb or two. There are two strains of the disease. For both we have cures of a sort, but slightly different cures. For strain *A* we can give the mother the drug and the child will not have a problem. For strain *B* we can tell the mother to wait until she has recovered and to have her children only then. Since the disease has produced no symptoms in the mother, testing is required to see whether she is infected. The government has two programs in place for preventing each strain of the disease. Program *A* tests women for whether they have strain *A* and if they do gives them the pill. Program *B* tests women for whether they have strain *B*, but if they do, they are not treated (there not being any treatment), but simply told to wait a month before conceiving, until the disease has had a chance to disappear. The first program forestalls about a thousand problem births per year. The second program forestalls about 2,000 problem births per year. If the government had to cut one of them, which should it cut? Why, clearly says Parfit it should cut Program *A* which only forestalls 1,000, not 2,000, problem births. If we took Donald Schwartz's view instead, we would have to reason thus: if we cut Program *A*, there will be 1,000 children who can say that but for what we did they would be uninjured, whereas if we cut Program *B*, there will *not* be a single child who can say that but for what we did they would be uninjured: the 2,000 children thus afflicted would not have been born if the government had pursued its old policy.

Parfit's hypothetical is inspired, but hardly clinches the matter. I do not, however aim to solve the problem here. My only purpose in expounding on it is to show the close connection between a narrow question of causation in the criminal law and that broad question of intergenerational ethics.

Another perennial doctrinal question of the criminal law, with broad philosophical import, is the distinction between acts and omissions. One can cause death by an act or by omitting to save someone's life. Ordinarily, in both law and morality we only consider the former to be murder. There are exceptions: If I bear a special relationship to someone, if I'm his father or doctor, I might be found guilty of murder for deliberately or recklessly failing to save him when I could. In some jurisdictions, I might even be considered guilty of murder, absent such a relationship, if I was nearby when the victim got in trouble and could have saved him with incredible ease. But, generally speaking, omitting to save is not murder.

This doctrine has gained special significance in the courts' treatment of euthanasia. Most jurisdictions do not permit a doctor to kill a terminally ill patient (regardless of the patient's wishes or those of his family). They do however permit him to not apply extraordinary measures to prolong the life of such a patient (at least provided the patient or his family have so indicated). What this means is that different standards are applied to the doctor depending on whether he causes his patient to die by an act or an omission. He simply may not cause the patient's death by an act, however hopeless and painful the patient's plight appears to be. He may, however, cause the patient's death by an omission, at least if his patient's plight appears sufficiently hopeless and painful. Thus a lot hinges on a quintessentially philosophical issue whether a particular way of causing death is to be regarded as causing death by an act or as causing death by an omission. Perhaps the best way to get the philosophical flavor of that issue is to construct a little imaginary dialogue that might erupt between a prosecutor and a defendant in such a case. Imagine that a doctor has just unplugged the life-support system of an irreversibly comatose patient. Let us suppose further that if this measure could be described as an omission to save, we would deem it appropriate. Not so if it amounts to an act of killing. So which is it?

Prosecutor: (*to doctor*) You disconnected the life-support system that kept the patient going and the patient died. Therefore you clearly killed the patient.

Doctor: I did not. Each pulsation of the respirator and each drop of fluid introduced into the patient's body by intravenous feeding devices is comparable to a manually administered injection or item of medication. Hence disconnecting the mechanical devices is really the same as withholding such injection or medication.

Prosecutor: Nonsense. Suppose the patient's worst enemy had walked into the hospital and done what you did here. Suppose, that is, he had just simply disconnected the patient. He owes no special duty and he has killed by omission. Thus by the logic of your argument he should not be found guilty. And that seems preposterous.

Doctor: You've got things wrong. Suppose a child is drowning. I am about to save it. The child's worst enemy tackles me and thus *prevents* me from saving the child. *I* will have killed that child by an omission. But *he* will have killed it by an action, inasmuch as he prevented me from saving it. The same thing can be said about your hypothetical about the patient's worst enemy. When the doctor disconnects, he is behaving as I am when I fail to go out to save the drowning child and thus only kills by omission. But when the enemy unplugs the equipment, he is preventing the doctor from treating the patient and thus behaving just like the fellow who is tackling me to prevent me from swimming out to save the drowning child. He is causing death by an act. He is a killer.

Prosecutor: I agree with your analysis of the case of the drowning child. But I don't think you are applying it correctly to the situation of the terminal patient. Wouldn't it be more accurate to say that when a doctor disconnects the life-support equipment which is in the process of keeping the patient alive he is behaving like the person who tackles a would-be rescuer and prevents him from saving the child? So he really is killing by an act rather than an omission.

Doctor: You are stretching the notion of prevention all out of shape. By that token one could say that the person who passed by a desperately thirsty man in the desert but who failed to open his waterhose to him was preventing the water from reaching the man and thus was killing him.

Prosecutor: Look, suppose this man were living in a comatose state without support systems. But some other patient needed kidneys. Could you remove this man's kidneys on the grounds that they are basically the same as a dialysis machine, each pump of which is equivalent to some manually administered treatment, which it is legitimate to withhold?

Doctor: If you insist on being commonsensical, don't introduce misleading metaphors like kidney dialysis. The fact is that there was here a sick man. If we intervene to save him, he lives. If we do not, he dies. We leave him no worse off than he would be without us. That's a classic case of letting die, not killing.

Prosecutor: What do you mean by saying "If we intervene to save him, he lives. If we do not, he dies. We leave him no worse off than he would be without us." If you had never started to help him in the first place, he would have ended up in the care of some other doctors, who would have saved him. He would thus not have died. So in fact he would be better off if you had never intervened in the situation. You did leave him worse off than he would be without you. That can hardly be described as a mere case of letting die.

Doctor: But how do you know those other doctors wouldn't have proceeded just as I did?

Although the debate is hardly at an end, we shall here cut it short. It has served its purpose, to illuminate the kinds of arguments that go into deciding whether to characterize conduct as an act or an omission.

Like my earlier AIDS hypothetical, the somewhat technical issue of the act–omission distinction connects up rather easily with all kinds of burning and concrete issues of practical ethics, the abortion controversy, for instance. This was famously illustrated with a celebrated hypothetical by the philosopher Judith Jarvis Thomson (Jarvis Thomson, 1971). Imagine, Thomson wrote, a hospital patient wakes up one morning only to discover that while asleep he has been "hooked up" to a renowned violin virtuoso. The virtuoso is afflicted with a strange blood disease and will die unless he is able to remain continuously hooked up to a compatible, healthy blood donor for the next nine months. Are you obligated to make the sacrifice the virtuoso asks of you? Must you remain hooked up to him for the next nine months? Your judgment of this issue will largely depend on how firmly you believe in the ethical underpinnings of the act–omission distinction. If you are convinced by the ethical force of the distinction, if you think there is a world of an ethical difference between killing someone and letting him die (notwithstanding the prosecutor's arguments to the contrary in the above dialogue), then you probably also judge the hospital patient entitled to disconnect from the virtuoso – and the pregnant woman entitled to abort.

For a final example of a doctrinal question with broad philosophical import, consider the law of complicity. If you help someone commit a crime, you are his accomplice. That sounds like a straightforward enough idea. What possible complications could arise in the course of implementing it? Plenty, it turns out. The most puzzling aspect of the concept of complicity is this basic question: What kind of contribution does it take to become an accomplice? The problem is neatly posed by a case like *Wilox* v. *Jeffery* [1951] 1 All ER 464. In 1949, a man named Coleman Hawkins, described by the court as a "celebrated professor of the saxophone," arrived in London to give a jazz concert at the Prince Theatre. He did so without having a work permit. Among the people greeting him at the airport was one Herbert Wilcox, the owner of a magazine called *Jazz Illustrated*. Wilcox attended the concert and gave it an enthusiastic review. Then, no doubt to his great surprise, he was prosecuted for the crime of aiding and abetting someone (namely, Coleman Hawkins), in violating the immigration law provision prohibiting foreigners from working in England without a permit.

The court explained:

> [Wilcox] paid to go to the concert and he went there because he wanted to report it. He must, therefore, be held to have been present, taking part, concurring or encouraging, whichever word you like to use for expressing this conception. It was an illegal act on the part of Hawkins to play the saxophone or any other instrument at this concert. [Wilcox] clearly knew that it was an unlawful act for him to play. He had gone there to hear him, and his presence and his payment to go there was an encouragement. He went there to make use of the performance . . . he went there . . . to get "copy" for his newspaper. It might have been entirely different . . . if he had gone there and protested, saying: "the musicians' union do not like you foreigners coming here and playing and you ought to get off the stage." If he had booed, it might have been some evidence that he was not aiding and abetting. If he had gone as a member of a claque to try to drown the noise of the saxophone, he might very likely be found not guilty of aiding and abetting. In this case, it seems clear that he was there, not only to approve and encourage what was done, but to take advantage of it by getting "copy" for his paper. [Thus we can say that] he aided and abetted. (Wilcox v. Jeffery [1951] 1 All ER 464)

Given the logic of the court's opinion, it is quite likely that it would have found all the other spectators to qualify as accomplices as well. Is this a sensible outcome? Many think not. Surely, they say, a more substantial contribution is needed to make someone an accomplice than something as insignificant as attending and applauding? On the other hand, together the various spectators did make a substantial contribution, one without which Hawkins's performance would not have taken place.

This sort of problem is quite common. We can shed light on it by thinking about a related phenomenon in economics: when you add up the marginal contributions of every worker in some enterprise (the amount of the total product that would not have been produced if that worker were absent), you will generally find that these contributions do not add up to the enterprise's total output. After all every corporation would pretty much run on as it does if any one of its employees were to be cut. That employee's absence would only subtract a smidgeon at most from the corporation's total output. Add up the smidgeons of all employees and their sum is still less than the total product the corporation turns out. This is just a special manifestation of the principle of diminishing marginal returns, which should perhaps more revealingly be called the principle of increasing marginal redundancy: in group activities everyone is more or less redundant and becomes increasingly so as the size of the group increases. Therefore adding up the amounts that would not have been achieved but for any individual's presence do not add up to the total.

With this in mind, it's pretty easy to think of lots of cases that are like *Wilcox v. Jeffery*. Imagine that A, B, C, and D, jointly issue some stock. As the law requires, they prepare a prospectus describing the stock, to be given to every potential purchaser. Many people buy. Then it turns out that the prospectus contained four egregious misrepresentations, falsehoods deliberately inserted to boost the value of the stock. When the truth comes out, the stock price falls. Some injured shareholders sue A, B, C, and D. The trial reveals that each of the four defendants contributed one of the misrepresentations. A study is conducted to assess the damages and it determines them to be $1,111. The study also concluded that had there been only one misrepresentation, damages would have been $1,000, had there been two, they would have been $1,100, and had there been three they would have been $1,110. In other words, one misrepresentation did $1,000 worth of damages, a second added only $100 to that total, a third only $10, and a fourth only $1.

It is now easier to understand the purpose of the law of complicity. Under traditional non-complicity doctrines, everyone is only liable if, but for him, some substantial harm would not have happened. Under that approach most members of a vicious group would be let off. Like the lying stock issuers, they would get off by reason of redundancy.

Once one has decided that it is possible to be an accomplice both to good and to bad deeds without actually making a difference, and certainly without making a substantial difference, one confronts a further problem. How is one going to distinguish bona fide accomplices from everyone else who did not made a difference to the outcome either? If I shout encouragement at a would-be assassin, I am an accomplice, even though the assassin was already determined to go ahead without my encouragement. If I shout encouragement at a deaf assassin, or at the television set depicting the assassination Jack Ruby-style, I am *not* an accomplice. Yet in both cases I shouted encouragement which made no difference. Why in the former case am I an accomplice and not in the latter case?

The answer is that there are different ways of *not* making a difference. Just think about a firing squad shooting at a lone target. Suppose that the execution is witnessed by a silently approving onlooker. Every single soldier in that firing squad as well as the onlooker is superfluous to the deadly outcome. But only the soldiers qualify as accomplices, not the onlooker, because they are superfluous in very different ways. The soldiers are superfluous by reason of redundancy: if we subtracted other soldiers from the scene, a given soldier's contribution to the outcome would eventually come to make a difference. The same cannot be said for the onlooker: he is superfluous by reason of his sheer ineffectuality. However many other actors we subtract from the scene, the onlooker's contribution will never make a difference to the outcome.

This problem too rather easily connects up with a larger issue: the question of collective responsibility for the atrocities said to be committed by one country upon another. Understanding complicity helps us sort out the contradictory impulses that beset our thinking about the responsibility of entire communities. It tells us that we are right to discount the frequent objection members of such communities make on the ground that their contribution to the atrocity made no difference: redundancy is a feature of all collective action and is the very feature the doctrines of complicity were meant to cope with. Of course, the analysis of complicity also makes it clear that one must carefully distinguish different ways of making no difference: one must distinguish the redundancy of the soldier from the redundancy of the onlooker. And those two won't always be easy to keep apart. This, then, is the legitimate part of our discomfort with collective responsibility.

We have looked in the last two sections at two of the three basic problem areas that have aroused the attention of philosophers of criminal law: the purposes of punishment and the problems of the General Part. The third and final area I will take up is the criminal law's so-called special part, problems associated with the particular crimes that make up a criminal code. A question that arises with surprising frequency is the moral justification for criminalizing one or another form of perceived misconduct. The question does not merely arise as to such well-publicized bones of contention as prostitution, pornography, homosexuality, or the printing of classified information. It has proved if anything more vexing and philosophically intriguing in connection with various property offenses. It is three of these offenses which I propose to take up next.

Consider the crime of blackmail. The archetypical blackmail scenario of course runs like this: Busybody says to Philanderer, "Give me $10,000 or I will reveal your secret love life to your wife." What is odd, puzzling, and intriguing about the fact that we criminalize this threat is that there would be nothing criminal about

90

Busybody just going ahead and telling Philanderer's wife about her husband's affairs. Generally, when I have a right to do or not do something it means I am free to agree not to use that right in return for some remuneration. Suppose Busybody owned some undeveloped land, on which he were thinking of erecting an office building. Suppose Philanderer and others of Busybody's neighbors would rather have it left as it is, perhaps so they might use it as a park or country club. They offer Busybody some money in return for a long-term lease, or maybe even the outright sale of the land. Busybody is, of course, free to desist from his initial plans. He is free not to exercise his right to use the land as he wants to in return for the offered remuneration. How is what Busybody is doing in the archetypical black-mail case any different? Why isn't his right to tell Philanderer's wife about her husband's infidelities exactly like his right to build an office building on land he owns, and why therefore doesn't his right to tell her entail the right not to tell her in return for a fee, just as his right to build entails the right not to build in return for a fee? That is the paradox of blackmail. Innumerable scholars have tried their hands at resolving this puzzle and have in the course only proved how wonder-fully intractable it is.

Let us examine just a few of the proposed solutions. The philosopher Robert Nozick has made the appealing suggestion that blackmail is different from a regu-lar bargain and really more like a robbery, because whereas in a regular bargain we are thrilled that the other party is available to do business with, in blackmail as in robbery we would be happiest if the other party didn't exist! At first glance that seems eminently correct: we are benefited by the existence of the butcher, the baker, and the groceryman: they are people we *want* to do business with. We are hurt by the existence of the robber and the blackmailer. So let's put them out of commission! At second glance, however, the suggestion no longer works. Just think about a pedestrian whom you negligently hit with your car, and who threat-ens to sue you unless you pay for his medical expenses. Surely he is not blackmail-ing you, but simply asking for the minimum of what he is entitled to from you. Yet you are certainly not benefited by his existence. By Nozick's account, however, the pedestrian is blackmailing you.

Another explanation has been advanced by the legal scholar James Lindgren. Commenting on the archetypical blackmail scenario sketched out above, he writes:

Here the blackmailer threatens to tell others damaging information about the black-mail victim unless the victim heeds the blackmailer's request, usually a request for money. The blackmailer obtains what he wants by using extra leverage. But that leverage belongs more to a third person than to the blackmailer. The blackmail vic-tim pays the blackmailer to avoid involving third parties; he pays to avoid being harmed by *persons other than the blackmailer*. When the reputation of a person is damaged, he is punished by all those who change their opinion of him. They may "punish" him by treating him differently or he may be punished merely by the knowl-edge that others no longer respect him.

Thus when a blackmailer threatens to turn in a criminal unless paid money, the blackmailer is bargaining with the state's chip. The blackmail victim pays to avoid the harm that the state would inflict; he pays because he believes that he can thereby suppress the state's potential criminal claim . . . Likewise, when a blackmailer threatens to expose damaging but noncriminal behavior unless paid money, he is also turning third-party leverage to his own benefit. What makes his conduct blackmail is that he interposes himself parasitically in an actual or potential dispute in which he lacks a sufficiently direct interest. What right has he to make money by settling other people's claims?

At the heart of blackmail, then, is the triangular nature of the transaction, and particularly this disjunction between the blackmailer's personal benefit and the interests of the third parties whose leverage he uses. In effect, the blackmailer attempts to gain an advantage in return for suppressing someone else's actual or potential interest. The blackmailer is negotiating for his own gain with someone else's leverage or bargaining chips. (*Lindgren, 1984*)

Like Nozick's explanation, this account seems very compelling at first. But then counter-examples crop up that quickly generate considerable unease: "Pay me $10,000, or I will persuade your son that it is his patriotic duty to volunteer for combat duty in Vietnam"; "Pay me $10,000, or I will give your high-spirited, risk-addicted 19-year-old daughter a motorcycle for Christmas"; "Pay me $10,000, or I will hasten our ailing father's death by leaving the Catholic church"; "Pay me $10,000, or I will reveal to the world what a lousy lover you are." These examples reek of blackmail, but under Lindgren's account they wouldn't seem to qualify: it is hard to think of them as involving the misappropriation of somebody's bargaining chip.

Elsewhere I have propounded my own solution to the blackmail paradox. Its essential strategy is to point out how the paradox is just one member of a large family of puzzles surrounding the role of consent in the criminal law. Each of these other puzzles, though basically ignored to date, is at least as interesting as the original blackmail puzzle. Here is just one illustration which I have dubbed the "punishment puzzle":

One night, Smithy, the burglar, breaks into the house of Bartleby. He finds very little of value. As he is about to leave, he discovers a safe, which he is unable, however, to open. Wielding a club, he wakes up Bartleby and asks him for the combination. But Bartleby refuses to tell him. "Look here," says the exasperated Smithy, "unless you tell me the combination, I am going to beat you to a pulp," But Bartleby is adamant. "What's in that safe really isn't very valuable. Just some cheap family jewelry. But it has enormous sentimental value for me, having been passed through the generations for ages. I simply cannot give it up." But Smithy persists: "Tell me the combination, or I'll make you regret it." Bartleby quite sincerely replies: "Much as I fear physical violence, I'd rather you give me a savage beating than give up what's inside that safe." "As you wish," says Smithy and proceeds to administer a fairly severe pummelling.

Another night, another burglar, let's call him Louie, breaks into Bartleby's house. Like Smithy, he finds very little of value. As he is about to leave, he too discovers Bartleby's safe, which he too is unable to open. Wielding a club, he wakes up Bartleby and asks him for the combination, but Bartleby refuses to tell him. "Look here," says the exasperated Louie, "unless you tell me the combination, I am going to beat you to a pulp." But Bartleby is adamant. "What's in that safe really isn't very valuable. Just some cheap family jewelry. But it has enormous sentimental value for me, having been passed through the generations for ages. I simply cannot give it up." But Louie persists. "Tell me the combination, or I swear I'll make you regret it." Bartleby quite sincerely replies, "Much as I fear physical violence, I'd rather you give me a savage beating than give up what's inside that safe." "As you wish," says Louie, and is about to launch into the beating, when his eyes fall on a slip of paper lying at Bartleby's bedside. He takes a closer look and realizes that this is the combination to the safe. He is about to open the safe when Bartleby implores him, "Please, it's just like I said, I am really attached to those trinkets inside the safe and I would rather you beat me to a pulp than strip me of those trinkets." Louie remains unmoved, opens the safe, takes what he finds inside and makes off.

Both Smithy and Louie are caught. You are the judge. Which of them should you punish more harshly?

What the law would do is reasonably clear – punish Smithy, the batterer, worse than Louie, the thief. The batterer would probably be found guilty of aggravated robbery, the thief of simple robbery. But that could vary. What is unlikely to vary is the significantly graver treatment of batterers than thieves. But does that make sense? (*Katz, 1996*)

A good case exists on both sides. Arguing for treating the batterer more leniently than the thief is the fact that ordinarily we think harm is in the eye of the victim. After all, the very conduct that would constitute a crime if done without his consent is regarded as perfectly innocent if he has consented. Add consent, and what otherwise would be a theft becomes a gift, what otherwise would be an assault becomes surgery, what otherwise would be a rape becomes love-making. Of course, in the punishment puzzle the victim did not give his free and voluntary consent to any kind of harm. But it would still seem to follow that, as between different harms, those the victim likes least are most harmful, and those the victim can tolerate most are least harmful. And that would suggest that the thief in my "punishment puzzle" is worse than the batterer.

On the other hand, there are strong arguments for a contrary position. Imagine the case of a man about to rape a woman. As he holds the knife to her throat, the woman declares "I would rather die than be violated." If he kills her, will he be able to argue that he should be punished no more harshly than he would be for a rape, since this victim preferred being killed to being raped? If we view the batterer more leniently than the thief on account of the victim's preferences, wouldn't we have to accept that argument as well?

Working one's way through the punishment puzzle and its various cousins turns out to lead to a solution of the original blackmail puzzle and to help one more generally to make sense of the strange ways of consent in the criminal law. Indeed it even helps one make sense of various problems surrounding the two offenses I shall take up next: insider trading and evasion.

Like blackmail, insider trading is something everyone is against and no one knows why. The archetypical case of insider trading looks as follows. The CEO of a large company learns that his company has just hit an oil mine. Before the news leaks out and causes the stock price to rise, he quickly buys up a substantial block of shares. When the news gets out he is able to resell it at a handsome profit. This is the sort of thing the law against insider trading forbids. It will seem so viscerally unfair to most people as to scarcely require any further justification. But if we do try to justify it nonetheless, we are in for real problems. One problem surfaces when we ask ourselves who has been hurt by the insider's behavior. Who is the insider's victim? First impressions notwithstanding, it is not the shareholder who is selling his shares while the insider is buying and who will be kicking himself when he finally sees its value go up. If the insider had abstained from trading, that shareholder would still have been selling his stock. It's just that the stock would have gone to someone other than the insider. It is this would-be buyer who loses out as a result of the insider's activities: the person who *would* have bought stock but did not buy stock because the insider was buying. This potential buyer – we will in fact never know who he is – hardly looks like a victim deserving either of special protection or compensation. After all, what kind of duty does the insider owe him in the first place? But without a victim deserving of protection and compensation, how can we be upset about insider trading? Could it be that insider trading is a victimless crime like drug use or prostitution? That seems like a very strange claim. This, moreover, is just one of many problems that beset any attempt at justifying the ban on insider trading. It does not follow that the ban is without merit. As with blackmail, enough effort will eventually turn up a satisfactory justification. It's just that doing so is a surprisingly challenging project. (One solution is proposed in Katz, 1996.)

Another set of puzzles is posed by crimes of evasion, sometimes referred to as a "fraud on the law." What makes this offense puzzling is that it implicates behavior that sometimes gets held up as exemplary of skilful lawyering and at other times is castigated as a fraud. Here are some typical cases: a 30-year-old foreigner who would ordinarily have to wait years to qualify for an immigrant visa arranges for a strategic marriage to his 70-year-old landlady. Has he committed a fraud upon our immigration laws? A depositor who wants to keep his assets secret and who realizes that banks must file reports about all deposits in excess of $10,000 puts $9,999 in 20 different banks. Has he committed a fraud on the bank reporting laws? A debtor who is about to declare bankruptcy uses what money he still has to buy an apartment, because basic necessities, like one's dwelling, cannot be seized by creditors even in a bankruptcy. Has he committed a fraud on the bankruptcy laws? A taxpayer who realizes that he cannot deduct the annual $1,000 gifts he is making to his son from his income tax embarks upon the following maneuver: he presents his son with a $10,000 cash gift, then asks him for a $10,000 business loan, and then proceeds to pay him $1,000 by way of interest every year. This $1,000 he then deducts from his income as a business expense. Has he committed tax fraud?

What I said about the criminal law's General Part also holds true for the special part. Its significance transcends the specific criminal law doctrines it purports to deal with. Coercion, deception, and trickery play a role throughout the law. Wherever they arise, the lessons taught by an examination of blackmail, insider trading, or evasion are apt to have relevance.

References

Alexander, L. 1980: The doomsday machine: proportionality, punishment and prevention. *The Monist*, 63 (23), 65–92.

Dressler, J. 1987: *Understanding Criminal Law*. New York: Matthew Bender.

Duff, R. A. 1987: *Trials and Punishments*. Cambridge: Cambridge University Press.

Fletcher, G. 1978: *Rethinking Criminal Law*. Boston: Little, Brown & Co.

Gescheider, G. A. et al. 1982: Psychophysical measurement of the judged seriousness of crimes and severity of punishment. *Bulletin of the Psychonomic Society*, 82, 275.

Hart, H. L. A. 1968: *Punishment and Responsibility*. Oxford: Oxford University Press.

Husak, D. 1987: *Philosophy of Criminal Law*. Totowa, NJ: Rowman & Littlefield.

Jarvis Thomson, J. 1971: A defense of abortion. *Philosophy and Public Affairs*, 1, 47–66.

Kadish, S. H. 1987: *Blame and Punishment*. New York: Macmillan.

Katz, L. 1987: *Bad Acts and Guilty Minds: conundrums of the criminal law*. Chicago and London: University of Chicago Press.

—— 1996: *Ill-Gotten Gains: evasion, blackmail, fraud and kindred puzzles of the law*. Chicago and London: University of Chicago Press.

Lindgren, J. 1984: Unraveling the paradox of blackmail. *Columbia Law Review*, 670, 702.

Moore, M. 1993: *Act and Crime*. Oxford: Oxford University Press.

—— 1996: *Placing Blame*. Oxford: Oxford University Press.

Parfit, D. 1987: *Reasons and Persons*. Oxford: Oxford University Press, Part IV.

Schwartz, T. 1978: Obligations to posterity. In R. I. Sikora and B. Barry (eds), *Obligations to Future Generations*, Philadelphia: Temple University Press.

Sellin, T. and Wolfgang, M. E. 1964: *The Measurement of Delinquency*. New York: John Wiley & Sons.

Williams, G. 1961: *Criminal Law: the general part*. London: Sweet & Maxwell, 2nd edn.

5

Public international law

PHILIP BOBBITT

The term "international law" first appears in an essay by Jeremy Bentham, *The Introduction to the Principles of Morals and Legislation*, written in 1789. The timing and the definition of this term are significant; not only has "international law" developed as a result of the development of the state itself, but 1789 is usually taken as a turning point in the structure of the state. In that year, the state began to change from the dynastic, monarchical structures that had dominated Europe to a more abstracted structure that drew its legitimacy from its relationship to the nation, rather than to a royal family. Accordingly, although Bentham claims to be doing no more than renaming what had been called "the law of nations," in fact he makes two important distinctions between that law and the new subject of international law. While the law of nations held that suits by a state against a private citizen of another state, and also suits between two citizens from different states, lay in the domain of the law of nations, Bentham excludes such cases and assumes that they properly belong to domestic rather than international law. For Bentham, as for us, international law has to do with relations among states, within a society of states that is distinct from the relationships among rulers and their subjects that hitherto prevailed. This article examines the applicability and sources of international law, both of which are distinct from that of domestic jurisprudence. This distinction lies in the society that gives rise to international law – a society of states rather than individuals. There are, nevertheless, profound links between domestic and international law such that one might well say that international law is constructed out of the assumptions of constitutional law. Different assumptions about the ground of legitimacy for the state, the bases for constitutional law, will ultimately yield a different international law; this transition is in fact already underway.

The subject matter of international law

The subject matter of international law thus concerns the various legal relationships of that society (and not simply those of states, per se). These are principally: (1) those matters that arise among states because they do not fall within the authoritative scope of a single state, such as questions arising as to territory, jurisdiction, nationality, migration, and other trans-state subjects; (2) issues that concern a state's behavior in relation to other states, such as the use of force, the construction of treaties, the operation of intergovernmental organizations; and (3) aspects of the state itself, including its definition, liability and immunity, relationship to its own nationals, especially its respect for their human rights.

Territory

Whether territory has been legally acquired is a matter for international law to determine. It is thus more than a coincidence that the first scholarly commentary that we may count as reflecting a modern perspective on the legal relations among states occurs in Spain at about the time Europe was struggling with the legal and moral issues arising from the discovery and exploration of the New World. Pope Gregory XIII's "line of demarcation" that divided up South America between the Portuguese and the Spanish more properly belongs to the medieval, religious function of the universal church rather than to the Renaissance displacement of that function which turned to legal relations among states as providing the defining rule for territorial legitimacy. The modes of legitimate acquisition of territory include: discovery, occupation, prescription (as by long and peaceful possession), purchase from another state, or cession by another state, conquest, disposition by treaty, and assignment by an international organization (including assignment in trust, as was frequently done by the UN in the aftermath of World War II). The content of such transfers is by no means limited to the right to control activity within a defined border, but extends also to airspace, subsoil rights, and authority over the continental shelf and the deep sea bed. Moreover, international law recognizes special domains that do not merely concern simple, absolute territorial rights but include various servitudes, demilitarized zones (such as those that divide North and South Korea), transit corridors (as once connected the Weimar Republic with East Prussia), free cities (such as Danzig), customs-free zones (such as the Coal and Steel Community of 1950s Europe) and concessions (such as those accorded Western powers by China in the latter part of the nineteenth century). Because territorial contiguity is one of the defining characteristics of the modern state – as opposed to the often widely separated inherited holdings of feudal domains – international law has taken this as a crucial subject for its development.

Jurisdiction

The competence of a state to prescribe, adjudicate, and enforce its domestic law is primarily a matter of its territorial extent, with the rare exceptions where there are persons within its territory who are immune from its jurisdiction, and rare occasions in which a state may exercise jurisdiction beyond its territory. To this territorial principle, must be added four other principles that support jurisdiction: nationality, security (or protective), universality and passive personality. These principles are used to resolve those situations in which more than one state claims jurisdiction. Thus, although, typically, events occurring within a single state's territorial boundaries give that state a basis for the application of its laws, some

97

offenses may be committed within the territory of one state that cause injury in another state. Most controversially, this has occurred when one state seeks extra-territorial jurisdiction beyond its borders, as for example when the United States seeks to apply its anti-trust laws to the actions of companies situated abroad whose anti-competitive behavior has effects within the United States. More than one state may legitimately claim jurisdiction; no rule of international law grants a state exclusive jurisdiction, even over matters that occur solely within its borders. In addition to jurisdiction arising from territoriality, states often exercise their authority based on the nationality of the party. A state may exercise jurisdiction over its nationals wherever they may be and with respect to offenses committed anywhere. Also a state may exercise jurisdiction over non-nationals whose offenses occur abroad but the effects of which are injurious to the security of the state. On this basis a state might claim jurisdiction over persons plotting to overthrow its government, although strictly speaking no "effects" had occurred within the target state, and the conspiracy took place abroad among non-nationals. British efforts to gain jurisdiction over IRA terrorists could rely on this basis even if the criminal acts took place outside the United Kingdom, were carried out by non-UK nationals, and were thwarted before any injuries could be accomplished. While this protective or security basis for state jurisdiction is typically relied upon when the acts are either not criminal in the state where they occur, or are unlikely of prosecution, the universality principle is invoked with respect to offenses that are crimes that are universally recognized as such or are crimes pertaining to the whole of humanity. The idea of a universal crime over which all states could exercise jurisdiction regardless of the offender's nationality or the place of incidence arose from the efforts to combat piracy; today, war crimes and acts of genocide also support universal jurisdiction. Whether torture also supports this jurisdiction is at present unclear. Finally, a state may exercise jurisdiction over its non-national with respect to acts that, although they occurred beyond the territory of the state, inflicted harm on that state's national. This basis for jurisdiction – the passive personality principle – is vigorously contested by states in the Anglo-American tradition and was not included in the 1935 Draft Convention that recognizes the four other principles.

Nationality

International law is the law for a society of states; thus it does not confer nationality on any individuals – including those born within the territory of a state – but it can be said to restrict the discretion of states to grant or withdraw nationality and to give rules by which contested versions of a single person's individuality can be resolved. For example, the conferment of naturalization by a state depends on the acquiescence of the individuals – since to hold otherwise risks infringing the rights of the previous state of national origin; nor does a state have any duty to admit former nationals whom it has denationalized, expecting insofar as such refusal amounts to an effort to deprive the current state of residence of the right of expulsion. Similarly, the very freedom of states to determine the identity of their own nationals leads to two kinds of problems: the stateless person, from whom all nationality has been withdrawn, and the plural national. Statelessness is the absence of nationality, and its consequence is that a state that inflicts injury on a stateless person cannot be challenged by any other state attempting to invoke its protection for that person. With respect to plural nationals, every state whose nationality a person possesses may regard him as a national and no state can invoke the protection of its nationals against a state to whom those persons are also nationals. The *Nottebohm* case – in which a German national, long resident in Guatemala, sought to avoid belligerent status at the time of World War II through a hasty and attenuated claim of Liechtenstein nationality – illustrates, however, the movement toward a realistic examination of a claimant's links with a particular state as determinative of the claims of protection asserted by one state against another with respect to a claimed national. In an effort to forestall the asserted protection of its nationals by certain states, "Calvo" clauses – named after a distinguished Argentine jurist and statesman – were frequently included in agreements between Latin American states and foreigners, purporting to waive the protection sought by nationals of foreign states. This ploy has been ineffective owing to the reason that international law recognizes such protection as a right of states and, thus, not alienable by a person.

International movement of persons

As a general matter, states have the right to determine whom to admit within their borders, and whom to expel. If nationals of a state are expelled from another state, however, the state of nationality is obliged to receive them unless they are willing to go to another state that will admit them. It was in acknowledgment of this rule of international law that the United Kingdom in 1972 admitted all East African Asians who were not Ugandan nationals, following their despicable expulsion from Uganda. States are, however, free to repatriate aliens whom they regard as undesirable – although, as the Mariel exodus of Cubans to the United States showed, this is not always easy – and states are also absolutely free to admit persons seeking asylum, though they are not required under international law to do so. Under the 1951 Convention Relating to the Status of Refugees and the 1967 Protocol Relating to the Status of Refugees, the Contracting Parties promised to accord refugees treatment no less favorable than that accorded aliens generally and agreed that no refugee once admitted could be expelled to territory "where his life or freedom would be questioned."

Global areas

The very territorial basis of the modern state, and its association with nationality and jurisdiction, mean that vast areas will be the subject of international law when this territorial basis is absent. Thus, the law of the sea, polar regions, air and outer space, as well as the global ecology that transcends any particular territory, are all important dimensions of international law. How would we determine the scope of a state's territorial sea, particularly in cases where offshore islands or the waters of a bay bounded by more than one state give rise to overlapping claims? How would we devise consistent rules for safe passage, the transit through international straits, and duty to aid vessels of a foreign flag in distress? Such subjects are not amenable to the decision of a single state alone. The continental shelf, which varies from region to region but is everywhere a potential source of minerals and sea life, is but one example of the legal difficulty posed by oceanic resources that are not obviously within the political borders of a system of states organized by borders. The Grotius–Selden debate of the seventeenth century was resolved in favor of freedom of the high seas and ever since international law has governed this subject. The high seas are defined by international law and are open to all commercial navigation, but only vessels that are associated with a particular state have such freedom – another reflection of the state-based nature of international law. A vessel that does not display a state flag may be detained and searched by any governmental vessel, and there must be a genuine link between the vessel and its state of origin. It was at first thought that the high seas would provide a model for the legal treatment of airspace, but the military use of the air to deliver lethal fire has led to the assertion of national airspace. Each state has sovereignty as to the airspace over its territory, and indeed this has also led to the assertion of aerial defense zones, extending hundreds of miles out to sea beyond a state's borders. But the most significant contemporary development in international law over subjects that are necessarily not amenable to a territorial treatment has been the growing consciousness of the need for rules to protect the global ecology. International law will embrace such problems as marine pollution, climatic change, air quality and the protection of the ozone layer, the by-products of development, and the export of hazardous materials; the competitive nature of the state system puts the system itself at risk if there is a fragmentary application of national law to such subjects.

Use of force

Before there was international law, there were doctrines on the legitimate use of force. A "just war," St Augustine wrote, was one to avenge injuries that "the nation or city against which war-like action is to be directed has neglected either to punish wrongs committed by its own citizens or to restore what has been unjustly taken by it." Thus for a very long time, violence and legitimacy have been intertwined; one might say that current doctrines on the use of force, however, are so completely different in their makeup as to suggest that pre-state notions represent a vestigial line that has been largely replaced. "Just war" doctrine was a theological idea, whereas the state system did not emerge until the universal political authority of the European Church had been shattered. When this happened, the right to use force was considered an attribute of every sovereign state, and the law of nations placed no restraints on the resort to war (though there were customs regarding permissible tactics in war). During pauses in the wars that began in 1914 and ended in 1990, there were efforts to outlaw war as an instrument of state policy. In 1928, the international community agreed on a comprehensive ban on war (except in self-defense). Sixty-three states signed the Kellogg–Briand

Pact for the Renunciation of War that year. In 1945, the United Nations Charter banned the threat or use of force (except in self-defense or as authorized by the United Nations itself). But it is only since 1990 that there has been a consensus within the society of states – which is to say among the great powers of that system – to rely on the rules and procedures of the Charter. It is thus far too soon to say whether this will be an effective rule of international law, but one can say that, at present, it is the law even if, as in the wars in the former state of Yugoslavia, it has been difficult to generate the moral and physical resources to enforce that law.

Article 2(4) of the UN Charter prohibits the use of force and, thus, is not limited to war alone but embraces all threats and acts of international violence by states. There are three exceptions to this proscription: states may use force: (1) in self-defense on behalf of themselves (as for example when Iran responded to the Iraq invasion in 1981) or in aid of other states (as when the US sent forces to assist South Vietnam); or (2) as part of a collective enterprise taken pursuant to UN authorization (as was the case in Korea in 1949), or if the use of force is specifically endorsed by the UN Security Council (as was the case when Coalition forces invaded Iraq and Kuwait in 1990 and also with the barely averted US invasion of Haiti in 1995). "Self-defense," however, is not self-defining. The *Caroline* rules articulated by the US Secretary of State, Daniel Webster, provide that the state resorting to force in self-defense must demonstrate that the need for action was "instant, overwhelming, and leaving no choice of means, and no moment for deliberation"; moreover, it is also generally accepted that the extent of the force used must be commensurate with the aggression it seeks to repel. But what of anticipatory retaliation, such as the Israeli attack on the United Arab Republic in 1967, that seeks to pre-empt an imminent aggression? And what of acts of force on behalf of state nationals abroad? The US mission to rescue hostages held in Iran in 1980, and the Israeli raid on Entebbe in 1976, provide instances of states acting without UN endorsement to intervene when the host state has either failed to protect foreign nationals on its territory or, as in the case of Iran, has illegally held them as hostages. What of humanitarian intervention, perhaps the most vexing case of all, in which a state uses force to protect another state's nationals against that state itself? It is very difficult to reconcile the flat prohibitions of Article 2(4) with transborder uses of force to support democratic self-determination or democratic processes when these have been hijacked, to suppress crimes against humanity including genocide, even to provide humanitarian aid where there is no constituted authority to request aid and the context of assistance is contested by force.

Construction of treaties

"Treaty" is the general term used to describe conventions, agreements, protocols, and exchanges of notes between or among states and governed by international law. International law does not distinguish between agreements identified as treaties and other agreements. The interpretation of treaties, including even those interpretive agreements such as the 1969 Vienna Convention of the Law of Treaties, is based on customary international law. As with other subjects of international law, the interpretation and application of treaties and interstate agreements necessarily cannot be confined to the domestic law of a single state, anymore than the construction of a contract can be left to the opinion of a single party. Moreover, the importance of treaties is greater than ever before. Although the commercial movement of goods and services is largely governed by private international law, the international law of trade is largely treaty based. Tariffs, quotas, contraband rules, subsidies, anti-dumping provisions, free trade zones, export controls on weapons technology and fissile material, all are governed by treaties.

To some extent, treaties are an effort to escape customary international law, much as statutory codification is an effort to escape the common law. But it would be erroneous to conclude that treaties privatize law; on the contrary, treaties depend upon international law because their construction depends on international law. Subjects such as treaty accession (by which a non-signatory state may subsequently become bound by treaty provisions), reservation (which apply to multilateral agreements), amendment and modification (which apply to all agreements), interpretation and termination are all matters of international law.

Operation of intergovernmental organizations

Organizations such as the United Nations and its predecessor the League of Nations were created as permanent congresses, not unlike the Congresses of Vienna, Verona, and Troppau, with representatives from member states. Other organizations, like the Red Cross and the World Health Organization, deal with governments but are not representative bodies. Still others, like the International Law Commission and the International Labor Organization, have state representatives but have a specialized function. All these organizations are created by international law, which determines their competence, functions, immunities, and legal status. Whereas formerly only states could bring claims against another state, make treaties, appear before international tribunals, or violate international law for that matter, today intergovernmental organizations can also do all these things. The role of NGOs (non-governmental organizations), such as Greenpeace, World Wildlife, Amnesty International, and the World Council of Churches, is becoming increasingly influential owing to the ability of such groups to influence the publics of the democracies. Their status in international law, however, is still unclear.

State

By far the most important subject for international law is the state itself. The international order is composed of states; international law only became a reality once there was a society of states self-conscious enough to be constituted in a particular way. International law is built out of the most fundamental assumptions of constitutional law, since the state is a constitutional idea. The principal constitutional characteristics of the state – sovereignty, recognition, personality, continuity, integrity – all supply subjects for international law because they provide the constitutive elements of the society of states that is governed by that law.

Sovereignty Of these constitutional ideas, the most influential and profound is the idea of sovereignty. Essentially, international law rests on the assumption of European constitutional concepts of sovereignty. Like American ideas of sovereignty, these concepts provide a universal role for international law and an egalitarian status for states. That is, since as a constitutional matter jurisdiction is taken to be fundamentally a matter of territorial extent, and since the society of states territorially exhausts the globe, international law is universal. And since all states are equal with respect to the rights of sovereignty, they are equal with respect to the rules of international law. The historical sources of this equality and universalism are, however, quite different for the American and European approaches. European sovereignty proceeds by descent from that of princes whose dynastic legitimacy was inherited by the states which they called into being; for this reason all states, like all princes, are equal with respect to the law. Similarly, the society of European princes was encompassed by the universality of the Christian Church, and this provides the model for the universality of the society of states and international law. American sovereignty, by contrast, derives its legitimacy from its relationship to popular consent with similar consequences for the universality of international law and the equality of states, but for different reasons and, potentially, with somewhat different consequences.

For example, international law – owing to its origin in European constitutional ideas – accords absolute authority to the state over internal, domestic affairs. Indeed, we owe the term "sovereignty," in this context, to an essay by Jean Bodin in 1577, entitled *De la republique* which took the familiar idea of *le souverain*, (meaning that from which there was no higher appeal) and applied it to the state itself. Both Bodin and Hobbes, who were influential constitutional theorists, agreed that the sovereignty of a state cannot be restricted by a constitution. By contrast, if we derive the legitimacy of the state from the consent of its people, then certain domestic and internal practices by the state would effectively de-legitimate it, even to the extent of inviting intervention. One account of the US invasion of Panama depicts the Panamanian regime, which had usurped authority from a democratically elected government, as having lost its legal status as a legitimate government. This view would justify the resulting armed intervention that restored the legitimate regime, whereas on the conventional view of international law the invasion appears to be illicit.

Recognition The society of states must have a means of recognizing legitimate members of that society. The international community is in constant flux, as new states appear and new regimes come to power. The 1933 Montevideo Convention on Rights and Duties of States codifies the three criteria for the recognition of a state: (1) effective control of a defined territory with a permanent population; (2) capacity to conduct international relations; and (3) independence from other countries. Recognition is thus a purely factual matter and is to be distinguished from "relations" which are a discretionary matter and can be accorded by a state to another state for a variety of political and moral reasons.

103

Personality   The possession of international personality means that an entity is capable of possessing international rights and obligations under international law and that it has the capacity to maintain its rights by bringing international claims. As late as 1912, Oppenheim could write, "States solely and exclusively are the subjects of international law." This is no longer so. States alone may be parties to actions in the International Court of Justice (ICJ), but today not only states but also confederations, insurgents, the inhabitants of a territory placed in trusteeship, international organizations, certain individuals, and even the Holy See and the Knights of Malta (for anomalous historical reasons) have international legal personality. International organizations, by which I mean organizations whose principal members are states – unlike states – enjoy *varying* degrees of personality. Like states they may have the capacity to enter into agreements with states, and if so this is evidence of some degree of international personality; such organizations may pursue legal remedies under international law to enforce those agreements. International organizations, most notably the UN, have been deemed to have sufficient international personality even to press claims against states outside an enforceable agreement, for example, for reparations as a result of damages to the organization or its agents. Other examples include the European Union which has the capacity to make treaties, and also receives and accredits diplomats, and posts delegations to other international organizations. Individuals have limited personality. It is no longer the case that only states can assert the human rights of persons; for example, the European Convention on Human Rights provide that individuals can initiate claims against their national state for breaches of that Convention. Nor is it still true that only states can be held responsible for breaching international law. Genocide and war crimes are now recognized as acts for which individuals can be held responsible.

Continuity   Change in the attributes of a state may have legal consequences. Changes in territory (as by partition or unification), in population (through mass migration), in regime (through normal political processes or on account of a revolutionary overthrow of the pre-existing constitution), or in independence (as by an occupying force or treaty arrangement) all call into question whether the new situation carries with it all the rights and obligations of the previous state of affairs. Although the *Restatement Third of Foreign Relations Law* and the 1978 Vienna Convention on State Succession take inconsistent positions, it may be that a consensus is emerging in the turmoil that has accompanied the collapse of the Soviet Union and the disintegration of Yugoslavia. Prior to this period, the minds of international commentators were focussed on the problems of continuity that are manifested in decolonization, as, for example, in the case of Hong Kong. What treaties entered into by the United Kingdom will be retained by Hong Kong? Does it get to choose some and reject others? Is the fresh consent of its treaty partners required? These questions can now, in light of experience, be seen to be problems largely, though not entirely, of continuity. If the new state is a successor state, then it inherits all the rights and obligations of the previous state. For example, Russia was treated as a successor and thus retained the Security Council seat of the Soviet Union. If the new state is a breakaway, such as a former colony, it is entitled to a clean slate. The obligations previously maintained are not automatically incumbent on the new state, which has the option of assuming the treaties of its predecessor where these are appropriate. For example, Lithuania may succeed to the fishing rights maintained in the Baltic *vis-à-vis* other Baltic states on a proportionate basis. If the new state is the product of a dissolution, then no state is a true successor but all parties to the dissolution take the obligations of the former state, as was the case with the dissolved UAR and is, arguably, the matter with the states of the former Yugoslavia. Finally, some kinds of treaty undertakings are fundamental to the essential continuity of the state system itself – especially boundary treaties, but also it may come to be recognized, certain arms control treaties and environmental undertakings – so that whatever the continuity of the particular state, the treaty obligations are necessarily imposed and remain intact.

Integrity   A state may lack integrity if the territorial composition of the state renders it unable to exist as a coherent entity. For example, the Vance–Owen proposals for the state of Bosnia-Herzegovina, the so-called ink-spot plan, posited a state with disparate provinces connected only by narrow corridors in the control of other states. This raises the question whether, as a legal matter, such a revised entity is a union, like the combined states of Colombia and Venezuela, or Denmark and Norway in the nineteenth century, or is in reality a dismembered state whose various parts are entitled to be treated separately.

State liability

Under international law, a state can be held liable for the consequences of its torts, breaches of contract, and non-payment of debts, much as other juridical entities. What distinguishes the state in this respect is its unique duties to aliens and the authority it possesses over the instruments of the state. Thus, states can be held liable for the failure to prevent harm to aliens, the failure to prosecute persons who wrongfully injure aliens, and the judicial denial of justice to aliens. This follows from the duty a state owes to the society of states, since aliens are presumably (though not always) nationals of some other state. On a somewhat different basis, states can be held responsible for acts that are incident to state sovereignty, such as nationalization and expropriation of foreign property, the malign consequences of weapons testing or maneuvers by fleets at sea or the non-combat activities of its armed forces.

The most formidable state defense against any legal action is the invocation of the doctrine of sovereign immunity – according to which a state may not be sued without its consent, since no other state has legal authority over any other state and, thus, cannot assert jurisdiction over the latter (*par in parem non habat imperium*). This doctrine has been substantially modified as twentieth-century states have become involved in commercial enterprises, eventually putting such enterprises in a privileged competitive position. A distinction is now drawn between the acts of a *state qua state* (*jure imperii*) and its non-governmental, proprietary acts (*jure gestionis*). Immunity is granted only with respect to the former, and is typically denied a state's trading and commercial activities. Other defenses asserted by the state include distress, necessity, self-defense, and, particularly, the sort of waivers embodied in the Calvo clauses discussed above.

Human rights

Prior to the UN Charter, human rights per se were not a subject for international law. Certain minority groups – racial, ethnic, religious – were guaranteed certain rights by way of special treaties, such as those concluded in Albania, Finland, and Poland, and customary international law had long recognized freedom from slavery, but there was no general attempt to regulate human rights. This was owing to the assumption of complete sovereignty that underlay the society of states. How a state treated its own citizens was, as a legal matter, no other state's affair.

The signing of the Charter marked the beginning of a new era in international law, although not perhaps quite the era its signatories had in mind. For while it is easy to see the UN as a second-generation League of Nations, with all the legalism of parliamentarianism on the march, the development of a human rights agenda, largely enforced by non-governmental organizations against the state-parties themselves was probably unforeseen by even its most visionary authors. The Charter calls for "universal respect for, and observance of, human rights and fundamental freedoms for all without distinction as to race, sex, language and religion" and announces as one of the purposes of the UN "to achieve international cooperation in promoting and encouraging respect for human rights and for fundamental freedoms for all without distinction as to race, sex, language or religion." Nevertheless, it was the consequence of a series of developments that work against the vitality of the nation-state – international communications; multinational markets and financial consortia; instant and pervasive publicity; religious, ethnic, gender, and racial sectarianism; in other words the increasing impossibility of governance – made the effective promotion of human rights a subject of international law. Whatever the case, various multilateral conventions have been widely ratified that provide rights to minimal sustenance, freedom of opinion, freedom of peaceful assembly, habeas corpus, public trial of crimes, the right to marry and procreate, to be educated, to work and own property and, what is more important than any of these declarations, institutions have been constructed to vindicate such rights, including a reporting system (provided for by both the Covenant on Civil and Political Rights and the Covenant on Economic, Social and Cultural Rights) and, in an optional protocol, for individual, non-state, communication to the Human Rights committee that receives the reports. Perhaps the most dramatic step has been taken in Europe, where the European Convention for the Protection of Human Rights and Fundamental Rights (1950) has led to the creation of a European Commission on Human Rights, and a Court of Human Rights, a structure that has been mirrored in the 1976 American Convention on Human Rights. The importance of these institutions, which have little enforcement power, is to bring to light matters that, once public attention is engaged, take on a political life of their own. This reflects a profound shift in the assumptions of sovereignty, not only piercing the territorial veil of the state, but activating those non-state elements that, increasingly, play a role in governance itself.

The sources of international law

Article 38 of the Statute of the International Court of Justice lists the sources of international law available to the Court in deciding cases. These are essentially the same sources for all international legal institutions, much as the forms of constitutional argument used by the US Supreme Court are the same forms as those of other American constitutional deciders. Article 38 directs the Court to:

(1) international conventions, whether general or particular, establishing rules recognized by the contesting states;
(2) . . . international custom. as evidence of a general practice accepted as law;
(3) the general principles of law recognized by civilized nations;
(4) judicial decisions and the writings of publicists.

The "sources" of law show what the system of laws regards as legitimate kinds of reasons; in US constitutional law, its sources are the text of the constitution, the history of its proposal to and ratification by the people, the practices of American courts and other authoritative deciders who believe themselves to be compelled by constitutional norms, cost–benefit (or welfare) assessment; constitutional structure and ethos in no particular hierarchy. In international law, the sources are the texts of treaties, the intentions of the parties (but not the history of the ratification of the treaty), decisions by international courts, widespread practices by national authoritative deciders who believe themselves guided by the norms of international law, the common judicial ethos of civilized states. The hierarchy is: texts (treaties), doctrine (custom), ethos (general principles of states), and decisions (which are evidence of doctrine, but do not supply it). These differences largely reflect two facts: (1) that international law is made out of the constitutional assumptions of European states that are fully sovereign (instead of the partial sovereignty of the United States) and thus need not, indeed cannot, rely on the ratification of a provision in derogation of the text; and (2) that there is no overarching world governmental structure whose sovereignty supersedes that of states and to whom the welfare of the society of states has been entrusted. Thus, some of the sources of argument for constitutional law simply drop out (structure and prudence, for example) and some are changed (historical argument shifting to the intentions of the signatories, and not of the domestic actors that ratify). This fact may mislead commentators on international law to conclude that it is not actually "law" since it varies from our expectations about the sources of national law; this is usually expressed as arising from the lack of enforceability and/or the lack of an authoritative sovereign. But once we realize that national law also varies in the availability of sources (as for example, the absence of historical argument in European models) and the nature of the sovereign, this question resolves itself into a factual one about actual reliance on the norms of international law. And once we realize that the forms of legal argument in national law are only invoked necessarily as justifications for decisions (rather than as guides to decisions), this factual question about reliance seems to have a clear answer. To a very great extent, and to an increasing extent for some centuries, states have justified their decisions by invoking the rules of international law. There is no sublime mechanism beyond this that amounts to "law."

Treaties

The phrase "any international conventions whether general or particular" refers to treaties. Sometimes treaties are analogized to legislation and sometimes to contracts. Multilateral conventions – to which there are more than two parties – may have such a broad effect owing to the large number of signatories that they seem to encompass as general an application as legislation. Provisions of such treaties are, it was argued in the North Sea Continental Shelf Cases, of such broad adoption that they become customary international law and are thus binding on all states. Bilateral agreements look more like contracts: they expressly take the parties out of the background context of customary international law, just as a contract takes the signatories outside the market. Perhaps the best way to conceptualize the legal role of treaties is to think of their origin as contracts among princes, before the state superseded the princely function; and thus to adapt such a contractual approach to the unique status of the state. Treaties are contracts (they are not legislation) but they are contracts among states, and since they are among states, they can have the general application of law (since the state, unlike typical parties to a contract, has a role in providing law). And, since they are among states, when breached they are not enforced by third parties but rather by the adjusted expectations of the "market" – which will exact higher costs the next time a breaching state attempts to negotiate a treaty.

No state has ever disputed the principle that treaties are legally binding, the legal imperative *pacta sunt servanda*. That is because the binding nature of treaties is a dimension of statehood, and to disavow this principle would strike at the legitimacy of the state itself. States, of course, from time to time may break their treaty obligations, or repudiate treaties entered into by former governments, but there is no instance of a state suggesting that treaties are not, as a matter of law, binding. Treaties are the paramount method of determining what has been agreed to by states and, thus, if a treaty and a customary rule exist simultaneously on an issue in dispute, the treaty provision will govern, as illustrated in the *Wimbledon* case. There, the PICJ accepted the argument that customary international law prohibited the passage of armaments through the territory of a neutral state, but nevertheless upheld a provision of the Treaty of Versailles that designated the Kiel Canal as "free and open to the vessels of commerce and war of all nations at peace with Germany." In stopping a vessel flying a neutral flag, Germany had breached her obligations.

If the factual context within which a treaty was supposed to operate changes so radically that its purposes cannot be served by adherence to its provisions, then the doctrine *clausula rebus sic stantibus* can be invoked to relieve the parties of obligations that do not make sense in the new context. In these circumstances, a contracting party may unilaterally withdraw from a treaty. Some writers, notably Kelsen, disparage this doctrine because, unlike similar national rules that allow for the modification of contract in domestic law, there is no objective and impartial authority to determine the validity of claims of changed circumstance, but it is clearly an overstatement to claim that "it is hardly possible to prove that the clausula is part of positive international law." Rather, let us say that the effect of changed circumstances on treaty obligations is a matter of judgment, which judgment is ratified – like those of so-called objective authorities – by the acceptance and legitimacy accorded them.

Customary international law

The customary practices of states have the status of international law when they are of such duration, are sufficiently widespread among the states of the international community, and are observed with the requisite consistency. Most importantly, such practices must be followed by states who believe themselves to be legally obliged to do so. Thus, custom is to be distinguished from mere comity, the consequence of an interruption of which would not produce legitimate sanctions.

But what precisely is the required duration – or sufficient consensus or consistency – is a matter of context. There is no minimum time limit, and practices that have been observed for only a short period may, nevertheless, achieve the status of international law if the practice is both extensive and virtually uniform, particularly where the subject matter of the practice is relatively novel. Inconsistency also, however, is not necessarily a bar: factors such as subject matter, the identity of the states involved and their number, are also relevant. A practice can be regarded as general, even if it is not of universal adoption; it is more important that the practices of those states likely to be affected by the rule are consistent. If a rule is to be derived from a practice, the leading states concerned with the practice in the international community must concur. All this is a way of determining when the society of states has tacitly adopted a legal rule because a society of equal sovereigns is defined by its common adherence to rules. Since a paramount constitutive rule of this society however is that its members are equal, and are sovereign, it follows that customary international law does not bind the state that – from the time of the inception of the rule – consistently rejects the practice. Change with respect to well-established rules occurs only when a state deliberately alters its practices, in the knowledge that to do so represents an illegal act: to change customary international law, a state must break it. If a sufficiently large number of influential states do so over time, a new rule comes into being. Like the rules of etiquette, an initial departure is always illicit, but may, if ratified by time, retrospectively be the first act of a new and successful custom. Just as a practice of states cannot become a legal rule unless it is obeyed under the belief that international law imposes such an obligation (the requirement of opinion *juris sivi necessitatis*), so the rule can only be changed by states that acknowledge they are refusing to obey a legal rule, rather than simply adopting a contrary one, as if through inadvertence or disagreement as to what the law requires. A practice that is generally followed but that states feel free to disregard as a legal matter can neither attain the status of a rule of customary international law, nor, if disregarded, serve as a basis for a new contrary rule. Failure to establish this self-consciousness is fatal to the claim of custom as rule. In the *Lotus* case, for example, a French ship collided with a Turkish ship, killing eight Turkish seamen. A Turkish prosecution of the French captain was challenged by France who invoked the rule that matters occurring on a ship came exclusively within the jurisdiction of the state under whose flag the ship sailed. The PICJ held, however, that instances of states refraining from prosecution under similar circumstances did not demonstrate that states were aware of a legal duty requiring them to do so. Thus, a new practice can overtake an old one when the novel behavior dissents from custom in the full awareness that the state is otherwise required to conform; and other states adopt the new practice in the expectation that the new rule – as it purports to be – requires them to behave in a certain way.

General principles

The principles contemplated by this phrase are not those of international law, in the sense of rules of international behavior commonly adhered to by civilized states. That definition would better comport with customary international law. Rather the "general principles" referred to are principles of domestic law that civilized states have in common. Such principles, applied by the ICJ, its predecessor the PICJ, and other international tribunals, include: the responsibility of principal for acts of its apparent agent, collateral estoppel, reparation for damage, and so on. Relying on just such principles, the ICJ held, faced in *Barcelona Traction* with a Canadian corporation doing business in Spain but owned largely by Belgians, that the reality of Belgian control did not confer standing on Belgium to sue Spain for unpaid debts to the company. Where one might have supposed, in light of *Nottebohm* cited above, the "reality" of actual links between the state and the party seeking protection might be dispositive, the Court instead looked to the general principles that might be derived from the domestic courts of states that, as a usual matter, deal with corporate residence when this diverges from the residence of the shareholder. This too has a certain practicality – for such "principles" are the result of innumerable encounters with similar legal problems, and thus supply international law with a resource of useful legal rules. While these rules are typically procedural in nature, the resort to principles of equity can, on occasion, enter international law by this route. This is distinguishable from the agreement by the parties to decide a case *ex aequo et bono* – which will permit the reliance on equity as a decisive factor only with the consent of the parties.

Judicial decisions

Article 38 also provides the subsidiary means of "judicial decisions and the teachings of the most highly qualified publicists of the various nations" as evidence of what the content of international law is, that is, not as the content itself but as providing direction in determining that content. Thus, the arguments that derive from this source are not "doctrinal" in the usual sense of that term, and there is no rule of *stare decisis* in international law. Indeed it would be more accurate to say of customary international law that *it* follows the pattern of stare decisis. especially with respect to the requirement of *opinio juris*, since the binding nature of a precedent only strictly adheres in those situations germane to reason why the rule was invoked in the allegedly governing case.

Conclusion

The relationship between constitutional law and international law promises certain changes in the foreseeable future. As the American paradigm of constitutional sovereignty becomes more widespread, an international order of limited sovereigns may replace the current legal order, with profound consequences for state responsibility and intervention. This comes at a time in the history of the state system when many threats to sovereignty are pressing the state – transborder environmental problems, migration, terrorism – and which will invite, therefore, the strategic change that invariably accompanies legal changes of this magnitude.

Bibliography

Bull, H., Kingsbury, B., and Roberts, A. (eds) 1990: *Hugo Grotius and International Relations.*
D'Amato, A. 1971: *The Concept of Custom in International Law.*
—— 1984: Is international law really law?, *Northwestern University Law Review*, 79, 1, 293.
de Vattel, E. 1863: *Le Droit des Gens*, ed. Pradier-Fodere.
Franck, T. M. 1970: Who killed Article II (IV). *AJIL*, 74, 809.
—— M. 1990: *The Power of Legitimacy among Nations.*
Grotius, H. 1833: *De Jure Belli Esti Pacis*, tr. Whewell.
Henkin, L. 1979: *How Nations Behave.*
Kelsen, H. 1952: *Principles of International Law.*
Lauterpacht, H. 1946: The Grotian tradition in international law. *BYIL*, 23, 1.
MacDougall, M. et al. 1960: *Studies in World Public Order.*
MacDougall, M., Laswell, H., and Riesman, W. M. 1967: The world constituted process of authoritative decision. *Journal of Legal Education*, 19, 403.
Lowenfeld, A. 1989: US law enforcement abroad: the constitution of international law. *AJIL*, 83, 880.
Nussbaum, A. 1954: *A Concise History of the Law of Nations.*
Oppenheim, L. 1912: *International Law: a treatise*, 2nd edn.
Paust, J. 1991: The reality of jus cogens. *Connecticut Journal of International Law*, 7, 81.

Reisman, W. M. 1984: International incidents: introduction to a new genre in the study of international law. *Yale Journal of International Law*, 10, 1.

—— 1987: The cult of custom in the late 20th century. *California Western International Law Journal*, 17, 133.

Schachter, O. 1989: Self-defense and the rule of law. *AJIL*, 83, 259.

Vagts, D. 1991: State succession: the codifier's view. *Virginia Journal of International Law*, 33, 275.

Vitoria, F. 1917: in J. B. Scott (ed.), *Classics of International Law*.

Zoller, E. 1984: *Peacetime Unilateral Remedies*.

6

Constitutional law and religion

PERRY DANE

The encounter of religion and law excites both theology and jurisprudence. Religion and law are each potent, ancient forces in human life. Their dialogue is abiding, but culturally contingent. It is profound, but, sometimes, refreshingly mundane.

This entry will devote most of its attention to the efforts of contemporary secular law to draw a picture of religion and determine its place in the civil state. That, however, is only one piece of a larger conversation on the relation of law and religion. It will do well, to give the topic breathing room, to begin with some of those other pieces.

Religion and law both have many layers. They are, for one, movements in human history – social, cultural, intellectual, and institutional phenomena. In some societies, law and religion merge. Even when they are distinct, they grip each other. Religious values, directly or through the conduit of moral sensibility, obviously influence legal traditions. But legal doctrines also affect religious thought. In the Hebrew Bible, the covenant between God and Israel echoes ancient Near Eastern treaty law. Patristic accounts of the efficacy of Christ's redemptive sacrifice drew on the Roman legal doctrine of "satisfaction."

The communal dramas of religion and law also mirror each other. Legal institutions take on religious trappings, to the point that they are sometimes accused of engaging in idolatry. Religious institutions and communities not only take on legal trappings, but also often see themselves in juridical terms, and govern themselves through ecclesiastical law.

Nevertheless, in Western history, the effort of the legal order, in particular, to define itself as distinct from the religous order has long been a powerful theme. At its most realized, this effort helps mark the spirit of modernity. The story is not just one, however, of civil institutions escaping religious domination. Harold Berman (1983) has, to the contrary, linked the Western tradition of legal rationalism and separated competencies to the eleventh-century Papal revolution, as the Church articulated grounds for its autonomy from secular powers.

In other cultures, the story has played out differently, but not more simply. Even in Iran, stereotyped as a theocracy, jurists subtly struggle with the proper relation between civil governance and religious order.

Law and religion, however, are not only movements. They are also each modes of thought, ways of negotiating reality. Like other modes of thought – science and art, for example – they are frames of reference, ideational and affective approaches to subjects both in and beyond their literal domain.

At one level, the resemblance between law and religion, as modes of thought, is powerful. They are both hermeneutic activities. Both find efficacy in ritual. They each live a dialectic between a commitment to authority and tradition and a commitment to objective truth. They are both obsessed with questions of right and wrong, sin and crime. And both set that inquiry into a larger, structural, often hierarchical, frame.

A question for both law and religion, however, has been whether their resemblance implies a true bond, or is just a snare and a distraction. The question, whether asked from the perspective of religion or that of law, exposes deep debates about the nature of both.

For some religious traditions, including Judaism, Islam, and Hinduism, law is a central religious category. Traditional Judaism focusses on the halakhah, Jewish law. The halakhah is more than ritual law. It is a complete body of law, encompassing also tort, property, and all the rest. More important, the law is, in classical Judaism, an expression of divine love. To study and obey the law is to join with God in creating the world. Rabbi Joseph Soloveitchik explained Judaism's "this-worldliness," despite belief in afterlife, by emphasizing that "here, in this world, man is given the opportunity to create, act, accomplish, while there, in the world to come, he is powerless to change anything at all" (Soloveitchik, 1983, p. 32).

Other religious traditions have defined themselves against the world-view of law. Forms of Pauline Christianity are obvious examples. Classic Confucianism is another. For these traditions, "legalism" is a dangerous temptation. In antinomian Christianity, law is an impediment to grace. In classic Confucianism, law obstructs the internalization of norms of conduct and deference that are the true sign of virtue and character-building.

For religious traditions that define the spiritual sensibility against law and its mode of thought, two questions remain. One is how to make sense of whatever place law retains in the religious community itself. For Christianity, this is the locus for the long debate over what Christian thinkers have historically labeled "Judaizing."

The second question is how to make sense of the place of law in the general social order. John Calvin ([1535] 1956, p. 46) argued that civil government was a response to human evil, designed to protect church and society and "establish general peace and tranquility" in this "mortal and transitory life" as an "aid necessary to our pilgrimage" to the "true country" in the Kingdom of God. Law is necessary, even "excellent," but second best.

Put another way, Calvin and Soloveitchik agree that law is a distinctly human, material enterprise; paradise is not a place for law. The difference is that, for Calvin, this is so much the worse for us; for Soloveitchik, it is so much the worse for paradise.

These contrasting religious perspectives on the place of law continue in contemporary secular culture's effort to think through the role of law. Is it a redemptive enterprise, or a mere accessory, even an impediment, to more authentic forms of temporal salvation? Consider, on one side, the perfectionist impulse in the common law tradition and in American constitutionalism. On the other side, consider the antinomian impulses apparent even in Anglo-American legal thinking, in the claimed disjunction, transplanted from theology to jurisprudence, between the "letter" and "spirit" of the law.

Two contemporary authors capture this debate, and its layers of paradox, with words whose religious resonance is obvious. Robert Cover (1983, p. 9), amid his critique of the state of the law (and the law of the state), nevertheless, described the enterprise of law as the creation of normative worlds, fragile but lofty bridges between the real and the ideal:

> Our visions hold our reality up to us as unredeemed. By themselves the alternative worlds of our visions – the lion lying down with the lamb, the creditor forgiving debts each seventh year, the state all shriveled and withered away – dictate no particular set of transformations or efforts at transformation. But law gives a vision depth of field, by placing one part of it in the highlight of insistent and immediate demand while casting another part in the shadow of the millennium.

Grant Gilmore (1977, pp. 109, 110–11), in contrast, despite his affection for law and its history, nevertheless ended one of his books with these words:

> As lawyers we will do well to be on our guard against any suggestion that, through law, our society can be reformed, purified, or saved . . .
>
> Law reflects, but in no sense determines, the moral worth of a society. The values of a reasonably just society will reflect themselves in a reasonably just law. The better the society, the less law there will be. In Heaven there will be no law, and the lion will lie down with the lamb. The values of an unjust society will reflect themselves in an unjust law. The worse the society, the more law there will be. In Hell there will be nothing but law, and due process will be meticulously observed.

As religion has struggled with the place of legal modes of thought, the law has struggled, as intensely, with the place of religious modes of thought. Appropriately, a classic site for this struggle has been religious law itself. Jewish tradition has generally insisted that the meaning of halakhah is to be found in the art of interpretation and not in divination or prophetic charisma. A powerful expression of this doctrine is the famous tale of the sage who, dissenting on a question of law, successfully summons the voice of heaven to support his position. His opponents, however, declare that, though God revealed the law, it is no longer "in heaven" (*Baba Metzia*, 59b). Its meaning is not to be decided by God, but by the hermeneutic authority of the sages.

In the contemporary secular legal conversation, questions about the autonomy of law arise in at least two guises. One is the debate between positivists and natural lawyers. This is not the place to explore that debate. But worth note is that among the issues it raises are both the largely religious one of the existence of

115

transcendent normative truths, and the more directly jurisprudential one of the relevance of such truths to law.

Debate over the autonomy of law also arises in another form more resonant with the rabbis' tale. This is the disagreement, at least as important as the arid quarrel over legal positivism, about whether law has the resources, in its own hermeneutic traditions, to fulfill its social and intellectual mission, or whether it should look, unmediatedly, to the methods of economics, moral theory, or other disciplines.

These two dimensions of legal autonomy can configure themselves in various combinations. Part of the power of Ronald Dworkin's (1986) work, for example, is that he rejects legal positivism, but also embraces legal hermeneutics, and rests both views on a commitment to the "integrity" of law.

The discussion so far has stressed the breadth of meaning of both "law" and "religion," and the dimensions of their discourse. These insights will recur. Nevertheless, as noted, the bulk of this entry will look to a more specific instance of the encounter, in the relationship between actual communities of faith and one type of legal order – the state.

This discussion will begin with constitutional law, the obvious focus for the civil inquiry into the place of religion. Equally interesting issues arise, however, in subconstitutional and non-constitutional contexts. Tort, tax, zoning, and corporation law, and other fields, all encounter the difficulties of fitting religion into their conceptual schemes. Some of those topics will be treated, briefly, later.

In the United States, the First Amendment to the Constitution treats the legal place of religion in two clauses: "Congress shall make no law respecting an establishment of religion or prohibiting the free exercise thereof." The Establishment Clause controls the involvement of government in religion, through sponsorship of religious acts and symbols, as in organized prayer in the public schools, or through material aid, as in subvention of parochial schools. The Free Exercise Clause guarantees a measure of liberty for religious practice. A central problem in free exercise debate has been whether religious conviction should be a ground for exemption from otherwise generally applicable laws – compulsory education, drug laws, tax laws, and many others. Both religion clauses figure, as a doctrinal matter, in two other sets of problems: discrimination among religions, and the state's role in adjudicating disputes within religious institutions or arising out of disagreements about religious governance.

One question of philosophical interest about both religion clauses is their precise relation to other constitutional and political principles. Some have argued for a close link between the religion clauses and other enumerated constitutional protections. Others, particularly authors of modern liberal theory, have read them as pointers to a more rigorous vision of the place of government in a true liberal state. Neither of these approaches necessarily rejects the idea that religion deserves heightened legal interest. But both seem incredulous at the idea that the calculus of rights would treat religion as fundamentally different from other realms of human life and to that extent reflect very similar impulses.

116

In the first view just cited, which links the religion clauses to other provisions of the Bill of Rights, the free exercise clause is often cast as a protection of religious expression (for example, Marshall, 1983). It is part of a constellation of rights that also includes freedoms of speech and association. The establishment clause, meanwhile, is sometimes read as a specialized application of principles of equal protection (for example, Kurland, 1962). It guarantees non-discrimination, both among religions and between religion and non-religion.

That the religion clauses are, in part, instances of more general constitutional principles is certain. Nevertheless, this reductionist hypothesis is radically incomplete. By tying the clauses so closely to other features of the constitutional order, it fails to account for the most interesting, theoretically excruciating, questions that they raise.

The profound and difficult problem in free exercise law is religion-based exemptions. Most constitutional civil liberties protections definably limit either what government can do, or how it can do it. The gravamen of a usual constitutional challenge is that there is something objectively wrong with a statute or policy. It is stifling speech, or invading privacy, or denying due process, or making forbidden distinctions.

Emblematic claims to religion-based exemptions do something different. They seek relief from a government action that is not defective itself, but happens to conflict with the religious obligations of the claimant. For example, a statute requiring drivers to have photographs on their licenses is not constitutionally suspect, as such. But it might happen to conflict with the views of persons who are trying to obey the biblical restriction on graven images. For that matter, *any* statute or government action, however ordinarily benign, is potentially subject to challenge under the free exercise clause.

This property of religion-based exemptions raises obvious difficulties. Justice Scalia, in *Smith* v. *Employment Division*, 494 U.S. 872, a 1990 Supreme Court case restricting such claims, called them "a constitutional anomaly," "not remotely comparable" to other types of constitutional claims (p. 886). Arguments for religious exemptions do not merely raise substantive questions of constitutional meaning; they challenge the rule of law itself by positing "a private right to ignore generally applicable laws" (*Smith* v. *Employment Division*). Chief Justice Waite, writing about 110 years earlier in rejecting Mormon challenges to bigamy statutes, wrote that to allow such exemptions would be "in effect to permit every citizen to become a law unto himself" (*Reynolds* v. *United States*, 98 U.S. 145, 167 (1878)).

Nevertheless, religion-based exemptions have a long history, in many jurisdictions. In 1963, in *Sherbert* v. *Verner*, 374 U.S. 398 (1963), the Supreme Court read the free exercise clause to require religion-based exemptions from generally applicable laws unless the government could show a compelling interest in enforcing the law. When the Supreme Court, in *Smith*, gutted *Sherbert*, Congress responded with the Religious Freedom Restoration Act, 42 U.S.C. § 2000bb, which created a statutory para-constitutional right that effectively overruled the Court and reinstated the *Sherbert* test.

Whether *Sherbert* or *Smith* represents the better view of the matter, what is

117

undeniable is the appeal of religion-based exemptions in the argumentative structure of free exercise. That appeal requires a theory, which will not be found in the more conventional civil liberties provisions of the Constitution (cf. Sandel, 1989).

The problems raised by the effort to assimilate the Establishment Clause to principles of non-discrimination are as acute, if less jurisprudentially charged. To begin with, the analogy does not explain why the clause requires, not only neutrality among persons but also, within its domain, neutrality among ideas. The Bill of Rights does not forbid the "establishment" of welfare liberalism, supply-side economics, or anti-communism, as long as that "establishment" does not entrench on individual liberties. But it does forbid the establishment of Presbyterianism, or of atheism.

Moreover, the clause forbids outright a range of government involvements with religion, discriminatory or not. The clause would bar official prayer in the public schools even if the prayers were rotated among every faith, or even interspersed with humanist texts. And the clause forbids direct aid to parochial schools, even if that aid is part of a general program extending to non-religious institutions. If anything, the clause mandates discrimination as often as it forbids it, by denying to religious beliefs and institutions access to government favor available to their secular counterparts.

Even putting all these doctrinal issues to one side, there are two mysteries that a theory of the establishment clause must confront. One is the basic vision of the clause. The equal protection clause only limits the actions of government. But its vision, if only by analogy, is more general. It forbids, for example, official racism. But it also encourages, or at least points to, an end to racism in society. The establishment clause is different. It mandates secular government. But it does so for the purpose of allowing, even nurturing, a religious society.

A second mystery of the Establishment Clause is its cultural specificity. Most constitutional liberties reflect principles shared, in spirit if not in detail, by other democratic legal traditions. The free exercise clause is no exception. But the Establishment Clause is. Many Western democracies do fine without separation of church and state, or with radically different versions of separation. England, for example, has an established Church, but that does not prevent it from being broadly tolerant of other faiths. Many nations give aid to religious schools, convinced it furthers religious freedom rather than inhibiting it.

A final defect of efforts to assimilate the religion clauses to other parts of the constitutional fabric is that they do not effectively connect the two clauses to each other. The free exercise clause seems to "favor" religion, by granting religious persons entitlements and immunities not available to others. The establishment clause seems to "disfavor" religion, by denying to religious persons, institutions, and ideas, rights, and favors available to their secular counterparts. Presumably, these characterizations, and the apparent contradiction they generate, are too crude. But to go beyond them will take more than simple analogies to other parts of the Constitution.

As noted above, though, there is a second way to connect the religion clauses to broader themes. This solution, attractive to the architects of resurgent liberal

118

theory, is to understand the religion clauses as foundations for a more rigorous account of the liberal state and its relation to the individual. John Rawls (1971, §§ 33–4) treats free exercise of religion as part of a larger notion of "equal liberty of conscience," subject to "the common interest in public order and security" (p. 212) but extending to both "moral and religious" claims (p. 206). Similarly, Bruce Ackerman (1984, p. 359) understands the separation of church and state to exemplify the thoroughgoing "neutrality" to which a just state should adhere among conceptions of the good. David A. J. Richards (1986) elaborates on both these themes.

This is not the place to discuss at length contemporary philosophical liberalism and its arguments. As readings of the religion clauses, however, these analyses, though more interesting and powerful than readings that merely link the clauses to other parts of the existing constitutional logic, are still both too sweeping and too narrow.

That the new liberal analysis is too sweeping is evident from the theoretical and practical distance between the religion clauses, in themselves, and the liberal effort to extend their principles beyond religion. A general "right of conscience" would radically revise, both jurisprudentially and substantively, the relationship between law and the individual. The free exercise clause, as limited to religious claims, does, to be sure, raise its own problems. But its narrow scope is what makes it more an island in a world of legal obligation than an overarching challenge to the notion of such obligation.

A generalized notion of "neutrality" among conceptions of the good raises similar problems. Some critics of the new liberal analysis have argued that aspirations to such neutrality are self-contradictory. Even if neutrality is coherent, it still suggests a thinness to the vision of the state that many critics find pernicious. Some of these critics have turned to neoclassical republicanism or other alternatives to the modern liberal vision.

The place of religion does figure in this debate. Some commentators have argued, on republican grounds, for a more forthright role for religion in the public square (for example, Carter, 1993; McConnell, 1985). But strict disestablishment is, unapologetically, itself a thick, non-neutral, vision of government and the common space of political discourse.

So much for why the liberal reading of the religion clauses is too sweeping. Even more revealing is the degree to which it is too narrow.

Again, one problem is the inability to explain the "no-aid" instincts of establishment clause law. A less obvious, but more profound, problem, is that "liberty of conscience" is in some ways a more restrictive idea than "freedom of religion." "Conscience" is a peculiarly deep, personal, sensation, different from mere preference or convention. The impetus to religious behavior, on the other hand, often is a matter of habit or social conformity. It is not always deep. It is often subject to doctrinal and personal conditions and contingencies. Nevertheless, the law treats that impetus as different in kind from other reasons for action, however intensely felt. To extend this regime, by analogy, beyond religion would require more than "liberty of conscience."

All this is not to say that the liberal arguments for liberty of conscience or strict neutrality are wrong. But whatever the merits of these ideas, they are not simple, linear, extensions of the principles underlying the religion clauses. Nor do they capture the distinct, long-held, intuitions supporting those principles.

For all the genuine links between the constitutional treatment of religion and broader issues in constitutional and political theory, those connections cannot be the whole of the matter. The constitutional treatment of religion is also an extension of the specific conversation between law and religion, which was the subject of the earlier part of this entry.

A full constitutional theory of religion would have to take much into account. In the American context, one part of the story, as historian Mark DeWolfe Howe (1965) has pointed out, has been the confluence of two opposing but complementary traditions: rationalist anti-clericalism, which feared the divisive and tyrannical potential of religion, and radical Baptist theology, which feared the corrupting influence of the state on salvation.

A precis of the story, however, might focus on two overlapping principles that animate much of American legal thinking on law and religion. One principle is separation. The other is deference. The Constitution separates the religious and secular realms, however much they might overlap. And it seeks to defer to religion's understanding of its own demands.

The notions of separation and deference are neither obvious nor uncontroversial. But they do help to make sense of the puzzling aspects of the law's understanding of both disestablishment and free exercise. They also help dissolve the apparent contradictions between the two principles.

The establishment clause expresses the imperatives of separation and deference at the "wholesale" level. It broadly defines the respective jurisdictions of religion and civil state. This does require non-discrimination. But it also requires avoidance of state involvement with religion, both to protect the state from religious encroachment, and to protect religion from the subordinating, homogenizing, influences of state sponsorship. That "deference" is at stake besides "separation" is evident to the extent that the state forgoes aspects of its sovereignty, such as certain potent symbols and rites, that could serve secular ends, but only at the expense of religion's institutional and ideological autonomy.

The establishment clause is more than a civil liberties provision. It is a structural component of the constitutional order, more akin to federalism than to equal protection. This helps explain the two mysteries noted earlier. Structural provisions of the Constitution, unlike civil liberties provisions, have little to say, even by analogy, about the morality of social relations. It should therefore not surprise that the establishment clause's vision of a secular government does not imply an accompanying vision of a secular society. And there should be no surprise at the establishment clause's cultural specificity, much as we do not expect all Western democracies to have American-style federalism or tripartite government.

If the establishment clause draws a general, "wholesale," set of boundaries between the domain of the state and the domain of religion, the free exercise clause expresses the imperatives of separation and deference at the "retail" level. It adjusts the boundaries to fit the perspectives and demands of particular faith traditions. Regulating drug use, or requiring photographs on drivers' licenses, or imposing taxes, do not violate the establishment clause; they are legitimate subjects of secular interest. But the law might still, by providing religion-based exemptions, accommodate the insistence of some faiths that these are profoundly religious questions.

Religion-based exemptions are analogous to the deference that a court shows when it invokes choice of law rules to apply the law of a foreign state to a case before it. Exemptions do not "permit every citizen to become a law unto himself." They do recognize that religious persons might, sometimes, legitimately be governed by a law other than the law of the state.

To invoke separation and deference as governing principles in the jurisprudence of both religion clauses is not to answer every doctrinal difficulty that those clauses raise. For the establishment clause, a central question remains how to distinguish impermissible involvement with religion from the permissible accommodation of individual religious exercise (see McConnell, 1985). This problem becomes particularly acute as the role of government expands. Two hundred years ago, it would have been easy to imagine a scrupulously secular government leaving room for a devoutly religious society. In today's world, however, how much is left to "society" once "government" has taken its bite?

In the free exercise context, many important remaining questions are methodological. A recurring theme in the *Sherbert* era, which might also figure in the working out of the Religious Freedom Restoration Act, is the play between ad hoc "balancing" and more categorical criteria. Even within the realm of balancing, there are doctrinal puzzles. For example, should "state interests" in the balance be measured in toto? Or should they be measured only at the margin, as they apply to the persons seeking exemption? The state's general interest in compulsory education might be enormous. But its interest in enforcing compulsory education laws against a small group of Amish might be minimal. The paradox is this: to measure state interests in toto is beside the point. But to measure state interests only at the margin suggests that the number of persons seeking an exemption would be a factor in whether that exemption should be granted. This dilemma is a direct result of the special dynamic of religion-based exemptions; it affirms, for better or worse, their singular place in the constitutional order.

Finally, it is worth note that the principles of separation and deference do not always converge. One example arises in the secular law's treatment of church property and governance disputes. American law has long held that secular courts may not resolve such disputes by interpreting for themselves the substantive content of theology or ecclesiastical law. That, though, leaves two alternatives. One is to bow to the pronouncements of authoritative religious tribunals, much as one court recognizes the judgments of another. The other is to ignore the religious element, and decide the dispute by sole reference to secular legal instruments such as deeds and contracts. The first approach emphasizes deference, but compromises separation by requiring the secular court to decide, at the threshold, where the locus of religious authority is. The second approach is better at maintaining distance, but it deprives the church of the ability to project its own normative apparatus and vocabulary.

One task of constitutional discourse about religion is to describe its subject. This requires articulating formal "definitions" of religion, a topic less interesting than is sometimes supposed. It also, though, requires fitting the picture of religion into the larger legal landscape.

The importance of such imaginative composition is even more apparent in the range of sub-constitutional and non-constitutional contexts in which the law confronts religion. A few examples will suffice.

Consider first the corporate form of churches. Legal theory usually treats corporations as creatures of the state, fundamentally different from natural persons. As Carl Zollmann (1917) pointed out decades ago, however, religious corporate identity is different. For religious entities, taking corporate form is only sometimes a constitutive act. It is more often a mediating act, putting a secular face on an existing reality.

For a church, corporate form might be the least important part of what it is. From the state's perspective, though, hard choices abound, each with practical and symbolic significance. Some American jurisdictions assimilate churches into their general law of non-profit enterprise. Others have distinct provisions for religious corporations. Some, remarkably, or not so, have distinct statutory provisions specifying separate structures for different, named, denominations. Some state codes provide for legal forms, such as the "corporation sole" (used by Catholic and Episcopal bishops, among others), that are generally unavailable outside the religious context.

Religious institutions pose distinct problems for the theory of non-profit enterprise. Corporate and tax codes distinguish between "public benefit" and "mutual benefit" non-profits. Arguably, religious congregations are classic mutual benefit societies, like country clubs. The law, however, usually treats them, either as sui generis, or as public benefit societies, with charities and schools. If that is to be, however, what, strictly speaking, is their "public" benefit?

Modern English courts take this question seriously. They have, for example, denied property tax exemption to the London Mormon Temple, because it was not open to the general public (*Church of Jesus Christ of Latter-Day Saints*, [1963] 2 All ER 733, [1963] 3 WLR 88). Similarly, they have struck down charitable trusts for cloistered religious orders (as against active religious orders), holding that those trusts conferred no "public" benefit (*Gilmour v. Coats*, [1949] 1 All ER 848, [1949] WN 188).

No modern American court would reach such results. But that only confirms the original question: what, from the view of the law of non-profits, is the "public benefit" of a church? Maybe the best answer is that treating churches as public benefit societies is more a recognition of their awkward place in the legal order than of their subjection to it.

The law's treatment of religious individuals must consider whether religious conduct is essentially voluntary, or is akin to status or obligation. Bankruptcy law, for example, asks whether religious tithing is, for various purposes, a legitimate expense of the bankrupt. To treat it as such is to allow less money to creditors. On the other hand, it is not clear why God is less of a "creditor" than a furniture store.

A similar dilemma arises when tort law confronts Christian Scientists and others who refuse to seek medical treatment after an accident. Should their awards be reduced for failure to mitigate damages? At first glance, it seems that not doing so would unfairly saddle tortfeasors with the cost of tort victims' religious choices. On the other hand, as Guido Calabresi (1985, pp. 45–52) points out, it is also plausible to analogize the Christian Scientist to the proverbial victim with an "eggshell skull" whose unexpected but expensive injuries are, under settled doctrine, charged to the tortfeasor.

Finally, the law must often choose between treating all religions alike, or treating religion like other things. In general tax law, employees who live in company-provided housing as a condition of employment need not count the value of that housing as income. This rule would cover Catholic priests who live in a rectory. It would not, however, cover the housing allowances paid to clergy of faiths who are free to pick their own home. Thinking this distinction unfair, Congress included in the tax code a special provision (26 U.S.C. § 107), which allows all active clergy to exclude or deduct the value of their housing. By keeping theological differences from determining tax burdens, however, the law treats clergy as a special class distinct from other workers. The choice between these two forms of discrimination is inevitably unsatisfactory.

All the issues noted here can be shoehorned into constitutional analysis. But that ignores the genuine puzzles that these problems pose in their own right to theories of tort, tax, nonprofits, and the like. It also overlooks that these are issues that the legal imagination must face regardless of any particular constitutional structure.

As this essay has emphasized, the encounter of religion and law goes both ways. Fully appreciating the legal issues just discussed, constitutional and not, requires realizing that many of those issues have mirror images in questions that religious traditions ask about the state.

This entry will not discuss in detail the theological effort to draw a picture of the state, and find a place for it. It did note one piece of that effort earlier, in the citation from John Calvin. Other traditions have struggled with the same questions, and reached different conclusions. Almost all, however, recognize both the basic legitimacy of state power and the need to draw lines beyond which obedience to that power must not go.

The civil effort to find a place for religion and the religious effort to find a place for the state do not only parallel each other. They also intersect. Consider, as a coda to this essay, one example, a composite of several actual cases:

A mother of young children enters a hospital, critically ill. Her doctors tell her that only a blood transfusion can save her life. She refuses to consent to the transfusion, citing her adherence to a religion that considers transfusions sinful, and a bar to eternal salvation.

The hospital seeks a court order forcing a transfusion. A judge comes to the

123

woman's bedside. She repeats her objections. She also says several times, however, that if the court orders the transfusion, it would be out of her hands, and her salvation would not be at risk. She repeats that she does not want to die, or abandon her children, but cannot consent to receive blood.

In these facts, a constitutional scholar will see issues of autonomy and legal competence. A choice of law scholar will hear echoes of the problem of "renvoi": what should a court do when the choice of law rules of the forum, X, require application of the law of Y and the choice of law rules of Y, in turn, require application of the law of X? A theologian will see complex questions of sinfulness, volition, and the choice between passivity and resistance in the face of persecution. A psychologist might discern an agonized effort to find an escape from a sea of internal conflicts, some beneath the surface.

The challenge in grappling with the immemorial conversation between religion and the law is neither to choose among these perspectives, nor to reconcile them. It is to take them each seriously, and find some way, haphazard and tentative, of navigating among them.

Bibliography

Ackerman, B. A. 1984: *Reconstructing American Law.* Cambridge, Mass.: Harvard University Press.

Berman, H. 1983: *Law and Revolution.* Cambridge, Mass.: Harvard University Press.

Calabresi, G. 1985: *Ideals, Beliefs, Attitudes, and the Law: private law perspectives on a public law problem.* Syracuse, NY: Syracuse University Press.

Calvin, J. [1535] 1956: *Institutes of the Christian Religion.* Translated and excerpted in J. Calvin, *On God and Political Duty,* ed. J. T. McNeil, Indianapolis: Bobbs-Merrill Co.

Carter, S. L. 1993: *The Culture of Disbelief.* New York: Basic Books.

Choper, J. H. 1980: The religion clauses of the First Amendment: reconciling the conflict. *University of Pittsburgh Law Review,* 41, 673–701.

Cover, R. 1983: The Supreme Court, 1982 term – foreword: nomos and narrative. *Harvard Law Review,* 97, 4–68.

Dworkin, R. 1986: *Law's Empire.* Cambridge, Mass.: Belknap Press.

Gilmore, G. 1977: *The Ages of American Law.* New Haven CT: Yale University Press.

Howe, M. DeW. 1965: *The Garden and the Wilderness: religion and government in American constitutional history.* Chicago: University of Chicago Press.

Kurland, P. 1962: *Religion and the Law of Church and State and the Supreme Court.* Chicago: Aldine Publishing Co.

Laycock, D. 1990: Formal, substantive, and disaggregated neutrality toward religion. *De Paul Law Review,* 39, 993–1,018.

Marshall, W. P. 1983: Solving the free exercise dilemma: free exercise as expression. *Minnesota Law Review,* 67, 545–94.

McConnell, M. 1985: Accommodation of religion. *Supreme Court Review,* 1–59.

Murray, J. C. 1960: *We Hold These Truths: catholic reflections on the American proposition.* New York: Sheed and Ward.

Rawls, J. 1971: *A Theory of Justice.* Cambridge, Mass.: Belknap Press.

Richards, D. A. J. 1986: *Toleration and the Constitution.* New York: Oxford University Press.

Sandel, M. J. 1989: Freedom of conscience or freedom of peace. *Utah Law Review*, 597–615. Reprinted in James Davison Hunter and Os Guinness (eds), *Articles of Faith, Articles of Peace: the religious liberty clauses and the American public philosophy*, Washington, DC: Brookings Institution, 1990.
Soloveitchik, J. B. 1983: *Halakhic Man*. Philadelphia: Jewish Publication Society.
Zollmann, C. [1917] 1969: *American Civil Church Law*. New York: AMS Press.

7

Constitutional law and interpretation

PHILIP BOBBITT

Constitutional interpretation is the subject of those who study how the Constitution is applied. When this study is a matter of actual legal decision making, as, for example, by an American court addressing a constitutional question, the court is constrained to rely on certain forms of argument, developed over the centuries of such decision making. When this study is an academic matter, it usually amounts to the application of various extra-legal disciplines to the analysis of this peculiarly American method of constitutional decision making. Constitutional interpretation is distinguished from constitutional discourse, which is the means by which various interpretations are compared when not constrained by the context of making decisions according to law. Let us consider these two dimensions of constitutional interpretation: the application of the Constitution by government officials; and the analysis of this application by academic commentators.

Official interpretation

This activity – decision according to law – is practiced daily by government officials in all branches, and at all levels, and by private lawyers appealing to those officials for such decisions. Because the American Constitution is the sole source of law for the United States, every act by government must have a legitimating ground in the Constitution. Any act that is inconsistent with the Constitution is simply not law in the American system, and no legal claim is enforceable unless that enforcement is compatible with the Constitution. Thus it may be said that every legal question depends, initially, on an interpretation of the Constitution.

The United States was created by the American people to be a state under law – and that law is the US Constitution. This striking political innovation, the state of limited sovereignty expressly created as such, required another innovation, the written Constitution. For so long as the state is the embodiment of sovereignty, written instruments can be no more than codes, changeable at the will of the sovereign state. A written Constitution is neither necessary nor plausible. It is only when sovereignty is detached from the state, that it makes any sense to have a written Constitution, and it is only when this detachment takes place that it is necessary to have a written Constitution. Only then can a state be held to account for departing from the terms of its creation. For this reason Thomas Jefferson wrote that "Our peculiar security is in the possession of a written constitution."

It is possible of course to have a limited government without a written Constitution (for example, Great Britain) or a written Constitution without a limited government (for example, the Third Reich); but it is very difficult to have a limited sovereign without a written instrument, though of course the promises of a written instrument cannot always forestall a government that usurps the sovereignty it claims to lie in the people (for example, the Soviet Union.) But a limited sovereign, acting by means of a government under the written constraints of a wholly superior legal instrument, will at least face the embarrassment of illegitimacy, when it contravenes that instrument.

One consequence of the decision to embody the Constitution in a text is the necessity to construe that text. Of greater importance, however, is the decision to put the state under law; this means that the text that accomplishes this will be construed along legal lines, and thus that the modalities of legal argument will structure decisions that determine the legitimate power of the state. Although it is often taken for granted, it is noteworthy that the ways in which the American Constitution can be legitimately interpreted are similar to the ways in which Anglo-American lawyers and judges construe legal documents. By relying on a written instrument to perfect the constitutional understanding of sovereign people endowing a state of limited sovereignty, the framers of the Constitution introduced the habits and style of Anglo-American legal argument into the politics of the state. The ways in which the Constitution is interpreted could have been different; indeed they are different in other societies. In the United States, however, the familiar methods of the common law – the ways in which the texts of contracts, wills, promissory notes and deeds were construed – became the methods of constitutional construction once the state itself was put under law.

These methods may be characterized as the forms of constitutional argument, or the *modalities* of constitutional interpretation. They determine whether a proposition of constitutional law is true from a legal point of view, and thus they also determine whether reliance on that proposition to support a legal decision is legitimate. These modalities might be categorized slightly differently, or subdivided, but the following six are generally accepted as composing the standard model of constitutional interpretation: (1) history – which relies on the original intentions of the ratifiers of the Constitution; (2) text – which looks to the meaning of the words of the Constitution as they would be interpreted by an average contemporary American today; (3) structure – which infers rules from the relationships that the Constitution mandates between the structures it sets up; (4) doctrine – which generates and applies rules from precedent; (5) ethos – which derives rules from those moral and political commitments of the American ethos that are reflected in the Constitution; (6) prudence – which balances the costs and benefits of a proposed rule. "Strict Construction" consists of an exclusive reliance on the first three forms.

It is an open question – and a hotly contested one in constitutional theory – whether there must be some rules that are generated outside these six modalities, such that would enable us to choose among them when they conflict, and justify

127

them when we rely on them. As Ronald Dworkin has observed, "Some parts of any constitutional theory must be independent of the intentions or beliefs or indeed the acts of the people the theory designates as framers. Some part must stand on its own political or moral theory; otherwise the theory would be wholly circular" (Dworkin, 1981). By contrast, Philip Bobbitt argues that such a resort to an external theory would de-legitimate the system of decision making (Bobbitt 1991) and in any case only deepens the problem of circularity (Bobbitt, 1979). Bobbitt uses that point to support his conclusion that the forms are modalities – determining the truth of a proposition (for example, that the equal protection clause may be used to protect the rights of whites) but neither true nor false in themselves (for example, that the Constitution ought to be construed according to the intentions of the ratifiers because they alone endowed the Constitution with authority.) "There is no constitutional legal argument outside these modalities. Outside these forms, a proposition about the US. Constitution can be a fact, or be elegant, or be amusing or even poetic; and although such assessments exist as legal statements in some possible legal world, they are not actualized in our legal world."

We will return to this debate when we consider the academic commentary on the standard model. First let us explore more carefully these six forms, that are said to constrain legal decision making when construing the Constitution.

History

Arguments in this form attend to ascertain the intentions of the people, the ratifiers of the Constitution, when they delegated their constitutive authority to the state over a particular matter. One way to think of the Constitution is to imagine it is a trust agreement, created by the people in their role as grantors. The Constitution specifies what powers the government, the trustees, are to have and endows these agents with the authority to accomplish the goals of the trust, subject to various limitations explicitly in the agreement or implied by it or inherent in the very nature of such a delegation (for example, the grantors could not irrevocably or permanently give away their "inalienable rights" to sovereignty since these, by definition, can merely be delegated to a limited government). Since the grantors created the trust, it is they who provided the authority to dispose of the corpus of powers with which they endowed the trust and it is to their purposes and intentions that we must look in interpreting the trust agreement, especially the powers of the trustees. If the trustees act beyond these intentions, they are altering the trust agreement and acting ultra vires. As with a trust agreement, the governing text will only constrain the grantor's agents if the methods of interpreting that text compel such constraints.

Consider the following question: does the Equal Protection Clause of the 14th Amendment protect whites from discrimination on the basis of their race when this discrimination is an effort to compensate African–Americans for the effects of slavery? Arguments that take a historical approach might be framed as follows. Did the ratifiers of the 14th Amendment intend to eradicate race discrimination, as evidenced by the statements of some of the drafters of that amendment when they were arguing for its adoption, and on which statements the public can be presumed to have relied? Or did they intend that the amendment be used exclusively to eradicate the race discrimination that attended black slavery, as was also urged by some of the drafters of the amendment, and which provided the historical context in which ratification took place? Or is it simply unclear what their intentions might have been, since race discrimination in favor of African–Americans was rare and largely unconsidered?

The method of historical argument is difficult – as the methods of history are difficult, and for the same reasons. The more remote the period of ratification, the more elusive is the intention of the ratifiers, and the more likely that an unwanted anachronism will corrupt our efforts to retrieve that intention. Although Justice Rehnquist once sarcastically wrote that, "if those responsible for [the Bill of Rights and the 14th Amendment] could have lived to know that their efforts had enshrined in the Constitution the right of commercial vendors of contraceptives to peddle them to unmarried minors through such means as window displays and vending machines located in the men's rooms of truck stops . . . it is not difficult to imagine their reaction," in fact it is difficult to imagine their reactions. What is altogether too easy, is to imagine our reactions and then transpose them to parties who would themselves be different were they thinking and writing today. Indeed, since we can never wholly free ourselves of our own expectations and emphases when we study the past, we should not place too much confidence in our ability to understand even the articulated motives of the ratifiers, to say nothing of the problems of mixed motives, misunderstood objectives, absent evidence and the like that bedevil the historian.

Alexander Bickel has suggested one way of coping with this difficulty: he proposes that we attend to the larger principles enshrined in the constitutional language as evidence of the purpose of the ratifiers, while permitting flexibility as to the actual policies that will serve those principles. Based on the facts available to them, it may well have been that the ratifiers of the Equal Protection Clause believed it could co-exist quite undisturbed with the racial segregation of schools; but we, who have learned a great deal about the harm such segregation works on both races, and who have learned to respect and admire the intellectual achievements of the descendants of slaves, could only give effect to the purposes of the Equal Protection Clause by applying it in the context of our knowledge, not simply that of its framers. To confine ourselves to the latter would actually frustrate the intentions of the ratifiers, just as if one were to mindlessly execute Leonardo's design for a helicopter in defiance of twentieth-century lift equations. This, however, merely throws us back to a question of at least equal difficulty: how do we know that the ratifiers wished us to proceed in this way? Felix Frankfurter has suggested that we may infer this command from the relative precision of the text: the more vague the language, the more we are free to execute principles and ignore the actual policies. This seems like a valid and helpful inference: but how do we know that it is one the ratifiers would have endorsed, and not just a move to vacuous generalities that will efface their intentions? After all, how can we understand a principle when it is entirely stripped of policies?

129

Jefferson Powell has attacked this problem and shown that the framers and ratifiers of the original text and Bill of Rights intended to have the Constitution construed by the entire range of legal arguments, that is, the full group of the modalities discussed above. His powerful arguments are a rebuff to those who would confine constitutional interpretation to a determination of original intent: the original intent, it seems, was not to be confined in this way.

Text

Textual approaches are easily confused with historical approaches. Consider the determination by Chief Justice Roger Taney in *Dred Scott* v. *Sanford* whether the diversity jurisdiction granted in Article III, which provides for suits in the federal courts by the citizens of one state against the citizens of another, could encompass a suit brought by a slave. In construing the term "citizen," Taney wrote,

> We must inquire who, at that time [1787–9, that is, the time of ratification] were recognized as the citizens of a state, whose rights and liberties had been outraged by the English government and who declared their independence, and assumed powers of Government to defend their rights by force of arms.

In contrast to this historical approach, Taney might have adopted a textual form. He might have asked: does the text of the Constitution, to the average contemporary person, appear to declare that a former slave can bring suit in federal court because the text does not qualify the word citizen by race? Or does the text appear to deny this jurisdiction because the word *citizen* is used instead of *person*, a difference that implies a distinction by race? Or is the text simply non-committal on this point? The answer in Taney's day, the mid-nineteenth century, might well have been different from the one he hypothesized for the late eighteenth century; the answer today would certainly be different.

The rationale for our attention to the contemporary construction of the words of the Constitution is also based on the sovereignty of the people. Since they alone can consent to the actions of government, a text granting powers to that government cannot exceed the understanding of the people. Their ongoing acquiescence – in contrast to those of the generation "who declared their independence, and assumed the powers of Government," – amounts to an ongoing consent, but they cannot be presumed to consent to terms that differ from their own common use of those terms.

Textual approaches, despite their connection to contemporary life, can have their own anachronistic qualities. Should Congress be able to authorize an air force? The text speaks only of an army and navy. Consider, for example, the Supreme Court's interpretation of the Fourth Amendment, which guarantees the "right of the people to be secure in their persons, houses, papers and effects, against unreasonable searches and seizures." Chief Justice William Howard Taft relied on textual argument when federal prohibition officers wire-tapped a telephone without seeking a warrant. Taft wrote:

The amendment itself shows that the search is to be of material things – the person, the house, his papers or his effects. The amendment does not forbid what was done here for there was no seizure. The evidence was secured by the sense of hearing and that only. There was no entry of the houses. (Olmstead v. United States, *1928 at 464*)

But the greatest impact of textual argument on constitutional interpretation has been in the area of the 14th Amendment. Its demands drove the doctrine of incorporation by which the various texts of the Bill of Rights were "incorporated" in the 14th Amendment and their guarantees applied against the states. This was principally the work of the great jurist, Hugo Black who used the legitimacy conferred by textual approaches, and their popular appeal, to effect a dramatic change in human rights. Black's textual jurisprudence was also felt in his construction of the terms of the Bill of Rights and his insistence that these terms were often "absolute." Black cited the First Amendment's provision that "Congress shall make no law . . . abridging the freedom of speech" as an example of a textual absolute when read with the expectations of the ordinary citizen. "No law," he often said, "means no law," an unwelcome and surprising interpretation to the lawyers and commentators who pointed out that this would strike down all obscenity laws, defamation and anti-incitement statutes, conspiracy laws, and the like. Black conceded that some texts did not contain absolutes because they did not state their prohibitions quite so categorically. The Eighth Amendment, for example, bars "cruel and unusual punishments" but does not specifically bar any particular punishment. But whatever such punishments are determined to be, Black wrote, they are absolutely prohibited because that is what the language of the amendment would mean to the ordinary American reading it today. Thus textual approaches can be made to stand as a bulwark against the prudential and doctrinal approaches that tend to balance such texts against necessity or provide a lawyerly construction of the terms.

Structure

Structural arguments depend on the fact that the Constitution sets up quite specific relationships among the governmental entities it endows with power. Rather than focussing on the complete sovereignty of the people, which is the basis for textual and historical argument, structural argument focusses on the limited sovereignty of the government and demands that these limitations be observed. Perhaps the most celebrated example of this form of argument is found in Part II of *McCulloch v. Maryland*. In determining whether a Maryland tax on the federally chartered Bank of the United States could be enforced, Chief Justice John Marshall declined to rely on any specific text, and explicitly rejected reliance on historical argument. Instead he offered a rationale based on inferences from the structure of federalism and representative government. A federal structure could not be maintained, he argued, if the states, whose officials are chosen by a state's constituency only, could tax the agencies of the federal government and thereby levy a tax on the entire national constituency which was represented by Congress only. Such an argument made the state tax unconstitutional in principle, and not, as is often thought, because it carried with it "the power to destroy" the federal instrumentality. The constitutional structure would not tolerate such a practice even though the text and the ratification debates did not explicitly condemn it.

Structural arguments follow a deceptively simply form. They rely on an uncontroversial statement about the institutions of government, from which inferences are drawn regarding the relationship among such institutions or between those institutions and the people. For example, in *National League of Cities* v. *Usery*, Justice William H. Rehnquist addressed the legal question whether a state may be required by Congress to observe minimum wage laws with respect to state employees. His rationale was entirely structural: first he asserted that the Constitution sets up a federal system in which some matters are left to state determination; second, he argued that at least some matters must therefore be left to the states or their sovereignty would be entirely merged into the federal government and the federal *system* would cease to exist; finally, he concluded that the decision as to how much to pay certain state employees, if made by the federal government, would effectively remove a state's ability to make its own policies – since some policies would become more or less expensive depending on the decisions of Congress – and thus that this must be one of those matters committed to the states without which the federal system would collapse.

Many celebrated examples of this form of argument can be found in the recent jurisprudence of the Supreme Court. *Bowsher* v. *Synar* struck down an attempt to use an officer, who was in fact responsive to the legislative branch, as a key executive official. *INS* v. *Chadha* struck down the legislative veto on the grounds that it represented a new and additional process by which laws could be created, despite the limited sovereignty of the government.

Although structural argument is one of the classic modalities, and was much relied upon by Marshall during the early period of American constitutional interpretation, it fell into disuse during the first half of the twentieth century. Its renaissance may be credited to an important lecture given in 1968 by Charles L. Black, Jr, entitled "Structure and relationship in constitutional law," which described a mode of constitutional interpretation based on "inference from the structure and relationships created by the constitution in all its parts or in some principal part." Black argued against "Humpty-Dumpty textual manipulation" in place of a reliance on "the sort of political inference which not only underlies the textual manipulation but is, in a well constructed opinion, usually invoked to support the interpretation of the cryptic text."

Prudence

"The Constitution," Justice Jackson wrote in the most famous single sentence expression of prudential argument, "is not a suicide pact." By this he meant that, whatever the commands of other forms of constitutional interpretation, a conclusion from those commands that was fatal to the state and its people was unacceptable. Of course, usually it does not come to that; indeed prudential argument entered the jurisprudence of constitutional interpretation by the modest avenue of judicial restraint.

Justice Louis Brandeis, most notably in his concurrence in *Ashwander* v. *TVA*, introduced prudential argument on this limited basis into judicial opinions in the twentieth century. His opinion provides various rules by which the Supreme Court can avoid unnecessarily deciding constitutional cases. Many of these derive from the restriction that the courts decide only "cases or controversies," but the effect, as Brandeis intended, is to enable the Court to better govern its own role, avoiding becoming embroiled in political conflicts that undermine the authority of the Court. "The most important thing we do," he said, "is not deciding." The means of avoiding decisions are crucial, Alexander Bickel wrote, "because [they] are the techniques that allow leeway to expediency." Moreover, insofar as a judge may decide to decline to hear a case on the basis of expediency – preferring to leave the issue, for example, to other branches to decide – prudential techniques are more than simply methods. If the rationale for prudential argument is that the ends can sometimes justify the means, such arguments also provide the means by which such a rationale is brought to bear. As a consequence, these sorts of arguments open the door to a wide range of policy considerations.

Prudential arguments introduce the calculus of costs and benefits into constitutional decision making, and ask that the practical effects of a decision be weighed as part of constitutional interpretation. A striking example occurred when, in the depths of the midwestern farm depression of the 1930s, the Minnesota legislature passed a statute declaring a moratorium on mortgage payments as a relief measure for hard-pressed farm debtors. On its face the statute seemed an example of the sort of law the framers feared would threaten democracy when legislatures wished to confer economic benefits on the majority of voters at the expense of capital holders – debtors usually outnumbering creditors. To prevent this, and to prevent the destruction of the national capital market, Article I includes the Contracts Clause. Nevertheless the Court recognized the political expediency of the state's action, upheld the statute and concluded,

> It is manifest . . . that there has been a growing appreciation of public needs and of the necessity of finding ground for a rational compromise between individual rights and public welfare. The settlement and consequent contraction of the public domain, the pressure of a constantly increasing density of population, the interrelation of the activities of our people, and the complexity of our economic interests, have inevitably led to an increased use of the origination of society in order to protect the very bases of individual opportunity . . . [T]he question is no longer merely that of one party to a contract as against another, but of the use of reasonable means to safeguard the economic structure upon which the good of all depends. (Home Building and Loan Association v. Blaisdell)

Similarly, another national crisis provided the background for *Bowles* v. *Willingham* (1944). Congress enacted the Emergency Price Control Act, providing for administrative actions to freeze or reduce rents for housing adjacent to defense plants and bases. The Court upheld the statute in frankly prudential language:

Congress was dealing here with conditions created by activities resulting from a great war effort. A nation which can demand the lives of its men and women in waging that war is under no constitutional necessity of providing a system of price control on the domestic front which will assure each landlord a "fair return" on his property . . . Congress . . . has done all that due process under the war emergency requires. (*at 519*)

But prudential arguments are by no means confined to emergencies. One can see their distinctive watermark in a number of ordinary constitutional situations. The characteristic reliance on facts, and the weighing of consequences, identifies these arguments.

Doctrine

In a mature juridical system, cases of first impression – where the subject matter comes for a decision absent prior decisions on the same subject – are relatively rare. In highly adjudicated areas, like those of the First Amendment's guarantees of free speech, and freedom of religion, or the Fifth Amendment's bar against involuntary self-incrimination, the weight of past decisions is heavy. These areas have become so heavily doctrinalized that the characteristic questions and cues looked for by the decider are likelier to come from prior decisions than from the Constitution itself. The American doctrine of stare decisis, however, does not accord prior decisions ultimate authority, and though given presumptive weight, they may be modified or overruled by a subsequent decider. This follows naturally from the limited sovereignty of the state, which must constantly check its actions against the grant of power from the people, so that even the most respected precedent is vulnerable to re-evaluation.

With respect to decisions by judges, doctrine is created out of judicial opinions – precedents. But all official deciders are guided to some extent by precedent, and there is much constitutional doctrine in the prior practices of Congress and the President that is little commented on by scholars.

When a judge states that a neutral, general principle derived from case law construing the Constitution is "on all fours with the instant case" and therefore governs it, or, instead, that no precedent can be found, or that the case law is divided such that no clear rule can be inferred, these arguments are drawn from a doctrinal mode. This mode relies on common law legal reasoning from the rationales offered by previous deciders. Thus it does not rely on dicta, which are mere expressions of opinion not crucial to the holding of the prior case. Only the rationale that leads to a decision may govern a later decision by serving as the basis on which the rule is determined. "Adjudication is meaningless unless the decision is reached by some rational process . . . [and] if a decision is to be rational it must be based upon some rule, principle or standard," wrote Hart and Sacks. On this view, constitutional interpretation is essentially a common law function, arising from the Court's processes to deciding cases.

Doctrinal argument is assessed not only by the rigorous standards of inference from precedent, but also by two other requirements: that is, in addition to being principled, such argument must be neutral as to the parties (such that no rule systematically favors any particular class or group, but treats those similarly situated with respect to the rule, similarly) and general as to applicability (such that new cases governed by the rule are not routinely distinguished away, thereby confining a precedent to its facts.)

Ethos

This modality of constitutional interpretation denotes an appeal to the very ethos of the American Constitution, an ethos that is clearly reflected in the superstructure of the political and legal system itself. The fundamental commitment of this ethos is to limited government and limited sovereignty, which presume that all residual authority remains in the private sphere and that the ultimate nature of that authority means that it cannot be delegated. A corollary to this idea is reflected in the ethos of self-government and representative institutions. The proto-constitutional document, the Declaration of Independence, manifests these ethical commitments.

Arguments from this modality can be called ethical arguments; they are defined by their appeal to those rights of individual choice that are beyond the power of government to compel. This contrasts with some European Constitutions that, though they depend upon popular sovereignty, do not create limited states, so that personal rights are granted, rather than confirmed, by the constitutional instrument.

Ethical arguments are perhaps most evident where unremunerated human rights are at stake. Thus they are associated with the open-textured language of the 9th and 10th Amendments, as well as the undeveloped privileges and immunities clause of the 14th Amendment. Ethical arguments are also sometimes called arguments of substantive due process, because they attempt to give substantive, rather than procedural content to the due process clauses of the Constitution.

Structural and ethical arguments share some similarities: each is essentially an inferred set of arguments, and neither depends upon any particular text but rather on the necessary relationships that can be inferred from the overall arrangements expressed by the text. Structural argument, however, infers rules from the powers granted to governments; ethical argument, by contrast, infers rules from the powers retained by the people and thus denied to the government. Finally, while structural arguments can yield different results for the state and federal governments, respectively, ethical arguments apply to both equally. Those means that are denied to the federal government on ethical arguments are also denied to the states.

Sometimes ethical arguments are said to rely on natural law, which is correct only to the extent it can be said that the fundamental division in American constitutional life between the public and private is itself derivative of notions of natural law; and sometimes ethical arguments are equated with moral and political arguments, which is largely incorrect save in those cases where the constitutional ethos reflects a specific moral or political commitment (for example, the bar against involuntary servitude).

Academic commentary

Commentary on constitutional interpretation has long been a fertile field for academic and political controversy. The dramatic Supreme Court decisions that restricted the New Deal, and then, after World War II, that were associated with the Warren Court – the desegregation, criminal procedure and abortion decisions, for example, sparked the current debate, which has largely concerned itself with the legitimacy of judicial review. This was famously stated by Alexander Bickel as arising from the Counter-majoritarian Objection – the claim that when an unelected court overturned the decisions of a legislature the court was acting without the legitimacy conferred by representation and was thus vulnerable, even suspect (Bickel, 1962).

Although the analysis of constitutional interpretation in terms of the modalities of argument is relatively new (Bobbitt, 1979, 1982), academic commentary in response to this objection can be seen to reflect positions derived from each of the forms of argument, and indeed has been evident to do so since the New Deal controversy brought the issue of legitimacy into play. Thus jurists like Hugo Black developed a jurisprudence based on textual approaches (Black, 1960) which sought to deny an independent role to the judiciary in interpreting the clear commands of the Constitution. Charles L. Black, Jr, in a remarkable series of lectures (Black, 1969) and an influential article on Brown and the desegregation decisions (Black, date), outlined structural argument and defended the Court's role in face of attacks from a doctrinalist perspective (Wechsler, 1959). Doctrinalists generally were hesitant about the Brown decision, which overturned considerable precedent without actually offering the rationale that has later become apparent (see Hand, 1958) and were greatly distressed by the opinion in *Roe* v. *Wade* on similar grounds. One objective of the Legal Process School was to rescue the legitimacy of official constitutional interpretation from the consequences of legal realism and the politicization of the Court (Hart, 1959) that the New Deal crisis had brought into high relief.

> [The Court] does not in the end have the power either in theory or in practice to ram its own personal preferences down other people's throats. Thus, the Court is predestined in the long run not only by the thrilling tradition of Anglo-American law but also by the hard facts of its position in the structure of American institutions to be a voice of reason, charged with the creative function of discerning afresh and of articulating and developing impersonal and durable principles of constitutional law.

By contrast, Judge Robert Bork spoke for many adherents to the mode of historical argument when he testified that,

> The judge's authority [to interpret the constitution] derives entirely from the fact that he is applying the law and not his personal values . . . [The only legitimate way to find the law] is by attempting to discern . . . the intentions of . . . those . . . who ratified our Constitution and its various amendments. The judge's responsibility is to

discern how the framers' values, defined in the context of the world they knew, apply in the world we know. If a judge abandons intention as his guide, there is no law available to him and he . . . goes beyond this legitimate power. (*Bork, 1987*)

Bickel himself developed a sophisticated, prudential defense of judicial review (Bickel, 1961). A later generation pushed these rationales further, articulating highly intricate theories that legitimated judicial review on structural (Ely, 1980), prudential (Ackerman, 1991), historical (Berger, 1977), textual (Linde), ethical (Grey, 1987) and doctrinal (Brest and Levinson, 1983) grounds, and this was furthered enriched by still later commentators (Amar/structural, 1991), (Tushnet/prudential, 1988), (Powell/historical, 1985), (Levinson/ethical, 19), (Balkin/textual, 1987) who tended to write more self-consciously in the awareness that each preferred modality was only one among many (Tribe, 1985; Griffin, 1994).

Thus the debate moved from controversies like the Meese/Brennan exchange, which was still principally concerned with legitimating judicial review, to a new set of questions, such as "How can any of these forms of argument maintain legitimacy when each is not objective?", "How does one choose among the forms when they conflict?", "What is the role of collateral disciplines in clarifying the operation of these forms, or in providing ideal models for decision making?" (Post, 1990; Fallon, 1987). In the mid-1980s Edwin Meese, US Attorney-General in the Reagan Administration, had maintained that judicial review was confined to the strict construction modalities (history, text, and structure) while Justice William Brennan had taken a more expansive view, stressing the prudential and ethical forms of argument. By the end of the decade, all the forms of argument were assimilated into a standard model that denied a privileged position to any particular modality of constitutional interpretation (Bobbitt, 1992), although the implications of this model remained highly contested.

Bibliography

Ackerman, B. 1991: *We The People*.
Amar, A. 1991: Taking Article III seriously. *Northwestern University Law Review*, 85, 443.
Balkin, J. M. 1987: Deconstructive practice and legal theory. *Yale Law Journal*, 96, 743.
Berger, R. 1977: *Government by Judiciary*.
Bickel, A. 1961: The passive virtues. *Harvard Law Review*, 75, 40.
—— A. 1962: *The Least Dangerous Branch: the Supreme Court at the bar of politics*.
Black, C. 1969: *Structure and Relationship in Constitutional Law*.
—— 1981: *The Decision according to Law*.
Bobbitt, P. 1982: *Constitutional Fate: theory of the Constitution*.
—— 1991: *Constitutional Interpretation*.
Bork, R. 1987: Original intent: the only legitimate basis for constitutional decision making. *Judge's Journal*, 13, summer.
Brest, P. and Levinson, S. 1983: *Processes of Constitutional Decision-Making*, 2nd edn.
Dworkin, R. 1988: *Law's Empire*.
Ely, J. H. 1980: *Democracy and Distrust*.

Fallon, R. 1987: A constructivist's coherence theory of constitutional argumentation. *Harvard Law Review*, 100, 1,189.

Grey, T. 1987: A constitutional morphology: text, context and pretext in constitutional interpretation. *Arizona State Law, Journal*, 19, 587.

Griffin, S. 1989: What is constitutional theory? *Southern California Law Review*, 62, 493.

Hand, L. 1958: *The Bill of Rights.*

Hart, H. 1959: The time chart of the justices. *Harvard Law Review*, 73, 84.

Meese, E. 1985: The Attorney General's view of the Supreme Court: toward a jurisprudence of original intention. In Symposium construing the constitution, *UC Davis Law Review*, 19, 1.

Monaghan, H. 1981: Our perfect constitution. *New York University Law Review*, 56, 353.

Post, R. 1990: Theories of constitutional interpretation. *Representations*, 30, 13.

Powell, J. 1985: The original understanding of original intent. *Harvard Law Review*, 98, 885.

Tribe, L. 1985: *Constitutional Choices.*

Tushnet, M. 1988: *Red, White, and Blue: a critical analysis of constitutional law.*

Wechsler, H. 1959: *Toward Neutral Principles of Constitutional Law.*

Wellington, H. 1990: *Interpreting the Constitution.*

8

Constitutional law and privacy

ANITA L. ALLEN

Introduction

The concept of privacy plays a significant role in constitutional thought and practice. Particularly in the United States, privacy's sometimes controversial role extends far beyond the ideals of private property and a political order comprised of separate public and private spheres. It extends broadly to ideals of limited and neutral government; and to moral conceptions of human beings as bearers of dignity, autonomy, or interests, by virtue of which they ought to have lives and ties substantially of their own choosing.

The expressions "privacy" and the "right to privacy" each have more than one usage in the law. For example, in US tort law, the "right to privacy" refers, individually and collectively, to four distinguishable rights (Prosser, 1960). Tortfeasors compensate plaintiffs for unauthorized: (1) intrusion into seclusion; (2) publication of private or embarrassing facts; (3) publicity placing another in a false light; and (4) commercial use of another's name, likeness, or identity. This collection of legal rights relating to interests in seclusion, reputation and personality, suggests that adequate privacy obtains where restrictions on access to persons and personal information accords freedom from intrusion and public exposure.

Like US common law, US state and federal statutes ascribe privacy rights. New York and several other states have legislated versions of one or more of the common law privacy torts. Moreover, a wide array of state and federal statutes limit disclosure of information contained in medical, school, adoption, tax, library, video rental, financial, and criminal records. Statutes also regulate potentially invasive practices such as polygraph testing and wire-tapping.

Most US privacy statutes implicitly define "privacy" much as tort law implicitly defines it, as restrictions on access to people and information. However, some legislation denominated as "privacy" legislation implies a broader definition. In the name of "privacy" some statutes establish qualitative standards for the collection, use, transfer, and storage of information. Policymakers call these standards "fair information practices." Fair information practices require that data collectors: (1) protect personal information from public exposure; (2) take reasonable steps to verify and update information; (3) allow individuals access to records of which they are the subject; and, finally, (4) obtain consent prior to otherwise

139

unauthorized uses of personal information. Fair information practices are mandated by the federal Privacy Act of 1974, 5 U.S.C.A., Section 552a, a statute governing information held in United States government record systems. Where privacy is conceived as a set of fair information practices, respecting privacy entails policies that grant the individual a degree of control over acquirable personal information.

The term "privacy" in US constitutional law often means what it means in US tort and statutory law, except that the fair information practices conception of privacy has not figured prominently in constitutional discourse. Constitutional uses of "privacy" include two that overlap those routinely found elsewhere in law. They are: (1) privacy used in a *physical* sense, to denote seclusion, solitude, security, or bodily integrity, at home and elsewhere; and (2) privacy used in an *informational* sense, to denote confidentiality, secrecy, or anonymity, especially with respect to correspondence, conversation, and records. But constitutional uses of "privacy" include a third one that is not yet characteristic of tort and statutory law: (3) privacy used in a *decisional* sense, to denote liberty, freedom, choice, or autonomy in decision making about sex, reproduction, marriage, family, and health care. The constitutional law or equivalent basic law of many nations incorporates protections for physical, informational and decisional privacy.

World Constitutions

In countries around the world, protecting a broad range of privacy interests is deemed a core function of government. Virtually every country's Constitution provides for a degree of physical, informational and decisional privacy by limiting government access to homes, possessions, and persons (Blaustein and Flanz, 1994). Under Article 10 of the Charter of Fundamental Rights, a citizen of the Netherlands has "the right to respect for his privacy." Chapter 2, Article 6, of the Swedish Constitution provides for physical and informational privacy, declaring that: "Every citizen shall in relation to the community be protected against forced encroachment on his body . . . [and] shall be protected against any bodily search, search of his home or similar encroachment as well as against any examination of letters or other confidential correspondence and against eavesdropping or recording of telephone conversations or other confidential communication." The democratic nations of the former British Empire, including Australia, Britain, Canada, and Ireland, may lack comprehensive written constitutions and/or express constitutional privacy provisions, but, nevertheless, protect important forms of physical, informational, and decisional privacy.

The Constitutions of Columbia, at Article 15, and Peru, at Article 2(5), contain explicit privacy language. The same is true of the Constitutions of several Eastern European countries, whose Constitutions date back only to the 1980s and 1990s. Article 26 of the 1992 Estonian Constitution provides for "the right to the inviolability of family life and privacy." Article 23 of the Constitution of the Russian Federation, adopted in 1993, provides for a "right to privacy, to personal and family secrets, and to protection of one's honor and good name." Privacy rights are explicit in the 1992 Constitution of the Slovak Republic, Section 2, Article 16; and the 1991 Constitution of the Republic of Slovenia, Article 34. The 1993 Constitution of post-apartheid South Africa, and the Constitutions of Nigeria and Sierra Leone include explicit privacy language. Article 40 of the Constitution of the People's Republic of China contains a provision protecting the "freedom and privacy of correspondence of citizens," as does the Constitution of the Republic of Korea, Chapter 2, Article 18.

The bare text of many national Constitutions promises robust legal protection for privacy. But little can be gleaned from a document of formal and hortatory principle. In the United States and elsewhere getting an accurate picture of constitutional protection for privacy requires a close look at courts, law enforcement agencies, and cultural milieu.

Focus: the United States

The specific idea of a constitutional right of privacy did not emerge until the twentieth century, when it sprang to life in American law. Well before its explicit emergence, however, provisions of the US Constitution, along with constitutionally mandated structural features of the US government, implied rights of privacy for free individuals and male heads of households and their families (O'Brien, 1979; Flaherty, 1972). The constitutional law of the United States illustrates that the concept of privacy can play a major, complex role in a constitutional framework, whether or not "privacy" and a "right to privacy" are recognized explicitly.

Americans have nearly always assumed inherent moral and political limits on the power of state and federal government to dictate the terms of individual lives. They have nearly always embraced the principle that government may not arbitrarily or unduly curtail physical, informational and decisional forms of privacy. *The Federalist* (1788) omits explicit mention of privacy as a principle of good government. Yet, this collection of political essays written by Alexander Hamilton, James Madison, and John Jay to the people of New York urging adoption of a US Constitution with a strong central government, presupposes a division between a politically prior private people and a created public government.

Throughout, *The Federalist* makes reference to the people as the possessors of the "ultimate authority" and as the "only legitimate fountain of power" (Cooke, No. 45, p. 315; No. 49, p. 339). Along the same lines, it depicts the Constitution as creating a national government with specific, limited powers: "the people surrender nothing and as they retain everything, they have no need of particular reservations [of rights]" (Cooke, No. 84, p. 581). In explaining why a separate bill of rights was not necessary, Hamilton wrote that: "The truth is . . . that the constitution is itself . . . a Bill of Rights" (Cooke, No. 84, p. 581). Rights of privacy are not set forth in *The Federalist*, but the papers refer to "private rights of particular classes of citizens" (Cooke, No. 78, p. 528). They appeal to "public and private confidence" (Cooke, No. 78, p. 529), and "certain immunities and modes of

141

proceeding, which are relative to personal and private concerns" (Cooke, No. 84, p. 581).

The word "privacy" appears nowhere in the original eighteenth-century US Constitution or its amendments. Yet one finds in US constitutional law broad doctrines relating to the protection of physical, informational, and decisional privacy. Most notably, Justices of the Supreme Court interpreting the text and logic of the Fourth Amendment have determined that a right to a "reasonable expectation of privacy" limits government search and seizure. The Court has also held that a fundamental "right of privacy" derived interpretatively from the 14th Amendment limits government interference with autonomous personal decision making respecting birth control and abortion. The well-developed Fourth Amendment "reasonable expectation of privacy" doctrine and the controversial 14th Amendment "right of privacy" doctrine are only part of the story of privacy in American constitutional jurisprudence. Constitutional case law and theory link privacy with the First Amendment (the privacy of conscience and group association), the Third Amendment (the privacy of the home), the Fifth Amendment (the privacy of thought and personality), and the Ninth Amendment (unenumerated privacy rights reserved to the people).

Privacy as a distinct legal value and right entered the mainstream of American tort law in the late nineteenth century, following the publication of "The right to privacy," in the 1890 *Harvard Law Review*. The work of Boston lawyers Samuel Warren and Louis Brandeis, the famous article successfully argued for the recognition of a new common law invasion of privacy tort. Although Warren and Brandeis made no claim for privacy as a constitutional value in the 1890 article, their work arguably laid the intellectual groundwork for the eventual development both of constitutional and statutory privacy rights. As a member of the Supreme Court dissenting in *Olmstead* v. *United States*, 277 U.S. 438 (1928), Brandeis himself drew on the language of the 1890 tort article to defend privacy as a civilized value fit for a modern constitutional jurisprudence.

The federal Constitution does not include the word "privacy" or a cognate expression. But at least ten state Constitutions include express protections for "privacy," "private life," and "private affairs." Since 1974, privacy has been one of the "inalienable rights" specifically enumerated in Article I, Section 1, of the California Constitution. Under Article I, Section 22, of the Constitution of Alaska, "The Right of the people to privacy is recognized and shall not be infringed." The Constitutions of South Carolina, Illinois, Louisiana provide for a right against "unreasonable invasions of privacy." In Hawaii, California, Florida, and Louisiana, case law holds that state privacy guarantees are stronger or broader than federal guarantees. The state of Washington interprets its Constitution's protection of "private affairs" as offering "heightened" protection regarding search and seizure law as compared to federal constitutional law, but "no greater" protection than the federal Constitution with respect to other forms of privacy.

States that do not have express privacy provisions in their Constitutions, nonetheless, protect aspects of privacy. The courts have inferred a right of decisional privacy from the equal protection clause of the Massachusetts Constitution.

Michigan and New York courts protect privacy through interpretations of their due process clauses. In New Jersey, judges acknowledge a right of privacy under a "natural and Unalienable rights" provision of the state constitution; in Pennsylvania, judges acknowledge privacy rights as among the "Inherent rights of Mankind."

The judicially developed "right to privacy" doctrines associated with state and federal constitutions concur that privacy interests are strong without being absolute. Even jurisdictions that elevate privacy interests to the level of fundamental, inalienable, or natural rights do not treat them as invariably superior to other interests. In practice, courts weigh and balance privacy interests against other important interests. Thus, to cite a series of illustrative examples, courts weigh the interests of prison inmates in freedom from cell searches and body-cavity searches against the state interest in law enforcement, corrections, and prison security. They weigh the interests of high school students in control over their lockers, handbags, hairstyles, and clothing against the interests of public school administrators in discipline, security, and education. They weigh the interests of highway motorists in unmolested travel against the interest of the public police in crime detection and traffic safety.

To cite additional examples, courts weigh the interest in choosing one's own spouse against the state interest in family stability, child welfare, and inheritance. They weigh interests in collecting sexually explicit materials in the home, against a state interest in regulating the manufacture and sale of obscenity. They weigh patients' interests in confidentiality against the health data-collection needs of state agencies and insurance companies. Courts weigh the "right to die" of people with incurable diseases against the state interest in preventing coercion and disrespect for life. Judges balance interests of employees in avoiding drug, alcohol, and AIDS testing against employers' interest in efficiency and workplace safety. They balance the interests of corporations in the confidentiality of competitive business strategies and practices against the public interest in checking fraud and regulatory violation. Lastly, courts weigh the privacy interests of the President in his notes, papers, and sound recordings against the national interest in preserving the separation of powers and the integrity of the executive branch.

Some state Constitutions that confer privacy rights specify how privacy considerations are to be weighed in the light of competing social concerns. In Montana, for example, a constitutional privacy right may be overcome only by a "compelling" state interest. The US Supreme Court does not always require the showing of a compelling state interest in cases that relate to constitutional privacy interests. In *Cruzan* v. *Missouri Department of Health*, 497 U.S. 261 (1990), the Court considered whether parents of an automobile accident victim in a permanent vegetative state were entitled to make a "private" decision on her behalf to terminate hydration and nutrition. The Court recognized an important 14th Amendment liberty interest in private medical decision making; but held that the state has a "legitimate interest" in erecting procedural barriers to family decision making.

The Supreme Court applied a "compelling interest" standard in cases scrutinizing the regulation of abortion, beginning with *Roe* v. *Wade*, 410 U.S. 113 (1973).

Under this highest of standards of review, a governmental regulation that inter-feres with the decision to abort is presumed invalid; to overcome the presumption, the government must show that its regulation constraining personal choice is narrowly drawn to further a legitimate and compelling state interest. The Court no longer applies the compelling state interest requirement of *Roe* in all abortion cases. In *Planned Parenthood* v. *Casey*, 112 Sup.Ct. 2791 (1992), the Court re-quired only that the government establish that challenged abortion restrictions did not "unduly burden" the important constitutional right to choose.

Theorizing about privacy

Theoretical accounts of privacy, including constitutional privacy, are plentiful. This was not always so. In the nineteenth century, the concept of privacy received focussed attention in the writings of few theorists. British utilitarian John Stuart Mill did not label liberty from collective and government regulation of decision making about personal life as "privacy." Yet Mill's *On Liberty* (1859) stands out as a compelling libertarian effort to delineate a defensible zone of personal privacy.

For Mill, the appropriately private sphere is the domain of what he termed "self-regarding" or "purely personal" conduct. Self-regarding conduct is conduct that "neither violates any specific duty to the public, nor occasions perceptible hurt to any assignable individual except himself" (Mill, 1859, p. 80). Phrased differently, an individual's conduct is self-regarding when it "affects the interests of no per-sons besides himself, or need not affect them unless they like" (Mill, 1859, pp. 73–4). Mill offers a utilitarian rationale for the libertarian principle that people should be let alone when their conduct is self-regarding. Mill argues that each individual is ultimately the best determiner of his or her own utility or interest. Consequently, "[t]he strongest of all the arguments against the interference of the public with purely personal conduct is that, when it does interfere, the odds are that it inter-feres wrongly and in the wrong place" (Mill, 1859, p. 81). This is because, "with respect to his own feelings and circumstances the most ordinary man or woman has means of knowledge immeasurably surpassing those that can be possessed by anyone else" (Mill, 1859, p. 74). Collective interference with individual judgment about self-regarding behavior "must be grounded on general presumptions which may be altogether wrong and, even if right, are as likely as not to be misapplied to individual cases, by persons no better acquainted with the circumstances of such cases than those are who look at them merely from without" (Mill, 1859, p. 74).

Using these arguments, Mill drew a line between public and private realms. But the realm of privacy he marked has parameters many would reject. In the US, marriage, childbearing, and childrearing are often regarded as quintessentially private matters. Mill saw the issue differently. He did not consider behavior re-specting one's own children "self-regarding" behavior. Mill thought government ought to regulate marriage and childbearing heavily: "[t]he laws which . . . forbid marriage unless the parties can show that they have the means of supporting a family do not exceed the legitimate powers of the State . . . [and] are not objection-able as violations of liberty (Mill, 1859, p. 107). Mill observed that "to bestow a life which may be either a curse or a blessing[,] unless the being on whom it is to be bestowed will have at least the ordinary chances of a desirable existence, is a crime against that being" (Mill, 1859, p. 106). In an overpopulated or potentially overpopulated country, "to produce children, beyond a very small number, with the effect of reducing the reward of labor by their competition is a serious offense against all who live by the remuneration of their labor" (Mill, 1859, pp. 106–7).

In *Liberty, Equality and Fraternity* (1873) Mill's critic James Fitzjames Stephen disputed the possibility of doing what Mill tried to do – to clearly delineate a zone of privacy. Actually employing the term "privacy," Stephen maintained that to "define the province of privacy distinctly is impossible" (Stephen, 1873, p. 160). What we can say is that it pertains to "the more intimate and delicate relations of life" (Stephen, 1873, p. 160). Stephen went on to assert that "[c]onduct which can be described as indecent is always in one way or another a violation of pri-vacy" (Stephen, 1873, p. 160). Similarly, effete images of privacy's "delicate" realm emerged from the jurisprudential writings of Americans Samuel Warren and Louis Brandeis (1890), who, following C. Cooley (1880), sometimes characterized pri-vacy vaguely as "being let alone."

Until the final third of the twentieth century, sustained discussions of privacy per se were rare in the academic law, humanities and social science publications. By contrast, theoretical discussions of concepts such as "equality," "freedom," "liberty," and "democracy" have been commonplace for centuries. Expositions of "private" property have been frequent occurrences in post-Enlightenment schol-arly literatures. Numerous expositions of the public/private distinction have been published since classical antiquity, both in law and in political science. Political theorists Hannah Arendt (1958) and Jürgen Habermas (1962), for example, illu-minated conceptual links among Greek conceptions of *polis* and *oikos*, Roman conceptions of *res publicae* and *res privatae*, and modern conceptions of public and private.

In response to developments in law, though with largely unarticulated linkage to the concept of private property or the public/private distinction, "privacy" and the "right to privacy" significantly entered scholarly lexicons in the 1960s. Build-ing on the contributions of nineteenth-century lawyers, Milton Konvitz (1966) and Alan Westin (1967) were among the first to provide systematic accounts of privacy as a philosophical concept with a place in law. Citing biblical sources, Konvitz identified privacy with the concealment of the true, transcendent self. In a more pragmatic vein, Westin emphasized the respects in which the privacy of individuals and entities concerns control over information.

Meaning and definition

Detailed analyses of the meaning of "privacy" appear in the scholarly writings of contemporary academic philosophers seeking to illuminate conceptions of privacy found in law, medicine, and politics (Inness, 1992; Schoeman, 1992; Wacks, 1989; Allen, 1988). Philosophers have had a mix of descriptive and prescriptive ambitions. They have sought to describe prevailing linguistic usages; and to prescribe ideal ones. Prescriptive definitional analyses have sought to show why particular uses of " privacy" and the "right to privacy" ideally would be eliminated from legal and moral discourse. Rather than simply make points about how "privacy" is and ought to be used, philosophers have also attempted to illuminate cultural dimensions of privacy broadly (Young, 1978; Pennock, 1971).

No definitional analysis of "privacy" boasts universal acceptance. One large family of definitions has had a particularly diverse following and energetic critics (Inness, 1992). Those definitions of privacy in which the idea of *restricted access* to people and personal information play a role have been especially popular (Allen, 1988). For example, privacy has been defined as *limitations on others' access* to the individual (Gavison, 1980); to an individual's life experiences, and engagements (O'Brien, 1979); to certain modes of being in a person's life (Boone, 1983); and to an entity that possesses experiences (Garrett, 1974). It has also been defined as the condition of being *protected from unwanted access* by others (Bok, 1983); as *lack of access to information* related to intimacies (Dixon, 1965); as selective *control over access* to oneself or to one's group (Altman, 1976); and as the *exclusive access of a person to a realm of his own* (Van den Haag, 1971).

Philosophers commonly characterize seclusion, solitude, anonymity, confidentiality, secrecy, intimacy, and reserve as particular forms of physical or informational privacy rather than as wholly independent concepts. Seclusion and solitude can be plausibly cast in popular "restricted access" privacy terms as restrictions on physical access to persons. Anonymity, secrecy, confidentiality, and reserve can be characterized plausibly as restrictions on access to personal information.

Limiting access to people and information is an evident goal of constitutional law. It is also a major theme in the constitutional jurisprudence of the courts. For example, the privacy theme figures importantly in First Amendment jurisprudence. The First Amendment provides that "Congress shall make no law . . . abridging the freedom of speech . . . or the right of the people peaceably to assemble." The Supreme Court has held that this provision guarantees a right of free association for individuals, and a right of privacy for groups: individuals may form exclusive political, social or civic groups whose meeting places and membership lists are beyond the reach of state and federal government. Writing for the majority in *NAACP* v. *Alabama*, 357 U.S. 449, 462 (1958), Justice Harlan explained that the "[i]nviolability of privacy in group association may in many circumstances be indispensable to preservation of freedom of association." Restricted access to meeting places is the demand of physical privacy; restricted access to membership lists, the demand of informational privacy. Group privacy rights under the constitution have been successfully claimed from time to time by groups seeking to end discrimination (for example, the NAACP) and by groups seeking to preserve it (for example, social clubs with membership criteria that exclude non-whites, Jews, or women).

In the words of the eighteenth-century thinker James Otis: "A man's house is his castle; and while he is quiet, he is as well guarded as a prince in his castle" (Wroth and Zobel, 1965, p. 142). This conception of the physical privacy of the home is reflected in Third Amendment strictures on access to private houses: "No Soldier shall, in time of peace be quartered in any house, without the consent of the Owner, nor in time of war, but in a manner to be prescribed by law." The British Parliament enacted the Quartering Act of 1774, authorizing the housing of British soldiers anywhere in the American colonies, including private dwellings. The ubiquitous soldiers were not subject to the authority of household patriarchs, whose "castles" were forceably breached (Gross, 1991, pp. 219–20). The Third Amendment appears in the Constitution as a direct result of England's refusal to treat the American colonists' homes as unbreachable safe havens. The Third Amendment "carved out a sharp distinction between public and private . . . [and] symbolized an emergent sense of privacy among the Revolutionary generation" (Gross, 1991, p. 220).

The privacy norms that motivated the Third Amendment are highly consonant with the privacy norms that underlay the Fourth Amendment. Also carving out a sphere of physical household privacy, the Fourth Amendment asserts that: "The right of the people to be secure in their persons, houses, papers, and effects, against unreasonable searches and seizures, shall not be violated, and no Warrants shall issue, but upon probable cause, supported by Oath or affirmation, and particularly describing the place to be searched, and the persons or things to be seized." Fourth Amendment cases since *Katz* v. *United States*, 389 U.S. 347, 351 (1968), have ascribed a right to a "reasonable expectation of privacy." To fall under the protection of the Fourth Amendment's limit on search and seizure: "[A]person must . . . exhibit . . . an actual (subjective) expectation of privacy and . . . the expectation [must] be one that society is prepared to recognize as 'reasonable.'" Traditionally private areas such as homes and public restrooms are not the only places with respect to which a person may have a reasonable expectation of privacy. What a person "seeks to preserve as private, even in an area accessible to the public, may be constitutionally protected." When the government intrudes in an area where a person has "justifiably relied" upon a sense of privacy, its intrusion is a "search and seizure." The "reasonable expectation of privacy" formula invites philosophic speculation as to the relevance in Fourth Amendment law of competing individual, judicial, and societal understandings of privacy. It also invites criticism for the implicit positivism of purporting to hang constitutional privacy rights on people's actual expectations rather than on considered judgments about the optimal distribution of power between government and citizen (Seidman and Wasserstrom, 1988).

The Fifth Amendment restricts access to personal information by limiting the government's power to compel persons to provide evidence against themselves that would lead to their prosecution in a criminal proceeding: "[N]or shall any person . . . be compelled in any criminal case to be a witness against himself." The Fifth Amendment privilege "respects a private inner sanctum of individual feeling and thought and proscribes state intrusion to extract self-condemnation" *Couch* v. *United States*, 409 U.S. 322, 327 (1973). On the face of things, it not clear how

147

being asked to speak the truth could be considered demeaning. Yet, human personality arguably is compromised by compulsory self-disclosure: "Personal dignity and integrity, both intimately tied to the ability to keep information about ourselves from others, are demeaned when the state is permitted to use tactics that make the unwilling incriminate themselves" (Berger, 1978, p. 213). Also compromised are the non-totalitarian ambitions of liberal democratic society. The Amendment "enables the citizen to create a zone of privacy which government may not force him to surrender to his detriment." *Griswold* v. *Connecticut*, 381 U.S. 479, 484 (1965).

The claim that the Bill of Rights privacy jurisprudence relates both to physical and informational privacy raises an interesting conceptual question. Is physical privacy reducible to informational privacy? The Fourth Amendment restricts access to people, households, and other private areas, while also restricting access to information of the sort that might be contained in a person's papers, effects, and conversations. Since physical contact can yield new information, one might take the view that concerns about restricting physical access ultimately boil down to concerns about information learned through sensory exposure.

A reason to be wary of a purely informational approaches to the First, Third, and Fourth Amendment is this. From the point of view of the person whose privacy is at issue, uncovering information about a person and uncovering the person can be invasions of different dimensions. For example, although both invasions are offensive, it is probably less assaultive to have one's sexual orientation revealed as a result of unauthorized access to medical records (an informational invasion) than as a result of unauthorized access to one's bedroom during a sex act (a physical invasion).

In any case, the "restricted access" definition of privacy can capture both the physical and informational senses of privacy at play in the jurisprudence of the First, Third, Fourth, and Fifth Amendment privacy doctrine. The same is not true of the "decisional" sense of privacy at play in the jurisprudence of the Ninth Amendment, the Fourteenth Amendment, and the penumbral privacy doctrine of *Griswold* v. *Connecticut*, 381 U.S. 479 (1965). One can speak of restricted access to decisions or to a zone of private decision making, but this use of "restricted access" is metaphorical in a way that definitional uses were not.

Acknowledging that the expression "privacy" is used in current constitutional law to refer to autonomous decision making (Feinberg, 1983), some philosophers argue that that usage is in error. They say that decisional privacy is not a sense of privacy at all, and therefore that a defensible definition of privacy – whether of the popular "restricted access" variety or otherwise – would not embrace decisional usages. Philosophers have proposed definitions of privacy that capture many shared intuitions about paradigmatic forms of physical and/or informational, and intentionally exclude decisional conceptions of privacy (Parent, 1983; Gavison, 1980).

Scholars sometimes condemn the idea of decisional privacy as a colossal conceptual blunder perpetuated by the courts. Ruth Gavison (1980) seems to view it that way. Her influential restricted access definition of privacy includes, in her words: "such 'typical' invasions of privacy as the collection, storage, and computerization of information; the dissemination of information about individuals; peeping, following, watching, and photographing individuals; intruding or entering 'private' places; eavesdropping, wiretapping, reading of letters, drawing attention to individuals, required testing of individuals; and forced disclosure of information" (Gavison, 1980, pp. 438–9). Her definition deliberately excludes: "prohibitions on conduct such as abortions, use of contraceptives and unnatural sexual intercourse . . . [and] regulation of the way family obligations should be discharged" (Gavison, 1980, pp. 438–9). What Gavison chooses to include and exclude is to some extent arbitrary. But the reason she gives for rejecting decisional privacy is one of considerable interest to philosophers who value the project of offering distinct, consistent accounts of major moral and political concepts; or to lawyers who value conceptual rigor and clarity in the law.

Gavison argues that a lack of rigor and clarity is the inevitable consequence of using "privacy" as a shorthand for autonomous decision making, or for liberty or freedom from outside interference with private choice. She maintains that once a decisional usage of "privacy" is adopted, it becomes impossible to give a philosophic account of the concept that distinguishes privacy from the concepts of liberty, freedom, and autonomy. The objection has also been raised that the idea of a right to be free from interference is absurd among a people with respect for the rule of law. So much interference with individual judgment and whim must be tolerated that the idea even of a *prima facie* right of private choice is untenable. This objection calls for attempts like John Stuart Mill's to give a principled account of legitimate and illegitimate collective interference with "private" decision making.

Criticisms like Gavison's have not prevented the idea of decisional privacy from taking hold in ordinary language, philosophy, and constitutional jurisprudence (Rubenfeld, 1989; DeCew, 1987; Feinberg, 1983). It is a fact of current linguistic practice and law that "privacy" will sometimes mean restricted access to people and information, and at other times mean limits on government regulation of decision making. The United States Supreme Court's best known decisional privacy cases – *Griswold* v. *Connecticut* and *Roe* v. *Wade* – reflect judicial confusion about the meaning of privacy. It is not always clear whether by "privacy" the justices have in mind physical privacy or informational privacy, in addition to or instead of personal decision making. Over time, the Supreme Court has learned to write about privacy with clarity. In *Whalen* v. *Roe*, 429 U.S. 589, 589–90 (1977), the Court itself distinguished physical and informational privacy ("interest in avoiding disclosure of personal matters") from decisional privacy ("interest in independence in making certain kinds of important decisions"), affirming that each is protected by constitutional law.

Philosophical objections to advancing personal liberties under a privacy rubric are to be distinguished from lawyerly objections based on interpretations of judicial role, textual meanings, and broad constitutional purposes. Some scholars of the US Constitution worry that the document cannot be coherently interpreted as providing protection for so indefinite a category as "privacy" (Henkin, 1974). Some argue that the category of privacy simply cannot be narrowed or defined without appeal to the values of the particular justices charged with deciding

149

particular cases, or, at best, their interpretations of social values. Appeal to privacy is thus charged as moralistic "natural law" jurisprudence; as illegitimate "judicial activism" or as "substantive due process." To strike down a state law because it violates "privacy" is to misunderstand the 14th Amendment as an invitation for the courts to second-guess the states or Congress on matters of substantive policy about which the Constitution itself has nothing to say (Ely, 1973).

Theoretical debates about decisional privacy have become intertwined with political advocacy. In the North American political arena, being for decisional privacy rights signifies being for women's rights and gay and lesbian rights. Being against decisional privacy rights signifies being against *Roe* v. *Wade* and in sympathy with *Bowers* v. *Hardwick*, 478 U.S. 186 (1986). In *Bowers* the Supreme Court held that a selectively enforced Georgia law criminalizing sodomy was constitutional. Some constitutional scholars continue to defend a decisional understanding of privacy, whether or not they hold the liberal views on abortion and gay rights, because they believe such an understanding is at the heart of notions of marital, family, and heterosexual sexual privacy. Other scholars have distanced themselves from decisional privacy jurisprudence. Cass Sunstein (1992) announced a preference for equal protection over privacy arguments for abortion that appears to be based in part on the definitional view that decisional privacy has nothing to do with "conventional" privacy; and in part on the strategic assessment that privacy arguments have a history of being confusing and unpopular.

Questions of value

A number of books survey normative moral and legal theories about privacy (Inness, 1994; Schoeman, 1994; Allen, 1988). As they reveal, one way to understand "privacy" is as a term of approbation referring to highly, even intrinsically, valued conditions or states. The thinking goes something like this. An anthropologist or cultural outsider can coherently ask what an unfamiliar social group treats as private; but it makes no sense for a cultural insider to ask whether privacy is a good or desirable thing. Such questions misunderstand the grammar of privacy. Typical statements about privacy, including, (1) "He needs his privacy!", (2) "They invaded her privacy!", and (3) "This is private!", presuppose a judgment on the part of the speaker that privacy is a good thing, and that there is substantial social consensus about the significance and value of privacy. The grammar of privacy suggested by the above examples, is that of a term whose function in language is to evoke basic, shared norms concerning approved modes of intimacy and separation. The precise nature of these norms is not revealed by statements like (1), (2), and (3), and is amenable to theoretical disagreement. Privacy norms are arguably explicable variously as norms of etiquette, civility, decency, morality, justice, or nature. But the value of privacy is not something it makes sense to debate.

A more commonly held view than the one just described, assumes that whatever "privacy" denotes, it denotes something that *can* be judged good or bad, useful or useless, depending upon the facts of the matter. Under this view, "privacy" is not inherently a term of approval, even though within a culture speakers often can presume shared privacy values.

Judith Thomson (1975), who argues that privacy can be judged good or bad, also argues that privacy interests are an amalgam of interests in property, the person, and confidentiality. She maintains that the value of privacy depends upon the value of undisturbed possession of and control of property, personal safety and peace of mind, and information non-disclosure. The libertarian who attaches a high value to property, safety, and peace, must also attach a high value to privacy.

For John Stuart Mill (1859) the value of privacy is that it promotes the greater balance of happiness over unhappiness in society – it promotes social utility. Many theorists similarly evaluate privacy by reference to its capacity to further specified ends. For some, the relevant ends recommending privacy are political goods that may or may not have value of the sort utilitarians care about. These presumed goods include neutrality (tolerating all and privileging no one's conception of the good) and democracy (letting each unique individual have an equal voice in government). To view privacy as a good relative to the ends of neutral, democratic government is to view rights of privacy as formal limits on government power, and as expressions of collective tolerance for individuality and conscience (Richards, 1986). Several scholars have emphasized that privacy is an important constitutional value relative to the goal of limiting totalitarian government (Rubenfeld, 1989).

S. I. Benn (1988) and other philosophers (Schoeman, 1984; Pennock, 1971) explain the value of privacy by direct deontological appeal to conceptions of human dignity and personhood. In connection with the normative underpinnings both of tort law and constitutional law, privacy has been accorded high value for its supposed capacity to further respect for human personhood (Bloustein 1967; Feinberg, 1983). In both cases, philosophers depict human personhood as consisting of unique, morally autonomous, and metaphysically free personalities. Without privacy and private choices, individuals become uniform and repressed. Individuals with these traits are incapable of flourishing as unique and morally independent persons. Although the "personhood enhancement" account of the value of privacy has been enormously influential, it has been criticized as exaggerating human individuality and wrongly turning individual choice into an unqualified good (Rubenfeld, 1989; Boone, 1983).

The value of privacy sometimes receives explanation in relation to its supposed capacity to enhance relationships. Thus, privacy is defended as a boon both to love and friendship and to merely civil ties with strangers (Post, 1989; Rachels, 1975; Fried, 1970). The repose that can come from periods of voluntary seclusion and control over personal information have important psychological benefits, and benefits for social life. Involuntary privacy losses can result in shame, embarrassment, humiliation, tension, and aggression; they can degrade and debilitate (C. Schneider, 1977). All cultures have privacy practices on which successful relationships depend (Moore, 1984). These practices promote individual and societal well-being.

Legal economist Richard Posner (1977) raises a dissenting voice on the question of the social value of one kind of personal privacy: informational privacy. Posner argues that people generally use privacy to conceal "bad" facts about themselves. The concealment of bad facts gives a person potentially undesirable "market" advantages over those with whom he or she deals. Stressing the value of accurate mutual knowledge on moral rather than economic grounds, Judith Andre (1986, p. 315) concludes that "there is no right to privacy nor to control over it" since "a society without mutual knowledge would be impossible."

Many normative accounts of privacy are premised on individualistic moral and political theories. In response, the "personhood enhancement" and the "relationship enhancement" accounts of privacy's value can be given a frank and communitarian twist. The communitarian account of privacy's value assumes that men and women are embedded in social worlds replete with responsibilities for others and obligations to contribute up to one's capacities. Without privacy for purposes of rest, rejuvenation, experimentation, and independent action, men and women would be less fit for performing their responsibilities (for caring for children, for example) and fulfilling social obligations (to cultivate artistic talent, for example). Privacy facilitates the flourishing of productive and responsible persons.

Criminal abortion statutes, sexual harassment, and rape stem in part from a disregard of the importance of women's privacy. The realization of this fact has turned some feminists into solid proponents of strong privacy rights throughout the law. Yet, leading feminists have been ambivalent about privacy as a regulative ideal in constitutional law. Catharine MacKinnon (1987), and other feminist legal theorists have argued that decisional privacy doctrines in constitutional law reinforce an ideal of lives free from government intervention, thereby legitimating community neglect of women and children (Olsen, 1989; Colker, 1989; Colker, 1992; Schneider, 1991). Feminists argue that the Supreme Court rejected arguments for public abortion funding for poor women because the abortion right was won under the banner of privacy. So long as abortions are treated as private rights, government is not likely to be assigned an obligation to pay for them.

How much "letting alone" can a just society permit? With autonomy comes risk. Harm to self and others is a decided risk when government closes the door to public intervention or assistance. In *Wisconsin* v. *Yoder*, 406 U.S. 205 (1972), the Supreme Court permitted an Amish family to truncate its children's formal education at the eighth grade, out of respect for the freedom – the privacy – of the Amish religion. Abandoned to their parents, the Yoder children are likely to have done reasonably well in their peaceful, insular community. *Deshaney* v. *Winnebago County Department of Social Services*, 489 U.S. 189 (1989), enacts the opposite possibility for the dependent and vulnerable among us. They may fail to survive abandonment to others in the name of privacy. Joshua Deshaney was left severely brain damaged after being repeatedly beaten by his father. When he sued, the Supreme Court held that he had no right to seek compensation for his injuries from the public agency responsible for removing children at risk of abuse from their family homes.

A personal tragedy for the people involved, *Deshaney* quickly became a symbol of the violence of privacy as a constitutional ideal (Schneider, 1991). But *Deshaney* is not the whole story of privacy as a regulatory ideal within constitutional law in the US. Privacy norms can facilitate violence; but they also facilitate romance. *Loving* v. *Virginia*, 388 U.S. 1 (1967), the historic decision that validated the marriage of a poor Virginia couple ordered to leave their home for violating miscegenation laws, is a symbol of the romance of privacy. Categorical condemnations of privacy as a constitutional value appear less tenable the more one recalls about the very large and often positive role privacy norms have played in constitutional law.

Conclusion

The absence of the word "privacy" from the text of the US Constitution has not prevented American judges from articulating the most extensive law of constitutional privacy in the world. Recent controversies over abortion and gay rights, leave doubts about whether the American approach to constitutional privacy merits more than partial emulation. A widely shared reverence for felt boundaries of public and private shaped the Constitution and Bill of Rights. Americans understand better today than in the nation's founding moment that a sharp distinction between public and private is something of a fairy tale (Radest, 1979); that they must rely on government to secure the privacy that they define, in part, as the absence of government (Kennedy, 1982). This irony – or incoherence – in American thought about constitutional privacy may help to explain why the nation has been unable to settle upon a jurisprudence that mediates basic concerns about the roles of judges in disputes about collective influence over individual lives.

Bibliography

Allen, A. L. 1988: *Uneasy Access: privacy for women in a free society.* Totowa, New Jersey: Rowman and Littlefield.
—— 1995: The proposed equal protection fix for abortion law. *Harvard Journal of Law and Public Policy*, 18, 419.
Altman, I. 1976: Privacy – a conceptual analysis. *Environment and Behavior*, 8, 7–8.
Andre, J. 1986: Privacy as a value and as a right. *Journal of Value Inquiry*, 20, 309–17.
Arendt, H. 1958: *The Human Condition.* Chicago: University of Chicago Press, 38–78.
Benn, S. I. 1988: *A Theory of Freedom.* Cambridge: Cambridge University Press, 292–3.
Berger, M. 1978: The unprivileged status of the Fifth Amendment privilege. *American Criminal Law Review*, 15, 191.
Blaustein, A. P. and Gisbert, H. F. 1994: *Constitutions of the countries of the world.* Dobbs Ferry, NY: Oceana Publications, Inc.
Bloustein, E. 1967: Privacy as an aspect of human dignity: an answer to Dean Preosser. *New York University Law Review*, 39, 34.
Bok, S. 1983: *Secrets: on the ethics of concealment and revelation.* New York: Random House.
Boone, C. K. 1983: Privacy and community. *Social Theory and Practice*, 9(1), 6–24.
Colker, R. 1989: Feminism, theology, and abortion: toward love, compassion and wisdom. *California Law Review*, 77, 1,017–75.

—— 1992: *Abortion and Dialogue*. Bloomington: Indiana University Press.

Cooke, J. (ed.) [1788] 1961: *The Federalist*. Middletown, Conn.: Wesleyan University Press.

Cooley, T. 1880: *A Treatise on the Law of Torts*. Callaghan & Co., 1st edn., 29.

DeCew, J. 1987: Defending the "private" in constitutional privacy. *The Journal of Value Inquiry*, 21, 171–84.

Dixon, R. 1965: The Griswold penumbra, constitutional charter for an expanded law of privacy. *Michigan Law Review 1964*, 197–231.

Ely, J. H. 1973: The wages of crying wolf: a comment on *Roe* v. *Wade*. *Yale Law Journal*, 89, 920.

Feinberg, J. 1983: Autonomy, sovereignty and privacy: moral ideals in the Constitution. *Notre Dame Law Review*, 58, 445–90.

Flaherty, D. H. 1972: *Privacy in Colonial New England*. Charlottesville: University Press of Virginia.

Fried, C. 1970: *An Anatomy of Values*. London: Oxford University Press.

Garrett, R. 1974: The nature of privacy. *Philosophy Today*, 18, 263–84.

Gavison, R. 1980: Privacy and the limits of law. *Yale Law Journal*, 89, 421, 428, 438–9.

Gross, R. A. 1991: Public and private in the Third Amendment. *Valparaiso University Law Review*, 26, 215.

Habermas, J. 1962: *The Structural Transformation of the Private Sphere*. Cambridge, Mass.: MIT Press, 3–4.

Henkin, L. 1974: Privacy and autonomy. *Columbia Law Review*, 74, 1,410.

Inness, J. 1992: *Privacy, Intimacy, and Isolation*. New York: Oxford University Press.

Kennedy, D. 1982: The stages of the decline of the public/private distinction. *University of Pennsylvania Law Review*, 130, 1,349.

Konvitz, M. 1966: Privacy and the law: a philosophical prelude. *Law and Contemporary Problems*, 31, 272.

MacKinnon, C. 1987: *Feminism Unmodified: discourses on life and law*. Cambridge, Mass.: Harvard University Press, 96–102.

Mill, J. S. [1859] 1978: *On Liberty*. Elizabeth Rapaport (ed.), Indianapolis: Hackett Publishing Co.

Moore, B. 1984: *Privacy: studies in social and cultural history*. New York: M. E. Sharpe.

O'Brien, D. 1979: *Privacy, Law and Public Policy*. New York: Praeger.

Olsen, F. 1989: Unraveling compromise. *Harvard Law Review*, 103, 105–35.

Parent, W. A. 1983: A new definition of privacy for the law. *Law and Philosophy*, 2, 305–38.

Pennock, J. R. and Chapman, J. W. (eds) 1971: *Privacy: Nomos XIII*. New York: Atherton Press.

Posner, R. 1977: *The Economic Analysis of Law*. Boston: Little, Brown, 2nd edn.

Post, R. 1989: The social foundations of privacy: community and self in the common law of tort. *California Law Review*, 77, 957.

Prosser 1960: Privacy. *California Law Review*, 48, 383–422.

Rachels. J. 1975: Why privacy is important. *Philosophy and Public Affairs*, 4, 323–33.

Radest, P. 1979: The public and private: an American fairy tale. *Ethics*, 89, 280–8.

Richards, D. A. J. 1986: *Toleration and the Constitution*. New York: Oxford University Press.

Rubenfeld, J. 1989: The right to privacy. *Harvard Law Review*, 102, 737–807.

Schneider, C. 1977: *Shame, Exposure and Privacy*. Boston: Beacon Press.

Schneider, E. 1991: The violence of privacy. *Connecticut Law Review*, 23, 973–98.

Schoeman, F. 1984: *Philosophical Dimensions of Privacy: an anthology*. Cambridge: Cambridge University Press.

——1992: *Privacy and Social Freedom*. Cambridge: Cambridge University Press.

Seidman, L. M. and Wasserstrom, S. 1988: The Fourth Amendment as constitutional theory. *Georgetown Law Journal*, 77, 19–112.

Stephen, J. F. [1873] 1967: *Liberty, Equality and Fraternity*. London: Cambridge University Press.

Sunstein, C. 1992: Neutrality in constitutional law (with special reference to pornography, abortion and surrogacy. *Columbia Law Review*, 92, 1–52.

Thomson, J. 1975: The right to privacy. *Philosophy and Public Affairs*, 4 (4), 295–314.

Van den Haag, E. 1979: On privacy. In J. R. Pennock and J. W. Chapman (eds), *Privacy: Nomos XIII*, New York: Atherton Press, 149.

Wacks, R. 1989: *Personal Information: Privacy and the law*. Oxford: Clarendon Press.

Warren, S. and Brandeis, L. 1890: The right to privacy. *Harvard Law Review*, 4, 193–220.

Westin, A. 1967: *Privacy and Freedom*. New York: Atheneum.

Wroth, L. K. and Hiller B. Z. (eds) 1965: *Legal Papers of John Adams*, 2. Cambridge, Mass.: Belknap Press.

Young, J. (ed.) 1978: *Privacy*. New York: John Wiley and Sons.

9

Constitutional law and equality

MAIMON SCHWARZSCHILD

No two people (or things) are exactly alike. In that sense, none is equal to another. Yet all share points in common. At a minimum, all people are people (as, for that matter, all things are things). To that extent, at least, they are equal. Whatever the ways people might be equal or unequal, they can be *treated* equally or unequally in a wide variety of different ways. They might receive equal respect, or equal rights at law, or equal opportunities to distinguish themselves, or equal property and other resources, or equal welfare and happiness. Equality might be reckoned by individuals, or it might be by groups. There might be absolute equality: the same for everyone, regardless of what is thought to be deserved or otherwise proper. Or equality might be proportional: the same for everyone according to what is deserved or otherwise proper.

These different kinds of equality, it is fairly obvious, can often be mutually exclusive. Equal opportunity to distinguish oneself amounts to an equal opportunity to become unequal. Equal rights for people whose skills or whose luck is unequal may ensure unequal possession of property and other human resources. To ensure equality of possessions, conversely, may require unequal rights, by way of equalizing or "handicapping" people with unequal abilities. Equal possessions are apt to mean unequal welfare and happiness for people with different needs, tastes, and personality types; equal welfare may require unequal resources. Individual equality, at least of some kinds such as equality of opportunity, is apt to mean group inequality, since groups – almost however defined – will have differing distributions of skills, luck, and ambition. Absolute equality and proportional equality are sharply different: honors or possessions or prison sentences for all, say, as against honors or possessions or prison sentences according to a scale of who deserves them.

Equality, in truth, might mean almost anything. The crucial questions are "who is to be equal to whom? With respect to what?" Yet as an ideal, equality exerts great moral force, especially in modern places and times. What are the sources of equality's power as an ideal? And toward what sorts of equality ought people and their laws to strive?

156

The Enlightenment and its antecedents

Envy of those more fortunate than oneself is no doubt something as old as humanity, and surely it is one source of some people's passion for equality. But envy as such is generally considered a vice, not a moral imperative. The roots of equality as an ideal reach back to the Stoic idea that by sharing a common humanity all people are equal, alike the children of God. It was not an idea that found much echo in Aristotle or other classical writers. Aristotle was more concerned with proportional equality: treating likes alike, with emphasis on the many ways in which people are unalike.

At least two Aristotelian ideas have special resonance for modern egalitarianisms, however. The first was more prudential than moral: that whenever people for good reasons or bad come to expect equality – whether sameness of rights, or goods, or whatever – the conspicuous absence of that equality can make for dangerous social turbulence. The second was the suggestion that human friendship can hardly exist between people whose condition is greatly unequal, with the implication again that social solidarity might presuppose some degree of social equality.

The Jewish and Christian sides of the Western heritage are a complex tangle of egalitarian and inegalitarian tendencies. At least in some moods, Jews and Christians have perennially seen themselves as communities of believers equal before God. Hence the prophetic and New Testament denunciations of the rich, and the allusions in the New Testament to believers holding their goods in common. There is also an element of equal rights for all before the law: Leviticus commands "one manner of law, as well for the stranger, as for one of your own country." Then again, there are important inegalitarian themes in Judaism and Christianity: distinctions between Jew and Gentile, saved and damned, priest and people, man and woman. At the beginnings of modernity, there was surely a levelling thrust to the Protestant Reformation, which abolished priesthood and hierarchy, and opened the Bible to all believers. And from some of the early Protestant sectaries, there was a whiff of more radical equality, social and economic as well as religious: "When Adam delved and Eve span / Who was then the gentleman?"

But the secular Enlightenment was the most important source for modern ideals of equality. For Hobbes, Locke, and Rousseau, men are equal in the state of nature. Hume – echoing Diderot and Adam Smith – wrote that all mankind are "much the same in all times and places." The American Declaration of Independence, perhaps the greatest political document of the Enlightenment, proclaimed it a self-evident truth that all men are created equal. And the French Revolutionaries, calling for *égalité*, claimed the mantle of the Enlightenment, as did the nineteenth- and twentieth-century socialist movements.

If equality was a salient Enlightenment idea, what sort of equality, among the myriad conflicting possibilities, was meant? As an intellectual and social movement, the Enlightenment arose to repudiate what it saw as the backwardness, superstition. and intolerance of medieval Christianity, and the frozen, hierarchical

157

society of medieval Christendom. The Enlightenment rejected the idea that a person's worth, identity, and destiny should be overwhelmingly bound up in birth and kinship. In Sir Henry Maine's later expression, the Enlightenment was a great step away from the "society of status."

Instead, the Enlightenment thinkers put a high value on the individual, endowed as a person with natural rights. The supreme natural right is the right to pursue happiness, each person in his own way, according to his own faculties. Natural rights attach to every person, regardless of birth. As such, they are equal rights.

But for the Enlightenment, including the American founders, this meant equal rights before the law. It did not mean equal outcomes in life. On the contrary, life's happiest outcome is to achieve enlightened reason, and the Enlightenment accepted that people's capacities for this are unequal. Moreover, trying to ensure equal human happiness would mean that people could not pursue their own ideas of happiness: there would have to be a collectively imposed definition of happiness in order to administer an equal distribution of it.

As for any idea of equal wealth or resources, the American founders followed Locke in emphasizing the right to property as a fundamental human right, with the recognition that property rights inevitably mean differences in wealth. For these Enlightenment thinkers, property rights were important in at least two ways: first, they encourage industriousness and hence promote prosperity; and second, they afford each person a practical opportunity to pursue personal goals, a personal idea of happiness, independent of any collective orthodoxy about what constitutes a good life. (The paradigm orthodoxy, of course, was that of the Church, against which the Enlightenment defined itself in the first place.) The characteristic social ideal of the Enlightenment was the *carrière ouverte aux talents*: equal opportunity to pursue various (and hence unequal) careers, for unequal rewards, without legal disabilities founded on irrelevant accidents of birth.

Equal rights and American constitutional law

The Enlightenment idea of equality exerts great influence on American constitutional law, which tends to treat discrimination on the basis of hereditary status as the model of what equality forbids. Historically, this has evolved somewhat fitfully. There is no mention of equality as such in the original Constitution and Bill of Rights. Instead, the Constitution prohibits titles of nobility, and the First Amendment guarantees government neutrality toward religion – religious discrimination having been a prime source of hereditary civil inequality in the seventeenth and eighteenth centuries. The US Constitution's only explicit provision for equality is the 14th Amendment, adopted after the American Civil War. It prohibits the denial to any person of "the equal protection of the laws," and its point was to abolish government discrimination against blacks, who had been held in slavery on a hereditary, racial basis and flagrantly denied equal rights before the law.

From the time it was adopted until nearly the mid-twentieth century, however, the "equal protection" clause was virtually a dead letter in American constitutional jurisprudence. The courts upheld most kinds of racial discrimination, relying on the fiction of "separate but equal"; Oliver Wendell Holmes dismissed the equal protection clause as "the usual last resort of Constitutional arguments." All this began to change only after World War II – a war that had been fought at least in part against Nazi racialism, after all – and in the 1950s the Supreme Court made equal protection the constitutional cornerstone for the civil rights revolution in the United States. The Justices did this by creating a kind of double standard: routine legal classifications or discriminations would continue to receive "minimal scrutiny" from the courts and would almost always be upheld, but "suspect" classifications – racial discriminations above all – would now be "strictly scrutinized" under the equal protection clause, and nearly always struck down.

The Supreme Court's school desegregation decisions were the prototype for "strict scrutiny." Racially segregated schools, established by law in many parts of America, had meant drastically reduced opportunity in life for black pupils, based on hereditary status. Race ought to be irrelevant to one's legal status, the Court now declared. School segregation was therefore condemned as a violation of equal protection. Within a few years after the famous decision in Brown v. *Board of Education*, the courts went on to condemn any law or government action – having to do with anything whatever, not just schooling – that treated people differently because of the color of their skin.

More recently, the courts adopted a kind of analogy between race and sex. Most sex discriminations nowadays receive something near "strict scrutiny," and are disallowed as denials of equal opportunity. Yet the courts stop short of holding that sex (unlike race) can never be a relevant difference that might justify different legal rights and duties.

Even where race and sex are concerned, moreover, the courts interpret the Constitution to bar the government only from "intentional" discrimination. This has a clear link to the idea that equality is a matter of individual rights, rather than of group outcomes, under the Constitution. To condemn a law (or any government action) as violating equal protection, it is not enough to show that racial groups, or the sexes, fare unequally under the law. The court will only intervene if persuaded that the government's *purpose* was to treat people differently on these bases. After all, the races and sexes fare unequally under many laws, perhaps under most of them. If blacks and whites have different average levels of education, for example, educational requirements for civil service jobs will affect the races differently. If they have different average incomes, fees and taxes will affect them differently. By scrutinizing intent, rather than effects, the courts turn the focus away from the group, and avoid trying to prescribe the massive social engineering that would be required to make every law and public policy affect every different group alike.

Court decisions in American civil rights cases routinely emphasize that equal protection means individual equality of opportunity, equal rights before the law, not equal outcomes or group rights. There are counter-tendencies, however, particularly in the "affirmative action" or "reverse discrimination" cases of recent decades. These reflect, quite obviously, the pressures created by the great racial disparities in America's past, disparities that continue into the present.

"Affirmative action" means quotas and preferences for people because of their group membership. It has roots, paradoxically, in the Enlightenment idea of individual equality before the law. If all individuals have a right to be free of racial discrimination by the government, say, it seems a natural step to test whether such discrimination is actually occurring by looking at how many people of each race are hired into government offices, offered government contracts, or whatever. Yet this step puts the focus straightaway on numerical outcomes for the group, rather than on the question of individual discrimination. Furthermore, since there is no way of knowing how many people of each race there would be in the absence of discrimination, any benchmark figure is bound to be more or less arbitrary. The desire to compensate for past discrimination gives reason to set the benchmarks higher rather than lower. And there is a strong incentive to meet any such benchmark, since doing so will tend to exonerate one from charges of discrimination. Hence, to achieve numerical outcomes, the society comes to apply different standards and qualifications to people depending on their group membership.

The decisions of the courts about all this, especially the Supreme Court, suggest that "affirmative action" is something of an exception that proves the rule about American constitutional doctrine. The judgments are often inconsistent, allowing and disallowing various "affirmative action" programmes in situations that are essentially indistinguishable. The Court often decides these cases by patchwork plurality rather than by majority. Altogether, the decisions have an air of equivocation about them. Even when the Justices uphold or prescribe "affirmative action," they tend to justify it in the language of equal opportunity and individual rights rather than group rights and equal outcomes.

Where racial (or sexual) discrimination is not at issue, the American courts do not read the equal protection clause to interfere with most of the ways government differentiates people. This too is linked to the idea of equal rights under law. Any constitutional principle of equality must grapple with the fact that in almost every law there is an element of equality, but also an element of inequality. The element of equality is that any general rule, by virtue of being a rule, applies equally in equal cases. Thus, insofar as a rule authorises or forbids certain people to do certain things in certain situations, all persons within the stipulated category are equally within it. But there is an element of inequality as well, because most rules also "classify" or make distinctions amongst people. Criminal laws distinguish the culpable from the non-culpable; budgets spend money on some things (and people) but not on others; the laws of tort and contract create rights and liabilities for people in some situations but not in others, and so forth.

If it is in the nature of laws to "classify" or discriminate, equality before the law cannot mean equality without such discrimination. Ideally, it must therefore mean something like "treating likes alike." One way that lawyers assess how well a rule treats likes alike is to consider how the classification corresponds to the legitimate purpose of the rule. To take an example that most Americans are now ashamed of: if the purpose of the internment of Japanese–Americans during World War II was to round up disloyal people, the round-up was both "over-inclusive," since the overwhelming majority of Japanese–Americans were loyal, and "under-inclusive", because members of the German–American Bund, say, were not rounded up.

A drawback of this way of reasoning is that the statement of a rule's purpose can often be manipulated to minimize over- or under-inclusiveness. If the purpose of the Japanese–American internment is said to be "to round up people with personal or family roots in any country that has actually attacked the territory of the United States," for example, then the policy is not under-inclusive in exempting the German–American Bundists. Moreover, it is almost impossible for any law to achieve a perfect fit between its purpose and its scheme of classification. Any minimum age fixed by law for acquiring a driving license, for example, will be both over- and under-inclusive: some under-age people would undoubtedly be model drivers, whereas some people who meet the age requirement will be childish and irresponsible on the road.

"Equal protection" cannot mean that all legal classifications are improper, nor has it meant that the courts assume the power to decide which likes are alike or how much over- or under-inclusiveness is too much. According to the American Supreme Court, drawing distinctions by way of law-making is what democracy is all about. What civic equality forbids is discrimination on the basis of hereditary status, like race and sex. Other legal differentiations amongst people and their activities get "minimal scrutiny" under the equal protection clause and are routinely upheld.

As for the ways in which people differentiate themselves economically and in their ideas of a good life, the American courts have never adopted the equal protection clause as a charter for promoting equality of wealth or happiness. "Minimal scrutiny" extends to the laws of property, and to the legal framework for economic markets generally. The Supreme Court disavows the idea that "equal protection" requires the state to provide even a minimum standard of welfare subsistence. There is nothing whatever in American constitutional history to suggest any requirement of actual equality of resources or of human happiness.

Liberty and equality under the Constitution

A great strength of the Enlightenment idea of civic equality is that it allows for a large measure of personal freedom under the Constitution. All freedoms, after all, entail the freedom to differentiate oneself from others. Political, artistic, or religious freedom, for example, is needed only by people who wish to differ politically, artistically, or religiously. It requires no exercise of freedom to conform. But to differentiate oneself is to make oneself unequal in one's condition, be it political, artistic, or religious. So, likewise, economic freedom – economic endeavor being most people's daily endeavor – means the freedom to differentiate oneself economically, freedom to become economically unequal. Economic freedom is also

161

related to other freedoms, since a degree of economic independence allows one to differ politically, artistically, or religiously in the face of pressures to conform. The ideal of equality before the law can coexist with the inequalities of condition that freedoms foment.

Hence the close link throughout American history, emphasized by de Tocqueville, between this idea of equality and the idea of individual liberty embodied in the Bill of Rights. The Enlightenment thinkers' rationale for equal rights before the law is the supreme worth of the individual. Every individual, regardless of birth or ancestry, is a bearer of natural rights by virtue of being an individual. Respect for equal rights therefore entails respect for the unequal outcomes produced by the exercise of equal rights. Since every individual has unique abilities, luck, ambition, and so forth, the exercise of equal rights will mean different possessions and different levels of well-being for different individuals. (There will be different outcomes for groups as well, since groups, almost however defined, are not identical in their distributions of abilities, luck, and so forth.) Only by curtailing or suppressing the exercise of equal rights could the state create and preserve an equality of possessions or of welfare.

The Enlightenment idea of equality, which has been so decisive for American constitutional law, has surely had great attraction for many people over the generations, in America and elsewhere. But there has also been considerable dissatisfaction with it, a dissatisfaction which lies near the heart of much nineteenth- and twentieth-century radicalism. In fact, the Enlightenment idea of equality itself carries the seeds of many of the political and philosophical objections raised against it.

The radical critique and the radical dilemma

There are at least two important objections. First, equality of rights does not prevent – to some extent it promotes – great inequality of condition. But the very success of the Enlightenment rejection of feudal inequality creates a moral sensitivity to inequalities of other kinds. Equality of rights implies equal dignity for every person, which inequality of condition seems to mock. If all people were not of equal dignity, after all, why should they have equal rights? Yet it seems a pious fraud to claim that there really is equal dignity for the rich and the poor, the happy and the miserable, those who enjoy the best of everything and those who scramble for cast-offs. Modern life abounds in individual and group inequalities of resources, success, and happiness. Unease with these inequalities, a sense that they are wrong, is encouraged both by the wide popular acceptance of the Enlightenment proclamation of equality and by the ambiguity of what that proclamation might mean. Once it is accepted as a self-evident truth that all men are created equal, and without great pedantry about what is intended, there is a natural recoil from glaring human inequalities of any kind.

Second, there is a double edge to the association between equality of rights and the idea of freedom. As has been suggested, equality of rights respects the inequality of outcomes that liberty produces, whereas to keep people equal in their condition would require curtailing or suppressing the liberties that people would exercise to differentiate themselves if they were free to do so. The trouble is that equal rights cannot be exercised equally (sometimes they can scarcely be exercised at all) by people of greatly unequal condition. Just as it can be jeered that "the law in its majesty forbids rich and poor alike to sleep under bridges," so freedom of speech, for example, is not the same for the rich, who can own a newspaper or a television franchise, and the poor who cannot. Likewise, the Enlightenment's fundamental egalitarian idea of careers open to talent gives an obvious unequal advantage to those with greater talents.

The ideology that inspired much nineteenth- and twentieth-century radicalism was Marxism, and it might be expected that Marxist thought would offer a well-developed body of ideas about equality, by way of an alternative to the Enlightenment ideas that tolerate such inequality of condition. Equality was surely a heartspring of Marxism, but Marx's writings actually have little to say on the subject. This turns out to be consistent with the logic of Marx's intellectual system. To be sure, equality – or rather, the principle "from each according to his ability, to each according to his needs" – is the goal of history in the Marxist scheme. But there can be no equality so long as there are economic classes. And class conflict is the key characteristic of human life according to Marx, once people progress past "primitive communism" and until at the final synthesis they reach the Communist millennium. The definition of that millennium, however, is that when it is reached, problems of distribution will no longer exist. Once communism is achieved and the problem of distribution solved, the question of equality, therefore, becomes moot.

If Marxist "scientific socialism," although inspired by the ideal of equality, had so little to say on the subject, the various strands of "utopian socialism" tended more toward yearning for equality, or struggling for it, than toward systematic philosophical speculation about it. The tension between liberty and equality of condition already dogged radical egalitarianism, however, as early as the Babeuf conspiracy during the French Revolution. The Babeuf manifestos proclaimed that all men by nature have the same right to earthly goods, that private property is the source of inequality and must therefore be done away with, that in order to ensure equality all men must be compelled to live in the same manner and to do physical work. "Let all the arts perish, if need be, so that we may have true equality." It was clear to the Babouvists that "true" equality of condition would require a regime of compulsion, not of freedom.

Can there be equality of condition, in practice, without giving up constitutional freedoms? This is the crucial question for any radical theory of equality and of what "equal protection" ought to mean under the Constitution.

History, as opposed to philosophy, does not give reason for great hope about this. Voluntary "utopian socialist" communities, it is true, have appeared throughout the nineteenth and twentieth centuries in various places around the world, with equality of possessions and often with a sincere effort at free and equal participation

163

in governance as well. But – with perhaps the single exception of the Israeli kib-butzim – all have been short lived: experiments begun in hope that break up quickly, usually in rancor.

Marxist "scientific socialism," on the other hand, has enjoyed (if that is the right word) longer sway in various countries, and a greater opportunity to put an alternative vision of equality into actual practice. True equality of condition was never achieved for the peoples under Communist government, nor did the governments ever claim that it was: as a matter of theory, complete equality must always await the final synthesis, on a golden dawn yet to come. Still, in the most intense periods, in the Soviet Union in the 1930s and in China during the Cultural Revolution, there was perhaps something near equality of condition for all but the *vozhd*, Stalin himself, and for Mao, the Great Helmsman: an equality of terror, the haunting knowledge that no one, high or low, however conformist, was safe for even a moment from denunciation, arrest, and destruction. For the rest, the Communist regimes attained the sort of equality best expressed on George Orwell's *Animal Farm*: "All animals are equal, but some animals are more equal than others." The ruling castes had their privileges which were kept partly hidden, there was a shabby equality of possessions for everyone else, and there was rigid suppression of any "inequality" or distinction of political, artistic, or religious expression. It was all leavened with corruption, and bought at the price of tens of millions of dead and untold suffering.

At the philosophical level, any theory of equality that offers itself as an alternative to the Enlightenment's equality before the law – any theory that seeks to satisfy the sense of injustice brought on by great inequalities of human condition – must presumably find ways of escaping the fragility of utopian socialism and the various drawbacks of "real, existing" Marxist socialism. At least, such a theory must do so if it is to hope for widespread acceptance and a chance to influence constitutional law.

John Rawls leads the way amongst contemporary academic philosophers in trying to develop such a theory. Ronald Dworkin is also an influential philosophical advocate of the idea that justice requires equality of resources. Although they differ on various points, both Rawls and Dworkin argue that economic egalitarianism is consistent with individual liberty, and perhaps essential to it. Michael Walzer is an example of a liberal writer with egalitarian sympathies who, nonetheless, accepts a range of inequalities in various spheres of life. Many academic feminists and like-minded "postmodern" radicals, on the other hand, more or less openly repudiate the liberal idea of individual freedom.

Rawls

John Rawls's book, *A Theory of Justice*, appeared in 1971, and reflected to some degree the resurgence of egalitarian radicalism that had rocked America and much of the Western world at the time. Philosophically sophisticated and complex, this book and Rawls's subsequent writings have provoked enormous interest, by no means only among philosophers. Rawls achieved at least three important things. First, he brought political philosophy back into the mainstream of academic philosophy at a time when analytic philosophy – prevalent in English-speaking countries – had appeared to turn away from social thought. Second, he insisted on the question of equality as a central issue for liberalism. And third, he succeeded in casting his argument (and much of the ensuing academic debate) in terms of the ways in which equality and liberty might reinforce each other, turning the spotlight away from the tensions between equality and freedom.

Rawls argues that justice requires two principles:

1   Every individual in a just society has an equal right to a fully adequate scheme of equal basic liberties consistent with a similar scheme for everyone.
2   Social and economic inequalities must satisfy two conditions. First, such inequalities must be attached to offices and positions open to all under conditions of fair equality of opportunity; and second, they must be to the greatest benefit of the least advantaged members of society.

The first principle is very close to the Enlightenment idea of natural rights and equality before the law. The second principle (known as the "difference principle") adds a requirement that there should be considerable (but not necessarily total) equality of property and other resources for all individuals, presumably throughout their lives. Inequalities are justified only as incentives or rewards which promote such increases in the society's wealth that actually make the poorest better off.

Rawls derives these principles from a hypothetical social contract. Suppose that a group of people meet to lay the framework for their society, and that they are behind a "veil of ignorance" as to what individual places they will have in that society. They do not know their race, sex, social class, talents, personal characteristics, or ideas of what makes for a good life. Rawls argues that they would adopt his principles in order to ensure that, when the "veil" is lifted, even the worst positions in society are as good as possible, and that all will be able to exercise their "moral powers" to pursue their ideas of a good life, whatever those ideas might turn out to be.

Much of the appeal of Rawls's theory comes from the way it links equality to liberty. Rawls insists, in fact, on the "lexical priority" of liberty, by which he means that liberty must not be exchanged for other economic or social advantages, including greater equality. In Rawls's social contract, equality is esteemed not for its own sake, but so that all persons will have the best practical opportunity to exercise their freedoms in pursuit of their individual ideas of the good life. Thus, Rawls's equality principle avows its adherence to Enlightenment ideas about liberty, individual autonomy, and the supreme worth of the individual, while appealing to the egalitarian ethic which the Enlightenment has tended to foster in modern men and women.

Actually, it is not clear how much equality of economic outcome is really required by Rawls's "difference principle." If inequality of resources could only be justified insofar as it improves the position of the single worst-off individual in society, then no inequality whatsoever could be justified, since the life of an utterly dysfunctional derelict, say, is probably not improved by any net improvement in the wealth of society. Rawls suggests that inequalities are justified if they improve the lot of a "representative member of the least advantaged class." But then the size of that class is crucial. If by the "least advantaged class" one means the poorer 50 percent of society, say, then great inequalities might be justified: the poorer 50 percent of Americans are probably better off now on average than they would be in a society with significantly fewer incentives for the creation of national wealth. Yet Rawls surely implies that he intends something close to equality of property and other resources as his governing principle of distributive justice.

An objection frequently raised against Rawls's scheme is that his parable of the social contract assumes great risk-aversion on the part of those behind the "veil of ignorance." He pictures them agreeing to forbid inequalities of economic outcome that do not benefit the least advantaged (or the least advantaged class), because any of them might turn out to be the least advantaged when the "veil" is lifted. But suppose in a society with more inequality, and more incentive to produce wealth, many people – perhaps most people – would be better off (although the worst off would be worse off) than they would be in a society where property is equal. Might people not wish to risk greater inequality – the possibility of being amongst the few who would be worse off than otherwise – in hopes of being amongst the many who would be better off?

This objection has implications that go beyond the niceties of social contract theory. The stated goal of Rawls's theory of justice is that everyone should be enabled to pursue an individual idea of the good life. For many intellectuals, and perhaps for many religious people, that pursuit might be a matter of adhering to a particular theory, cause, or faith. But for many non-intellectuals, economic activity is the grist of daily life, and the idea of a good life is bound up with achieving economic distinction for oneself and one's family. Yet economic distinction means economic inequality, and much of it might be forbidden by Rawls's theory of justice.

The question of risk-aversion suggests that even behind the veil of ignorance, there might be no consensus for Rawls's principles. And once the veil is lifted, talented, lucky, or ambitious people might surely chafe. It is not clear how a notional agreement "behind the veil" would compel actual agreement in real life. In the absence of such agreement, a society intent upon Rawls's equality principle might have to use considerable compulsion in order to maintain it. Rawls insists that his theory gives "lexical priority" to liberty, even over equality. But a society really intent on equality – persuaded, perhaps, that if people stand out too much in their attitudes, outlook, or ideas, that they are apt to try to stand out economically as well – might relegate freedom to a priority that is "lexical" in the other sense: merely verbal or nominal, best honored in the breach.

Dworkin

Ronald Dworkin is a lawyer and philosopher, and probably the leading intellectual heir to Rawls. He derives his egalitarianism not from any parable of a social contract, but rather from an ethical theory that would judge people by how they meet the ethical challenges they set themselves in life. Since all are equal in having to face such challenges, justice requires that they should have equal resources with which to face them. Moreover, ethics are apt to be frustrated by unjust circumstances, so each person's ethical life is best led under conditions of justice, with equal resources for all. Freedom is essential for such equality, because to define equal resources in a complex world, and to allocate them fairly, there must be ongoing freedom of discussion; likewise, people must have liberty to develop their ideas of a good life in order for resources appropriate to those ideas to be distributed equally.

Equality of resources, for Dworkin, means that people's unequal talents and luck should not be permitted to produce inequalities of wealth. Dworkin is more radical than Rawls about this, inasmuch as he would not even tolerate inequalities that improve the condition of the worst off. On the other hand, Dworkin accepts that once everyone has received an equal initial bundle of resources, those people who choose to engage in valuable activities ought to be entitled to acquire and to keep what others are prepared to pay – so long as the ensuing inequality is the result of a person's choice of occupation and hard work, rather than a result of unequal talent or luck. And Dworkin calls for equality of resources, but not for a government effort to create equal welfare or happiness, because on his ethical model people ought to be responsible for pursuing their own, autonomous ideas of welfare.

Dworkin does not propose that people's talents and luck should actually be made identical – that those favored by birth should be forced to undergo physical or mental amputation of some kind. Instead, he envisions an insurance scheme, carried out in practice by redistributive taxation, which would compensate for inequalities of luck and ability. The goal would be to compensate for handicaps, but not for expensive tastes or other moral choices, whose consequences a person should rightly live with on Dworkin's "challenge model" of ethics.

One objection to this is that it is difficult to know where handicaps, talents, and luck might end and where matters of moral choice begin. If one is conditioned by one's upbringing to choose a valuable occupation and to work hard at it, is that one's luck or one's moral choice? Moreover, if handicaps are difficult to distinguish from expensive tastes and other personal choices, an egalitarian society might be driven towards a policy of compensating for expensive tastes as well as for handicaps, which tends to convert the principle of equality of resources into a policy of trying to ensure equal welfare or happiness for all.

A deeper objection is that equality of resources might not after all promote Dworkin's goals of ethical autonomy and responsibility. Dworkin's argument is that equal resources give people the best chance to choose (and to try to meet) their own individual ethical challenges in life. But darker possibilities suggest themselves. Perhaps many people would not feel they can "afford" to be ethical individualists in conditions of general poverty – and in a society that enforces equality of resources there would be little incentive to create wealth and hence, it is fair to predict, little wealth. (There is evidence, surely, that ethical attention to human rights is greater in affluent countries than in poor ones.) Then again, there is the danger that when society enforces a sameness of resources or conditions, it may foster a human sameness as well – a climate of conformity and lack of imagination. People may be most apt to develop independent ethical ideals where there is wide human diversity, and there tends to be wider human diversity when human conditions differ, not when they are the same. Still another possibility is that, far from promoting ethical responsibility, a society that ensures equal resources might create a sense that no urgent ethical obligations remain, or that it no longer matters very much how any individual behaves.

Finally, it might be questioned how much liberty there could really be in a society committed to Dworkin's equality of resources. Unlike Rawls, who says that equality is necessary for autonomy and freedom, Dworkin suggests that freedom is valuable primarily because it is needed to achieve justice, meaning a genuinely equal distribution of resources. If freedom is not valuable for its own sake, but only as a means towards equality, it is not clear why there should be freedom for people who do not believe that justice requires such equality, and who would use their freedom to work against equality of resources.

Equality unmodified or spheres of justice

One possible reaction to the avowedly liberal egalitarianism of Rawls and Dworkin can be seen in the writing of many academic feminists, proponents of "critical race theory", and other "post-modern" radicals. These hearken back to the eighteenth-century Babeuf manifestos and denounce liberalism in all its forms as inconsistent with true equality.

In the view of many of these writers, individual autonomy, legal rights, the artifacts of civilization, even rationality and language, are all means of acquiring unequal power, and hence sources of sexual, racial, or class oppression. Although equality is taken to be a transcendent virtue, the suggestion is that equality can scarcely even be defined within a society (and in a language) so corrupted by inequality of power.

The only way to try to achieve equality, on this view – or even to find out what equality might mean – is through a radical new form of democracy that gives "voice" and "power" to the disadvantaged. In particular, the best that the law can do is to "listen empathically to the powerless," to abandon "false neutrality," and to "empower the oppressed."

One thing that these feminist and other writers surely illustrate is how readily various ideas of equality can be at war with one another. Equality in the sense of generality is probably basic to most ideas of law: law, that is, means creating general rules, to be applied "without regard to persons," and specifically without regard to any person's wealth or status. By contrast, the strong implication in much of the recent radical legal writing is that legal rules (and judges) should above all "take account of persons" and favor those deemed to be "oppressed", in the name of equality, of course, and hence in the name of constitutional "equal protection."

Michael Walzer represents a very different reaction to Rawls and Dworkin. Walzer is a democratic socialist. Nonetheless, his book, *Spheres of Justice*, begins with the recognition that it is the human way for people to differentiate themselves from one another, unless prevented by overwhelming force from doing so. Walzer accordingly rejects any principle of equality of resources or equality of condition that would try to prevent people from differentiating themselves economically.

Rather, Walzer suggests that the nub of equality, the basic thing that egalitarians want, is that life should not be a matter of domination by some people with subordination for others. The best way to have less dominance is to recognize that there are many different spheres of life, and to ensure that there are opportunities for dignity and success in each. Walzer's goal is what he calls "complex equality," whereby people are able to face each other as equals, not because all are required to be the same in any particular respect, but because all have a real chance to achieve dignity in one or other sphere of life.

Thus, for Walzer, the market is one legitimate sphere, but politics is another, kinship is another, the sphere of basic human needs is yet another. In some of these spheres there will inevitably, and rightly, be a hierarchy of achievement and success. Economic activity is a sphere in which some people will be more successful than others. But success in one sphere ought not, in justice, to spill over into another. For example, there are many things that money cannot buy, and in Walzer's view there are many more – including political power – that it should not be able to buy. Provision for basic human needs, according to Walzer, should itself be considered a sphere separate from the market. So, like political power, a basic level of welfare should not be a matter of what money can buy, although money inequality need not otherwise offend "complex equality".

As a socialist, Walzer might favour "blocking" a variety of money exchanges that most people in market economies might not find objectionable. But "complex equality," as a general idea of justice, has strong affinities to the Enlightenment idea of equality before the law. Unlike Rawls and Dworkin, Walzer does not see human dignity as requiring equality of economic outcome. Rather, like the Enlightenment thinkers, Walzer intends his spheres of justice as a way for people to differ from each other – with as much equal status as possible, but short of creating pressures for human sameness that are apt to overwhelm all freedom to be different.

Is equality a value?

Equality is shorthand for many values, some of which conflict with one another, and some of which conflict with other values such as freedom.

169

Two ideas of equality, however, probably command broad support in most developed countries today. The first is that, whatever inequalities of condition there might be, these inequalities should not be permanent and hereditary, and that social policy ought to do what it can to promote opportunities for "mobility" and success. This is essentially the Enlightenment idea: that the law should not treat people differently on the basis of accidents of birth, and more generally, that race or caste or status should not overwhelmingly govern a person's destiny.

The second idea is that, in relatively wealthy societies "no one ought to starve": that there ought to be some minimum of social insurance and alleviation of need. Strictly speaking, this is not an idea of equality at all. It stipulates a minimum, and in no way forbids inequalities of condition above that minimum. Still, what underlies it is an idea of equality, not equality of condition but equality of respect: that to be respected as a person, and to have any real opportunity to take advantage of equal rights, one must be above a certain threshold of want.

These two ideas do not fully answer the radical egalitarian objections, namely that great inequalities of condition ought always to be a source of moral unease, and that equal rights cannot really be exercised equally by unequal people. Yet there is a paradoxical, perhaps even self-defeating, aspect to radical egalitarianism. The source of almost every kind of egalitarianism, after all, is something like the liberal idea of the supreme worth of the individual. Were it not for that idea, why would it matter that all should be equal and that no individual should be slighted? Yet the tendency of radical egalitarianism – of trying to achieve anything like equality of condition – is to efface the differences that distinguish one person from another, that make each person individual.

An important reason that the Enlightenment idea of equal rights is widely accepted is that it coexists fairly well with other widely held values, including the idea of individual freedom. More radical ideas of equality, it is true, are deeply held by some people, and have an influence in the popular culture. But these ideas are far from displacing the Enlightenment idea of equal rights. Outside the academic world, for example, there is little public resonance even to Rawls's and Dworkin's avowedly liberal egalitarianism. The same is surely true of radical feminism and other "postmodern" radical theory. Equality as a matter of constitutional law continues to mean equal rights, not equal resources or a requirement that the government should try to ensure an equally happy life for everyone. This is perhaps unlikely to change very much under liberal constitutions, at least until equality of human condition can be persuasively reconciled with human freedom to be different.

Bibliography

Aristotle 1941: *Nicomachean Ethics*, tr. W. D. Ross; and *Politics*, tr. B. Jowett; *Basic Works of Aristotle*, ed. R. McKeon, New York: Random House.

Berlin, I. 1980: Equality. In H. Hardy (ed.), *Concepts and Categories*, Oxford: Oxford University Press, 81–102.

Berns, W. 1986: Equally endowed with rights. In F. S. Lucash (ed.), *Justice and Equality Here and Now*, Ithaca: Cornell University Press, 151.

Daniels, N. (ed.) (n.d.): *Reading Rawls*. New York: Basic Books.

Dworkin, R. 1987: What is equality? Part 3: the place of liberty. *Iowa Law Review*, 73, 1–54.

—— 1988: Foundations of liberal equality. In G. B. Peterson (ed.), *Tanner Lectures on Human Values*, Salt Lake City: University of Utah Press, 3–119.

Flew, A. 1989: *Equality in Liberty and Justice*. London: Routledge.

Gutmann, A. 1980: *Liberal Equality*. Cambridge: Cambridge University Press.

Rawls, J. 1971: *A Theory of Justice*. Cambridge, Mass.: Harvard University Press.

—— 1993: *Political Liberalism*. New York: Columbia University Press.

Tocqueville, A. de 1961; tr. H. Reeve, *Democracy in America*. New York: Schocken Books.

Walzer, M. 1983: *Spheres of Justice: a defense of pluralism and equality*. New York: Basic Books.

Westen, P. 1990: *Speaking of Equality*. Princeton: Princeton University Press.

10

Evidence

JOHN JACKSON AND SEAN DORAN

Although problems of truth and knowledge have raised philosophical questions throughout the centuries, there has been little theorizing about such problems in legal contexts until relatively modern times. Much of the reason for this may be attributed to the fact that in the Middle Ages questions of fact were not determined by forms of proof that appealed to evidence. Instead, legal procedures prescribed methods of proof, such as ordeal, battle, or compurgation, which did not require a tribunal of fact to come to conclusions on the basis of evidence (Berman, 1983). Even when these methods came to be replaced and the production of evidence ceased to be a matter for God, Anglo-Saxon and Roman-canon procedure became governed by highly technical rules of proof based on the authority of the church, the early scholastic writers and writers of classical antiquity. Only gradually when the theories of the Enlightenment suggested that individuals could make their own inquiries about the nature of the world did legal systems allow the courts to estimate for themselves the probative value of the various claims made by the parties.

It took some time, however, for this principle of "universal cognitive competence," as it has been called (Cohen, 1983), to be reflected in a theory of legal proof. Through the development of jury trial, the English legal system came to embrace this principle earlier than continental systems, but it was not until the work of Jeremy Bentham (1827) in the early nineteenth century that the principle was applied in a rigorous and consistent manner toward English legal procedure. Although not widely recognized for his writings on evidence, his theory of evidence and proof is still the most developed in the history of legal thought. The first section of this article assesses the legacy left by Bentham to the field of evidence scholarship. The article then goes on to examine the regulation of the process of proof and the competing values which underpin the formulation of rules to effect this regulation. The next section considers the development of the "new" evidence scholarship, whose adherents have focussed attention on the indeterminate nature of the process of proving facts rather than on the rules themselves, which dominated the realm of evidence scholarship until recent times. Finally, the article looks at the implications of this break with tradition for the future development of the law of evidence.

The Benthamite legacy

Bentham's views were controversial and were not universally accepted, but his work has influenced thought about evidence in the legal process in three very significant ways. First of all, Bentham articulated a cognitivist, empirical episte-mology which laid the foundation for many of the epistemological and logical assumptions of standard evidence discourse in the Anglo-American world. Twin-ing (1990), the leading theorist on the intellectual history of evidence scholarship, has called this the "rationalist tradition of evidence scholarship." Although Bentham did not invent this epistemology – it had its roots in the English empiri-cist philosophy of Bacon and Locke – he was one of the first legal theorists to articulate these ideas. According to Twining, one of the key tenets of the ration-alist tradition was the belief in a correspondence theory of truth. This theory pos-tulates that events and states of affairs occur and have an existence which is independent of human observation and that true statements correspond with these facts. Present knowledge about past facts, which is what much adjudication is concerned with, is possible, but because it is based on incomplete knowledge, evid-ence establishing the truth about the past is typically a matter of probabilities, and the characteristic mode of reasoning is inductive by which one starts with certain basic data and moves by way of inductive generalization towards a probable con-clusion. Twining remarks that nearly all leading Anglo-American writers on evid-ence have adopted these views, although more often than not *sub silentio*.

Bentham's second and more distinctive contribution to evidence scholarship was to commit adjudication to truth finding. Twining (1985) has concluded that to this day Bentham's theory of evidence represents the most fully developed and unequivocal form of a truth theory of adjudication. Inspired by the ideas of the French revolution and the need for the will of the legislator to be done, Bentham believed that the object of legal procedure must always be the vindication of rights and the enforcement of the law. Although the substantive laws may not in them-selves maximize the principle of utility, it was essential that laws were enforced in the interest of security so that expectations raised by law should not be dis-appointed. Hence the need to put priority on rectitude of decision. Bentham con-ceded that there were constraints on the achievement of this goal. Due regard was to be had to the avoidance of vexation, expense, or delay. But he had little time for values which do not so much constrain truth finding as conflict with it. So he was opposed to rules of privilege designed to protect marital harmony or confidential information and was particularly critical of the lawyer–client privilege and the privilege against self-incrimination.

These ideas were controversial in their day and remain so. Even accepting Bentham's famous principle of utility, there is room for argument about the im-portance that should be placed on rectitude of decision making. In certain kinds of adjudication, dispute settlement is seen as more important than strict enforce-ment of the law, particularly where the parties have a continuing interest in maintaining a relationship. Other theorists not so wedded to the principle of utility

173

can argue that Bentham gave insufficient attention to the notion of procedural rights, such as the right to be heard, the right to legal advice and assistance and the right of silence (Galligan, 1988). But the very fact that these issues are debated within a general consensus about the importance of truth finding illustrates the continuing significance of Bentham's ideas. Twining has commented that given the vastly different context in which litigation takes place today, the extent to which Bentham's central concerns and themes still have resonance is remarkable. Indeed the growing unpopularity in many jurisdictions of certain privileges, most notably the privilege against self-incrimination, is a testament to the continuing appeal of Bentham's concern for truth finding.

Bentham's third contribution to the field of evidence scholarship has been his approach toward the law of evidence itself. For Bentham not only championed the importance of truth finding in adjudication; he developed a model of adjudication to achieve this goal. His preference was for what he called a natural as opposed to a technical system of proof, by which he meant that all relevant evidence should be admitted and evidence should be weighed solely on the merits of the individual case without reference to rigid rules. This "anti-nomian" thesis, as it has been called (Twining, 1985, pp. 66–75), may be regarded as a logical consequence of his attachment to the principle of universal cognitive competence and the importance of truth finding in adjudication. If it is the case that individuals can reason for themselves about evidence (without the need to rely on authoritative rules) and that such individuals are not to be fettered by values unrelated to the discovery of truth, which may require that certain relevant evidence is not taken into account, then there is no need for rules of evidence at all.

The regulation of proof

The effect of Bentham's anti-nomian thesis was to lay down the gauntlet to the law of evidence, challenging it to justify its continuing existence. Instead of the law of evidence being viewed as an all embracing set of rules for the regulation of proof in legal procedures, it has come to be viewed as a series of disparate exceptions to the Benthamite principle of free proof. This is best encapsulated in Thayer's (1898) famous depiction of the law of evidence as based on two principles: that nothing is to be received which is not logically probative of some matter to be proved, and that everything which is probative should be received unless a clear ground of policy of law excludes it. Unlike Bentham, Thayer did not favour a complete absence of rules but he led the way toward a rationalization of the rules of evidence and the result has been a gradual diminution in their scope. This theme of rationalization continued to resonate throughout the work of leading twentieth-century evidence scholars such as Wigmore, Maguire, McCormick, and Morgan. In the same spirit of reductionism, one of the century's leading expositors of the law of evidence on the other side of the Atlantic, Sir Rupert Cross, is reputed to have remarked: "I am working for the day when my subject is abolished" (Twining, 1990, p. 1).

Yet the anti-nomian thesis can be taken too far. No matter how highly a system of proof values rectitude in decision making, it is impossible to have a system of adjudication without *some* rules regulating proof. In any system of adjudication a decision must be reached on the issues in dispute and this requires a decision rule to determine when a party has won and when it has lost. In a typical case scenario, the facts as presented are gauged by reference to a rule of law. In turn, the application of that rule to those facts which the rule deems to be material produces a resolution of the central issue, namely whether the defendant is guilty or liable (MacCormick, 1978). But if it cannot be shown that these facts occurred, it does not follow that the defendant is not guilty or not liable. To enable a decision to be reached, provision must be made for what should happen when the material facts have not been shown to have occurred.

Furthermore, it follows from the imperative to reach a decision that it may not be possible to prove the material facts to a degree of absolute certainty. The decision will then have to be made under conditions of uncertainty. The rationalist tradition assumes that knowledge is a matter of probability and not certainty and this is particularly the case in the kind of institutionalized setting in which litigation is conducted. In addition to rules determining who wins in the event of the material facts being proved, there is therefore a need for rules to determine what standard of proof is necessary to enable the material facts to be considered proved or not proved. The standard required must be a degree of probability but it need not be the same degree for all kinds of litigation, as it should take account of the magnitude of the harm that will be caused if a decision is wrong. What is required here is an essentially political and moral judgment concerning the extent to which the various parties should be exposed to risks of error (Zuckerman, 1989, pp. 105–9). So standards of proof are conventionally different in civil and criminal cases. Since civil litigation has traditionally been viewed as a dispute between private parties, it has been considered wrong to favor one party over another and the standard has thus been guided by the principle that the risk of errors should be allocated as evenly as possible between the parties. In criminal cases, on the other hand, it is considered preferable to allocate the risk of error in favour of the defendant because the risk of a person being wrongly convicted is considered much graver than the risk of a person being wrongly acquitted. The value judgment involved here is often expressed in the aphorism that it is better that ten guilty persons go free than that one innocent person be convicted. The state must therefore bear the burden of proving guilt beyond reasonable doubt, but it is worth noting that the standard is not stretched to one of beyond *all* doubt as this would make it practically impossible to convict anyone. Hence the phrasing of the above aphorism in tens rather than, say, thousands, although the position of the standard of proof beyond reasonable doubt on this scale cannot be precisely located.

As well as rules specifying when the material facts will be proved, there is also a need for rules determining *how* the facts are to be proved. This involves making value judgments as to how proof is best determined, but it also involves making moral and political judgments as to what is a fair procedure. Legal decisions have to inspire confidence in their impartiality and fairness. One question is whether

175

the task of proof should be put into the hands of the courts, as happens in so-called inquisitorial systems, or whether it should be put into the hands of the parties (Damaska, 1986). This question cannot be determined solely on the basis of which method is better able to aid truth finding. If, for example, there is mistrust of official decision making, then there may be a reluctance to give the courts too large a role in the resolution of the dispute. The parties will be given more control over the process and lay decision makers may be brought in to assist in the resolution of the facts. In this event there will be a need for further rules to specify which parties bear the burden of proof on the issues in dispute and to regulate the presentation of proofs.

If the anti-nomian thesis underestimates the extent to which rules of proof are *necessary* in any adjudication system, the thesis also underestimates the extent to which rules may be thought to be *desirable*. The judgments about risk allocation and procedural fairness that have to be made in constructing any adjudicative system may be thought in certain contexts to require the kind of exclusionary rules and rules regulating the weight of evidence that Bentham most disapproved of. Adversary adjudication has encouraged parties to produce direct oral evidence in support of the claims they are making in order that their evidence can be cross-examined by opposing parties. Hence the traditional ban on hearsay evidence. In addition, parties cannot be allowed to protract proceedings endlessly. Thayer's first principle requires that nothing should be adduced which is irrelevant, but it may be considered that rules of relevance are required to regulate the admissibility of *insufficiently* relevant kinds of evidence.

In the context of criminal adjudication, Zuckerman (1989) has argued that apart from the need to discover the truth there are in addition two important principles, the principle of protecting the innocent and the principle of maintaining high standards of propriety throughout the criminal process. The principle of free proof is founded, as we have seen, on the belief that human beings are competent to find the truth, but it does not deny that errors may be made in the evaluation of evidence. In particular, there has been a concern that certain kinds of evidence, such as evidence of an accused's convictions or confession evidence, or identification evidence, may be over-valued by particular tribunals of fact. Such concern is accentuated when this tribunal is a jury, due to the perception that the lay mind is particularly vulnerable to the influence of prejudicial evidence and particularly ill equipped to identify potential deficiencies in certain genres of evidential material which appear on face value to be reliable. It follows that given the prominent place which the jury has occupied in the Anglo-American legal tradition, the development of the law of evidence has been shaped to a significant extent by the dictates of jury trial.

Returning to the allocation of the risk of error, if this is to be accomplished on an even basis between the parties then it may be argued that each party must bear the risk of evidence being improperly evaluated against them. But if particular weight is to be given to the principle of protecting innocent defendants in criminal procedure, then evidence which might have the effect of increasing this risk when it is evaluated may have to be excluded or regulated. This would seem to explain in part the continuing use of rules which restrict admission of an accused's character, the strict rules governing the admissibility of confessions and rules requiring corroboration of certain kinds of evidence. Similarly, the principle of maintaining high standards of propriety in the criminal process may be thought to justify the use of exclusionary rules. The principle against self-incrimination and the rules regulating confession evidence, for example, arguably stem as much from concern about maintaining a proper balance between the power of law enforcement officials and the accused as from a concern about the risk of false confessions. To the three principles considered there might indeed be added a fourth, which veers even further from pure truth-finding concerns and which extends to legal procedures generally. It has been argued that the entire legal process, including the rules of evidence, has, at its core, the goal of promoting the acceptability of verdicts (Nesson, 1985). On this view, for example, the actual effectiveness of instructions to the jury on how to deal with certain kinds of potentially suspect evidence would be subordinate to the cathartic and morally legitimizing role which such instructions play in the context of the trial process.

The discussion until now has characterized evidential rules as mandatory in form. It is, however, undeniable that there has been increasingly less reliance on mandatory rules to protect the principles of adversary and criminal adjudication. Rather, the prevailing view is now that these are better protected by means of judicial or statutory discretion or by means of guidelines and rules of practice. Bentham himself made a distinction between rules addressed to the will of the judge to which he was opposed and instructions addressed to the understanding, general guidelines which he sometimes referred to as rules. While the scope of the rules of evidence has therefore declined throughout the twentieth century, there has been a movement in favor of flexible standards, guidelines, balancing tests and rules of practice to deal with particularly problematic kinds of evidence. So, for example, exclusionary rules such as the hearsay rule have been relaxed and replaced by guidelines to judges or in jury cases by judicial instructions and warnings to juries. Juries are also given warnings on the evidential significance to be attached to character evidence, identification evidence, and the accused's lies and silence. It might be argued in this connection that just as we have seen that the development of mandatory exclusionary rules was inextricably linked to mistrust of the jury, so the transition to more flexible guidelines and instructions may reflect a heightened faith in the capacity of the lay tribunal to weigh certain forms of evidential material which was traditionally withheld from its sphere of deliberation.

The "new" evidence scholarship

Much of the law of evidence has therefore moved in an anti-nomian direction and if Bentham somewhat underestimated the importance of values external to truth finding in adjudication, it has appeared that these can be given force without the need for exclusionary rules. Just as Bentham's anti-nomian thesis would seem to have been realized, however, a more fundamental challenge has been mounted in the late twentieth century to the entire rationalist tradition which is calling into question this reductionist approach towards the law of evidence. Outside mainstream evidence scholarship, there has been increasing skepticism about the possibility of objective knowledge. As Nicolson (1994, p. 729) has noted, "the apparent failure of the Enlightenment project to deliver its promise of a social utopia through continuous scientific advance has led to a questioning of its epistemological assumptions." In particular, it is being questioned whether it is ever possible to see the world except as shaped by our world experience and culture. This challenge to the rationalist tradition has been manifested in philosophy, the humanities and science, but is also breeding a societal malaise with many established institutions. In the legal world this has meant a skepticism about the courts' ability to achieve truth or justice.

Much of this prevailing mood would seem to have passed evidence scholars by (Nicolson, 1994; Seigel, 1994). But there has in recent years been a shift in the focus of their interest away from the rules of evidence toward the process of proof. This "new" evidence scholarship, as it has been dubbed (Lempert, 1988), can be traced back to the early twentieth-century evidence scholar, J. H. Wigmore, but it did not attract much interest until the 1960s and 1970s when a number of scholars became embroiled in a dispute about the application of probability theory to legal processes after an erroneous attempt was made to use statistical reasoning to resolve problems of evidence in a celebrated Californian case (*People* v. *Collins*, 68 Cal. 2d, 438 P.2d 33 (1968); contrast Finkelstein and Fairley, 1970, with Tribe, 1971; and Williams, 1979, 1980, with Cohen, 1980). Although this debate was conducted largely within the spirit of the rationalist tradition, it provided the stimulus for evidence scholars to examine the process of proof and this exposed evidence scholarship to ideas which have gained ground in other disciplines.

The rationalist tradition assumed that it is possible to start with certain basic items of evidence which correspond with reality and then reason from these toward a probability judgment of a past event. But some of the new evidence scholars are now arguing that we do not collect bits of evidence as one might collect shells from the sand (Tillers, 1988; Schum, 1986). Instead evidence is gathered according to the relevance of the investigation in hand and this involves considering and testing hypotheses from the beginning. Furthermore, it is highly questionable whether we will all reach the same conclusion on the presentation of the same evidence. When we test evidence we do not test it against a universally available stock of knowledge about the common course of events but, according to certain cognitive scientists, by reference to particular schemas or stories that form the basis of our knowledge structures (Pennington and Hastie, 1986). It is questionable how far these ideas question the rationalist tradition. Certain scholars believe that theoretical structures are as much dependent on facts and evidence as facts and evidence are dependent on theoretical structures (Tillers, 1988). No evidence is presented in a form which is free from theoretical shaping, but it remains possible that external events as well as subjective ideas shape the evidence we see. Others, however, have gone further and advocated a coherence theory of truth instead of a correspondence theory of truth so that instead of determining the truth of what happened, all we can do is to fit the evidence to a theory or story about what happened (B. Jackson, 1988a).

Future directions of the law of evidence

The implication of these ideas for adjudication and the rules of evidence is quite startling. To say that we can never reach a universal consensus on truth claims is not to say that we have to take the extreme relativist position that one method of truth finding is as good as any other. If we take this position, we may as well either abandon the goal of truth finding and search for other methods of dispute settlement or permit those whose verdicts are likely to be most acceptable to the community to decide questions of fact (taking the fourth principle mentioned above to its logical extreme). In fact, of course, there is much on which we can reach agreement; it is just that we have to be aware that biases can easily creep into our schematic processing of evidence. The anti-nomian thesis associated with the rationalist tradition assumed that because every normal and unbiased person will come to the same conclusion about the evidence, there was little need to regulate the proof process. Questions of fact were matters of common sense to be distinguished from rules of evidence which were treated as exceptional and artificial constraints on free inquiry. As Thayer (1898, p. 264) put it, "The law furnishes no test of relevancy. For this, it tacitly refers to logic and general experience." But if our knowledge is conditioned by our particular perspectives and biases, then we need to be much more careful about our truth finding procedures. Far from this suggesting we need no rules; it suggests we need *more* rules.

First of all, it would seem that we need to open up the process of discovery of evidence to as much scrutiny as the process of justification, which means that we need to focus as much on the process of proof before trial as on the process of proof at trial (Jackson, 1988b). Any justification at trial will appeal to selective information, so we need to examine how that evidence was selected. Furthermore, the process of obtaining information is interactive and information will change as it is reported to others. We therefore need to regulate the evidentiary process at as early a stage as possible. We also need to ensure that all those who are interested parties in the dispute are able to participate in the fact-finding enterprise so that their perspective is not excluded from consideration. This requires fair disclosure of existing evidence to the relevant parties but it also requires that parties are able to put forward their stories in a manner that does justice to them. Much attention has rightly focussed already on the conditions under which defendants are questioned by police officers and elaborate codes of conduct have been drawn up to govern this process, but there needs to be as much attention given to the way in which evidence is elicited from other witnesses.

Second, the existing procedures for evaluating evidence need to be fundamentally reviewed. It is now argued that triers of fact conceptualize evidence holistically by constructing stories or episodes from the evidence that is heard rather than atomistically in terms of whether the items of evidence adduced add up to proof to a certain standard. It would seem to follow that triers of fact should be asked to decide between competing versions of reality specified by the parties rather than whether each of the elements of guilt or liability have been proved to a required standard of proof (Allen, 1991, 1994). If we can no longer be sure that our commonsense assumptions are universal, we also need to scrutinize rules that are supposedly based on common sense but may in fact reflect stereotypical assumptions and discriminatory generalizations about certain kinds of people (MacCrimmon, 1991). The rule, for example, that evidence of sexual complaint should be admissible has tended to focus attention on whether a complaint was made on the assumption that a victim of sexual abuse will wish to make a complaint. It is also now recognized that the traditional rules of competence and hearsay have prevented the courts from having access to children's evidence. This does not necessarily mean that we should abandon all exclusionary rules. There is a danger that if we leave questions of relevance and probative value exclusively to judges, they may discriminate against particular classes of people with whom they have had no experience. One example is the way in which it would seem that the sexual history of rape complainants has in certain jurisdictions been allowed to seep into the trial on the ground that it has some relevance to the case (Adler, 1987). One solution is to issue statutory guidelines on the relevance of certain difficult issues such as sexual history evidence. Another is to allow greater use of expert evidence to enable a better understanding to take place of persons whose experience may not be within the experience of trial decision makers.

Third, we may need to reconsider the role of the parties and adjudicators at trial. In the adversary system the tribunal of fact has traditionally occupied a passive role and it is assumed that triers of fact do not need to engage in the cut and thrust of argumentative debate with the parties before reaching their conclusions. But since evidence is no longer conceived as a set of individuated items which is absorbed by the tribunal of fact but is instead a dynamic process which involves fitting information within a more global framework, then presenters of evidence and triers of fact could both benefit from greater interaction between each other. Advocates could be given more feedback as to how the evidence is being interpreted and triers of fact could question advocates and witnesses more on what they are finding it difficult to understand. Indeed since the stories and schemas used by fact finders to make sense of the evidence are inevitably used by them to reach their conclusions, there is an argument that parties should be entitled to engage in debate with the tribunal of fact on the processes of reasoning that are being used by the triers of fact to reach their decision. This suggests that we may need to reshape the conventional roles which participants have in the trial process in order to introduce a more formal channel of communication between the parties and triers of fact. There is a danger that this may result in a risk of certain prejudicial information coming to the knowledge of the tribunal of fact. But it is arguably better that any risk of prejudice is exposed openly during the trial than allowed to fester silently behind closed doors. To such reformatory ideas should be added a cautionary note. While logic may point toward an enlarged participatory role for the finder of fact in the process of proof, the constraints imposed by the adversary system in general and by the jury in particular cannot be overlooked. First, the adversarial trial is founded on the notion of party control over the process of proof and it may be objected that an intrusive fact finder will have the effect of skewing this process and in so doing *impeding* the discovery of truth. Second, the jury, as we presently know it, is not ideally placed in practical terms to engage in active debate with trial participants. Both of these reservations, however, invite broader questions which stray far beyond the remit of the present work, relating to the general desirability of the adversarial model and to the claim to primacy of the jury as a finder of fact.

Whatever view we may form on such questions, the foregoing discussion suggests that far from shrinking into nothingness, the law of evidence has a vital role to play in the preparation, presentation, and evaluation of evidence. The law of evidence has tended to be seen in a negative way as imposing constraints on free proof, often in the interests of fairness to the accused or other parties. But modern conceptions of truth finding suggest that there is not such a dichotomy between truth and fairness as is sometimes thought. If there are no objective criteria against which to match our conclusions of fact, we must test them out against others who are making claims about what has happened. In a legal claim this will invariably mean the participants in the case. It is therefore not merely fair to give such participants a chance to respond to the claims that have been made, it becomes important to enable them to participate in order that a more informed decision is reached. So while we may say that a procedure is fair only if both sides to a dispute are permitted to be heard, we can also say that such a procedure is likely to assist in the pursuit of truth finding. But this means that positive steps need to be taken to ensure that the parties and witnesses affected by litigation are able to participate in telling their stories in as effective a way as they can, and that those who ultimately have to reach decisions of fact understand the evidence presented and justify the conclusions that are reached.

At present, however, there is a growing perception that procedures throughout the common-law world are failing to give satisfaction to participants who become embroiled in adjudication. Much of this has to do with the failure of the legal system to provide outcomes that are considered fair and accurate. But there is, in addition, growing concern about the cost and delay of existing procedures, much as there was in Bentham's day. Litigants are in consequence turning away towards alternative procedures, and conventional legal procedures are slowly being displaced by alternative forms of dispute resolution such as negotiation, mediation, and arbitration which do not count truth finding amongst their primary goals (Seigel, 1994). For certain kinds of disputes where the parties are in a continuing relationship and it is more important to look forward than to look back, truth finding may not be as important. For other disputes, however, particularly those which involve issues of public importance, truth finding is of great importance and here it is vital not only that there is access to justice but that an outcome is reached that is as fair and accurate as it can be within the constraints of litigation. In this sense the goals that Bentham defined are as relevant today as they were in his day, and the challenge for evidence scholars is still to design procedures which do justice to these goals.

Bibliography

Adler, Z. 1987: *Rape on Trial*. London: Routledge & Kegan Paul.

Allen, R. J. 1991: The nature of juridical proof. *Cardozo Law Review*, 13, 373–422.

—— 1994: Factual ambiguity and a theory of evidence. *Northwestern Law Review*, 88, 604–40.

Bentham, J. [1827] 1978: *Rationale of Judicial Evidence*. New York: Garland.

Berman, H. J. 1983: *Law and Revolution: the formation of the Western legal tradition*. Cambridge: Harvard University Press.

Cohen, L. J. 1980: The logic of proof. *Criminal Law Review*, 91–103.

—— 1983: Freedom of proof. In W. L. Twining (ed.), *Facts in Law*, Wiesbaden: Steiner Verlag, 1–21.

Damaska, M. 1986: *The Faces of Justice and State Authority*. New Haven: Yale University Press.

Finkelstein, M. O. and Fairley, W. B. 1970: A Bayesian approach to identification evidence. *Harvard Law Review*, 83, 489–517.

Galligan, D. 1988: More scepticism about scepticism. *Oxford Journal of Legal Studies*, 8, 249–65.

Jackson, B. S. 1988: *Law, Fact and Narrative Coherence*. Merseyside: Deborah Charles Publications.

Jackson, J. D. 1988: Theories of truth finding in criminal procedure: an evolutionary approach. *Cardozo Law Review*, 10, 475–527.

Lempert, R. 1988: The new evidence scholarship: analysing the process of proof. In P. Tillers and E. D. Green (eds), *Probability and Inference in the Law of Evidence: the uses and limits of Bayesianism*, Dordrecht: Kluwer, 61–102.

MacCormick, D. N. 1978: *Legal Reasoning and Legal Theory*. Oxford: Clarendon Press.

MacCrimmon, C. 1991: Developments in the law of evidence: the 1989–90 term – evidence in context. *Supreme Court Law Review (2d)*, 385–450.

Nesson, C. 1985: The evidence or the event? On judicial proof and the acceptability of verdicts. *Harvard Law Review*, 98, 1,357–92.

Nicolson, D. 1994: Truth, reason and justice: epistemology and politics in evidence discourse. *Modern Law Review*, 57, 726–44.

Pennington, N. and Hastie, R. 1986: Evidence evaluation in complex decision making. *Journal of Personality and Social Psychology*, 51, 242–58.

Schum, D. 1986: Probability and the process of discovery, proof and choice. *Boston University Law Review*, 66, 825–76.

Seigel, M. 1994: A pragmatic critique of modern evidence scholarship. *Northwestern University Law Review*, 88, 995–1,045.

Thayer, J. B. [1898] 1979: *A Preliminary Treatise on Evidence at Common Law*. Boston: Little Brown.

Tillers, P. 1988: Mapping inferential domains. In P. Tillers and E. D. Green (eds), *Probability and Inference in the Law of Evidence: the uses and limits of Bayesianism*, Dordrecht: Kluwer, 277–336.

Tribe, H. L. 1971: Trial by mathematics: precision and ritual in legal process. *Harvard Law Review*, 84, 1,329–93.

Twining, W. L. 1985: *Theories of Evidence: Bentham and Wigmore*. London: Weidenfeld & Nicolson.
—— 1990: *Rethinking Evidence: exploratory essays*. Oxford: Basil Blackwell.
Williams, G. 1979: The mathematics of proof. *Criminal Law Review*, 297–308, 340–54.
—— 1980: A short rejoinder. *Criminal Law Review*, 103.
Zuckerman, A. A. S. 1989: *The Principles of Criminal Evidence*. Oxford: Clarendon Press.

11

Comparative law

RICHARD HYLAND

Comparative law is the field of study devoted both to describing the content and style of local, national, and religious legal systems and to exploring the similarities and differences among them. Comparative legal scholarship has contributed to law revision, to the unification and harmonization of law across national boundaries, and to the delineation of a fund of ideas common to many legal systems. The terms *comparative legislation* and *comparative jurisprudence* are often used as synonyms for *comparative law*, though occasionally with the different nuances that the terms themselves suggest.

Comparative research that reports the substantive content or particular style of a foreign legal system is called *descriptive* comparison. Most authors believe that comparative law involves more than a description of foreign law. *Theoretical* comparison focusses on the similarities and differences among legal systems. *Applied* comparative law is concerned with finding the best norm for a given social or economic situation.

Comparative research can be done on different scales (Zweigert and Kötz, 1987, vol. 1, pp. 4–5). *Macrocomparison* focusses on general questions, such as the differing styles of codification and statutory interpretation, the value of precedent, the importance of the scholarly doctrine in the development of the law, and the decisional styles of the courts. *Microcomparison* is concerned with how specific legal problems are resolved in the various jurisdictions.

Some scholars have suggested that, since comparative law, unlike torts and contracts, does not represent a particular substantive field of the law, it does not contain a separate body of knowledge and therefore should be considered to be simply one of many methods by which the law may be studied (Gutteridge, 1949, p. 1). Others, however, have argued that comparative law provides the only means by which the study of law may become a science – the scholarly doctrine in any one country is generally concerned only with the application of that country's legal norms, while comparative analysis permits a more general study of the nature and operation of legal systems (Zweigert and Puttfarken, 1978, pp. 2–3). The relation between the methodological and scientific aspects of comparative law has been explored in considerable depth (Constantinesco, 1972–83).

From the point of view of legal theory, two aspects of comparative research are particularly worthy of note. The first is that comparativists have frequently adopted

184

their methodological ideas from jurisprudence and have proven particularly imaginative in translating philosophical and sociological ideas into research programs. As a result, the data that comparative legal scholarship has amassed may prove to be useful in the evaluation of jurisprudential theories. Second, students of comparative law have not yet settled on a single method to achieve its goals. Comparative law seeks to grasp both the similarities and the differences among the various legal systems, yet none of the available comparative methodologies is able to perform both aspects of the task. Throughout much of the modern history of comparative law, the dominant comparative paradigm has focussed on the similarities, attempting in various ways to identify a set of ideas or practices common to all developed legal orders. The differences among the systems have been examined chiefly in terms of the proper "family" classification, an approach that analyzes the differences among a small number of legal families rather than the particularities of the numerous individual legal systems themselves. A minority voice, beginning perhaps with Montesquieu, has emphasized that each legal system presents a different vision of justice and that the examination of these myriad differences should be the goal of comparative research. This position is beginning to gain adherents, though it has as yet advanced little beyond a call to action.

Because a unifying paradigm is lacking in this field of research, the contributions of modern comparative law can best be understood – and will be presented here – in terms of the sum of its major achievements and the spectrum of its principal methodologies.

Universalism

Laws were already compared in antiquity – the ancient sources report, for example, that the Romans sent a delegation to Athens before drafting the XII Tables. (For the history, see Hug, 1932.). Comparative study was also instrumental when Roman law was received into the European legal systems. The theorists of Latin natural law, particularly Grotius and Pufendorf, developed their ideas by comparing the laws of ancient societies. Montesquieu's contribution to comparative constitutional analysis is particularly noteworthy (Montesquieu, 1748). Comparative methodology has also been employed in the Anglo-American tradition, from Lord Mansfield to Joseph Story and James Kent, especially in the effort to import notions from the law merchant into the common law. The unification of law in a national context – examples include the drafting of the French Civil Code, the German Commercial Code, and the Uniform Commercial Code – has often been preceded by a comparison of local laws.

Modern comparative law is said to date from 1869, the year both of the founding of the French Société de Législation Comparée and of the appointment of Sir Henry Sumner Maine to the Corpus Chair of Historical and Comparative Jurisprudence at Oxford (Brown, 1971, pp. 232–3). Maine's *Ancient Law*, published in 1861, applied to the study of law a process of comparison similar to that employed by Darwin in his *Origin of Species*. Modern comparative law, like comparative anatomy and comparative philology, thus began as one of the comparative disciplines based on evolutionary ideas. "Comparative legal investigation deals with the evolutionary side of the law; by no means, however, with that desolate and sterile kind of evolution which derives each development from an accidental and external coincidence of particular facts; but, on the contrary, with the spiritual point of view which assumes that the world-process involves an inherently reasonable course of development, an evolutionary struggle which employs mechanical factors only for the attainment of its ends" (Kohler, 1887, p. 6). The comparative method was considered by the Victorians to be one of their most significant intellectual achievements. A well-known result of this research is Maine's hypothesis that legal relations universally evolve from the status of family dependency to the contractual form of individual obligation – "*from Status to Contract*" (Maine, 1861, pp. 172–4).

The initial phase of modern comparative scholarship culminated in the discussion regarding the nature and purpose of comparative law at the Congrès international de droit comparé, held in Paris in conjunction with the World's Fair of 1900. The orators at the Paris Congress generally endorsed a universalist conception of the law. The universalist thesis is perhaps best understood not as a systematic theory of the law but rather as an effort to temper the effects of two particularist tendencies in nineteenth-century law – widespread national codification, with the resulting breach in the unity of the Roman law tradition, and the Romantic conception of the individuality of each national culture, an idea formulated by Herder and introduced into jurisprudential thought by Savigny and the Historical School. Though universalist theorists recognized that legal systems differ, they were confident that, due to "the profound unity of human nature of which the law is a necessary manifestation," universal legal principles would one day govern all of humanity (del Vecchio, 1910, p. 65). The universalists pointed to a number of phenomena to justify their optimism, including the convergence of national laws toward common principles and the frequency with which legal institutions created in one system are adopted by another.

From the universalist point of view, the mission of comparative law was to cull from the various domestic-law formulations an ideal law that could be adopted and applied in all countries. As the idea was explained by Edouard Lambert, one of the founders of modern comparative law, the purpose of the comparative enterprise is

> to discover the common fund of institutions and conceptions beneath the apparent statutory diversity, to collect maxims common to these legal systems, and thereby constantly to encroach on the domain of particularism. The unifying force attributed to comparative law . . . results in the progressive effacement of the accidental diversity that prevails among legal systems located in countries of similar development and economic condition and the reduction of statutory differences that are not justified by political, moral, or social reasons and which, therefore, are due to historical accident or to transitory and superficial causes. (*Lambert, 1905, p. 37*)

The universalist convictions of the turn-of-the-century comparativists were a powerful force for the joining of hands among legal scholars at the close of a century of national codification. Nonetheless, the universalist theories have frequently been criticized. To begin with, the universal legal principles that the universalists believed they had discovered were derived from Christianity, Roman law, and natural law theories rather than from a thorough examination of the world's legal systems. Moreover, though the universalists were aware of difference, they wholly failed to acknowledge its role in the comparative process. In line with turn-of-the-century historiography, the universalists considered diversity to be a remnant of historical accident rather than a suggestion that the world's legal systems may actually differ.

Functionalism

After World War I, comparative scholarship gained a new perspective when efforts were undertaken to unify certain areas of the private law. It was thought that the dissimilarity of domestic laws impedes international commerce and that comparative law should therefore contribute to the unification of commercial law. In particular, the International Institute for the Unification of Private Law (UNIDROIT), located in Rome, asked a number of leading comparative scholars to participate in drafting a uniform law for the international sale of goods. As a preliminary to the drafting, Ernst Rabel, perhaps the outstanding comparativist of this century, together with his associates at the Kaiser Wilhelm Institute in Berlin, produced a survey of the world's domestic sales laws. The work is considered to be one of the great achievements of modern comparative law (Rabel, 1936–58).

Rabel believed that the process of unification begins by an examination of how the various domestic legal systems resolve the practical issues involved. He hypothesized that, if the legal constructions and characterizations particular to each legal system were ignored and if attention were instead directed exclusively to the actual consequences of the judicial decisions, a common or best solution would generally emerge from the comparison, and unification could be achieved with little or no normative discussion.

> By and large, the most important part of the uniform law will arise and take form, as one might say, by itself, on the basis of a comparison of laws. The form in which substantive legal ideas have until now been hidden, the technical-juridical constructions, are to be discarded. The practical solutions deserve the more intense interest, and a comparison of those solutions will be richly rewarded with regard to most legal issues. When viewed in this manner, the similarities will prove to be extraordinarily strong and thoroughly profound. (*Rabel, 1936–58, vol. 1, p. 67*)

A major aspect of comparative research continues to be its contribution to the unification of law, particularly in the area of international commerce (David et al., 1973–, vol. 2, ch. 5).

187

Max Rheinstein, one of Rabel's close collaborators, suggested that the functionalist method could be generalized and applied beyond the context of the unification of law to the entire comparative process. (Rheinstein, 1934, pp. 248–50). The generalization of the functionalist method is related to theories of sociological jurisprudence and particularly to Roscoe Pound's arguments in favor of a functionalist program for legal research (Pound, 1931, pp. 710–11). Similar ideas were suggested by Rudolph von Jhering and developed in German jurisprudence by the theorists of *Interessenjurisprudenz* and the *Freirechtsschule* (Zweigert and Kötz, 1987, vol. 1, pp. 44–5). Functionalist comparison is also related to the legal realist conception of the law as an instrument for channeling or modifying human behavior. "Law is 'social engineering' and legal science is a social science" (Zweigert and Kötz, 1987, vol. 1, p. 44). Because of the importance of functionalism, both in terms of its exceptional contributions and the intensity of the criticism it has provoked, its method, particularly as presented by its leading proponents, Konrad Zweigert and Hein Kötz, repays careful examination. (For a summary of the criticism, see Frankenberg, 1985.)

Functionalist comparison begins by the choice of the particular practical problem that is to be the subject of study. The legal systems to be compared are then selected and examined with regard to how they resolve such problems. Following Rabel's lead, functionalist method disregards differences in doctrinal construction and legal concept and, instead, directs its attention almost exclusively to the practical consequences of the norms, and particularly to the remedy provided in the specified fact situation. "For the comparative process, this means that the solutions we find in the different jurisdictions must be cut loose from their conceptual context and stripped of their national doctrinal overtones so that they may be seen purely in the light of their function, as an attempt to satisfy a particular legal need" (Zweigert and Kötz, 1987, vol. 1, p. 42).

The disregard of legal construction yields obvious benefits in the endeavor in which Rabel employed it, namely, the production of a uniform law. It has also served as a much-needed corrective to the rule-orientation of turn-of-the-century comparative theorists. Nonetheless, the functionalist focus on the law's practical consequences neglects much of what might profitably be included as the object of comparative research. For one, there is the rigorous and systematic conceptual structure employed in most developed legal systems to order legal understanding and to ensure that like cases are decided alike. Functionalism also neglects an essential element of daily legal activity, the work done by lawyers and legal scholars everywhere, namely, the careful preparation of a legal construction to resolve the issues in dispute.

Functionalism is particularly concerned with how to compare the law's practical consequences across legal systems. The *tertium comparationis* that is believed to permit comparison is *functionality*. "Incomparables cannot usefully be compared, and in law the only things which are comparable are those which fulfill the same function" (Zweigert and Kötz, 1987, vol. 1, p. 31). Since the actual function and effect of legal institutions is a matter of sociological concern, one might imagine that an empirical investigation would be a necessary prelude to functionalist research in comparative law. The functionalists avoid this step by means of a central premise, namely that the practical problems that the law is asked to resolve are similar or even [in] identical across different cultures. "If law is seen functionally as a regulator of social facts, the legal problems of all countries are similar. Every legal system in the world is open to the same questions and subject to the same standards, even in countries of different social structures or different stages of development" (1987, vol. 1, p. 45). For example, children are born, and everywhere their names and civil status must be determined. Similarly, in most countries, individuals purchase at least some of their necessities, and the law is called on to regulate those transactions.

Despite its widespread acceptance, the idea that the social issues the law is asked to resolve are so similar as to present a constant across legal systems is, for several reasons, highly questionable. First, there are institutions for which equivalents are not found in all systems. Polygamous marriages are permitted in some societies, for example, and not in others. Moreover, in every society, the issues of practical life are already shaped by history, culture, religion, and language before they are posed as legal questions. Though economics also plays a role, the economic aspect is not necessarily primary. For example, every nation confronts the problem of providing for the poor. But welfare is not simply an economic issue. It raises moral and social questions that, in the particular constellation in which they arise, are often particular to the society in question. Furthermore, the influence of a society's vision extends beyond complex political issues and affects the way even the simplest activity is perceived – and regulated by the law. A good example is the giving of gifts, which, though largely unregulated in some societies, in others is viewed as an act so fraught with risk that it must be carefully policed (Hyland, 1996).

There is yet another difficulty with the presumption that life situations are everywhere the same. In order to find a basis for comparison, functionalist research often abstracts from the concrete details of the situations prevailing in different jurisdictions. "Thus instead of asking, 'What formal requirements are there for sales contracts in foreign law?' it is better to ask, 'How does foreign law protect parties from surprise, or from being held to an agreement not seriously intended?'" (Zweigert and Kötz, 1987, vol. 1, p. 31). The question presumes that a particular legal norm is designed to fulfill this specific purpose, and, even more importantly, that the law is exclusively an instrument crafted to achieve certain ends. In other words, in the process of formulating generalizations such as this, the differences that complicate the analysis are excluded and the answer is smuggled in as one of the presuppositions to the question.

A further methodological premise of functionalist comparative research is the *praesumptio similitudinis* (Zweigert and Kötz 1987, vol. 1, p. 36). Functionalism presumes that legal systems tend to resolve practical questions in the same way. "[D]ifferent legal systems give the same or very similar solutions, even as to detail, to the same problems of life, despite the great differences in their historical development, conceptual structure, and style of operation" (1987, vol. 1, p. 36). Zweigert

189

and Kötz have called this the "basic principle of comparative law" (1987, vol. 1, p. 36). In practice, the presumption often determines the result of a functionalist comparative study.

> [T]he same presumption acts as a means of checking our results: the comparatist can rest content if his researches through all the relevant material lead to the conclusion that the systems he has compared reach the same or similar practical results, but if he finds that there are great differences or indeed diametrically opposite results, he should be warned and go back to check again whether the terms in which he posed his original question were indeed purely functional, and whether he has spread the net of his researches quite wide enough. (*Zweigert and Kötz, 1987, vol. 1, p. 36*)

In other words, the *praesumptio* suggests that comparative research is not complete until it has been demonstrated that the legal systems under consideration reach similar results in similar circumstances. Should a case of actual difference occur, comparativists influenced by functionalist methodology often assume that the major legal systems tend, over time, to converge toward the same solution.

The presumption of similarity has great heuristic value. It suggests that legal systems that differ on one level may, nonetheless, function similarly on another level and that comparative research is not complete until the aspects of similarity have been uncovered. Benefiting from this insight, the adherents of the functionalist method have produced highly significant contributions to comparative study. Perhaps the most suggestive has been the attempt to delineate a *common core* of questions that legal decision makers in widely diverse regimes will, as a practical matter, decide in the same manner (Schlesinger, 1961). The method has been used to great advantage in uncovering regularities with regard to the formation of contracts (Schlesinger, 1968).

Nonetheless, there are difficulties with the *praesumptio*. For one, it encourages reductionism. Differences among legal systems are neglected when, in the main, the solutions from the different systems coincide. Second, the presumption operates to remove from view one of the most important issues in the law, namely the question of the relationship between the law, on the one hand, and norms that arise outside of a legal context, such as conventional morality, on the other. Legal systems take different positions on the question of the extent to which the law should provide a legal sanction for social norms. The *praesumptio* encourages the view that legal and extra-legal regulation fulfill the same function, and, therefore, are essentially the same. "[O]ften the comparatist must go beyond the purely legal devices, for he finds that the function performed in his own system by a rule of law is performed in a foreign system not by a legal rule at all, but by an extra-legal phenomenon" (Zweigert and Kötz, 1987, vol. 1, p. 34). Yet, in legal and moral theory, it makes a great deal of difference whether individuals are free to discover their obligations for themselves or whether their obligations are imposed by the law.

Families of legal systems

Discussion of difference in comparative law has focussed principally on the proper classification of legal systems into a small number of *families*. Comparativists vary widely in their assessment of the number of extant legal families and the criteria to be used when grouping legal systems together.

Turn-of-the-century theorists resorted largely to extra-legal criteria. Sauser-Hall, for example, proposed grouping the legal systems of the world into four families on the basis of the race of the members of the societies in which the legal systems operated (Sauser-Hall, 1913). Geography, language, and cultural affinity were also suggested as criteria. Wigmore concluded that only 16 cultural groupings had managed to elaborate durable legal systems (Wigmore, 1928). A contemporary version of Wigmore's classification distinguishes five legal groupings on the basis of their differing cultural contexts – the law of primitive peoples, ancient law, Euro-American law, the religious legal systems, and the laws of the Afro-Asiatic peoples (Schnitzer, 1961, vol. 1, pp. 133–42).

More recently, however, the criteria have focussed on the historical sources and systematic characteristics of the legal systems themselves. Numerous classifications have been developed. René David, the author of the leading treatise in this tradition, suggested two criteria. The first is whether a lawyer educated in one system would be capable, without undue effort, of practicing in another system. If so, the two systems may be considered to be members of the same family. The second criterion focusses on whether the systems in question are founded on similar philosophical, political, and economic principles (David and Brierley, 1985, pp. 20–1). Based on these criteria, David distinguished three principal groupings – the Romano-Germanic family, socialist legal systems, and the common law – together with a miscellaneous category composed of other conceptions. Another respected treatise, adopting a classification scheme modeled on comparative linguistics, considers as a family those legal systems derived from a common source and distinguishes seven such families – French, German, Scandinavian, English, Russian, Islamic, and Hindu (Arminjon et al., 1950, pp. 47–9). Related results have been reached on the basis of criteria such as characteristic modes of legal thought, distinctive institutions, the nature of the legal sources, and the ideology of the legal system (Zweigert and Kötz, 1987, vol. 1, pp. 68–75).

One of the benefits of family theory in comparative law is that it permits a concurrent investigation of difference and similarity. Those working in this tradition have illuminated the differential workings of the civil and common law traditions (Merryman, 1985; von Mehren and Gordley, 1977). They have also debated the relationship between capitalist and socialist law – in particular, whether, due to differences in social formation, capitalist and socialist legal systems are so different as to render comparison nugatory (Knapp, 1962), or rather whether the two systems are converging (Tunc, 1962).

Family theory, however, also has its limitations. One problem is that the families of legal systems are characterized almost exclusively with regard to a country's system of private law. Since many countries have adopted private law rules from one source and constitutional norms from another, the family approach is unable to explore the uniqueness of the vision presented by each of the individual legal systems. A further difficulty with family theory is that it shifts the focus from a comparison of actual legal systems to an examination of theoretical constructs,

191

such as the proper distinction between the civil and common law traditions. When the question is posed in this manner, there is a risk of transforming multiplicity into polar opposition and the further temptation to select one of the two solutions as the "better" rule.

In practice, family classification has served a largely pragmatic purpose – it renders the task of comparison manageable, since, frequently, only a few representative members of each family are included in a comparative study.

> Mature legal systems are often adopted or extensively imitated by others; as long as these other so-called "affiliated" legal systems maintain the style of the parent system, they usually do not possess to the same degree that blend of originality and balanced maturity in solving problems which characterizes the "significant" legal system. While they are at this stage of development, the comparatist may ignore the affiliate and concentrate on the parent system. (*Zweigert and Kötz, 1987, vol. 1, p. 39*)

The major contribution of family theory – indeed, probably the most ambitious comparative law project ever undertaken – is the *International Encyclopedia of Comparative Law* (David et al., 1973–). Each of the 17 volumes of the *Encyclopedia* examines one of the principal topics of private law, and each in turn is subdivided into a dozen or more book-length chapters. The project's German-language predecessor, Schlegelberger's *Handwörterbuch* (Schlegelberger, 1927–39), surveyed topics in terms of the solutions of the historically most important representatives of the major family traditions. In contrast, the authors of many chapters in the *Encyclopedia* have occasionally highlighted those solutions that present especially interesting characteristics (Drobnig, 1969, p. 225).

Ideal types

Some of the most creative aspects of comparative legal scholarship have been inspired by Max Weber's sociology of law. In Weber's view, the law differs from conventional normative orders by the fact that it depends on a class of professional jurists for its administration and enforcement. Economic and social factors influence the law only indirectly – through the training received by legal practitioners (Weber, 1922, p. 776). This Weberian insight has suggested to comparativists that the differing styles of the various legal systems may be partially due to the social origin and education of their legal notables (*honoratiores*) (Rheinstein, 1970).

Weber distinguished legal systems that are principally concerned with substantive results from those oriented toward the production of formal rules. He also believed that legal systems may possess a high or low degree of rationality. The permutations of these four categories produce four *ideal types* or stages of legal systems: charismatic legal revelation through law prophets, empirical law finding by means of the jurisprudence of legal notables, the imposition of law by secular monarchs or religious authority, and the systematic elaboration of law by professional jurists (Weber, 1922, p. 882).

Following a Weberian methodology, Mirjan Damaska has demonstrated that differences with regard to institutional setting and judicial practice produce differences in substantive and procedural rights (Damaska, 1986, p. 1). Damaska's work is generally regarded as a major achievement of contemporary comparative research. His analysis focusses on the political factors that, regardless of the wording of the laws, largely determine the rendering of justice in a particular legal system. Damaska classifies legal systems into four ideal types, which, like Weber's, result from the permutations of two sets of criteria. As far as the organization of governmental authority is concerned, Damaska distinguishes between the *hierarchical* authority of a classical bureaucracy applying technical standards and the *co-ordinate* authority of nonprofessional decision makers applying community standards. Damaska argues that the first is a useful model of adjudication in the civil law, while the second reflects essential attributes of the common law. The second set of criteria, which concerns the perception of the legitimate ends of government, distinguishes between the adversarial mode of adjudication, designed chiefly for *conflict resolution*, and the inquisitorial mode of judicial process, which is better suited for *activist policy implementation*. The four resulting categories permit Damaska to explore both the differences and the similarities among such diverse forms of adjudication as criminal procedure in Mao's China (activist and hierarchical), Roman–canonical civil procedure (conflict resolving and hierarchical), trials before lay English justices of the peace in the eighteenth century (conflict resolving and co-ordinate), and public interest litigation in the United States (activist and co-ordinate).

Damaska has organized a large amount of comparative and historical material into an understandable pattern, uncovered structural similarities in legal systems of quite different provenance, and demonstrated that the governmental and political context of the law significantly influences the application of its norms. Damaska's work represents a significant advance over traditional family theories that characterize chiefly in terms of the historical source of a system's rules. Nonetheless, Damaska's ideal types are unable to focus on the actually functioning legal systems and the differential visions they contain. Both family theory and the notion of ideal types subsume existing legal systems under a small number of conceptual categories. Those categories can reveal important structural similarities, but, since they tend to emphasize commonality over difference, they ultimately oversimplify complexity (Frankenberg, 1985, p. 422).

Difference theory

A number of contemporary comparative theorists argue that the potential of comparative research is to discover the particular vision of justice and the conception of life under law that is implicit in each individual legal system (Hyland, 1990). These theorists suggest that this potential can be fully realized only if it is acknowledged that legal systems may actually differ – in other words, that no level may be discoverable at which, in any meaningful sense, the differences disappear. The differences relate to features of a legal system that endure over time – and that generally survive even legislative revision.

> The legislators may, indeed, with a stroke of the pen modify the actual legal rules, but these other elements and features nonetheless subsist. They cannot be so arbitrarily changed because they are intimately linked to our civilisation and ways of thinking. The legislators can have no more effect on them than upon our language or our reasoning processes. (*David and Brierley, 1985, p. 19*)

The concern with difference has been present throughout the modern period of comparative scholarship, even though it has played a subsidiary role. For example, René David noted that, when viewed in the perspective of difference, "law appears less as a collection of norms, and more as the expression of a certain civilization, the manner of satisfying a certain conception of the organization of human relations and a certain sentiment of justice" (David, 1961, p. 58). The evolutionary theorists too understood that individual legal systems provide a source of knowledge.

> Every nation has abilities and tasks that it fulfills within its sphere; it has a particular understanding of life and its own conception of the law. For this reason, it will – indeed, it must – achieve something particular. Nonetheless, every nation is also affected by the forces of world development. As a nation develops its particularity, it simultaneously brings all of humanity a step forward. (*Kohler 1901, p. 18*)

The recent focus on difference in contemporary French philosophy, feminist thought, and poststructuralist literary theory has reinvigorated this approach to comparative research. Moreover, critical legal theory suggests that a focus on difference in comparative law may provide jurists with the critical distance needed for the preparation of change in the legal order (Frankenberg, 1985; Legrand, 1995).

The basic methodological postulate for difference-oriented comparative research is that all levels of difference among legal systems – whether in terms of concepts or results – should be acknowledged rather than suppressed. In particular, the marginal differences, which are generally ignored in comparison designed to discover similarities, must be brought to the foreground. Only they permit a careful delineation of the understanding contained in each system. Moreover, it becomes especially important to note which problems are handled within the law and which are regulated by means of extra-legal norms. All reductionist assumptions are to be abandoned, including, for example, the notion of family relationships. In fact, in order to assure that no potential source of wisdom is left unexplored, difference theorists presume that every legal system is different and contains a unique understanding from which we may benefit. In other words, the effect of difference theory in comparative law is a *praesumptio* – or, in good Latin, a *conjectura – dissimilitudinis*.

Difference theorists have advanced several methodological proposals. They suggest, first of all, that comparativists should acknowledge that they are participant

– they observe from the point of view of a particular legal system (Frankenberg, 1985, pp. 441–5). Productive comparison requires of an individual researcher not merely an attempt to avoid prejudice, but also a self-critical awareness of the relationship between self and other. A second tenet of difference theoretical comparison involves a re-examination of the nature of the object of study. The law is conceived not as a collection of doctrines and rules but rather as an aspect of the culture that produced it (Legrand, 1995). Cultural differences are central to any attempt to explain why individual legal systems differ from each other. In particular, the language in which a system is formulated may exercise a decisive influence – the law can be understood as the elaboration of the notion of justice each language contains (Hyland, 1990).

Rodolfo Sacco's conceptual scheme for evaluating differences among legal systems may well represent the most significant contribution to the understanding of difference in recent comparative law (Sacco, 1991). Sacco suggests that what jurists in one system perceive as a unitary rule of law is, in fact, a set of competing and conflicting norms that emerge differently from a close analysis of statutes, case law, and doctrinal discussion. Borrowing from the study of phonetics, Sacco employs the concept of *legal formants* to distinguish these differing conceptions of a legal rule within an individual system. One particularly important insight is that some legal formants are never explicitly formulated as norms. The unformulated formants – which Sacco calls *cryptotypes* – describe the legal mentality of jurists working in a particular legal system. Cryptotypes are often discernible only from a comparative point of view. As a result of the multiplicity of legal formants, a rule codified similarly in two legal systems may, nonetheless, differ in application. After painstaking research, Sacco has documented the subtleties of difference that survive in otherwise similar legal environments.

Merryman has proposed additional concepts for the purpose of analyzing legal systems that resemble each other with regard to the statement of their rules (Merryman, 1981, pp. 379–85). The *extension* of a legal system refers to the location of the boundary between social convention and the law. By a legal system's *penetration* is meant the extent to which the law actually governs matters in a particular society. Legal *culture* refers to the deeply rooted attitudes about the nature and role of the legal system. Other differentiating aspects include legal *structures*, legal *actors*, and legal *processes*.

The increased focus on difference is necessary to fulfill the universally held goals of comparative research, namely the examination of both similarity and difference among the world's legal systems. In this regard, the contribution of contemporary difference theory is to have discovered the reductionism at the core of many comparative methodologies. Difference theorists have also challenged the fundamental – yet largely unevaluated – assumption of much previous applied comparison, namely that the unification of law is always superior to the inconvenience that occasionally results from difference. In fact, the elimination of difference in the law narrows the possibilities for creativity and experimentation and may be compared to the extinction of animal and plant species that results from the destruction of natural habitat. "Actually, both uniformity and particularity among legal systems have their pros and cons. The greater the number of particular legal institutions existing at a given time, the greater may be the probability of certain types of progress" (Sacco, 1991, p. 2).

Despite these contributions, the difference theoretical approach to comparison has not yet fulfilled its promise. To begin with, difference theory has only rarely been employed in actual comparative studies. Moreover, difference theorists are only beginning to delineate a method for achieving their goals. For example, they have not fully clarified what it means to locate the wisdom contained in an individual legal system. Difference theory's expansive definition of the object of comparative study also yields a difficult question of method. From the point of view of difference, a legal system seems to constitute an element of the tapestry of the surrounding culture and to form merely another element of cultural diversity. The question then becomes whether there is any basis for the separate comparison of legal systems, or whether the most appropriate unit of comparison would instead be the entirety of a national or local culture. Difference theory produces a particular theoretical conundrum when it encounters critical legal theory. If difference in the law is largely determined by difference in the larger cultural context, it is difficult to understand how, as critical difference theorists suggest, comparative law will be able to emancipate jurists from the illusion that particular rules are necessary. (See Legrand, 1995, p. 265.)

Perhaps the most difficult problem with regard to difference theory is a political one. It is the need for a politically acceptable solution to the challenge posed in contemporary society by the notion of difference. Though difference is accepted and even celebrated in today's multicultural environment, one of the essential convictions of contemporary intellectual life is that national stereotypes and group characterizations are to be avoided. In order to circumvent this problem, the comparative study of the law has tended to avoid research programs that focus on the particular features of individual legal systems and the differences among them. When differences are discovered, gentility seems to require that the differences be dissolved. The *praesumptio similitudinis* is one obvious product of this concern about difference. Unification of law, as a goal of comparative study, is another. Both the presumption and the effort devoted to the unification of law may be due more to a commitment to original unity than to the necessities of international commerce. In this regard, the task of difference-oriented comparison will be to demonstrate that the pursuit of the wisdom anchored in particularity need not produce politically unacceptable stereotypes.

The current state of the comparative law debate about difference is perhaps best exemplified by the discussion concerning the question of when it is appropriate for one legal system to borrow norms from another. In light of the difference theorists' suggestions that legal systems are rooted in the cultures that created them, some comparativists have argued that norms should be borrowed only cautiously and after a painstaking examination of their actual meaning and effect in the system in which they originated (Kahn-Freund, 1974). Montesquieu had already noted that many laws are so specific to a particular people that they rarely would be suitable in another context (Montesquieu, 1748, bk 1, ch. 3).

In response to this position, Alan Watson reminds us that laws have been borrowed with great frequency and that the borrowing has proven beneficial even when the borrowers were largely unaware of the effect of the norms in their original context (Watson, 1993). As examples, Watson points to the reception of Roman law in early modern Europe, the widespread adoption of the French Civil Code during the nineteenth century, and the more recent importation of other European codes into non-Western nations. To Watson, the prevalence of borrowing suggests that a legal system is not as closely associated with a particular culture or political structure as the difference theorists have suggested.

In evaluating the debate, it has been pointed out that, though some of the borrowings have proven to be beneficial, others have produced results that differ significantly from the source systems, and others still have proven unsuccessful and were eventually abandoned (Merryman, 1981, pp. 367–9). The debate is of exceptional interest and will certainly intensify as the question is posed whether provisions of uniform laws developed by international organizations – such as the Convention on Contracts for the International Sale of Goods (Sponsored by the United Nations Commission on International Trade Law (UNCITRAL)) and UNIDROIT's Principles of International Commercial Contracts – should be adopted into domestic law. It is important to note that the two positions in the debate differ chiefly with regard to their conception of the nature of law. The Watsonian position conceives of a legal system as a set of rules, together, perhaps, with their doctrinal elaboration. Kahn-Freund has suggested that law is an expression of the vision of justice contained in a particular culture or setting. In other words, the questions raised in the course of comparative research coincide with those that are central to the philosophy of law.

Bibliography

Arminjon, P., Nolde, B., and Wolff, M. 1950: *Traité de droit comparé* [*Treatise on Comparative Law*], 3 vols. Paris: LGDJ.

Brown, L. 1971: A century of comparative law in England: 1869–1969. *American Journal of Comparative Law*, 19, 232–52.

Constantinesco, L.-J. 1983: *Traité de droit comparé* [*Treatise on Comparative Law*], 3 vols. Paris: LGDJ, 1972–4; Economica, 1983.

Damaska, M. 1986: *The Faces of Justice and State Authority*. New Haven and London: Yale University Press.

David, R. 1961: Existe-t-il un droit occidental? In Nadelmann et al. (eds), *XXth Century Comparative and Conflicts Law: legal essays in honor of Hessel E. Yntema*, Leyden: A. W. Sythoff, 56–64.

David, R. and Brierley, J. 1985: *Major Legal Systems in the World Today*. London: Stevens & Sons, 3rd edn.

David, R., et al. (eds) 1973–: *International Encyclopedia of Comparative Law*, 17 vols. Tübingen: J. C. B. Mohr; The Hague, Boston, London: Martinus Nijhoff.

del Vecchio, G. [1910] 1915: Science of universal comparative law. In A. Kocourek and J. Wigmore (eds), *Primitive and Ancient Legal Institutions*, Boston: Little, Brown, 61–70.

Drobnig, U. 1969: Methodenfragen der Rechtsvergleichung im Lichte der *International Encyclopedia of Comparative Law*. In E. von Caemmerer et al. (eds), *Ius Privatum Gentium: Festschrift für Max Rheinstein*, Tübingen: J. C. B. Mohr, vol. 1, 221–33.

Frankenberg, G. 1985: Critical comparisons: re-thinking comparative law. *Harvard International Law Journal*, 26, 411–55.

Gutteridge, H. 1949: *Comparative Law*. Cambridge: Cambridge University Press, 2nd edn.

Hug, W. 1932: The history of comparative law. *Harvard Law Review*, 45, 1,027–70.

Hyland, R. [1990] 1994: Babel: A *She'ur*. *Cardozo Law Review*, 11, 1,585–1,612. Reprinted in D. Patterson (ed.), *Postmodernism and Law*, Aldershot, Singapore, Sydney: Dartmouth, 127–54.

—— 1996: Gifts. In R. David et al., *International Encyclopedia of Comparative Law*, vol. 8, ch. 6.

Kahn-Freund, O. 1974: On uses and misuses of comparative law. *Modern Law Review*, 37, 1–27.

Knapp, V. 1962: Verträge im tschechoslowakischen Recht: Ein Beitrag zur Rechtsvergleichung zwischen Ländern mit verschiedener Gesellschaftsordnung. *Rabels Zeitschrift für ausländisches und internationales Privatrecht*, 27, 495–518.

Kohler, J. [1887] 1915: Evolution of law. In A. Kocourek and J. Wigmore (eds), *Primitive and Ancient Legal Institutions*. Boston: Little, Brown, 3–9.

—— [1901] 1978: Über die Methode der Rechtsvergleichung. In K. Zweigert and H.-J. Puttfarken (eds), *Rechtsvergleichung* [*Comparative Law*], Darmstadt: Wissenschaftliche Buchgesellschaft, 18–29.

Lambert, E. [1905] 1978: Conception générale et définition de la science du droit comparé, sa méthode, son histoire. In K. Zweigert and H.-J. Puttfarken (eds), *Rechtsvergleichung* [*Comparative Law*], Darmstadt: Wissenschaftliche Buchgesellschaft, 30–51.

Legrand, P. 1995: Comparative legal studies and commitment to theory. *Modern Law Review*, 58, 262–73.

Maine, H. [1861] 1909: *Ancient Law: its connection with the early history of society and its relation to modern ideas*, ed. F. Pollock, London: John Murray.

Merryman, J. 1981: On the convergence (and divergence) of the civil law and the common law. *Stanford Journal of International Law*, 17, 357–88.

—— 1985: *The Civil Law Tradition: an introduction to the legal systems of Western Europe and Latin America*. Stanford: Stanford University Press, 2nd edn.

Montesquieu, C.-L. [1748] 1977: *The Spirit of the Laws*, 2 vols, ed. D. Carrithers, Berkeley, Los Angeles, London: University of California Press.

Nadelmann, K., et al. (eds) 1961: *XXth Century Comparative and Conflicts Law: legal essays in honor of Hessel E. Yntema*. Leyden: A. W. Sythoff.

Pound, R. 1931: A call for a realist jurisprudence. *Harvard Law Review*, 44, 697–711.

Rabel, E. [1936–58] 1964: *Das Recht des Warenkaufs: Eine rechtsvergleichende Darstellung* [*The Law of the Sale of Goods: a comparative survey*], 2 vols. Berlin and Leipzig: Walter de Gruyter & Co.

Rheinstein, M. 1934: Comparative law and conflict of laws in Germany. *University of Chicago Law Review*, 2, 232–69.

—— 1970: Die Rechtshonoratioren und ihr Einfluß auf Charakter und Function der Rechtsordnungen. *Rabels Zeitschrift für ausländisches und internationales Privatrecht*, 34, 1–13.

Sacco, R. 1991: Legal formants: a dynamic approach to comparative law, parts I and II. *American Journal of Comparative Law*, 39, 1–34, 343–401.

Sauser-Hall, G. 1913: *Fonction et méthode du droit comparé* [*The Function and Method of Comparative Law*]. Geneva: A. Kündig.

Schlegelberger, F. (ed.) 1927–39: *Rechtsvergleichendes Handwörterbuch für das Zivil und Handelsrecht des In- und Auslandes*, 7 vols. Berlin: Franz Vahlen.

Schlesinger, R. 1961: The common core of legal systems: an emerging subject of comparative study. In K. Nadelmann et al. (eds), *XXth Century Comparative and Conflicts Law: legal essays in honor of Hessel E. Yntema*, Leyden: A. W. Sythoff, 65–79.

Schlesinger, R. (ed.) 1968: *Formation of Contracts: a study of the common core of legal systems*, 2 vols. Dobbs Ferry: Oceana; London: Stevens & Sons.

Schnitzer, A. 1961: *Vergleichende Rechtslehre* [*Comparative Jurisprudence*], 2 vols. Basel: Verlag für Recht und Gesellschaft, 2nd edn.

Tunc, A. 1962: La possibilité de comparer le contrat dans des systèmes juridiques à structures economiques différentes. *Rabels Zeitschrift für ausländisches und internationales Privatrecht*, 27, 478–94.

von Mehren, A. and Gordley, J. 1977: *The Civil Law System*. Boston and Toronto: Little, Brown, 2nd edn.

Watson, A. 1993: *Legal Transplants: an approach to comparative law*. Athens and London: University of Georgia Press, 2nd edn.

Weber, M. [1922] 1978: *Economy and Society*, ed. G. Roth and C. Wittich, tr. E. Fischoff et al., Berkeley, Los Angeles, London: University of California Press.

Wigmore, J. 1928: *A Panorama of the World's Legal Systems*, 3 vols. Saint Paul: West.

Zweigert, K. and Kötz, H. 1987: *Introduction to Comparative Law*, 2 vols, tr. T. Weir, Oxford: Clarendon Press, 2nd edn.

Zweigert, K. and Puttfarken, H.-J. 1978: Einleitung. In K. Zweigert and H.-J. Puttfarken (eds), *Rechtsvergleichung* [*Comparative Law*]. Darmstadt: Wissenschaftliche Buchgesellschaft, 1–9.

Zweigert, K. and Puttfarken, H.-J. (eds) 1978: *Rechtsvergleichung* [*Comparative Law*]. Darmstadt: Wissenschaftliche Buchgesellschaft.

12

Interpretation of statutes

WILLIAM N. ESKRIDGE, JR

After a lengthy period of slumber, statutory interpretation has, since 1982, enjoyed a renaissance among scholars of public law. Most human rights protections in the United States today involve the interpretation of statutes rather than the Constitution, and the ordinary business of lawyers is overwhelmingly statutory. The topic is central to an understanding of American public law. The following is a mini-history of "legisprudence," the jurisprudence of interpreting statutes.

The positivist era, 1890s to 1930s: eclecticism and specific intent

Before the 1890s, American theories of statutory interpretation largely tracked English theory, following the plain meaning of the statute, except in the rare case where the plain meaning is absurd (Sutherland, 1891). Thus American theory was in the main positivist: follow the rules enacted by the legislature. But it contained a safety valve – the exception for absurd results – that was jurisprudentially ambiguous. An absurd meaning should not be imputed to the legislature because it was probably not the legislature's intent (positivism) *or* because it is not right, just, or fair (natural law). In a celebrated case, the Supreme Court interpreted a sweeping federal prohibition against prepaying transportation of people immigrating to the United States, not to bar a church's payment of travel expenses for a rector it had engaged (*Holy Trinity Church*, 1892).

Holy Trinity Church was a prolegomenon to an era in which the Court expressed a constitutional hostility to socio-economic regulatory statutes which displaced old common-law rules. The judicial philosophy scorned as "mechanical jurisprudence" (Pound, 1908a) was one nostalgic for the economic libertarian values of the common law, that judges felt were under assault from the new regulatory statutes (Pound, 1908b). The conservatives of the bench and bar in that period expressed their arcadian philosophy through statutory as well as constitutional interpretation (for example, *Caminetti*, 1916). The common law had long been a natural law surrogate in statutory interpretation (for example, statutes in derogation of the common law should be narrowly construed), and an avuncular Supreme Court episodically pursued that theme for two generations (1892–1938).

The rallying cry of anti-Court progressives during this period was distinctly positivist: they contended that the common law was no longer sufficient to the needs of a complex, strife-ridden society, that the legislature was in a better position to gather the facts and make the judgments necessary for such a society, and that the role of courts was to follow these progressive commands of the legislature and give up their *Lochnerian* obduracy. Roscoe Pound argued that the libertarian values imported into statutes by mechanical jurisprudence was "spurious" statutory interpretation, and a betrayal of the proper role of courts in a democracy (Pound, 1907). According to Pound, the proper method of statutory interpretation is "imaginative reconstruction" of the legislature's specific intent.

Justice Oliver Wendell Holmes, Jr, asserted that statutory interpretation is usually just an exercise in determining the statute's plain meaning (Holmes, 1899). Like Pound, Holmes was a positivist who believed in the separation of law and morals, rejected as spurious a judge's effort to read his own values into statutes, and under the banner of legislative supremacy was willing to swallow virtually any silly thing the legislature was willing to enact. Unlike Pound, Holmes emphasized plain meaning, not only for reasons of democratic theory, but also for rule of law reasons. For our polity to be a "government of laws and not men," legal rules must be objectively determinable and "external" to the decision maker. For the same reasons that Holmes favored a "reasonable man" standard in torts cases, he advocated a "normal speaker" theory of plain meaning.

In contrast to both Holmes and Pound, the legal realists in the 1920s and 1930s debunked the possibility of objectivity in statutory or any other kind of interpretation, arguing that judges had enormous law-making discretion, a discretion that was little confined by statutory plain meaning or imaginative reconstruction (Llewellyn, 1934; also Gray, 1921). For example, Judge Benjamin Cardozo defended a decision, questioned by Pound, in which the New York Court of Appeals held that a murdering heir cannot inherit as a result of his crime under state inheritance law (Cardozo, 1921, defending *Riggs* v. *Palmer*, 1884). Max Radin defended such creative interpretation within positivist premises, on the grounds that there is no coherent "original" collective intent embedded in statutes and that any such intent is not binding on the constitutionally independent judiciary (Radin, 1930). These realists unsettled the statutory interpretation debate, for they rejected the legislative positivism of Pound and Holmes as well as the natural law of *Holy Trinity*. Though positivists, the realists viewed the sovereign's rules as the results of the judicial and not the legislative process. And because judges had great leeway in reading their own policy preferences into statutes, the realists emphasized instrumental, policy-driven considerations.

The New Deal ensured the complete defeat of mechanical jurisprudence and offered the prospect of a very attractive positive law regime in which smart young judges and administrators (many of whom were prominent realists) were making policy. Yet at the very moment of progressive positivism's electoral triumph over *Lochnerian* natural law, positivism found itself intellectually vulnerable. The more American intellectuals learned about fascism in Europe, the more they became restive over positivist separation of law and morals (Fuller, 1940; cf. Muller, 1993). Were Nazi decrees "law" in the same way that New Deal statutes were? If not, what gave US law a legitimacy denied to Nazi law?

WILLIAM N. ESKRIDGE, JR

The legal process era, 1938–69: purposive interpretation

American law faced a severe intellectual challenge on the eve of World War II. The insufficiency of both formalism and realism gave rise to a demand for a theory of statutory interpretation that tied law to reason as well as democracy and rules. Judges as well as statutory interpretation theorists grappled with this conundrum, and a tentative answer emerged in the period 1939 to 1942: "law" is the purposive rules devised to facilitate the productive co-operation of interdependent humans in society, and statutory interpretation is therefore the carrying out of the legislature's instrumental purposes (de Sloovere, 1940; Jones, 1940; Nutting, 1940; Radin, 1942).

The new generation of scholars and judges accepted the realist argument that non-elected officials engage in lawmaking, but they suggested that such lawmaking must have some direction from democratic sources. "Legislation has an aim," asserted Justice Felix Frankfurter; "it seeks to obviate some mischief, to supply an inadequacy, to effect a change of policy, to formulate a plan of government" (Frankfurter, 1947, at 538–9). Hence statutory interpretation should be guided by "the principle that in determining the effect of statutes in doubtful cases judges should decide in such a way as to advance the objectives which, in their judgment, the legislature sought to attain by the enactment of the legislation" (Jones, 1940, at 757). By tying statutory interpretation to legislative purpose, these thinkers established a link to democratic theory, and they further argued that this contributed to the rule of law. Remarkably, at the same time an academic consensus was forming against the plain meaning rule and in favor of interpreting statutes to fulfill their purposes, the New Deal Court was filling the US Reports with the fruits of that consensus (*American Trucking*, 1940). Additionally, young scholars were incorporating this view of law into teaching materials that would in the 1950s be published under the same title: "The Legal Process" (see Garrison and Hurst, 1940–1; Feller, Gellhorn, and Hart, 1941–2).

After World War II, legal academics developed a full-fledged "legal process" theory of law and statutory interpretation. The most important early effort was Lon L. Fuller's "The case of the Speluncean explorers," a collection of hypothetical opinions applying a murder statute to explorers who cannibalized one of their number in order to survive while trapped in a cave (Fuller, 1949). The debate among the hypothetical judges sharply contrasted the legislative positivism of holmesian Judge Keen and the judicial positivism of realist Judge Handy, with the New Deal law-as-purpose approach, which is laid out in the opinion of Judge Foster. Foster's opinion maintained, first, that law is premised upon the possibility of human interdependence and that the conditions for that interdependence vanished when the explorers became stuck in the cave. In any event, Foster argued that murder statutes should be interpreted in light of their deterrent purpose, which would not be served by convicting people killing in self-defense or by necessity.

Fuller's jurisprudence provided legal scholars in the emerging legal process school with a political theory on which to rethink statutory interpretation. In the 1950s,

Fuller's colleagues at the Harvard Law School, Professors Henry M. Hart, Jr, and Albert M. Sacks, dilated Hart's pre-war teaching materials into more than 1,400 pages about *The Legal Process* (Hart and Sacks, 1958). Following the views of Foster's opinion, Hart and Sacks's intellectual starting point was the interconnectedness of human beings, and the usefulness of law in helping us coexist peacefully together. "Law is a doing of something, a purposive activity, a continuous striving to solve the basic problems of social living," they asserted (1958, p. 166). Because the legitimacy of law rests upon its purposiveness and not upon abstract social contract principles, Hart and Sacks further asserted that "[e]very statute must be conclusively presumed to be a purposive act. The idea of a statute without an intelligible purpose is foreign to the idea of law and inadmissible" (1958, p. 1,156.)

Hart and Sacks emphasized that the process of law-making hardly ends with the enactment of a statute and that law is a process of reasoned elaboration of purposive statutes by courts and agencies (Hart and Sacks, 1958, ch. 1). Because "every statute . . . has some kind of purpose or objective," ambiguities can be intelligently resolved, first, by identifying that purpose and the policy or principle it embodies, and then by deducing the result most consonant with that principle or policy (1958, chs 1, 7). Hart and Sacks not only rejected the plain meaning rule in favor of a rule of reasonable interpretation, but rejected imaginative reconstruction as well. Their theory of interpretation was a dynamic one, as revealed in their analysis of the "Female juror cases" (Hart and Sacks, 1958, ch. 7). After ratification of the 19th Amendment ensuring women the right to vote, state courts addressed the question whether statutes requiring all eligibile voters to be available for jury service included women, who had been excluded when the statutes were enacted. Hart and Sacks were scornful of opinions refusing to update such statutes to reflect 19th Amendment values and the underlying citizenship purposes of the jury service laws. Similarly, Hart and Sacks echoed Cardozo's endorsement of the dynamic, principle-based result in *Riggs* v. *Palmer* (Hart and Sacks, 1958, ch. 1).

Hart and Sacks's purposive theory of statutory interpretation has remained widely influential and inspired the leading works on statutory interpretation (for example, Dickerson, 1975; Hurst, 1982; Mermin, 1973). The Supreme Court in the 1950s generally followed the approach (for example, *Schwegmann Brothers*, 1951, which contains an excellent debate among the Justices as to whether the Court's responsibility is to apply the statute's purpose, its plain meaning, or the original legislative expectations), and the Warren Court in the 1960s followed a very liberal version of this approach. The plain meaning rule became a virtual dead letter in the 1960s, as the Warren Court invoked statutory purpose to update statutes relating to antitrust, habeas corpus, selective service, consumer welfare, and civil rights. Overruling 100 years of contrary precedent and strongly contradictory legislative history, the Court reinterpreted the Civil Rights Act of 1866 to provide a cause of action for racial discrimination in property and contract transactions (*Jones* v. *Mayer*, 1968). The Warren Court in cases like this one went well beyond Hart and Sacks, who were reluctant to override clear statutory directives in the name of purpose or principle.

Post-legal process theories: 1969–present

Although legal process theory was the dominant mode of thinking about law from the 1940s to the 1960s, since about 1969 it has been under siege. Legal process theory remains fundamentally important and perhaps even pre-eminent, but it has fragmented, partly in response to these new challenges.

Revival of positivism: formal theories of interpretation

The ascendancy of legal process coincided with a period of sustained growth and expansion in American society, a period that ended no later than 1973. After a generation of economic and legal binging, America rediscovered scarcity in the 1970s, and statutory interpretation in both theory and practice reflected this and the concomitant interest in economic theories of interpretation. Economics-inspired scholars saw statutes as precisely delineated deals, rather than as mini-constitutions evolving to satisfy broad purposes (Posner, 1977). Such scholars also tended to view statutes as deals that were wont to distribute rents to specific groups, rather than as measures in the public interest, as Hart and Sacks assumed them to be (Easterbrook, 1984). This engendered a more beady-eyed approach to statutory interpretation, emphasizing either original intent (Posner, 1985) or text (Easterbrook, 1983).

The Supreme Court of Chief Justice Warren Burger amply reflected this develop-ment, and indeed did so ahead of the academy. The milestone was Chief Justice Burger's opinion in *TVA v. Hill* (1976). The issue was whether the Endangered Species Act of 1973 precluded the completion of a $100 million dam to ensure the survival of a species of snail darter. Although the cost was lavish and the result unreasonable to him, Burger applied the statute's plain meaning to the letter – and sided with the snail darter against TVA. This opinion was an important turn-ing point, giving the plain meaning rule new life after a generation of desuetude. In the 1980s, a group of "new textualist" judges and scholars pressed the plain meaning rule as the only legitimate mode of statutory interpretation, and Justice Antonin Scalia has been the leading exemplar of the plain meaning rule on the Rehnquist Court (Eskridge, 1994, ch. 7). The new textualism takes a harder line than plain meaning cases such as *TVA v. Hill* against considering either legislative history or reasonable results. Its motto would be that a judge should consider the text, the whole text, and nothing but the text.

The new textualism is inspired by a particularly dogmatic positivism (Scalia, 1988): under Article I, § 7, of the Constitution, all that is "law" is the text actually adopted by the legislature and presented to the chief executive (Scalia, concurring in *Bock Laundry*, 1989). Nothing else should count. For essentially the same rea-sons suggested by Radin, the new textualists posit that legislative intent and pur-pose are spongy and incoherent concepts that cloud rather than illuminate statutory meaning. "Imagine how we would react to a bill that said, 'From today forward, the result in any opinion poll among members of Congress shall have the effect of law.' We would think the law a joke at best, unconstitutional at worst.

This silly 'law' comes uncomfortably close, however, to the method by which courts deduce the content of legislation when they look to the subjective intent" (Easterbrook, 1988). Additionally, the new textualists believe that any freedom judges feel to consult legislative history or evaluate the reasonableness of results, will increase the ambit of judicial discretion, an unhealthy development in a democracy (Scalia, 1985–6). Finally, leading exemplars of the new textualism are inspired by traditional liberal presumptions against state interference in the private sphere (for example, Easterbrook, 1983).

Critical scholarship and normativism

The legal process vision of law as reasoned elaboration of legitimate legislative activity was persuasive in the 1950s in part because of society's çonsensus about what is "reasonable" and who is "legitimate." That consensus shattered in the 1960s, as it became clear that most Americans – women, people of color, gays and lesbians, people living in poverty, non-English-speaking citizens – had not been consulted as to what is reasonable and who is legitimate. When these were heard from in the 1960s, consensus died, and it remained dead for a generation of identity politics. Critical scholars have developed anti-legal process insights into public law out of this experience.

Hart and Sacks implicitly claimed that all law, legislative as well as judicial, is (or can be) rational, objective, and neutral. Formalist scholars assert a dichotomy between rational, objective, neutral principles the judiciary is obliged to enforce and irrational, subjective, partisan rent-seeking which the legislature is entitled to adopt. Critical scholars, in turn, claim that *all* law, legislative as well as judicial, is ultimately arational, subjective, and ideological; they further claim that the difference between neutral principles and partisan politics is hard to divine and impossible to apply (Brest, 1982; Peller, 1985).

> It is as much a myth that courts can determine whether a statute fit when it was passed, or fits today, as it is a myth that prescient courts can use the perceived values of tomorrow's majority in a value-neutral way. As much as shaping the present by predicting the future, courts will shape the present by interpreting the past. (*Hutchinson and Morgan, 1982*)

Critical scholars are skeptical about the premises or operation of pluralist positivism (Unger, 1975). For example, they reject the concept that "interests" are exogenous facts and claim that interests are socially constituted and subject to change through politics (Brest, 1982). Attitudes and values are, similarly, subject to change; and much of the critical agenda is a call to transform our society by alerting it to inhuman modes of oppression and anomie. Hence, some of the critical scholars who have set forth a positive vision of government have urged a redefinition of what "law" does. Law's agenda should not be determinacy, objectivity, or certainty (the legal process, pluralist hallmarks of statutory law), but rather "edification" (Singer, 1984). The law is pulled toward formalism and its concomitant certainty, apparently because of fears that uncertainty about what exactly the law is will leave us without fair means of regulating private conflicts, or even of knowing how to behave, and will encourage predatory conduct by the government and private power centers. Legal rules do not protect us against these horribles and that, in truth, the main value of legal rules is constitutive: the formulation of rules is how we create and express shared values.

For these and other reasons, at least some critical scholars insist that statutory interpretation be explicitly normativist, because law itself rests upon social justice rather than following the rules laid down. A decision that reflects unjust racial or sexual power alignments is unacceptable. Stated less strongly, a normativist viewpoint could maintain that all statutes be interpreted as though they had been enacted yesterday, and therefore normatively updated to reflect current values (Aleinikoff, 1988).

The new legal processes: positivism, principles, and pragmatism

Legal process theory remains important in American law, but for recent generations of lawyers process theory has taken on new meanings and nuances. The relatively traditional process thinkers emphasize the positivist features of that philosophy: its commitment to neutrality and neutral principles, the principle of institutional settlement, and the importance of continuity, precedent, and tradition in law (for example, Farber, 1989; Redish, 1991; Maltz, 1991). This group of thinkers is on the whole eclectic but formalist in its approach to law, emphasizing legislative supremacy and, with it, the importance of both textual plain meaning and legislative intent.

At the other side of the spectrum, but still within the legal process tradition, are the progressives, who emphasize law's purposivism, the fidelity owed by officials to reason, and the central role of public values (Calabresi, 1982; Eskridge, 1994, ch. 5; Sunstein, 1990). Common themes tie together these process progressives. One is anti-pluralist: legislation must be more than the accommodation of exogenously defined interests; law-making is a process of value creation that should be informed by theories of justice and fairness. Another theme is that legislation too often fails to achieve this aspiration and that creative law-making by courts and agencies is needed to ensure rationality and justice in law. A final theme is the importance of dialogue or conversation as the means by which innovative law-making can be validated in a democratic polity and by which the rule of law can best be defended against charges of unfairness or illegitimacy (Minow, 1987).

The distinction between progressive and progressive process theorists may be captured in Ronald Dworkin's distinction between a pluralist "rulebook community," in which citizens generally agree to obey rules created by the government, and a "community of principle," in which citizens see themselves governed by basic principles, not just political compromises (Dworkin, 1986). The latter is a worthier sense of community, Dworkin argues, and legislation as well as adjudication must be evaluated by its contribution to the principled integrity of the community. Thus, in Dworkin's ideal community of principle, "integrity in legislation" requires law-makers to try to make the total set of laws morally coherent. Like justice and fairness, integrity in the law contributes to the sorority/fraternity of the body politic, the moral community that bonds the nation together. The role of courts is to interpret authoritative statements of law in light of the underlying principles of the community. In the "hard cases" of statutory interpretation, like *TVA* v. *Hill*, the best interpretation is the one that is most consonant with the underlying values of society and makes the statute the best statute it can be, within the limitations imposed by the statutory language.

In between the process formalists and the progressives lie a centrist group, which travels under the banner of "pragmatism" (Eskridge and Frickey, 1990; Patterson, 1995; Posner, 1990; Radin, 1989). These thinkers emphasize the eclectic and instrumental features of the process tradition: legal reasoning is a grab bag of different techniques, including not just textual analysis, but also sophisticated appreciation of the goals underlying the legal text and the consequences of adopting different interpretations. Law involves a balance between form and substance, tradition and innovation, text and context. Pragmatism probably best captures the actual practice of courts and agencies, but provides little normative direction for that practice.

References

Aleinikoff, T. A. 1988: Updating statutory interpretation. *Michigan Law Review*, 87, 20.
Bork, R. H. 1990: *The Tempting of America*.
Brest, P. 1982: Interpretation & interest. *Stanford Law Review*, 34, 765.
Calabresi, G. 1982: *A Common Law for the Age of Statutes*.
Cardozo, B. N. 1921: *The Nature of the Judicial Process*.
de Sloovere, F. 1940: Extrinsic aids in the interpretation of statutes. *University of Pennsylvania Law Review*, 88, 527.
Dickerson, R. 1975: *The Interpretation and Application of Statutes*.
Dworkin, R. 1986: *Law's Empire*.
Easterbrook, F. H. 1983: Statutes Domains. *University of Chicago Law Review*.
—— 1984: The Supreme Court, 1983 term – foreword: the Court and the economic system. *Harvard Law Review*, 98, 4.
—— 1988: The role of original intent in statutory construction. *Harvard Journal of Law and Public Policy*, 11, 59, 65.
Eskridge, W. N., Jr, 1994: *Dynamic Statutory Interpretation*.
—— and Frickey. P. P. 1990: Statutory interpretation as practical reasoning. *Stanford Law Review*, 41, 321.
Farber, D. 1989: Statutory interpretation and legislative supremacy. *Georgia Law Journal*, 78, 281.
Feller, A. H., Gellhorn, W., and Hart, Jr, H. M., 1941–2: *Materials on Legislation*.
Frank, J. 1947: Words and music: some remarks on statutory interpretation. *Columbia Law Review*, 47, 1,259.
Frankfurter, F. 1947: Some reflections on reading statutes. *Columbia Law Review*, 47, 527.
Fuller, L. L. 1940: *The Law in Quest of Itself*, 122–5.
—— 1949: The case of the Speluncean explorers. *Harvard Law Review*, 62, 616.
Garrison, L. and Hurst, W. 1940–1: *Law in Society*.

Gray, J. C. 1921: *The Nature and Sources of Law.*

Hart, H. M., Jr and Sacks, A. [1958] 1994: *The Legal Process: basic problems in the making and application of law,* ed. W. N. Eskridge, Jr and P. P. Frickey.

Holmes, O. W., Jr 1899: The theory of legal interpretation. *Harvard Law Review,* 12, 417, 419.

Hurst, J. W. 1982: *Dealing with Statutes.*

Hutchinson, A. and Morgan, D. 1982: Calabresian sunset: statutes in the shade. *Columbia Law Review,* 82, 1,752, 1,772–3.

Jones, H. W. 1940: Extrinsic Aids in the Federal Courts. *Iowa Law Review,* 25, 737.

Landes, W. and Posner, R. A. 1975: The independent judiciary in an interest-group perspective. *Journal of Law and Economics,* 18, 875.

Llewellyn, K. 1934: The Constitution as an institution. *Columbia Law Review,* 34, 1.

Maltz, E. M. 1991: Rhetoric and reality in the theory of statutory interpretation. *Boston University Law Review,* 71, 767.

Minow, M. 1987: The Supreme Court, 1986 term. *University Law Review. Harvard Law Review,* 101, 10.

Nutting, C. B. 1940: The ambiguity of unambiguous statutes. *Minnesota Law Review,* 24, 509.

Patterson, D. M. 1995: *Law and Truth.*

Peller, G. 1985: The metaphysics of American law. *California Law Review,* 73, 1,152.

Posner, R. A. 1985: *The Federal Courts.*

—— 1990: *The Problems of Jurisprudence.*

Pound, R. 1907: Spurious interpretation. *Columbia Law Review,* 7, 379.

—— 1908a: Common law and legislation. *Harvard Law Review,* 21, 383, 384–5.

—— 1908b: Mechanical jurisprudence. *Columbia Law Reivew,* 8, 605.

Radin, M. J. 1989: Reconsidering the rule of law. *Boston University Law Review,* 69, 781.

Radin, M. 1930: Statutory interpretation. *Harvard Law Review,* 43, 863, 870–1.

—— 1942: Short way with statutes. *Harvard Law Review,* 56, 388.

Redish, M. H. 1991: *The Federal Courts in the Political Order.*

Scalia, A. 1985–6: Speech delivered at various law schools.

—— 1989: The rule of law as a law of rules. *University of Chicago Law Review,* 56, 1,775.

Singer, J. 1984: The player and the cards: nihilism and legal theory. *Yale Law Journal,* 94, 1.

Sunstein, C. R. 1990: *After the Rights Revolution.*

Sutherland, J. 1891: *Statutes and Statutory Construction.*

Unger, R. 1975: *Knowledge and Politics.*

Cases

Church of the Holy Trinity v. *United States,* 143 U.S. 457 (1892).

Caminetti v. *United States,* 242 U.S. 470 (1917).

United States v. *American Trucking Associations, Inc.,* 310 U.S. 534 (1940).

Schwegmann Bros. v. *Calvert Distillers Corp.,* 341 U.S. 384 (1951).

Jones v. *Alfred H. Mayer Co.,* 392 U.S. 409 (1968).

TVA v. *Hill,* 437 U.S. 153 (1976).

Green v. *Bock Laundry Machine Co.,* 490 U.S. 504 (1989).

13

Conflict of laws

PERRY DANE

Conflict of laws, or "private international law," adjudicates the private law effects of the awkward fact that the world consists of distinct jurisdictions. Choice of law, a branch of conflict of laws, decides the relevance of foreign law to a case heard in one jurisdiction, but having connections to others. For example, a New York driver takes a Turkish passenger on a car trip in Ontario. The car crashes. The passenger sues the driver in a British court. In deciding whether the driver is immune from suit by the passenger, should the court look to the law of New York, Turkey, Ontario, or England?

William Prosser, the tort systematizer, wrote in 1953 that choice of law "is a dismal swamp, filled with quaking quagmires, and inhabited by learned but eccentric professors who theorize about mysterious matters in a strange and incomprehensible jargon. The ordinary court, or lawyer, is quite lost when engulfed and entangled in it" (Prosser, 1953, p. 971).

More recently, choice of law has sometimes resembled the law's psychiatric ward. It is a place of odd fixations and schizophrenic visions. It abounds with purported cures to alleged diseases, and questions about which are crazier.

The scolding tone of both these metaphors, however, obscures the real difficulties of choice of law, and the opportunities it provides to legal theory. In truth, choice of law is a psychiatric ward *in* a swamp, a jurisprudential wilderness encounter group. It is an exercise that forces the law to reveal its deepest assumptions, and to rub raw its contradictions and demons. Moreover, it is an urgently practical challenge, a rare genuine example of applied jurisprudence.

Choice of law has long been a scene of struggle. In the United States, and to a degree elsewhere, this century has seen an epic battle between two very different views.

The first is classical choice of law, drawn most fully by Joseph Beale in the 1930s in his treatise (1935) and in the *Restatement of Conflict of Laws* (American Law Institute, 1934). Like most "classical" outlooks, it lasted, in its most refined formulation, for only a slice of time, and was both the culmination of, and a reaction to, earlier trends.

The second view – or set of views – might be called modernist choice of law. It began, even before classicism reached its peak, with Walter Wheeler Cook (1942) and others. Its influence grew in the 1950s and 1960s with the work of Brainerd

Currie (1963) and the drafting of the *Second Restatement* (American Law Institute, 1971). It grew into a powerful academic and judicial revolution, with dissonant branches. That revolution has become choice of law's new orthodoxy. It remains to be seen whether more recent scholarship, and judicial disenchantment, will spark a counter-revolution.

Most of this article is organized around the dispute between the classical and modernist outlooks. First, it outlines the premisses of classicism. Then it discusses the modernist challenges to most of those premisses. In its concluding sections, the article turns to other debates, inside each of these traditions, or transcending the differences between them.

Classical choice of law rested on seven pillars. It was not always fully faithful to each. Some were matters of degree. Together, however, these propositions defined the classical commitment.

(1) The first pillar was so ingrained it was rarely noticed. In common with the prevailing imagination, classical choice of law assumed that the only sources of effective legal norms were nation-states and their juridical divisions. Some legal theories recognize the independent authority of religious or other non-state communities. Classical choice of law had no use for such pluralism. It grudgingly accepted tribal law, but only as sanctioned by the territorial law of a state.

(2) The classical thinkers also assumed that choice of law was typically not a matter of international law or, among states in the United States, federal law. Nor was it grounded in the self-executing reach of one sovereign's law in another sovereign's courts. It was the law of individual forums, each adjudicating the rights of litigants before it. Classical authors often said that a forum was not bound by, nor did it enforce, foreign law as such. Rather, when appropriate, it enforced foreign-created rights.

Nothing in the classical view precluded control of choice of law from beyond or outside the forum. (This is not the place to discuss more practical aspects of the international or federal dimensions of choice of law.) Notable, however, is how classicism combined a commitment to state autonomy with an account of how distinct sovereigns might make sense of each other's role in the definition of rights.

(3) This leads to the third, most jurisprudentially laden, pillar of classicism, which might be called "vestedness." (See Dane, 1987.) Classical choice of law insisted that substantive legal rights vested, on the basis of real-world, primary events, and behaviors. A court's job was to find those pre-existing rights. Choice of law was not like tort or contract law or the like, which applied legal norms to primary behavior. It did not reflect an *exercise* of law-making authority, but an effort, from the perspective of the forum, to *allot* that authority. It was a second-order process, the law that found which law would apply.

The operational meaning of vestedness is that a forum should not, in doing choice of law, take its own identity as a variable (Dane, 1987, pp. 1,205–7). To do so would be to assume that a party's pre-existing rights change when the party enters a particular forum. Thus, a tort choice of law rule that looks to the "law of the place of injury" is consistent with vestedness. So is a rule that looks to the "law of common domicile" or even "the law favoring recovery." But a rule that specifies the "law of the forum," as forum, is not.

Vestedness did not require that outcomes be identical whatever the forum in which a case was brought. For one thing, different forums could have different choice of law regimes, each itself consistent with vestedness. Even if forums did have the same choice of law rules, that would not, in the classical conception, require identical results. Substantive law created vested rights. Adjective law, even if outcome-determinative, did not, and classicism was unperturbed by that. Finally, vestedness did not require that a forum with jurisdiction always enforce even substantive rights. Doctrine treated some causes of action as non-transitory; their enforcement was left to the jurisdiction that created them (American Law Institute, 1934, §§ 610–11). More generally, the classical view recognized a forum's power to decline to enforce foreign norms that violated its own "public policy" (American Law Institute, 1934, § 612). Traditionally, though, this idea only referred to the forum's prerogative to dismiss a case without reaching the merits. It was not a general warrant for a forum to apply its own law.

Because vestedness could not, and was not designed to, produce uniformity of result, it was not just a strategy to deter forum-shopping or advance another purely instrumental goal. Rather, it reflected a particular vision of adjudication, to which we will have to return.

(4) The fourth pillar of classical choice of law is often called "territorialism." This label is misleading, however. Any choice of law theory grounded in the division of the world into territorial states will be "territorial." The question is *which* territorial variables the theory finds relevant.

Western choice of law since the middle ages has struggled with two forms of territorialism. One form – call it person-territorialism – looks to where actors come from, as defined by domicile, citizenship, or similar notion. The other, which is what most commentators mean when they speak of "territorialism," but could more rightly be called act-territorialism, looks to where relevant events, such as an injury or the making of a contract, occurred.

Classical American choice of law doctrine, except in matters of status, rejected domicile or citizenship as variables in choice of law. Even contractual capacity, for example, was governed, not by domicile, as in Continental doctrine, but by the law of the place where the contract was made.

Leading advocates of classical American choice of law admitted, though, the contingent character of their emphasis on act-territorialism. They thought personal law archaic (Beale, 1935, § 5.2 at 52). Their American sensibility affirmed an ethic of mobility and the fluidity of political and legal affiliation. But, in contrast to their view of other aspects of their system, they never claimed that looking to domicile would be incoherent, or violate any axioms of jurisprudence.

(5) The fifth pillar of classical American choice of law was an effort to frame choice of law rules that were independent of substantive issues. This commitment was multilayered, and very much a matter of degree.

At the least, it meant that choice of law rules should not prejudge substantive outcomes. Its rules specified which law would apply, not which result would prevail.

The substance-independence of classical choice of law meant more than out-come-neutrality, however. It also meant that their rules – "place of injury" for tort, "place of making" for contracts, and so on – did not depend on particularized assessments of state interests in specific legal rules. This attitude might be called formalism, except for the vagueness and disutility of the term. It is better to say that the classical view relied on general, unmodulated, ideas about how the nor-mative concerns of jurisdictions translated into the creation of legal rights.

Nevertheless, classical choice of law did not claim to escape substance entirely. It had to, even at the second-order level on which it operated, reach conclusions about what tort law was about, what an "injury" was, where a contract was "made." Indeed, on this last question, it relied on a set of rules, including a "mailbox" rule, that were explicitly drawn from "general contract law." These second-order rules did not predetermine first-order outcomes, even on the exact same issues. But their justification and provenance, within the classical logic, was never fully explained.

(6) The sixth commitment of classical choice of law, apparent from the examples already cited, was to a regime of rules. Classical choice of law strove for objective, automatic, simple, criteria.

Like most regimes of rules, this one did not always live up to its billing. As critics long ago complained, it elided some hard questions for which its rules were little help. More interesting, there were some instances in which classicism explicitly recognized a place for more "practical" standards, not susceptible to simple rules (for example, American Law Institute, 1934, § 358, Comment b).

(7) Finally, classical choice of law rested on what might be called instantaneity. Not only did rights vest. And not only did they vest on act-territorial, bright-line rules. They also vested from facts at an instant in time. For torts, for example, the magic instant was the injury – the "last event" necessary to the cause of action. Thus, even if all the conduct causing an injury occurred in state X, and all the consequences of that injury were felt in Y, if the injury occurred in Z, the law of Z governed.

Again, instantaneity had its wrinkles. But the determination to find a magic instant for the creation of every right, and to collapse complex narratives into that instant, was, as much as anything, the source of what most observers, even other-wise sympathetic, have thought to be the frequent arbitrariness of the classical scheme.

These seven ideas joined into a single picture of choice of law. In that picture, the occurrence of a specific event, in a defining moment, in a given place, led the law of that place to fix a set of rights. The self-imposed duty of a forum was to search for the act and the moment and the place and the rights.

There is, however, a crucial point rarely made by either friends or foes of classicism. The pieces of this picture, though they fit together, were also analytically distinct. Vestedness does not require act-territorialism. Rules do not require instantaneity. And so on. To be sure, there are connections. But in a different history, all these issues could have configured themselves in any number of other combinations.

Oddly, choice of law modernists have not questioned the first two premises of classical doctrine – the exclusivity of states and the limited relevance of international or federal law. If anything, modernist trends have reinforced both these ideas.

The modernists have, however, mounted sustained attacks on each of the other five pillars of classicism. These attacks intertwine. The following discussion wrenches them apart, to study the significance of each. We are more interested in particular arguments than in identifying all the modernist factions. Also, some themes are postponed that a more doctrinal account of modernist choice of law would put first. The order of presentation instead will be, roughly, from the least to the most interesting.

(1) The least surprising element of modernist choice of law, echoing other fields of law, has been its retreat from a regime of rules. This retreat has never been wholesale. But the basic claim under it is a matter of modernist consensus: the connections between legal regimes and facts in the world are not on–off, logically exclusive couplings, but are matters of degree, like gravitational attraction.

From this basic insight have come diverse approaches. These include impressionistic searches for a legal issue's "center of gravity," multi-factor inquiries into which state has the "most significant relationship" to an issue (American Law Institute, 1971, §§ 145, 188), and single-factor balances (Baxter, 1963, pp. 8–20). Putting aside such specifics, though, the progress of rule-skepticism in the field has matched similar stories elsewhere: tentative incursions into the old rules, bouts of liberated anarchy, efforts to reduce the anarchy to formulas, reduction of the formulas to generalizations (or new rules), a breakdown of those generalizations, and so on.

(2) The modernist attack on instantaneity has tracked the attack on rules. Its intellectual resonance, however, is distinct.

Various fields of law – contracts comes to mind – assumed, in their own, contemporaneous, classical ages, that rights vested in an instant. Before that instant, no right existed. After that instant, everything that happened just unwound the spring.

The modern trend has been to relax such strictures. Rights can mature and evolve. Moreover, the retrospective adjudication of rights can understand them to arise out of a set of events, without the need to pinpoint the moment of their creation.

213

Choice of law has taken a similar, if more radical, turn. In contract law, the idea that contracts form at an instant is still alive, if struggling. But instantaneity in choice of law, the magic moment that locks everything in place, has lost almost all its currency. The instant has given way to a full-scale narrative, a set of defining events over time and space.

The pregnant question, though, is how to cabin that narrative. A revealing example is the problem of "after-acquired domicile." Consider a choice of law regime that, as many modern approaches do, emphasizes domicile. What if, after an accident, or analogous event relevant to a cause of action, one of the parties establishes a new domicile? Is this after-acquired domicile germane to the choice of law inquiry? Many courts and theorists, whose methodologies might otherwise lead them to answer yes, have held back. However they articulate their reasons, the intuition at work seems to be that there is some proper boundary to the events that tell the story of a cause of action. After-acquired domicile falls outside that story.

(3) Mention of after-acquired domicile anticipates the next point of the modernist attack. This is the shift, albeit relative, from act-territorialism to person-territorialism.

Many modernist authors cast their criticism of act-territorialism as an attack on formalism and reification. Cook, in a famous discussion of married women's contracts, argued that the classical view that a woman could lose her contractual disability by just crossing a border was unrealistic and arbitrary (1942, pp. 434–8). Building on Cook, Currie based much of his system on a claim that there was a category of "false conflicts" that classical choice of law overlooked, and for which its rules could only produce correct results by sheer chance (1963, pp. 107–10).

Currie's "false conflicts," however, were just cases of common domicile. Through the lens of person-territorialism, such cases will, naturally, be easy. But from an act-territorial perspective, there is an exactly analogous set of "false conflicts" in which all the relevant events of an interaction take place in one jurisdiction.

The real dispute between act- and person-territorialism was not about formalism, but over accounts of legal jurisdiction and personal affiliation, accounts whose implications extend to the great issues of war and peace ravaging the present age. Critics of act-territorialism argue that polities are composed of people, not plots of land. The defenders of act-territorialism reply that, however true this is, the people of a polity still create a legal regime whose reach is territorial (Twerski, 1971). Expectations are territorial. So are entitlements. Persons who cross into a state come under the protection and control of that state.

Moreover, choice of law modernists do a good deal of reifying themselves. Domicile, and related concepts such as residence or citizenship, are all legal constructs. It is unclear whether any of them can capture the full texture of the links between persons and states.

(4) Modernism has challenged the classical claim to substance-independence. That challenge has been as multi-layered as the claim itself.

At one level, almost all modernists agree that choice of law must look to the particulars of state interests in legal questions. In this consensus lurk vital differences, some of which will be taken up later. At the root of the consensus, though, is the conviction that the abstract sureties of the old regime must be tested by this question: which states would care about the outcome of a case, and why?

The modernists have never quite resolved, however, to what extent their account of state "interests" is descriptive or normative. As Lea Brilmayer demonstrates, this has led some devotees to invoke "interests" not grounded in any empirical inquiry into the actual policies of real states (Brilmayer, 1995, pp. 101–9).

A more serious problem is that some schools of interest analysis have yet to give a satisfactory account of the theoretical limits to legitimate state interests. Modernist purists disdain certain half-way approaches, such as those that look to "centers of gravity" or "most significant relationships," that leaven their concern for "interests" with a search for relevant "contacts" between states and the facts of a case. The purists argue that these approaches perpetuate, if with a broader palate, the classical tendency to ignore questions of "policy." Nevertheless, looking for relevant "contacts" at least implicitly recognizes the normative dimensions of the problem. If "contacts" without "interests" are vacuous, "interests" without "contacts" are unanchored.

A more controversial strain of modernism has argued that choice of law analysis should give up, not only its indifference to substance, but its neutrality too. Some authors have urged specific substantive preferences in choice of law, such as one favoring tort victims over tortfeasors. Others, including Robert Leflar (1966), have argued that courts should undertake an explicit, objectively defined, search for the "better law."

Such proposals sometimes seem the most severe departures yet from classical choice of law. But they actually raise rich and useful questions from the classical perspective.

Recall that a friend of the other pillars of classical choice of law, specifically vestedness, would not object, in principle, to abandoning outcome-neutral choice of law rules. To say that choice of law is a second-order law about laws is not to say that it can have no substantive content. The question is where the content comes from.

Outcome-oriented methods, such as the one favoring tort plaintiffs, can reflect a view that states share certain underlying policies despite their differences on details of law. Similarly, the "better law" approach can rest on a sense that the reach of a legal norm depends, at least in part, on its fit into the shape and trajectory of general legal culture. These accounts are fascinating, if only for their echoes of long lost views of a "general common law." But they do not contradict the second-order character of choice of law.

It is a different matter if the reason for introducing substantive concerns into choice of law is the infiltration of the forum's own, first-order, substantive views. Interestingly, the proponents of outcome-driven choice of law have never quite settled between these two types of argument.

215

(5) These thoughts lead to the question of vestedness itself. That question has been put off so far, so that its glare would not overwhelm the other elements of the battle between the classical and modernist schools. Nevertheless, the attack on vestedness has been the most powerful part of the modernist program, which most sharply illuminates larger issues in legal theory.

The crucial moment in the modernist attack on vestedness came when Brainerd Currie moved from "false conflicts" to his solution of "true conflicts." A true conflict exists when both the forum and another state have a genuine, serious, interest in a case. Currie rejected, head on, the notion that a forum should not treat its own identity as a variable in the choice of law calculus. Instead, he wrote, the "sensible . . . thing for any court to do, confronted with a true conflict of interests, is to apply its own law" (Currie, 1963, p. 119). To understand the profound implications of this statement, however, requires some perspective.

Vestedness in the classical scheme rested on two distinctions built into a traditional, norm-based, view of law and adjudication (Dane, 1987, pp. 1,218–23). The first distinction is between the existence of legal rights and their enforcement. With this distinction in hand, the classical model could describe choice of law as a second-order search for rights that existed, in some objective sense, independent of the forum in which a case was brought.

The second distinction is between the reason for a legal norm and the reason for enforcing the rights created by that norm. Even if the reason for a legal norm is one or another substantive policy, the reason for enforcing the norm is to vindicate the system of rights itself, apart from that policy. With this distinction, the classicists could justify how a forum with one set of substantive convictions would be willing to enforce rights established under legal norms expressing radically different substantive convictions.

One way of appreciating the history of the choice of law revolution is to notice that Walter Wheeler Cook took aim at the first of these distinctions, and Brainerd Currie at the second.

Cook pressed the claim that, when a court engaged in choice of law, it was not, despite appearances, applying foreign law. All it was doing was enforcing a "right created by its own law," but incorporating, in the definition of that right, "a rule of decision identical, or at least highly similar though not identical, in scope with a rule of decision found in the system of law in force in another state or country" (Cook, 1942, p. 20).

This argument, or "local law" theory, seems at first to be mere quibbling. If anything, it resembles the classical mantra that a court cannot, strictly, enforce foreign law, but only, by operation of its own law, foreign-created rights.

Cook, however, had more in mind. He was a leader of American legal realism. His project, beyond choice of law, was to advance and refine the nominalist and behaviorist strain of legal realism, which – contrary to norm-based jurisprudence – argued that law was nothing more than the behavior of legal institutions engaged in the exercise of power. Courts, in this view, could do right by parties. But they were not in the job of finding "rights," at least distinctly legal rights, in the sense of entitlements with a real, objective, juridical existence apart from their enforcement.

216

Cook's view collapsed the distinction between first-order and second-order decisions. Classicism required courts to rise above themselves, so to speak, to find the proper law. But in a behaviorist jurisprudence, what counted was what courts did. If a court, to do right by the parties, incorporated a foreign "rule of decision," this was no different in principle from what it did in a purely domestic case. Thus, in a tort case, a court might consider, as relevant data, the legal standards in effect where certain acts were done, and bring those standards to bear. But this would be the forum's tort law at work, not a second-order effort to referee between the forum's law and foreign law.

Currie accepted Cook's view that a court doing choice of law was only doing "local law." But that still left the question of when it should incorporate foreign "rules of decision." Currie's answer, that it should not do so if it had a genuine interest in a case, rested on a simple observation. If a forum applies its own law, "it can be sure at least that it is consistently advancing the policy of its own state" (Currie, 1963, p. 119). Put another way, Currie – in violent contrast with the classical view – assumed that the only persuasive reason for enforcing a legal norm was to advance the policy or substantive moral vision underlying the norm.

Thus, the quarrel between classical and modern choice of law is also a quarrel between radically different visions of law. How this quarrel will work out remains unclear. The legacy of legal realism persists. A new jurisprudence of rights has appeared, but it is only beginning, tentatively and sporadically, to influence choice of law.

Nevertheless, Currie's solution to true conflicts, though it shaped the modernist conversation, has, in its purest form, only had very partial successes. Sometimes the resistance has been grounded in classical premises, but often it has found new formulations, as will be discussed below. Vestedness, if only as an instinct, retains a surprising hold on the legal culture.

Not all the great issues in choice of law track the conflict between classicism and modernism. Within the modernist program, important issues remain. We have already seen debates about "contacts" and "interests," and about outcome-neutrality. Another set of questions concerns the content of state "interests" themselves. Three particular issues stand out.

The first problem involves the nature of the interests that states have in their domiciliaries. Currie, anticipating "public choice" theories, assumed that states enact legal norms to benefit favored classes of persons. He then argued, in a powerful and formative departure from more traditional accounts of domiciliary connection, that, when the parties to a controversy were domiciled in different states, a state would only be interested in applying its law if application of that law would benefit its own domiciliary, but not otherwise. Thus, if state X had a pro-plaintiff rule on an issue, and its domiciliary was the plaintiff, it had interest in applying its law. But if its domiciliary was the defendant, then it had no interest.

The implications of Currie's account are starkest in the so-called "unprovided-for case." Assume that state X has a pro-plaintiff rule and state Y has a pro-defendant rule, but the domiciliary of X is the defendant and the domiciliary of Y

is the plaintiff. According to Currie's view at its most rigorous, *neither* state has a real interest in applying its law.

For Currie's supporters, the unprovided-for case is a charming puzzle, which calls for supplementary rules. For his detractors, it is the loose end that unravels the whole fabric. Other choice of law theories have "unprovided-for" cases. In traditional person-territorialism, stateless persons pose a problem. For classicism, torts on uncharted territories pose a problem. But Currie's "unprovided-for case" is neither of these. It suggests that there are ordinary legal controversies outside the normative field of *any* jurisdiction. That, to many, seems to run counter to what the idea of law-making jurisdiction is about.

The flaw in Currie's view, according to his critics, is that he ignores the extent to which laws reflect, not a state's wish to confer largesse, but its judgment of corrective justice. Law-makers do not only legislate entitlements; they also legislate correlative duties (Ely, 1981, pp. 196–9). A state making judgments of corrective justice has as much of an interest in penalizing its domiciliaries when they have done wrong as in benefiting them when they have been wronged.

Currie's view of state interests raises a second problem. Currie recognized that, in addition to party-directed interests, states might have more systemic interests, including legal predictability, comity with other states, and so on. He argued, however, that those interests were too remote and speculative to excuse a forum facing a true conflict from applying its own law. He also argued that it was unfair to put on a forum's domiciliaries the cost of vindicating those systemic interests.

Many of Currie's modernist successors have been, however, more congenial to systemic interests. In particular, there is a tradition of suggesting that states might have a long-term selfish interest in selectively deferring to the laws of other jurisdictions, in the expectation that those other jurisdictions will in turn sometimes defer to its law. A popular analytic tool to which this tradition has turned in recent years has been game theory, with its demonstrations that tacit co-operation can, under certain conditions, be the most effective long-term strategy for maximizing self-interest (Kramer, 1990, pp. 341–44; cf. Brilmayer, 1995, § 4.2).

The consequence of some of these views is to resurrect forms of forum-neutrality under the guise of self-interest. Given the complexity of game theory, this may be too much of a coincidence. As noted earlier, it sometimes appears that what is really at work are the same instincts, in sublimated form, that committed the classical authors to vestedness in the first place.

The decline of classicism left issues hanging that might otherwise have engaged its interest, and which would be important in any renewal of classicism. Three of these issues hold particular jurisprudential interest.

First, as noted earlier, classicism never frankly assessed the role of substantive legal ideas in the authority-allocating task of choice of law. If a classical perspective would urge some modernist theories to be more explicit about the warrant for their substantive commitments, it can ask no less of itself.

Second, the classical tradition never fully defined what it meant to "apply" foreign law. The legal realists had their own, reductionist, answer to this question.

But for an anti-Realist, it remains a rich and important puzzle, related to the problem of adequacy of translation in philosophy of language. To what extent, for example, even putting aside legal realist behaviorism, is the practical meaning of law relevant to its translation across jurisdictions? If state *X* imposes liability for an act, but its juries never award substantial damages, should that be relevant to a court in state *Y* that is applying the law of *X*?

A third challenge that a renewed classicism might have to face is to refine the distinction between first-order and second-order legal processes. Modernists since Cook have argued that choice of law is necessarily a first-order process, no different in principle from tort or contract. The general classical view is that it is a second-order process, an effort to *allot* rather than *exercise* legislative jurisdiction.

Within the classical model, however, there might be room to recognize that *some* of choice of law *is* a first-order exercise of authority. The First Restatement implicitly suggests this possibility at several points. For example, although it provided that the law of the place of injury would govern most questions in a tort suit, including the standard of care (negligence, strict liability, or some other), it also held that the specific law of the place of tortious conduct could determine if a given standard had been satisfied (American Law Institute, 1934, § 380(2)). The meaning of this rule is obvious. The place of injury has legislative jurisdiction. It can use that jurisdiction any way it likes. But the Restatement assumes that the place of injury would, under its own tort law, look to the prevailing norms in the place of conduct as data relevant to its assessment of whether an alleged tortfeasor has acted properly. The problem is that, by not making this point explicitly, the Restatement never developed the machinery with which to work out the implications of that assumption.

This entry concludes with an issue that transcends the differences between classical and modernist choice of law. That issue is the relevance to choice of law of the normative authority of non-state legal regimes. The aim here is not to discuss the merits of legal pluralism, but rather to chart its implications for the shape of choice of law.

Classical choice of law's rejection of legal pluralism is explainable by both the tenor of its times, and by its own tendency to conceptual rigidity. Less immediately obvious is why modernist choice of law would have, for all its revolutionary zeal, left these assumptions untouched.

Part of the answer lies in modernism itself. Although there have been other trends in modern jurisprudence, modernist choice of law has been, in form as well as belief, profoundly statist. It has relied on an account of law that looks to institutions rather than norms, and it has tied the duties of courts to the "interests" of states. Thus, it has deprived itself of the imaginative capacity to see what Robert Cover (1983, pp. 15–16, 26–40) has called the "jurisgenerative" power of myriad human communities outside the formal boundaries of the state.

It remains unclear whether legal pluralism is a mortal challenge to choice of law modernism. It is also unclear whether a renewed classicism, should it arrive, will effectively devote its own intellectual resources to the problem. What is clear is that, as the ideology of state exclusivism, and the nation-state itself, come under increasing theoretical and practical attack, choice of law will have to find a place in that conversation too.

Bibliography

American Law Institute 1934: *Restatement (Second) of Conflict of Laws.* St Paul, Minn.: American Law Institute Publishers.
—— 1971: *Restatement of the Law of Conflict of Laws Second.* St Paul, Minn.: American Law Institute Publishers.
Baxter, W. 1963: Choice of law and the federal system. *Stanford Law Review,* 16, 1–42.
Beale, J. 1935: *The Conflict of Laws.* New York: Baker, Voorhis, & Co., 3 vols.
Brilmayer, L. 1995: *Conflict of Laws.* Boston: Little, Brown, & Co., 2nd edn.
Cavers, D. 1965: *The Choice-of-Law Process.* Ann Arbor: University of Michigan Press.
Cook, W. W. 1942: *The Logical and Legal Bases of the Conflict of Laws.* Cambridge, Mass.: Harvard University Press.
Cover, R. 1983: The Supreme Court, 1982 term – foreword: nomos and narrative. *Harvard Law Review,* 97, 4–68.
Currie, B. 1963: *Selected Essays on the Conflict of Laws.* Durham, NC: Duke University Press.
Dane, P. 1987: Vested rights, "vestedness," and choice of law. *Yale Law Journal,* 96, 1,191–1,275.
Ehrenzweig, A. 1962: *A Treatise on the Conflict of Laws.* St Paul, Minn: West Publishing Co.
Ely, J. H. 1981: Choice of law and the state's interest in protecting its own. *William & Mary Law Review,* 23, 173–217.
Kramer, L. 1990: Rethinking choice of law. *Columbia Law Review,* 90, 277–345.
Laflar, R. 1966: Conflicts law: more on choice-influencing considerations. *California Law Review,* 54, 1,584–98.
Prosser, W. 1953: Interstate publication. *Michigan Law Review,* 51, 959–1,000.
Twerski, A. 1971: Enlightened territorialism and Professor Cavers – the Pennsylvania method. *Duquesne Law Review,* 9, 373–93.

PART II

CONTEMPORARY SCHOOLS

14

Natural law theory

BRIAN BIX

Natural law theory has a long and distinguished history, encompassing many and varied theories and theorists – though there are probably no points of belief or methodology common to all of them. In legal theory, most of the approaches dubbed "natural law" can be placed into one of two broad groups, which I call "traditional" and "modern" natural law theory, and will consider in turn below. Some modern natural law theorists who do not fit comfortably into either group will be noted in summary at the end.

Traditional natural law theory

We take it for granted that the laws and legal system under which we live can be criticized on moral grounds; that there are standards against which legal norms can be compared and sometimes found wanting. The standards against which law is judged have sometimes been described as "a (the) higher law." For some, this is meant literally: that there are law-like standards that have been stated in or can be derived from divine revelation, religious texts, a careful study of human nature, or consideration of nature. For others, the reference to "higher law" is meant metaphorically, in which case it at least reflects our mixed intuitions about the moral status of law: on one hand, that not everything properly enacted as law is binding morally; on the other hand, that the law, as law, does have moral weight. (If it did not, we would not need to point to a "higher law" as a justification for ignoring the requirements of our society's laws.)

"Traditional" natural law theory offers arguments for the existence of a "higher law", elaborations of its content, and analyses of what consequences follow from the existence of a "higher law" (in particular, what response citizens should have to situations where the positive law – the law enacted within particular societies – conflicts with the "higher law").

Cicero

While one can locate a number of passages in ancient Greek writers that express what appear to be natural law positions, including passages in Plato (*Laws*;

Statesman; Republic) and Aristotle (*Politics, Nicomachean Ethics*), as well as Sophocles' *Antigone*, the best known ancient formulation of a Natural Law position was offered by the Roman orator Cicero.

Cicero (*Laws, Republic*), wrote in the first century BC, and was strongly influenced (as were many Roman writers on law) by the works of the Greek Stoic philosophers (some would go so far as to say that Cicero merely offered an elegant restatement of already established Stoic views). Cicero offered the following characterization of "natural law":

> True law is right reason in agreement with nature; it is of universal application, unchanging and everlasting; it summons to duty by its commands, and averts from wrongdoing by its prohibitions. And it does not lay its commands or prohibitions upon good men in vain, though neither have any effect on the wicked. It is a sin to try to alter this law, nor is it allowable to attempt to repeal any part of it, and it is impossible to abolish it entirely. We cannot be freed from its obligations by senate or people, and we need not look outside ourselves for an expounder or interpreter of it. And there will not be different laws at Rome and at Athens, or different laws now and in the future, but one eternal and unchangeable law will be valid for all nations and all times, and there will be one master and ruler, that is, God, over us all, for he is the author of this law, its promulgator, and its enforcing judge. Whoever is disobedient is fleeing from himself and denying his human nature, and by reason of this very fact he will suffer the worst penalties, even if he escapes what is commonly considered punishment.

In Cicero's discussions of law, we come across most of the themes traditionally associated with traditional natural law theory (though, as might be expected in the first major treatment of a subject, some of the analysis is not always as systematic or as precise as one might want): natural law is unchanging over time and does not differ in different societies; every person has access to the standards of this higher law by use of reason; and only just laws "really deserve [the] name" law, and "in the very definition of the term 'law' there inheres the idea and principle of choosing what is just and true."

Within Cicero's work, and the related remarks of earlier Greek and Roman writers, there was often a certain ambiguity regarding the reference of "natural" in "natural law": it was not always clear whether the standards were "natural" because they derived from "human nature" (our "essence" or "purpose"), because they were accessible by our natural faculties (that is, by human reason or conscience), because they derived from or were expressed in nature, that is, in the physical world about us, or some combination of all three.

As one moves from the classical writers on natural law to the early Church writers, aspects of the theory necessarily change and therefore raise different issues within this approach to morality and law. For example, with classical writers, the source of the higher standards is said to be (or implied as being) inherent in the nature of things. With the early Church writers, there is a divine being who actively intervenes in human affairs and lays down express commands for all mankind – though this contrast overstates matters somewhat, as the classical writers referred to a (relatively passive) God, and the early Church writers would sometimes refer to rules of nature which express divine will. To the extent that the natural law theorists of the early Church continued to speak of higher standards inherent in human nature or in the nature of things, they also had to face the question of the connection between these standards and divine commands: for example, whether God can change natural law or order something which is contrary to it, a question considered by Ambrose and Augustine (among others) in the time of the early Church and by Francisco Suarez more than a thousand years later.

Aquinas

The most influential writer within the traditional approach to natural law is undoubtedly Thomas Aquinas (*Summa Theologiae*), who wrote in the thirteenth century. The context of Aquinas's approach to law, its occurrence within a larger theological project that offered a systematic moral system, should be kept in mind when comparing his work with more recent theorists.

Aquinas identified four different kinds of law: the eternal law, the natural law, the divine law, and human (positive) law. For present purposes, the important categories are natural law and positive law.

According to Aquinas, (genuine or just) positive law is derived from natural law. This derivation has different aspects. Sometimes natural law dictates what the positive law should be: for example, natural law both requires that there be a prohibition of murder and settles what its content will be. At other times, natural law leaves room for human choice (based on local customs or policy choices). Thus while natural law would probably require regulation of automobile traffic for the safety of others, the choice of whether driving should be on the left or the right side of the road, and whether the speed limit should be set at 55 miles per hour or 65, are matters for which either choice would probably be compatible with the requirements of natural law. The first form of derivation is like logical deduction; the second Aquinas refers to as the "determination" of general principles ("determination" not in the sense of "finding out," but rather in the sense of making specific or concrete). The theme of different ways in which human (positive) law derives from natural law is carried by later writers, including Sir William Blackstone (*Commentaries on the Laws of England*, Vol. I (1765)), and, in modern times, John Finnis (discussed below).

As for citizens, the question is what their obligations are regarding just and unjust laws. According to Aquinas, positive laws which are just "have the power of binding in conscience." A just law is one which is consistent with the requirements of natural law – that is, it is "ordered to the common good," the law-giver has not exceeded its authority, and the law's burdens are imposed on citizens fairly. Failure with respect to any of those three criteria, Aquinas asserts, makes a law unjust; but what is the citizen's obligation in regard to an unjust law? The short answer is that there is no obligation to obey that law. However, a longer answer is warranted, given the amount of attention this question usually gets in discussions of natural law theory in general, and of Aquinas in particular.

The phrase *lex iniusta non est lex* ("an unjust law is not law") is often ascribed to Aquinas, and is sometimes given as a summation of his position and the (traditional) natural law position in general. While Aquinas never used the exact phrase above, one can find similar expressions: "every human law has just so much of the nature of law, as it is derived from the law of nature. But if in any point it deflects from the law of nature, it is no longer a law but a perversion of law"; and "[unjust laws] are acts of violence rather than laws; because, as Augustine says, a law that is not just, seems to be no law at all." (One also finds similar statements by Plato, Aristotle, Cicero, and Augustine – though, with the exception of Cicero's, these statements are not part of a systematic discussion of the nature of law.)

Questions have been raised regarding the significance of the phrase. What does it mean to say that an apparently valid law is "not law," "a perversion of law" or "an act of violence rather than a law." Statements of this form have been offered and interpreted in one of two ways. First, one can mean that an immoral law is not valid law at all. The nineteenth-century English Jurist John Austin (*The Province of Jurisprudence Determined* (1832)) interpreted statements by Sir William Blackstone (for example, "no human laws are of any validity, if contrary to [the law of nature]") in this manner, and pointed out that such analyses of validity are of little value. Austin wrote,

> Suppose an act innocuous, or positively beneficial, be prohibited by the sovereign under the penalty of death; if I commit this act, I shall be tried and condemned, and if I object to the sentence, that it is contrary to the law of God . . . the Court of Justice will demonstrate the inconclusiveness of my reasoning by hanging me up, in pursuance of the law of which I have impugned the validity.

Though one must add that we should not conflate questions of power with questions of validity – for a corrupt legal system might punish someone even if shown that the putative law was invalid under the system's own procedural requirements – we understand the distinction between validity under the system's rules and the moral worth of the enactment in question.

A more reasonable interpretation of statements like "an unjust law is no law at all" is that unjust laws are not laws "in the fullest sense." As we might say of some professional, who had the necessary degrees and credentials, but seemed nonetheless to lack the necessary ability or judgment: "she's no lawyer" or "he's no doctor." This only indicates that we do not think that the title in this case carries with it all the implications it usually does. Similarly, to say that an unjust law is "not really law" may only be to point out that it does not carry the same moral force or offer the same reasons for action as laws consistent with "higher law." This is almost certainly the sense in which Aquinas made his remarks, and the probable interpretation for nearly all proponents of the position. However, this interpretation leaves the statement as clearly right as under the prior (Austinian) interpretation was clearly wrong. One wonders why such declarations have, historically, been so controversial.

226

To say that an unjust law is not law in the fullest sense is usually intended not as a simple declaration, but as the first step of a further argument. For example: "this law is unjust; it is not law in the fullest sense, and therefore citizens can in good conscience act as if it was never enacted; that is, they should feel free to disobey it." This is a common understanding of the idea that an unjust law is no law at all, but it expresses a conclusion that is controversial.

There are often moral reasons for obeying even an unjust law: for example, if the law is part of a generally just legal system, and public disobedience of the law might undermine the system, there is a moral reason for at least minimal, public obedience to the unjust law. This is Aquinas's position (he stated that a citizen is not bound to obey "a law which imposes an unjust burden on its subjects" if the law "can be resisted without scandal or greater harm"), and it has been articulated at greater length by later natural law theorists (for example, by John Finnis).

Finally, it should be noted that the proper interpretation of certain basic aspects of Aquinas's work remains in dispute. For example, there is debate within the modern literature regarding whether Aquinas believed moral norms could be derived directly from knowledge of human nature or experience of natural inclinations, or whether they are the product of practical understanding and reasoning by way of reflection on one's experience and observations.

Natural law in early modern Europe

In the period of the Renaissance and beyond, discussions about natural law were tied in with other issues: assertions about natural law were often the basis of or part of the argument for individual rights and limitations on government; and such discussions were also often the groundwork offered for principles of international law. Hugo Grotius and Samuel Pufendorf (writing in the early and late seventeenth century, respectively) were prominent examples of theorists whose writings on natural law had significance in both debates. (Grotius and Pufendorf, along with other prominent seventeenth-century theorists, Francisco Suarez, Thomas Hobbes, and John Locke, were also central in developing the concept of individual rights in the modern sense of that term.)

A further significance of Grotius' work was its express assertion that natural law, the higher law against which the actions of nations, law-makers and citizens could be judged, did not require the existence of God for its validity. (However, one can find hints of such a separation of natural law from a divine being at least as far back as the fourteenth-century writings of Gregory of Rimini.) From that time to the present, an increasingly large portion of the writing on questions of natural law (and the related idea of "natural rights") was secular in tone and purpose, usually referring to "the requirements of reason" rather than divine command, purpose, will, or wisdom.

Perspective

It is normally a mistake to try to evaluate the discussions of writers from distant times with the perspective of modern analytical jurisprudence.

227

Cicero and Aquinas and Grotius were not concerned with a social–scientific-style analysis of law, as the modern advocates of legal positivism could be said to be. These theorists were concerned with what legislators and citizens and governments ought to do, or could do in good conscience. It is not that these writers (and their followers) never asked questions like "what is law?" However, they were asking the questions as a starting point for an ethical inquiry, and therefore one should not be too quick in comparing their answers with those in similar-sounding discussions by recent writers, who see themselves as participating in a conceptual or sociological task.

Natural law has, from time to time and with varying degrees of importance, escaped the confines of theory to influence directly the standards created and applied by officials. For example, natural law (or standards and reasoning that appear similar to natural law, but which are characterized as "substantive due process", "natural justice" or simply "reason") has been offered as the source of legal standards for international law, centuries of development in the English common law, and certain aspects of United States constitutional law. Natural law also appears to have played a significant role in American history, where its reasoning, or at least its rhetoric, has been prominent (among other places) in the Declaration of Independence, the Abolition (anti-slavery) movement, and parts of the modern Civil Rights movement.

John Finnis

In modern times, the traditional approach to natural law has been advocated by a number of theorists, most of whom were self-consciously writing in the tradition of Aquinas. For example, the French writer Jacques Maritain (*Man and the State* (1951)) has had significant influence in the area. Among the English-language writers, the most prominent advocate of the traditional approach is arguably John Finnis (*Natural Law and Natural Rights* (1980)).

Finnis's work is an explication and application of Aquinas's views (at least, of one reading of Aquinas, a reading advocated by Germain Grisez, among others): an application to ethical questions, but with special attention to the problems of social theory in general and analytical jurisprudence in particular.

Finnis's ethical theory has a number of levels. The foundation is the claim that there are a number of distinct but equally valuable intrinsic goods (that is, things one values for their own sake), which he calls "basic goods." In *Natural Law and Natural Rights*, Finnis lists the following as basic goods: life (and health), knowledge, play, aesthetic experience, sociability (friendship), practical reasonableness, and religion (Finnis's list of basic goods changes somewhat in later articles). These are "intrinsic" goods in the following sense: one can value, for example, health for its own sake, but medical treatment only as a means to health. If someone stated that she was buying medicine, not because she or someone she knew was sick or might become sick, and not because it was part of some study or some business, but simply because she liked acquiring medicines and having a lot of them around, one might rightly begin to question her sanity.

However, the difference between right and wrong cannot be drawn at the level of basic goods. At this level, one can only distinguish the intelligible from the unintelligible. We *understand* the person who is materialistic, greedy, malicious or unfair, however much we disapprove of such attitudes and actions. The greedy person is seeking the same basic goods as we, though in a way we would consider out of balance (and thus wrong).

Finnis describes the basic goods he identifies, and other principles identified in his moral theory, as "self-evident," but he does not mean this in the sense that the truth of these propositions would be immediately obvious to all competent thinkers. For Finnis, what it means for a (true) proposition to be "self-evident" is that it cannot be derived from some more foundational proposition; thus, "self-evident" is here the opposite of syllogistically demonstrable. (However, while these propositions cannot be thus demonstrated, they can be supported by consistent data of experience and by dialectical arguments, for example, from consistency.) Nor does the claim about "self-evidence" suggest that everyone will be equally adept at reaching these propositions. People of substantial experience, who are able and willing to inquire and reflect deeply may be better able to discover the "self-evident" truths than would others (Aquinas wrote that some propositions, including the first principles of practical reason and natural law, were only self-evident to the wise).

Much of what is conventionally considered to be ethics and morality occurs at a second level in Finnis's theory. Because there are a variety of basic goods, with no hierarchy or priority among them, there must be principles to guide choice when alternative courses of conduct promote different goods. (This is one basis for contrasting Finnis's position with utilitarian moral theories, under which all goods can be compared according to their value in a single unit, for example, promoting happiness.) On a simple level, we face such choices when we consider whether to spend the afternoon playing soccer (the value of play) or studying history (the value of knowledge). The choice is presented in a sharper form when someone (say, a medical researcher) must choose whether to kill (choosing against the basic good of life), in a situation where the person believes that doing so would lead to some significant benefit (perhaps saving more lives at some future time) or avoid a greater evil. Morality offers a basis for rejecting certain available choices, but there will often remain more than one equally legitimate choice (again, there is a contrast with most utilitarian theories, under which there would always be a "best" choice).

For Finnis, the move from the basic goods to moral choices occurs through a series of intermediate principles, which Finnis calls "the basic requirements of practical reasonableness." Among the most significant, and most controversial, is the prescription that one may never choose to destroy, damage or impede a basic good regardless of the benefit one believes will come from doing so. In other words, the end never justifies the means where the chosen means entails intending to harm a basic good.

Other intermediate principles listed in *Natural Law and Natural Rights* (the list changes somewhat in Finnis's later writings) include that one should form a rational plan of life; have no arbitrary preferences among persons; foster the common good of the community; and have no arbitrary preferences among the basic goods.

Law enters the picture as a way of effecting some goods – social goods which require the co-ordination of many people – that could not be effected (easily or at all) without law, and it also enters as a way of making it easier to obtain other goods. Thus, the suggestions Finnis makes about law and about legal theory are derivative from the ethical code which is, in a sense, his primary concern. As to questions regarding the obligation to obey the law, Finnis follows Aquinas: one has an obligation to obey just laws; laws which are unjust are not "law" in the fullest sense of the term, and one has an obligation to comply with their requirements only to the extent that this is compatible with moral norms and necessary to uphold otherwise just institutions.

Even though Finnis's theory might be seen as primarily a prescriptive account – a theory of how we should live our lives – the analysis also has implications for descriptive theory, including a descriptive theory of law. Finnis argues that a proper ethical theory is necessary for doing descriptive theory well because evaluation is a necessary and integral part of theory formation. For example, while he agrees with the legal positivist, H. L. A. Hart, that a descriptive theory of a social practice like law should be constructed around the viewpoint of a participant in the practice, Finnis proposes a significant amendment to Hart's approach. He argues that, when doing legal theory, one should not take the perspective of those who merely accept the law as valid (Hart would include those who accept the law as valid for a variety of reasons, including prudential ones); rather, the theory should assume the perspective of those who accept the law as binding *because* they believe that valid legal rules (presumptively) create moral obligations. The difference may seem minor, but it means crossing a theoretically significant dividing line: between the legal positivist's insistence on doing theory in a morally neutral way and the Natural Law theorist's assertion that moral evaluation is an integral part of proper description and analysis.

Modern natural law theory

As has been noted, the concept of "natural law" or the "natural law approach" to analyzing law has deep historical roots. It is fair to speak of the "natural law tradition," but the meaning and significance of the earlier works are sufficiently ambiguous that many different perspectives have claimed to be part of that tradition. What criteria should be used in identifying a theorist's affiliation, and which theorists one includes under a particular label, will generally not be important, as long as one understands the moral or analytical problems to which the various theorists were responding, and the answers the theories are proposing.

While it may not be useful to try to adopt the role of gatekeeper, saying which theories are properly called "natural law theories" and which not, there may be some point, for the purpose of greater understanding, to identify similarities among those theorists who have defined themselves (or have been defined by later commentators) with that label. One such division is as follows: there are two broadly different groups of approaches that carry the label "natural law" theory. The first group includes the theorists already discussed: Cicero, Aquinas, Grotius, Pufendorf, and Finnis, among many others. The second group reflects debates of a different kind and a more recent origin; the second approach focusses more narrowly on the proper understanding of law as a social institution or a social practice. (The two types of approaches are by no means contradictory or inconsistent, but they reflect sets of theoretical concerns sufficiently different that it is rare to find writers contributing to both.)

The second (or "modern") set of approaches to natural law arises as responses to legal positivism, and the way legal positivists portrayed (and sometimes caricatured) traditional natural law positions. While attacks on the merits of natural law theory can be found in the works of John Austin, O. W. Holmes, and Hans Kelsen, a large portion of the recent discussions of "natural law theory" derive from the 1958 "Hart–Fuller Debate" in the *Harvard Law Review*. In this exchange, H. L. A. Hart laid the groundwork for a restatement of legal positivism (which he more fully articulated in *The Concept of Law* (1961)). Part of his defense and restatement involved demarcating legal positivism from natural law theory, and the demarcation point offered was the conceptual separation of law and morality. Lon Fuller argued against a sharp separation of law and morality, but the position he defended under the rubric of "natural law theory" was quite different from the traditional natural law theories of Cicero and Aquinas (as will be discussed in detail below).

In part, because of responses to legal positivists like Hart, a category of "natural law theories" has arisen which is best understood by its contrast to legal positivism, rather than by its connection with the traditional natural law theories of Cicero and Aquinas. While the traditional theories were generally taking a particular position on the status of morality (that true moral beliefs are based in or derived from human nature or the natural world, that they are not relative, that they are accessible to human reason, and so on), a position which then had some implications for how legislators, judges, and citizens should act (as well as for all other aspects of living a good life); this second category of "natural law theories" contains theories specifically about law, which hold that moral evaluation of some sort is required in describing law in general, particular legal systems, or the legal validity of individual laws.

Lon Fuller

Lon Fuller (*The Morality of Law* (1964)) rejected what he saw as legal positivism's distorted view of law as a "one-way projection of authority": the government gives orders and the citizens obey. Fuller believed that this approach missed the need for co-operation and reciprocal obligations between officials and citizens for a legal system to work.

Fuller described law as "the enterprise of subjecting human conduct to the governance of rules." Law is a form of guiding people, to be contrasted with other forms of guidance, for example, managerial direction. Law is a particular means to an end, a particular kind of tool, if you will. With that in mind, one can better understand the claim that rules must meet certain criteria relating to that means, to that function, if they are to warrant the title "law." If we defined "knife" as something that cuts, something which failed to cut would not warrant the label, however much it might superficially resemble true knives. Similarly, if we define law as a particular way of guiding and co-ordinating human behavior, if a system's rules are so badly constructed that they cannot succeed in effectively guiding behavior, then we are justified in withholding the label "law" from them.

Fuller offered, in place of legal positivism's analysis of law based on power, orders, and obedience, an analysis based on the "internal morality" of law. Like traditional natural law theorists, he wrote of there being a threshold that must be met (or, to change the metaphor, a test that must be passed) before something could be properly (or in the fullest sense) be called "law." Unlike traditional natural law theorists, however, the test Fuller applies is one of function rather than strictly one of moral content; though, as will be noted, for Fuller these questions of procedure or function have moral implications.

The internal morality of law consists of a series of requirements which Fuller asserted that a system of rules must meet – or at least substantially meet – if that system was to be called "law." (At the same time, Fuller wrote of systems being "legal" to different degrees, and he held that a system which partly but not fully met his requirements would be "partly legal" and could be said to have "displayed a greater respect for the principles of legality" than systems which did not meet the requirements.)

The eight requirements were:

1 laws should be general;
2 they should be promulgated, that citizens might know the standards to which they are being held;
3 retroactive rule-making and application should be minimized;
4 laws should be understandable;
5 they should not be contradictory;
6 laws should not require conduct beyond the abilities of those affected;
7 they should remain relatively constant through time; and
8 there should be a congruence between the laws as announced and their actual administration.

Fuller's approach is often contrasted with that of traditional natural law positions. Fuller at one point tried to show a connection, writing that "Aquinas in some measure recognized and dealt with all eight of the principles of legality." On the other hand, Fuller also realized that there were significant differences: he once referred to his theory as "a procedural, as distinguished from a substantive natural law." However, he chafed at the dismissal of his set of requirements as "merely procedural": an argument frequently made by critics that his "principles of legality" were amoral solutions to problems of efficiency, such that one could just as easily speak of "the internal morality of poisoning." Such criticisms misunderstand the extent to which our perceptions of justice incorporate procedural matters. This is a matter Fuller himself brought up through an example from the former Soviet Union. In that system, there was once an attempt to increase the sentence for robbery, an increase also to be applied retroactively to those convicted of that crime in the past. Even in the Soviet legal system, not known for its adherence to the rule of law, there was a strong reaction against this attempt to increase sentences retroactively. It is a matter of procedure only, but still it seemed to them – and it would seem to us – a matter of justice. Following the rules laid down (just one example of procedural justice) is a good thing, and it is not stretching matters to characterize it as a moral matter and a matter of justice.

On the other hand, there were times when Fuller overstated the importance of his "principles of legality." When critics argued that a regime could follow those principles and still enact wicked laws, Fuller stated that he "could not believe" that adherence to the internal requirements of law was as consistent with a bad legal system as they were with a good legal system. There are various ways that this "faith" can be understood. One argument could be that a government which is just and good will likely also do well on procedural matters. Additionally, when proper procedures are followed (for example the requirement that reasons publicly be given for judicial decisions), some officials might be less willing to act in corrupt ways. The contrary claim, that governments which are evil will be likely to ignore the procedural requirements, also has some initial plausibility. There have been regimes so evil that they have not even bothered with any of the legal niceties, with establishing even the pretense of legality, and to some extent Nazi Germany is an example. However, there have also been regimes, generally condemned as evil, which have at least at times been quite meticulous about legal procedures (South Africa before the fall of apartheid or East Germany before the fall of Communism may be examples). Since the principles of legality can be understood as guidelines for making the legal system more effective in guiding citizen behavior, wicked regimes would have reason to follow them.

Thus, on one hand, one might say: first, that following the principles of legality is itself a moral good; second, the fact that a government follows those principles may indicate that it is committed to morally good actions; and third, that following such principles may hinder or restrict base actions. On the other hand, it is probably claiming too much for those principles to say that following them would guarantee a substantively just system. However, one should not conclude, as some critics have, that the evaluation of Fuller's entire approach to law should turn on the empirical question of whether there have ever been (or ever could be) wicked governments which, for whatever reason, followed the rules of procedural justice. (Like the question of whether there can ever be, over the long term, "honor among thieves", the ability to maintain procedural fairness amidst significant iniquities, is an interesting topic for speculation, but little more.) The main points of Fuller's position – that a value judgment about the system described is part of the way we use the word "law"; and that there is analytic value to seeing law as a particular

233

kind of social guidance, which is to be contrasted with other forms of social guidance, and which can be more or less effective according to how well it meets certain criteria – would not be undermined by pointing out legal systems which were substantively unjust but which seemed to do well on questions of procedural justice.

Those who approach natural law through the Hart–Fuller debate sometimes overemphasize the question of when a rule or a system of social control merits the label "law" or "legal". There is a danger with such a focus, in that debates about proper labeling (not just whether something is "law" or not, but also whether an object is "art" or not, whether a particular form of government is "democratic" or not, and so forth) often smother real moral, sociological, or conceptual arguments beneath line-drawing exercises. It is always open to theorists to stipulate the meaning of the terms they use, even for the limited purpose of a single discussion. To say that it is important that the products of a wicked regime be called "law" or not indicates that there is something further at stake (for example, whether and when citizens have a moral obligation to obey the law, and whether punishment is ever warranted for people who had been acting in accord with what the law at the time required or permitted), but the burden must be on the advocate to clarify what the further point is. It is probably preferable to bypass questions of labeling and line-drawing, to face directly whatever further substantive issues may be present.

Ronald Dworkin

Ronald Dworkin is probably the most influential English-language legal theorist now writing. Over the course of thirty years, he has developed a sophisticated alternative to legal positivism. Though his theory has little resemblance to the traditional natural law theories of Aquinas and his followers, Dworkin has occasionally referred to his approach as a natural law theory, and it is clearly on the natural law side of the theoretical divide set by the Hart–Fuller debate.

In Dworkin's early writings (collected in *Taking Rights Seriously* (1978)), he challenged a particular view of legal positivism, a view which saw law as being comprised entirely of rules, and judges as having discretion in their decision making where the dispute before them was not covered by any existing rule. Dworkin offered an alternative vision of law, in which the resources for resolving disputes "according to law" were more numerous and varied, and the process of determining what the law required in a particular case more subtle.

Dworkin argues that along with rules, legal systems also contain principles. As contrasted with rules, principles do not act in an all-or-nothing fashion. Rather, principles (for example, "one should not be able to profit from one's own wrong" and "one is held to intend all the foreseeable consequences of one's actions") have "weight," they favor one result or another; there can be – and often are – principles favoring contrary results on a single legal question. Legal principles are moral propositions that are grounded (exemplified, quoted or somehow supported by) past official acts (for example, the text of statutes, judicial decisions, or constitutions).

There is still a legal positivist-like separation of law and morality in this view of law, in that judges are told to decide cases based not on whatever principles (critical) morality might require, but rather based on a different and perhaps inconsistent set of principles: those cited in, or implicit in, past official actions.

Dworkin argued for the existence of legal principles (principles which are part of the legal system, which judges are bound to consider where appropriate) by reference to legal practice (in the United States and England). Particularly telling for Dworkin's argument are those "landmark" judicial decisions where the outcome appears to be contrary to the relevant precedent, but the courts still held that they were following the "real meaning" or "true spirit" of the law; and also, more mundane cases where judges have cited principles as the justification for modifying, creating exceptions in, or overturning, legal rules.

With the conclusion that there were legal principles as well as legal rules, it would seem to follow that there are fewer occasions than previously thought where judges have discretion because there are "gaps" in the law (that is, places where there is no relevant law on the subject). However, now the likely problem was not the absence of law on a question, but its abundance: where legal principles could be found to support a variety of different results. how is the judge to make a decision? Dworkin's answer is that judges should consider a variety of views of what the law requires in the area in question, rejecting those (for example, "in tort cases, the richer party should lose") which do not adequately "fit" past official actions (statutes, precedent, constitutions). Among the theories of what the law requires that adequately fit the relevant legal materials, the judge would then choose that theory which was morally best, which made the law the best it could be. This final stage of judicial decision making is where moral (or partly moral, partly political – the characterization is neither obvious nor crucial) factors take a central role in Dworkin's view of how judges do (and should) decide cases. Two tenets of Dworkin's early writings were thus related: that law contained principles as well as rules; and that for nearly all legal questions, there was a unique right answer.

In his later writings, Dworkin (*Law's Empire* (1986)) offered what he called "an interpretive approach" to law. (While Dworkin has said little about the relationship between his earlier writings and his later work, the later work is probably best seen as a reworking of earlier themes within a philosophically more sophisticated analysis.) He argued that "legal claims are interpretive judgments and therefore combine backward- and forward-looking elements; they interpret contemporary legal practice as an unfolding narrative."

According to Dworkin, both law (as a practice) and legal theory are best understood as processes of "constructive interpretation." (He believes that constructive interpretation is also the proper approach to artistic and literary works, and his writings frequently compare the role of a judge with that of a literary critic. Both the applicability of constructive interpretation to art and literature and the treatment of legal interpretation as analogous to artistic or literary interpretation, are controversial claims.) One can think of constructive interpretation as being similar to the way people have looked at collections of stars and seen there pictures of mythic figures, or the way modern statistical methods can analyze points on a graph (representing data), and determine what line (representing a mathematical equation, and thus a correlation of some form between variables) best explains that data. Constructive interpretation is both an imposition of form upon the object being interpreted (in the sense that the form is not immediately apparent in the object) and a derivation of form from it (in the sense that the interpreter is constrained by the object of interpretation, and not free to impose any form she might choose). Dworkin also described the concept of "Integrity": the argument that judges should decide cases in a way which makes the law more coherent, preferring interpretations which make the law more like the product of a single moral vision.

For Dworkin, the past actions of legal officials, whether judges deciding cases and giving reasons for their decisions or legislators passing statutes, are data to be explained. In some areas, there will be little doubt as to the correct theory, the correct "picture." The answer seems easy because only one theory shows adequate "fit."

Often, however, there will be alternative theories, each with adequate "fit". Among these, some will do better on "fit", others on moral value. In making comparisons among alternative theories, the relative weighting of "fit" and moral value will itself be an interpretive question, and will vary from one legal area to another (for example, protecting expectations – having new decisions "fit" as well as possible with older ones – may be more important regarding estate or property law, while moral value may be more important than "fit" for civil liberties questions). The evaluation of theories thus takes into account (directly and indirectly) a view about the purpose of law in general, and a view about the objectives of the particular area of law in which the question falls. Dworkin wrote, "Judges who accept the interpretive ideal of integrity decide hard cases by trying to find, in some coherent set of principles about people's rights and duties, the best constructive interpretation of the political structure and legal doctrine of their community."

Dworkin's writings (both earlier and later) can be seen as attempts to come to terms with aspects of legal practice that are not easily explained within the confines of legal positivism. For example:

1 the fact that participants in the legal system (regularly, if not frequently) argue over even basic aspects of the way the system works (for example, the correct way to interpret ambiguous statutes, and how one should apply constitutional provisions to new legal questions), not just over peripheral matters or the application of rules to borderline cases;
2 even in the hardest of hard cases, lawyers and judges speak as if there were a unique correct answer which the judge has a duty to discover; and
3 in landmark cases, where the law seems on the surface to have changed radically, both the judges and commentators often speak of the new rule having "already been present" or "the law working itself pure."

A standard response to Dworkin's work (both to his early writings and to the later "interpretative" work) is that judges and legal theorists should not look at law through "rose-colored glasses," making it "the best it can be"; rather, they should describe law "as it is." The key to understanding Dworkin, in particular his later work, is to understand his response to this kind of comment: that there is no simple description of law "as it is"; or, more accurately, describing law "as it is" necessarily involves an interpretative process, which in turn requires determining what is the best interpretation of past official actions. Law "as it is," law as objective or non-controversial, is only the collection of past official decisions by judges and legislators (which Dworkin refers to as the "pre-interpretive data," that which is subject to the process of constructive interpretation). However, even collectively, these individual decisions and actions cannot offer an answer to a current legal question until some order is imposed upon them. And the ordering involves a choice, a moral–political choice among tenable interpretations of those past decisions and actions.

Dworkin, like Fuller, is a natural law theorist in the modern rather than traditional sense of that label, in that he denies the conceptual separation of law and morality, and asserts instead that moral evaluation is integral to the description and understanding of law.

General considerations

Within this second type of natural law debate, as exemplified by the works of Fuller and Dworkin (and their critics), it is not always immediately clear what the nature or status is of the claims being made. Some of them could be merely sociological or lexicographical: that is, statements about the way we actually use the label "law." For example, one could plausibly interpret Fuller as arguing that, for better or worse, the way most people use the word "law" includes a moral claim (in other words, that we tend to withhold the label from wicked laws or wicked regimes).

At other times, for example, with some of Dworkin's arguments, the claims regard the best description of our practices, but not merely our linguistic practices in how we use terms like "law," but also our practices in how we act within or react to the legal system. In a different sense, Dworkin's theory also (tacitly) presents a normative claim: that law and legal theory seen as Dworkin would have us see them are (morally) better than the same practices as viewed through the alternative characterizations of other theories.

A different set of problems arise when students of legal theory try to understand traditional natural law theories (such as the works of Aquinas and Finnis). The difficulties come because the issues central to many of these theorists (for example, the extent to which moral truths are "self-evident"; the extent to which various goods, claims, or arguments are incommensurable; whether a moral theory can be constructed or defended independent of a belief in God; and the like) bear little resemblance to what normally passes for legal theory. This, of course, is not a criticism of the traditional natural law theorists; if anything, it is a criticism of the way such material is often presented to a general audience, glossing over the differences in concern and focus between traditional natural law theorists and (many) modern analytical legal theorists.

237

Other modern writers

A number of other modern writers have written works offered as "natural law" theories, some of which do not fit comfortably in either of the two broad subcategories considered above.

Michael Moore has discussed various aspects of law in the light of a Platonist (metaphysically realist) approach to language, morality, and legal concepts. Moore's analysis might be best understood as responding to the question: how do we determine the meanings of legal terms like "valid contract," "criminal malice," and "due process." On one extreme is the ("conventionalist") response that like all language, the terms mean whatever we want them to mean, or whatever meaning they have gained from our practices and conventions over generations. Moore's response is at the opposite extreme: simple descriptive terms ("bird", "tree"), legal terms ("malice," "valid contract"), and moral concepts ("due process," "equal treatment") all have meanings determined by the way the world is, not by our changing, and often erroneous beliefs about those objects. Moore has shown how this approach to metaphysics (and language) has numerous repercussions for the way we should interpret constitutions and statutes and analyze problems of the common law and precedent.

Lloyd Weinreb (*Natural Law and Justice* (1987)) has offered an interesting characterization of the natural law tradition (that is, the tradition of Cicero and Aquinas) that varies from the way it is seen by most commentators and advocates today. In particular, Weinreb sees the works of the ancient classical theorists and Aquinas (among others) as having been concerned, each in his own way, with the problem of explaining the possibility of human moral freedom in a world that otherwise appears determined by fate or fortune (in classical thinking) or by divine providence (in the view of the early Church). In Weinreb's view, recent natural law writers like Finnis and Fuller are missing the basic point of natural law theory when they try to distance their claims from earlier arguments about normative natural order, which can now be understood as addressing generally the problem of the ontology, or reality, of morality.

Ernest Weinrib sees law as having an "immanent moral rationality." For Weinrib, one can speak of the essence or the nature of law, of various parts of the law (for example, tort law) and of doctrines within the law. This view of law is contrasted with approaches which assert or assume that law is basically a kind of politics, or that it is a means of maximizing some value (for example, utility or wealth). In Weinrib's words, "legal ordering is not the collective pursuit of a desirable purpose. Instead, it is the specification of the norms and principles immanent to juridically intelligible relationships." The essence of law can be worked out to particular normative propositions, and therefore what the law requires is not merely identical with the rules legislatures (and judges) promulgate. While Weinrib generally does not use the label "natural law" for his approach (provocatively choosing instead "legal formalism," a label modern theorists usually apply pejoratively), he has noted the overlap of his arguments with those put forward by Aquinas and other traditional natural law theorists.

Deryck Beyleveld and Roger Brownsword (*Law as a Moral Judgment* (1986)) have constructed an approach to legal theory around Alan Gewirth's argument for objective moral principles. Gewirth's argument states that engaging in practical reasoning itself presupposed a commitment to a number of moral principles. Beyleveld and Brownsword use this analysis to argue against value-free social theory; in the context of legal theory, they argue that Gewirth's analysis requires a rejection of legal positivism in favor of an equation of law with morally legitimate power.

Conclusion

A diverse family of theories carries the label "natural law." Within legal theory, there are two well-known groupings which cover most (but not all) of the writing that has carried the label "natural law": (1) "traditional natural law theory" sets out a moral theory (or an approach to moral theory) in which one can better analyze how to think about and act on legal matters; and (2) "modern natural law theory" argues that one cannot properly understand or describe the law without moral evaluation.

Bibliography

Aquinas, T. 1993: *The Treatise on Law*, ed. R. J. Henle, Notre Dame, Indiana: University of Notre Dame Press (text of *Summa Theologiae*, I–II, pp. 90–7, with translation, commentary and introduction).

Blackstone, Sir W. 1765: *Commentaries on the Laws of England, Volume I: Of the Rights of Persons*. Oxford: Clarendon Press.

Cicero, Marcus Tullius 1988: *De Re Publica; De Legibus*, tr. C. W. Keyes, Cambridge, Mass.: Harvard University Press.

Dworkin, R. 1978: *Taking Rights Seriously*. London: Duckworth (the 1978 edition contains as an appendix, "A reply to critics").

—— 1986: *Law's Empire*. Cambridge, Mass.: Harvard University Press.

Finnis, J. 1980: *Natural Law and Natural Rights*. Oxford: Clarendon Press.

Finnis, J. (ed.) 1991: *Natural Law*, 2 vols. New York: New York University Press (a wide-ranging collection of law review articles on natural law theory).

Fuller, L. 1958: Positivism and fidelity to law – a response to Professor Hart. *Harvard Law Review*, 71, 630–72.

—— 1969: *The Morality of Law*. New Haven: Yale University Press, rev. edn (the revised edition contains a helpful reply to critics).

George, R. (ed.) 1992: *Natural Law Theory*. Oxford: Clarendon Press (a collection of relatively recent articles on natural law theory).

Grotius, H. 1925: *De Jure Belli ac Pacis Libri Tres*, tr. F. Kelsen, Oxford: Clarendon Press.

Hart, H. L. A. 1958: Positivism and the separation of law and morals. *Harvard Law Review*, 71, 593–629.

Kelly, J. M. 1992: *A Short History of Western Legal Theory*. Oxford: Clarendon Press.

Moore, M. 1985: A natural law theory of interpretation. *Southern California Law Review*, 58, 277–398.

Pufendorf, S. 1991: *On the Duty of Man and Citizen according to Natural Law*, ed. J. Tully, tr. M. Silverthorne, Cambridge: Cambridge University Press.

Weinreb, L. 1987: *Natural Law and Justice*. Cambridge, Mass.: Harvard University Press.

15

Legal positivism

JULES L. COLEMAN AND BRIAN LEITER

Along with natural law theory, legal positivism is one of the two great traditions in legal philosophy. Its adherents include important nineteenth-century figures like John Austin and Jeremy Bentham, as well as twentieth-century thinkers like Hans Kelsen, H. L. A. Hart, and Joseph Raz. All positivists share two central beliefs: first, that what counts as law in any particular society is fundamentally a matter of social fact or convention ("the social thesis"); second, that there is no necessary connection between law and morality ("the separability thesis"). Positivists differ among themselves, however, over the best intepretation of these core commitments of positivism. (Indeed, the definitions offered here of the social and separability theses are broader than the ones offered by those who coined the terms (Raz, 1979, p. 37; Coleman, 1982, p. 29). Legal positivists also share with all other philosophers who claim the "positivist" label (in philosophy of science, epistemology, and elsewhere) a commitment to the idea that the phenomena comprising the domain at issue (for example, law, science) must be accessible to the human mind. This admittedly vague commitment does little to convey the richness of positivism as a general philosophical position, but it serves to indicate that the label, though acquiring a very special meaning in legal philosophy, is not utterly discontinuous with its use elsewhere in the philosophical tradition.

Jurisprudence: method and subject-matter

Hart (1961) has done more than anyone else to define methodology in the positivist tradition. Hart wrote his seminal work when "linguistic" philosophy was still dominant in the English-speaking world; he, in turn, adopted its method of "conceptual analysis" for questions in legal philosophy. On this approach, jurisprudence aims to give a satisfactory analysis of the uses to which the concept of "law" is put in various social practices (for example, legal argument in courts, in legislatures, in everyday settings). Such an analysis must account, in particular, for two features of the concept: first, our sense that of all the various norms in a society (moral, aesthetic, social) only some subset are norms of "law"; second, our sense that "legal" norms provide agents with special reasons for acting, reasons they would not have if the norm were not a "legal" one. A satisfactory analysis of the concept of law, then, must account for these two features, what we may call, respectively, "the criteria of legality" and the "normativity" or "authority" of law.

Conceptual analysis is not a mere exercise in lexicography. As Hart observed: "the suggestion that inquiries into the meanings of words merely throw light on words is false" (1961, p. v). Rather, "a sharpened awareness of words . . . sharpen[s] our perception of phenomena" (1961, p. 14, quoting John Austin). Thus, Hart describes his inquiry as a kind of "descriptive sociology" (1961, p. v), that is, an analytic taxonomy of the uses to which the concept is actually put in real social practices (for example, how activities referred to as law relate to and differ from other activities, such as those referred to as morality). Later writers in the positivist tradition have also emphasized that the "sociological" inquiry can be detached from the "linguistic" one (cf. Raz, 1979, p. 41: "we do not want to be slaves of words. Our aim is to understand society and its institutions. We must face the question: is the ordinary sense of 'law' such that it helps identify facts of importance to our understanding of society").

Invariably, positivists and natural lawyers are treated as a contrasting pair. Unlike, say, the legal realists, who made empirical claims about adjudication, positivists and natural lawyers have focussed primarily on the concepts of legality and authority and they are typically thought to express diametrically opposed views about both (roughly, natural lawyers reject both the social thesis and the separability thesis).

Ronald Dworkin, positivism's most eloquent critic, presents a special case. His earliest objections to positivism were built around the claim that moral principles can be legally binding in virtue of the fact that they express an appropriate dimension of justice or fairness. This rejection of the separability thesis has led many commentators to characterize him as a natural lawyer. Dworkin's work (1986), however, introduces an important distinction between the conditions of legality (or legal validity) and the meaning of a valid legal rule. Dworkin does not claim that the validity of legal principles depends on their morality, but he does believe that in *interpreting* the meaning of valid legal rules it is often necessary to consult moral principles. Insofar as Dworkin does not claim that morality is a criterion of legality, he appears to reject one of the classic commitments of natural law.

Perhaps the most distinctive feature, however, of Dworkin's jurisprudence – certainly when compared with positivism and natural law theory – is its focus on adjudication. For Dworkin, a jurisprudence, above all else, must provide a plausible account of certain features Dworkin finds in adjudication: for example, that judges disagree not only about what recognized legal rules or principles require, but also about what principles and rules are really "legal" ones; and that even in hard cases, judges argue as though there are legally binding standards, rather than writing as though they are exercising discretion. For Dworkin, then, the accounts of legality and authority grow out of his theory of adjudication. While for the positivist, the central legal figure is the law-maker or legislator, the central figure for Dworkin is law's interpreter, the appellate judge.

Legality and authority

Hart has expressed positivism's central tenet as the claim that there is a difference between the way the law is and the way it ought to be (1983, pp. 49–87). This tenet is expressed by the account of legality given by the social and separability theses. The resulting account of the criteria of legality, however, has received differing interpretations. On a "restrictive" construal, favored by Joseph Raz, positivism holds that it can never be a criterion of legal validity that a norm possess moral value; the criterion of legality must simply be some determinate social fact: for example, that the norm has a particular social source (for example, it was passed by the legislature) (Raz, 1979, pp. 37–52; Raz, 1985, pp. 311–20). On a more "inclusive" construal (sometimes called "incorporationism"), favored by H. L. A. Hart, Jules Coleman, and several other writers, positivism is only committed to two weaker claims: first, that it is not *necessary* in all legal systems that for a norm to be a legal norm it must possess moral value (what Coleman has dubbed "negative positivism"); and second, that what norms count as legal norms in any particular society is fundamentally a matter of *social conventions*. The latter can include a convention among relevant officials to make the moral value of a norm a condition of its legal validity (see Coleman, 1982; Hart, 1994; Lyons, 1977; Soper, 1977; Waluchow, 1994).

Note that positivists do not deny that there may be a great deal of overlap between a community's law and its morality, both its positive and critical morality. Many of morality's most urgent demands are typically enacted into law; indeed one might hold that an even greater convergence of the demands of morality and law should be seen as law's ultimate aspiration. Even complete convergence between the demands of morality and law would not violate the separability thesis, however, for this thesis involves only a claim about the conditions of legal validity, not about the extent to which moral and legal norms overlap in practice.

Accounts of legality are often driven by accounts of authority. Indeed, positivism has often proved attractive because of natural law theory's failure to account adequately for either. The moral value of a norm, for example, cannot be a necessary condition of its being a legal norm (as the natural lawyer would have it) since we all recognize cases of binding laws that are morally reprehensible (for example, the laws that supported apartheid in South Africa).

Natural law fares no better as an account of the authority of law. A practical authority is a person or institution whose directives provide individuals with a reason for acting (in compliance with those dictates). If Brian accepts Friedrich as an authority, then the fact that Friedrich commands Brian to do something gives Brian a reason for doing it, *without assessing how good Friedrich's reasons are for having commanded it*. If what Friedrich commands is something Brian ought to do on its own merits, then Brian has a reason for doing what Friedrich commands independent of the fact that Friedrich commanded it. On the other hand, if Friedrich is an authority, then Brian has a reason for doing what Friedrich commands independent of the substance of that command.

243

Now we can see the problem with the natural lawyer's account of authority. For in order to be law, a norm must be required by morality. Morality has authority, in the sense that the fact that a norm is a requirement of morality gives agents a (perhaps overriding) reason to comply with it. If morality has authority, and legal norms are necessarily moral, then law has authority too.

This argument for the authority of law, however, is actually fatal to it, because it makes law's authority redundant on morality's. Consider, for example, the moral prohibition against intentional killing. Individuals have a good reason, *as a matter solely of morality*, not intentionally to take the lives of others. Now suppose that a law proscribing intentional killings is enacted. For law to be authoritative, it must provide citizens with a reason for acting that they would not otherwise have. But if all legal requirements are also moral requirements (as the natural lawyer would have it) then the fact that a norm is a norm of law does not provide citizens with an additional reason for acting. Natural law theory, then, fails to account for the authority of law.

The failure of natural law theory to account adequately for legality and authority makes positivism an attractive possibility, though it plainly does not imply that positivism is correct. We must now explore in greater detail positivist accounts of legality and authority.

Positivism: Austin vs. Hart

It is natural to begin any discussion of positivist theories of legality and authority with John Austin's so-called, "will" or "command theory of law." According to Austin, law is the order of a "sovereign" backed by a threat of sanction in the event of non-compliance. A norm is law, then, only if it is the command of a sovereign. Legality, on this account, is determined by its *source* – that is, the will or command of a sovereign – not its substantive merits. The criteria of legality are matters of fact, not value.

If law is a matter of fact, not value, then what can explain its normative force? How can we derive a normative conclusion (about law's authority) from a factual premise (its legality)? Recall that on Austin's account, a command is not law unless it imposes a threatened sanction in the event of non-compliance with its demands. Without sanctions, commands would really be no more than requests. Agents act in compliance with law's demands, then, in order to avoid imposition of sanctions. It is the threat of sanction that gives agents a (prudent) reason to act and thus the sanction accounts for law's normativity.

Hart (1961, pp. 18–77) famously critiqued each aspect of Austin's theory: the picture of the sovereign as a distinct individual; the conception of law as commands and as primarily prescriptive in nature; and finally, the emphasis on sanctions as the explanation of law's normativity.

For Austin, the sovereign is a particular person, namely that individual who, as a matter of fact, happens to have secured the habit of obedience, but who herself is not in the habit of obeying anyone. Hart rightly notes that, by treating the sovereign as a person, Austin's account is unable to explain other salient features of law, namely the fact that legal rules remain valid or binding even after a sovereign dies or is otherwise disempowered, even, in other words, when that particular person no longer enjoys the habit of obedience. It fails as well to explain the fact that the commands of a new "sovereign" can be law even though she has not yet secured a habit of obedience.

To remedy this failing, Hart reformulates Austin's conception of the sovereign so that the sovereign is not a person but an office. The authority to legislate vests in the office, not in the person, except insofar as one is a legitimate occupant of the office. But the office is an institution, and institutions are created by rules. The rules that create offices are plainly not orders backed by threats. Instead, they are rules that empower or authorize certain actions by public officials.

Thus, not all laws are liberty limiting in the way in which Austin envisions; rather, some laws expand liberty. They are enabling, or what Hart calls power conferring – expanding rather than contracting the scope of individual freedom by giving legal effect or force to personal choices, for example, the distribution of one's holding through wills, the decision to bind oneself to future actions by contract or marriage, and so on. Some rules confer power on private individuals while those that create offices confer power and authorize public persons. So Austin is wrong to emphasize law's prescriptive nature to the exclusion of its power-enhancing functions.

If not all laws are commands backed by threats, then the existence of sanctions cannot be the source of law's normativity, for laws that confer power are presumably authoritative though they do not impose sanctions. Sanctions may lead people to comply with law's demands, but they cannot explain the sense in which law might be thought to impose an obligation of compliance. Rather than explaining the obligations law imposes, sanctions are a sign that the law has failed fully to motivate compliance on its own terms. In order to understand the authority of law, we need to understand how law might motivate compliance in the absence of sanctions.

For Hart, law consists of rules of two distinct types: primary rules that either limit or expand liberty; and secondary rules that are *about* the primary rules. Hart distinguishes among three different kinds of secondary rules: those that create a power to legislate; others that create a power to adjudicate; and finally a rule of recognition. The rule of recognition is not a power-conferring rule. Instead, it sets out the conditions that must be satisfied in order for a norm to count as part of the community's law. So we might say that Hart really believes that there are three kinds of legal rules: those that obligate, those that enable and the rule of recognition that sets out validity conditions.

In contrast to Austin, Hart maintains that wherever there is law, there are primary rules that impose obligations and a rule of recognition that specifies the conditions that must be satisfied for a rule that imposes obligations to be a legal rule. These are the minimal conditions for the existence of a legal system.

In place of Austin's reliance on sanctions as a source of law's authority, Hart emphasizes the idea that law consists in *rules*, in particular, *social rules*. There is a difference between what people do *as a rule* and what they do when they are *following a rule*. In the latter case, the rule provides them with a reason for doing what they do. Social rules have both normative and descriptive dimensions. Rather than being mere descriptions of what individuals are in the habit of doing (as, for example, the habit of obeying the commands of a sovereign), rules provide agents with reasons for doing what they do (as a rule), and with grounds for criticizing those who fail to follow suit. Rules, when accepted from an "internal point of view," provide reasons for acting apart from the mere reasons of prudence that threats supply. Social rules, in short, are normative in a way that habits of obedience are not – or so Hart argues. If law is normative, it is because it consists in rules. (Threats, by contrast, can only explain the sense in which one feels *obliged* to comply, not the sense in which one feels one has an obligation of obedience.)

The *content* of a social rule depends on the scope of convergent behavior, and its *normativity* depends on its being accepted from an internal point of view by the majority of individuals. There is an essential behavioristic dimension to both aspects of social rules. Its content is fixed by behavior, and its normativity depends on acceptance, which is not simply a psychological state or disposition, but a pattern of behavior related to that state or disposition: namely, the reflective practices of justification and criticism by appeal to the rule. Just as Austin identifies law with social facts – the orders or commands of sovereigns – Hart also advocates understanding law in terms of social facts – in his case, social rules: that is, normative practices whose content and normative force depend on actual behavior.

We can distinguish social from other kinds of normative rules, including those of *critical morality*. A requirement of critical morality need not describe or correspond to a prevailing practice; in fact it may be inconsistent with prevailing practice. At the other extreme are descriptions of existing practices – accounts of what individuals do as a rule. The rules of critical morality have normative force in a way in which rules that are mere descriptions of behavior do not, but their force is independent of social practices. It should be clear that the concept of a social rule is designed to fit between Austin's habits of obedience and the view that law consists in rules of critical morality. If Hart is correct, the former are inadequate to explain the normative force of law, whereas the latter explain the normative force of law by rooting it in the demands of critical morality in violation of the separability thesis.

The authority of law

Hart advances two distinct views about the role of social rules in explaining the authority of law. In the earlier sections of *The Concept of Law*, he argues that law is authoritative because it consists in social rules. The social rule theory does not represent Hart's ultimate view about legal authority, however. Often legal rules are enacted to promote social practices where none exist, or to mediate between conflicting social practices, or even to eliminate an undesirable, but nevertheless widespread social practice. In each of these cases, the law's validity does not depend on the existence of the corresponding social practice. Being a social rule, then, is not a necessary condition of legal validity. If law is authoritative, it cannot be because all laws are social rules.

Once Hart correctly, albeit not explicitly, abandons the view that law consists in social rules, he needs an account both of legality and authority that does not depend on the claim that the distinctive feature of legal rules is that they are social rules. The view he comes to is roughly this: the rule of recognition is a social rule whose authority depends on its being accepted from the internal point of view by the relevant officials, that is, judges. Rules subordinate to the rule of recognition may or may not be social rules. Their status as law is independent of that fact and so is their authority. Instead, their authority derives from their being valid under the rule of recognition. The authority of the rule of recognition is transferred to rules whose legality depends on their standing in the relationship of being valid under the rule of recognition.

There are two problems with this account of legal authority. Even if we accept that the rule of recognition is authoritative in virtue of its being a social rule, it does not follow that rules valid under the rule of recognition are authoritative in virtue of their validity under the rule of recognition. The rule of recognition applies only to the behavior of relevant officials. It provides officials with very narrowly defined reasons for acting – that is, grounds for applying certain criteria as standards for assessing the validity of other "legal" actions. These reasons simply have nothing to do with the reasons legal rules in general might be said to provide ordinary citizens. Whereas the validity relationship is truth preserving, it is not authority transferring.

Second, the authority of the rule of recognition does not derive from its being a social rule, that is, its being accepted from an internal point of view. Acceptance from an internal point of view is expressed through the behavior of appealing to the rule as a grounds of criticism and justification. The claim that the authority of a social rule derives from the internal point of view thus amounts to the view that what makes a norm reason giving is the fact that the majority of individuals treat it as such. But the authority of a rule (its reason-giving capacity) cannot be grounded in the mere fact that individuals treat it as reason giving.

Typically a normative social practice will be accepted from an internal point of view. That is, if a rule or practice is normative, individuals are likely to appeal to it as providing them with justifications for what they do and grounds for criticizing the non-compliance of others. Acceptance from an internal point of view is likely to be a reliable indicator of the normativity of a social practice. But if acceptance from an internal point of view is inadequate to explain the normative force of a social rule, what does?

Social rules have two components: the description of what individuals do as a rule and their being accepted from an internal point of view. If the internal point of view does not explain the rule's normative authority, the only remaining possibility is the fact of convergent behavior. Accounts of legal authority rooted in convergent behavior have been ignored ever since Hart devastated Austin's version of it in *The Concept of Law*. How, after all, can the mere fact that individuals do something as a rule provide someone with a reason for doing the same thing?

Here are two ways in which merely convergent behavior can be reason giving. Suppose Newt is self-interested. Then the fact that everyone drives on the right side of the road gives Newt a reason for doing the same thing. Newt's interests often require him to co-ordinate his behavior with others, and when they do, Newt has a reason to do what others do simply because they do what they do. The fact of convergent behavior, then, provides a *prudential* reason for treating law as authoritative.

Alternatively, suppose that Emma is motivated to do the right thing but is uncertain about what morality requires of her. If Emma believes that others are similarly motivated, then Emma has a reason to do what they are doing – not because in doing so Emma co-ordinates with others but rather because, on the (plainly contestable) assumption that others are trying to do what morality requires, by following their lead, Emma is more likely to be doing what she ought to do, that is, the right thing. Here, then, the fact of convergent behavior provides an *instrumental* reason of morality for treating the law as authoritative.

Some officials believe that the rule of recognition provides something like the right standards for evaluating the validity of norms subordinate to it. For them, compliance with what other officials do may be required in order that they all do what is required (morally or otherwise). Still other officials are motivated largely by a desire to co-ordinate their behavior with other officials – quite apart from their views about the substantive merits of the rule of recognition itself. The avoidance of confusion and mayhem, as well as the conditions of liberal stability require co-ordination among officials. Whether motivated by political or private moral virtue, or even by brute self-interest, the mere fact that many judges act in a certain way – that is, apply certain standards to determine legal validity and reason from those standards in certain ways – can provide particular officials with a compelling reason to do what others do – just because they do it. Convergent behavior, not acceptance from the internal point of view, is the key to understanding the authority of the rule of recognition.

What becomes, then, of Hart's notion of the internal point of view? We can take what Hart offers as an analysis of a social rule as in fact a stipulative definition of the term: a norm cannot be a social rule unless it is accepted from the internal point of view. In that case, the internal point of view is a necessary condition of a norm's being a social rule. Acceptance, then, from the internal point of view may be both a necessary condition of a normative practice constituting a social rule and a reliable indicator that a practice or rule is normative. But it is not this fact about social rules that explains their normative force. Instead, convergence does the normative work – at least with respect to the rule of recognition. We still require, however, an account of the authority of rules subordinate to the rule of recognition.

To develop such an account, we need to say more about the positivist conception of legality. Hart correctly rejected Austin's conception of law as the commands of a "sovereign" backed by threatened sanctions. In its place, we have acknowledged a distinction between the rule of recognition and other kinds of (primary) rules: those that confer power and those that impose obligations. The centerpiece of this conception of legality is the rule of recognition. One useful way of developing this conception of legality is to examine Dworkin's objections to it. Once we have this conception of legality in place, we can then take up the question of what explains the authority of law so conceived.

Judicial discretion

Dworkin (1977, pp. 14–45) describes Hart's position in terms of four basic tenets: (1) the rule of recognition; (2) the model of rules, that is, the claim that all legally binding norms are rules; (3) the separability thesis; and (4) judicial discretion, that is, the constrained authority of judges to appeal to standards other than those legally binding on them in order to resolve controversial legal disputes. We have discussed each of these except the argument for judicial discretion.

Why is judicial discretion unavoidable? Hart suggests two general lines of argument: one having to do with the rule of recognition, the other with the "open texture" of language. As Hart understands it, a rule of recognition sets forth the conditions necessary and sufficient for a norm's counting as part of a community's law. The set of norms satisfying these conditions will be finite. It is conceivable that a dispute will arise in which no norm satisfying the rule of recognition applies or controls the outcome. In such a case, the judge has no option but to go beyond the set of binding legal norms and consult a non-legally binding standard.

Even where there are binding legal norms, discretion may still be required. Legal rules, after all, are expressed in general terms (for example, "No vehicles in the park"). General terms have a core of accepted meaning and a penumbra of uncertain or controversial meaning. A man without hair is "bald"; a Rolls-Royce is a "vehicle." But is a man with a hundred hairs bald? Is a motor scooter a "vehicle"? Rational individuals who are competent speakers of the language cannot disagree about whether a hairless man is bald, or a Rolls-Royce is a vehicle; but they can disagree about whether a man with thinning hair is bald and whether a motor scooter is a vehicle.

Terms like "bald" and "vehicle" are general (or sortal) terms and they appear everywhere in the law. Cases arise in which the question is whether the general term applies to the facts at hand. Hart's idea is that there is a distinction between easy and hard cases that parallels the distinction between the core and penumbra of a concept. Legal rules are binding with respect to their core instances: no rational, competent speaker of the language could deny that the rule applies in such cases. However, with respect to the penumbra of a concept, rational disagreement is possible and the law dictates no particular answer. The judge must exercise discretion and, in effect, legislate meaning. In doing so, he typically appeals to norms of fairness as well as to the policies that the law could be seen as aspiring to implement. In doing so, judges typically appeal to moral principles and social policies that are not themselves binding legal standards. This view of discretion, then, grows out of a particular theory of meaning.

Dworkin's objections to Hart exploit his theory of adjudication, especially its commitment to discretion. Dworkin agrees with Hart that in hard cases judges will appeal to moral principles to resolve disputes. Unlike Hart, however, he argues that such norms are not extra-legal standards, but are instead binding legal standards. His evidence for the claim that they are binding legal standards is, moreover, that judges so regard them. They are part of the law though they are not rules in Hart's sense, nor is their status as law a matter of their being identified as law by a rule of recognition. They are part of the law because they express a dimension of justice or fairness suitable to law. If Dworkin is right, *contra* Hart: (1) law is not simply a matter of rules (law includes moral principles); (2) moral principles are law though they are not identified as such under a rule of recognition; (3) moral principles are law *in virtue* of their expressing a dimension of morality, thus violating the separability thesis; and (4) instead of exercising discretion, judges appeal to binding legal standards that are not rules. All four tenets of Hart's positivism must be abandoned.

Though many positivists have taken up the task of responding to Dworkin's objections, the centerpiece of many of these has been the idea that ("inclusive") positivism can allow moral principles to be legally binding standards provided their being law depends on their satisfying a condition in the rule of recognition (cf. Sartorious, 1971; Hart, 1994). The idea is that moral principles can figure in the law as binding standards only if they are identified as such under a rule of recognition. In that case, it is not their morality as such that makes them law; rather, it is the *fact* that they meet the demands set forth in the rule of recognition. Allowing moral principles to be legally binding in this way saves both the separability thesis and the rule of recognition. The separability thesis is saved because what makes even moral principles binding law is that they are recognized as such under a rule of recognition, not their truth. The rule of recognition is saved just because the legality of all norms – including moral principles – depends on establishing that they satisfy the demands set forth in the rule of recognition.

Some positivists, notably Raz (1979) and his followers (for example, Marmor, 1992), take a different tack: they claim there are far better explanations for why judges might argue *as if* moral principles are legally binding than that they really are legally binding. Politically, for example, it behooves unelected judges to act as though they are "constrained" by law rather than owning up to their exercise of discretion.

If a positivist incorporates into law moral principles that are not rules, the positivist must abandon the model of rules. This is not a problem, however, since no positivist – not even Hart – advances this model. Hart's point has always been that law is a rule-governed (that is, a normative) practice, where rule-governed is always intended to be broadly construed so as to include customary practices and other norms (cf. Hart, 1994). Dworkin's objection is based on a narrow and uncharitable reading of Hart. Positivists are prepared to accept that a variety of different kinds of norms can count as law. What they insist on is that the legality of those norms be established by a rule of recognition.

What about the positivist's apparent commitment to judicial discretion? By allowing moral principles to count as law the number of binding legal standards increases. This suggests that the number of occasions on which a judge will face a case without the benefit of guiding or controlling legal standards will decrease significantly. That means that the extent of judicial discretion resulting from the paucity of available legal standards will diminish. At some point, it may be reduced to an insignificant fraction of the total number of cases litigated. Increasing the absolute number of binding legal standards affects only this argument for discretion, however. More standards suggests more cases involving the penumbra of general terms. Indeed, moral principles are especially contestable in just this way. Concepts like "justice" and "fairness" are likely to be even vaguer and more contestable than terms like "bald" and "vehicle" are. So increasing the set of binding legal standards by incorporating controversial moral principles into law may actually increase the extent of discretion owing to problems of vagueness and controversy. In short, Dworkin's objections do not appear decisive against a sympathetic reformulation of Hart's positivism.

Incorporationism and legality

Even if moral principles can sometimes be binding on officials, inclusive positivism or incorporationism claims that this fact about moral principles can be explained by the rule of recognition. The legality of moral norms is not a function of their morality, but their validity under a rule of recognition; the rule of recognition in a particular community asserts, in effect, that certain norms are law provided they meet the demands of justice, or that they cannot be law unless they do so, and so on. Incorporationism depends on a rule of recognition incorporating morality into law. Dworkin denies that legal positivists can be incorporationists in this sense, and offers four different objections to a positivist's attempt to incorporate morality into law through the rule of recognition. (Note that some of these objections would also be accepted by positivists who are not incorporationists; cf. Raz, 1985.)

First, a rule of recognition that includes reference to moral principles will violate the separability thesis. Second, positivism is committed to the idea that what makes something law depends on its history or the form and manner of its enactment: legality, for a positivist, cannot depend on the substantive value of a norm or the truth of a moral principle. Incorporationism violates this requirement. Third, positivism is committed to the rule of recognition serving an epistemic function: that is, by consulting it, individuals can determine for themselves what the law is and what it requires of them. Incorporationism allows morality into law in a way that makes it impossible for the rule of recognition to serve its epistemic function. Fourth, positivism is committed to the rule of recognition being a social rule. Incorporationism renders the rule of recognition incapable of being a social rule. How might the incorporationist respond to these objections?

Coleman (1982) has argued that the core of the separability thesis is given by what he calls negative positivism: the claim that there is no *necessary* connection between law and morality. This does not preclude a rule of recognition from incorporating morality into law. It only precludes positivism from claiming that law must necessarily incorporate morality into law – everywhere, in all possible legal systems.

Is positivism committed to pedigree, historical or non-contentful criteria of legality? In fact, incorporationism does not entail the absence of a pedigree or non-contentful criterion of legality. A rule of recognition might hold, for example, that a principle is part of the law to the extent it is appealed to in preambles to legislation, judicial opinions and the like. Under such a rule, it is the fact that a moral principle is cited that contributes to its legality, not the fact that the principle is true or expresses a dimension of justice, or the like. (Some incorporationists go further and argue that moral principles can count as law in virtue of their truth, though this position is quite controversial among positivists. Cf. Coleman, 1995.)

Does incorporationism undermine positivism's commitment to the idea that the rule of recognition serve an epistemic function? The worry is this: a rule of recognition should allow individuals to determine which norms are binding law; the rule of recognition is, after all, a rule of *recognition*. Hart himself introduces it by discussing the role it plays in reducing uncertainty about the law of a community. Unfortunately, a rule that makes morality a criterion of legality fails to reduce uncertainty, because moral principles are inherently controversial.

We can distinguish, however, between two different epistemic functions the rule of recognition might be asked to serve: validation and identification. The rule of recognition is the standard in virtue of which *officials*, especially judges, validate the legality of norms. Legal positivism is committed to the rule of recognition's serving a validation function. Nothing in incorporationism threatens the rule of recognition's ability to serve that function. That a rule of recognition may be controversial in its instantiations, however, does not entail that judges disagree about what the rule is. They disagree, perhaps, only about what it requires. In that case, they do not disagree about what the validation standard is, only about what it validates.

Finally, Dworkin claims that a rule of recognition that incorporates morality into law cannot be a social rule. A social rule requires a pattern of convergent behavior. A rule of recognition that incorporates morality will generate disagreement because officials will disagree about its requirements or instantiations. So the element of convergent practice will be missing. As just noted, however, disagreement about a rule's instantiations is compatible with agreement about what the rule is. Officials can agree that the rule of recognition requires incorporating some moral principles into law, while disagreeing among one another about what those principles are. Nevertheless, their behavior converges in the requisite way.

Incorporationism responds to Dworkin's earlier objections to positivism. Its plausibility depends on understanding the rule of recognition in a way that permits it to incorporate moral principles into law. Dworkin offers four arguments to the effect that such a rule of recognition would be incompatible with positivism's most fundamental commitments. Arguably, however, Dworkin either misunderstands positivism's commitments or underestimates the resources available to the incorporationist to meet the objections. Interestingly, positivists like Raz share many of

Dworkin's worries. These worries become most apparent when we consider whether incorporationism can provide a plausible positivist conception of law's authority.

Raz's theory of authority

Recall that we distinguished between the authority of the rule of recognition and the authority of rules subordinate to it. The authority of the rule of recognition, it was suggested, depends on the convergent behavior of relevant officials. What matters, in this view, is that officials converge, not what norm their behavior converges on; they might even converge on the kind of rule of recognition incorporationism favors. Thus, nothing in the account of the authority of the rule of recognition is incompatible with the incorporationist's conception of legality. The question remains whether incorporationism is compatible with the best available positivist conception of the authority of rules subordinate to the rule of recognition. In considering the authority of rules subordinate to the rule of recognition, we have already ruled out Austin's account in terms of sanctions and Hart's account of authority in terms of the internal point of view. What alternatives remain?

The most influential positivist account of legal authority is due to Joseph Raz (1979, 1985). Yet Raz believes that his account of authority is incompatible with incorporationism. So can incorporationism be reconciled with the Razian account of authority?

We can begin by outlining the central features and key insights of Raz's view. Each of us asks ourselves, on various occasions: what ought I to do? What we ought to do depends on the reasons that apply to us – reasons that would ground or justify one or another course of conduct. We can suppose that there are good moral reasons and good prudential reasons, and that the balance of reasons will, typically, settle for us what we ought to do. Of course, we may be unclear from time to time about the proper weight to assign to various reasons and there will be conflicts that may, from time to time, seem unresolvable by reason alone. Setting these problems aside for now, we may suppose that the set of reasons that apply to us settles the issue of what we ought to do even if we are not always altogether clear about the answer that reason supplies.

We can refer to the answer reason supplies as the requirements of "right reason." To say that the law is a practical authority is to say that it provides an independent and different reason for acting that figures in the decisions of agents as to what they ought to do. Our concern is with the relationship between the reasons that law supplies and those that already apply: the demands of right reason. There are three possibilities: (1) the reasons law supplies might be generally unrelated to the demands of right reason, thus giving us more reasons to think about; (2) they might, in general, conflict with the demands of right reason; or (3) they might generally coincide with those demands.

The Austinian view is that law provides distinct and altogether different reasons for acting than those that already apply (in the absence of law). Avoiding legal sanction gives us something else to think about when we are contemplating what

253

we ought to do. Hart, however, convincingly argues that sanctions do not adequately explain the claim that law makes to being a practical authority, a claim whose truth or falsity would not hang on whether particular legal directives were backed by threats.

That leaves us with options (2) and (3). The reasons law provides can either generally coincide with those of right reason or stand in conflict with them. If the reasons law provides conflict with the demands of right reason, then it would not be rational for individuals to act on the basis of law's reasons. Law leads agents away from right reason, and, therefore, away from what they ought to do. Legal authority appears to require that law's reasons generally coincide with the demands of reason. If law's reasons, however, merely reiterate or reaffirm the demands of right reason, law's reason is otiose. Law's reason merely confirms what we ought to do; it does not provide us with a reason for acting different (in any way other than logically) from the reasons we already have. It appears that either the law is irrational or otiose; either interpretation fails to provide a basis for a plausible claim to authority. How, then, can law be a practical authority when the reasons it supplies coincide with those of right reason?

One's directives are authoritative only if individuals acting on the basis of them are likely to comply more fully with the reasons they already have for acting. Somewhat more precisely, in order for law to be a practical authority, it must be the case that for each agent for whom law is an authority, that agent would more fully or satisfactorily comply with the demands of right reason that apply to him by acting on the basis of the reasons law supplies than he would do otherwise. Raz calls this the normal justification thesis (1985, p. 299). Thus, the authority of law depends on its efficacy in this sense.

How can one do better by complying with the demands of right reason by following legal directives than one would do by following the demands of reason directly? There are two possibilities. Even when we have access to the relevant reasons and can assess adequately their weight in the balance of reasons, we may be unable to co-ordinate our behavior with others in ways that are necessary to bring about what we all have good and sufficient reasons for doing. Suppose we will all benefit from the provision of certain services – for example, police, schools, health care, and so on. Each of us has prudential or self-interested reasons for creating the institutions that provide these benefits, but none of us is capable either of creating the institutions individually or of organizing the large-scale collective efforts that would otherwise be necessary. Thus, we are much more likely to succeed in creating these institutions if we follow legal directives that tax us for the purposes of funding and establishing these institutions than we would be by acting on the basis of the reasons we have. In this kind of case, law's claim to authority is connected to its co-ordination function. (Notice that co-ordination arguments can be extended beyond the standard case of providing public goods. Suppose each of us had a reason for acting that required us to ensure that no one in the relevant political community of which we were members fell below a certain minimum level of income. We would be much more likely to succeed in meeting the demands of right reason by putting in place some sort of welfare state than we would by trying to meet the demands of reason individually. Our individual efforts, however well motivated, would be overcome by various epistemic and free-rider problems that only a legally created welfare state can overcome.)

Now consider an argument for legal authority that is not based on law's co-ordination function. Suppose that right reason requires that all of us be act-utilitarians. Very few of us are actually in a particularly good position to determine which course of conduct is required of us all the time. We do not have access, for example, to most people's benefit and damage schedules. At least with respect to some of the larger scale projects to which we might be required to contribute, we would probably do better as utilitarians if we followed the judgments of democratically elected public officials. Their legislative decisions are reached after gathering information that we are not in a position to secure. In such cases, law's authority would derive from its special epistemic role.

In short: there are times when each of us would do better following the law than we would acting directly on the basis of right reason. Typically, these are cases involving problems of co-ordination or uncertainty. The claim to legal authority is based on the thought that the reasons law provides replace the reasons that otherwise apply to us because acting on the former will enable us more fully to comply with the demands of the latter than we will by acting on the basis of them directly. To the extent to which it is generally true that one will do better acting on the basis of law's reason than by acting on the basis of the reasons law provides, it is rational for us to accept law as an authority over us. There will always be areas, of course, in which we have a special expertise, and cases in which the law makes clear mistakes. Its authority will therefore be incomplete at best.

Incorporationism and authority

Raz believes that his account of authority presupposes the "sources thesis": the thesis that a norm is law only if it has a social source (for example, being duly enacted by the legislature). Incorporationism, however, allows that sometimes the legal validity of a norm could depend on its moral truth rather than on its having a social source. Thus, the sources thesis appears to be incompatible with incorporationism.

Does authority require the sources thesis? And are the underlying motivations for the sources thesis really incompatible with incorporationism? Before answering these questions, it is worth noting the relationships among incorporationists, Dworkin and Raz.

Dworkin and Raz both believe that legal positivism cannot allow incorporationism. Dworkin draws this conclusion from considering various deep commitments of positivism, for example, the separability thesis, the social thesis and the rule of recognition's epistemic function. In contrast, Raz draws the same conclusion from considerations drawn from a positivist account of legal authority. Incorporationists and Dworkin believe that modern legal democracies incorporate moral principles into law without regard to their social source, and in that way both disagree with Raz. Incorporationists claim that this is accomplished through the rule of recognition; Dworkin argues that this is achieved through the practice of adjudication.

The burden for the Razian is to explain the role of moral principles in law without resorting to incorporationism; the burden for the incorporationist is to provide a theory of authority that is positivistic in spirit and compatible with incorporationism. And that is why Raz represents a more formidable challenge to the incorporationist than Dworkin does. (Notice, in this regard, that Hart (1994) decided, wrongly it seems, to spend most of his time responding to Dworkin rather than to Raz.)

According to the sources thesis, legality depends on a norm's social source, not its substantive content or underlying justification. What in the theory of authority appears to require this constraint? What would be problematic for the Razian theory of authority if the legality of a moral norm depended in some way on aspects of its moral merits? The idea is this: suppose that determining whether or not a norm constitutes part of a community's law meant engaging in substantive moral argument of the sort incorporationism appears to envision and allow. In determining whether a norm was valid law, one would be forced to uncover the underlying justificatory (moral) reasons that already apply to individuals. In determining, for example, whether a norm against murder was valid law one would be looking to see what justifies the prohibition against murder and thus why one has a reason not to murder. Doing that, however, would be incompatible with treating law as an authority. To treat law as an authority is to forego assessing the underlying or justificatory reasons. Authority presupposes foregoing precisely the sort of inquiry incorporationism appears to invite.

Suppose, however, that the rule of recognition has a clause to the effect that no norm can count as part of the community's law if it violates due process or equal protection, or even more generally, fairness. In this sense, the validity of the law depends on aspects of its morality. Determining whether or not a norm counts as law would require us to explore aspects of its moral value, in particular, its fairness. But that inquiry does not lead us to uncover the moral reasons that would justify the prohibition in the first place – the reasons that would already explain to us why we ought to act in a particular way or forebear from acting in certain ways.

An example might be helpful. The legislature passes a prohibition against certain forms of intentional killings. We all know the kinds of reasons that would justify such a prohibition. Suppose the rule of recognition says that a legislative enactment can be valid law only if it meets the demands of fairness. If a court is asked to determine the validity of the legislative enactment, it will inquire into a range of matters. The court will no doubt be looking to questions about the form and manner of enactment. Once it moves beyond those matters, it might take up the question of whether the law meets the requirements of fairness, a moral requirement of legal validity. At no time, however, in inquiring into the validity of the enactment must the court look to the underlying moral reasons for having a prohibition against certain forms of intentional killings. At least, without further argument, it does not follow from the fact that a rule of recognition makes reference to substantive moral considerations as a condition of legal validity that inquiries into legal validity will lead to the underlying justificatory reasons of legislation in a way that is incompatible with the concept of authority.

A related argument against incorporationism would go something like this: if the law is to be an authority, the rule of recognition must serve an identification and not merely a validation function. The kind of rule of recognition that incorporationism allows is incompatible with its serving this kind of identification function.

The rule of recognition must serve an identification function for the following reason: law is an authority only if individuals acting on the basis of it will do better in complying with the demands of right reason than they would do otherwise. For individuals to act on the basis of law's directives, however, they have to be aware of what the law requires of them. That means that the rule of recognition must make the law accessible to them – it must fulfill the *epistemic* function of *identifying* what the law is.

Moreover, even if the rule of recognition served an identification function, it would not follow that the considerations brought to bear on the question of identification would coincide entirely with those that are relevant to justification. The moral reasons that bear on identifying the rule as law need not coincide with those that figure in its justification, that is, those that establish the way in which it is connected to the demands of right reason.

This is an argument for the sources thesis. After all, the considerations of morality that justify the prohibition against certain intentional killings and those that specify the content of fairness, due process, and equal protection may be controversial. This means that if moral principles are essential to the practice by which ordinary citizens come to recognize which of the community's norms count as binding law, then the rule of recognition (as conceived by the incorporationist) will not discharge its epistemic function.

Incorporationists have two possible lines of response. Hart (1994) concedes the centrality of the rule of recognition's epistemic function, and concedes that incorporating morality into law makes law more uncertain. But, Hart contends,

> the exclusion of all uncertainty at whatever costs in other values is not a goal which I have ever envisaged for the rule of recognition . . . A margin of uncertainty should be tolerated, and indeed welcomed in the case of many legal rules, so that an informed judicial decision can be made when the composition of an unforeseen case is known and the issues at stake in its decision can be identified and rationally settled. (*pp. 251–2*)

Thus, the positivist might argue that Raz is mistaken to think that the authority of law requires that there be no margin of uncertainty that results from incorporating morality into law.

Other incorporationists question whether incorporating morality into law really renders law uncertain (as Hart seems to suppose) (cf. Coleman, 1995). Recall the distinction between validation and identification. The rule that officials must use to determine legal validity need not be the same rule that ordinary·citizens employ in order to identify the law that applies to them. Indeed, ordinary citizens tend to either know what the law is (especially the criminal law) or to find out what the law is from lawyers. In both cases, the law provides authoritative guidance without citizens being able to formulate themselves the relevant rule of recognition!

The argument for authority we are considering now depends on ordinary citizens being in a position to identify and act upon the law that applies to them. That requires that citizens have access to a reliable indicator of what the law in their community is. That indicator may or may not be the rule of recognition; empirically, it seems it probably is not. If the rule that citizens typically turn to in order to determine the law that applies to them is not the rule of recognition, then it does not matter what kinds of constraints the rule of recognition imposes. All that is required of the rule of identification is that it be a reliable indicator of what turns out to be valid law. (It still remains, however, a significant problem for the incorporationist to explain how it is that a rule of identification can be a reliable indicator of what the law is if it is different from the rule of validation.)

It might turn out (as an empirical and not a conceptual matter) that the only kinds of rules that ordinary citizens can appeal to in determining the law that applies to them are ones that satisfy the sources thesis: that is, ones in which the law is identified by its source. In that case, we could view the sources thesis only as a *constraint on the theory of authority, not on the theory of validity*. What makes something law, in other words, need not depend on its social source. Incorporationism, then, would be compatible with validity and thus with any plausible conception of legality. All law, however, also claims authority. In order for that claim to be true, most, if not all, legal norms must be identifiable as such in light of their social sources. Only then can individuals appeal to them in ways that might prove fruitful from the point of view of their interest in complying with the reasons that apply to them. So understood, the sources thesis would be a condition of legitimate authority and not a constraint on the standards of legal validity.

This would impose a constraint on the rule of recognition were it necessarily an identification rule, that is, were it the case that ordinary citizens had to appeal to it in order to identify the law that applies to them. In fact, all that positivists really require is that there exist some practice that enables ordinary citizens reliably to determine the law. *That* practice need not coincide with the rule of recognition (cf. Coleman, 1995). The sources thesis, then, would impose a constraint on the rule of identification and not the rule of validation. For there to be law there must be a validation rule – one that is as broad as incorporationism allows. For law to be authoritative, however, there must be an identification rule – one that may not be so broad. There is a problem for incorporationism only if those two rules must be the same rule.

The same general strategy of argument connects the two elements of the account of legal authority developed so far. The authority of the rule of recognition depends ultimately on considerations of co-ordination and knowledge. The same is true with respect to the authority of rules subordinate to the rule of recognition. With respect to the rule of recognition, officials have reason to comply with what others do as a rule if they want to co-ordinate their behavior with what others do, or if they believe that the behavior of others reflects an understanding of what the appropriate standards of validity are. The link is between individual action and the convergent behavior of other officials.

That link is unavailable as a general explanation of the authority of rules subordinate to the rule of recognition. Here the link is between the reasons that already apply to agents and the agents' grounds for believing that the law's reasons provide a better avenue for complying with them than they otherwise would have. The agent's confidence is a function of the law's expertise and its abilities to co-ordinate human action. So while the account given so far draws a distinction between the authority of the rule of recognition and the authority of rules subordinate to it, the same general account is at work in both.

Conclusion

An adequate jurisprudence should include accounts of the concepts of legality and authority, as well as providing a theory of adjudication. As a rule, positivists have focussed primarily on issues pertaining to the concepts of legality and authority. Central to positivism's analysis of legality is the institutional nature of law; central to its analysis of authority is the idea of efficacy. Individual positivists, as the foregoing has made clear, differ significantly on how the details of legality and authority are best explained.

Bibliography

Austin, J. 1955: *The Province of Jurisprudence Determined*. London: Weidenfeld & Nicolson.
Coleman, J. L. [1982] 1983: Negative and positive positivism. *Journal of Legal Studies*, 11, 139–64. Reprinted in M. Cohen (ed.), *Ronald Dworkin and Contemporary Jurisprudence*, London: Duckworth.
—— 1995: Reason and authority. In R. George (ed.), *The Autonomy of Law: essays on legal positivism*, Oxford: Oxford University Press.
Dworkin, R. 1977: *Taking Rights Seriously*. Cambridge. Mass.: Harvard University Press.
—— 1986: *Law's Empire*. Cambridge, Mass.: Harvard University Press.
Hart, H. L. A. 1961: *The Concept of Law*. Oxford: Clarendon Press.
—— 1983: *Essays on Jurisprudence and Philosophy*. Oxford: Clarendon Press.
—— 1994: Postscript. In P. Bulloch and J. Raz (eds), *The Concept of Law*, Oxford: Clarendon Press, 2nd edn.
Kelsen, H. 1968: *The Pure Theory of Law*. Berkeley: University of California Press.
Lyons, D. 1977: Principles, positivism and legal theory. *Yale Law Journal*, 87, 415–35.
Marmor, A. 1992: *Interpretation and Legal Theory*. Oxford: Clarendon Press.
Postema, G. J. 1986: *Bentham and the Common Law Tradition*. Oxford: Clarendon Press.

Raz, J. 1979: *The Authority of Law*. Oxford: Clarendon Press.
—— 1985: Authority, law and morality. *The Monist*, 68, 295–324.
Sartorious, R. 1971: Social policy and judicial legislation. *American Philosophical Quarterly*, 8, 151–60.
Soper, E. P. 1977: Legal theory and the obligation of a judge: the Hart/Dworkin dispute. *Michigan Law Review*, 75, 473–519.
Waluchow, W. 1994: *Inclusive Positivism*. Oxford: Clarendon Press.

16

Legal realism

BRIAN LEITER

"Legal realism" refers to an intellectual movement in the United States that coalesced around a group of law professors and lawyers in the 1920s and 1930s, including Karl Llewellyn, Jerome Frank, Felix Cohen, Herman Oliphant, Walter Wheeler Cook, Underhill Moore, Hessel Yntema, and Max Radin. These writers thought of themselves as taking a *realistic* look at how judges decide cases, at "what the courts . . . do in fact," as Oliver Wendell Holmes, Jr (a major intellectual forebear) put it (Holmes, 1897, p. 461). What judges really do, according to the realists, is decide cases according to how the facts of the cases strike them, and not because legal rules require particular results; judges are largely "fact-responsive" rather than "rule-responsive" in reaching decisions.

How a judge responds to the facts of a particular case is determined by various psychological and sociological factors, both conscious and unconscious. The final decision, then, is the product not so much of "law" (which generally permits more than one outcome to be justified) but of these various psycho-social factors, ranging from the political ideology to the institutional role to the personality of the judge. Thus, the legacy of realism in both the practice and teaching of law consists of phenomena like these: lawyers now recognize that judges are influenced by more than legal rules; judges and lawyers openly consider the policy or political implications of legal rules and decisions; law texts now routinely consider the economic, political, and historical context of judicial decisions. In this sense, it is often said that "we are all realists now."

The realists are by now the subject of a substantial historical literature (see the bibliography to Fisher, 1993, pp. 325–6). This article will concentrate, by contrast, on the largely neglected, but substantial, contributions of realism to a philosophical theory of law and adjudication, one at odds with the mainstream of the jurisprudential tradition. The realists, unfortunately, often expressed hostility to systematic theorizing and even denied the existence of a "realistic" school of thought; their own theoretical efforts were, at the same time, hindered by a lack of philosophical sophistication and control. These features of their work have led to a highly critical treatment of the realists in the work of later, more philosophically acute jurisprudents (cf. Hart, 1961). Almost despite themselves, however, the realists succeeded in developing a powerful and coherent theoretical view of law and adjudication.

Jurisprudential methodology

Realists have a fundamentally different conception of methodology in jurisprudence, and it is this that puts them at odds with the mainstream of the tradition. Modern legal philosophy has, like most of twentieth-century Anglo-American philosophy, employed the method of *conceptual analysis*: hence the title of the seminal work of this genre (Hart, 1961). In its simplest form, the method of conceptual analysis calls for the explication of the meaning of concepts ("morality," "knowledge," "law") that figure in various human practices; it is an essentially armchair inquiry. Such an approach does, however, aim to illuminate real social institutions, for "the suggestion that inquiries into the meanings of words merely throw light on words is false" (Hart, 1961, p. v); rather one seeks "a sharpened awareness of words to sharpen our perception of phenomena" (Hart, 1961, p. 14, quoting J. L. Austin). In analyzing the concepts, then, we illuminate the social phenomena they describe – for example, our moral, epistemic or legal practices.

Among the features of the *concept* of law thought to require philosophical explication, two are generally taken to be central: (1) of all the various norms in a society, only some subsets are norms of "law" ("criteria of legality"); and (2) that a particular norm is a "legal" norm provides agents with special reasons for acting ("normativity of law"). An account of the criteria of legality demarcates the boundary (if any) between norms of law and all other norms in the society (especially norms of morality), and at the same time defines the scope of judicial obligation: judges must abide by and enforce the norms *of law*. An account of the normativity of law, by contrast, explains how or why law changes our reasons for action. It thus helps demarcate the boundary between group behavior that is merely habitual and that which is genuinely rule governed; in the latter case, but not the former, the norm describing the behavior provides a standard of conduct to which people can legitimately appeal in justifying conformity with or criticizing deviation from the norm. Only when we understand norms from this "internal" point of view – that is, as providing agents with these special reasons for action – can we begin to understand the norms that comprise "law" (Hart, 1961, pp. 54–5). (See Article 15, LEGAL POSITIVISM.)

Realism has often been construed by its critics as a conceptual theory – what might be called "the predictive theory," often attributed to Holmes (1897, pp. 458, 461; see also, Llewellyn, 1930, esp. at pp. 3–4; Frank, 1930, p. 46; Cohen, 1935, pp. 828–9, 839). According to the predictive theory; a norm is a norm of law just in case it constitutes an accurate prediction of what a court will do; the claim that it is the law that a particular exchange of promises constitutes a contract is, on the predictive theory, equivalent to a prediction that a court will enforce these promises when called upon to do so by one of the parties. If a court declines to find an enforceable contract in the case at hand, then, on the predictive theory, there is, as a matter of law, no contract. Thus, the final criterion of legality, for the predictive theory, is what courts do in the particular case, and an accurate statement of law is equivalent to an accurate prediction of what the court will do. Because the predictive theory understands by the concept "law" nothing more than a prediction of what courts will do, the only reason for action provided by the theory comes from the prudent concern of those subject to the "law" to avoid or engage the power of the courts. The statement, "As a matter of law, Mr Jones, you are bound to do *X* by this contract," provides, on the predictive theory, only one reason for action for Mr Jones: namely, his prudent desire to avoid sanction by the courts for failure to perform. The only normativity of law, then, is the type of normativity present for the person Holmes calls "the bad man" "who cares only for the material consequences which . . . knowledge enables him to predict" (Holmes, 1897, p. 459).

The predictive theory, so construed, was famously attacked by H. L. A. Hart (1961, pp. 101–2, 132–44). According to Hart, to conceive of the normativity of law as the Holmesian "bad man" does is to adopt an "external point of view" on the law, "recording and predicting the decisions of courts or the probable incidence of sanctions"; but this is to miss precisely the internal aspect of rules which is distinctive of a legal system, namely that people "continuously express in normative terms their shared acceptance of the law as a guide to conduct" (Hart, 1961, p. 134). This particular criticism, however, seems to miss the mark: for why not see Holmes as also characterizing law from an "internal point of view" and simply contesting how the rules of law look from that point of view? On this Holmesian account of the "internal point of view," norms of law are seen by agents as providing – *contra* Hart – only *prudential* reasons for action (cf. Perry, 1995).

Hart is more successful in his attack on the predictive theory as an account of the criteria of legality. We may summarize the two central difficulties as follows. First, the predictive theory has no satisfactory account of judicial *mistake*; by equating the law with what the court does (or will do), it makes it impossible – indeed unintelligible – to complain that a court is mistaken about the law. Second, the predictive theory simply fails as a conceptual analysis of "law." Take, for example, a judge trying to decide what the "law" is on some point; according to this theory, what she is really trying to do is decide what it is she will do, since the law on this point is equivalent to a prediction of what she will do!

The manifest absurdity of the realists' purported conceptual theory might have suggested that Hart had misinterpreted the realists; yet, on the whole, Hart's criticisms have been widely embraced. In fact, however, there is a better explanation for the absurdity: as a methodological matter, the realists were not engaged in conceptual analysis. Indeed, Holmes makes clear on the very first page of "The path of the law" that he is talking about the meaning of law *to lawyers*, who will "appear before judges, or . . . advise people in such a way as to keep them out of court" (1897, p. 457), and not aiming for a generally applicable analysis of the concept of law. So, too, Frank cautions that he "is primarily concerned with 'law' as it affects the work of the practicing lawyer and the needs of the clients who retain him" (Frank, 1930, p. 47 n.). (Hart's criticisms may be more apt with respect to Cohen, 1935.) In fact, it will become clear as we consider the realist arguments for legal indeterminacy (below) that the realists are, in *conceptual* matters, tacit legal positivists with respect to the criteria of legality.

If the realists are not engaged in conceptual analysis, what methodology are they employing? Interestingly, conceptual analysis has fallen out of favor in philosophy since the late 1960s, except in jurisprudence. This general development marks what might be called "the naturalistic turn" in philosophy, and it is here that we will find the key to realist methodology: for the realists are not bad legal philosophers, as Hart's analysis might suggest, but prescient ones, philosophical naturalists before their time.

Naturalists in philosophy all share the following methodological view: philosophical theorizing ought to be continuous with and dependent upon empirical inquiry in the natural and social sciences. It will not do to seek an acount of phenomena through an armchair analysis of concepts; we must begin, instead, with the relevant empirical data about these phenomena provided by the various sciences, and construct our philosophical theory to accommodate them.

W. V. O. Quine ("Epistemology naturalized" in Kornblith, 1994) provides one important contemporary paradigm of philosophical naturalism, what we may call "Replacement Naturalism." According to Quine, epistemology studies the relationship between evidence (in the form of sensory input) and our various theories about the world (the cognitive "output" as it were). Traditional (non-naturalized) epistemology wants to find a normative, foundational relationship between evidence and theory: it aims to show which of our theories are really *justified* on the basis of indubitable evidence. Quine argues that the foundationalist program is impossible, in part because evidence always underdetermines the choice among theories, and thus does not *justify* only one of them. From the failure of the normative, foundational project, Quine draws the conclusion that the only fruitful study of the relation between evidence (sensory input) and theory (cognitive output) is a descriptive account of what input causes what output, of the sort provided by psychology. Thus, says Quine, "Epistemology . . . simply falls into place as a chapter of psychology" (Kornblith, 1994, p. 25). The science of human cognition *replaces* armchair epistemology: we naturalize epistemology by turning over its central question – the relation between theory and evidence – to the relevant empirical science.

The dominant strand of naturalism in realism is a type of replacement naturalism. Indeed, Quine's famous slogan – "Epistemology . . . simply falls into place as a chapter of psychology" – echoes Underhill Moore's own jurisprudential credo 25 years earlier; his work he says "lies within the province of jurisprudence. It also lies within the field of behavioristic psychology. It places the province within the field" (Moore and Callahan, 1943, p. 1). Jurisprudence – or more precisely, the theory of adjudication – falls into place, for the realist, as a chapter of psychology (or social science generally); we abandon the normative ambition of telling judges how they *ought* to decide cases in order to undertake the *descriptive* study of the causal relations between input (facts and rules of law) and outputs (judicial decisions). This yields a fully naturalized *descriptive* theory of adjudication, rather than a conceptual theory of the criteria of legality or a conceptual theory of adjudication, as a by-product of the former (cf. Hart, 1961).

Yet Moore, it may seem, does not speak for all realists, some of whom appear to

264

retain the ambition of formulating a *normative* theory (as do many naturalistic epistemologists; cf. the essays by Alvin Goldman in Kornblith, 1994). All the realists endorse the following *descriptive* claim about adjudication: in deciding cases, judges respond primarily to the stimulus of the facts. The question, to which we return below, is whether this descriptive claim can be parlayed into a *normative* theory, the traditional ambition of jurisprudence (to tell judges how they *ought* to decide).

Legal indeterminacy

Why abandon the normative ambitions of traditional jurisprudence in favor of replacement naturalism? Here we need to understand the influential realist arguments about the indeterminacy of law.

The law on some point is *rationally* indeterminate when the "class of legal reasons" (hereafter "the class") is insufficient to justify a unique outcome on that point. The class encompasses those reasons that are proper justificatory grounds of judicial decision: for example, that prior, analogous cases have held a similar way or that a relevant statute requires the outcome are legitimate reasons for a judicial decision. The law is *locally* indeterminate when it is indeterminate only in some select range of cases (for example, those cases that reach the stage of appellate review). The law is *globally* indeterminate when it is indeterminate in all cases. (Strictly speaking, we are concerned only with the *under*determinacy of law, not its indeterminacy: we are concerned that the class justifies more than one, but perhaps not simply any, outcome.)

The law is *causally* indeterminate if the class is insufficient to *cause* the judge to reach only one outcome in that case. More precisely, suppose that relevant "background conditions" obtain: judges are rational, honest and competent, and they do not make mistakes. The law is causally indeterminate just in case the class together with relevant background conditions is still insufficient to cause the judge to reach only one outcome in that case. One reason this might be true is, for example, because the law is rationally indeterminate on that point: if the class justifies more than one outcome, then even rational, honest and competent judges will not be caused by applicable legal reasons to reach the decision they reach; we must look elsewhere to find out what caused them to do what they did. (On this way of conceiving the varieties of indeterminacy, see Leiter, 1995.)

All realists defend the following two theses about indeterminacy: (1) the law is rationally indeterminate locally not globally; and (2) the law is causally indeterminate in the cases where it is rationally indeterminate. Some realists defend this additional thesis: (3) the law is causally indeterminate even where it is rationally determinate and the background conditions obtain.

Rational indeterminacy

The class includes legitimate *sources* of law (such as statutes, prior court decisions) and legitimate ways of *interpreting* and reasoning from those sources (for example, interpreting statutes by the "plain meaning", reasoning by analogy). Someone might think the law is indeterminate because there are too few sources of law (so that there are no *legal* reasons for decision on some points) or too many conflicting sources (so that the conflicting sources provide legal reasons for conflicting decisions). The realists, however, argue that rational indeterminacy results from there being too many conflicting but equally legitimate ways of interpreting and reasoning from the sources, thus yielding conflicting legal rules. Thus, for example, Llewellyn argues that it is equally legitimate for a court to treat precedent "strictly" or "loosely." On the strict view,

> a later court can reexamine the [earlier] case and can invoke the canon that no judge has power to decide what is not before him, can, through examination of the facts or of the procedural issue, narrow the picture of what was actually before the court and can hold that the ruling made requires to be understood as thus restricted. In the extreme form this results in what is known as expressly "confining the case to its particular facts". (*1930, p. 72*)

The strict view of precedent, says Llewellyn, "is applied to *unwelcome* precedents" (1930, p. 73), as a way of distinguishing them from the case at hand. But there is another approach to precedent, the "loose view," which "is like the other, recognized, legitimate, honorable" (1930, p. 74). On this view the earlier court "has decided, and decided authoritatively, *any* points or all points on which it chose to rest a case" so that in "its extreme form this results in thinking and arguing exclusively from *language* that is found in past opinions, and in citing and working with that language wholly without reference to the facts of the case which called the language forth" (1930, p. 74). But if "each precedent has not one value [that is, stands for not just one rule], but two, and . . . the two are wide apart, and . . . whichever value a later court assigns to it, such assignment will be respectable, traditionally sound, dogmatically correct" (1930, p. 76), then precedent, as a source of law, cannot provide reasons for a unique outcome, because precedent can be interpreted to stand for more than one rule, and so justify more than one outcome.

As with precedent, Llewellyn argues that with respect to the interpretation of statues, "there are 'correct,' unchallengeable rules of 'how to read' which lead in happily variant directions" (1950, p. 399). By mining the cases, Llewellyn shows that courts have endorsed contradictory "canons of construction" like "A statute cannot go beyond its text" but also "To effect its purpose a statute must be implemented beyond its text" (1950, p. 401; Llewellyn adduces 28 contradictory canons at 401–6; cf. Llewellyn, 1930, p. 90). But if a statute can properly be construed in contradictory ways to stand for different rules, then reasoning from the statute will not justify a unique outcome in the case at hand (cf. Radin, 1930).

Indeterminacy enters not just in the interpretation of statutes and precedents, but also in the wide latitude judges have in how to characterize the facts of a case. After all, rules – what we get by interpreting precedents and statutes – must be applied to facts; but the facts of a case do not come with their own descriptions, and must be characterized in terms of their legal import. Many realists argued here, as well, that judges could legitimately characterize the same facts in differing ways, and thus even with a definite rule, the judge could still be justified in reaching more than one decision depending on how he characterized the facts. (See Frank, 1930, pp. 108–10; Frank, 1931, p. 28; Llewellyn, 1930, p. 80.)

Local indeterminacy

The Realists, unlike the later writers of critical legal studies, defended only the view that the law was *locally* indeterminate, that is, that the class only failed to provide a justification for a unique outcome in some circumscribed class of cases. Most, but not all, realists were concerned with appellate litigation, and with the opinions of appellate courts; all confined themselves to cases that were actually litigated before courts at some level. Thus, Llewellyn explicitly qualified his defense of the indeterminacy of law by saying that "*in any case doubtful enough to make litigation respectable* the available authoritative premises . . . are at least two, and . . . the two are mutually contradictory as applied to the case at hand" (1931, p. 1,239, emphasis added).

Now the evidential base of cases actually litigated clearly could not support the inference that the law is *globally* indeterminate, for it would omit all those "easy" cases in which a clear-cut legal rule dictates a result, and which, consequently, no one (typically, at least) bothers to litigate. In any event, it is far less controversial, and certainly familiar to all practicing lawyers, that the law is locally indeterminate, even if this fact conflicts both with the popular perception in the realists' own day as well as our own. Moreover, if the law is locally indeterminate *in some or most of the cases actually litigated* that still raises the troubling specter of judges deciding cases unconstrained by law. The realists, unlike many contemporary political and legal philosophers, were not concerned with this issue, and in some respects even endorsed the practice unguardedly (see Cohen, 1935).

Causal indeterminacy

All the realists make the point that the law (as the putative cause of decision) is causally indeterminate where it is rationally indeterminate. Indeed, this follows immediately given two assumptions: first, that law exercises its causal influence through reasons; and second, assuming the background conditions obtain, that reasons cannot be the sole cause of a decision if they do not uniquely justify that decision. But if the law is rationally indeterminate on some point, then legal reasons justify more than one decision on that point: thus we must look to additional factors to find out why the judge decided as he did. As Radin remarked, "somewhere, somehow, a judge is impelled to make his selection" of an outcome (1930, p. 881). And as Holmes observed more than 30 years before: "You can give any conclusion a logical form. You always can imply a condition in a contract. But why do you imply it?" Holmes is quick with an answer: the basis for the decision is to be found in "a concealed, half-conscious battle on the [background] question of legislative policy" (1897, pp. 465–6, 467; cf. Llewellyn, 1931, p. 1,252). Other

267

realists, as we shall see shortly, looked to an array of psychological and sociological factors as the *real* causal determinants of decision.

Some realists made the point that the law was causally indeterminate with respect to how a court would rule on a particular dispute precisely because the background conditions often do not obtain (for example, Frank, 1931, p. 240). This raises very different sorts of questions about the legitimacy of the adjudicatory process, and to the extent it is true (and it often is), it is of considerable importance to lawyers and litigants.

But some realists held a further, more startling thesis: that the law is causally indeterminate even where it is rationally determinate *and* the background conditions obtain – precisely because reasons *per se* are causally inefficacious! This view is clearest in Moore, who took most seriously the naturalistic imperative to make jurisprudential theorizing continuous with empirical inquiry in the social sciences (see his 1923, 1929, 1943). For Moore, the relevant science was (usually) psychology, in particular Watsonian behaviorism, which viewed human beings, like rats and dogs, as complex stimulus-response machines.

For the behaviorist, the content of the mind is a black box, not to be invoked in explaining behavior. On this view, reasons are causally relevant only as certain types of (aural, visual) stimuli, but are *not* causally relevant in virtue of their rational content or meaning! ("[A] proposition of law," says Moore "is nothing more than a sensible object which may arouse a drive and cue a response" (1943, p. 3).) So, for the behaviorist, the fact that reasons *justify* a decision is not a causally significant fact, because *justification* involves a relation between the rational content of different propositions, and such content is off-limits for the behaviorist. The law is causally indeterminate on this picture even when it is rationally determinate, because rational determinacy (that is, justification via rational contents) is causally irrelevant for the behaviorist. Thus, Moore can say that the "logical processes of the institution of law . . . throw[ ] no light on any pertinent question as to what the institution has been, is or will be" (1923, p. 611) – that is, such rational processes make no causal difference. Similarly, Moore complains that to move "[f]rom necessary logical deduction to necessary behavior" is "an easy step" but a misstep, presumably because rational determinacy does not entail causal determinacy for the behaviorist (1929, p. 704). And even Llewellyn observed that for Moore's account of adjudication, "all reference to the actor's own ideas is deprecated or excluded" (1931, p. 1,245). This final thesis about indeterminacy is not only the most unfamiliar but also the least important for purposes here.

Notice now that the realist argument for indeterminacy turns on a conception of what constitute *legitimate* members of the class, that is, what count as legitimate *legal* reasons. This, of course, is just to presuppose some view of the criteria of legality, and it is a deficiency of realist jurisprudence that it has no explicit theory on this score. Yet when Holmes chalks up judicial decision not to law but to a half-conscious judgment of policy, he is plainly presuming that such considerations of policy are not legitimate sources of law. And in demonstrating the indeterminacy of *law* by concentrating on indeterminacy in the interpretation of *statutes and precedents* the realists seem to be supposing that these exhaust the authoritative sources of law, a thesis easiest to justify on positivist grounds. Indeed, Llewellyn even says at one point that judges take rules "in the main from authoritative sources (which in the case of the law are largely statutes and the decisions of the courts)" (1930, p. 13). The realists did not develop a conceptual analysis of "law," but it appears they may actually need the positivist analysis!

Finally, we are now in a position to see the motivation for replacement naturalism in jurisprudence. Recall that Quine had argued for replacement naturalism as follows: the central concern of epistemology is the relationship between evidence (input) and theory (output); if a normative, foundational account of this relationship is unrealizable (because, for example, evidence underdetermines theory), then there is only one fruitful account of this relationship to be given: namely, the purely descriptive, causal account given by the science of human cognition.

But now we can see that the realists have made the very same argument about the theory of adjudication. Its central concern is the relation between facts, rules of law, and legal reasoning (that is, the class) – the "input" – and judicial decision – the "output." If the law is always rationally indeterminate, then no normative, foundational account of this relationship is possible; there is no normative, foundational relationship between the class and a particular decision, because the class is able to justify more than one decision (that is, it *underdetermines* any particular decision). Given the failure of the traditional normative project, the realists propose seeking a fruitful *descriptive* account of what input causes what decisions, by subsuming the theory of adjudication within a scientific account of judicial behavior.

Descriptive theory of adjudication

The realists, as philosophical naturalists, sought to make their theorizing about adjudication continuous with scientific inquiry. While all the realists were scientific in attitude and method, only Moore pursued the link with social–scientific inquiry systematically. Indeed, Llewellyn aptly described Moore's position as "semibehaviorist, via cultural anthropology" (1931, p. 1,243 n. 50). Note, however, that the model of psychology, anthropology and social science at work in Moore and in realism more generally is positivistic (in the scientific, not legal, sense), not hermeneutic: we seek to study human (or judicial) behavior as we study the rest of the natural world, relying on detached observation in order to formulate causal laws. The hallmark of the naturalistic impulse in realism is this attempt to "formulat[e] laws of judicial behavior" (Moore and Hope, 1929, p. 704) based on actual observation of what it is courts do in particular cases. As Cook put it: legal scholars must eschew *a priori* methods and "observe concrete phenomena first and . . . form generalizations afterwards" (1924, p. 460).

The central proposition that issued from this inquiry is what we may call the "core claim" of realism: in deciding cases, judges respond primarily to the stimulus of the facts of the case. Observation of court decisions, in other words, shows that judges are deciding based on their response to the facts of the case – what they think would be "right" or "fair" on these facts – rather than because of legal rules

269

and reasons. (Recall that because of the rational indeterminacy of law, judges can justify *post hoc* the decision that strikes them as "fair" on the facts.) The challenge for at least some realists was to correlate facts ("input") with decisions ("output"), in order to "observ[e] and stat[e] the causal relation between past and future decisions" (Moore and Sussman, 1931, p. 560).

The core claim is stated neatly by Oliphant: judges "respond to the stimulus of the facts in the concrete case before them rather than to the stimulus of over-general and outward abstractions in opinions and treatises" (1928, p. 75). Similarly, Llewellyn cautions that, in looking at the pronouncements of appellate courts, one must understand "how far the proposition which seems so abstract has roots in what seems to be the due thing on the facts before the court" (1930, p. 33). Later Llewellyn would speak of "the fact-pressures of the case" (1931, p. 1,243; cf. 1960, p. 122) and "the sense of the situation as seen by the court" as determining the outcome (1960, p. 397). Max Radin suggested that the decision of a judge was determined by "a type situation that has somehow been early called up in his mind" (1925, p. 362), where "type situations" were simply "the standard transactions with their regulatory incidents [which] are familiar ones to [the judge] because of his experience as a citizen and a lawyer" (1925, p. 358) (for example: "the situation of a person bargaining for actual wares, agreeing to pay a certain amount for them and carrying them off on a promise to pay at a future time, is a common situation" (1925, p. 357)).

Federal District Court Judge, Joseph Hutcheson, affirmed that "the vital, motivating impulse for the decision is an intuitive sense of what is right or wrong for that cause" (1929, p. 285). Frank cited "a great American judge, Chancellor Kent" who confessed that, "He first made himself 'master of the facts.' Then (he wrote) 'I saw where justice lay, and the moral sense decided the court half the time; I then sat down to search the authorities . . . but *I almost always found principles suited to my view of the case*'" (1930, p. 104 n.). The same view of judging is presupposed in Llewellyn's advice to lawyers that, while they must provide the court "a technical ladder" justifying the result, what the lawyer must really do is "on the facts . . . persuade the court your case is sound" (Llewellyn, 1930, p. 76). As Frank pointed out, the very same advice had been offered by a former president of the American Bar Association (Frank, 1930, pp. 102–3 n.). It is no small virtue of the realists' core claim that it constitutes what every practicing lawyer knows.

Notice that the core claim forms the crux of the realists' notorious "rule-skepticism" (Hart, 1961, pp. 132–44). The realists were skeptical not about the existence or conceptual coherence of rules, but about whether rules make any significant causal difference in judicial decision making. It is what judges think would be "right" or "fair" on the facts of the case – and not legal rules – that generally determines the course of decision according to the realist. (It is striking, too, that on this central issue Hart can do no better than assert what the realists deny: "*it is surely evident* that for the most part decisions . . . are reached either by genuine effort to conform to rules consciously taken as guiding standards of decision or, if intuitively reached, are justifed by rules which the judge was antecedently disposed to observe and whose relevance to the case in hand would be generally acknowledged" (1961, p. 137, emphasis added). The *real* dispute between Hart and realism, then, is not conceptual, but empirical: it concerns how often rules do or do not matter (causally) in adjudication.)

While all realists accepted the core claim, they divided sharply, however, over the issue of what determines how judges respond to the facts. One wing of realism, represented by Frank and Hutcheson, held that what determines the judge's response to the facts of a particular case are idiosyncratic facts about the psychology or personality of the individual judge (the "idiosyncrasy wing"). Another wing of realism, represented especially by Llewellyn and Moore, held that judicial response to the facts was "socially" determined such that these responses fall into very particular patterns, making generalization and prediction possible (the "sociological wing"). Over time, there has been a gradual "Frankification" of realism, with the views of the idiosyncrasy wing coming to stand for realism itself; but, in fact, prominent realists had a very different view about the determinants of judicial decision.

The idiosyncrasy wing

Judge Hutcheson's confession that he reached his decisions by getting a "hunch" about what would be right or fair on the facts of a given case (1929, p. 278) provided the foundation for the idiosyncrasy wing of realism. Frank specifically endorsed Hutcheson's view and declared: "the way in which the judge gets his hunches is the key to the judicial process" (1930, p. 104). While conceding that "rules and principles are one class of . . . stimuli" producing decisions, Frank claimed that it is "the judge's innumerable unique traits, dispositions and habits" which are decisive, which "shap[e] his decisions not only in his determination of what he thinks fair or just with reference to a given set of facts, but in the very process by which he becomes convinced what those facts are" (1930, pp. 110–11). Political and economic biases, often thought to be important in adjudication, in fact only "express themselves in connection with, and as modified by, these idiosyncratic biases" (1930, p. 106). Thus, concludes Frank, "the personality of the judge is the pivotal factor in law administration" (1930, p. 111; cf. 1931, p. 242). (Note, however, that no one in the idiosyncrasy wing adhered to the view, often wrongly attributed to realism, that "what the judge ate for breakfast" determines the decision.)

But if "the ultimately important influences in the decisions of any judge are the most obscure, and are the least easily discoverable" (1930, p. 114) precisely because they are these idiosyncratic facts about the psychology of the individual judge, then how will it be possible to formulate laws of judicial behavior? In fact, Frank repudiates this ambition of the behaviorists when he declares that, "The truth is that prediction of most specific decisions . . . is, today at any rate, impossible" (1931, p. 246; cf. 1930, *passim*). The qualification ("today at any rate") is important: for the problem is *not* that there are no determinants of decision (Frank does accept a type of Freudian psychic determinism) but rather that such determinants are epistemologically opaque: we have no reliable way of knowing what they are. But even Frank allowed that if judges became suitably self-aware – undergoing, say, psychoanalysis – then they could provide us with the information about their personalities that would make prediction possible (1930, p. 163).

Even if later images of realism seem to conform to the Frankian model, Frank himself was aware that his was a minority view, both among lawyers and among realists. Fond of armchair Freudian speculations, Frank charged that the continued demand for certainty (via predictability) in law was the product of an infantile longing for the protection of a father-figure (1930, p. 34). More interestingly, he suggested that the reason he and Hutcheson had "far less belief in the possibility of diminishing the personal element in the judge than Oliphant or Llewellyn" was due to his and Hutcheson's greater experience with trial courts, where, Frank suggested, the personal element was omnipresent (1931, p. 30, n. 31).

The sociological wing

Writers in the sociological wing of realism did not deny the relevance of the fact that judges are human beings with individual personalities (see Llewellyn, 1930, pp. 80–1, 1931, pp. 1,242–3); rather they insisted that the relevant facts about judges *qua* human beings were not primarily idiosyncratic ones. As Cohen aptly put it (in answer to Hutcheson and Frank): "Judges are human, but they are a peculiar breed of human, selected to a type and held to service under a potent system of government controls . . . A truly realistic theory of judicial decision must conceive every decision as something more than an expression of individual personality, as . . . even more importantly . . . a product of social determinants" (1935, p. 843). If writers like Frank emphasized the psychological profile of the individual judge, writers like Llewellyn, Cohen and Moore emphasized the "sociological" profile of the judge, one he had in common with many others. Judicial decision is still primarily explicable in terms of psycho-social facts about judges (that determine how they respond to the facts of particular cases), it is just that these psycho-social facts are held to be general and common, rather than idiosyncratic.

Unfortunately, the realists did not have a rich sociological theory of judicial personality. Their strongest argument was an inference to the best explanation: given that judicial decisions can be correlated with the underlying facts of the cases decided, it must be the case that there are "social" determinants of decision that force decisions of individual judges into these predictable patterns.

The realists tended to draw their best examples of this point from the commercial realm (rather, say, than constitutional law). Here they commonly advanced two sorts of claims: with respect to the underlying facts of the case (whether stated in the opinion or not), what judges do is either (1) enforce the norms of the prevailing commercial culture; or (2) do what is best socio-economically under the circumstances.

Oliphant gives this example: looking at a series of conflicting court decisions on the validity of contractual promises not to compete, Oliphant observed that, in fact, the decisions tracked the underlying facts of the cases:

All the cases holding the promises invalid are found to be cases of employees' promises not to compete with their employers after a term of employment. Contemporary guild [that is, labor union] regulations not noticed in the opinions made their holding eminently sound. All the cases holding the promises valid were cases of promises by those selling a business and promising not to compete with the purchasers. Contemporary economic reality made these holdings eminently sound. (*1928, pp. 159–60*)

Thus, in the former fact-scenarios, the courts enforced the prevailing norms (as expressed in guild regulations disfavoring such promises); in the latter cases, the courts came out differently because it was economically best under *those* factual circumstances to do so.

Llewellyn provides a similar illustration (1960, pp. 122–4). A series of New York cases applied the rule that a buyer who rejects the seller's shipment by formally stating his objections thereby waives all other objections. Llewellyn notes that the rule seems to have been rather harshly applied in a series of cases where the buyers simply may not have known at the time of rejection of other defects or where the seller could not have cured anyway. A careful study of the facts of these cases revealed, however, that in each case where the rule seemed harshly applied what had really happened was that the market had gone sour, and the buyer was looking to escape the contract. The court in each case, being "sensitive to commerce or to decency" (1960, p. 124) applies the unrelated rule about rejection to frustrate the buyer's attempt to escape the contract. Thus, the commercial norm – buyers ought to honor their commitments even under changed market conditions – is enforced by the courts through a *seemingly* harsh application of an unrelated rule concerning rejection. It is these "background facts, those of mercantile practice, those of the situation-type" (1960, p. 126) which determine the course of decision.

Moore tried to systematize this approach as what he called "the institutional method" (1929, 1931). Moore's idea was this: identify the normal behavior for any "institution" (for example, commercial banking); then identify and demarcate deviations from this norm quantitatively, and try to identify the point at which deviation from the norm will *cause* a judicial decision that corrects the deviation from the norm (for example, how far must a bank depart from normal check-cashing practice before a court will decide against the bank in a suit brought by the customer?). The goal is a predictive formula: deviation of degree X from "institutional behavior (that is, behavior which frequently, repeatedly, usually occurs)" (1929, p. 707) will cause courts to act. Thus, says, Moore: "the semblance of causal relation between future and past decisions is the result of the relation of both to a third variable, the relevant institutions in the locality of the court" (1931, p. 1,219). Put differently: what judges respond to is the extent to which the facts show a deviation from the prevailing norm in the commercial culture.

The theory of the sociological wing of realism – that judges enforce the norms

273

of commercial culture or try to do what is socio-economically best on the facts of the case – should not be confused with the idea that judges decide based, for example, on how they feel about the particular parties or the lawyers. These "fireside equities" (Llewellyn, 1960, p. 121) may sometimes influence judges; but what really determines the course of decision is the "situation-type", that is, the general pattern of behavior exemplified by the particular facts of the disputed transaction, and what would constitute normal or socio-economically desirable behavior in the relevant commercial context. The point is decidedly not that judges usually decide because of idiosyncratic likes and dislikes with respect to the individuals before the court (cf. Radin, 1925, p. 357).

But why would judges, with some degree of predictable uniformity, enforce the norms of commercial culture as applied to the underlying facts of the case? Here the realists did little more than gesture at a suitable psycho-social explanation. "Professional judicial office," Llewellyn suggested, was "the most important among all the lines of factor which make for reckonability" of decision (1960, p. 45); "the *office* waits and then moves with majestic power to shape the man" (1960, p. 46). Echoing, but modifying Frank, Llewellyn continued:

> The place to begin is with the fact that the men of our appellate bench are human beings . . . And one of the more obvious and obstinate facts about human beings is that they operate in and respond to traditions . . . Tradition grips them, shapes them, limits them, guides them . . . To a man of sociology or psychology . . . this needs no argument. (*1960, p. 53*)

Radin suggested that "the standard transactions with their regulatory incidents are familiar ones to him [the judge] because of his experience as a citizen and a lawyer" (1925, p. 358). Cohen, by contrast, simply lamented that "at present no publication [exists] showing the political, economic, and professional background and activities of our judges" (1935, p. 846), presumably because such a publication would identify the relevant "social" determinants of decision.

Of course, by the time of *The Common Law Tradition*, Llewellyn had actually repudiated many of the naturalistic ambitions of early realism, remarking, for example – and with Moore obviously in mind – that the judge is not a "Pavlov's dog" (1960, p. 204). The final collapse of naturalism in realist jurisprudence comes with Llewellyn's introduction of "situation-sense," a mysterious faculty that permits judges to detect the "natural law which is real, not imaginary . . . [that is] indwelling in the very circumstances of life" (1960, p. 122, quoting Levin Goldschmidt). Plainly, though, the ambition of making theories of adjudication continuous with social scientific inquiry has been abandoned in favor of rank mysticism when the explanation for the correlation of decisions with underlying facts is the operation of a non-naturalistic faculty, "situation-sense"! (But for a different understanding of later Llewellyn, see Kronman, 1993, pp. 209–25.)

One final difficulty may seem to plague the realists' descriptive theory. For surely it is obvious that some cases that come before courts are easy (the rules clearly dictate a certain outcome), that judges often appear to strive to conform to the demands of rules, and that judges often decide in ways that are consistent with rules being causes of decision. Call these phenomena "the rule truisms." How can the core claim of realism be compatible with the rule truisms?

The key here is to remember that the central naturalistic commitment of realism is to explain judicial decision in terms of the psycho-social facts about judges that account for how they make decisions. But judges, as the sociological wing emphasizes, are a special breed of human being, and this too counts as a relevant psycho-social fact. "Judges," says Cohen, "are craftsmen, with aesthetic ideals" (1935, p. 845) – surely a relevant fact about the psychological profile of the judge. And Llewellyn concedes that in trying to get a court to decide in your favor, " 'rules' loom into importance. Great importance. For judges think that they must follow rules, and people highly approve of that thinking" (1930, p. 4). Judges, in short, are guided according to the realists by "a certain ideal of judicial craftmanship" (Kronman, 1993, p. 214). Let us call this the idea of "the normative judiciary" – of how judges ought ideally to decide cases. To the extent that human beings *qua* judges have a conception of the normative judiciary, then to that extent *the psychological fact about them* explains why they are sometimes rule-responsive in the way the rule truisms suggest. Theoretical coherence, a virtue not much prized by the realists, is, nonetheless, preserved in the face of the rule truisms – by showing that even "rule-responsiveness," however infrequent, is, nonetheless, explicable within a naturalistic account of judicial decision.

The attack on formalism

Whatever their differences among themselves, the realists were united in their opposition to a very different descriptive theory of adjudication, often called "formalism" or "mechanical jurisprudence." According to the formalist, "the judge begins with some rule or principle of law as his premise, applies this premise to the facts, and thus arrives at his decision" (Frank, 1930, p. 101). Judges, of course, write their opinions in this "formalistic" mode, but the realists want to insist precisely that, "the decision often may and often will prove to be inadequate if taken as a *description* of how the decision really came about and of what the vital factors were which caused it" (Llewellyn, 1930, p. 37; cf. Cohen: "The traditional language of argument and opinion neither explains nor justifies court decisions" (1935, p. 812)).

"Formalism" as an epithet has actually been widely applied. In a very strict sense, the formalist holds that decisions flow (or ought to flow) from certain axiomatic definitions. Thus, in the notorious (formalistic) opinion in *United States* v. *E. C. Knight Co.* (156 U.S. 1 (1895)), the US Supreme Court held that the regulation of a sugar manufacturer (responsible for 90 percent of sugar production in the United States!) was not within the power of Congress to regulate "interstate commerce," since, *by definition*, interstate commerce did not include manufacturing, which takes place only within a state.

In a looser sense, formalism names any view in which authoritative legal sources

275

together with the "methods" of legal reasoning are sufficient to provide a water-tight justification for a unique outcome to any dispute. The deductive model of decision just described by Frank is the most familiar form.

The realists were intent to deny the descriptive adequacy of formalism on both counts. We shall return momentarily to the realist attitude toward formalism as a normative theory.

Formalism owed its intellectual underpinning to the work of Christopher Langdell, Dean of Harvard Law School in the late nineteenth century, who, along with certain followers (like Joseph Beale), was a figure for whom the realists reserved a special antipathy. Langdell aimed to make law "scientific" in a different sense than the realists. As one commentator explains:

> To understand a given branch of legal doctrine in a scientific fashion, one must begin . . . by first identifying the elementary principles on which that field of law is based (for example, in the case of contract law, the principles that the minds of the parties must meet for a contract to be formed and that each must give or promise to give something of value to the other in return). These elementary principles are to be discovered by surveying the case law in the area. Once they have been identified, it is then the task of scholars to work out, in an analytically rigorous manner, the subordinate principles entailed by them. When these subordinate principles have all been stated in propositional form and the relations of entailment among them clarified, they will . . . together constitute a well-ordered system of rules that offers the best possible description of that particular branch of law – the best answer to the question of what the law in that area *is* . . . [I]ndividual cases that cannot be fit within this system must be rejected as mistakes. (*Kronman, 1993, p. 171; for an eloquent discussion of Langdell and realism, see generally pp. 170–99*)

The realists, as we have seen, rejected this picture wholesale. In particular, they denied that the sort of categories adduced by the Langdellian scholar were really descriptive of the bases of decision. Notice, however, that the realists repudiate primarily the methodology, not the aspiration, of Langdell: they object to Langdell's notion that decisions track abstract principles of law, rather than particular patterns of facts (cf. Oliphant, 1928; Llewellyn, 1931, p. 1,240). The mistake of Langdell is in thinking we can learn the law, in the sense the lawyer needs to learn it (that is, in order to be able to predict what courts will do), by examining the opinions and the reasons given therein; rather, the realists *qua* naturalists discover that decisions track underlying fact patterns ("situation-types"), not published rationalizations (or the "axioms" to be adduced from them).

Normative theory of adjudication

All realists share a commitment to the core claim: in deciding cases, judges respond primarily to the stimulus of the facts. If this is a true descriptive thesis about adjudication, what room does it leave for a *normative* theory of adjudication? The realists are not always clear on this issue, but the majority of them endorse a type of view we may call "quietism."

276

Quietists hold that since the core claim reports some irremediable fact about judging, it makes no sense to give normative advice – except perhaps the advice that judges "ought" to do what it is that they will do anyway. So if judges, as a matter of course, enforce the norms of commercial culture or try to do what is socio-economically best under the circumstances, then that is precisely what realists tell them they ought to do.

Thus, Holmes complains that "judges themselves have failed adequately to recognize their duty of [explicitly] weighing considerations of social advantage." But having just noted that what is really going on in the opinion of judges anyway is "a concealed, half-conscious battle on the question of legislative policy," it follows that this "duty" is in fact "inevitable, and the result of the often proclaimed judicial aversion to deal with such considerations is simply to leave the very ground and foundation of judgments inarticulate, and often unconscious" (1897, p. 467). Thus, what Holmes really calls for is for judges to do explicitly (and perhaps more carefully) what they do unconsciously anyway. (Contrast the non-quietistic Cohen (1935, p. 810), who recommends that judges address themselves to questions of socio-economic policy *instead* of the traditional doctrinal questions that they often address.)

In a similar vein, Radin suggested that the decisions judges make on the basis of the type-situations into which they put facts essentially track the sorts of decisions one would get by demanding explicitly that judges do the "economically or socially valuable thing" (1925, p. 360). Frank observed that with respect to what he dubbed "Cadi justice" – justice by personal predilection essentially – "[t]he true question . . . is not whether we should 'revert' to [it], but whether (a) we have ever abandoned it and (b) we can ever pass beyond it" (1931, p. 27). Advocating a " 'reversion to Cadi justice' . . . is as meaningless as [advocating] a 'reversion to mortality' or a 'return to breathing' " (1931, p. 31). This is because "the personal element is unavoidable in judicial decisions" (1931, p. 25).

The most important example of normative quietism in realism comes from Llewellyn's work on Article 2 of the Uniform Commercial Code. For how can a realist, one might wonder, tackle the enterprise of designing rules for what ought to be done in commercial disputes? The answer should be obvious: tell judges that they ought to do what it is they will do anyway, that is, enforce the norms of commercial culture, of the prevailing mercantile practice. Thus, the Code imposes an obligation of "good faith" in all contractual dealings (Sec. 1-203) which means besides honesty, "the observance of reasonable commercial standards of fair dealing in the trade" (Sec. 2-103). But for a court, then, to enforce the rule requiring "good faith" is just for that course to enforce the relevant norms of commercial culture! The reliance of the Code throughout on norms of "good faith" and "reasonableness" is a constant invitation to the judge to do what he would, on the realist theory, do anyway: enforce the norms of the prevailing commercial practice.

A final worry might arise about this normative "program." For the motivation for the quietism is the thought that since judges will decide in accordance with the core claim anyway, it would be futile or idle to tell them they "ought" to decide in some other way. But why think judges *must* be fact-responsive? One possibility is

277

that the core claim of realism is supposed to report a brute psychological fact about human judgment: indeed, Frank often presents it that way (1930, p. 100). A perhaps more plausible hypothesis is that the core claim is inevitably true of common-law judges, who, by role and tradition, are invited to examine and re-work the law in ways that are responsive to the changing circumstances in which legal problems arise. Thus, it is not because of a "deep" wired-in fact about the human psyche that the core claim is true, but rather a contingent, but still obsti-nate, fact about adjudication in the common-law system. Indeed, we may detect a further, non-quietistic, normative element in realism: namely, to the extent, however small, that judges are *not* fact-responsive and fairness-driven in their decisions (to the extent, for example, that they are sometimes formalistic or Langdellian in their mode of decision), then to that extent they *ought* to decide as the core claim says most of them ordinarily do. This additional, more ambitious, normative demand does not, however, receive the sustained defense one would hope to find.

Other themes from realism

Writers often associated with realism have been the source of other intellectual themes that have recently overshadowed the distinctive realist contributions in philosophy of law. Primary among these is the purported argument against the public/private distinction generally attributed to the economist Robert Hale and the philosopher Morris Cohen (both contemporaries of the realists) (see the selec-tions in Fisher et al., 1993; cf. Llewellyn, 1930, p. 10; Cohen, 1935, p. 816), and brought to prominence by the critical legal studies (CLS) movement in the 1970s and 1980s (see the introduction to chapter 4 in Fisher, 1993, a volume which generally views realism through a CLS lens). The argument runs as follows: since it is governmental decisions that create and structure the so-called "private" sphere (that is, by creating and enforcing a regime of property rights), there should be no presumption of "non-intervention" in this "private" realm (for example, the mar-ketplace) because it is, in essence, a public creature. There is, in short, no natural baseline against which government cannot pass without becoming "intervention-ist" and non-neutral, because the baseline itself is an artifact of government regulation.

This general argument has been widely influential (see, for example, Sunstein, 1987, pp. 917–19); unfortunately, it is based on a *non sequitur*. From the fact that a "private" realm is a creature of government regulation it does not follow that government action in that realm is normatively indistinguishable from govern-ment action in the "public" realm: for the key issue is the normative justification for drawing the baseline itself, not simply the fact that one has been drawn by an exercise of public power. If the underlying normative reasons for the baseline are sound (that is, for demarcating a realm of "private" transactions), then *these rea-sons* provide an argument *against* intervention. Hale and many of his contempor-ary followers are, of course, correct that many proponents of the baseline (wrongly) regard its existence *per se* as a reason against government action (cf. Sunstein, 1987); but this is simply to repeat in reverse the *non sequitur* of those who think the regulability of the "private" sphere follows from recognizing that its very existence depends on public regulation.

References

Cohen, F. 1935: Transcendental nonsense and the functional approach. *Columbia Law Review*, 35, 809–49.

Cook, W. W. 1924: The logical and legal bases of the conflict of laws. *Yale Law Journal*, 33, 457–88.

Frank, J. 1930: *Law and the Modern Mind*. New York: Brentano's.

—— 1931: Are judges human? Parts I & II. *University of Pennsylvania Law Review*, 80, 17–53, 233–67.

Holmes, Jr, O. W. 1897: The path of the law. *Harvard Law Review*, 10, 457–78.

Hutcheson, Jr, J. 1929: The judgment intuitive: the function of the "hunch" in judicial decision. *Cornell Law Quarterly*, 14, 274–88.

Llewellyn, K. 1930: *The Bramble Bush*. New York: Oceana.

—— 1931: Some realism about realism – responding to Dean Pound. *Harvard Law Review*, 44, 1,222–64.

—— 1950: Remarks on the theory of appellate decision and the rules and canons about how statutes are to be construed. *Vanderbilt Law Review*, 3, 395–406.

—— 1960: *The Common Law Tradition: deciding appeals*. Boston: Little, Brown & Co.

Moore, U. 1923: Rational basis of legal institutions. *Columbia Law Review*, 23, 609–17.

Moore, U. and Hope, T. 1929: An institutional approach to the law of commercial banking. *Yale Law Journal*, 38, 703–19.

Moore, U. and Sussman, G. 1931: Legal and institutional methods applied to the debiting of direct discounts – I. Legal method: banker's set-off; II. Institutional method; VI. The decisions, the institutions, and the degree of deviation. *Yale Law Journal*, 40, 381–400, 555–75, 1,219–50.

Moore, U. and Callahan, C. 1943: Law and learning theory: a study in legal control. *Yale Law Journal*, 53, 1–136.

Oliphant, H. 1928: A return to stare decisis. *American Bar Association Journal*, 14, 71–6, 107, 159–62.

Radin, M. 1925: The theory of judicial decision: or how judges think. *American Bar Association Journal*, 11, 357–62.

—— 1930: Statutory interpretation. *Harvard Law Review*, 43, 863–85.

Bibliography

Fisher, W. W. et al. (eds) 1993: *American Legal Realism*. New York: Oxford University Press.

Hart, H. L. A. 1961: *The Concept of Law*. Oxford: Clarendon Press.

Kornblith, H. (ed.) 1994: *Naturalizing Epistemology*. Cambridge, Mass.: MIT Press, 2nd edn.

Kronman, A. 1993: *The Lost Lawyer*. Cambridge, Mass.: Harvard University Press.

Leiter, B. 1995: Legal indeterminacy. *Legal Theory*, 1.

Perry, S. 1995: Interpretation and methodology in legal theory. In A. Marmor (ed.), *Law and Interpretation*. Oxford: Oxford University Press.

Sunstein, C. 1987: *Lochner*'s Legacy. *Columbia Law Review*, 87, 873–919.

17

Critical legal studies

GUYORA BINDER

Critical legal studies is a movement in legal scholarship associated with the Conference on Critical Legal Studies, an organization inaugurated by a small conference at the University of Wisconsin in 1977 (Schlegel, 1984). By the early 1990s the *movement* had come to influence the work of an enormous number of legal scholars, particularly in the fields of legal and constitutional theory, while the *organization* had diffused into new non-existence.

As an intellectual movement, critical legal studies combined the concerns of legal realism, critical Marxism, and structuralist or post-structuralist literary theory. Many of its members identified with the leftist politics of the student movements of the 1960s.

Critical legal studies as analytic jurisprudence: the critique of liberal rights theory

A few critical legal scholars have shown interest in the traditional concerns of analytic jurisprudence. These scholars have largely followed in the footsteps of legal realists Wesley Hohfeld, Walter Wheeler Cook, Robert Hale, and Morris Cohen, criticizing liberal rights theory by stressing the economic and social interdependence of legal persons (Hofeld, 1913; Cook, 1981; Hale, 1943; Cohen, 1927). This perspective reinterprets rights as:

> [R]elations among persons regarding control of valued resources . . . Legal rights are correlative; every legal entitlement in an individual implies a correlative vulnerability in someone else, and every entitlement is limited by the competing rights of others . . . Property rights are interpreted as delegations of sovereign power to individuals by the state; these rights should therefore be defined to accommodate the conflicting interests of social actors. (*Singer. 1993. p. 20*)

If property rights are understood to confer power it similarly follows that contractual bargaining is never truly equal and all contractual consent is coerced through the exercise of superior bargaining power.

Because they identify entitlements with power over others, critical legal scholars argue that the liberal ideals of freedom to act without harming others, and freedom to transact with consenting others, are self-defeating. Accordingly, these ideals cannot be realized in a legal regime and efforts to realize them will yield doctrinal systems that are structured by recurrent, irresolvable debates. Doctrinal systems that are "liberal" in this sense will include rules, but the rules will generally confront, or even contain, counter-rules that contradict them. Accordingly, in such a system, the rules do not determine results and cannot explain whatever ability legal practitioners have to predict results (Kennedy, 1991; Balkin, 1986). Liberal rights theory, then, is not formally realizable. Judicial application of a liberal rights regime involves political discretion; it can never be the mere formality demanded by the liberal ideal of the rule of law.

This "indeterminacy thesis," as it has come to be called, is a claim about classical liberalism and its aspiration to secure liberty through a rule of law. The claim is that no determinate rule system can secure liberty, a claim that is more true than new.

Yet observers have mistakenly ascribed to critical legal scholars a categorical claim that all legal rules are necessarily indeterminate. Confusion has arisen on this point because critical legal scholars have identified additional sources of indeterminacy in American legal doctrine beyond its embodiment of liberal rights theory. Critical legal scholars also argue that doctrinal standards requiring identification of the interests of legal actors are indeterminate. This second claim takes critical legal scholars beyond their legal realist predecessors; indeed it implies a critique of the instrumentalist approach to legal decision making embraced by many legal realists. This second "indeterminacy thesis" is the more original and interesting contribution of critical legal studies.

Taken together, critical legal scholars' indeterminacy critiques of liberal rights theory and of the jurisprudence of interests attribute indeterminacy to a good deal of American legal doctrine. Yet they do not amount to a categorical claim that no rule or rule system can yield determinate results.

Critical legal studies as social theory

The indeterminacy critique of interests developed by critical legal scholars is best seen as a contribution to social and political theory rather than analytic jurisprudence. It is essentially a claim that society and politics are legally constructed. Thus it is an original and philosophically important claim about the relationship between law and society. Critical scholars don't see legal language as indeterminate *relative to* the social context to which it refers. Rather, they see legal language as indeterminate *because of* the indeterminacy of the social context to which it refers (Kennedy, 1973). The indeterminacy of the social world frustrates instrumentalist efforts to explain or prescribe legal rules on the basis of their service to certain interests.

The remainder of this article will explicate this critique of instrumentalism by reviewing the work of several critical legal scholars. As we shall see, critical legal scholars have deployed this critique not only against existing legal institutions, but also against instrumentally driven proposals to reform or overthrow them.

The critique of instrumentalism

Legal realists tended to see legal doctrine as an empty shell, covertly determined by social context; they sought only, by means of policy analysis, to make that contextual determination overt and self-conscious. Critical scholars, like most modern legal scholars, have so internalized the realist characterization of doctrine that they equate legal doctrine with the policy analysis that the realists advocated. Unlike the realists, critical legal scholars do not treat legal doctrine as a special or even a distinct case among forms of social knowledge, uniquely lacking in truth or determinacy. Instead, they treat it as a typical instance of the use of social science methods to promote policy ends; so that its indeterminacy simply exemplifies the indeterminacy and value-laden quality of the social knowledge on which it is based.

Accordingly, much influential critical legal scholarship is properly seen as a critique of legal realism rather than a recapitulation of it. In "The metaphysics of American law," Gary Peller made this rejection of realism explicit, while making clear that it by no means entailed a return to the formalism of liberal rights theory (Peller, 1985). Instead, he argued that realism perpetuated the basic flaw of formalism: its commitment to determinacy. Instead of seeing the social world as determined by law, realism insisted that legal decisions are and should be determined by their social context. Instead of subordinating facts to rules, Peller argued, legal realism subordinated rules to facts. Each involved the same structure and the same faith in the ability of experts to know and control the social world. In the "deconstructive" cultural criticism of Foucalt and Derrida, Peller finds an elegant device for equating the legal analysis embraced by liberal formalists with the policy analysis embraced by legal realists; both are simply "discourses" or "disciplines" – practices of observation, classification, argument, and judgment which do not simply describe human beings, but also shape them. Accordingly, these concepts seemed to encompass both the formal legal analysis and instrumental policy analysis that critical legal scholars link.

One of the key arenas in which this link was forged was in the critics' transformation of legal history. This revision began with Morton Horwitz's *The Transformation of American Law* (Horwitz, 1977). This study of antebellum jurisprudence demonstrated that by the middle of the nineteenth century the jurisprudence of natural law had been replaced by the sort of instrumentalist jurisprudence that the realist scholars favored. By arguing that this instrumentalist regime served the interests of a merchant and industrial elite, Horwitz challenged the assumptions of realists that this style of jurisprudence was necessarily more democratic than a jurisprudence of natural rights. Other critical scholars, most prominently Duncan Kennedy and Robert Gordon, have extended the attack on realism implicit in Horwitz's work by questioning some of the instrumentalist premisses implicit in his method. Thus, Gordon has questioned the possibility of explaining doctrinal change in terms of elite interests, when legal doctrine and legal thought are partly constitutive of those interests (Gordon, 1984). Kennedy, in the meantime, has severely complicated our notion of doctrinal change by presenting liberal legal doctrine as a contradictory framework embracing positivism and natural rights, instrumentalism and formalism. In this context, the selection of one or another pole by a legal decision maker deploys, but does not alter, the doctrinal framework (Kennedy, 1976, 1979). Because doctrinal frameworks are so malleable, Kennedy and Gordon are inclined to say that doctrine expresses, articulates, even constitutes conflicting interests, but does not serve them.

Other critical scholars have stressed the malleability of the notion of interest itself as a barrier to doctrinal determinacy. Writing about decision criteria that call for the balancing or representing of interests, Al Katz has argued that the concept of interest disguises but does not resolve the tension between "natural rights" and "popular sovereignty" in liberal jurisprudence. Moreover, the interests balanced or represented are products of the techniques by which they are measured or observed. Accordingly, the modern decision maker's practices of balancing and representing may be characterized as disciplines that constrain the identities of individuals and groups in the process of recognizing their "interests." The realists' incorporation of these social scientific techniques into legal doctrine insured that doctrine could remain no more determinate than policy analysis (Katz, 1979, 1987, 1983).

Several critical scholars have used the indeterminacy of interests as a basis for attacking the policy analysis that dominates post-realist legal scholarship. Most such scholarship explores three models of social choice: the adversary process, the electoral process, and the market. These models all involve attempts to reconstruct the normative certainty on which classical liberalism rested without adopting its naive assumption that social actors can exercise freedom without infringing the freedom of others. Each of them rests on an image of society as a competition among antagonists. Nevertheless, each of these models identifies normative truth as the fairly compiled aggregate of the subjective preferences of "interests" of these antagonists. Thus, even though adjudication, efficiency, and majority rule might reach different results, each rests on the same assumptions and each makes a similar claim to truth. Post-realist legal scholarship focusses on three issues: (1) which of these models should be employed for the resolution of a particular controversy; (2) how these models can be reconciled; and (3) how the decision-making process modeled by each can be made more fair. Critical legal scholars, by contrast, reject the notion that the interests of individuals and groups develop independently of the processes which aggregate them. Accordingly, they are convinced that no mere combination of the adversary process, the electoral process, and the market can automatically produce legitimate social choice.

William Simon's work on the adversary process undermines the notion of interests in the context of representing individuals and groups. In *The Ideology of Advocacy*, he argued that lawyers cannot represent their clients without attributing to them "interests" that are recognized by the legal system as legitimate and realizable

283

(Simon, 1978). In this way lawyers – poverty lawyers especially – can socialize and co-opt their clients in the very process of zealous representation. They learn to live with this because the "ideology of advocacy" reassures them that truth is the outcome of the adversary process. At the same time, this conception of truth allows their opponents to abdicate moral responsibility for the reprehensible causes they advance. The adversarial ethic allows lawyers for both the poor and the rich to act on the basis of "interests" manufactured by the legal system itself, rather than their own values.

Critical legal scholars have similarly attacked economic analysis of law, on the grounds that it mistakenly treats individual economic preferences as independent of legal rules. Thus, their objection is not so much to the substitution of efficiency for justice as a criterion of adjudication, but to the belief that the two criteria can be separated at all. Where economic analysts of law have urged that courts should allocate resources to those who value them more in order to escape transaction costs, Edwin Baker, Mark Kelman, and Duncan Kennedy have argued that how much each party to a dispute values a resource depends heavily on whether or not she already possesses it and may depend even more on what else she possesses. Thus, resources cannot be distributed on the basis of calculations of allocative efficiency because such calculations always depend on prior assumptions about the distribution of resources. Accordingly, the critics argue, questions of allocative efficiency can never be separated from questions of distributive justice (Baker, 1975; Kelman, 1979; Kennedy, 1981).

Critical scholars have similarly objected to scholarship that invokes political science in an effort to reconcile adjudication with majoritarian decision making. By treating voter preferences as given, such scholarship is able to treat the problem of democratic decision making as a matter of aggregating those preferences, without exploring how they are arrived at. By contrast, critic Richard Parker has argued that even a judicially supervised electoral process cannot represent the "interests" of the poor because poverty precludes people from formulating and pursuing their own political goals (Parker, 1981).

The critique of instrumental reformism

There is little point in improving the ability of the market, the electoral process, and the adversary system to represent interests if those interests are constituted in the very process of representation. Accordingly, the critical scholars' anti-instrumentalism is aimed not only against these institutions, but also against liberal reforms designed to improve them.

Such criticism of liberal reform movements appears to follow one of two paths. One such path is exemplified by Alan Freeman's "Legitimizing racial discrimination through antidiscrimination law" (Freeman, 1978) and Karl Klare's "Judicial deradicalization of the Wagner Act" (Klare, 1978). These pieces criticize decisional law (anti-discrimination law since *Brown*) and legislation (the National Labour Relations Act) that are commonly thought to be major achievements of progressive politics. They criticize these products of progressive politics as ineffectual

284

because, while they made minor adjustments to provide the appearance of protection for persons of color and working people, these legal changes have, in practice, left the decision-making institution of the market intact. Many readers have understood these articles to imply that it is the market that chiefly oppresses the poor, whose ranks include substantial numbers of workers and persons of color. Many readers go on to assume that such Marxist scholarship takes the institution of a market as a given, and that until capitalism is overthrown, struggles for civil or labor rights are futile and misdirected.

In fact, however, these pieces celebrate the political struggles that brought about these liberal reforms. What they lament is the exhaustion of such political movements as a result of their embodiment in institutions, specifically in adjustments to the ground rules for bargaining within a market. According to Klare and Freeman, these movements did not fail because they accepted the institution of the market; to the contrary, they challenged the institution of the market by embodying a form of association and decision-making inconsistent with it. These movements were contained by the market, however, when their struggles were embodied in legal institutions. The labor movement was the setting for collective participation in political decision making about the meaning and shape of work; labor law reduced it to a common economic interest. The civil rights movement was a forum for passion, participation, interracial understanding, solidarity and sacrifice; civil rights law eventually reduced it to a right to governmental indifference. In short, these articles do not urge contempt for the labor and civil rights movements as irrelevant because they did not pursue world revolution against capitalism. They celebrate these movements as forms of association and decision making that were, in and of themselves, good and sufficient alternatives to instrumentalism.

This perspective is perhaps a little clearer in a second pattern of critique of liberal reformism. This pattern, exemplified by William Simon's "Legality, bureaucracy and class in the welfare system" (Simon, 1983) and Derrick Bell's "Serving two masters" (Bell, 1976), directs critical attention at the strategic decisions made by liberal reformist lawyers on the basis of distorting assumptions about their client groups' "interests." In each case the lawyers are criticized not so much for interfering with a situation better left alone but for allowing abstract conceptions of their clients' interests to blind them to their clients' potential to contribute to the process of social change.

Accordingly, Derrick Bell has argued that integrationist lawyers failed to recognize one black community's desire for quality neighborhood schools over which they could exert some control and which could serve as vehicles of opportunity for black educators. The result was that these lawyers were so busy pursuing their clients' interests that they ignored their desires. They also failed to learn from their clients to the detriment of the lawyers' own political vision. Finally, they squandered an opportunity to mobilize an aroused community to define its own goals, not only in the litigation process, but also in the administration of its own schools.

William Simon has revealed a related problem encountered by poverty lawyers endeavoring to render welfare bureaucracies more generous and less degrading by formalizing their decision-making procedures. It could hardly have surprised

285

anyone that the result was to make the welfare bureaucracy more bureaucratic. But what lawyers had failed to consider was the impact of bureaucratization on welfare workers and on the future possibilities for welfare recipients to influence those workers. Removing the discretion of welfare workers degraded their work and destroyed opportunities for them to pursue civil vocations, even as it destroyed opportunities for arbitrariness, condescension, and discrimination. It dehumanized welfare recipients' contact with the welfare bureaucracy, which perpetuated the dehumanization of welfare recipients in a new, more impersonal form. It sometimes created new forms of personal degradation as well, substituting inflexible skepticism for invasive curiosity. While recipients "received" new rights to constrain agency behavior, they found that they could not avail themselves of these rights without the indulgence of other poverty professionals – lawyers. Thus poverty lawyers solved the problem of welfare worker abuse of welfare recipients by disempowering welfare workers instead of by empowering welfare recipients. As a result, they foreclosed the possibility that welfare recipients would have found in such a transformed relationship with welfare workers a political resource rather than a liability. By assuming that the interests of recipients and workers were opposed, poverty lawyers ignored the possibility that those interests could evolve and converge as a result of political activity. And by taking for granted that the recipients' interests could be pursued without the recipients' participation, poverty lawyers ignored the possibility that welfare recipients might have a non-economic interest in political participation and control over their circumstances.

These four critical assessments of legal strategies for liberal reform suggest serious misgivings about the desirability of social reforms planned, directed, and institutionalized by experts. Thus, the problem with the civil rights movement, the welfare reform movement, and the labor movement was not their failure to attack capitalism. There is no such central cause or single accurate description of oppression in the world. The problem with these reform movements was that they made too many assumptions about the problem to be solved and involved too few people in the decision-making process. In short, they were not sufficiently democratic. Critical legal scholars' attack on instrumentalism is inspired by their commitment to participatory democracy.

The critique of revolutionary instrumentalism

Critical legal scholars have the same misgivings about ambitiously radical programs for social change that they have about liberal reformist programs. If they are planned and conducted by experts based on fixed assumptions about the "interests" of the oppressed, they are as undemocratic and misguided as the movements for liberal reform.

This caveat is made explicit in Edwin Baker's "The process of change and the liberty theory of the First Amendment" (Baker, 1981). Here Baker identifies instrumentalism as the separation of means and ends. Arguing that the distinction is artificial and cannot be maintained, he attacks the notion that the end of progressive social change justifies violent or coercive means. Baker's chief purpose is to argue that even the radical change to a collectivist or communal society is compatible with, even requires, strict protection of individual freedom of opinion.

Critical legal scholar Roberto Unger has argued that the Marxist theory of revolution is undermined by its reliance on the same kind of instrumental reasoning that informs mainstream policy analysis.

Marx identifies revolution as the change from one mode of production to another. But how does Marx define the concept of capitalism, the paradigm for all modes of production? At least three factors are crucial for the identification of a "capitalist" economy: (1) a predominance of "free labor," understood as the condition in which a laborer owns all of her own labor and none of the means of production; (2) commodity production for private accumulation of wealth; and (3) sufficient accumulation of wealth to enable industrialization. But Unger points out that there is no necessary connection between commodity production and the development of a labor market, or between a labor market and industrialization, or between industrialization and private accumulation. Any criterion for recognizing capitalist societies based on these criteria will be both under- and overinclusive (Unger, 1987).

The crucial assumption underlying Marx's conception of capitalism is that "free labor" is economically necessary to industrialization. This assumption is undermined by the irreparable ambiguity of the concepts of free labor and economic necessity. Each of these concepts is analytically related to the concept of desire, a variant of the concept of interest. To say that the "free laborer" has property in her labor, is to say that her labor can only be utilized with her consent. To say that a "free labor" market makes possible industrialization by utilizing labor more efficiently is to say that it better fulfills desires. Because Marx's theory of revolution is a variant of economic determinism, it shares the tendency of liberal economics to treat individual desire as an independent variable. A market is a means of aggregating desires. If one claims that the introduction of a free labor market better fulfills desires, one wrongly assumes that desires are independent of the means by which they are aggregated into social choice.

The instability of desire over time renders the concept of free labor indeterminate. Are specifically enforceable contracts for personal service expressions of "free labor" or involuntary servitude? In respecting the laborer's freedom at the time of contracting, we must sacrifice her freedom at the time she wishes to leave service, thereby designating her former self custodian of her later self's interests. In recognizing the laborer's freedom at the time of leaving service, we reduce her freedom at the time of contracting, effectively designating her later self custodian of her former self's interests. The instability of desire precludes us from simply respecting the preferences of the laborer. Because we cannot uncontroversially identify individual preferences, we can give no determinate meaning to the concept of free labor that underlies Marx's concept of capitalism.

The instability of desire also undermines the determinacy of concepts like economic efficiency that aggregate individual desires. Thus even if Marx could define free labor, he would have difficulty demonstrating that free labor was economically necessary to industrialization. And this claim is crucial to Marx's conception of capitalism as both a system and a necessary stage in the development of the "productive forces."

Marx would have denied that his conception of economic necessity was based on any notion of desire. For Marx, economic life consisted in production rather than consumption, and the value of products was a function of labor rather than consumer demand. Thus "economic necessity" would have meant "necessary to production," not "necessary to the satisfaction of consumer demand." "Free labor" then, was "necessary" in the sense of necessary to the development of industrial production.

Yet the "necessity" of "free labor" to industrialization depends on culturally contingent "consumer" preferences. In characterizing bondage as a "fetter" on the development of the productive forces, Marx meant that it inhibited production by misallocating labor: bound laborers have no incentive to seek more productive tasks. And less production means less social surplus to invest in the development of industry.

But unless we specify the "consumer" preferences of laborers and employers for different labor relations, we cannot conclude that a market in free labor will allocate work more efficiently than a market in bound labor. This follows from the familiar Coase theorem that, absent transaction costs, allocative efficiency does not depend on the distribution of entitlements (Coase, 1960). From the standpoint of efficiency, the choice of remedy for personal service contracts is as irrelevant as the choice of remedy for any contract.

The choice between free and bound labor is simply a choice between a damage remedy and a specific performance remedy for contracts for personal service. It follows that the distribution to employers of a property right in their laborer's services doesn't prevent the efficient allocation of those resources. A worker learning of a more productive position can buy her employer out, leaving both better off. Similarly, an employer discovering a more productive use for an employee can lease her services to another employer, or to the employee herself.

We can only conclude that bondage allocated labor inefficiently by viewing labor as a consumer good rather than a factor of production. Many masters refused to manumit their slaves at market price, or to permit them to hire their time. Few masters invested in the education and skilling of their slaves, or permitted their slaves to so invest. Many masters felt that it demeaned their authority to bargain with their slaves. And masters correctly feared that slaves allowed to wander in search of productive employment would run away. But this means that the slave system failed to allocate labor efficiently because neither the master nor the slave regarded the slave merely as a factor of production, to be valued according to the income she might yield. Masters owned slaves partly for the consumption value of the attendant honor, just as slaves were often willing, though not always able, to pay more than their own market value to consume the honor of self-ownership. Thus Marx's concern with the efficient allocation of labor for production cannot be separated from the question of its efficient allocation for consumption.

We have seen that critical legal scholars argue that the concept of efficiency is

288

thoroughly indeterminate when applied to the allocation of resources for consumption. Because we often incorporate our possessions into our sense of self, how much we value a good often depends on whether we already have it. This point applies to property in labor. Employers whose identities are already invested in master status are more likely to pay a premium for slave labor; penniless slaves could offer little for their freedom, while we would be surprised to learn of freed slaves selling themselves back into slavery at any monetary price. Thus the efficient allocation of the entitlement to dispose of labor depends in part on how the law distributes it.

The contingency of allocative efficiency on legal and cultural norms means that legal and cultural changes can make an efficient allocation inefficient and vice versa. Robert Steinfeld has shown that indentured servitude ceased to be a profitable way to employ labor when workers would no longer stand for it, and courts became less willing to enforce it (Steinfeld, 1991). Rather than economic rationality ending bound labor, the cultural rejection of bound labor made it economically inefficient.

What made bondage a "fetter" on the productive forces was the fact that the productive forces included laborers who saw it as demeaning. What binds "free" wage labor to the service of industrialization and accumulation to form "capitalism" is culture. This means that capitalism can never be separated from the "superstructure" it is supposed to explain. It also means that there is no necessary connection among any of the defining elements of a mode of production, and no necessary incompatibility between what are supposed to be elements of different modes of production. The indeterminacy of interests renders the Marxist conception of revolution incoherent.

The indeterminacy of interests, as developed by critical legal studies, undermines the instrumental conception of society that informs policy analysis across the political spectrum. Although the indeterminacy critique of liberal rights theory is better known, the indeterminacy critique of instrumentalism is critical legal studies' most important philosophical claim.

Bibliography

Baker, C. E. 1975: The ideology of the economic analysis of law. *Philosophy and Public Affairs*, 5, 3.
—— 1981: The process of change and the liberty theory of the First Amendment. *Southern California Law Review*, 55, 293.
Balkin, J. 1986: The crystalline structure of legal thought. *Rutgers Law Review*, 39, 1.
Bell, Jr, D. A. 1976: Serving two masters: integration ideals and client interests in school desegregation litigation. *Yale Law Journal*, 85, 470.
Coase, R. 1960: The problem of social cost. *Journal of Law and Economics*, 3, 1.
Cohen, M. 1927: Property and sovereignty. *Cornell Law Quarterly*, 13, 8.
Cook, W. W. 1981: Privileges of labor unions in the struggle for life. *Yale Law Journal*, 27, 779.

Freeman, A. D. 1978: Legitimizing racial discrimination through antidiscrimination law: a critical review of Supreme Court doctrine. *Minnesota Law Review*, 62, 1,049.

Gordon, R. W. 1984: Critical legal histories. *Stanford Law Review*, 36, 57.

Hale, R. 1943: Bargaining duress and economic liberty. *Columbia Law Review*, 43, 603.

Hofeld, W. 1913: Some fundamental legal conceptions as applied in judicial reasoning. *Yale Law Journal*, 28, 16.

Horwitz, M. J. 1977: *The Transformation of American Law, 1780–1860*. Cambridge and London: Harvard University Press.

Katz, A. 1979: Studies in boundary theory: three essays in adjudication and politics. *Buffalo Law Review*, 28, 383.

—— 1983: Mythologies of political representation. Unpublished manuscript.

—— 1987: Balancing. *In the Public Interest*, 7, 18.

Kelman, M. 1979: Consumption theory, production theory and ideology in the Coase theorem. *Southern California Law Review*, 52, 669.

Kennedy, D. 1973: Legal formality. *Journal of Legal Studies*, 2, 351, 381.

—— 1976: Form and substance in private law adjudication. *Harvard Law Review*, 89, 1,685.

—— 1979: The structure of *Blackstone's Commentaries*. *Buffalo Law Review*, 28, 205.

—— 1981: Cost benefit analysis of entitlement problems: a critique. *Stanford Law Review*, 33, 387.

—— 1991: A semiotics of legal argument. *Syracuse Law Review*, 42, 75.

Klare, K. E. 1978: Judicial deradicalization of the Wagner Act and the origins of modern legal consciousness, 1937–1941. *Minnesota Law Review*, 62, 265.

Parker, R. D. 1981: The past of constitutional theory – and its future. *Ohio State Law Journal*, 42, 223, 239–46.

Peller, G. 1985: The metaphysics of American law. *California Law Review*, 73, 1,151.

Schlegel, J. H. 1984: Notes toward an intimate, opinionated and affectionate history of the conference on legal studies. *Stanford Law Review*, 36, 391.

Simon, W. H. 1978: The ideology of advocacy: procedural justice and professional ethics. *Wisconsin Law Review*, 29.

—— 1983: Legality, bureaucracy, and class in the welfare system. *Yale Law Journal*, 92, 1,198.

Singer, J. 1993: *Property Law: rules, practices, policies.* 20.

Steinfeld, R. 1991: *The Invention of Free Labor: the employment relation in English and American law and culture, 1350–1870.* Chapel Hill and London: University of North Carolina Press.

Unger, R. 1987: *Social Theory: its situation and its task.* Cambridge and New York: Cambridge University Press.

18

Post-realism and legal process

NEIL DUXBURY

Introduction

During the past two decades, the intricacies of American legal realism seem to have been relentlessly explored. Finding an American law professor who does not have his or her peculiar "take" on the subject would be something of a minor miracle. Depending on whose commentaries one reads, legal realism may be seen to represent a variety of turning points in American legal thought. Accordingly, realism marked the birth of social scientific legal study (Schlegel, 1979, 1980); it demonstrated the essentially political nature of the legal process (Horwitz, 1992); it even – in the eyes of certain of its detractors – constituted a jurisprudence of nihilism and tyranny (for an account of this critique, see Purcell, 1969; Duxbury, 1992). This essay will not assess these or any other interpretations of realist jurisprudence. Rather, its purpose is to analyze the ways in which certain post-realist jurisprudential tendencies have either built upon or departed from basic realist insights.

Modern legal theory and the impact of realism

In the United States, interest in realist jurisprudence was revived significantly with the emergence of critical legal studies in the late 1970s. While there are certain fundamental differences between the realist and critical traditions in American jurisprudence, legal realism never embodied a commitment to grand-scale social and legal transformation which has been espoused by at least one major proponent of critical legal studies (Unger, 1987a, 1987b, 1987c). However, realists and critical legal theorists alike acknowledge the inevitability of indeterminacy in law. Whereas legal realists recognized and generally lamented the existence of legal indeterminacy, representatives of critical legal studies have endeavored to demonstrate the peculiar consequences of indeterminacy. According to critical legal theorists, it is owing to the existence of indeterminacy, that law is an ineluctably political practice. Unlike their realist forebears, proponents of critical legal studies have shown a greater eagerness to uncover the political implications of indeterminacy in law.

Law and economics – particularly as developed at the University of Chicago – is commonly regarded as methodologically and ideologically very different from critical legal studies. Yet certain commentators on law and economics have tended to treat it just as critical legal studies has been treated: that is, as an outgrowth of the realist jurisprudential tradition. "In the law schools," Edmund Kitch has claimed, "law and economics evolved out of the agenda of legal realism. Legal realism taught that legal scholars should study the law as it works in practice by making use of the social sciences, and economics was one of the social sciences to which academic lawyers turned" (Kitch, 1983, p. 184). Whereas Kitch treats law and economics as a continuation of the realist legal tradition, Arthur Allen Leff regarded it as "an attempt to get over, or at least to get by, the complexity thrust upon us by the Realists" (Leff, 1974, p. 459). My own view is that the law and economics tradition ought to be regarded neither as an attempt to develop nor to undermine the lessons of realist jurisprudence. For a proper understanding of the development and the jurisprudential impact of law and economics requires that the tradition be understood primarily in relation to developments in economic as opposed to legal theory (see Duxbury, 1995, ch. 5).

Although one of the most incisive and sympathetic studies of realist jurisprudence is the product of a British legal scholar (Twining, 1985), it is worth noting that legal philosophers in the United Kingdom have tended to be indifferent, if not hostile, to the realist tradition. British critical legal theorists, for example, appear to have been little inspired by realist jurisprudence. While British legal theory has hardly failed to flourish owing to the general disinclination of its representatives to consider realism as a subject deserving of sustained attention, it is worth speculating on the reason for this disinclination. My own suspicion is that the reason British legal theorists tend not to treat realism seriously may be traced to H. L. A. Hart's assessment of the subject in his classic positivist text, *The Concept of Law* (1961). In that book, Hart criticizes realist rule-skeptics – and Jerome Frank in particular – for focussing only on the duty-imposing function of rules in the process of judicial decision making and ignoring those secondary rules which confer judicial and legislative power. According to Hart, it is crucial to appreciate – and legal realists appeared not to appreciate – that there must exist specific power-conferring rules which facilitate the appointment of legal officials. Realists tended to consider rules as if they were nothing more than manipulable tools to be used arbitrarily in the process of adjudicating disputes. They said little if anything about the fact that there must exist a definite body of rules which confer on certain people the capacity to adjudicate disputes in the first place. Those legal philosophers – and this includes the majority of British legal philosophers – who have been educated primarily in the positivist jurisprudential tradition appear generally to accept Hart's criticism of realist legal thought.

Not surprisingly, it is to the United States that one must look in order to understand how jurisprudence has developed directly in response to the lessons of realism. During the latter half of this century, there have emerged, I believe, two distinct traditions of "post-realism" in the United States. The first of these traditions might conveniently (if somewhat vaguely) be labeled *policy science*. The second, and more significant, of these traditions is commonly termed *legal process*. I shall consider each of these traditions in turn.

Policy science

Policy science, as a form of jurisprudence, was the joint creation of the political scientist, Harold D. Lasswell, and the Yale law professor, Myres S. McDougal. In the late 1930s, Lasswell and McDougal began teaching a course together at the Yale Law School in which they explored the possibility of expanding upon the lessons of legal realism. Their particular concern was to develop the law school curriculum in such a way as to facilitate the promotion of democratic values. Whereas legal realists tended not to explore the political implications of their arguments (indeed, this is precisely why realism suffered from so much political misinterpretation), Lasswell and McDougal endeavored to outline an explicitly pro-democratic approach to the development of legal policy. The framework for this approach is set out in their oft-cited article, "Legal education and public policy," first published in 1943. According to one commentator, this article marks "the clear beginning of the post-realist period" in American legal scholarship (Stevens, 1971, p. 530).

One of the objectives behind Lasswell and McDougal's article is to highlight what they considered to be the shortcomings of realist jurisprudence. They focus especially on the inability of most realists successfully to utilize social scientific methods for the purpose of legal study. "Heroic, but random, efforts to integrate 'law' and 'the other social sciences,'" they observe, "fail through lack of clarity about *what* is being integrated, and *how*, and *for what purposes* ... The relevance of 'non-legal' materials to effective 'law' teaching is recognized but efficient techniques for the investigation, collection and presentation of such materials are not devised" (Lasswell and McDougal, 1943, p. 263). Whereas so-called realists had been concerned merely with integrating law and the broader social sciences, Lasswell and McDougal were more concerned with demonstrating how such integration could be made to serve a specific purpose.

But what purpose? Lasswell and McDougal's answer to this question is very specific. The purpose of integration is to demonstrate to legal decision makers, present and future, that the social sciences constitute an invaluable source of normative guidance. Legal realists, they argued, made the mistake of assuming the possibility of a value-free social science. In fact, they insisted, far from providing some sort of value-free framework, the social sciences constitute a collection of conceptual tools to which legal decision makers of the future will be able to resort in order to make legal values explicit. Enlightened by the social sciences, in other words, lawyers of the future will come to acknowledge that they are dealing not only with law but also with policy (hence the term "policy science").

For Lasswell and McDougal, the study of law along scientific lines would require of law students not that they embrace any old values, but that they affirm explicitly the values to which they ought already to be committed, that is, the individualistic values of American liberal democracy. Realist jurisprudence – indeed, American jurisprudence in general – had remained conspicuously inarticulate on the matter of how to relate "legal structures, doctrines, and procedures . . . clearly and consistently to the major problems of a society struggling to achieve democratic values" (Lasswell and McDougal, 1943, p. 205). The spread of despotism throughout Europe offered a sharp reminder that the acceptance of democracy can never be taken for granted; and it was recognition of precisely this fact that led Lasswell and McDougal to develop their argument that the fundamental goal of post-realist jurisprudence ought to be "the better promotion of democratic values" (Lasswell and McDougal, 1943, p. 264). They outline their argument thus:

> We submit this basic proposition: if legal education in the contemporary world is adequately to serve the needs of a free and productive commonwealth, it must be conscious, efficient, and systematic *training for policy making*. The proper function of our law schools is, in short, to contribute to the training of policy-makers for the ever more complete achievement of the democratic values that constitute the professed ends of American polity. (*Lasswell and McDougal, 1943, p. 206*)

Thus, in Lasswell and McDougal's view, the primary reason for developing an interdisciplinary approach to legal education is to use the social sciences as a medium through which to immerse the law student in those values which are deemed to represent the values of democracy.

But how is this immersion to be achieved? That is, how is the law student to be exposed to these values? And still more importantly, what are these values? It is to Lasswell and McDougal's credit that they do not sidestep these questions. However, their effort to answer them reveals the basic problems inherent in their perspective.

The pivotal value to which law students ought to be exposed, they assert, "is the dignity and worth of the individual," for it is only through respect for this value that students may come to recognize that "a democratic society is a commonwealth of mutual deference – a commonwealth where there is full opportunity to mature talent into socially creative skill, free from discrimination on grounds of religion, culture or class" (Lasswell and McDougal, 1943, p. 212). Apart from this basic respect for the distinctness of the individual, law students will also be encouraged to recognize other "general values in which they participate as members of a free society" (Lasswell and McDougal, 1943, p. 246). These values are the shared values of "power, respect, knowledge, income, and safety (including health)" (Lasswell and McDougal, 1943, p. 217). In later writings, Lasswell and McDougal gradually modified and expanded this list: "knowledge" was replaced by the separate categories of "enlightenment" and "skill"; "income" was broadened to "wealth"; "safety" to "well-being"; and "morality" – later changed to "rectitude" – was added to their list. These values, for Lasswell and McDougal, constitute the basic values of human dignity. The primary purpose of post-realist jurisprudence, they claimed, was to demonstrate to students that their recognition of these values as self-evident is of fundamental importance for the maintenance and furtherance of a properly democratic order.

How, then, was policy science supposed to work? That is, how might Lasswell and McDougal's basic values of human dignity ever come to feature centrally in the law school curriculum? Their answer to this question seems to be that one can do little more than proselytize: law professors must be encouraged to reorient their teaching along policy science lines. New courses must be devised, and old ones revised, along policy science lines. All curricular revision ought to be guided by one simple criterion: whether or not current doctrines and practices in particular areas of law serve to promote or to retard the basic values of human dignity (Lasswell and McDougal, 1943, pp. 248–62). The fundamental obstacle facing the policy science proposal, however, was that it bore little resemblance to anything that either students or teachers actually wanted from legal education. Lasswell and McDougal wrote in high-falutin terms about the need for radical pedagogic change in the American law schools. But no one was prepared to seize the initiative with them. Indeed, at most law schools less prestigious than Yale, resources simply did not exist which would have permitted the seizing of such an initiative, even if anyone should have wished to do so. Another Yale law professor has recently hailed their 1943 article as "a forgotten classic" in the history of modern American legal scholarship (Kronman, 1993, p. 202). To my mind, however, the article is more eccentric than classic. It offers a highly idiosyncratic vision of legal education perfected. If policy science had not hailed from Yale, it is doubtful that it would have generated even marginal academic interest.

Perhaps the greatest shortcoming of all concerning policy science as a form of jurisprudence is that it did not improve significantly upon the lessons of legal realism. I would argue, indeed, that Lasswell and McDougal offered little more than a version of realist jurisprudence for good times. Like their realist forebears, they recognized that law is a political phenomenon. But their argument seemed to be that so long as an educational framework was established which would ensure that future lawyers subscribed to the right kind of politics, the use of law to promote political objectives ought not to be discouraged. That law might be used to serve both good and bad political ends seemed not to concern Lasswell and McDougal. For them, the integrity of a law school curriculum redesigned to promote the basic values of human dignity would be enough of a safeguard to ensure that the legal profession did not stray into murky political waters. If law students were provided with a good political education, then they would eventually develop into good legal policymakers. The matter, in Lasswell and McDougal's eyes, really was as simple as that.

Legal process

As compared with Lasswell and McDougal, many American law professors in the post-World War II era were remarkably less sanguine about the prospects for the development of law as a political tool. The tradition of American jurisprudence known as "legal process' epitomizes the sense of disquiet which various law professors of this period expressed regarding the politicization of law. While it would be inappropriate strictly to characterize legal process as a post-realist tradition – the development of process jurisprudence in the United States parallels if not predates the advent of realism (see Duxbury, 1993, pp. 607–22) – it seems not inaccurate to claim that it was only as legal realism began to wane that the process tradition came to acquire a distinctive identity. Legal process, in short, came alive in response to the challenges of realist legal thought.

What is meant when we speak of "legal process' as a form of jurisprudence? It seems to me that "process," in this context, can be seen to denote two things. First, there is the legal process itself. The process tradition in American jurisprudence presents a very distinctive account of the elements which make up the legal process. Secondly, "process" denotes a specific process of legal reasoning which most process theorists believe ought to dominate constitutional adjudication (or indeed, some would argue, adjudication in general). Let us take these different dimensions of process in turn.

Who should do what?

One of the issues at the heart of the process tradition in American jurisprudence is that of institutional competence: viz., within the legal process, which institution should be deemed competent to do what? From the mid-1930s onwards, various law professors – virtually all of them associated in one way or another with the Harvard Law School – turned their attention to this question. In the 1930s, Felix Frankfurter and Henry Hart had written a series of articles in which they warned against the dangers of blurring the distinction between adjudication and legislation. If this distinction does become blurred – and it appeared, during the New Deal era, that this is precisely what was happening – then the integrity of the Supreme Court can no longer be guaranteed:

> A Court the scope of whose activities lies as close to the more sensitive areas of politics as does that of the Supreme Court must constantly be on the alert against undue suction into the avoidable polemic of politics. Especially at a time when the appeal from legislation to adjudication is more frequent and its results more far-reaching, laxity in assuming jurisdiction adds gratuitous friction to the difficulties of government . . . Inevitably, fulfilment of the Supreme Court's traditional function in passing judgment upon legislation, especially that of Congress, occasions the reaffirmation of old procedural safeguards and the assertion of new ones against subtle or daring attempts at procedural blockade-running. (*Frankfurter and Hart, 1935, pp. 90–1*)

The message which Frankfurter and Hart were endeavoring to promote was simple: adjudication is a peculiar type of institutional activity which ought not to embrace policy-making; and if the integrity of the adjudicative process is to be preserved, judicial self-restraint must dominate the activity of the courts. Within the legal process tradition, nobody took more care in developing the idea that adjudication is somehow a "special" form of juristic activity than did Lon Fuller. For Fuller, "adjudication is a form of social ordering institutionally committed to 'rational' decision" (Fuller, 1978, p. 380). This thesis is elaborated by Fuller in this article, "The forms and limits of adjudication." (Although published in 1978, shortly after his death, this article was circulated in draft form by Fuller among members of the Legal Philosophy Discussion Group at Harvard Law School as early as 1957.) Fuller argues in this article that "the distinguishing characteristic of adjudication lies in the fact that it confers on the affected party a peculiar form of participation in the decision, that of presenting proofs and reasoned arguments for a decision in his favor" (Fuller, 1978, p. 364). As a legal activity – as opposed, say, to the refereeing of a sport or the judging of a competition – adjudication demands, indeed, that decisions be "reached within an institutional framework that is intended to assure to the disputants an opportunity for the presentation of proofs and reasoned arguments" (Fuller, 1978, p. 365). Given that adjudication requires that an affected party be able to participate in the process of reaching a decision, that person, "if his participation is to be meaningful," must "assert some principle or principles by which his arguments are sound and his proofs relevant" (Fuller, 1978, p. 369). Only by resorting to principles might disputing parties convincingly assert their rights within the adjudicative process. Indeed, for Fuller, principles and adjudication go hand-in-hand. He attempts to illustrate this point by constructing a particular scenario:

> We may see this process . . . in the case of an employee who desires an increase in pay. If he asks his boss for a raise, he may, of course, claim "a right" to the raise. He may argue the fairness of the principles of equal treatment and call attention to the fact that Joe, who is not better than he, recently got a raise. But he does not have to rest his plea on any ground of this sort. He may merely beg for generosity, urging the needs of his family. Or he may propose an exchange, offering to take on extra duties if he gets the raise. If, however, he takes his case to an arbitrator he cannot, explicitly at least, support his case by an appeal to charity or by proposing a bargain. He will have to support his demand by a principle of some kind, and a demand supported by principle is the same thing as a claim of right. (*Fuller, 1978, p. 369*)

Within the literature of the legal process tradition, this passage is, in my opinion, fairly crucial. Fuller manages here to draw together three distinct process themes: that adjudication is a special form of legal-institutional activity; that the court is a forum of principle; and that principles serve to protect rights. These themes – especially the second and third themes – would, in due course, come to be associated primarily with the legal philosophy of Ronald Dworkin. Before the advent of Dworkin, however, these three themes were developed very gradually by a variety of writers within the legal process tradition. The history of this development is by no means neat, and in an article of this nature it is possible only to sketch what is in fact a fairly complex intellectual history. Any summary of this history would be thoroughly deficient, however, if account were not taken of Henry Hart and Albert Sacks's unpublished manuscript, "The legal process" (1958).

At the core of "The legal process" rests the observation that law is a purposive process. The basic purpose of legal institutions, according to Hart and Sacks, is to maximize the total satisfactions of valid human desires. "Almost every, if not every, institutional system gives at least lip service to the goal of maximizing valid satisfactions for its members generally" (Hart and Sacks, 1958, p. 115). For Hart and Sacks, this observation may be taken for granted. What is far less obvious, however, is the matter of how the legal process might best pursue the goal of maximization. Successful pursuit of this goal, according to Hart and Sacks, demands an efficient legal system; and one can only have an efficient legal system if most issues of social ordering are left to private individuals and groups, if the law is allowed to intervene in the process of private ordering only when it is required, and if – once the law is permitted to intervene – there exists no confusion as to which legal institution ought to do the intervening. An efficient legal process, in other words, is one which intervenes in the process of private ordering only when necessary and which demonstrates a general awareness of which legal institution is competent to do what. Accordingly, a proper distribution of institutional responsibility between, say, the courts and the legislature demands the recognition that each must refrain from trying to perform functions for which it is not competent.

While Hart and Sacks examine the institutional competence of both legislatures and courts (and other law-applying bodies, for that matter), it is their reflections on the courts in particular which feature most significantly within the history of the legal process tradition. Integral to adjudication, they argue, is "the power of reasoned elaboration" (Hart and Sacks, 1958, p. 161). In other words, courts are expected to reach decisions on the basis of rationally defensible principles. It is not enough that a court should reach welcome or popular decisions; it is more important that those decisions be principled – that they be sound. But were the American courts of the 1950s and 1960s fulfilling this expectation? Were they adjudicating in a principled fashion? The decisions of the Supreme Court under the Chief Justiceship of Earl Warren indicated that the requirement of soundness was not being taken seriously. Given that many of these decisions were meeting with a good deal of popular support, the question arose as to why this requirement ought to be treated seriously. That is, if a judicial decision seems like a good decision, why should it matter that it is not backed up explicitly by principle? This question Hart and Sacks failed to confront. Refinement of the process tradition in American jurisprudence demanded that someone else speak where Hart and Sacks had fallen silent.

The affirmation of principle

The question which Hart and Sacks failed to confront – the question of why principles matter – was tackled head-on by Herbert Wechsler in his classic article, "Toward neutral principles of constitutional law" (1959). In that article, Wechsler argues that during the first half of this century, and especially during the New Deal era, the Supreme Court paid little attention to principles. Indeed, in decisions such as *Lochner* v. *New York* (198 U.S. 45 (1905)) and other famous early twentieth-century liberty of contract cases, the Court had demonstrated a commitment to judicial activism by reading policy preferences into the 14th Amendment of the United States Constitution. Activist constitutional adjudication, Wechsler observed, was equally prevalent in the Supreme Court during the 1950s. Between the early decades of this century and the 1950s, however, something had changed. The early twentieth-century liberty of contract cases are generally considered to represent the unwelcome face of judicial activism. By reading an economic preference – a preference for *laissez faire* and Social Darwinism rather than for economic interventionism – into the Constitution, the Supreme Court of the *Lochner* era was demonstrating just why political adjudication may be considered undesirable. But by the 1950s, political adjudication appeared to be serving good rather than bad ends. For Wechsler, the segregation decisions – and *Brown* v. *Board of Education* (347 U.S. 483 (1954)) in particular – demonstrated this point. Those decisions, he believed, had "the best chance of making an enduring contribution to the quality of our society of any . . . in recent years" (Wechsler, 1959, p. 27). Yet he also believed that those decisions were, in a peculiar way, unsatisfactory. They were unsatisfactory because they were not sufficiently principled.

In elaborating this point, Wechsler focussed specifically on the case of *Brown* v. *Board of Education*, in which the Supreme Court held that racial segregation in American public schools denies black children equal protection of the laws as guaranteed by section 1 of the 14th Amendment. The Supreme Court had reached its decision in *Brown*, he observed, "on the ground that segregated schools are 'inherently unequal,'" having "deleterious effects upon the colored children in implying their inferiority, effects which retard their educational and mental development" (Wechsler, 1959, p. 32). Yet there existed no evidence to support this argument. Indeed, Wechsler suggested, the reality may be that integrated schools are racially hostile schools in which blacks suffer by being made to feel inferior. It may even be the case that, where segregation does exist, blacks enjoy a "sense of security" in their own schools (Wechsler, 1959, p. 33). In offering this argument, Wechsler was not attempting to justify racial segregation. Rather, he was attempting to demonstrate that the Supreme Court needed to do rather more than it had done in order to justify integration. But what should the Court have done? According to Wechsler, the Court ought to have demonstrated that the constitutional invalidation of state-enforced segregation was founded on a principle which would favor the interests of neither blacks nor whites – a principle such as that the state ought not to impede freedom of association.

Even Wechsler himself seemed not entirely convinced that freedom of association was the principle at stake in *Brown*. But then, the hesitancy of his conclusion is not especially important. What is far more important, for the purpose of understanding the legal process tradition as a strand of post-realist legal thought, is an estimation of why Wechsler felt that resort to principles is crucial in the context of constitutional adjudication. His argument is perhaps most easily grasped if one contrasts the *Lochner*-type liberty of contract decisions with the segregation decisions. In the former set of decisions, the Supreme Court was adjudicating in an activist fashion, using the 14th Amendment to validate a preference for *laissez faire* over economic interventionism. In the latter set of decisions, the Supreme Court was again engaging in judicial activism, this time using the 14th Amendment to validate a preference for racial integration over segregation. Both sets of decisions were political: the first set was welcomed, the second set castigated. For Wechsler, these two sets of decisions illustrate that where a politically appointed judiciary reaches decisions on the basis of policy preference, one must expect judicial preferences to change with the political climate. Where political change occurs, in other words, the political objectives behind judicial activism are likely also to change. The consequence of this is that while the decisions of an activist Supreme Court may be welcomed when the politics of the Court are considered to be favorable, its decisions are equally likely to cause outcry when the political perspective of the Court appears to change for the worse. Judicial activism thus turns out to be a constitutional jurisprudence for good times. For Wechsler, however, a jurisprudence for good times is an unsound basis for constitutional adjudication: it would be hypocrisy, after all, if one were to applaud activism when the courts are engaging in good politics and then to cry foul once the courts begin to pursue political objectives with which one disagrees. To put the point very simply, if one wishes to welcome the political adjudication which produced *Brown*, one must also accept the political adjudication which produced *Lochner*.

Hence, for Wechsler, the importance of principles. If guided by general neutral principles, constitutional adjudication is likely to exhibit a greater degree of consistency, and in consequence command a greater degree of respect, than if it were guided by considerations of policy. This faith in principle marks off the legal process tradition from the realist tradition in American jurisprudence. So-called realists recognized the problem of judicial indeterminacy; but they had little idea as to how such indeterminacy might be controlled or eradicated. Within the process tradition, we find a solution to this problem: indeterminacy can be controlled through the constraining force of principle. It almost goes without saying that there exist plenty of objections to this solution. Perhaps the main objection is that the solution overlooks the fact that principles themselves may be indeterminate – they may appear sometimes to conflict (for example, where a claim to privacy is pitted against the right to freedom of speech) – and that, in cases of such indeterminacy, there exists no principled way of determining which principle should prevail. Despite this objection and others, however, process writers after Wechsler – writers such as Alexander Bickel, John Hart Ely, and Ronald Dworkin – have continued to refine the legal process perspective (see, for example, Bickel, 1961; Ely, 1980; Dworkin, 1986). As with the criticisms of this perspective, consideration of these refinements lies beyond the scope of this essay. Rather than consider the various twists and turns of the legal process tradition, my aim here has been to demonstrate how process jurisprudence constituted a response – a highly problematic response, but, nevertheless, a response – to a problem which legal realism did little more than acknowledge and which policy science basically glossed over: the problem, that is, of how to monitor and control the impact of politics on law.

Bibliography

Bickel, A. M. 1961: The Supreme Court, 1960 term – foreword: the passive virtues. *Harvard Law Review*, 75, 40–79.

Duxbury, N. 1992: The reinvention of American legal realism. *Legal Studies*, 12, 137–77.

—— 1993: Faith in reason: the process tradition in American jurisprudence. *Cardozo Law Review*, 15, 601–705.

—— 1995: *Patterns of American Jurisprudence*. Oxford: Oxford University Press.

Dworkin, R. 1986: *A Matter of Principle*. Oxford: Clarendon.

Ely, J. H. 1980: *Democracy and Distrust: a theory of judicial review*. Cambridge, Mass.: Harvard University Press.

Frankfurter, F. and Hart, H. M. 1935: The business of the Supreme Court at October Term, 1934. *Harvard Law Review*, 49, 68–107.

Fuller, L. L. 1978: The forms and limits of adjudication. *Harvard Law Review*, 92, 353–409.

Hart, H. L. A. 1961: *The Concept of Law*. Oxford: Clarendon.

Hart, H. M. and Sacks, A. M. 1958: The legal process: basic problems in the making and application of law. Cambridge, Mass.: Harvard Law School unpublished mimeograph.

Horwitz, M. J. 1992: *The Transformation of American Law, 1870–1960: the crisis of legal orthodoxy*. New York: Oxford University Press.

Kitch, E. W. 1983: The intellectual foundations of "law and economics." *Journal of Legal Education*, 33, 184–96.

Kronman, A. T. 1993: *The Lost Lawyer: failing ideals of the legal profession*. Cambridge, Mass.: Belknap Press.

Lasswell, H. D. and McDougal, M. S. 1943: Legal education and public policy: professional training in the public interest. *Yale Law Journal*, 52, 203–95.

Leff, A. A. 1974: Economic analysis of law: some realism about nominalism. *Virginia Law Review*, 60, 451–82.

Purcell, Jr, E. A. 1969: American jurisprudence between the wars: legal realism and the crisis of democratic theory. *American Historical Review*, 75, 424–46.

Schlegel, J. H. 1979: American legal realism and empirical social science: from the Yale experience. *Buffalo Law Review*, 28, 459–586.

—— 1980: American legal realism and empirical social science: the singular case of Underhill Moore. *Buffalo Law Review*, 29, 195–323.

Stevens, R. 1971: Two cheers for 1870: the American law school. *Perspectives in American History*, 5, 403–548.

Twining, W. 1985: *Karl Llewellyn and the Realist Movement*. London: Weidenfeld & Nicolson.

Unger, R. M. 1987a: *False Necessity: anti-necessitarian social theory in the service of radical democracy. Part I of "Politics", a work in constructive social theory*. Cambridge: Cambridge University Press.

—— 1987b: *Plasticity into Power: comparative–historical studies on the institutional conditions of economic and military success. Variations on themes of "Politics," a work in constructive social theory*. Cambridge: Cambridge University Press.

—— 1987c: *Social Theory: its situation and its task. A critical introduction to "Politics," a work in constructive social theory*. Cambridge: Cambridge University Press.

Wechsler, H. 1959: Toward neutral principles of constitutional law. *Harvard Law Review*, 73, 1–35.

19

Feminist jurisprudence

PATRICIA SMITH

Since the 1980s a substantial amount of challenging and creative legal scholarship has come to be known as feminist jurisprudence (see Smith, 1993). The character of this scholarship is quite diverse. Just as it has been noted that there is not one feminism, but many; so there is not one feminist legal theory, but many. The question is what is feminist jurisprudence and what makes it worth attending to? What (if anything) do all these divergent views have in common that binds them together and distinguishes them from all other theories? (What makes them all feminist?) Second, what do they tell us about law? (What makes them jurisprudence?) Third, what is important about this form of legal analysis? Supposing that there is a distinctively feminist jurisprudence, why is law in need of it? These questions are derived from the major objections leveled against feminist jurisprudence, namely: (1) it is not distinctively feminist; (2) it is not "properly" jurisprudence; and (3) it is not philosophically interesting. These objections challenge the very existence or legitimacy of feminist jurisprudence as a philosophical discipline. So it is worth considering each question (or objection) separately.

Let's start with the easiest question. What makes feminist jurisprudence jurisprudence? Since jurisprudence is the analysis of fundamental legal relations, concepts, and principles, and the feminist legal theory that identifies itself as jurisprudence is, in fact, engaged in such analysis, the real question is why there should be any objection to classifying it as jurisprudence? It is claimed that feminist jurisprudence is a contradiction in terms. Jurisprudence, it is argued, is supposed to be the neutral analysis of universal legal principles, so given that feminism is self-interested, it produces a self-interested jurisprudence, which is a contradiction in terms. But this argument is misguided in both of its central premises: (1) it assumes that feminism is somehow unfairly self-interested, which is false; and (2) it assumes that jurisprudence is neutral (meaning non-moral or apolitical) which is also false.

The feminist answer to (1) is that feminist jurisprudence is no more self-interested than supposedly universal jurisprudence, which, in fact, is patriarchy masquerading as the objective analysis of neutral legal principles and concepts. In fact, much feminist jurisprudence is dedicated to proving that traditional jurisprudence and law are not neutral or universal, but biased in favor of the dominant

302

culture, at the expense of all others (see Smith, 1993; Minow, 1990; Rhode, 1989). So this objection to the legitimacy of feminist jurisprudence relies on denying or ignoring the central claim of feminists about the nature of jurisprudence and law. Thus, it embodies a fundamental misconception about the object of feminist jurisprudence, which is not intended to reconstruct legal institutions so as to favor women. It is intended to reconstruct legal institutions so as not to disfavor women. That is, it is intended to eliminate bias against women. So, while feminism is self-interested, it is self-interested in the sense that self-defense is self-interested, which is to be interested in promoting justice, not privilege. Therefore, the assumption that feminism is illegitimately self-interested is false.

As to point (2), that jurisprudence is neutral, this objection relies on a particular interpretation of what counts as jurisprudence. The idea of jurisprudence in common usage today can be divided into a broad and a narrow sense. Broadly speaking, jurisprudential theories are political theories which have legal ramifications. For example, liberal, Marxist, and socialist political theories spawn jurisprudential views (that is, legal theories) that follow from and reflect their implications. When people talk about liberal jurisprudence or Marxist jurisprudence, that is what they are talking about. Clearly, this broad sense of jurisprudence does not entail neutrality in its theories. Quite the contrary.

Much (although not all) feminist jurisprudence is associated with one or more of these political theories. For example, liberal feminists since Mary Wollstonecraft have always argued that liberal values should be applied equally to women as in Gutmann (1980). Marxist feminists argue that marxist class analysis applies equally to gender as in Davis (1981). Socialist feminists argue that socialist principles should be used to alleviate the oppression of sexism as in Jaggar (1983). Feminist theories often point to the omission of women or the presence of gender discrimination within the general political theories with which they are associated. And feminist jurisprudence can be combined with any number of other political views. It can be pragmatic as in Radin (1990), postmodern (Frug, 1992), purely radical (MacKinnon, 1989), or not associated with any other particular theory (Minow, 1990; Rhode, 1989). There is no single feminist jurisprudence, no single political view associated with feminism, except feminism itself, which is also a political view (the view that advocates freedom and justice for women.) So, all feminist theory is political. Its form varies depending on the other theories with which it is combined. Yet, all these views fit within the broad sense of jurisprudence that informs all feminist work.

But there is also a narrow, technical sense of jurisprudence, however, which is sometimes equated with all jurisprudence. Thus, the legitimacy of the broad sense is sometimes questioned, and that is the ground for denying that feminist jurisprudence is "really" jurisprudence. It does not fit the narrow sense of jurisprudence. But the narrow sense of jurisprudence – at least in the form that denies the legitimacy of feminist jurisprudence – is itself open to question.

The narrow sense of jurisprudence has traditionally been concerned with the question: what is law? Addressing this question, philosophers have focussed on the concept of law as such, on legal concepts and relations, and legal functions,

303

particularly legal reasoning. Historically, three major theories were advanced to deal with these issues.

The oldest, natural law, commonly defined law as a precept of reason promulgated for the common good by those in authority to do so. Natural law holds, among other things, that there is a necessary connection between law and morality, such that an immoral law is invalid or not binding.

The second view, legal positivism, which became predominant in the nineteenth century, objected to the natural law view as confusing what law is with what law ought to be, and attempted to construct a value-neutral definition of its own. Positivists today generally define law as a system of rules promulgated by authorized procedures, recognized as binding by officials and obeyed by the bulk of the population.

The third theory, legal realism, a twentieth-century development, objected to the natural law approach as too obscure and metaphysical, and to the positivist approach as too rigid and abstract. Arguing that law is fundamentally and inescapably political, the realists defined law roughly as a method of dispute settlement by appeal to the authority of an office, especially a court; or to put it more succinctly, they claimed that law is what judges say it is. These well-known theories continue to debate the fundamental nature of law and the appropriate function of jurisprudence to this day.

Given this history we can see that traditional jurisprudence was not always divided, but has long been divided into two major subcategories: normative and descriptive jurisprudence. This division was instituted by John Austin, the nineteenth-century positivist who dedicated his famous lectures to "determining the province of jurisprudence, properly so called." According to Austin, the proper domain of jurisprudence was the descriptive analysis of the positive law, its basic concepts and relations. Normative analysis of law, he thought, was the proper domain of legislation, not jurisprudence, and the two should not be confused, just as law and morality should not be confused.

The powerful influence of this view can be seen in the official definition of jurisprudence found today in *Black's Law Dictionary*:

> that science of law which has for its function to ascertain the principles on which legal rules are based, so as not only to classify those rules in their proper order ... but also to settle the manner in which doubtful cases should be brought under the appropriate rules. Jurisprudence is more a formal than a material science. It has no direct concern with questions of moral or political policy, for they fall under the province of ethics and legislation.

Notice that this definition conveniently settles the long and continuing controversy between positivists and natural law theorists, by making positivism the only true jurisprudence. Unfortunately, philosophical questions are not often answered so easily, and presumably those who find natural law insightful will not have their questions answered by *Black's Law Dictionary*. Nevertheless, the dictionary entry does show the power of positivist influence in American legal thought, as well as the problematic nature of the approach taken by Austin to define natural law out of existence. And it is precisely this view which provides the grounding for the objection that feminism, not being neutral, is contradictory to jurisprudence.

According to *Black's Law Dictionary* natural law theory is not jurisprudence (and legal realism is not jurisprudence either) so perhaps feminists should not be disturbed if their theory is not considered to be jurisprudence for the same reasons. But the important point is that *Black's Law Dictionary*, in its attempt to be neutral, is blind to its own bias against all theories but one, which it assumes by adopting a positivist definition of what qualifies as jurisprudence: hardly a neutral definition.

What this demonstrates is that given the nature of law as *arguably* political, jurisprudence cannot be made neutral in any way and certainly not by stipulative definition, because arguing and examining the political implications of law, or lack of them is a central issue of jurisprudence. So jurisprudence is not and cannot be neutral, and that shows that both the assumptions that underlie the objection to the legitimacy of feminism as jurisprudence are false. So feminist jurisprudence is indeed jurisprudence or else natural law is not. This is not to say that they cannot both be wrong. Positivists can claim that natural law is wrong, but not that it is not jurisprudence. Similarly, feminist detractors.

The more difficult question is what makes feminist jurisprudence feminist? The great diversity within feminism has led some critics (and even some feminists) to argue that there is no common feminist perspective. There is no feature that distinguishes feminist jurisprudence from all other legal philosophy. All feminism is actually reducible, or so it is argued, to those theories that inform its many facets. Liberal feminism is reducible to liberalism; postmodern feminism is reducible to postmodernism, and so on. Thus, it is claimed, feminism provides no new idea, or distinctive theory. It is simply the application of old theories to the particular problem of women's oppression.

Furthermore, it is claimed, there is no point of view of all women. Feminism, if it can be identified as one view, is the view of a few women who are seeking to impose it on everyone else. The fact is that the majority of the women of the world either disagree with the views of feminists, or else never thought about the issues feminists raise. So it is highly problematic for feminists to represent themselves as speaking for all women. These are serious charges.

It is true without question that women are as diverse as human beings can be. Women can be rich, poor, weak, strong, dominating, passive, upper class, lower class, rational, irrational, the list could go on indefinitely. Women are members of every race, religion, nationality, class, or ethnic group. So what is the supposed perspective of all women that is the putative foundation of feminism? What do all women have in common?

What do I have in common with the homeless women I walk past in Grand Central Station, or the invisible ones that I do not see in my home town? What do college professors have in common with prostitutes, or drug addicts, society women, or corporate executives, cashiers, or the lonely invalids who inhabit the nursing homes? How can anyone presume to speak for all of them? The women of South

Africa, Bangladesh, former Yugoslavia, China, the Brazilian rainforests, and the Australian outback are all women. Can they possibly all have something in common?

When I think of the problem in these terms it reminds me of when I was trying to figure out exactly what it is that makes human beings human. It turns out that there is no set of necessary and sufficient conditions that delineates the classification and distinguishes it from all others. There is no property common to all and only human beings. And I think that is true about women as well.

Nevertheless, I was not willing to conclude that therefore there is no such thing as a human being or a woman. Isolating necessary and sufficient conditions is not the best approach to solving all problems or answering all questions. So, I intend to cling to the intuition that there is something we share that makes us all human, even if we cannot say exactly what it is with logical precision. Similarly, I still think that there is something common to all women that feminism addresses, despite our profound differences. Even if we are unable to specify it precisely, we can indicate generally what this is.

So what is it? What do all women have in common regardless of race, class, religion, station, nationality, ethnicity, or background? All women live in a patriarchal world. All women function within an environment that is patriarchal. It is unavoidable, like the air. We eat, sleep, and breathe it (as do men.) But all women hold a certain position within that world (despite the qualification of our other differences) because it is precisely the function of patriarchy to specify that position and preserve it. Thus, all women operate within a world-view that constitutes a certain picture of reality – a picture that is profoundly and systematically gendered, even if that picture is beginning, just beginning, to crack and dissolve. That is the insight of radical feminists, that gender itself is a social construction based on and reflecting sexism: that is, male dominance and female subordination – supposedly justified as the result of natural needs and differences – male autonomy and female restriction – supposedly justified as the protection of women – and male glorification and female devaluation – supposedly justified as a value-neutral description of the world (see MacKinnon, 1989). This theory is not reducible to any other.

Now, this description of patriarchy as sexism is an oversimplification. One of the problems all feminists face is that any description of patriarchy will inevitably be an oversimplification because patriarchy is an entire world-view. It is enormously complex. By comparison, if you asked ten people for a description of, say, the United States (or any complex entity), you would get ten different descriptions. They could all be true. They would all be incomplete. No one of them could be the best description for all purposes. And they could all disagree with one another and still be accurate because they would differ in focus, purpose, characterization, and so forth. But patriarchy is much more complex than any single nation or culture. It is an entire world-view, with a million implications and effects, which has structured reality since the prehistory of human existence without any serious objection, challenge, or change until the second half of the twentieth century. This is a profoundly effective world-view, as Catherine MacKinnon put it, the most perfect ideology ever invented. It structures virtually everything that exists in its own image of reality. There is almost nothing that it does not touch. A comprehensive description of something like that is utterly impossible. So it is hardly surprising that different feminists provide different descriptions of it and different approaches to it. In fact, it would be very surprising if that were not the case.

It does not follow, however, that because patriarchy is a complex world-view that cannot be described comprehensively, that there is no such thing as patriarchy or that women are not subject to it. Patriarchy is the systematic subordination of women to men, and that is the experience that all women share. The point of view of all women is the point of view of those who are subordinated on the basis of their sex regardless of what else may be different about them. Even if some individual personal relationships deviate from this norm, systematic social organization still conforms to it everywhere.

So the one experience common to all women is living in the subordinated half of a patriarchal world, and the one feature common to all feminism is the rejection of that world-view. The focus and result of this rejection may vary a great deal. Feminists may disagree with one another about what constitutes a rejection of sexist domination, or about which approach is likely to improve the condition of women, or is most susceptible to abuse or misinterpretation. They may disagree about which element gets to the essence of the problem, or even whether there is an essence to this problem. Nevertheless, all feminist theories are intended to liberate women from sexist domination in one form or another.

Sexist domination comes in many forms. It is found in social attitudes about rape, wife battering, sexual harassment, employment practices, educational expectations, workplace design, advertising, entertainment, and family responsibilities, to name just a few. Most of these social attitudes are reflected in law. They are part of the million effects and implications of patriarchy. And all these effects and implications are the legitimate domain of feminist theory. That is what makes it so interesting. Thus, the diversity of feminist theories is in part a reflection of the pervasiveness of patriarchy and the great variation of its effects.

The diversity is also due to other perspectives on which feminists diverge. That is, feminists adopt many different approaches to patriarchy. For example, some have focussed on political and social institutions that create barriers to equal participation in the public sphere as in Taub and Williams (1985). Others have focussed on the disadvantage caused by hierarchical economic structures, and particularly the division between the home and the market as in Olsen (1983) or Williams (1989). Yet others have concentrated on the value structures associated with traditional male and female roles, to challenge the hierarchy of values imposed by patriarchy on society as in West (1988). Still others have challenged the structure of knowledge and the nature of gender itself, as presented by the patriarchal picture of reality (Minow, 1990; MacKinnon, 1989; Cornell, 1991). All these theories are partial, and all are helpful, except insofar as any might claim to be universal or comprehensive. Each addresses some aspect of the pervasiveness of patriarchy.

Yet it does not follow that feminist theories share no common, distinctive feature. To see what makes feminist theories distinctive, we should compare them not with each other, but with anti-feminist or non-feminist views. These differences make clear that what is common to all feminist theories is also what is distinctive about them.

Consider the debate between Catherine MacKinnon and Phyllis Schlafly over the ERA as an example of the feminist anti-feminist dispute (see MacKinnon, 1987). What was that debate about? It was, at bottom, a disagreement over whether the traditional roles of men and women should be changed or preserved. How these traditions are described depends on the point of view. The feminist describes the effects of these traditional roles and institutions as sexist domination. The anti-feminist describes them as the preservation of family values. But the feminist is arguing that patriarchy should be changed and the anti-feminist that it should be preserved. Both agree that this issue is crucially important.

The non-feminist theory on the other hand either argues that patriarchy is not important or simply does not address it. But a feminist generally thinks the implications and effects of patriarchy are relevant to many more subjects than the non-feminist recognizes. In fact, a significant part of the feminist project is to educate the non-feminist, so to speak, to make clear the significance of patriarchal influences where they commonly go unrecognized. For example, the major source of dissatisfaction among Marxist feminists with Marxism is its failure to recognize the effects of patriarchy across and within classes (Sargent, 1981). Or, in legal theory, a central project of feminists is to make clear that certain institutional structures – such as equal protection law founded on male norms as the standards of comparison (Littleton, 1987), concepts – such as force and consent in rape law (Estrich, 1987), or customs – such as non-interference with family violence as respect for privacy (Allen, 1988), or judicial review based on the intent of the framers (Minow, 1990) are biased or value laden, when they are assumed to be neutral.

Overall then, the anti-feminist supports patriarchy. The non-feminist overlooks or ignores patriarchy. And the feminist opposes patriarchy. So the one feature that defines or identifies a theory as feminist is that it takes the changing of patriarchy as its central focus. That is precisely what makes feminist jurisprudence feminist, despite all its variations.

So feminist jurisprudence is jurisprudence because it is the analysis of fundamental legal relations, concepts and principles. It is feminist because it examines and opposes patriarchy. But why is that project central to jurisprudence as a whole, rather than a specialized topic for a small subgroup? The formulation of the question betrays its answer. The feminist claims that patriarchy unfairly structures all social arrangements, and is dedicated to reforming that structure. Anyone who denies the broad significance of that sort of project is like the feudal lord who denied that the industrial revolution was relevant to him because his fief was in the country. If you think the claim is narrow it is because you do not believe it, or perhaps do not understand it because it is undertaken incrementally and peacefully.

Yet, for the unbeliever, instrumental arguments can also be given. First, law, given its nature, tends to preserve the status quo. Law is a system of order intended to provide stability. That is its value; but that also makes it poorly suited to deal with change, especially broad based, systemic social change. Second, law naturally embodies the values, attitudes, expectations and presumptions of the dominent culture (which it generally represents as universal values and/or neutral descriptions of facts of nature). This feature makes law badly suited to deal with diversity in a truly open and equitable manner. Yet in a world of fast paced social change, pressing pluralism and global diversity these limits are serious.

But if law is supposed to promote the general welfare it must be able to accommodate social change and cultural diversity better than its current structure and tradition allow. The dominant culture – those who hold power, make law and public policy, and influence institutional development – have no stake in solving these problems, and their training, background, and position militate against their being able to recognize such problems as central, to see them, let alone deal with them.

If law stands for justice, it must be justice for all. But the fact is that law has been notoriously bad at providing justice for those outside the dominant culture. Blacks, Indians, and Chinese (to mention three of the most infamous examples) as well as all women did not get the same standard of justice that the founding fathers set up for themselves and those who were much like them, even as they called it "justice for all." Nor is this deficiency yet corrected. Our blind spots are still significant. Feminist analysis is one of the best corrective lenses available today because it speaks from the position of the outsider. This enables it to be more creative, less tied to the tradition, less blinded by its own prominence.

Feminists have enormous motivation to find ways to accommodate change and diversity in law, because the feminist program is part of the new development that will otherwise be left out, and because women are among the legal outsiders who are vying for recognition. In fact, some feminist work has provided unusually insightful observations about whether norms are neutral or biased, and about how legal mechanisms might be revised and developed to increase its flexibility and responsiveness. Feminists are very good gadflies.

For these reasons feminist jurisprudence is clearly of general interest. It is the only legal philosophy that currently confronts patriarchy as a central issue. Contrary to the objection that this is not philosophically interesting, it provides a vantage point for truly creative and insightful analysis of the most basic structures of law and society. We have hardly begun to explore its implications.

References

Allen, A. 1988: *Uneasy Access: privacy for women in a free society*. Totowa, NJ: Rowman & Littlefield.

Cornell, D. 1991: *Beyond Accommodation*. New York: Routledge.

Davis, A. 1981: *Women, Race, and Class*. New York: Random House.

Estrich, S. 1987: *Real Rape*. Cambridge, Mass.: Harvard University Press.

Frug, M. J. 1992: *Postmodern Legal Feminism*. New York: Routledge.

Gutmann, A. 1980: *Liberal Equality*. New York: Cambridge University Press.

Jaggar, A. 1983: *Feminist Politics and Human Nature*. Totowa, NJ: Rowman & Allenheld.

Littleton, C. [1987] 1993: Reconstructing sexual equality. *California Law Review*, 75, 1,279. Reprinted in P. Smith (ed.), *Feminist Jurisprudence*, New York: Oxford University Press.

MacKinnon, C. 1987: *Feminism Unmodified: discourses on life and law*. Cambridge, Mass.: Harvard University Press.

—— 1989: *Toward a Feminist Theory of the State*. Cambridge, Mass.: Harvard University Press.

Minow, M. 1990: *Making All the Difference*. Cambridge, Mass.: Harvard University Press.

Olsen, F. [1983] 1993: The family and the market. *Harvard Law Review*, 96, 1,497. Reprinted in P. Smith (ed.), *Feminist Jurisprudence*, New York: Oxford University Press.

Radin, M. J. [1990] 1993: The pragmatist and the feminist. *California Law Review*, 63, 617. Reprinted in P. Smith (ed.), *Feminist Jurisprudence*, New York: Oxford University Press.

Rhode, D. 1989: *Justice and Gender*. Cambridge, Mass.: Harvard University Press.

Sargent, L. (ed.) 1981: *Women and Revolution*. Boston: South End Press.

Smith, P. (ed.) 1993: *Feminist Jurisprudence*. New York: Oxford University Press.

Taub, N. and Williams, W. [1985] 1993: Will equality require more . . . *Rutgers Law Review*, 37, 825. Reprinted in P. Smith (ed.), *Feminist Jurisprudence*, New York: Oxford University Press.

West, R. [1988] 1993: Jurisprudence and gender. *Chicago Law Review*, 55, 1. Reprinted in P. Smith (ed.), *Feminist Jurisprudence*, New York: Oxford University Press.

Williams, J. C. [1989] 1993: Deconstructing gender. *Michigan Law Review*, 87, 797. Reprinted in P. Smith (ed.), *Feminist Jurisprudence*, New York: Oxford University Press.

20

Law and economics

JON D. HANSON AND MELISSA R. HART

Introduction

Law and economics, as it has been succinctly defined by Richard Posner, one of its most prolific and influential exponents, entails "the application of the theories and empirical methods of economics to the central institutions of the legal system" (1975, p. 759). Although scholars have long applied economic analysis to some fields of law, such as antitrust and commercial law, the "new" law and economics that Posner has in mind applies economic principles to virtually every legal problem, even in less obvious fields such as criminal and family law.

Although economic analysis has now been widely applied, nowhere has its application been more fruitful or influential than in tort law. (See Article 3, TORT LAW.) As George Priest (1992) explained,

> there are few articles within the last ten years and no articles of importance within the last five years written about modern tort law that have not addressed . . . this new approach to the law . . . This trend is highly likely to continue for the future . . . [T]here is no future lawyer, no future academic, no future judge that can believe that one can adequately understand modern tort law without taking seriously the economic analysis of its effects. (p. 704)

Equally, an adequate understanding of modern economic analysis requires an appreciation of the impact that tort law has had on its development.

To see why, it is necessary first to consider two general modes of analysis within law and economics: the *positive* mode, which is descriptive or predictive; and the *normative* mode, which is prescriptive or judgmental. Legal economists have asked two types of positive questions. First, all legal economists ask: What are a policy's behavioral effects, and would that policy lead to the efficient – that is, the cost minimizing – outcome? Second, some legal economists also ask: what would the law look like if efficiency were its sole purpose, and does the law, in fact, look like that? This second type of question is asked by scholars – positivists – testing the hypothesis that judge-made law is currently structured as if efficiency were its sole purpose (for example, Landes and Posner, 1987; Easterbrook and Fischel, 1991). Asserting and testing that positive hypothesis was once the central project of law and economics and was largely responsible for the rapid rise of the new law and economics. The positive hypothesis appears to have lost some adherents in recent years, but it was the positivists' impressive initial successes that seemed to convince many scholars and judges to take efficiency seriously as a legal goal. It was in part because of the positivists' striking empirical support for the claim that "the logic of the law *is* really economics," (Posner, 1975, p. 764 (emphasis added)) that scholars and some jurists leapt to the normative view that the logic of the law *ought* to be economics. (Michelman, 1978, pp. 1,038–9). And, thus, the following two *normative* questions of law and economics surfaced: First, should efficiency be the goal of law?; and, second, if so, how should the law be reformed to best serve that goal? The former question provoked comment from the likes of Ronald Dworkin and Richard Posner in one of the more famous and subtle legal debates of this century (see generally, *Journal of Legal Studies*, 9 (1980); *Hofstra Law Review*, 8 (1980)). Now, however, the vast majority of law and economics scholarship assumes without hesitation that the goal of law should be efficiency. Today's legal economists most commonly inquire into the effects of different policies (the first positive issue) and recommend reforms in light of those effects (the second normative issue). To understand how we got here, it is helpful to examine more closely the positivist hypothesis.

In one of the earliest and most significant contributions to the positivist project, Richard Posner (1972) reviewed 1,500 American appellate court decisions to test his "theory of negligence" (p. 29). The sample appeared to confirm his hypothesis that, "the dominant function of the fault system is to generate rules of liability that if followed will bring about, at least approximately, the efficient – the cost-justified – level of accidents and safety" (1972, p. 33). No matter that the courts did not speak in terms of efficiency, for

> the true grounds of legal decision are often concealed rather than illuminated by the characteristic rhetoric of judicial opinions . . . Indeed, legal education consists primarily of learning to dig beneath the rhetorical surface to find those grounds. It is an advantage of economic analysis as a tool of legal study rather than a drawback that it does not analyze cases in the conceptual modes employed in the opinions themselves. (*Posner, 1972 (2nd edn), p. 18*)

Perhaps, but even Posner seemed to sense the strain in his argument that a single goal, efficiency, explained all of negligence law and yet no court, in a sample of 1,500 opinions, once mentioned efficiency. Fortunately for the hypothesis, the strain was relieved by the rhetoric contained in "Judge Learned Hand's famous formulation of the negligence standard [in *US* v. *Carroll Towing Co.*, 159 F.2d 169 (2d Cir. 1947)] – one of the few attempts to give content to the deceptively simple concept of ordinary care," (1972, p. 32). Although the case fell outside of Posner's data set, he characterized it as an "attempt to make explicit the standard that the courts had long applied" (p. 32).

To a considerable degree, therefore, the early success of the positivist project can be attributed to the suggestive language in *Carroll Towing*. To better understand the issue that Judge Hand was addressing, consider the context as legal economists commonly describe it. The defendant, Carroll Towing Co., was readjusting a line of barges moored in New York Harbor. One of the barges, the *Anna C*, broke loose and crashed into a tanker. The tanker's propeller damaged the hull of the *Anna C*, and she sank. The plaintiff, the owner of the *Anna C*, sued Carroll Towing Co. for the damages. The question before the appellate court was whether the tug owner, who had been deemed negligent at trial, could avoid paying the damages to the owner of the *Anna C*. The defendant argued that the barge owner was partially to blame for the accident because he failed to keep a bargee on board. Judge Hand agreed. Hand reasoned – and this is the jurisprudentially significant aspect of the opinion – that a defendant should be deemed negligent, and a plaintiff contributorily negligent, whenever the cost to the party of preventing an accident is less than the *expected cost* of the accident. According to his pithy algebraic formulation, a party's duty is a function of three variables: the probability of an accident's occurring, (P); the gravity of the resulting loss or injury if an accident occurs, (L); and the burden of precautions adequate to avert the accident, (B). Applying the formula, Hand found that the barge owner was contributorily negligent because the cost of leaving a bargee on the barge, (B), was less than the probability of a loss, (P), times the gravity of the loss, (L). According to Posner, Hand's reasoning made explicit the otherwise implicit "economic meaning of negligence" (1972, p. 32).

As Posner highlighted, the "Hand Formula" appears consistent with the efficiency goal of minimizing the total cost of accidents, including the cost of preventing accidents. If $B < PL$, then an additional or *marginal* investment in accident prevention (B) will have positive net returns in terms of a marginal reduction in expected accident costs (PL). Efficiency requires that such investments be made. By holding a party liable for whom $B < PL$, tort law will encourage efficient investments in accident prevention. Put in the language of legal economists, tort law will induce parties to "internalize their externalities." (*Externalities* are the costs that an actor's actions impose on others but that the actor excludes from his or her decision-making calculus. Much of tort law can be understood as an attempt to force individuals to take into account – to *internalize* – the costs that their actions impose on others.) If, however, $B > PL$, an investment in accident prevention will yield negative net returns. Put differently, society is better off, in economic terms, by incurring lower accident costs instead of higher accident-prevention costs.

An economic model of *Carroll Towing*

To identify more clearly whether and under what circumstances the Hand Formula is efficient, we turn now to a simple model using the facts in *Carroll Towing*. As with all law and economics models, ours is premissed upon a series of assumptions, many of which are indisputably unrealistic. So that readers unfamiliar with economic analysis might suspend incredulity, it is worth noting at the outset the purpose of this type of model. Economists hope that through a set of simplifying

Table 20.1 *Carroll Towing* hypothetical

Tug owner's care (1)	Expected benefit to tug owner ($) (2)	Expected cost to barge owner ($) (3)	Net gain ($) (2 – 3) (4)
Tow rapidly	150	125 (on)	25 (on)
		145 (off)	5 (off)
Tow moderately	100	50 (on)	50 (on)
		70 (off)	30 (off)
Tow slowly	50	20 (on)	30 (on)
		40 (off)	10 (off)

Source: Polinsky, 1989, p. 48

abstractions, useful insights can be gleaned about otherwise intractably complex problems – insights that maintain some validity even in the messy real world. By first examining the *Carroll Towing* case through the lens of an abstract model and then evaluating the effects of relaxing many of the model's underlying assumptions, we hope to illustrate both the nature of economic reasoning and its potential benefits and costs. The initial assumptions of our non-technical model are as follows:

1   The barge owner and tug owner are rational (they pursue consistent ends by efficient means) and perfectly informed (they know the costs outlined in table 20.1).
2   *Transaction costs* (more specifically, the *ex ante* (pre-accident) costs to the parties allocating liability or setting care levels by contract) are prohibitively high.
3   The parties' *activity levels*, the frequency and duration of their actions, are irrelevant in that they do not affect the total cost of accidents. Only the level of care the parties take when they act is relevant.
4   All of the liability standards are costless to administer.
5   Both parties are risk neutral. *Risk-neutral* individuals care only about the expected value of an option. The *expected value* of a risky situation is the absolute magnitude of the risk, should it occur, multiplied by the probability that it will occur. *Risk-averse* individuals, in contrast, care not only about the expected value, but also about the absolute magnitude of the risk. For example, suppose an individual is offered a 50 percent chance of winning $10,000 or a guarantee of winning $5,000. Both offers have the same expected value, $5,000. If the offeree is risk neutral, therefore, he or she will be indifferent between the two choices. If risk averse, he or she will prefer the $5,000 with certainty.
6   Both parties know the applicable legal rules.
7   Courts accurately measure the costs and benefits of each party's behavior– they too know the numbers in Table 20.1 – and perfectly apply the liability standard.

8   Neither party knows what level of care the other party will take.
9   All costs and benefits can be measured in terms of a single metric, dollars.
10 There are no spillover effects or third-party externalities. Each party's decision as to how much care to take has no effect on parties outside the model.

Consider now the specific terms of our example, as described in table 20.1 (which builds on an example developed by Professor Polinsky in his widely read introduction to the field (1989, p. 48). As column 1 indicates, the tug owner can take different levels of care by moving the boat line at one of three speeds. Column 2 describes the benefits to the tug owner of moving the barges at each speed. Towing at higher speeds enables the tug owner to maximize the amount of work she can complete in any day. Towing the barges more slowly forces the tug owner to forego additional revenue. Economists refer to this type of foregone benefit as an *opportunity cost* and treat it like any other cost. Column 3 shows that both of the parties can affect the expected accident costs to the barge. As indicated in the parentheses in columns 3 and 4 we have assumed for simplicity's sake that the barge owner can take either of two levels of care: he can either keep a bargee on the barge or allow the bargee to get off. Although not reflected in the table, we also assume that the cost of keeping a bargee on board is positive, but trivially small. Column 4 shows the total expected benefits less the total expected costs – the net social gain – of the parties' activities at different levels of care.

The efficient result – that is, the outcome that minimizes the costs of accidents and thus maximizes net social gain – requires that both parties take care. The tug owner must tow at moderate speed, and the barge owner must keep a bargee on board. While column 4 readily reveals the efficient result, to fully appreciate *why* this is the efficient result, it is useful to examine the problem by employing the sort of marginal analysis that is fundamental to economic reasoning. Rapid towing generates the greatest expected benefit to the tug owner ($150). From a social perspective, however, towing moderately is preferable because the marginal cost to the tug owner of towing moderately (B) is only $50 of opportunity costs ($150 – $100), while the marginal benefit of that investment in terms of the reduction in expected accident costs (PL) is $75 (depending on the barge owner's care level, $125 – $50 or $145 – $70). Because the cost of prevention is less than the expected accident costs ($B < PL$), efficiency mandates that the tug owner does not tow rapidly. Note that efficiency also requires that the tug owner does not tow slowly because the marginal cost of doing so is $50, while the marginal benefit is only $30 ($B > PL$). Thus, the efficiency criterion requires the tug owner to tug moderately. Similarly, the barge owner should keep a bargee on board because the marginal cost of doing so is, by assumption, always less than the marginal benefit. Having identified the efficient outcome, we turn now to the task of defining a set of possible liability standards and examining which of those standards, if any, would lead to that efficient outcome.

In light of its central role in defense of the positivist hypothesis, if there is one case that should confirm that hypothesis, it is *Carroll Towing*. Ironically, however, legal economists have neglected to examine whether the Hand Formula, as applied in *Carroll Towing*, actually was efficient. Instead, they have divorced the Hand Formula from its context and have suggested that because of its apparently beneficial efficiency consequences in the abstract, the Hand Formula leads to efficiency in specific factual settings. Because confirmation of the positivist hypothesis – that the common law is in fact efficient – requires more than a theoretically plausible abstraction, we will treat this as an opportunity to re-test the hypothesis by placing the Hand Formula back in context.

Rules 1–6, as depicted in figure 20.1, represent six possible tort liability standards. The question being answered in each of the two-by-twos is whether the parties took efficient levels of care. The named party in any given box – P (plaintiff) or D (defendant) – is the one who will bear liability in light of the indicated conduct. As specified in table 20.1, the efficient outcome – under any of the rules – is that both parties take care. The underlining indicates the likely result given the incentives created by the particular liability standard. Thus, from each two-by-two we can see: the actual result (that is, who will bear liability, and who will take efficient care) and whether the actual result is efficient. Each figure – or each liability rule – is named, somewhat didactically, according to the number of times that a court might be required to apply the Hand Formula.

The two rows are mirror images of each other, with the standards becoming increasingly pro-plaintiff moving in numerical order from rule 1 to rule 6. Under a "no-Hands" rule (commonly referred to as a *no liability* rule), the plaintiff pays costs of all accidents, while under a "reverse no-Hands" rule (*strict liability*), the defendant pays all accident costs. Under rule 3, a "one-Handed" standard (*negligence*), the defendant is liable whenever she fails to take efficient care, but otherwise the plaintiff is liable. Rule 4 represents a "reverse one-Handed" standard (strict liability with a defense of *contributory negligence*), in which just the reverse is true: The plaintiff is liable when he fails to take efficient care, but otherwise the defendant is liable. Under the "two-Handed" standard of rule 2, the defendant is liable if and only if the plaintiff takes efficient care but the defendant does not. (This standard, which Judge Hand applied in *Carroll Towing*, is commonly referred to as negligence with a defense of contributory negligence.) The opposite is depicted in rule 5, in which the plaintiff is liable if and only if the defendant takes care but the plaintiff does not. (This "reverse two-Handed" rule has no common name and, to our knowledge, has never been adopted by courts.)

Which of these rules would lead both parties to take efficient levels of care? As long as the accident context is *bilateral* – that is, as long as both parties can take effective accident prevention measures – we can immediately eliminate rules 1 and 6. Under a no-Hands rule, only the plaintiff will take efficient care. The tug owner will never be held liable for her negligence and, hence, will have no reason to internalize the costs her negligence will impose on the barge owner. She will gain the $50 of marginal benefits without having to pay the $75 in marginal expected accident costs. The opposite is true under a reverse no-Hands rule: Only the tug owner will take care, because the barge owner can externalize the $20 of costs associated with maintaining a bargee on the barge. Both rules, therefore, clearly fail the efficiency criterion under the circumstances. However, in *unilateral*

Figure 20.1 *Liability rules*

(1) No-Hands rule (no liability)

		P's care	
		Yes	No
D's care	Yes	P	P
	No	P	P

(2) Two-Hands rule
(negligence/contributory negligence)

		P's care	
		Yes	No
D's care	Yes	P	P
	No	D	P

(3) One-Hand rule (negligence)

		P's care	
		Yes	No
D's care	Yes	P	P
	No	D	D

(4) Reverse one-Hand rule (strict liability/contributory negligence)

		P's care	
		Yes	No
D's care	Yes	D	P
	No	D	P

(5) Reverse two-Hands rule

		P's care	
		Yes	No
D's care	Yes	D	P
	No	D	D

(6) Reverse no-Hands rule
(strict liability)

		P's care	
		Yes	No
D's care	Yes	D	D
	No	D	D

accident contexts, where only one party can make cost-justified investments in accident-cost reduction, even rules 1 and 6 can lead to efficient investments in accident reduction. Suppose, for example, that only the tug owner could take cost-justified steps to prevent the accident. Under rule 6, or absolute defendant liability, the tug owner will be liable regardless of its care level. Thus, rule 6 forces the tug owner to internalize fully the costs to the barge. While this result would occur in the unilateral accident context, most of the debate over appropriate tort liability standards centers around bilateral accidents, so we will focus the balance of our analysis on that context.

Under our initial assumptions, then, any of the rules with the exception of 1 and 6 will lead to an efficient result (Landes and Posner, 1987, ch. 3; Shavell, 1987, pp. 26–46). Under rule 2, a judge or jury will apply the Hand Formula first to the defendant. If the defendant is not negligent, the plaintiff will bear the costs. If the defendant fails the Hand test, then the court applies the same test to the plaintiff. If the plaintiff is contributorily negligent, he will be liable. The defendant will thus be liable only if she, but not the plaintiff, fails the Hand test. This rule will cause both parties to take efficient care. The plaintiff knows the following: If the defendant tows moderately, the plaintiff will be liable for $70 if he does not leave a bargee on the barge, or $50 if he does. The plaintiff therefore is better off leaving a bargee on the barge. If the defendant does not take care, the plaintiff will be liable for $145 if there is no bargee on board, and will bear no liability if there is a bargee on board. As these numbers illustrate, the plaintiff will be better off taking care regardless of the defendant's behavior. The defendant knows that the plaintiff, as a rational actor, will take care. The defendant will therefore compare her net benefits without care ($150 − $125, or $25) with those of taking efficient care ($100 − $0, or $100). Because $100 is greater than $25, the defendant will take care. The bottom row is simply the reverse of the top row, so the reasoning for rule 5 is the reverse of that for rule 2. Both parties will take care under this standard as well.

Under rule 3, the court will apply the Hand Formula only to the defendant. If she fails, she is liable for all accidents, regardless of the plaintiff's care level. The most she could benefit under this rule is $25 (or $150 − $125) if she does not take care. If she passes the Hand test, she is liable for nothing, and enjoys $100 of benefit. Weighing these options, the rational defendant will take care. The plaintiff knows that he will therefore be liable for all accident costs. The plaintiff, faced with $50 in expected costs if he does take care, and $70 in expected costs if he does not take care, will choose to take care. Rule 4 is the mirror image of rule 3, and hence will also lead to the efficient result.

As this analysis of the various liability rules demonstrates, the standard employed by Judge Hand – rule 2, or negligence with a defense of contributory negligence – appears to satisfy the efficiency criterion. Thus far, however, our analysis provides only weak support for the positivist hypothesis, because it fails to yield a unique prediction – that is, it is indeterminate as between rules 2–5 (Elster, 1993, p. 181). So the question we turn to next is: if some of the model's assumptions are relaxed, will it yield a more determinate result that more clearly supports, or threatens, the positivist hypothesis? The law and economics literature does not, as far as we can tell, include any discussion of how to evaluate assumptions – a surprising omission given that every economic conclusion ultimately turns on the economist's starting assumptions. In our view, there are at least two questions that should be asked when evaluating assumptions. First, is the assumption plausible? Some assumptions are less controversially accurate in the real world, while others are either more controversial or uncontroversially implausible. Second, how relevant is the assumption? That is, does the success of the model rest on the assumption – making it extremely relevant – or does relaxing the assumption have no real effect on the model – making it irrelevant? Or is the assumption's relevance indeterminate in the sense that there is currently too little empirical data available to allow a reasonably confident prediction as to the assumption's effect?

If an assumption is implausible, it can have one of three implications for the positivist hypothesis. If the assumption is implausible and irrelevant it will have no effect on the strength of the model. If it is implausible and its effect is indeterminate, it will present some threat to the model – it may not disprove law's efficiency, but it certainly should undermine the positivists' confidence when declaring the law efficient. Finally, if an assumption is implausible and very relevant to the model – that is, the model's success rests in some substantial part on the assumption – it presents a serious threat to the model's conclusion. We turn now to examining each of the model's assumptions according to those criteria.

Relaxing the model's initial assumptions

Transaction costs

We began by assuming that transaction costs were too high for the tug owner and the barge owner to assign the risk of damage between themselves by contract. Relaxing the assumption – supposing instead that the expected gains to contracting exceed the transaction costs – seems to confirm the positivist hypothesis by showing that the initial assumption was both plausible and relevant. This exercise also allows us to explore two of the most important insights of law and economics.

Legal economists commonly begin their analyses with the assumption that transaction costs are trivial. This analytical approach was first introduced by Nobel Prize winner Ronald Coase (1960) in his famous article "The Problem of Social Cost." Over-simplifying a bit, the so-called *Coase Theorem* posited that where no obstacles to bargaining exist between the parties involved, resources will be allocated efficiently regardless of who is initially assigned the rights to the resources and regardless of what form of legal protection those rights are provided. As economists sometimes put the point, where parties can contract with each other without cost, all accident costs will be internalized.

An example may clarify why in settings where transactions are costless, a court's choice of liability standards has no efficiency implications. Recall that the tug owner will earn an additional $50 and the barge will suffer an additional $75 in damages if the tug owner tows rapidly rather than moderately. If the law gives the barge owner the right to enjoin the tug owner from tugging rapidly, the tug owner would be willing to pay up to $50 to do so, but the barge owner would accept nothing less than $75 to permit it. Thus, the tug owner will be forced to tow moderately, as is efficient. If, on the other hand, the law gives the tug owner the right to tug rapidly, the tug owner will accept any amount greater than $50, and the barge owner will pay up to $75 for the tug owner to slow to a moderate speed. Therefore, if the parties could contract together costlessly, irrespective of who was buying and who was selling, the tug owner would end up tugging moderately.

In fact, legal economists posit that the likelihood of an efficient result in this context is even higher than it would be if a court applied the Hand Formula to determine liability. When parties contract together, each of them is making his or her own subjective judgment about the value of the relevant activity. The measurement of value is a fundamental issue in economics. A *subjective* valuation system is favored by most legal economists, because it allows each party to judge the effects of an outcome according to her or his own preferences. Where contractual negotiation is possible, legal economists therefore generally prefer contract-based, subjective allocations of costs to tort-based objective allocations.

However, transaction costs are almost never zero and are often rather high. These transaction costs might, for instance, include information costs (the parties must locate each other, learn the legal rules, evaluate the probability of different accidents and the possible accident costs) and "strategic behavior" (for example, one or both of the parties may try to hold out, refusing to bargain in the hopes that the other party will compromise his position). In circumstances where individuals cannot (or will not) contract to allocate the costs of accidents, the legal system may have to intervene and impose liability standards as a proxy for contractual allocation.

Here, a second important insight of legal economics becomes relevant. Guido Calabresi and Douglas Melamed (1972) observed in a classic article, "Property Rules, Liability Rules, and Inalienability: One View of the Cathedral," that once the legal system has defined and assigned an entitlement – a legal right – it still must decide what form of protection to provide the entitlement. When *property rule* protection is provided, the entitlement can change hands only by contract – that is, only if its holder agrees to sell. Hence, the transfer of entitlements protected by property rules depends on a holder's subjective valuations. When the entitlement is protected by a *liability rule*, a non-holder can take the entitlement as long as he or she is willing to pay *ex post* a state-determined price. The transfer of entitlements under liability rules depends therefore on objectively determined values.

The choice between property-rule and liability-rule protection, then, turns on trade-offs between two variables: first, the level of the contracting costs relative to the potential gains to contracting; and second, the extent to which a subjective means of valuation is superior or inferior to an objective means. In the *Carroll Towing* context, the case for liability rule protection seems reasonably strong. Contracting costs on a crowded day in New York Harbor may well have been prohibitively high, and the value of the loss – a barge and its cargo–can be measured fairly accurately using an objective measure. Thus, the assumption that transaction costs were high, which is plausible, and – given their effect on the choice of liability standards – relevant to the positivist hypothesis, seems to be supported by the context of the case.

Activity levels

We have thus far assumed that accident costs are a function of only one type of investment: care-level investments. However, it is possible – in fact, likely – that the parties' activity levels will also affect the costs of accidents. For instance, the tug owner's activity may have posed a risk to the barge not just as a result of how carefully she moved the barges, but also as a result of how often and how far she moved them. Thus, a liability rule can have two principal *deterrence effects*: first, as we have already indicated, the *care-level effect* is the change in the costs of accidents resulting from a change in the amount of care taken by a party; and second, the *activity-level effect* is the change in the total costs of accidents resulting from a change in the duration or frequency of a party's activity.

The efficient level of activity is that level beyond which the net marginal gains of an additional unit of activity (assuming efficient care) are no longer positive. To deter all accidents that could be cost-justifiably prevented, judges and juries would need to compare the benefits a party obtains from greater participation in the activity to the resulting increase in expected accident costs. Unfortunately, courts tend to ignore activity-level considerations, and most scholars believe that, as a practical matter, courts are *unable* to conduct the necessary activity-level calculus, because of the amount of information that they would need (Shavell, 1980, p. 25).

The addition of activity-level considerations to the *Carroll Towing* analysis could very well change its conclusions. Judge Hand appears to assume that the benefits to the tug owner of moving the barges will remain constant for every job she completes. However, the *law of diminishing marginal returns* suggests that the tug owner's net gains will eventually decline with each additional trip. For instance, the value to the tug owner of a trip (and if not the second, then the third or fourth or the fifth) is likely to be less than the value of the first. But, because courts do not, or cannot, consider whether the marginal benefits of an additional unit of activity would justify the costs, the negligence rule may cause the tug owner to tug too often, albeit moderately.

Consequently, any rule in which the plaintiff bears the costs when both plaintiff and defendant have taken care (rules 1–3) will lead the defendant to engage in too high a level of activity. And, for analogous reasons, the plaintiff will engage in an inefficiently high level of activity if the defendant is liable when both parties have taken care (rules 4–6). There is no liability standard that can force both defendants and plaintiffs to optimize their activity levels. The problem of non-optimal activity levels is therefore theoretically insuperable. And absent some empirical basis for believing that one party's activity levels are more significant in creating

321

accident costs other things equal, of that one party's activity levels are relatively inexpensive to reduce, there is no good way to choose among liability standards on activity-level grounds. Nor is there any basis for determining whether the introduction of activity levels will undermine entirely the claim that the common law is efficient.

Administrative costs

We began with the clearly implausible assumption that administrative costs – that is, the various costs of implementing a particular tort regime – were zero. No one denies that the administrative costs of the current regime are extremely high. Many studies have found that administrative costs eat up at least as much money on average as injured plaintiffs receive in compensation (Shavell, 1987, pp. 262–4). And while critics of the present tort system commonly point to that fact, no one has been able to show how it should affect the choice among liability standards. Because of the dearth of empirical evidence, it is not clear that the administrative costs of our current system exceed its benefits; that another liability standard would yield lower administrative costs without a more-than-offsetting increase in accident costs; or, finally, that there are not other means of lowering administrative costs independent of the liability standard (Shavell, 1987, pp. 262–5; Croley and Hanson, 1991, pp. 14–17).

The mere observation that the costs of administering the current tort regime are significant does not aid in the choice among liability standards. That those costs are so substantial, however, does suggest that any confidence one might have in the common law's efficiency should be tempered by how little is known about variables that likely matter a great deal.

Risk-neutrality

Contrary to our starting assumption, many individuals are concerned not only with expected losses but also with the absolute size of those losses – that is, many individuals are risk averse. Thus, the Hand Formula's implicit assumption, that negligence should turn on the expected value of costs and benefits without regard to the absolute magnitude of those costs and benefits, is implausible in a world of human decision making. To avoid the problem that risk aversion creates, legal economists typically assume that individuals have insurance, which, by transforming a potential loss of some absolute amount into premiums equal to the expected value of the loss, allows the insureds to behave *as if* they are risk neutral (Posner, 1992, p. 12). But while it is true that most individuals have some insurance, it seems unlikely that many have enough insurance to behave as the Hand Formula posits.

Insofar as the full-insurance assumption is empirically untrue, the possibility that one party is more averse to risk or faces greater insurance costs, may have significant implications for the choice among liability standards. Because the efficiency goal of minimizing the total costs of accidents is concerned in part with the costs of insuring against those accidents that cannot be cost-justifiably prevented, it matters who is liable for those accidents. In circumstances where plaintiffs typically have greater insurance costs, other things equal, courts should choose one of the liability standards on the bottom row. When insurance costs are higher for defendants, the opposite reasoning dictates that courts choose one of rules 1–3. Absent evidence regarding the relative preferences of plaintiff and defendant for tort-provided insurance, efficiency concerns do not dictate the choice of one liability standard over the others.

Legal knowledge

Where the law is unknown by the potential plaintiffs and defendants, it cannot have its desired deterrence effect (Kaplow, 1994, pp. 365–6). The assumption that parties know the legal rules is therefore clearly relevant to the positivist hypothesis. It may also be a somewhat implausible assumption, in light of mounting evidence

> that people often ignore or otherwise fail to respond to law, and, when they do try to be law-abiding, that they misconstrue legal signals . . . The reality that cognitive limitations impair the learning of law makes legal instrumentalism much more difficult. An analyst must become involved in the messy matter of the extent to which actors will respond to formal legal signals. (*Ellickson, 1989, p. 40*)

The extent of legal knowledge held by parties to a dispute will vary tremendously depending on the context of the suit and the identities of the parties involved (Latin, 1985, 1994). Therefore, the introduction of questions about legal knowledge complicates the model and, to some extent, undermines the grounds for believing that the common law is efficient.

Applying the Hand Formula

It is essential to the positivist hypothesis that courts not only apply the Hand Formula, but that they do so accurately, measuring the relevant marginal benefits and costs of each party's choices. While this assumption is clearly relevant to the model's success, it is in fact quite implausible (Gilles, 1994, pp. 1,020, 1,028). Above, we summarized the conventional view that courts and juries have too little information to competently apply the Hand Formula with respect to a party's *activity levels*. Positivists such as Posner do not deny this judicial shortcoming–indeed, they have employed it as a means of explaining certain areas of the law. However, a more general formulation of that shortcoming poses a real threat to the positivists. Some investments in accident prevention – such as, but by no means limited to activity-level investments may well have significant positive returns, but are not considered by courts applying the Hand Formula. Moreover, for those investments that courts and juries do consider, there is little reason to be confident that the relative costs and benefits are (or, indeed, can be) accurately measured (Croley and Hanson, 1991, pp. 67–75).

In *Carroll Towing*, Judge Hand reasoned that the cost of maintaining a bargee on the barge (*B*) must have been low because the bargee had offered a fabricated story as an excuse for his absence, and that *PL* must have been high because of the war-time bustle of New York Harbor. The balancing of *B* against *PL* seems rather rough, though understandably so in light of how little information judges and juries typically have. Hand himself recognized this difficulty, writing in another case, *Moisan v. Loftus*, 178 F.2d 148, 149 (2d Cir. 1949), that

> [t]he difficulties . . . in applying the rule . . . arise from the necessity of applying a quantitative test to an incommensurable subject-matter . . . [A]ll such attempts are illusory, and, if serviceable at all, are so only to center attention upon which one of the factors may be determined in any given situation.

Even Posner – a Seventh Circuit judge – has conceded the difficulty of accurately applying the Hand Formula. In *McCarty v. Pheasant Run, Inc.*, 826 F.2d 1554, 1557 (7th Cir. 1987), he noted that, "[f]or many years to come juries may be forced to make rough judgments on reasonableness, intuiting rather than measuring the factors in the Hand Formula." Why measurement problems constitute a mild qualification rather than a fundamental challenge to the positivist hypothesis is unclear.

Simultaneity or observability of parties' care-taking investments

The efficiency justification of the standard applied in *Carroll Towing* may be significantly undermined if we relaxed the assumption that each party behaves independently, taking as given the behavior of the other.

Contrary to our initial assumption, it seems plausible to assume that the tug owner could observe ahead of time whether the plaintiff had taken efficient care – that is, the tug owner likely knew whether the barge had a bargee aboard. Under the rule 2 standard applied by Judge Hand, if the tug owner sees that the barge owner has taken care, then she will have an incentive to take care because otherwise she will be liable for an amount greater than the costs of taking care. If, however, the tug owner sees that there is no bargee on board, she can take inefficiently low levels of care with impunity (as if she were acting in a no liability – rule 1 – regime), because she knows that the barge owner will be deemed contributorily negligent and therefore held liable. (Space constraints prohibit us from sketching the numerous explanations for why the plaintiff might behave negligently even when the Hand Formula is applied.) When the plaintiff fails to take efficient precautions, efficiency still requires that the defendant take care. That is, to maximize net gains (at $30), we still want the defendant to tow at a moderate speed. If the defendant tows rapidly, his own gains will be high, but net social gains will be only $5, which is the worst of all possible worlds. Thus, absent an assumption of simultaneity (or non-observability), the defendant who observes that the plaintiff has not taken care would have no tort-provided incentive to take the efficient level of care under the standard applied by Judge Hand.

This criticism of the rule applied in *Carroll Towing* assumes that the defendant could observe plaintiff's care level before deciding on her own how rapidly to tow. Of course, it may be that the defendant would act first, in which case the reasoning would be reversed. Given what we know about the facts of this case, however, that would not present the same problems, since in order to observe whether the defendant was behaving efficiently, the plaintiff would already be on the barge – that is, it would already have taken what Hand defined as the efficient level of care. In this case, therefore, the standard applied (rule 2) appears not to have been the most efficient.

Which rules will be more efficient than the two-Handed rule applied in *Carroll Towing*? Any rule that makes the defendant liable when both parties have been negligent will eliminate the sequential care problem that we have identified. So, for instance, a negligence rule (rule 3) would be efficient. Likewise, a reverse two-Handed rule (rule 5) would work, but a reverse one-Handed rule (rule 4) would not.

Efficiency as a norm

If, as we believe the previous section indicates, *Carroll Towing* did not reach the efficient result, is there any reason to believe that the other cases cited by Posner and his positivist compatriots have done so – or at least that they have done so with enough consistency that the claim that the common law *tends toward* efficiency could be supported? It seems unlikely. If, even when courts strive for efficiency, they fail, then there is little reason to be confident that courts avowedly motivated by non-economic considerations will reach decisions that satisfy the efficiency criterion.

The preceding analysis, however, should have done more than simply raise doubts about positivism: it should have implicitly offered a sample of the positivists' early striking successes and of several key insights that law and economics has brought to legal analysis. Though positivists now speak less often and less boldly than they once did, law and economics continues to thrive, largely because of the work of legions of normativists, who accept efficiency as the relevant goal of law and employ the tools of law and economics to identify how the law can best serve that goal.

The true benefits of law and economics, according to the normativists, exist in identifying and making clear to law-makers and judges the reforms that are – or are not – necessary for efficiency's sake. In pursuit of those benefits, legal economists have authored countless articles and books analyzing the efficiency of particular tort doctrines or decisions. And yet, while there are several excellent books introducing and summarizing the key law-and-economics insights for tort law (for example, Landes and Posner, 1987; Polinsky, 1989; Shavell, 1987), legal economists have offered very little in the way of direct instruction to courts interested in resolving cases with efficiency as a goal.

In this section, we build on lessons learned through our exploration of *Carroll Towing* to offer a tentative step toward providing a catalogue of questions that an efficiency-minded court might ask when faced with a tort claim. For reasons high-lighted in the next section, we are doubtful that any "how to" manual will yield significant benefits. Our efforts, however, should at least be heuristically useful as a means of reviewing some of the previous section's insights.

Imagine a modern-day judge confronted with a tort dispute. The judge must determine first where to set the legal entitlement and next what type of legal protection to accord that entitlement. If the transaction costs between the parties are low—and especially if the court's objective measure of damages is likely to deviate substantially from the subjective valuations of the parties – then the court should allocate the entitlement to the party who values it most and should en-courage the parties to contract to mutually beneficial arrangements by protecting the entitlement with a property rule (Posner, 1986, pp. 49–50). (But see Ayres and Tally, 1995.)

If, however, transaction costs are prohibitively high, such that liability rule protection is warranted, then the court must inquire into which of the liability standards would be most efficient. Initially, a court seeking efficiency might focus solely on the parties' care levels, inquiring whether one or both of the parties could make a care-level investment that would reduce the total cost of the accident. This question has two parts, one of which has been discussed at length by legal econ-omists, and the other of which has been largely ignored. The former is the ques-tion of *preventability* – that is, whether either party *could* make an adjustment in care level to prevent the accident. If both parties' care levels are relevant, the accident is bilateral; if only one party can effect the cost of an accident by adjust-ing his or her care level, the context is unilateral; and where neither party can adjust his or her care level to reduce the costs of an accident, the context might be called "non-lateral."

The latter question – the question of *deterrability* – asks whether tort liability will in fact have any beneficial effect on a party's conduct. There are two types of rea-sons why a party may be undeterrable. First, a party may externalize *ex ante* even the threat of tort liability. For instance, a party may not foresee or may underestim-ate the risk, a party may not know the law, or a party's insurance may substantially eliminate the impact of tort law. Second, tort liability may be wholly or largely redundant in that a party may be given adequate incentives to take care from sources other than tort law. A number of sources, such as administrative regulation and market forces – including well-functioning insurance markets – could provide those incentives. When tort law is a redundant or an ineffective means of deter-rence, its use may not be justifiable as a tool for preventing future accidents.

Imposing tort liability on a party will lead to efficient care-level investments only when the accident is preventable by that party (that is, $B < PL$) and that party is deterrable. When either of those necessary conditions is not satisfied, liab-ility will have no beneficial effect on a party's care levels. Therefore, if a judge is faced with a non-lateral accident context, he or she will have to choose liability standards using criteria other than deterrence or prevention. If the accident con-text is unilateral, the appropriate no-Handed rule – either liability or absolute liab-ility, depending on which party's behavior is relevant – will likely be most efficient.

Finally, if the accident context is bilateral, the efficiency-minded judge should choose from among liability standards 2 through 5.

Having narrowed the field to four, the judge might next ask whether one of the parties could have observed the other's care level before deciding whether to take care. Where the defendant can observe the plaintiff's care level, the court should choose a standard that holds the defendant liable when both parties were negligent (rules 3 or 5). Where, on the other hand, the plaintiff could observe the defendant, the court should adopt rules 2 or 4. Of course, where care is unobservable or the parties acted simultaneously, none of the four rules can be eliminated on efficiency grounds, so some other criterion will have to determine the choice.

The judge confronting the evidence in a tort dispute may, of course, reach the conclusion that neither the plaintiff nor the defendant could have prevented the accident cost-justifiably. In that context, the choice of a liability standard is going to necessitate a judgment about which party should pay the costs of non-negligent accidents. Rules 2 and 3 will leave those costs with the plaintiff, while rules 4 and 5 will shift them to the defendant. As should be clear from our discussion above, two possible conclusions suggest themselves from a court's finding that neither the plaintiff nor the defendant could have prevented the accident cost-justifiably. First, the court could be wrong. That is possible for two reasons, both stemming from information deficiencies: (1) courts cannot take a party's potential *activity-level* investments into account; and/or (2) courts cannot take all of a party's potential *care-level* investments into account. Consequently, if there are many potential but unverifiable cost-justified activity-level and/or care-level investments that a party could make, then that party should be held liable even in the absence of proven negligence. Again here, courts should be sensitive to deterrability, and not just preventability, of accidents.

The second possible conclusion that one might draw from a court's findings of non-negligence is that the court is correct. When an accident occurs in the absence of any negligent behavior, efficiency demands that courts allocate the costs of accidents to the party best able to bear those costs. Courts, in other words, should pick the row that best satisfies the insurance goal – that is, the row that allocates the risk of unprevented accidents to the party who can bear them at least cost. If the plaintiff has the greater aversion to risk, the court should apply one of the rules that will rest liability with the defendant. If the defendant is more risk averse, the plaintiff should be responsible for the costs of non-negligent accidents.

A final issue for the efficiency-minded court may be possible administrative-cost considerations. In the non-lateral accident context, if none of the other criteria proves more helpful than the care-level criterion, the judge might opt for a no liability standard since it will likely be least costly to administer. In the bilateral accident context, courts are unlikely to know the costs of any given rule, but it seems plausible that rules 3 and 4, where the Hand Formula is applied only once, will be less costly to administer.

While this catalog is by no means exhaustive, it highlights the questions that legal economists would have judges ask to channel the law toward efficient results. The reader may, however, have noticed a tension in this list. Though it is possible that each of these efficiency considerations will point toward the same liability standard in a particular accident context, it seems far more likely that different efficiency considerations will have conflicting implications for the choice among liability standards. A judge, or a legal economist, must then confront the task of somehow choosing among competing efficiency concerns.

Some limitations of law and economics

Much of law and economics scholarship is strikingly un-self-critical. We feel a special obligation, therefore, to highlight for the newcomer a few of the more common criticisms.

The fault line along which most of the critiques of law and economics rest can be exposed by re-examining the catalog of efficiency considerations provided in the previous section. While it is possible to list an array of considerations a judge might take into account, any such inventory will not – and, in our view, cannot – answer a set of questions having to do with how a court might measure each consideration or balance one consideration against the other. For instance, how does a court counterbalance care-level deterrence considerations against activity-level deterrence considerations? Or, assuming that all deterrence considerations point in the same direction, how does a court counterbalance insurance and de-terrence considerations where they are conflicting? What about administrative costs? Does any rule more strict than no liability (rule 1) create benefits exceeding administrative costs? Although those sorts of questions might be answerable at the level of theory, they are virtually unanswerable in practice. The problem fac-ing the legal economist is that, for efficiency to maintain any normative punch, all the significant efficiency effects of a rule (or its alternatives) must be taken into account. But the economist, just like the judge, is highly constrained by informa-tion costs and is, therefore, often unable accurately (or uncontroversially) to weigh countervailing efficiency considerations.

A legal economist trying to find a way out of this dilemma might take one of two routes – the first empirical, the second theoretical. First, the normativist can do the empirical research necessary to weigh properly the various efficiency considera-tions. That option has rarely, if ever, been taken since the costs of such research seem likely to outweigh the benefits. Instead, scholars typically attempt a cheap version of this approach by eyeballing the various efficiency considerations and offering their own view, together with a smattering of contestable empirical sup-port, of how the countervailing efficiency considerations stack up. The normative force of conclusions emerging from this form of analysis is strengthened inasmuch as more of the efficiency effects are considered, but weakened inasmuch as the analysis underlying the conclusion is less scientific. Second, the normativist can narrow the focus of the model until something unequivocal can be said about the model's simplified and stylized world. Efficiency analyses lose their normative force, however, inasmuch as they ignore potentially significant efficiency considerations. Thus, this approach sacrifices normative force by excluding potentially significant efficiency effects in return for the added normative force that comes from the claim to scientific rigor.

The normative force of any law and economics conclusion is, thus, limited by one or the other of those criticisms. As Amartya Sen (1985) has observed,

> the demands of tractability can conflict with those of veracity, and we can have a hard choice between simplicity and relevance. We want a canonical form that is uncomplicated enough to be easily usable in theoretical and empirical analysis. But we also want an assumption structure that is not fundamentally at odds with the real world, nor one that makes simplicity take the form of naivety. (*p. 341*)

It is perhaps unsurprising that the most common and potent criticisms of law and economics are either that its models are indefensibly unrealistic or that the analysis is insufficiently scientific.

In recent years, a number of prominent arguments have been made about the lack of realism of economic models. Many critics charge that focussing on money as a measure of damages over-simplifies the way that human beings value certain goods. Valuing human life in dollar terms is said to offend and compromise the fundamental social norm of valuing human life infinitely (Calabresi and Bobbitt, 1978). As Posner himself put it when discussing the sale of babies for adoption, "economists like to think about the unthinkable" (1986, p. 141). In response to that view, many defenders of the cost/benefit approach to policymaking point out that, like it or not, there is in everything we do an implicit monetary value that is placed on human life. To bury our heads in the sand and pretend that it does not happen is to ensure that it will be done in a haphazard and wasteful way. Millions spent to save one life, might be better used to save a dozen lives. The sufficiency of that response is hotly debated, and to some extent recalls the normative question of whether, or to what extent, efficiency should be the goal of the legal system. As Cass Sunstein has argued, "efforts to insist on a single kind of valuation and to make goods commensurable, while designed to aid in human reasoning, actually make such reasoning inferior to what it is when it is working well" (1993, p. 780).

A second argument about the lack of realism of law and economics is that the "rational actor" described by the legal economist bears no resemblance to a real person. As a result, any legal conclusions based on unrealistic expectations of human behavior may be useless or even harmful to real-life decision making. There is an emerging body of empirical evidence that people's behavior deviates systematically from the predictions of the rational actor model. In light of that sort of evidence, scholars, most notably, Robert Ellickson (1989), have begun to challenge legal economists to enrich the normative force of economic analysis by illuminating the rational-actor model with insights from sociology and psychology in order to introduce "more realism about both human frailties and the influence of culture" (1989, p. 25). Responding to these calls for realism, Posner observes, predictably, that although rationality may be a reductionist notion, reductionism is inherent in scientific inquiry (1992, pp. 16–17, 1989, pp. 60–2).

329

Perhaps the most common criticism of law and economics is that it overlooks or, worse, displaces questions of distribution or equity. When analyzing the efficiency of one or another area of the law, legal economists typically take as given the current distribution of wealth and treat distributional consequences as irrelevant. But as critics have pointed out, many people are less concerned with the total amount of social wealth (or utility) than with its distribution. Economists respond in part by observing that distributional questions taken by themselves fall outside the reach of economic science. Once again, law and economics faces a tension between, borrowing Amartya Sen's terms, simplicity and relevance.

Conclusion

As the above-mentioned criticisms suggest, law and economics is not without costs. The trade-off between the need for realism and the need for science is a genuine one, and it is one that future legal economists will have to confront. However, recognizing some weaknesses in law and economics is no reason to abandon it. Whatever its costs, law and economics also has benefits. After all, while the claim that efficiency should serve as *the* goal of the law might not find much support, many people – perhaps most people – still believe that efficiency should be *a* goal of the legal system. And, where a model's relevant assumptions are plausible, law and economics can contribute in important ways to our understanding of laws' effects, of how those laws might be altered to better serve the goal of efficiency, or, alternatively, of what the efficiency costs of pursuing different policy goals (such as equity) might be.

Bibliography

Ayres, I. and Tally, E. 1995: Solomonic bargaining: dividing a legal entitlement to facilitate Coasean trade. *Yale Law Journal*, 104, 1,027–117.

Calabresi, G. and Bobbitt, P. 1978: *Tragic Choices*. New York: W. W. Norton & Co.

Calabresi, G. and Melamed, A. D. 1972: Property rules, liability rules, and inalienability: one view of the cathedral. *Harvard Law Review*, 85, 1,089–128.

Coase, R. 1960: The problem of social costs. *The Journal of Law and Economics*, 3, 1–44.

Croley, S. and Hanson, J. 1991: What liability crisis? An alternative explanation for recent events in products liability. *Yale Journal on Regulation*, 8, 1–111.

Donohue, III, J. and Ayres, I. 1987: Posner's Symphony No. 3: thinking about the unthinkable. *Stanford Law Review*, 39, 791–812.

Easterbrook, F. and Fischel, D. 1991: *The Economic Structure of Corporate Law*. Cambridge, Mass.: Harvard University Press.

Ellickson, R. 1989: Bringing culture and human frailty to rational actors: a critique of classical law and economics. *Chicago–Kent Law Review*, 65, 23–55.

Elster, J. 1993: Some unresolved problems in the theory of rational behavior. *Acta Sociologica*, 36, 179–89.

Gilles, S. 1994: The invisible hand formula. *Virginia Law Review*, 80, 1,015–54.

Horwitz, M. 1980: Law and economics: science or politics?. *Hofstra Law Review*, 8, 905–12.

John M. Olin program in law and economics conference on "economic analysis of civil procedure." *The Journal of Legal Studies*, 23, 303–665.

Kaplow, L. 1994: The value of accuracy in adjudication: an economic analysis. *The Journal of Legal Studies*, 23, 307–401.

Kennedy, D. 1981: Cost–Benefit analysis of entitlement problems: a critique. *Stanford Law Review*, 33, 387–445.

Landes, W. and Posner, R. 1987: *The Economic Structure of Tort Law*. Cambridge, Mass.: Harvard University Press.

Latin, H. 1985: Problem-solving behavior and theories of tort liabilities. *California Law Review*, 73, 677–746.

—— 1994: "Good" warnings, bad products, and cognitive limitations. *UCLA Law Review*, 41, 1,193–295.

Michelman, F. 1978: Norms and normativity in the economic theory of law. *Minnesota Law Review*, 62, 1,015–48.

Polinsky, A. M. 1989: *An Introduction to Law and Economics*. Boston: Little, Brown & Co., 2nd edn.

Posner, R. 1972: *Economic Analysis of Law*. Boston: Little, Brown & Co., 2nd edn.

—— 1975: The economic approach to law. *Texas Law Review*, 53, 757–82.

—— 1986: *Economic Analysis of Law*. Boston: Little, Brown & Co., 3rd edn.

—— 1989: The future of law and economics: a comment on Ellickson. *Chicago–Kent Law Review*, 65, 57–62.

—— 1992: *Economic Analysis of Law*. Boston: Little, Brown & Co., 4th edn.

Priest, G. 1992: The inevitability of tort reform. *Valparaiso University Law Review*, 26, 701–7.

Sen, A. 1985: Goals, commitment, and identity. *Journal of Law, Economics, and Organization*, 1, 341–55.

Shavell, S. 1980: Strict liability vs. negligence. *Journal of Legal Studies*, 9, 1–25.

—— 1987: *Economic Analysis of Accident Law*. Cambridge, Mass.: Harvard University Press.

Sunstein, C. 1993: Incommensurability and valuation in law. *Michigan Law Review*, 92, 779–861.

Symposium on efficiency as a legal concern. 1980: *Hofstra Law Review*, 8, 485–770.

Cases

McCarty v. *Pheasant Run, Inc.*, 826 F.2d 1554 (7th Cir. 1987).

Moisan v. *Loftus*, 178 F.2d 148 (2d Cir. 1949).

United States v. *Carroll Towing Co.*, 159 F.2d 169 (2d Cir. 1947).

21

Legal formalism

ERNEST J. WEINRIB

Introduction

Rumor has it that legal formalism is dead. This rumor is false. Formalism reflects the law's most abiding aspiration: to be an immanently intelligible normative practice (Weinrib, 1988, 1995, pp. 1–55). The rumor will become true only with the passing of the aspiration.

This essay on formalism presents a voice from the empty sepulcher. The conception of formalism that I offer differs from the caricature current in contemporary legal scholarship, where formalism – usually identified as postulating the mechanical application of determinate rules – serves principally as a "loosely employed term of abuse" (Simpson, 1990, p. 835). The crucial issue, of course, is not the proper reference for formalism as a word but the most plausible conception of formalism as an idea. My own version claims fidelity to law's normative dimension, to juristic thinking, and to a philosophical tradition stretching back to classical antiquity.

The project of formalism

Formalism is a theory of legal justification. As a theory of *justification*, formalism considers law to be not merely a collection of posited norms or an exercise of official power, but a social arrangement responsive to moral argument. As a theory of *legal* justification, formalism focusses on the phenomena most expressive of the juridical aspect of our social lives: on interactions between parties who regard their interests as separate, and on the role of courts in resolving the consequent controversies. Thus, formalism's project is to elucidate the forms of moral argument appropriate to adjudication among mutually disinterested parties.

The basic unit of formalist analysis is the legal relationship. Law connects one person to another through the ensemble of concepts, principles, and processes that come into play when a legal claim is asserted. If, for instance, the claim is for breach of a contract, the legal relationship between the parties is defined by the doctrines and concepts of contract law and by its accompanying procedures of adjudication. Or if the claim concerns a non-consensual harm, the legal relationship of the injurer and victim is composed of the norms, concepts and institutions of tort law.

Formalism's interest is in the internal structure of such relationships. The relationship's components – its various doctrines, concepts, principles, and processes – are the parts of a totality. The formalist wants to understand how these parts relate to one another and to the totality that they together form. Is a legal relationship an aggregate of autonomous elements, so that these parts are connected to one another only through their contingent juxtaposition within the same legal relationship, like so many grains in a heap of sand? Or are the parts the interdependent constituents of an internally coherent whole?

Law's justificatory aspect provides the standpoint from which to address these questions. Underlying any element in legal relationships is some consideration that supposedly justifies it. The formalist concern with the structure of a juridical relationship is, therefore, a concern with the connection between justificatory considerations. Do the considerations that justify the various parts of a relationship play their justificatory role in isolation from one another? Or do they interlock into a single justification that coherently pervades the entire relationship?

The term "formalism" suggests a contrast between the formal and the substantive. That contrast lies at the core of the formalist methodology. The formalist approaches legal relationships by first discerning their necessary conditions, their internal principles of organization, and their presuppositions. These formal aspects then guide substantive determination.

To understand law as a justificatory enterprise, the formalist elucidates three features of justification: (1) its nature; (2) its structure(s); and (3) its ground. By the nature of justification, I mean the minimal conditions that any consideration must observe if it is to be justificatory. By the structure of justification, I mean the most abstract and comprehensive patterning of justificatory coherence. By the ground, I mean the presuppositions about agency that ultimately account for the normative character of any justification.

Let me turn to each of these features. The following discussion indicates how the consideration of formal aspects precedes the drawing of substantive conclusions. Throughout, I use tort law to illustrate. The illustration itself reflects the formalist insistence that private law is a distinctive mode of legal ordering and not merely a disguised form of public law. The formalist affirms, in other words, the categorical difference between justice between the parties, on the one hand, and justice in the pursuit of collective goals, on the other.

The nature of justification

A common criticism of tort law (for example, Franklin, 1967) goes as follows. In combining the goals of deterrence and compensation, tort law sets up a lottery for both litigants. From the plaintiff's standpoint, tort law recognizes a moral claim to compensation in the aftermath of injury. Yet instead of treating alike the sufferers

333

of like injury, tort law makes the victim's compensation depend on the fortuity of a tortious act. Similarly, from the defendant's standpoint, tort law is a mechanism for deterring carelessness. Yet tort law makes the occasion and scope of deterrence depend on the fortuity of the injury's occurrence and extent. The result of linking the compensation of victims to the deterrence of actors is that both compensation and deterrence work capriciously. The legal consequences for the litigants are normatively arbitrary.

Those who offer this criticism urge the abolition of tort law. They argue that because tort law cannot intelligibly combine deterrence and compensation, the law should replace tort law's treatment of personal injury with arrangements that aim at deterrence and compensation separately. The criticism assumes that deterrence and compensation are valid goals and then adjudges tort law incoherent in their light.

In the formalist view, the criticism is correct (though, as we shall see shortly, the dismissal of tort law does not follow from it). Goals, such as compensation and deterrence, that focus on each litigant independently cannot provide the moral underpinning for the relationship between plaintiff and defendant. In the context of tort law, such goals do not observe the minimal condition any consideration must observe if it is truly to function as a justification.

At stake is the nature of justification. A justification justifies: it has normative authority over the material to which it applies. The point of adducing a justification is to allow that authority to govern whatever falls within its scope. A consideration that functions as a justification must be permitted, as it were, to expand into the space it naturally fills. Consequently, a justification sets its own limit. For an extrinsic factor to cut the justification short is normatively arbitrary.

This is the arbitrariness to which the critics of tort law point. The goals of compensation and deterrence are independent of one another. Compensation addresses the needs of the injured party, and is indifferent to deterrence. Similarly, deterrence looks to the conduct of the injurer and is indifferent to compensation. Consequently, when juxtaposed within the tort relationship, compensation and deterrence are mutually truncating. What limits compensation is not the boundary to which its justificatory authority entitles it, but the competing presence of deterrence in the same legal relationship. Thus, tort law compensates victims only when damages serve the purpose of deterrence. In the same way, tort law artificially restricts deterrence, by tying deterrence to what is needed not to deter wrongdoers but to compensate victims. In this mixing of justifications, neither of them occupies the entire area to which it applies. Accordingly, neither in fact functions as a justification. Understood as composite of compensation and deterrence, tort law ceases to be a justificatory enterprise.

The formalist sees in the abolitionist critique of tort law an indication of what would answer the critique. In effect, the abolitionists point to the tension between the bipolarity of the tort relationship and the normative reach of the standard tort goals. Because each goal addresses the situation of only one of the parties, neither justifies the relationship as a whole. When combined they embrace both parties, but because the goals are mutually independent, the moral force of one artificially

limits the moral force of the other. In principle, the solution is to elaborate a justification that is bipolar in the same way that the tort relationship is.

The abolitionist position presupposes that justification takes the form of goals
such as compensation or deterrence. Abolitionists reason that since tort law cannot coherently satisfy such goals, it should be replaced. Ignored is the possibility
that the justification applicable to tort law is as relational as tort law itself. The
abolitionists assume that justifications refer to goals. The formalist assumes only
that justifications justify.

Formalism asserts that formal considerations are prior to substantive ones.
Accordingly, formalism's initial concern is not with a justification's substantive
merit, but with the minimal condition for its functioning *as* a justification, namely,
that it fill its own conceptual space. Purported justifications that do not respect
that condition are not so much villains as imposters: they are not doing something
wrong, but they are pretending to be what they are not.

It is worth noting at this stage what the formalist does *not* maintain. The formalist neither disputes the desirability of achieving compensation and deterrence
nor asserts the superiority of tort law to other mechanisms for handling injury.
The claim, rather, is that the goals of compensation and deterrence do not serve
a justificatory function in the tort context. Whether they serve such a function in
a different context is another matter.

The structures of justification

As this brief discussion of tort law indicates, justifications do not act as justifications unless legal relationships are coherent. Justificatory considerations provide
moral reasons for relating one person to another through a set of legal concepts
and consequences. Incoherence in the relationship reflects the presence of mutually independent justificatory considerations. Coherence, on the other hand, is the
interlocking into a single integrated justification of all the justificatory considerations that pertain to a legal relationship. A relationship is coherent when a single
justification animates it, so that the justification's moral force is congruent with
the relationship's boundaries. Coherence thus denotes unity.

At this point, the question arises: what are the different ways in which legal
relationships can express a single justificatory idea? Or, to put it another way,
what are the different structures of legal justification?

The classic treatment of justificatory structure is Aristotle's discussion of justice
(Aristotle, *Nicomachean Ethics*, V, 1,130a, 14–1,132b, 20, discussed in Weinrib,
1995, pp. 56–83). Aristotle outlines the patterns of justificatory coherence for
external relationships. To make their structural dimension salient, Aristotle represents these relationships at their most abstract, stripping away everything but
their unifying principles. From this emerge two justificatory structures: corrective
justice and distributive justice.

Corrective justice is bipolar, in that it relates the parties directly through the
harm that one of them inflicts on the other. Corrective justice treats the doer and

335

the sufferer of harm as the active and passive participants in a single relationship. Its unifying principle is the sheer correlativity of harm done to harm suffered. Neither the doing nor the suffering counts independently of the other. The doing of harm is normatively significant only because of the suffering that is correlative to it, and vice versa. For purposes of corrective justice, doing and suffering are not separate events but the correlative aspects of a single event.

Distributive justice, on the other hand, relates the parties not directly but through the medium of a distributive scheme. Under distributive justice, persons divide a benefit or burden in accordance with a criterion of distribution. This criterion, the collective purpose served by the distribution, is the distribution's principle of unity.

The two structures of justice have their respective notions of injustice. Corrective justice is the response to a wrong done to – and thus immediately implicating – a specific victim. In contrast, injustice in a distributive context consists in overdrawing a common resource, thereby diminishing the benefit available to other participants in the distribution. Such injustice affects the individual participants only derivatively: they each receive less because there is less for all to share.

Aristotle highlights the distinction between corrective justice and distributive justice by representing their structures in mathematical terms. He characterizes the direct relationship of the doer and sufferer in corrective justice as a quantitative equality in which the victim's loss is identified with the wrongdoer's gain. In contrast, he portrays distributive justice as an equality of proportions that relates the participants to their shares in accordance with the operative criterion of distribution. Just as the two kinds of equality are categorically different, so each form of justice is independent of the other and has its own integrity.

The contrast between the equalization of quantities in corrective justice and the equalization of proportions in distributive justice is especially evident in the number of parties that each can embrace. Because the transfer of a single quantity increases one amount at the expense of another, it can occur only between two amounts. Accordingly, the form of justice that Aristotle describes as an equalization of quantities is necessarily restricted to two parties at a time, with each interacting pair being treated discretely. In contrast, a series of equal proportions can be continued infinitely. Aristotle's mathematical representation of distributive justice mirrors the open-endedness of the number of parties that can participate in a distribution. Whereas the addition of parties in corrective justice is inconsistent with its structure, the addition of parties in distributive justice merely decreases the size of each person's share in the subject-matter of the distribution.

Moreover, the contrast between the two mathematical operations certifies the impossibility of integrating the two forms of justice into a broader form. No single mathematical operation combines proportionate and quantitative equality, because no single mathematical operation can have both a restricted and an open-ended number of terms. Similarly, there is no overarching form of justice into which corrective and distributive justice can be dissolved.

Corrective justice and distributive justice are structures of justificatory coherence. If justificatory considerations elaborate what the doer of harm owes to the sufferer of harm, they have the shape of corrective justice; if they point to the

336

grounds for dividing a benefit or burden among a group ("to or for each according to some criterion"), they have the shape of distributive justice. The terms "corrective" and "distributive" apply to a relationship between persons by applying to the type of justification that supports that relationship.

Because corrective and distributive justice are categorically different and mutually irreducible patterns of justificatory coherence, it follows that a single external relationship cannot coherently partake of both. No distributive justification coherently applies to the bipolar relationships of private law. Those relationships require justifications that connect the parties directly as doer and sufferer. Aristotle's contrast of corrective and distributive justice does not determine whether the law should treat an incident correctively or distributively. But if the positive law is to be coherent, any given relationship cannot rest on a *combination* of corrective and distributive justifications. When a corrective justification is mixed with a distributive one, each necessarily undermines the justificatory force of the other, and the relationship cannot manifest either unifying structure.

Tort law illustrates the drastic implications of this line of thinking. All the goals – deterrence, compensation, punishment, loss-spreading, wealth-maximization, cheapest cost avoidance – routinely adduced or proposed for tort law are inadequate because they interrupt the direct relationship of doer and sufferer. Such goals, accordingly, are incompatible with the coherence of the private law relationship. If tort law is to be a truly justificatory enterprise, we can disqualify them even without evaluating their substantive desirability.

The ground of justification

Implicit in legal justification is a conception of normativeness. What is that conception? The standard assumption of legal scholarship is that normativeness is rooted in the substantive desirability of certain goals. Tort theorists who emphasize deterrence, for instance, point to the desirability of reducing the number and severity of injuries. Similarly, the compensation rationale rests on the desirability of alleviating hardship in the aftermath of injury. The goals that validate legal regulation may, of course, be multiple and complex. At bottom, however, they represent aspects of human well-being that law is supposed to promote.

The phenomenon of private law precludes the formalist from sharing this conception of normativeness. Only inasmuch as they reflect the structure of corrective justice do the bipolar relationships of private law manifest justificatory coherence. Aspects of human well-being, however, are not intrinsically bipolar. In our tort example, for instance, the goals ascribed to tort law do not link the doer and the sufferer of harm: nothing about compensation as a justificatory consideration ties it to the action of a particular injurer; and nothing about deterrence ties it to the suffering of a particular plaintiff. Corrective justice therefore cannot presuppose aspects of well-being as the sources of its own normativeness.

The formalist account locates the ground of justification not in substantive goals that promote well-being but in the conceptual structure of free agency. Agency is

337

an exercise in purposiveness, in which the agent can reflect on the content of any particular purpose and spontaneously substitute one purpose for another. Accordingly, what characterizes agency is not the particular purposes that constitute the content of choice, but the form of choice evident in the capacity to abstract from any particular purpose.

Practical reason is the determining ground of agency so construed. Inasmuch as only a rational being can abstract, agency is rationality as it operates to change the world. Particular acts are most expressive of the agent's rationality not when they are determined by the givenness of inclination and circumstance, but when they express the universality inherent in the form of choice. At a minimum, this universality requires that the principle on which a purposive being chooses to act be capable of functioning as a principle valid for all purposive beings, whatever their inclinations or circumstances and whatever the specific purposes that might promote their well-being. In this conception of normativeness, particular choices are required to live up to the formal standpoint that characterizes the purposive activity of free agents. Normativeness is thus the expression of practical reason in its most literal sense: as a unity of reason and practice.

What I have briefly and inadequately described is the idea of free and purposive agency that figures in the great expositions of natural right by Kant and Hegel. Right is the totality of norms governing the interaction of free purposive agents. Just as the corrective and distributive justice provide the structures of justification and then insist that legal reasoning conform to those structures, so the philosophy of natural right elucidates the abstract structure of agency and then insists that particular actions conform to that structure. Because under natural right agents are conceived as morally accountable only by virtue of their capacity for self-determination, moral significance does not immediately attach to given particularities, whether of nature, inclination, or circumstance. Rather, such particularities are the material for the embodiment of abstract agency. Natural right regards rights, not well-being, as normatively fundamental, and it construes rights as the juridical manifestations of the agent's capacity for self-determination.

To locate the normative grounding of law in abstract agency, not well-being, is not to deny the significance of well-being. As an activity, agency takes place under certain empirical conditions, which for human beings include the working of one's will through the physical organism of the body, the sentience of the organism, the presence of satisfactions that motivate action, and so on. Of course, for such beings, well-being is normatively significant. The point, however, is that under natural right, well-being is not normatively *basic*. Well-being is significant to the extent that it embodies abstract agency and that natural right protects well-being in accordance with the norms of right implicit in such agency. In contrast to theories that look upon rights as labels attached to protected interests in well-being, natural right regards rights as the moral reasons for protecting them.

Corrective justice presupposes the natural right notion of agency. As Aristotle himself observes, corrective justice is a normative structure that abstracts from considerations of virtue or circumstance, so that all that matters is the correlativity of doing and suffering as such (*Nicomachean Ethics*, V, 1,132a, 2–7). Natural right

338

provides the abstract notion of agency that underlies the abstracted justifications of corrective justice and that makes sense of the sheer correlativity of doing and suffering. This means that the agent's particular purposes – even such morally plausible purposes as the promotion of welfare or of the good – are irrelevant to corrective justice. All that matters is that, whatever their particular purposes, agents should not exercise their free purposiveness in a way that is inconsistent with the free purposiveness of other agents. As operative within corrective justice, therefore, practical reason abstracts from the particularity of this or that purpose to the very idea of purposiveness itself. Hence the norms of corrective justice are geared to the prevention of wrongful interferences with rights rather than to the promotion of welfare.

Distributive justice also presupposes the fundamental values of natural right. By distributing things to persons in accordance with some criterion, distributive justice postulates a distinction between things and persons. Implicit in distributive justice is the Kantian idea that a thing (the subject matter of the distribution) can be a means to any end for which it is useful, whereas the nature of a person (the participant in the distribution) is to be an end and never only a means to an end. Similarly, the equal application of the criterion of distribution to all who fall under its justificatory force reflects their equal moral status as ends in themselves by certifying that they are not available for use according to the distributor's pleasure. The positive law may give effect to the Kantian values of personhood and equality that underlie distributive justice in a variety of ways: by incorporating these values into the techniques for construing statutes, by elaborating notions of natural justice or fairness for administrative procedures, or by enshrining specifications of personhood and equality into constitutional documents.

The immanent intelligibility of law

I mentioned at the beginning that formalism represents the law's aspiration to be an immanently intelligible normative practice. Immanence bespeaks a standpoint that is internal to law. How does formalism illuminate this immanence?

First, the components for the formalist analysis are not elements of an external ideal but merely the internal presuppositions of law as a justificatory enterprise. Formalism starts with the notion of legal justification and works backward to the preconditions of that notion and then backward to the preconditions of those preconditions, and so on. My discussion of the nature, structures, and ground of justification has summarily retraced this process of regression: implicit in justification is the coherent application of a justification to what it justifies; implicit in coherence is the unitary structure of what coheres; implicit in these structures is an abstracting notion of agency. Nowhere does the analysis assume an external standpoint.

Second, formalism tries to make sense of juristic thinking and discourse in their own terms. Formalism is attentive to the striving of sophisticated legal systems to their own justificatory coherence – to what Lord Mansfield (in *Omychund* v. *Barker*, (1744) 26 Eng. Rep. 15, at 23) called the law's attempt to work itself pure. Consequently, formalism takes seriously the concepts, principles and institutions through which the law expresses that coherence. The formalist treats the law's concepts as signposts of an internal intelligibility and tries to understand them as they are understood by the jurists who think and talk about them. The formalist, accordingly, regards law as understandable from within, not as an alien language that requires translation into the terminology of another discipline such as economics. Whereas the practitioner of economic analysis, for instance, might construe the plaintiff's cause of action in private law as a mechanism for bribing someone to vindicate the collective interest in deterring the defendant's economically inefficient behavior, the formalist interprets it simply as what it purports to be: the assertion of right by the plaintiff in response to a wrong suffered at the hands of the defendant.

Third, formalism highlights coherence, which is itself an internal notion. Coherence implies the presence of a unified structure that integrates its component parts. In such a structure the whole is greater than the sum of its parts, and the parts are interconnected through the whole that they together form. One understands the coherence of something by attending to the self-contained circle of mutual reference and support among its components. Justificatory coherence points not outward to a transcendent ideal but inward to a harmonious interrelationship among the constituents of the structure of justification.

Negligence law illustrates the coalescence of a number of concepts into a coherent justificatory ensemble (Weinrib, 1995, pp. 145–70). The concepts of negligence law instantiate corrective justice by tracing different aspects of the progression from the doing to the suffering of harm. Throughout, negligence law treats the plaintiff and the defendant as correlative to one another: the significance of doing for tort law lies in the possibility of causing someone to suffer, and the significance of suffering lies in its being the consequence of someone else's doing. Central to the linkage of plaintiff and defendant is the idea of risk, for, as Justice Cardozo observed in *Palsgraf* v. *Long Island R.R.*, 248 N.Y. 339, at 344 (1928), "risk imports relation." The sequence starts with the potential for harm inherent in the defendant's act (hence the absence of liability for non-feasance), and concludes with the realization of that potential in the plaintiff's injury (hence the necessity for factual causation). The further requirements of reasonable care and remoteness link the defendant's action to the plaintiff's suffering through judgments about the substantiality of the risk and the generality of the description of its potential consequences. Each category traces an actual or potential connection between doing and suffering, and together they translate into juridical terms the movement of effects from the doer to the sufferer. The negligence concepts form an ensemble that brackets and articulates a single normative sequence.

Although the formalist approach is internal to law, it is evaluative and not merely descriptive. The point of formalism is to discern standards of evaluation that are internal to the phenomenon being evaluated. Implicit in the conceptual and institutional apparatus of law, as well as in the activity of its jurists, is the claim to be a justificatory enterprise. Formalism asks what law would look like if it were true to this claim. Formalism thus has a critical standpoint, but one that emerges from law's own aspirations.

Conclusion

Over the last generation legal scholarship has both lengthened its reach and shortened its ambition. The lengthening of reach is evident in the appeal beyond law to other disciplines and modes of thinking: economics, literature, history, and so on. The shortening of ambition is evident in the assumption – shared by economic analysts, legal pragmatists, and critical legal studies scholars – that law is not systematically intelligible in its own terms. The lengthening and the shortening are parts of the same phenomenon: the richness of interdisciplinary work reflects the supposed poverty of the law's own resources.

In contrast, formalism retrieves the classical understanding of law as "an immanent moral rationality" (Unger, 1983, p. 57). This conception of law begins with Aristotle's sketch of the justificatory structures for legal relationships; it is elaborated in Aquinas's treatise on right; and it continues through the accounts of normativeness found in the great natural right philosophies of Kant and Hegel. By attending to the distinctive morality that marks coherent legal relationships, the version of formalism I have been presenting asserts the autonomy of law both as a field of learning and as a justificatory enterprise. Formalism thus claims to be the theory implicit in the law as it elaborates itself from within.

Half a century ago, in a fascinating but unjustly neglected article, Michael Oakeshott observed the chaos of what was then passing for jurisprudential explanation (Oakeshott, 1938)). After tracing the competing claims of historical, economic, and other jurisprudences, he pointed out that a truly philosophical jurisprudence could not simply accept the conclusions of special disciplines but must instead start with what we, in some sense, already know about law, and work back through the presuppositions of this knowledge to a clearer and fuller knowledge. This, he said, was the procedure followed by all great philosophers, including such figures as Aquinas and Hegel. Jurisprudence, Oakeshott concluded, must regain a sense of this tradition of inquiry. Unfortunately, the passage of time has not appreciably diminished the pertinence of his observations.

A previous version of this essay appeared in *Harvard Journal of Law and Public Policy*, 16 (1993), 583–95.

Bibliography

Aquinas, T. 1975: *Summa Theologiae, Volume 37, Justice (2a2ae. 57–62)*, tr. T. Gilby, New York and London: Blackfriars.
Aristotle 1962: *Nicomachean Ethics*, tr. M. Ostwald, Indianapolis: Bobbs-Merrill.

Franklin, M. A. 1967: Replacing the negligence lottery: compensation and selective reimbursement. *Virginia Law Review*, 53, 778–814.

Hegel, G. W. F. [1821] 1952: *The Philosophy of Right*, tr. T. M. Knox, Oxford: Clarendon Press.

Kant, I. [1797] 1991: *The Metaphysics of Morals*, tr. M. Gregor, Cambridge: Cambridge University Press.

Kress, K. (ed.) 1992: Symposium: corrective justice and formalism. *Iowa Law Review*, 77 (i–xii), 403–863.

Oakeshott, M. 1938: The concept of a philosophical jurisprudence. *Politica*, 203–22, 345–60.

Simpson, A. W. B. 1990: Legal iconoclasts and legal ideals. *Cincinnati Law Review*, 58, 819–44.

Unger, R. M. 1983: The critical legal studies movement. *Harvard Law Review*, 96, 561–675.

Weinrib, Ernest J. 1988: Legal formalism: on the immanent rationality of law. *Yale Law Journal*, 97, 949–1,016.

—— 1995: *The Idea of Private Law*. Cambridge and London: Harvard University Press.

22

German legal philosophy and theory in the nineteenth and twentieth centuries

ALEXANDER SOMEK

Considering the mainstream of early nineteenth-century legal thought in retrospect, there appears to have been a preoccupation with two major questions, both reflections of the idealistic temper of German philosophy. The first concerns the enigma of how the legitimate general will, representing the conditions of justice, can be realized on the level of individual actions. Assuming the perspective of the individual agent, it had to be explained why the realization of a genuinely free individual will implies the recognition of a generally acceptable and effective regime of coercion. The answer to this question lay in the acceptance of the state's predominance over civil society. The latter was seen as an unstable aggregation of social atoms, each with its own needs and unruly desires; their drives had to be contained and were at the same time protected through the enforcement of general laws. Given this resolution, a second question arose: what medium could lend the general will an adequate form of expression and implementation? While most philosophers were convinced that all legal constraints on individual action had to issue from the impartial and mechanical application of neutral and general legal rules, influential legal scholars pointed out that the mediation of general will and individual action presupposes the intervention of a conceptual apparatus, specifically designed to reveal the systematic significance of statutory provisions. It will be seen that the inherent difficulties in answering the first question reached to and affected the attempts to answer the second.

Nineteenth-century idealism

Certain writings of Immanuel Kant bear on our theme. Although they were published at the end of the eighteenth century, their impact on the later tradition calls for a brief sketch of the basic ideas.

Introducing the first of the questions, adumbrated above, Kant begins with a reconstruction of the necessary conditions for the legal appropriateness of individual action. Assuming a setting in which persons, equal and free, can select and pursue their goals as they wish, Kant applies the universal principle of moral judgment, that is, the categorical imperative, to determine the formal constraints on performing an act that one has freely chosen (*Willkür*). Hence, the general

343

principle of law is inferred from a moral point of view: an act is legally correct if it respects everyone's freedom of action according to a general rule of law. If this condition is met, people have rights (notably, the right to property) and obligations. Since infringements upon the freedom of others are incompatible with the general rule of freedom, Kant regards coercion (in the abstract) as an appropriate means of reinforcement. Thus, coercion is defined in terms of a double negative, as the "hindrance of a hindrance of freedom." Given the inherent uncertainty of the hypothetical state of nature, the powers of legislation and law enforcement must be exercised by the state, whose acts are subordinated to the ideal of republicanism. Along with the separation of those powers, this ideal requires that the legislature pass only those laws that could plausibly stem from the consent of "a people with mature reason." Although Kant is convinced that a government fulfilling the requirements of republicanism could only be sustained by an enlightened monarch, the ideal includes a morally charged principle of political autonomy: ideally, the members of such a republic would only be subject to those morally acceptable rules to which they had collectively given their approval. Thus, Kant's republicanism is an echo of the related notion, familiar from his moral philosophy, that all moral legislation must presuppose an ideal "kingdom of ends," in which reasonable beings would be associated by means of a systematic and coherent set of "communal laws."

The links Kant established between the morally acceptable form of legislation, "true" political autonomy and individual rights, were transformed by the philosophers of German Idealism into the idea that the legal system is a reflection of the organic unity of the citizens. As a result, the state was seen either as an indispensable institution for engendering the moral attitudes necessary for a kingdom of ends or as the highest expression of the communal morality (*Sittlichkeit*), whose institutional structure transcends the limited perspective of individual moral judgments. The former is clearly expressed in the legal philosophy of Johann Gottlieb Fichte; the latter can be found in Georg Wilhelm Friedrich Hegel's *Philosophy of Right*.

Although Fichte was deeply inspired by Kant's critical philosophy, his theory of legal relationships took a different course. Starting with the *a priori* evident principle of spontaneous subjectivity (that is, the exercise of free activity unconditioned by external circumstances or natural drives), Fichte is concerned with a reconstruction of the necessary conditions for the individual awareness (*Selbstbewußtsein*) of such unconditional freedom. His deductions reflect a double strategy: first, a progression from unconditional subjectivity to the conditions of self-awareness on the level of the individual self, and second, a regression to the circumstances under which those conditions would be met in the historical world.

Following the first strategy, Fichte argues that self-awareness consists of the identity of unconditional spontaneity and its reflection on itself. Since all reflection necessarily implies a distinction, the individual self can become aware of its subjective spontaneity only if it separates the latter from every kind of restricted activity (such as perception or volition aroused by certain objects of desire). It follows

344

that spontaneous subjectivity can become aware of its free activity on the level of the individual self only in a sphere of volition that is, by its very definition, neither determined by natural causes nor limited to specific acts of choice. Self-reflection, able to grasp that sphere, is prompted when the individual self is summoned to free self-determination by another individual self. Since the other self, in order to consistently deliver the respective summons (*Aufforderung*), must restrict its own activity, individuals can become aware of their freedom only if they mutually restrict their spheres of action. Thus, for Fichte the concept of law follows from the purely theoretical construction of conditions that allow the spontaneity of reason to enter into the individual experience of conduct. Far from being grounded in a moral principle or in the mutual restriction of self-interested behavior, legal relationships represent the conditions under which individuals partake of unconditional freedom.

Once the conditions for unconditional freedom have been deduced, the second step for Fichte is to identify the circumstances sufficient to motivate human beings to subordinate their freedom of action, provided that others are willing to do the same, to a system of rules. In this context, Fichte devises a set of governmental institutions whose operation is strictly mechanical. The basic structure of legal and political institutions is deduced from a series of hypothetical contracts; the most important among them is the "contract of unification" (*Vereinigungsvertrag*), which transforms the social perspective of the individual self into that of a member of the organic unity of the state. The latter has to guarantee each individual's sphere of activity, which implies a broad conception of rights, including rights to property and to work. In addition, Fichte stresses the state's responsibility to police mutual co-operation for the sake of the well-being and moral perfection of the citizens, in some respects a foreshadowing of socialist ideas. And his legal philosophy has its utopian moments, too. Particularly in his later writings, Fichte regards legal sanctions as having merely transitional significance, relevant only until humankind has been transformed into an "imprint of reason" (*Abdruck der Vernunft*). It comes as no surprise that Fichte's theory of the state has totalitarian connotations as well.

Whereas Fichte's philosophical argumentation departs from (alleged) self-evident premises, Hegel's philosophy is devoted to the discovery of the contradictory yet organic interplay of "moments' that represent a deeper trans-individual totality. Although for Hegel, too, the law stands for conditions for the creation of freedom, those conditions are reconstructed from the perspective of what he calls the "objective spirit" (*objektiver Geist*), which encompasses all ethically relevant social perspectives, actions, and institutions.

According to Hegel, freedom consists of the unification of two conflicting moments: "generality", understood as absolute independence and indeterminacy on the one hand, and "particularity," understood as conditioned determinacy in decisions, on the other. Specific forms of freedom partake of these moments in shifting constellations and therefore represent separate instances of the totality. Thus, to work out a statement of the rational basis of law and morality is to provide a coherent account of the internal composition and external juxtaposition of the forms of freedom. This methodological perspective explains the dynamic aspect of Hegel's dialectical analysis. The objective spirit is viewed as unfolding itself internally, this through the differentiation of forms, and representing its totality in each distinction. Since the synthesis of moments includes their simultaneous attraction and repulsion, the forms necessarily transcend their own limits. As their moments are obliterated, elevated and preserved (this is the triple meaning of "sublation", that is, *Aufhebung*) in the transition to a later form, the reality of freedom is ultimately conceived as the increasingly mediated totality of relationships between forms of freedom. This methodological approach is clearly reflected in the structure of Hegel's *Philosophy of Right*.

In the sphere of private legal relationships, freedom is first understood in terms of independent individual ownership. The decision to make a thing one's own stands for the unification of mutually accepted freedom of choice (indeterminacy) and distinctive acts of appropriation and exchange (determinacy). The unsubstantiated or, as it were, "abstract" character of such a synthesis of general and individual will is brought to the fore, when the respect for property is denied through acts of injustice. The resulting need to determine the objectively valid content of the general will is then addressed within the sphere of morality. Even though the particular will, in moral judgment, seemingly abides by a general principle (such as the categorical imperative), that which is to count as a correct application of the principle must ultimately be determined by individuals themselves. Hence, there are no shared criteria for determining whether moral judgments are carried out correctly and without deception or fraud. Thus, a stable reconciliation of individual and general will requires that the domain of individual moral judgment be transcended, that one move from it into the sphere of communal morality (*Sittlichkeit*). On this level the generality of the particular will, understood as independence from individual desires and arbitrary choices, is rendered stable through the belief that existing habits and institutions actually promote the well-being and socially acceptable self-assertion of individuals.

Sittlichkeit has different manifestations in different contexts. Whereas the individual will, within the family, is eventually subordinated to the integrity of the communal bond, the market relationships of civil society are dominated by an individualistic spirit. Even in this sphere, however, the common bond is knit unintentionally – on the one hand, through the fact of mutual economic dependencies (the pursuit of individual happiness increases the well-being of society as a whole), and, on the other, through professional and political groups to which members of civil society contribute on a voluntary basis. (So it is that they start to understand themselves as parts of a trans-individual whole.) However, the internal instability of a class-divided civil society must be remedied through the intervention of the state, whose acts acknowledge individual well-being as a right. Institutionally, the state is depicted as an organism whose three branches of government (monarchical, legislative, administrative) represent the unity of general and particular will in three different forms. As is well known, Marx and other left-wing Hegelians pointed to the fact that such an organic unity had not yet been attained in practice.

From idealism to nineteenth-century constructivism: the case of the historical school

Despite their apparent rejection of Hegel's glorification of the state, the major pro-ponents of the historical school (Savigny, Puchta, Jhering, Gerber) shared his conviction that legal institutions originate in the spirit of the people (*Volksgeist*), which lends to the universal principles of freedom and equality distinctively na-tional contours. In particular, Carl Friedrich von Savigny highlights both the evolutionary development and the "organic" coherence of legal institutions. In his early writings, legal history is framed within a three-stage model of legal culture. After the age of customary law and legislation, the development culminates in a period in which legal institutions, though still originating in the spirit of the peo-ple, find adequate representation in doctrinal categories. It follows that jurists must be regarded as the representatives of the legal consciousness of the people. Since the people's general will, at the very epitome of legal evolution, is most adequately represented within the categories of the science of law, it could never be captured by the authoritative issuance of a set of legal rules. Accordingly, members of the historical school were strictly opposed to codification.

This opposition is intriguing for another reason, too. It stems from the recogni-tion that statutory language is inherently indeterminate, from the rejection, then, of the enlightenment philosophers' notion that legal certainty could somehow be assured by means of the mechanical application of rules. Since no canon of inter-pretation offers a safeguard against indeterminacy, the representatives of the his-torical school consider the idea that legal doctrine essentially amounts to the application of rules as, in a word, wrong-headed. In their opinion, rules are but surface manifestations of a latent legal content, which is to be drawn out, made manifest, by means of a construction of the systematic meaning of legal institu-tions and rights. According to Georg Friedrich Puchta and Rudolph von Jhering, such a construction requires that one employ the inherited legal vocabulary in the conceptual dissection of the legal materials (statutes, cases) and, through and as a result of such an analysis, that one supplement and refine the evolving hier-archical system of legal concepts. Once the legal materials have been transmuted into manifestations of an "underlying" conceptual structure, the vocabulary en-ables the legal analyst to link the meaning of legal concepts to concrete events. In this respect it represents the grammar according to which a people expresses its general will on the level of detailed legal relationships. Furthermore, the legal vocabulary can also be used in a productive way, for it allows the extension of constructed principles to unprecedented cases.

From the turn of the century to World War II: disintegration and reconstruction

The constructivist method of the historical school was extremely influential for the subsequent development of German legal thought, not just in the field of civil law, but also in the area of constitutional and administrative law (Gerber, Laband, Jellinek). Nonetheless, it fell victim to relentless attacks by the so-called "free law movement" (Stampe, Ehrlich, Kantorowicz, Fuchs, Isay) at the turn of the century.

The idea underlying the movement's critique is fairly simple. The deductions of conceptual jurisprudence, which developed in the sequel of the historical school, exceed by far what could be claimed to follow from the language of the German civil code, enacted in 1900. Since those provisions are the only relevant source of authority, and since the constructivist method amounts to nothing more than a reminder of an opaque metaphysics, the results of this method are a sham. Accordingly, once one has abstracted from the doctrinal metamorphosis of the code, it can then be seen, as Ulrich Kantorowicz writes, that the code contains more gaps than regulations. In order to fill such gaps and to ensure the realization of social justice in processes of adjudication that is free from constraints (*freie Rechtsfindung*) one must appeal to the common sense of the people (*Kantorowicz*) or the living law of the community (*Ehrlich*). Since such a dramatic shift in orientation would have to be manifest in the legal curriculum, too, Ernst Fuchs proposes the establishment of "clinical programs." Others, such as Eugen Ehrlich, seek to replace the established style of legal analysis by a more sociological approach.

The challenge posed by the free law movement triggered two different historically significant responses: The "jurisprudence of interests" and the rise of what might be called "radical proceduralism."

The jurisprudence of interests attempts to restore the constructivist's idea of a latent legal content, but by reversing directions and proceedings in an empirical way. While constructivists held that elusive means-ends-relationships are only of marginal significance to the construction of the conceptual structure, scholars such as Philipp Heck and Heinrich Stoll adopt the idea (already expressed in Jhering's later work) that means-ends-relationships provide the rational basis of legal institutions, and contend that the true meaning of the statute can be elicited through research on the political and social circumstances of their enactment. However, the constructivist's favorite tools, legal concepts, are only useful as a means of organizing the legal materials into a conceptually neat "external system." The real task of the interpreter is to provide a reconstruction of the reconciliation of conflicting social interests that underlie the statutory regulations and, if possible, to go on to reconstruct from these efforts at reconciliation, the "internal system" of legislative evaluations of interests (*Interessenbewertungen*). Such a system would be true to the historical facts and, at the same time, would enable the judge to draw conclusions that transcend the sphere of statutory language. Still, the jurisprudence of interests is unworkable if the existing polity turns out to be riddled with contradictions and conflicts.

A very different response to the free law movement was chosen by proponents of what might be termed "radical proceduralism." Its emergence can be traced back to the writings of Oskar Bülow, and its most marked expression appears in the works of James Goldschmidt, Julius Binder, and Adolf J. Merkl. These writers point out that the law governs its own application. Since all law suits terminate in the stage of final decision, controversies about the proper method of statutory construction are eventually resolved through procedural inappellability (*Rechts-kraft*). Therefore, Goldschmidt holds that until a final decision has been reached, legal claims exist, during a law suit, only relative to the situation defined by procedural stages (*Rechtslagen*). Binder goes further. Any doctrine of law, he holds, that disregards the domain of procedure is completely pointless, for there simply is no law apart from procedure. Accordingly, the plaintiff and the defendant have rights only if they are able to prevail in a law suit. In a less radical way, Merkl tried to accommodate the free law movement's indeterminacy thesis in his "dynamic" model of the legal system. It became one of the building blocks of Hans Kelsen's pure theory of law.

According to Merkl, every "legal act" (a term referring to acts of parliament, administrative and judicial decisions) performs at the same time a (constrained) law-applying and an (unconstrained) law-making function. From the perspective of the conditions governing them, legal acts can be arranged hierarchically (such as constitution → legislative acts of parliament → judicial decision). Within the hierarchical structure each act is conditional upon the provisions of the conditioning act, inasmuch as the latter sets the limits for the former. According to both Merkl and Kelsen, the science of law (*Rechtswissenschaft*), drawing on the language of legal acts, can identify the constraints set by the conditioning act and single out those acts that violate the constraints. It cannot (and must not), however, purport to offer any additional guidance to the decision maker, for the choice among alternatives within the constraints established by the conditioning act is left to the decision maker's discretion.

In radicalizing the dynamic model of the pure theory of law, Kelsen's disciple Fritz Sander contends that authorized legal officials alone can make legally valid statements that a decision maker has exceeded his or her discretion. Sander believes that Merkl's hierarchical perspective on the legal system, though reflecting the official's feeling of constraint, is unable to describe purportedly objective limits to the law-making process. Constraints mean nothing more than what the officials say they mean. It follows, that in the process of its own reproduction the legal system paradoxically owes its hierarchical structure to a prior inversion of that structure. Related ideas will be expressed later in the century, albeit in a muted form, in the legal hermeneutics of Joseph Esser and in Niklas Luhmann's sociological theory of law.

Kelsen's pure theory of law is undoubtedly one of the most noteworthy species of legal positivism. Along with perspicuous statements about the identity of the law and the state, and claims about the ideological nature of legal subjectivity, the theory is perhaps still most famous for its rigorous separation of law and morality. While Kelsen regards all natural law theory as based on unwarranted premises, he did not subscribe to the traditional versions of legal positivism either (as found, for example, in the writings of Bierling and Bergbohm). In strictly separating "is" and "ought," Kelsen accuses traditional positivists of reducing the validity of legal norms to a matter of mere social fact (recognition, the power of the state, or whatever). Steering an arduous course between the pitfalls of natural law theory on the one hand and traditional legal positivism on the other, Kelsen tries to establish that the validity of any legal system is dependent on a "basic norm." This hypothetical rule demands that validity be ascribed to those legal regimes that are, by and large, effective. At the most sophisticated stage in the development of his theory, Kelsen conceived the basic norm as a "transcendental condition" for the description of the legal system.

The reference to "transcendental conditions" reflects the influence of neo-Kantianism, the most prominent philosophical school at the turn of the century, on legal theory. Interestingly, most neo-Kantian legal philosophers do not resort to Kant's *Rechtslehre* (which they regarded as evidence of Kant's increasing senility), but to his theory of knowledge. While Rudolf Stammler outlines a purely formal theory of natural law (*richtiges Recht*) and Hermann Cohen – the leading figure in the Marburg school – conceives of his "ethics" in terms of a theory of legal science, the members of the influential Heidelberg School (above all: Windelband, Rickert and Lask) are concerned with a reconstruction of the internal logic of the cultural sciences (*Kulturwissenschaften*). Their basic idea is that just as statements in the natural sciences are related to the value of truth, the validity of statements in the domain of the cultural sciences is dependent on a link to cultural values. Accordingly, all propositions of law turn on the "legal value" or "legal idea" (*Rechtswert* or *Rechtsidee*). Since, following Kant, the conditions of possibility of experience are at the same time the conditions of the possibility of the objects of experience, the "legal value" performs a constitutive function for the identification of valid legal materials. Formulating formal conditions of experience within a distinctive cultural sphere, neo-Kantian theory failed, however, to place any substantive constraints on the law. Although Gustav Radbruch, the most prominent legal philosopher in this context, singles out justice, purpose, and legal certainty as the necessary elements of the idea of law, these elements are all understood as formal characteristics of the law; its content is left to the political process.

The period 1933 to 1945: *"Völkische"* jurisprudence

Turning to Nazi jurisprudence, it must be noted that the Nazi jurist's extraordinary productivity in the field turned on a double-strategy, practical in nature. Whereas new regulations and, of course, the commands of the Führer had to be respected, the received body of statutes was seen as lending itself to extensive reinterpretation. From the enormous bulk of materials in which Nazi jurisprudence attempted to justify the second strategy, two examples are deserving of our attention.

In an influential essay written in 1934, Carl Schmitt offers a demarcation of the new millennium's style of legal reasoning by pitting *konkretes Ordnungsdenken* ("thinking in a concrete institutional order") against "normativism" on the one hand, and "decisionism" on the other. The former, with its hard and fast commitment to general rules, is seen as compensating for a lost sense of order. The latter, Schmitt holds, is based on the assumption that society has to be constantly rescued, by powerful sovereign rulers, from its tendency to lapse into disorder, marked by a normative vacuousness. By comparison, "thinking in a concrete institutional order" presupposes the existence and stability of institutions whose meaning and function cannot be reduced to the language of legal rules. In an institutional order the "normal situation" is prior to the rule governing its preservation. Hence, legal officials can reconstruct an already given statutory language and apply even seemingly vague "concrete legal concepts" (such as "brave soldier" or "dutiful public official") because of their familiarity with the (new) "normal situation."

A similar attempt to provide the Nazi's position on legal interpretation with a theoretical foundation was made by scholars coming from a neo-Hegelian background. Adapting earlier proto-fascist readings of Hegel to the officially favored style of *völkisches Rechtsdenken*, both Binder and Larenz emphasize that the existing legal materials have to be regarded as manifestations of the *völkisch* spirit of the law. Like Schmitt, Larenz holds that *völkisches Rechtsdenken* favors "concrete-general" (that is, vague) legal concepts. Their application provides the medium through which the political will of the *Volk* expresses itself in legal relationships.

The period 1945 to the present: from natural law to postmodernism

The immediate aftermath of World War II gave rise to a brief renaissance of natural law theory. Here the most famous contribution is Radbruch's, which differs from his earlier position in a single respect: as a component of the idea of law, the value of justice is not completely devoid of substantive constraints.

In assessing the validity of legal rules, according to Radbruch, law-applying officials have to balance the claims of legal certainty with those of justice. Legal certainty requires that personal political commitments be suppressed in the process of adjudication; under normal conditions the legislative decision will then prevail. Still, legal certainty is outweighed by considerations of justice if the elementary requirements of the latter are violated by a statue in an intolerable way. The examples provided by Radbruch clearly reflect the Nazi regime: laws contradicting substantive or procedural due process and laws based on a racist bias are evidently unjust and therefore void. It might be added that Radbruch's idea has been repeatedly used by the German Federal Constitutional Court for the retroactive invalidation of administrative decisions that were based on Nazi legislation.

Despite the resurgence of natural law theory, it seems that, on the whole, the Nazi past has had a stifling effect on the further development of German legal thought. Critical attitudes toward traditional legal analysis, re-established in the post-war period, have been challenged as undermining the rule of law. It comes, then, as no surprise that most critical approaches have been relegated to a separate compartment of legal studies, the sociology of law. Nonetheless, mainstream legal theory has changed a good deal in Germany; the field has paid increasing attention to the hermeneutical aspects of interpretation (Esser, Kaufmann, Müller) and has developed the jurisprudence of interest into the jurisprudence of values (Larenz, Canaris). According to the latter, the legal system is not simply the outcome of contingent power struggles, but reflects internal coherence within a hierarchy

351

of principles and sub-principles through which its different levels are connected. Adjudication should reconstruct the complex scheme of principles and appeal to it in contexts where "balancing" is called for. German jurisprudence, therefore, had been prepared for Dworkin's ideas when, in the late 1970s, the reception took place in the writings of Robert Alexy. Earlier, the same author had first introduced Jürgen Habermas's theory of rational discourse to jurisprudential readership, transforming it into a theory of legal argumentation.

Legal philosophers, today, obviously inspired by Rawls's example, have taken up contractarian theories of justice (Höffe). Others are engaged in an elaboration of the best interpretation of the eighteenth- and nineteenth-century tradition, and this replete with rich detail. Still others are studying applied ethics (in particular, in the fields of abortion, euthanasia, and animal rights). Habermas alone, in recent years, has offered a more comprehensive account of the philosophy of law.

For Habermas the law is an indispensable means of disseminating social solidarity in different spheres of social action. Through a reconstruction of the institutional design of modern constitutional democracies, he attempts to show how the private and public autonomy of citizens mutually presuppose each other. In this context, Habermas pays special attention to the relationship between the state and civil society: though functionally more or less independent, the political processes of the state serve as receptors for the major impulses for social change from the "communicative power" released in the public sphere of civil society. The entire legal system is, therefore, depicted as highly dynamic, being constantly nourished by the institutionalized "tension of facticity and validity." It follows that the historically established system of rights is always open to revision.

Instances of "postmodernist" approaches to law and society are currently being formulated under the guise (or should one say "banner"?) of social systems theory. Given postmodern conditions of "fragmentation", Karl-Heinz Ladeur, for example, holds legal decision making should not even attempt to follow a consistent pattern. On the contrary, the conflicting demands of the different subsystems of modern society can only be accommodated in situational acts of balancing. In a similar vein, Gunther Teubner and Helmut Willke, departing from problems of regulatory efficiency, recommend that the legal structure of the modern welfare state should undergo significant transformations. The state should refrain from regulatory intervention and, rather, facilitate the co-operative self-reflection of social systems on locally or functionally specified levels. By comparison, the catalyst for virtually everything in German social systems theory, Niklas Luhmann, claims that the subsystems of modern society necessarily coexist in a state of mutual indifference to each other. Hence, for its reproduction, the legal system depends on exclusive recourse to specific legal communications, whose binary code ("legal/illegal") marks them off from the languages of economy, politics, art, and so on. In order to reveal to itself its own identity, the legal system has to produce descriptions of its own operations. Since the system cannot step outside its own mode of operation, self-description involves a paradox: the line between inside and outside is drawn from the inside. What makes Luhmann's analysis appealing is his idea that most operations of the legal system are devoted to obscure ("invisibilize") paradoxes such as the one alluded to here. And in studying of paradoxes, obfuscations and modes of deparadoxication, Luhmann promotes the Germanic cause of legal deconstruction: a legal system is necessary, not despite the fact that it obscures the undecidability and contradiction of its own operation, but precisely because it does.

Bibliography

Alexy, R. 1986: *Theorie der Grundrechte* [*Theory of Rights*]. Frankfurt/Main: Suhrkamp, 2nd edn.
—— 1983: *A Theory of Legal Argumentation: The Theory of Rational Discourse as Theory of Legal Justification.* Oxford: Clarendon Press, New York: Oxford University Press.
Ellscheid, G. and Hassemer, W. 1974: *Interessenjurisprudenz* [*Jurisprudence of Interests*]. Darmstadt: Wissenschaftliche Buchgesellschaft.
Höffe, O. 1987: *Politische Gerechtigkeit. Grundlegung einer kritischen Philosophie von Recht und Staat* [*Political Justice. Groundwork of a Critical Philosophy of Law and State*]. Frankfurt/Main: Suhrkamp.
Kelsen, H. 1934: *Reine Rechtslehre. Einleitung in die Rechtswissenschaftliche Problematik.* Leipzig and Vienna; ed. S. L. Paulson, Aalen: Scientia, 1985; tr. B. L. Paulson and S. L. Paulson, *Introduction to the Problems of Legal Theory*, Oxford: Clarendon Press, 1992.
Kersting, W. 1993: *Wohlgeordnete Freiheit. Immanuel Kants Rechts- und Staatsphilosophie* [*Well-Ordered Liberty. Immanuel Kant's Philosophy of Law and the State*]. Frankfurt/Main: Suhrkamp, 3rd edn.
Krawietz, W. (ed.) 1976: *Theorie und Technik der Begriffsjurisprudenz* [*The Theory and Technique of Conceptual Jurisprudence*]. Darmstadt: Wissenschaftliche Buchgesellschaft.
Ladeur, K.-H. 1989: From universalistic law to the law of uncertainty: on the decay of the legal order's "totalizing teleology" as treated in the methodological discussion and its critique from the left. In C. Joerges and D. M. Trubek (eds), *Critical Legal Thought; an American–German debate.* Baden-Baden: Nomos, 567–90.
Larenz, K. 1979: *Methodenlehre der Rechtswissenschaft* [*Methodology of Legal Science*]. Berlin, Heidelberg, New York: Springer, 4th edn.
—— K. 1987: *Rechts- und Staatsphilosophie der Gegenwart* [*The Philosophy of Law and the State of the Present*]. Berlin: Juncker & Dünnhaupt.
Luhmann, N. 1985: *A Sociological Theory of Law.* London: Routledge & Kegan Paul.
Ogorek, R. 1989: Inconsistencies and consistencies in 19th century legal theory. In C. Joerges and D. M. Trubek (eds), *Critical Legal Thought: an American–German debate.* Baden-Baden: Nomos, 13–38.
Radbruch, G. 1973: *Rechtsphilosophie*, ed. E. Wolf and H.-P. Schneider [*Legal Philosophy*, which includes in addition to a revised 3rd edn. of *Legal Philosophy* (1933) major post-War articles]. Stuttgart: K. F. Köhler, 8th edn.
Riebschläger, K. 1968: *Die Freirechtsbewegung. Zur Entwicklung einer soziologischen Rechtsschule* [*The Free Law Movement. On the Development of a Sociological School of Jurisprudence*]. Berlin: Duncker & Humblot.
Rüthers, B. 1988: *Entartetes Recht. Rechtslehren und Kronjuristen im Dritten Reich* [*Degenerate Law*]. München: Beck.
Siep, L. 1992: *Praktische Philosophie im Deutschen Idealismus* [*Practical Philosophy of German Idealism*]. Frankfurt/Main: Suhrkamp.
Somek, A. 1992: *Rechtssystem und Republik. Über die politische Funktion des systematischen Rechtsdenkens* [*Legal System and Republic. On the Political Function of Systematic Legal Thought*]. Vienna and New York: Springer.

Teubner, G. 1992: *Law as an Autopoietic System*. Oxford: Blackwell.

Willke, H. 1986: Three types of legal structure. The conditional, the purposive, and the relational program. In G. Teubner (ed.), *Dilemmas of Law in a Welfare State*. Berlin and New York: de Gruyter, 280–98.

23

Marxist theory of law

ALAN HUNT

The object of Marxist theory of law

Marxist theory of law asks: what part, if any, does law play in the reproduction of the structural inequalities which characterize capitalist societies? It is thus a project which does not occupy the same field as orthodox jurisprudence; its agenda is necessarily different. Thus Marxist theory of law cannot simply replace elements within liberal legalism in order to produce an alternative theory and it does not address the same questions which motivate liberal jurisprudence. It has mainly played an oppositional role. Its most frequent manifestations have been directed toward providing a critique of liberal legal thought. The critique is "oppositional" in the sense that it has been directed at controverting the conventional wisdom of liberal legalism.

Marxist theory of law exhibits a number of general themes which have been reworked into new and variant combinations. In summary form the major themes which are present in Marx's own writing and in subsequent Marxist approaches to law are:

1　Law is inescapably political, or law is one form of politics.
2　Law and state are closely connected; law exhibits a relative autonomy from the state.
3　Law gives effect to, mirrors or is otherwise expressive of the prevailing economic relations.
4　Law is always potentially coercive and manifests the state's monopoly of the means of coercion.
5　The content and procedures of law manifest, directly or indirectly, the interests of the dominant class(es).
6　Law is ideological; it both exemplifies and provides legitimation to the embedded values of the dominant class(es).

These six themes are present in Marxist writings on law in a variety of different forms and, in particular, with very different degrees of sophistication and complexity. This point can be illustrated by taking theme 5, concerning the connection between law and class interests. In a simple version this finds expression in the

355

claim that law gives effect to the interests of the capitalist class and that law is thus an instrument through which the capitalist class imposes its will. This theme is also present in more sophisticated forms which stress that the content of law can be read as an expression of the complex dynamic of class struggle. As such it comes to include legal recognition of the interests of subordinated classes secured through struggle.

These themes raise issues excluded or ignored in orthodox jurisprudence; for example, the focus on the connection between law and politics or between law and class interests either adds to or redirects the concerns of jurisprudence. Other themes have more wide-ranging implications for legal theory. For example, the insistence on the ideological nature of law involves an entirely different way of looking at the texts, discourses and practices of law. Such a point of departure disallows a positivist acceptance of legal rules as the taken-for-granted primary reality of law.

Outline of a Marxist theory of law

What follows is an outline of a Marxist theory of law which concentrates on achieving an integrated theoretical structure from the main themes present in the diverse versions of Marxist theory of law. It is *not* an attempt to offer a précis of Marx's own writings on law. It is important to stress that Marx did not produce anything that could be called a "theory of law." Law was never a sustained object of Marx's attention although he did have much to say about law that remains interesting and relevant (Cain and Hunt, 1979; Vincent, 1993).

The selection of a starting point is the most important step in the development of any theory. Space does not permit a full defense of the starting point selected. The claim is that Marxism is a rigorously sociological theory in that its general focus of attention is on social relations. Law is a specific form of social relation. It is certainly not a "thing," nor is it reducible to a set of institutions. In one of many similar passages Marx stated his relational approach in the following terms:

> Society does not consist of individuals, but expresses the sum of interrelations, the relations within which these individuals stand . . . To be a slave, to be a citizen are social characteristics, relations between human beings A & B. Human being A, as such, is not a slave. He is a slave in and through society. (*Marx, 1973, p. 265*)

The relational approach to law posits that legal relations are first and foremost a variety or type of social relation that are identified by a specific set of characteristics that separates them from other types of social relations. Legal relations take the form of relations between "legal subjects." The legal subject does not coincide with the natural person; thus until relatively recently women were either not legal subjects or were constrained within a specific legal status which imposed duties whilst granting few rights. It should be noted in passing that there is an important connection between "legal subject" and "citizen," which is neither homologous nor opposed.

The most simple instance of the legal subject is that of the adult person recognized by a court as the bearer of rights and thus able to initiate litigation. Many social institutions are endowed with legal subjectivity or "legal personality," for example, the corporation is accorded the status of a legal subject. It is also important to emphasize the wide variety of legal statuses into which people and groups are interpellated; defendants, witnesses, trustees, beneficiaries, agents, owners, and a host of other legal statuses are summoned into being. Legal interpellation may itself be constitutive of a social relation as is the case with the formation of a corporation where law is performative (a legal act actually changing the position of the parties). In other circumstances the legal interpellation does not create a social relation but rather it affects the terms, conditions and limits under which that relationship is lived out and struggled around.

A legal relation always generates a potential "mode of regulation"; it is "potential" in the sense that many legal relations may be wholly or largely passive in that the legal dimension of the relation may play no part at all in the way the concrete social relations is lived out. Law provides a wide variety of different modes of regulation of social relations. In many instances this is directly apparent in the conventional classification of types of law; thus criminal law employs different agents (for example, police) and imposes different sanctions (for example, imprisonment) from those techniques associated with private law (for example, litigation, damages). The concept of a mode of regulation serves to focus attention on law as an ongoing set of practices which contribute to the reproduction and transformation of social relations.

The major ingredient of a legal mode of regulation is the form which flows from the attribution of rights to interpellated legal subjects. The discourse of rights needs to be understood as consisting of a bundle of rights/duties distributed between legal subjects located within social relations. Both rights and duties embrace a variety of different types of attributions whose significance is that they not only provide a relatively unified legal discourse which can handle a range of different social relations, but which also overlap with wider normative and moral discourses. This interface of legal and moral rights provides for both the authoritative determinations of rights/duties in litigation, a meta-discourse which provides legitimation and also a terrain, a contestation, and change in which new or variant claim-rights are articulated and asserted.

The significance of the rights-grounded discourse is that it provides an integrated field within which all forms of social relations can be made subject to a common discursive apparatus. This is not to suggest that rights discourse is or can be fully coherent or free from internal tensions or contradictions. One of the major contributions of the "critical legal studies" school has been to highlight the internal incoherence and contradictions within the discourse of rights (Hutchinson, 1989). It is important to note that rights-discourse figures in other forms of dispute handling outside litigation such as negotiation and public debate.

Law and legal process have the potential to change the relative positions of legal subjects within social relations; in this basic sense law is a distributive mechanism. Again it is necessary to stress "potential" since it does not follow that change in legal capacity necessarily effects positions within social relations. This is particularly obvious where law "fails", for example, in not achieving an adequate mechanism to enforce child support payments by deserting fathers. The general process of legal distribution is that interests and claims are transcribed into rights discourses, and in that process the capacities of legal subjects are confirmed or varied. Law is a major distributive mechanism by varying the relative positions and capacities of the participants in social relations. Thus one important dimension of legal regulation is that it regulates the boundaries or spheres of competence of other modes of regulation. This process frequently manifests itself in the never ending process in which legal discourse invokes and redraws the boundary between the public and the private.

It is important to emphasize the quest for consistency in legal doctrine. Engels formulated the issue clearly in his letter to Conrad Schmidt:

> In a modern state, law must not only correspond to the general economic conditions and be its expression, but must also be an *internally coherent* expression which does not, owing to internal conflicts, contradict itself. (*Cain and Hunt, 1979, p. 57; Marx and Engels, 1975, p. 399; emphasis in original*)

Two important points follow. First, it explains why law is rarely if ever the direct instrumental expression of the interests of a dominant class. Second, it is the persistent quest for coherence, rather than its realization that is significant. Indeed a necessary tension between competing versions of legal boundaries, such as that between public and private, ensures the flexibility and responsiveness of law to changing contexts and pressures.

Marxism's central concerns are: (1) to explain the relations of subordination or domination that characterize particular historical epochs; (2) to account for the persistence and reproduction of these relations; and (3) to identify the conditions for ending these relations and realizing emancipated social relations. The method and content of a Marxist theory of law will necessarily be concerned to explore the role of law in these three areas.

Alternative Marxist approaches to law

The characteristics of this relational theory can be illustrated by contrasting it with two other variants which have been influential in the history of Marxist work on law. The first draws on Marx's imagery of base and superstructure which distinguishes between "the economic structure of society," which forms the base or "real foundation," "on which rises a legal and political superstructure and to which correspond definite forms of social consciousness" (Marx, 1971, p. 21). Law is assigned to the "superstructure" which "reflects" the "base" or "economic structure." Thus it is the economic structure which determines or has causal priority in determining the character and content of the law (and all other features of the superstructure).

The base–superstructure thesis is problematic in a number of respects. The notion of base–superstructure is a metaphor; it seeks to advance our understanding of social relations by importing an analogy which involves imagery derived from thinking about society as if it were a building or a construction project. The base–superstructure metaphor runs the risk of committing Marxism to an "economic determinism"; the objection to which is that it proposes a causal law (analogous to classical scientific laws) which asserts the causal priority of the economic base over all other dimensions of social life (Williams, 1977, pp. 83–9). There is a "weaker" version of the idea of determination in which "determination" is conceived as a mechanism whereby "limits" are set within which variation may be the result of causal forces other than the economic structure. Thus the economic base is pictured as prescribing the boundaries or as setting objective limits for the different elements of the superstructure. This sense of determination is theoretically more attractive because it does not foreclose or pre-determine the causal relationship that exists between the different facets of social life.

Marx and Engels both occasionally came close to this softer version of "determination". Perhaps its best known formulation is provided by Engels's letter to Bloch (September 21, 1890):

> According to the materialist conception of history, the *ultimately* determining factor in history is the production and reproduction of real life. Neither Marx nor I have ever asserted more than this . . . The economic situation is the basis, but the various elements of the superstructure – political forms of the class struggle and its results, such as constitutions . . . juridical forms, and especially the reflections of all these real struggles in the brains of the participants, political, legal, philosophical theories . . . also exercise their influence upon the course of the historical struggles and in many cases determine their *form* in particular. There is an interaction of all these elements in which, amid all the endless host of accidents . . . the economic movement is finally bound to assert itself. (*Marx and Engels, 1975, pp. 394–5; emphasis in original*)

This version of the determination thesis is usually referred to as the "theory of relative autonomy"; its central idea is that law and other elements of the superstructure can have causal effects in that they "react back" upon the economic base which, however, still retains causal priority, but now only "ultimately." Marx and Engels also used phrases such as "in the last instance" and "in the final analysis" to express this long-run sense of the determination by the economic.

Many Marxist writers on law have been attracted to this "softer" version of determinism. Its merit is that it retains some sense of the causal weight or importance of the economic order while at the same time it provides an invitation to explore the intriguing specificity of law.

Despite the undoubted attractions of "soft determinism" plus "relative autonomy" it cannot provide a satisfactory starting point for Marxist theory of law. In its simplest form the objection is that it says both too much and too little. It says too much in that instead of providing a theoretical starting point it, rather, imposes a conclusion for each and every piece of investigation, namely, that the economic is determinant. But it says too little because it offers no account of the mechanisms whereby this ultimate or long-run causality is produced.

A quite different starting point for a Marxist theory of law was employed by the early Soviet jurist, Evgeny Pashukanis, who, in the 1920s, produced what still remains the most comprehensive Marxist theorization of law (Beirne and Sharlet, 1980; Pashukanis, 1978). Pashukanis set out to model his theory on the framework that Marx had employed in Volume I of *Capital* which opens with a rigorous discussion of the concept "commodity" (Marx, 1970, ch. 1); he sought to elucidate "the deep interconnection between the legal form and the commodity form" and for this reason his theory is often referred to as the "commodity form" theory (Pashukanis, 1978, p. 63). His key proposition was that "the legal relation between subjects is simply the reverse side of the relation between products of labour which have become commodities" (1978, p. 85). In its simplest form Pashukanis viewed the contract as the legal expression of this primary relationship of capitalism, namely the commodity exchange. "Commodity exchange" and "legal contract" exist in a homologous relation; they are mutually dependent.

The most succinct evaluation of Pashukanis is that while he correctly identified law as a social relation, he blocked that insight by reducing law to a single and inappropriate relation, the commodity relation. The root source of both his success and his failure was the rather simplistic reading of Marx, in general, and of *Capital*, in particular, on which he relied. He treated Marx's opening discussion of the commodity as if Marx was propounding an economic history of capitalism which traced its development from the general growth of "simple commodity production." For Marx the famous chapter on commodities was a means of approaching what he regarded as the most basic relationships constitutive of capitalism, namely, capitalist relations of production; for this reason the standard Marxist criticism of Pashukanis is that he reverses Marx's priority of production relations over commodity relations. Thus in grounding his analysis of legal relations upon the homology with commodity relations Pashukanis skewed his whole subsequent analysis.

That Pashukanis took this wrong turn can be readily explained. The most important feature of his work, both theoretically and politically, is his contention that law is irredeemably bourgeois; that is law is especially and distinctively associated with the existence of capitalism. Hence for Pashukanis there could be no post-capitalist law; thus the idea of "socialist law" was both unnecessary and contradictory. The alternative Marxist view is that socialism would involve the development of new sets of relationships and these in turn would necessitate new forms of legal relations. For example, socialism would be likely to accord increased importance to a range of semi-autonomous bodies which would operate with large measure of self-regulation whilst drawing its resources from public sources; such bodies would require new legal property forms. To recover the general relational orientation proposed by Pashukanis it is necessary to free Marxist theory of law from the narrow focus on commodity relations.

Ideology as law and law as ideology

Law is ideological in a double sense; law is ideologically constructed and is itself a significant (and possibly major) bearer of ideology. This can be expressed in two theses:

1 Law is created within an existing ideological field in which the norms and values associated with social relations are continuously asserted, debated, and generally struggled over.
2 The law itself is a major bearer of ideological messages which, because of the general legitimacy accorded to law, serve to reinforce and legitimate the ideology which it carries.

Ideology is not falsity or false consciousness, nor is it a direct expression or "reflection" of economic interests. Rather ideology is a contested grid or competing frame of reference through which people think and act. The dominant ideology is the prevailing influence which forms the "common sense" of the period and thus appears natural, normal, and right. The key project of every dominant ideology is to cement together the social formation under the leadership of the dominant class; it is this process which Gramsci called hegemony (Gramsci, 1971).

The content of legal rules provides a major instance of the condensation of ideology. Law has two important attributes as an ideological process. First, it offers a deep authoritative legitimation through the complex interaction whereby it both manifests a generalized legitimacy, separated from the substantive content of its constituent rules and, on the other hand, confers legitimacy. Modern democratic law involves a change in the form of legitimacy itself; it involves a movement towards impersonal, formal legitimation of social relations in which "law" becomes increasingly equated with "reason." Increasingly the legitimation of social order appeals to law simply because it is law, and, as such, provides the grounds for the obligations of obedience by citizens. Law also comes to be seen as the embodiment of the bond between citizen and nation, the people-nation, as law both constitutes and expresses the state's sovereignty.

The foregoing discussion of legal ideology makes no claim to completeness; it does, however, serve to put in place two major themes: first the doubly ideological character of law; and second the need for attention to the historical dynamic whereby the role and significance of legal ideology has expanded with modern democratic law (Collins, 1982, ch. 3; Hunt, 1985, 1991; Poulantzas, 1978, pp. 76–93; Sumner, 1979, chs 7 and 8).

Law and state

The relational approach highlights the importance of the law-state connection. It seeks to find a way of furthering our grasp of a connection which is on the one

361

hand close, but within which a significant degree of autonomy and separation of law from the state is manifest. Orthodox jurisprudence tends to be preoccupied with the issue of the identification and legitimation of the boundaries of legal control of individual conduct.

The state is an institutional complex whose dynamic emerges from the tensions within and between state institutions (Poulantzas, 1973; Jessop, 1990). Coexisting and competing projects are pursued by different state agencies. Whilst some are directed towards the cohesion of the state, such as those pursued in the course of the political projects of governments, it is equally common for agencies to operate in such a way as to create spheres of autonomy. The bureaucratic imperatives within state institutions frequently favour such functional separation. The legal system has a distinctive project of state unity whose ideological source stems from the theory of sovereignty. The unity of the state is always a project, but it is one which is never realized.

The most difficult feature of the law–state relationship to give an account of is the manner in which the state is both within and outside the law. It is not just a matter of pointing to the persistent reality of state illegality, but even more important of the large sphere of state action which is not unlawful but which is not subject to legal regulation. The really important issue is the way in which law marks out its own self-limitations. The ideological core of the modern state lies in the varieties of the idea of a state *based on law* (*Rechtsstaat*) epitomized by the constitutional doctrine of the rule of law. The considerable variation in the degree of judicial review of state action that exists between modern capitalist states should be noted.

It is within the law–state relationship that the important but difficult question of the relationship between coercion and consent needs to be posed. Marxists have historically stressed the repressive character of law; they have done so in order to redress the blindness of most liberal jurisprudence which has systematically played down the role of coercion and repression in the modern state. But in reacting against the omissions of liberal theory some Marxists have come perilously close to simply reversing liberalism's error by equating law with repression. The really difficult problem is to grasp the way in which repression is present in the course of the "normal" operation of modern legal systems.

One possible explanation along these lines posits a fall-back thesis: normally law operates more or less consensually, but in exceptional moments the repressive face of law is revealed. Such an account emphasizes the role of special powers and emergency legislation as providing the means for the legal integration of repression. This focus on legal exceptionalism is important, but potentially misleading. It draws attention to the capacity of the state to suspend the operation of democratic process. But it draws too stark a distinction between normal and exceptional conditions. A more adequate view draws attention to the fact that a wide range of legal procedures are coercive and where they are deployed systematically set up patterns of repression. For example, the role of courts as debt enforcement agencies, able to order repossession or grant seizure powers runs counter to the liberal image of civil law as a mechanism for resolving disputes.

362

Economic relations and the law

A core question for Marxist theory of law is: what part does law play in the production and reproduction of capitalist economic relations? A number of key legal relations form part of the conditions of existence for capitalist economic relations without which they could not function. Law provides and guarantees a *regime of property*. The expansion of the forms of capital and their complex routes of circulation require such a regime which protects multiple interests falling short of absolute ownership.

Legal relations have distinctive effects. The most important of these is the extent to which legal relations actually constitute economic relations. The most significant example is the formation of the modern corporation with limited liability; these are legal creations in the important sense that it is precisely the ability to confer a legal status which limits the liability of participants that makes the relationship not only distinctive but a viable vehicle for the co-operation of capital drawn from a range of sources (Hunt, 1988). Similarly, the modern contract must embrace contract planning for a range of potential variables. The same consideration affects the expansion of issues embraced in collective agreements between labor and capital which necessitates a level of detailed specification that cannot be sustained within traditional notions of custom and practice.

It is important to stress the complex interaction that exists between legal and economic relations. Some of these features can be briefly indicated. Legal doctrines and processes must make provision for the interrelations of capital, through commercial law, insurance, banking, and other financial services. One traditional way of identifying these activities is to speak of the conflict-resolution role of law. But it may be wise to avoid this formulation since it focusses too narrowly on litigation and the courts. It is probably more helpful to think of these mechanisms as background conditions which constitute the framework within which economic relations are conducted.

Law also provides the central conceptual apparatus of property rights, contract, and corporate personality which play the double role of both constituting a coherent framework for legal doctrine and, at the same time, provides significant components of the ideological discourses of the economy. Conceptions of rights, duties, responsibility, contract, property, and so on, are persistent elements in public discourses. The inter-penetration of legal and non-legal features of these discourses play a significant part in explaining the impact of legal conceptions on popular consciousness.

Legal relations and class relations

Another important question for Marxist theory of law is: what contribution, if any, does law make to the reproduction of class relations? This requires attention to the impact of law upon the pattern of social inequality and subordination. Two general theses can be advanced:

363

1   The aggregate effects of law in modern democratic societies work to the systematic disadvantage of the least advantaged social classes.
2   The content, procedures, and practice of law constitute an *arena of struggle* within which the relative positions and advantages of social classes is changed over time.

The important point to be stressed is that these two theses are neither incompatible nor contradictory; they are *both* true at one and the same time. The first thesis that law disadvantages the disadvantaged operates at all levels of legal processes. It will be assumed that these unequal consequences are either self-evident or so well evidenced in empirical studies as not to require support here. Substantive inequalities disadvantaging the working class (and other subordinate categories) are embedded in the content of legal rules. The procedures of law, the discretion of legal agents, the remedies and sanctions of law and other dimensions manifest unequal social effects. In order to produce a complete analysis of law's capacity to participate in and to reinforce the reproduction of social inequality it is necessary to trace the detailed interaction between the different processes involved.

The second thesis about law as an arena of struggle requires some means of registering and establishing the connection between economic interests and the categories of legal doctrine. Here attention needs to be directed toward the manner in which social interests are translated into rights-claims and the degree of "fit" between those claims and the prevailing form of law expressed in existing legal rights. Analysis of this type generates hypotheses such as: claims capable of translation into a discourse of individual rights and those interests congruent with existing rights categories are more likely to succeed than claims not matching these characteristics.

Conclusions

This essay has outlined a general framework for a Marxist theory of law. There are inevitably issues that have been omitted. Most significantly almost nothing has been mentioned about what Marx himself said about law, or about the history of Marxist writing and debate on law. Another omission concerns the relationship between Marxist theory of law and orthodox jurisprudence. The agendas of Marxist theory and jurisprudence overlap but do not converge. Marxism gives prominence to issues omitted or marginalized within jurisprudence such as the repressive role of law and the fundamentally political character of law. In these respects Marxism can provide a much needed supplement to jurisprudence by its stress on the rootedness or connectedness of law with social, cultural, and economic relations. It provides a powerful source of resistance to the prevalent tendency within orthodox jurisprudence to treat law as disconnected, even autonomous. Marxism further refutes the timeless or ahistorical quality of much liberal jurisprudence. Marxism insists that the role and place of law are always a consequence of a concrete and historically specific dynamic of the interaction of institutions and practices.

If Marxism supplements jurisprudence, it should not simply seek to negate or displace orthodox jurisprudence. The pervasive jurisprudential issues, such as the grounds for the obligations of citizens to obey law, the means of determining the proper limits of state action and the conditions under which it is permissible to restrain the conduct of citizens are also important questions for Marxism. The renewal of socialism requires, not the withering away of law, but the realization of a legal order that enhances and guarantees the conditions of political and economic democracy, that facilitates democratic participations and restrains bureaucratic and state power. The implication is that a Marxist approach to law will be concerned, on the one hand, with characteristically jurisprudential issues but will also be concerned about the potential contributions of legal strategies to achieving effective political strategies for the social movements that reflect the Marxist political and ethical commitment to the poor and the oppressed.

Bibliography

Althusser, L. 1969: *For Marx*. Harmondsworth: Penguin.

Althusser, L. and Balibar, E. 1970: *Reading Capital*. London: New Left Books.

Beirne, P. and Sharlet, R. (eds) 1980: *Pashukanis: selected writings on Marxism and law*. London: Academic Press.

Cain, M. and Hunt, A. 1979: *Marx and Engels on Law*. London: Academic Press.

Collins, H. 1982: *Marxism and Law*. Oxford: Oxford University Press.

Cutler, A., Hindess, B., Hirst, P., and Hussain, A. 1977: *Marx's "Capital" and Capitalism Today*. London: Routledge & Kegan Paul, 2 vols.

Gramsci, A. 1971: *Selections from the Prison Notebooks of Antonio Gramsci*, ed. Q. Hoare and G. Nowell-Smith, London: Lawrence & Wishart.

Hunt, A. 1985: The ideology of law. *Law & Society Review*, 19, 11–37.

—— 1988: On legal relations and economic relations. In R. N. Moles (ed.) *Law and Economics*, Stuttgart: Franz Steiner.

—— 1991: Marxism, law, legal theory and jurisprudence. In P. Fitzpatrick (ed.), *Dangerous Supplements: resistance and renewal in jurisprudence*, London: Pluto Press.

Hutchinson, A. (ed.) 1989: *Critical Legal Studies*. Totowa, NJ: Rowman & Littlefield.

Jessop, R. 1990: *State Theory: putting capitalist states in their place*. Cambridge: Polity Press.

Marx, K. 1970: *Capital*. London: Lawrence & Wishart, vol. I.

—— 1971: *A Contribution to the Critique of Political Economy*, ed. M. Dobb, London: Lawrence & Wishart.

—— 1973: *Grundrisse: introduction to the critique of political economy*. Harmondsworth: Penguin.

Marx, K. and Engels, F. 1975: *Marx–Engels Selected Correspondence*. Moscow: Progress Publishers.

Pashukanis, E. 1978: *Law and Marxism*, ed. C. Arthur, London: Ink Links.

Poulantzas, N. 1973: *Political Power and Social Classes*. London: New Left Books.

—— 1978: *State, Power, Socialism*. London: New Left Books.

Sumner, C. 1979: *Reading Ideologies*. London: Academic Press.

Vincent, A. 1993: Marx and law. *Journal of Law and Society*, 20 (4), 371–97.

Williams, R. 1977: *Marxism and Literature*. Oxford: Oxford University Press.

Further reading

Beirne, P. and Quinney, R. (eds) 1982: *Marxism and Law*. New York: John Wiley.

Fine, R. 1984: *Democracy and the Rule of Law: liberal ideals and Marxist critiques*. London: Pluto Press.

Geras, N. 1989: The controversy about Marx and justice. In A. Callinicos (ed.), *Marxist Theory*. Oxford: Oxford University Press.

Hirst, P. 1979: *On Law and Ideology*. London: Macmillan.

Sumner, C. 1979: *Reading Ideologies: an investigation into the Marxist theory of ideology and law*. London: Academic Press.

Sypnowich, C. 1990: *The Concept of Socialist Law*. Oxford: Oxford University Press.

24

Deconstruction

J. M. BALKIN

Deconstruction has a broader, more popular, and a narrower, more technical, sense. The latter refers to a series of techniques for reading texts developed by Jacques Derrida, Paul de Man, and others; these techniques, in turn, are connected to a set of philosophical claims about language and meaning. However, as a result of the popularity of these techniques and theories, the verb "deconstruct" is now often used more broadly as a synonym for criticizing or demonstrating the incoherence of a position.

Deconstruction made its first inroads in the United States through departments of literary criticism, which sought new strategies for interpreting literary texts. As a result, deconstruction became associated and sometimes confused with other trends, including reader response theory, which argues that a text's meaning is produced through the reader's process of encountering it.

In Europe, on the other hand, deconstruction was understood as a response to structuralism; it is therefore sometimes referred to as a "poststructuralist" approach. Structuralism argued that individual thought was shaped by linguistic structures. It therefore denied or at least severely de-emphasized the relative autonomy of subjects in determining cultural meanings; indeed, it seemed virtually to dissolve the subject into the larger forces of culture. Deconstruction attacked the assumption that these structures of meaning were stable, universal, or ahistorical. However, it did not challenge structuralism's views about the cultural construction of human subjects. Social theories that attempt to reduce human thought and action to cultural structures are sometimes called "antihumanist." Ironically, then, deconstruction suffered the curious fate of being an antihumanist theory that nevertheless was often understood in the United States as making the radically subjectivist claim that texts mean whatever a person wants them to mean. The misunderstandings that deconstruction has engendered are partly due to the obscurity of expression that often distinguishes the work of its adherents.

Despite Derrida's insistence that deconstruction is not a method, but an activity of reading, deconstruction has tended to employ discernible techniques. Many deconstructive arguments revolve around the analysis of conceptual oppositions. A famous example is the opposition between writing and speech (Derrida, 1976). The deconstructor looks for the ways in which one term in the opposition has been "privileged" over the other in a particular text, argument, historical tradition, or social practice. One term may be privileged because it is considered the general, normal, central case, while the other is considered special, exceptional, peripheral, or derivative. Something may also be privileged because it is considered more true, more valuable, more important, or more universal than its opposite. Moreover, because things can have more than one opposite, many different types of privilegings can occur simultaneously.

One can deconstruct a privileging in several different ways. For example, one can explore how the reasons for privileging A over B also apply to B, or how the reasons for B's subordinate status apply to A in unexpected ways. One may also consider how A depends upon B, or is actually a special case of B. The goal of these exercises is to achieve a new understanding of the relationship between A and B, which, to be sure, is always subject to further deconstruction.

Legal distinctions are often disguised forms of conceptual oppositions, because they treat things within a legal category differently from those outside the category. One can use deconstructive arguments to attack categorical distinctions in law by showing that the justifications for the distinction undermine themselves, that categorical boundaries are unclear, or that these boundaries shift radically as they are placed in new contexts of judgment (Schlag, 1988).

Perhaps the most important use of deconstruction in legal scholarship has been as a method of ideological critique. Deconstruction is useful here because ideologies often operate by privileging certain features of social life while suppressing or de-emphasizing others. Deconstructive analyses look for what is de-emphasized, overlooked, or suppressed, in a particular way of thinking or in a particular set of legal doctrines. Sometimes they explore how suppressed or marginalized principles return in new guises. For example, where a field of law is thought to be organized around a dominant principle, the deconstructor looks for exceptional or marginal counter-principles that have an unacknowledged significance, and which, if taken seriously, might displace the dominant principle (Unger, 1986; Frug, 1984; Dalton, 1985; Peller, 1985; Balkin, 1987).

Sometimes deconstructive analyses closely study the figural and rhetorical features of texts to see how they interact with or comment upon the arguments made in the text. The deconstructor looks for unexpected relationships between different parts of a text, or loose threads that at first glance appear peripheral yet often turn out to undermine or confuse the argument. A deconstructor may consider the multiple meanings of key words in a text, etymological relationships between words, and even puns to show how the text speaks with different (and often conflicting) voices (Balkin, 1990b, 1989). Behind these techniques is a more general probing and questioning of familiar oppositions between philosophy (reason) and rhetoric, or between the literal and the figural. Although we often see the figural and rhetorical elements of a text as merely supplementary and peripheral to the underlying logic of its argument, closer analysis often reveals that metaphor, figure, and rhetoric play an important role in legal and political reasoning. Often the figural and metaphorical elements of legal texts powerfully support or undermine the reasoning of these texts.

Deconstruction does not show that all texts are meaningless, but rather that they are overflowing with multiple and often conflicting meanings. Similarly, deconstruction does not claim that concepts have no boundaries, but that their boundaries can be parsed in many different ways as they are inserted into new contexts of judgment. Although people use deconstructive analyses to show that particular distinctions and arguments lack normative coherence, deconstruction does not show that all legal distinctions are incoherent. Deconstructive arguments do not necessarily destroy conceptual oppositions or conceptual distinctions. Rather, they tend to show that conceptual oppositions can be reinterpreted as a form of nested opposition (Balkin, 1990a). A nested opposition is an opposition in which the two terms bear a relationship of conceptual dependence or similarity as well as conceptual difference or distinction. Deconstructive analysis attempts to explore how this similarity or this difference is suppressed or overlooked. Hence deconstructive analysis often emphasizes the importance of context in judgment, and the many changes in meaning that accompany changes in contexts of judgment.

Deconstruction's emphasis on the proliferation of meanings is related to the deconstructive concept of iterability. Iterability is the capacity of signs (and texts) to be repeated in new situations and grafted onto new contexts. Derrida's aphorism "iterability alters" (Derrida, 1977) means that the insertion of texts into new contexts continually produces new meanings that are both partly different from and partly similar to previous understandings. (Thus, there is a nested opposition between them.) The term "play" is sometimes used to describe the resulting instability in meaning produced by iterability.

Although deconstructive arguments show that conceptual oppositions are not fully stable, they do not and cannot show that all such oppositions can be jettisoned or abolished, for the principle of nested opposition suggests that a suppressed conceptual opposition will usually reappear in a new guise. Moreover, although all conceptual oppositions are potentially deconstructible in theory, not all are equally incoherent or unhelpful in practice. Rather, deconstructive analysis studies how the use of conceptual oppositions in legal thought has ideological effects: how their instability or fuzziness is disguised or suppressed so that they lend unwarranted plausibility to legal arguments and doctrines. Because all legal distinctions are potentially deconstructible, the question when a particular conceptual opposition or legal distinction is just or appropriate turns on pragmatic considerations. Hence, deconstructive arguments and techniques often overlap with and may even be in the service of other approaches, such as pragmatism, feminism, or critical race theory. (See Article 19, FEMINIST JURISPRUDENCE AND THE NATURE OF LAW; Article 26, LEGAL PRAGMATISM.)

Deconstruction began to have influence in the legal academy with the rise of critical legal studies (CLS) and feminism. (See Article 17, CRITICAL LEGAL STUDIES.) However, deconstructive scholarship eventually became part of an emerging category of postmodern jurisprudence separate from critical legal studies (Balkin, 1989; Schlag, 1991b; Cornell, 1992). (See Article 25, POSTMODERNISM.) Deconstructive arguments in feminism have been more clearly understood as a development and critique of earlier feminist themes; they are best studied in the context of feminist jurisprudence. This difference may have something to do with the continuing vitality of feminism and the waning influence of critical legal studies at the end of the 1980s.

Critical legal scholars were originally attracted to deconstruction for three reasons. First, because deconstruction claimed that meanings were inherently unstable, it seemed to buttress the thesis that legal decision making was indeterminate. This, in turn, appeared to support the familiar critical legal studies (CLS) emphasis on the political character of legal decision making (Dalton, 1985; Frug, 1984). Second, because deconstruction discovered instability and indeterminacy everywhere, it seemed to support the notion that social structures were contingent and social meanings malleable and fluid. This supported CLS claims that legal ideology rested on claims of the "false necessity" of social and legal structures that seemed reasonable in theory but were oppressive in practice (Peller, 1985). Third, because deconstruction seemed to show that all texts undermined their own logic and had multiple meanings that conflicted with each other, deconstruction could be used for the purpose of "trashing" – that is, showing that particular legal doctrines or legal arguments were fundamentally incoherent.

Nevertheless, CLS's appropriation of deconstruction along these lines was problematic. First, the CLS argument seemed to assume an autonomous subject who was manipulating indeterminate language; this was in tension with deconstruction's antihumanist assumptions (Schlag, 1990a). If meaning is beyond the control of the subject, and the subject is socially constructed, it is hard to argue that legal reasoning is a disguise for political reasoning (Balkin, 1991). Second, if the conceptual oppositions of liberal legalism were deconstructible, so too would be the concepts that critical legal studies scholars would offer to replace those of liberal legalism. If deconstruction could be used to show the incoherence of liberal thought, it could equally be used to show the incoherence of any alternative to liberal thought. Third, the contingency and instability are separate concepts, and neither is identical with mutability. Even if legal concepts had multiple and unstable meanings, it did not follow that legal and social structures were easily manipulated and changed.

Similar problems arose in the attempt by British critical legal theorists (Goodrich, 1987, 1990; Douzinas et al., 1991) to use deconstruction to show how rhetorical figures created ideological support for injustice. Ironically, rhetoric becomes viewed with a certain degree of suspicion in this body of work, because rhetoric and figure grant legal writing and legal theory far more legitimacy than they deserve. The problem is that this critique does not seem to distinguish the present legal system and its doctrines from alternatives equally dependent on rhetoric and figural language.

A more promising line of attack for CLS rejected the claim that legal doctrine was unstable and easily malleable. It asserted that political and legal ideologies operated as a form of constraint on individuals. These ideologies constructed a way of thinking about society that prevented individuals from considering other alternative orderings of social and legal structures, and thus limited their thought (Gordon, 1982, 1987; Balkin, 1991). From this standpoint, the determinacy of legal doctrine was quite real, but was produced by the social construction of the subject. CLS's use of deconstruction was also more successful when it concentrated on showing how the justifications for specific legal doctrines and legal distinctions undermined themselves, or how the ideologies underlying legal doctrines marginalized or suppressed important features of human life (Unger, 1986).

Like critical legal scholars, feminists also found deconstruction useful as a method of ideological critique, directed in this case at patriarchal thought and institutions. Feminists could use deconstructive arguments to expose and critique the suppression and marginalization of things associated with women and femininity. Moreover, the iterability and instability of social meanings seemed to undermine any potentially pessimistic suggestions in radical feminism that patriarchy was a unconquerable monolith, or that patriarchy's control of social construction had been so successful that women's very desires and identities were nothing more than the products of male power and privilege. Because social meanings are iterable, they are fluid and unstable, and always present possibilities of interpretive variance and play. Thus, the deconstructive theory of meaning seemed to suggest potential avenues of resistance to patriarchy, and seemed to allow, if not guarantee, the possibility of feminist critique.

Unfortunately, deconstruction tends to destabilize not only patriarchy, but also femininity and feminine identity. Deconstructive arguments that "women's perspectives," "women's interests," or "femininity" have been suppressed or marginalized in existing culture beg two important questions: the first is whether there can be such relatively stable and determinate entities; the second is whether they do not already form nested oppositions with what they are claimed to oppose. Thus, feminists employing deconstructive critiques have been faced with two important, yet potentially conflicting, goals: to identify and honor the feminine that has been suppressed or marginalized, and to recognize the instability and contested nature of the identity so honored (Cornell, 1991). (See Article 25, POSTMODERNISM.)

In 1987 a major academic scandal erupted when Paul De Man's wartime journalism for a pro-Nazi newspaper was discovered. The revelations raised anew the question of deconstruction's relationship to ethics and politics. In literary circles, deconstruction had often been accused of political quietism, because no clear moral or political consequences could be drawn from an interpretive theory that asserted that all meanings were unstable and seemed to deny the certainty of all truths. Some critics even accused De Man of turning to obscurantism to assuage his guilty conscience over collaboration. These accusations particularly affected his close friend Derrida, a Jew, who was a teenager during World War II. Whether directly or indirectly as a result of the De Man affair, Jacques Derrida began to explore the question of the normative uses of deconstruction. In subsequent work (Derrida, 1990) he asserted that deconstruction had always been concerned with normative questions, and cryptically insisted that "Deconstruction is justice".

The connections between deconstruction and social justice were hardly questioned in earlier critical legal studies and feminist scholarship because it was simply assumed that deconstruction was an impressive analytical weapon that could be used to criticize politically regressive positions and "trash" liberal legal thought. Nevertheless, it was not difficult to see that deconstructive arguments could as easily be used by the political right as by the political left, and that they could serve many different political positions (Balkin, 1987, 1990b). By the 1990s several legal scholars began to examine the relationship between deconstruction and social justice more carefully.

Drucilla Cornell (1992) has addressed these questions through a combination of deconstructive and feminist legal theory. Basing her work on a synthesis of Derrida and Emmanuel Levinas, Cornell argues that deconstruction necessarily presupposes an ethical relationship to others; deconstruction requires us not only to recognize others as others but also to be open to them and their perspectives. Thus, deconstruction contains an ethical imperative both to question our own beliefs and to understand the situation and views of others. Cornell's redefinition of deconstruction as a "philosophy of the limit" attempts to make sense of Derrida's claim that deconstruction is justice by arguing that justice is an unpassable difficulty or paradox for any legal system rather than a transcendental ideal.

My own work (Balkin, 1994) argues that Derrida's attempted equation of deconstruction and justice is unsatisfactory. In order for deconstruction to be used for purposes of social and political critique, it has to presume a transcendental value of justice – an inchoate and indeterminate longing for justice that is never fully articulated or satisfied in human law, culture, or convention. Deconstruction is useful as a critical tool because it exposes the gap or inadequation between the transcendental value of justice and its concrete instantiations in human culture.

Pierre Schlag offers a marked contrast to these approaches; he emphasizes deconstruction's antihumanism. Schlag criticizes CLS's use of deconstruction as an intellectual tool employed to promote a normative agenda (Schlag, 1990a, 1991b) because it assumes that CLS scholars choose how deconstruction can be wielded. In fact deconstruction is not a tool but a predicament: legal doctrines are already deconstructed without any human choice or intervention. Moreover, Schlag argues that all normative legal theory – legal theory that purports to offer normative prescriptions about how society should be organized and regulated – is intellectually bankrupt. The rhetorical style of normative legal scholarship assumes that people are in control of what and how they think about normative problems, and that people offer normative directives to others who are persuaded by their cogency and coherence, and who carry them out because of the normative justifications given. Poststructuralism has already shown that this picture of human agency and human reason is inadequate; the goal of legal scholarship should henceforth be to study the stylistics of legal rhetoric and how they have contributed to the perpetuation of the fantasy of rational autonomy (Schlag, 1990b, 1991a).

At first glance, Schlag's attack on normative legal scholarship seems puzzling and even self-defeating, because Schlag appears to be employing the rhetorical form of normative prescription in his own writing. Moreover, if legal scholars are socially constructed to articulate their scholarship in normative rhetoric, why does their obedience to this social construction pose any difficulty? Schlag's position would have critical bite only if he assumed that there is something wrong about this way of thinking from which legal scholars should and could be liberated. In fact, Schlag's point seems to be more sociological and predictive than critical. He thinks that social forces are causing the enterprise of normative legal discourse to disintegrate before our eyes; hence he predicts that legal scholarship will be increasingly unable to engage in normative legal dogmatics without an increasing sense of dislocation (Schlag, 1990b, 1991a).

As the examples in this essay suggest, deconstruction has proven to be a surprisingly adaptable concept serving many different purposes and supporting many different types of legal scholarship. It first appeared in the American legal academy as an esoteric weapon of critical legal scholars. By the 1990s it had been instrumental in the rise of postmodern jurisprudence and some critiques of critical legal studies. Along the way it has fostered debates about ideological and social construction, the connections between post-structuralism and justice, the role of rhetoric in legal thought, the nature of feminine identity, and the health and direction of normative legal scholarship. The deconstructive dictum that "iterability alters" seems to apply particularly to deconstruction itself, for the meaning and importance of deconstruction in legal theory has continually changed as it has been employed in different contexts and situations. As a result, its future and its future applications in the legal academy remain – as a deconstructionist might say – indeterminate.

Bibliography

Balkin, J. M. 1987: Deconstructive practice and legal theory. *Yale Law Journal*, 96, 743.
—— 1989: The footnote. *Northwestern University Law Review*, 83, 275.
—— 1990a: Nested oppositions. *Yale Law Journal*, 99, 1,669.
—— 1990b: Tradition, betrayal, and the politics of deconstruction. *Cardozo Law Review*, 11, 1,113.
—— 1991: Ideology as constraint. *Stanford Law Review*, 43, 1,133.
—— 1994: Transcendental deconstruction, transcendent justice. *Michigan Law Review*, 94, 1,133.
Cornell, D. 1991: *Beyond Accommodation*. New York: Routledge.
—— 1992: *The Philosophy of the Limit*. New York: Routledge.
Dalton, C. 1985: An essay in the deconstruction of contract law. *Yale Law Journal*, 94, 997.
Derrida, J. 1976: *Of Grammatology*. Baltimore: Johns Hopkins University Press.
—— 1977: Ltd., Inc. abc. . . . *Glyph*, vol. II, Baltimore: Johns Hopkins University Press, 162–254.
—— 1990: Force of law: "the mystical foundation of authority." *Cardozo Law Review*, 11, 919.
Douzinas, C., Warrington, R., and McVeigh, S. 1991: *Postmodern Jurisprudence: the law of text in the texts of law*. London: Routledge.
Frug, G. 1984: The ideology of bureaucracy in American law. *Harvard Law Review*, 97, 1,276.
Goodrich, P. 1987: *Legal Discourse: studies in linguistics, rhetoric and legal analysis*. London: Macmillan.
—— 1990: *Languages of Law: from logics of memory to nomadic masks*. London: Weidenfeld & Nicolson.

Gordon, R. 1982: New developments in legal theory. In D. Kairys (ed.), *The Politics of Law.* New York: Pantheon Books, 281–93.

—— 1987: Unfreezing legal reality: critical approaches to law, *Florida Law Review*, 15, 196.

Peller, G. 1985: The metaphysics of American law. *California Law Review*, 73, 1,151.

Schlag, P. 1988: Cannibal moves: an essay in the metamorphoses of the legal distinction. *Stanford Law Review*, 40, 929.

—— 1990a: "Le Hors' de text, c'est moi:" the politics of form and the domestication of deconstruction. *Cardozo Law Review*, 11, 1,631.

—— 1990b: Normative and nowhere to go. *Stanford Law Review*, 43, 167.

—— 1991a: Normativity and the politics of form. *University of Pennsylvania Law Review*, 139, 801.

—— 1991b: The problem of the subject. *Texas Law Review*, 69, 1,627.

Unger, R. M. 1986: *The Critical Legal Studies Movement.* Cambridge, Mass.: Harvard University Press.

25

Postmodernism

DENNIS PATTERSON

Postmodernism is a topic which attracts attention. In fact, it probably attracts too much attention or, one might say, attention of the wrong sort. The discussion of postmodernism has fallen into the hands of those who use it as a vehicle for the propagation of specious ideas, principally about the relationship of language to the world and mind to culture. Often identified with recent French philosophy, in particular deconstruction (see Article 24. DECONSTRUCTION). postmodernism has by and large failed to enjoy the sort of careful attention an analytic treatment provides.

And what is the relevance of postmodernism to legal theory? This entry is devoted to this question. Before I discuss postmodernism and legal theory, I shall advance an analytic account of postmodernism. This account will, I hope, lay the foundation for a discussion of specific philosophical questions in legal theory, questions which are of interest in philosophy generally, and legal theory in more particular ways.

Modernism

In discussing postmodernism, it is helpful to observe two dichotomies: modern/postmodern and modernity/postmodernity. The modern/postmodern (modernism/postmodernism) dichotomy identifies philosophical positions (discussed below). By contrast, postmodernity is an epoch, one in which the defining features of modernity are no longer part of the terrain of human existence. Postmodernity is exemplified in culture by the presence of "pastiche" – the juxtaposition of unrelated elements in various cultural forms. One sees this point most easily in contemporary discussions of architecture. Whether or not we are in postmodernity is, of course, very much open to question. This entry is concerned with the first of these dichotomies, that between modernism and postmodernism.

Modernism is the form of thought identified with the spirit of the Enlightenment. Enamored of the power of science and its attendant control over nature, philosophy in the modern age replaced the medieval emphasis on custom, ritual, authority and cosmology with a self-conscious preoccupation with legitimacy, progress, civility, rationality, and human emancipation.

Modernism is exemplified by three axes which, taken together, provide a three-dimensional perspective (Murphy and McClendon, 1989, p. 191):

1   *Epistemological foundationalism.* This is the view that knowledge can only be justified to the extent it rests on indubitable foundations;
2   *Theory of language.* Language has one of two functions – it represents ideas or states of affairs, or it expresses the attitudes of the speaker;
3   *Individual and community.* "Society" is best understood as an aggregation of "social atoms."

These three components of the modernist picture should not be understood simply as parts of a whole. Each represents not an idea or element in a picture but an axis which, when taken with the others, enables one to see a broad range of thinkers as all-of-a-piece.

As the label suggests, epistemological foundationalism is an epistemological axis, with foundationalism at one end and skepticism at the other. The representative rationalist foundationalist is René Descartes. In essence, Descartes saw the problem of knowledge as a problem about certainty. Separating belief from illusion required a method. For this, Descartes invented the "method of doubt." The process of validating belief required that the belief be submitted to an inner (mental) tribunal for interrogation. Ideas which survived this process of questioning earned the label "clear and distinct." The emphasis on method and validation led, not surprisingly, to the valorization of mathematics, science, and geometry, for it was in these areas that Descartes found that which was most certain: axiom, system, and deduction.

The other foundationalist approach to knowledge is empiricism, which replaces the rationalist emphasis on the formal relations between and among ideas with an appeal to our ordinary, commonsense understanding of experience. When we see an object, we have a retinal impression of a thing which exists in space and time or, to put it more colloquially, we have an experience of another body. Providing an explanation of such an experience (for example, how it is possible, what is involved in "having" the experience) without resort to anything "in" the mind is the gravamen of empiricism. Empiricism is foundationalist in that, for the empiricist, the basis of all knowledge of the world is sense impressions.

Skepticism is not necessarily tied to either the rationalist or the empiricist account of knowledge. In other words, it is a mistake to see the skeptic as one who denies the rationalist or the empiricist account of knowledge. The skeptic does not deny that what is described (on either account) *as* knowledge is *in fact* knowledge. The skeptic denies that we ever *have* knowledge. For example, David Hume believed that, although we had to assume its existence, we could not *prove* the existence of the external world. All we have to base our knowledge of causation on is a constant conjunction of sense impressions. Sense impressions – raw input from the outside world – are the only available "ground" of knowledge. In sum, knowledge on the modernist view is foundational (rationalism or empiricism): for

376

modernists, the only question is whether the foundations are themselves adequate and whether the "logic of construction" from foundations is itself adequate.

The two poles of the language axis stand for the two functions of language: language refers to objects in the world, or is expressive of the attitudes, preferences, or emotions of the speaker. One end of the pole, that of representationalism, is closely linked with epistemological foundationalism. If language is a medium for referring to objects in the world, then knowledge of what something is can be gleaned from the object's representation in language. The point of studying language is to study the ways in which words refer to things.

In their philosophical heyday, modernist philosophers advanced theories of language that saw words as place holders or stand-ins for things. In the twentieth century, the work of Ludwig Wittgenstein before 1929 stands as the paradigmatic expression of the program of "logical atomism," which emphasizes the reduction of the elements of sentences to their constituent parts in the world.

If language is not a means of referring, then what else can it do? If one accepts the claim that language does refer to things in the world – the representationalist view – then what is one to do with ethical discourse? Logical positivists recommended that ethics, together with the whole of "Continental philosophy," be dismissed as "bad poetry." The only alternative was to develop an account of language as a mode of personal expression. Thus, according to logical positivists, moral judgments are not "true", do not "represent" the world; rather, they are expressions of preference, attitude or feeling.

Now to the third modernist axis. To the individualist, society is composed simply of "social atoms," each endowed with needs and desires the existence and identity of which are known (internally) to each. Political economy is best understood from the perspective of individual motivation. All talk of public values, group norms, or "structures" of all manner are eschewed. Methodological individualism is the explanatory model for understanding.

The collectivist (for example, Marxism: see Article 23, MARXIST THEORY OF LAW) counters that far more foundational than the individual is the *class* to which that person belongs. Class is one of many constitutive social facts which shape the individual – make her what she is. At its most radical expression, the individual is not in control of her fate, she is produced by forces beyond her control. At the individual level, agents are capable of making free and rational decisions with respect to their own preferences only to the extent they are able to become aware of and break free from the structures that shape their choices. Taken together, these three axes give us the picture of modern thought shown in figure 25.1.

Postmodern thought

Postmodern thought is any form of reflection which departs significantly from one or more of the three axes of modernist thought. Because different disciplines concentrate on one axis to the exclusion of others, departures from modernist premises are best viewed on a discipline-by-discipline basis. For example, modernist political

Figure 25.1

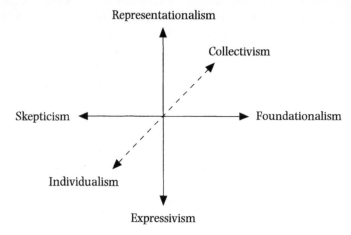

Source: Murphy and McClendon, 1989, p. 196

theory is a struggle between individualists at one end (for example, Hobbesians) and collectivists on the other (for example, Marxists or structuralists). The specific struggle is over the fundamental ontological unit: the individual or the group. The postmodernist departure is to reject those two categories in favor of "practices" as the basic unit of social analysis (Schatzki, 1996).

Before turning to law, let us consider how philosophy in the mid-twentieth century took a postmodern turn. The turn occurred in a place few would have thought to locate it, that of analytic philosophy. The work of the philosopher and logician Willard Van Orman Quine represents what in time will be seen as a radical break with previous thought.

In Quine's view, the modernist conception of knowledge as a process of building from the simple to the complex, and the concomitant notion that truth is a matter of resonance between word (concept) and world, could not be maintained. (In scientific practice, Quine thought, the conduct of research belied his conception of knowledge). Quine substituted holism for foundationalism.On a holist account, the truth of any one statement or proposition is a function not of its relationship to the world but of the degree to which it "hangs together" with everything else taken to be true. Quine stated his view this way:

> The totality of our so-called knowledge or beliefs, from the most casual matters of geography and history to the profound laws of atomic physics or even of pure mathematics and logic, is a man-made fabric which impinges on experience only along the edges. Or, to change the figure, total science is like a field of force whose boundary conditions are experience. A conflict with experience at the periphery occasions readjustments in the interior of the field. Truth values have to be redistributed over some of our statements. Reëvaluation of some statements entails reëvaluation of others, because of their logical interconnections – the logical laws being in turn simply certain further statements of the system, certain further elements of the field.

Having reëvaluated one statement we must reëvaluate some others, which may be statements logically connected with the first or may be the statements of logical connections themselves. But the total field is so underdetermined by its boundary conditions, experience, that there is much latitude of choice as to what statements to reëvaluate in the light of any single contrary experience. No particular experiences are linked with any particular statements in the interior of the field, except indirectly, through considerations of equilibrium affecting the field as a whole.

If this view is right, it is misleading to speak of the empirical content of an individual statement – especially if it is a statement at all remote from the experiential periphery of the field. Furthermore it becomes folly to seek a boundary between synthetic statements, which hold contingently on experience, and analytic statements, which hold come what may. Any statement can be held true come what may, if we make drastic enough adjustments elsewhere in the system. (*Quine, 1980, pp. 42–3*)

Quine's picture of knowledge of the external world changed the way people thought about the construction of knowledge. The breakthrough was to see knowledge not as a matter of foundations – building up from bedrock – but a function of one's being able to move about within a holistic web (be it a web of theory or intersubjective practice). It is in the move from simplicity, reductionism, and foundations to holism, network, and totality that Quine's epistemology is rightly described as "postmodern." Quine's embrace of holism, together with his pragmatism on questions of truth, invite comparison with the second of the three aspects of modernism which are displaced in postmodernity, that of the referential theory of language.

Language has been a central concern of philosophy in this century. In a postmodern approach to language, the modernist picture of sentence–truth–world is replaced with an account of understanding which emphasizes practice, warranted assertability, and pragmatism.

The principal contemporary exponent of the pragmatist approach to truth is Richard Rorty. He summarizes his position this way:

For the pragmatist, the notion of "truth" as something "objective" is just a confusion between

> (I) Most of the world is as it is whatever we think about it (that is, our beliefs have only limited causal efficacy)

and

> (II) There is something out there in addition to the world called "the truth about the world" (what James sarcastically called "this tertium quid intermediate between the facts *per se*, on the one hand, and all knowledge of them, actual or potential, on the other").

The Pragmatist wholeheartedly assents to (I) – not as an article of metaphysical faith but simply as a belief we have never had any reason to doubt – and cannot make sense of (II). When the realist tries to explain (II) with

> (III) The truth about the world consists in a relation of "correspondence" between certain sentences (many of which, no doubt, have yet to be formulated) and the world itself

the pragmatist can only fall back on saying, once again, that many centuries of attempts to explain what "correspondence" is have failed. (*Rorty, 1982, p. xxvii*)

So what can we glean from these passages from Quine and Rorty? The basic point is that the modernist distinction between two realms of discourse, the factual and the expressive, cannot be maintained. If that distinction cannot be maintained, then with what are we left? Rorty's suggestion is to follow the later Wittgenstein, specifically the Wittgenstein of *Philosophical Investigations*. The task of philosophy is the perspicuous elucidation of our linguistic practices. What are the implications of this postmodern critique for law?

Law and postmodernism

The investigation of truth in law turns out to be the effort to describe what lawyers *do* with language. The modernist, referential approach preoccupies itself with the ways in which legal language represents, depicts, and captures the world. Those who deny such a referring relation have left themselves little in the way of alternatives to relativism or crass conventionalism. We need not embrace these two unpalatable alternatives. But if jurisprudence is to be an account of what lawyers do, what is to be said of truth? Let us now turn to that question.

What postmodernism achieves is a shift from a concept of language as representation to language as practice (meaning as use). It is a move from picturing to competence, with competence being a manifested ability with and facility in a language. Of course, our immediate concern is with the special language of law.

Law is an activity driven by assertion. As Dworkin puts it so well, propositions of law – "statements and claims people make about what the law allows or prohibits or entitles them to have" (Dworkin, 1986, p. 4) can be quite general or quite specific. Propositions of law may range from "The 14th Amendment prohibits the denial of equal protection" to "Jones has violated the motor vehicle code by exceeding the speed limit." How in the law do we go from assertion to truth? To answer this question, we need to know something about the nature of legal argument.

Claims in law are assertive in nature. The claim "Ordinance S is unconstitutional" purports to assert a truth. To ask what it is about S which prompts one to assert its unconstitutionality is to ask for the *ground* of the claim "S is unconstitutional." Suppose S states the following requirement: "Any assembly of 12 persons or more requires a parade permit." This fact is the ground for the claim that S is unconstitutional. The ground is advanced in support of the claim.

But, one might ask, what connects the ground to the claim? This is to ask how the ground is *relevant* to the claim. What is sought is the *warrant*. In the case of S, the warrant is the First Amendment to the United States Constitution. The First Amendment, which provides for the right to peaceable assembly, is the warrant which provides the connection between the ground and the claim.

Of course, the text of the First Amendment is not self-executing. There is more to the move from ground to claim than resort to a warrant. In addition to invoking a warrant, the warrant must be used in the right way. This is where the forms of argument come into play. The forms of argument are culturally endorsed modes for the use of warrants. The forms of argument are the *backings* for warrants.

Philip Bobbitt's account of argument in constitutional law provides the best example of the role of argument in law. In brief, Bobbitt argues that the practice of constitutional interpretation is a matter of using six forms of argument (he refers to them as "modalities") to show the truth of propositions of constitutional law. The following six modalities are the forms of argument in constitutional law:

> [H]istorical (relying on the intentions of the framers and ratifiers of the Constitution);
> [T]extual (looking to the meaning of the words of the Constitution alone, as they would be interpreted by the average contemporary "man on the street");
> [S]tructural (inferring rules from the relationships that the Constitution mandates among the structures it sets up);
> [D]octrinal (applying rules generated by precedent);
> [E]thical (deriving rules from those moral commitments of the American ethos that are reflected in the Constitution); and
> [P]rudential (seeking to balance the costs and benefits of a particular rule). (*Bobbitt, 1992, pp. 12–13*)

Justification – the activity of showing the truth of a legal proposition – is a matter of employing the modalities. To be legitimate, a constitutional argument must remain within the modalities. The modalities themselves, either alone or in combination, can never be legitimate, for they are the means by which legitimacy is maintained (through their use in argument). The modalities are the constitutional grammar of justification.

Use of forms of argument to show the truth of legal propositions does not exhaust the argumentative activities of lawyers. What counts as a form of argument may itself be called into question. Additionally, lawyers debate the criteria by which they judge what is to count as an appropriate form of argument. Let us consider some examples.

Judge Richard Posner has challenged conventional beliefs about the status of facts of legislative history. Judge Posner has argued that the canons of statutory interpretation are an improper guide to the meaning of statutes because they are based on false assumptions regarding the nature of the legislative process. The basic assumption Posner calls into question is an imputation of omniscience to Congress:

> Most of the canons of statutory construction go wrong not because they misconceive the nature of judicial interpretation of the legislative or political process but because they impute omniscience to Congress. Omniscience is always an unrealistic assumption, and particularly so when one is dealing with the legislative process. The basic reason why statutes are so frequently ambiguous in application is not that they are poorly drafted – though many are – and not that the legislators failed to agree on just what they wanted the statute to accomplish in the statute – though often they do fail – but that a statute necessarily is drafted in advance of, and with imperfect application for the problems that will be encountered in, its application. (*Posner, 1985, p. 811*)

As an example of a canon founded on the assumption of legislative omniscience, consider that of *expressio unius est exclusio alterius* ([T]he expression of one thing is the exclusion of another.) Posner's point, one that is well taken, is that the canon would only make sense "if all omissions in legislative drafting were deliberate" (Posner, 1985, p. 813). As an example, Posner raises the Supreme Court's decision in *Touche Ross & Co.* v. *Redington*, 442 U.S. 560 (1979), where the Court used the canon as the basis "for refusing to create private remedies for certain statutory violations" (Posner, 1985, p. 813). Posner objects:

> Whether the result in the private-action cases is right or wrong, the use of *expressio unius* is not helpful. If a statute fails to include effective remedies because the opponents were strong enough to prevent their inclusion, the courts should honor the legislative compromise. But if the omission was an oversight, or if Congress thought that the courts would provide appropriate remedies for statutory violations as a matter of course, the judges should create the remedies necessary to carry out the legislature's objectives. (*Posner, 1985*)

By calling into question certain of the assumptions of the historical form of argument, Posner turns what is normally backing (historical argument) into something which *itself* requires backing.

What Posner calls into question are certain of the beliefs and assumptions of the historical form of argument. Posner is not rejecting legal argument *per se*, nor is he putting in question any other aspect of legal reasoning. His is a quite specific and localized complaint. In fact, much of the strength of his criticism is drawn from the fact that he is able to make his points about unrealistic historical assumptions without upsetting any other part of the system of beliefs.

We must take matters one step further to complete our account of the typology of argument in law. Consider a direct challenge to the efficacy of a form of argument. Let us stay with historical argument. Together with textual and doctrinal argument, historical argument is among the most common of the forms of argument. In American jurisprudence, lawyers often ask what motivated a legislature to draft the law as they did. The focus is often on a problem, issue, or set of historical circumstances to which the legislature or Congress was responding when the legislation in question was drafted. In short, appeal to history as a guide to purpose and intent is a cardinal move in the lawyer's argumentative framework.

In *United Steelworkers of America* v. *Weber*, 443 U.S. 193 (1979), the Supreme Court of the United States considered the legality of a private affirmative action plan for skilled workers. The case generated majority, concurring, and dissenting opinions. A central focus of each opinion was the legislative history of Title VII. There was much debate among the justices as to the meaning of various aspects of the record. The form of argument each employed was historical argument.

I want to consider William Eskridge's challenge to the conventional understanding of the historical form of argument at issue in *Weber*. In *Dynamic Statutory Interpretation*, Eskridge describes two perspectives that are usually brought to bear in the interpretation of statutes:

(1) the statutory text, which is the formal focus of interpretation and a constraint on the range of interpretive options available (textual perspective);
(2) the original legislative expectations surrounding the statute's creation, including compromises reached (historical perspective). (*Eskridge, 1987, p. 1,483*)

To these two perspectives, which we recognize as the textual and historical forms of argument, Eskridge adds a third, the "evolutive perspective," which he describes as:

> the subsequent evolution of the statute and its present context, especially the ways in which the societal and legal environment of the statute has materially changed over time. (*Eskridge, 1987, p. 1,483*)

In an effort to make his argument against the background of conventional understanding of legal argument, Eskridge notes that "[w]hen the statutory text clearly answers the interpretive question . . . it normally will be the most important consideration" (Eskridge, 1987, p. 1,483). Of course, the ordinary meaning of the text is not always dispositive, as was the case in *Weber*. When text is not dispositive, the door opens for dynamic statutory interpretation.

Why is *Weber* a good candidate for dynamic statutory interpretation? Eskridge regards the question in *Weber* as one particularly amenable to dynamic analysis because

> it recognizes not only that the very nature of the problem had changed since 1964, but also that the legal and societal context of Title VII had changed. In 1964, the legal culture – legislators, judges, administrators, and commentators – focused on how to root out discrimination inspired by racial animus. People thought that rooting out actual prejudice would create a color-blind society. The intellectual focus changed over the next fifteen years, as the legal community came to realize that discrimination could be just as invidious even when it could not be established that prejudice was at its root. The concept of the continuing effects of historical patterns of discrimination suggested that current institutions might perpetuate discrimination even though no one in those institutions remained personally prejudiced. This insight was not a historical concern of the 1964 Act, but it evolved into a current concern and was recognized in subsequent statutes, judicial decisions, and commentary. (*Eskridge, 1987, p. 1,493*)

While Eskridge labels his argument "evolutive," the argument is clearly historical in nature. The point of the argument is to put in question the conventional limits on historical argument, which preclude asking anything about history other than from the then-present perspective. Eskridge puts the historical form of argument in question by making the case for the legal significance of failed legislative aspirations. Where the text of a statute is unclear, as he argues it was in *Weber*, and history demonstrates a clear historical aspiration on the part of Congress, *subsequent* history (both social and legal) should play a justificatory role in cases like *Weber*.

Conclusion

In this entry, I have tried to provide an analytic account of postmodernism and show its implications for legal theory. Postmodernism represents a new way of understanding the development of analytic philosophy in the twentieth century. When we see modernism all-of-a-piece, composed of the three axes which comprise it, we cannot help but see analytic philosophy since mid-century as representing a significant departure from the concerns of modernism. This is not to deny that many philosophers carry on the modernist tradition. Nor is it to deny that many would dispute the characterization of philosophy just given. Rather, it is to argue for the proposition that postmodernism represents a compelling new way to approach the questions which animate analytic philosophy.

For legal theory, this means that its concerns may rightly be informed by general philosophical discussion. Philosophy of law or jurisprudence in the twentieth century has been largely uninformed by questions in metaphysics and epistemology, preferring to dispute the borders between legal discourse and ethical discourse. Little progress has been made in this latter endeavor. Postmodernism presents the opportunity to consider these other issues from the legal point of view.

Bibliography

Bobbitt, P. 1992: *Constitutional Interpretation*. Oxford: Blackwell.

Dworkin, R. 1986: *Law's Empire*. Cambridge: Harvard University Press.

Eskridge, Jr, W. N. 1987: Dynamic statutory interpretation. *University of Pennsylvania Law Review*, 135 1,479–555.

McGowan, J. 1991: *Postmodernism and Its Critics*. Ithaca: Cornell University Press.

Murphy, N. 1990: Scientific realism and postmodern philosophy. *British Journal for the Philosophy of Science*, 41, 291.

Murphy, N. and McClendon, J. 1989: Distinguishing modern and postmodern theologies. *Modern Theology*, 5, 191, 196.

Patterson, D. 1992: Postmodernism/feminism/law. *Cornell Law Review*, 77, 254–317.

—— 1996: *Law and Truth*. Oxford and New York: Oxford University Press.

Posner, R. 1985: *The Federal Courts*. Cambridge: Harvard University Press.

Quine, W. V. O. 1980: Two dogmas of empiricism. In W. V. O. Quine, *From a Logical Point of View*. Cambridge, Harvard University Press, 2nd edn, 20–46.

Rorty, R. 1982: *Consequences of Pragmatism*. Minneapolis: University of Minnesota.

Schatzki, T. 1996: *A Wittgensteinian Practice Theory: mind/action, intelligibility, and sociality*. Cambridge: Cambridge University Press.

Wittgenstein, L. 1958: *Philosophical Investigations*, tr. G. E. M. Anscombe, New York, Macmillan, 3rd edn.

—— 1961: *Tractatus Logico-Philosophicus*, tr. D. Pears and B. McGuinness, London: Routledge & Kegan Paul.

26

Legal pragmatism

RICHARD WARNER

Many legal scholars insist that they are pragmatists and that their pragmatic perspective crucially informs their vision of the law (see, for example, Lipkin, 1993). Are they right? Does pragmatism offer some important insight into the law, an insight that escapes other perspectives?

What is pragmatism?

The first step is to say what pragmatism is. As a philosophical position, pragmatism makes characteristic claims about justification and truth. We begin with justification and then turn to truth. The approach to justification is non-foundational. This is what many legal scholars find so appealing in pragmatism; legal pragmatism's most constant refrain is that justification lacks a foundation (West, 1991, p. 121).

But what exactly is non-foundationalist about justification? The answer begins by noting the obvious: namely, we accept and employ various *norms of justification* in deciding what to assert and how to act, and in evaluating the assertions and actions of others (we may, of course, employ such norms unreflectively and unconsciously). Such norms delineate what counts as a justification (and sometimes when one justification is better than another). *Cohen* v. *California* illustrates what we mean by a "norm of justification." Cohen was arrested for wearing a jacket on which the words "Fuck the draft" were clearly visible. The Court held that "[t]he ability of government, consonant with the Constitution, to shut off discourse solely to protect others from hearing it is . . . dependent upon a showing that substantial privacy interests are being invaded in an essentially intolerable manner." This is a norm of justification: it tells us what counts as justifying an invasion of privacy.

Intellectual history is, in part, the history of the rejection of old norms for new ones, so the question inevitably arises, "What makes the prevailing norms the right ones? How do we know that the assertions and actions they apparently justify *really* are justified?" Pragmatism provides a way to answer this question: we can turn our norms of justification on themselves. Of course, we cannot evaluate all our norms at once; some have to serve as the standard against which to assess the others. The important point is that such assessment is always *internal* to the norms in question. We assess how well our norms work by using *those very norms*. There is no *external* standard of evaluation: *our norms of justification neither have nor need a ground outside themselves*. This is the distinctive pragmatic claim about justification.

An essential point: the norms I mean are the norms we *actually* use day in and day out. These are the norms that neither have nor need a ground outside themselves. The focus on actually-in-use norms is a *Rortyan* version of pragmatism (Rorty, 1982, p. xxv). Not all pragmatists endorse this version. Some – notably C. S. Peirce – allow evaluation of actual norms in light of a standard that we do *not* use, an *ideal* norm that we do not have but could in principle construct (Burks, 1958, pp. 16–17). Peircean pragmatism makes sense against the background of Peirce's views about rational inquiry. Peirce envisions different inquirers beginning their investigations with different and conflicting views, and he contends that, if all inquirers follow correct methods of rational inquiry, their views will – in the infinite long run – converge on a single theory. According to Peirce, this theory will contain what we are ideally justified in believing. How could it not? It is the unique result of the correct application of rational methods of inquiry over the infinite long run; everything reason ultimately validates is in the theory, and everything reason ultimately rejects is not.

Now let us turn then to the pragmatist account of truth. We begin with what, according to pragmatists, truth is *not*. It is *not* a matter of "corresponding to the facts." This may – and should – seem puzzling; after all, it surely *seems* that, for example, the statement "The cat is on the mat" is true when it corresponds to the fact that the cat is on the mat. Pragmatists, nonetheless, reject the correspondence picture of truth as a profound misconception; Rorty, for example, does so emphatically (Rorty, 1991, p. 23). So how do pragmatists explain truth? Peirce provides the best starting point. Peirce envisions different inquirers beginning their investigations with different and conflicting views, and he contends that, if all inquirers follow correct methods of rational inquiry, their views will – in the infinite long run – converge on a single theory. According to Peirce, this theory will contain what we are ideally justified in believing. Peirce holds that what is ultimately justified in this way is true; this is how Peirce *defines* truth. What it means for a statement to be true simply *is* for it to be included in the final theory. This Peircean approach illustrates the general pragmatist strategy: Truth is not a matter of correspondence; rather, what is true is what ends up justified in the long run.

Now let us turn to *Rortyan* pragmatism. How do Rortyan pragmatists define truth? How do they implement the underlying pragmatist idea that truth is not a matter of corresponding to the facts, but a matter of justification? Rortyan pragmatism focusses on actually-in-use norms and does not recognize a Peircean ideal norm that emerges at the final infinite limit of rational inquiry, so Rortyan pragmatists cannot define truth, as Peirce does, by appeal to such an ideal norm; rather, the obvious strategy is to equate being true with being adequately justified under *current, actually-in-use* norms of justification. Indeed, what other answer could there be as long as we reject evaluation of actually-in-use norms in terms of ideal, *not*-actually-in-use, norms? (Rorty, 1989, p. 52).

This completes our sketch of the pragmatist approach – or, better, of the *two* pragmatist approaches – to justification and truth. The sketch leaves us with the question, which pragmatism is the one legal pragmatists endorse? Legal pragmatists are – or are best interpreted as – Rortyan pragmatists. The views of legal pragmatists are generally inconsistent with Piercean pragmatism. Most legal pragmatists would deny the existence of methods of rational inquiry whose consistent application would ensure that initially disagreeing inquirers ultimately converge on a single theory. Legal pragmatists emphasize diversity; they call attention to the divergent viewpoints and methods of different cultures, social classes, races, and genders (Minow and Spelman, 1991, p. 251). Divergence, not convergence, is the recurrent theme. But to deny that rational inquiry converges on a single theory is to tear the heart out of Peircean pragmatism, for such convergence is what *defines* the ultimately justified theory. Legal pragmatists cannot, therefore, consistently be Peircean pragmatists.

Foundationalist versus non-foundationalist views of the law

How does such abstract theorizing about justification and truth matter to the law? To see what is at stake, it is helpful to contrast the pragmatist/non-foundationalist position with a non-pragmatist foundationalist one. The positions of Catherine Wells and Richard Wright provide just such a contrast; Wells is a pragmatist/non-foundationalist while Wright endorses foundationalism and explicitly rejects pragmatism and non-foundationalism. A *caveat*: for us, Wells and Wright serve as exemplars of particular positions; and, to make them into clear examples, we will both simplify and supplement their positions. Our "Wells" and "Wright" are not precise portraits of the real Wells and Wright; the resemblance is close, however.

We begin with Wright. To understand Wright's rejection of pragmatism in favor of foundationalism, we must understand his objection to what he calls "pluralistic . . . normative theory." Pluralistic theories recognize no ultimate single norm "to resolve conflicts among competing sub-norms" (Wright, 1995, p. 160). Wright contends that such theories make the choice between the competing sub-norms "arbitrary" – in the sense that we cannot have a reason to choose one norm over another. On Wright's view, to have such a reason *is* to have a norm that decides between the sub-norms. The reason would have to identify some features of one sub-norm that make it superior to the competing sub-norm, and this means the reason *is* the conflict-resolving norm – the norm being that sub-norms with such-and-such features are superior to norms with so-and-so features.

Wright holds that *any* rationally acceptable normative theory *must* contain an ultimate single norm. Rortyan pragmatists disagree. Our actually-in-use norms develop and change over time; and one cannot say in advance of this development what the norms *must* look like; one cannot say whether there will be one ultimate norm or not. To insist that normative theories without an ultimate norm are irrational is to assess actually-in-use norms by a standard of rationality external to those norms. This is enough to make Wright count as a foundationalist. But he

387

goes further. He identifies the ultimate foundational norm. It is "the foundational norm of equal individual freedom." Wright explains: "Freedom ... is an ... attribute of each rational being. The possession of free will or freedom is what gives each rational being moral worth – an absolute moral worth that is equal for all rational beings" (Wright, 1995, p. 162). One must use one's freedom in a way consistent with a like freedom for others; otherwise, one claims that one's freedom is more important than the freedom of others, which is false, for "freedom is what gives each rational being moral worth – an absolute moral worth that is equal for all rational beings" (Wright, 1995, p. 162).

Turning from individuals to the state, Wright contends that the state has the right to coerce citizens to use their freedom in ways consistent with a like freedom for others. This right has limits, of course; suppose you take more than your share of the dessert and thereby use your freedom in a way inconsistent with a like use by others. Most of us – and Wright is among them – would not think the state has a right to coerce you to take only your fair share of dessert. State power does not – and should not – extend into every aspect of our lives. Let us put this issue aside and focus, as Wright does, on torts – an area in which the state clearly may, in appropriate circumstances, coerce behavior. Wright contends that the foundational norm of equal individual freedom explains how courts actually handle negligence cases. He considers cases in which "the defendant put the plaintiff at risk to benefit the defendant or some third party, and the plaintiff was not seeking to directly benefit from the defendant's risk-creating activity." Wright argues that "the actual test of negligence in such cases is . . . the defendant's creation of a significant, foreseeable and unaccepted risk to the person or property of others. A risk is significant . . . if it is a level of risk to which an ordinary person would be unwilling to be exposed without his consent" (Wright, 1995, p. 261). To impose such a risk is to use one's freedom in a way *not* consistent with a like freedom for others, and the state has a right to use its power both to deter such behavior and to compel compensation for the injuries it may cause.

The point to emphasize is that the state's position here is appropriately premised on the foundational principle of equal freedom. For Wright, this means citizens have an *obligation* to obey. This way of putting the point suggests – misleadingly – that Wright thinks that citizens have an obligation to obey the law when and only when the law can be appropriately derived from the norm of equal freedom. Wright's (the real Wright's) views are considerably more complex, but we can put the (intricate and interesting) details aside. The broad outline we have given is sufficient for a contrast with Wells. It is the point about obligation that turns out to be essential to the contrast.

Wells emphatically rejects foundationalism. Wells is a Rortyan pragmatist who advocates what Wright calls a "pluralist normative theory." She denies that any rationally acceptable normative theory must contain an ultimate single norm; rather,

> theory and practice evolve together with a context of human purpose and activity; the practice informs the theory while the theory, in turn, informs the practice. Thus

> the hallmark of a pragmatic method is its continual reevaluation of practices in the light of norms that govern them and of the norms in light of the practices they generate. (*Wells, 1992, p. 331*)

There can be no ultimate norm since any norm is subject to evaluation in light of others. Wells finds empirical confirmation of these claims in the actual practice of adjudication. She contends that legal decision-makers in fact work with *multiple* norms, no one of which is "ultimate." Legal decision makers "locate the controversy within a web (*or several different webs*) of relevant normative analysis" (Wells, 1992, p. 332), and "it is only by locating an issue within these *various theories* that a judge can understand the full extent of the controversy." Furthermore, the normative rules we find in theories – no matter how detailed – cannot capture the full basis of a judge's decision; decision making is also a matter of non-rule-guided intuitive understanding. The reason is that

> the rules utilized by legal reasoning contain many vague terms and unstated exceptions, and for this reason, application of a rule is not merely a matter of determining whether certain formal conditions apply. Application also requires that we have an intuitive grasp of the rule – an ability to determine which of many logically possible exceptions are in the "spirit" of the rule and also relevant to the case at hand. (*Wells, 1992, p. 330*)

This emphatically non-foundationalist and pluralist picture is a far cry from Wright. The contrast between Wright and Wells emerges clearly if we compare old laws enforcing slavery with current laws prohibiting sexual harassment. Wright and Wells would – we may safely assume – agree that we should not obey laws enforcing slavery and should obey laws prohibiting sexual harassment. The question is, why? Wright has a ready explanation. Slavery so grossly violates the fundamental right of equal freedom that there is no obligation to obey laws enforcing slavery. We are, on the other hand, obligated to obey the laws imposing strictures on sexual harassment – provided they can be appropriately derived from the foundational right of equal freedom.

Wells must, of course, reject this foundationalist explanation. In the case of slavery, this may not seem too worrisome. After all, our actually-in-use norms *now* prohibit slavery, so doesn't this at least provide a basis for explaining why we – those of us who now abhor slavery – would not *now* be obligated to obey laws enforcing slavery? This is a weak reply, however. To see why, turn to sexual harassment. No one will deny that norms of justification prevalent in our culture until very recently justified behavior that we now think of as sexual harassment, and no one will deny that such norms are still widespread in our contemporary culture. Wells does not – let us assume, for now – want to say that those who accept such norms are not obligated to obey laws about sexual harassment. The point of sexual harassment laws is to compel a certain kind of behavior in the workplace – *whether or not* those subject to the laws accept norms of justification that justify behaving in the compelled fashion. Of course, the temptation here is to say that norms that do not justify slavery and sexual harassment are *the right norms*, and that norms that do justify these things are simply wrong. But, as a Rortyan pragmatist, Wells cannot say this. Where norms of justification conflict, Rortyan pragmatism's anti-foundationalism about justification denies a neutral perspective independent of either set of norms from which both sets can be evaluated. Confronted with conflict, all we can say is that the assertions and actions our norms validate are justified *relative to those norms*. Those on the other side can say the same thing with respect to *their* norms. We are forced to a relativism about justification. There is no way to reject this relativist conclusion and remain a Rortyan pragmatist. (This does *not* mean that pragmatists must refrain from raising moral objections to, for example, slavery and sexual harassment; they can – they can insist that, *under the norms they accept*, slavery and sexual harassment should not be tolerated. The relativism of pragmatism need not be the sophomoric relativism of "anything goes.")

So what explanation can Wells give of why we should not obey laws enforcing slavery but should obey laws prohibiting sexual harassment? Wells rejects the demand that she give an explanation here. Before we consider this response, it is helpful first to consider the response of pragmatists who do *not* reject our explanatory demand. Joseph Singer is an excellent example. He addresses the general issue of which our particular question about slavery and sexual harassment is an instance. The general question is simply: what are the proper limits of state power? An answer to this general question would provide the basis for determining in particular whether laws about slavery and sexual harassment fall inside or outside the proper purview of state power. Legal pragmatism's answer is *not* the traditional one that we find in classical liberal political philosophy. Legal pragmatists typically reject the classical answer, and we can understand their pragmatic alternative by first looking at the answer they reject.

Pragmatism and legitimacy

In classical liberal political theory, a government is legitimate when (and only when) its citizens – at least most of them – have a *prima facie* general obligation to obey it. Such an obligation exists only when the state can justify (most of) its actions on grounds that *every reasonable citizen* would accept. Wright's views illustrate the idea. Wright contends that *every rational person* must assent to the foundational principle of equal freedom, and he derives the obligation to obey the law from that principle.

Joseph Singer, as we noted earlier, attacks the classical liberal conception of legitimacy. Singer notes that the possibility of a rational consensus is the fundamental premiss underlying liberal legitimacy, and he objects that the requisite consensus is not possible: "it is not possible to identify a 'common point of view' to answer normative questions that can be both based on shared values and sufficiently definite to generate answers in particular cases" (Singer, 1988, p. 536). Note that this is precisely what Wright thinks he *can* do; he intends, in his analysis of negligence in terms of equal freedom, to offer "a 'common point of view' [the foundational norm of equal freedom] . . . based on shared values and sufficiently definite to generate answers in particular cases." It would be interesting to adjudicate this disagreement between Wright and Singer; however, another task is more pressing here. Legal pragmatists do not merely criticize the classical liberal conception of legitimacy, they also offer an alternative conception, a conception that does not assume that a rational consensus is possible. This positive conception is our concern. We want to know whether it provides an adequate pragmatic explanation of why, for example, one should not obey laws enforcing slavery, but should obey laws prohibiting sexual harassment.

We will focus on the positive conception as Joseph Singer develops it. Singer sets himself the task of articulating a conception of the proper use of state power without assuming that a rational consensus is possible. Singer argues we need "a language that allows us both to understand alternative social visions and to judge them" (Singer, 1988, p. 542). Singer insists that "[t]here is no single best way to [judge competing social visions]," and that "[o]ur goal should be to generate competing visions of social justice . . . We must talk to each other about our competing visions of the good society" (Singer, 1988, p. 542). Singer thinks pragmatism helps us here. It helps us "affirmatively think about justice and to establish it in the world – to elaborate the democratic values embedded in our culture" (Singer, 1989, p. 1,757). We can accomplish this by focussing "on the ways in which our categories of discourse, and modes of analysis reinforce illegitimate power relationships by embodying the perspectives and concerns of those who are powerful and suppressing members of oppressed groups" (Singer, 1989, p. 1,769). As Singer says, "Truth and justice are both partly a matter of experimentation, of finding out what works and trying out different forms of life. *The process of discerning the truth is not passive*" (Singer, 1989, p. 1,757).

The crucial idea is that if we were to actively engage in "conversation" (talking to others, experimentation, analysis) – *carefully observing the appropriate pragmatic strictures such as paying attention to power relationships* – we would ultimately be led to see the "truth," to see what is and is not *really* justified. This idea yields a picture of the proper use of state power. In legitimate uses of state power, the agents of the state aim, as the basis for their action, at knowing what is really justified, and they carry out this aim by engaging in "conversation" *under the appropriate pragmatic constraints*. This is to participate in good faith in the "process of discerning the truth." One might suggest – although Singer does not take matters this far – that we *should* obey legitimate uses of state power, but are under *no obligation* to obey illegitimate uses. This would provide a pragmatic resolution of the problem we raised for Wells: namely, why should we not obey laws enforcing slavery yet should obey laws prohibiting sexual harassment? That is, it resolves the problem provided we think that laws enforcing slavery did not arise out the appropriately pragmatic conversation while laws banning sexual harassment did.

We need not investigate the merits of this suggestion, for – whatever its merits – *it is flatly inconsistent with Rortyan pragmatism*. Singer defines legitimacy in terms of a process that reveals the truth about what is and is not "really" justified. For a Rortyan pragmatist, our norms of justification neither have nor need any ground outside themselves: there is no "truth" to discern about what is and is not "really" justified. So we have not found an acceptable Rortyan-pragmatic solution to the question of the proper limits of state power. Of course, one possible response here is to abandon Rortyan pragmatism. But that would be to abandon the claim that Rortyan pragmatism provides some fundamental insight into the nature of the law.

Rejecting the demand

Singer, as we have interpreted him, tries to explain why, for example, one should not obey laws allowing slavery but should obey laws prohibiting sexual harassment. Wells, as we noted earlier, rejects this explanatory demand. Of course, she can – *in a sense* – explain why one should not obey laws allowing slavery but should obey laws prohibiting sexual harassment. She can point out that our actually-in-use norms prohibit both slavery and sexual harassment. However, "our" norms are not everyone's norms. Some adhere to norms that allow – what we regard as unjustifiable – sexual harassment. The demand was to explain why they ought to obey laws prohibiting sexual harassment. And – again *in a sense* – Wells can explain this; she can point out – again – that, from the point of view of "our" norms, sexual harassment is unjustified. What she cannot do is explain – from some neutral perspective – why those whose norms differ from ours should obey laws prohibiting sexual harassment. For Wells, there is no such neutral perspective. To recognize such a perspective is to overlook the basic pragmatist point: namely, our norms neither have nor need a ground outside themselves. To look for a "neutral perspective" from which to review norms and pass judgment on them is to look for such a non-existent ground. The pragmatic approach rejects any such explanatory task.

Some will find Wells's pragmatic non-foundationalism decidedly unpalatable; they will insist that – surely – there *must* be a way to show that *everyone* is obligated to obey laws prohibiting sexual harassment. For example, Wright, as we have seen, contends that an obligation to obey the law derives from the foundational norm of equal freedom, a norm to which all rational persons must assent. Our goal is not to resolve this difference, but to use the difference to make the nature of legal pragmatism clear. The key difference between the Rortyan pragmatist Wells and Wright is that she completely rejects the idea that there is anything all rational persons *must* assent to; moreover, unlike Singer (as we have represented him), Wells does not try to replace the ideal of necessary rational assent with an alternative explanation of why people should obey the law. Instead, she insists that we abandon the – in her eyes, futile – search for such an explanation. Instead, we should focus on the practices of argument and justification that comprise our actually-in-use norms. These norms do in fact incorporate a variety of ways to deal with conflicting points of view, and the good-faith practice of argument and justification often leads – not necessarily, but *in fact* – to agreement. Legal pragmatism urges us to understand the law by focussing on the practices that comprise our actually-in-use norms, on the pattern of actual conflict and conflict-resolution that we find displayed in the judicial decision making. This is the perspective pragmatism offers us. But is it a perspective we should adopt? The key issue here is anti-foundationalism. Are there norms any rational person *must* accept, as Wright – and many others – think? Or, are there no such norms, as Wells – and many others – think? The plausibility of legal pragmatism depends on the answer to this traditional philosophical question.

Bibliography

Burks, A. W. (ed.) 1958: *Collected Papers of Charles Sanders Pierce.* vol. 8.

Lipkin, R. J. 1993: Pragmatism – the unfinished revolution: doctrinaire and reflective pragmatism in Rorty's social thought. *Tulane Law Review*, 67, 1,561–630.

Minow, M. and Spelman, E. 1991: In context. In M. Brint and W. Weaver (eds), *Pragmatism in Law & Society*.

Rorty, R. (ed.) 1982: *Consequences of Pragmatism.*

—— 1989: *Contingency, Irony, and Solidarity.*

—— 1991: *Objectivity, Relativism, and Truth.*

Singer, J. 1988: Legal realism now. *California Law Review*, 76, 465–551.

—— 1989: Should lawyers care about philosophy?. *Duke Law Journal*, 1,752–87.

Wells, C. 1992: Improving one's situation: some pragmatic reflections on the art of judging. *Washington and Lee Law Review*, 49, 323–38.

West, C. 1991: The limits of neo-pragmatism. In M. Brint and W. Weaver (eds), *Pragmatism in Law & Society*.

Wright, R. 1995: Right, justice, and tort law. In D. Owen (ed.), *Philosophical Foundations of Tort Law*.

PART III

LAW AND THE DISCIPLINES

27

Law and anthropology

REBECCA REDWOOD FRENCH

Legal anthropology is the study of legal systems using the method and theory of cultural anthropology. It is centered in the analysis of law as a phenomenon inseparable from cultural context, the agent-actors, language, history, and traditions of the society in which it operates. With the late twentieth-century doubts about law – about its canons, about logical analysis, about the adequacy of legal systems in plural societies – together with the impact of international, global, and media transformations, legal scholars have turned increasingly to other methods of analysis and theory. The anthropological analysis of law and legal systems offers one such strong critique.

Legal anthropology grew out of the Victorian interest in the nature and origin of human beings and the societies which they formed and, as such, is essentially a product of the European engagement with the cultures of other lands. The jurist, Sir Henry Maine (*Ancient Law*, 1897), often considered the founder of the field, looked at the societies of England and India and posited an evolutionary theory for the development of law. His phrase, "from status to contract," influenced jurisprudential thinking in the late nineteenth century. Primitive folk moots were the topic of a study by George Lawrence Gomme in 1880. Another lawyer, Lewis Henry Morgan of Rochester, New York, observed the local Iroquois nation and developed an evolutionary theory of society based on technological change and material factors which passed through several stages from savagery and barbarism to civilization (*Ancient Society*, 1877). His ideas of unilinear evolution were used by Karl Marx and Friedrich Engels as the basis for their theory of the various stages of society between savagery and the withering of the state in Communism.

Anthropology, while retaining its links to the sociological theories of August Comte, Emile Durkheim, and Max Weber, developed into a separate discipline around the turn of the century. In both England and North America, trained physical scientists who branched off into considerations of human nature and the formation of societies began to call what they were doing "anthropology." W. H. R. Rivers and C. G. Seligman in England and Franz Boas and his students, Margaret Mead, Alfred Kroeber, Edward Sapir, and Ruth Benedict in North America emphasized the collection of information about other societies using a scientific research technique which they termed "ethnography." Individuals and teams of researchers went to live for long periods of time with small groups of hunting/

gathering and tribal peoples in Africa, Asia, and the Americas. Descriptions based on qualitative interviews, observation and participation in the culture, were then presented in ethnographic monographs, that is, stylized statements of the ecology, religion, economic production, political systems, law and world-views of the people studied. Cultural relativism – rather than a theory of evolutionary stages – was the underlying theme of these ethnographic projects in the first part of the twentieth century. The legal system of a group was collected as part of the general picture and often presented as equally sophisticated, formal and just in comparison to Anglo-American or Continental law.

Legal anthropology has a unified constellation of conceptual themes that have been maintained through much of its disputatious career and recently have begun to have a strong effect on the study of law:

1 A law system is an integral, inextricable part of a whole social system. Law is a "web of reciprocal obligations" (Malinowski, 1926) and must be understood within the context of the whole society.
2 All societies and groups have systems which operate to influence conflict and to exert social control. What these systems are and whether or not they are "legal" or "law" is a question for investigation.
3 A basic presumption of the sub-discipline is that legal systems exist in all groups and sub-groups of societies as well as at the local, state, national, and transnational levels. Legal anthropology does not look exclusively at the formal, state systems of law; in fact, until recently, it concentrated on the informal, non-state legal systems.
4 Groups and societies are situated within distinct historical, cultural, and social arenas which directly influence the legal systems of these groups. As a consequence, legal systems will vary widely both within and across societies.
5 Anthropological methods are employed to observe and describe – from the perspective of the insider – the local understandings of conflict, anti-social deviance, social control, and legal identity. Traditionally, the focus was on disputes, rule-formation, decision making, exercised authority, and sanctions within a group. More recently, other methods and subjects of focus have been used.
6 Anthropological theories about the nature and operation of culture and society provide the basis for analysis of legal phenomena. Anthropologists look at the interrelations (a) between components of the legal system, and (b) between the legal system and other aspects of the society.
7 Comparison between legal systems are contextually situated and attempt to avoid normative judgments. They often do not employ Anglo-American jurisprudential categories or legal systems as their basis for comparison.

Most of the monographs written in legal anthropology in the early twentieth century consisted of attempts to codify the rules of various groups using a Western legal framework. Early fieldworkers in this tradition were R. F. Barton in the Philippines (1919, 1949), and Gutmann (1926), Rattray (1929) and Holleman (1952) in Africa. Barton was a teacher among the Ifugao in the Philippines where he stayed for eight years, learning their language and social life. His book, *Ifugao Law* (1919), uses the case system of recording to elaborate their sophisticated system of substantive property laws.

Bronislaw Malinowski, perhaps more than any other anthropologist, established the tradition of extensive fieldwork and detailed empirical observation in combination with the competent use of the local language and sensitivity to shades of opinion from the insider point-of-view. He lived for several years among the Trobriand Islanders in Melanesia and authored many books based on their society including his famous work on law, *Custom and Conflict among the Savages* (1926). Malinowski rejected most Western notions of law. He argued that law is not "a special system of decrees," but an integral part of society – the "net of obligations" between people which is backed up by "social and psychological constraints . . . which make men keep to their obligations." Through his exploration of how social institutions, including law, function to fulfill human needs within a society, he founded the functionalist school of anthropology. Several of Malinowski's students, notably Isaac Schapera (1938), used his methods to observe other legal systems.

The study of legal anthropology was given a new format and structure by an American legal academic Karl Llewellyn and anthropologist E. Adamson Hoebel in a book called *The Cheyenne Way* (1941). Hoebel had done extensive fieldwork among the elders of the Cheyenne tribe, many of whom remembered disputes and settlements from earlier periods. Llewellyn was a very creative legal scholar who, in this and other publications, set about creating a new set of principles and a new vocabulary for examining law across cultures. This book was the first to champion the case method, a central technique for collecting the law of non-Western people.

In the year 1954 legal anthropology turned to recording the processes by which law operated. In England, Max Gluckman published *The Judicial Process among the Barotse* which set an enviably high standard for the process of reporting cases, this time observed while they were actually being tried. In the United States, Hoebel published *The Law of Primitive Man*. Two other books using the casuistic approach were published in that year, Watson Smith and John Roberts's *Zuni Law*, and *A Manual of Nuer Law* by P. P. Howell. With these studies, emphasis shifted from the reporting of the substantive law in terms of rules and principles to the processes and cultural practices of law. This shift to the study of behavior in the disputing process has been dominant ever since.

Several debates marked the progress of the subfield over these first several decades. The first, initiated by Malinowski, revolved around the correct model of law: law as the behavior of individuals, law as the operations of institutions such as the state, or law as the normative rules and principles of a group. To educe law from the behavior of individuals, a researcher looks at routine behavior in a society, socialization, psychological internalization, and social order. For the second model, institutional structure, organized power, authority, group membership, and sanctions are the focus of interest. For the final model of rules and principles, one collects cases of conflict, compares them to written versions and commentaries and then analyzes them for the legal principles evinced.

The second debate was over the insider/outsider perspective. Max Gluckman and Paul Bohannan (*Justice and Judgment among the Tiv* (1957)) engaged in a lively exchange in the 1950s over the use of the term "the reasonable man" to describe a standard for jurisprudential reasoning among the Barotse people in Africa. Gluckman stressed the importance of generalized concepts for cross-cultural comparison. Bohannan championed the use of concepts from the legal folk culture claiming that Western legal terminology de-emphasized and ultimately falsified the "native point-of-view." Bohannan's viewpoint was eventually successful and the result has been a beneficial emphasis on detailed ethnography and folk classifications. Legal anthropology now takes as an initial premiss the assumption that the legal system of the developed Western world does not serve as an adequate model for comparative studies of legal systems. This attention to the insider perspective has come at the expense of cross-cultural comparison and integration with Western legal terminology.

The third debate, over the nature and definition of law, continued into the 1970s. After Hoebel outlined universal characteristics for law, Leopold Pospisil and others debated these characteristics, in an attempt to find an adequate cross-cultural definition. Did law consist of: concepts, rules, principles, behavior, territoriality, sanction, authority, symbols, commands, social control? Pospisil, for example, derived four characteristic elements for legal systems which distinguish them from politics and religion: authority, intention of universal application, *obligatio* and sanction (1958, 1971). By the 1980s, there were many comments about the futility of this area of inquiry and it gradually ceased to be a central concern of legal anthropology.

From the 1920s to the 1980s, these debates marked the course of the discipline and determined its central questions, approaches and techniques of investigation and comparison. Legal anthropologists described, compared and contrasted examples of dispute resolution through village law studies in different societies and used them to create typologies of dispute resolution. Others rendered detailed descriptions of the process of law, used dramaturgical models or described the cathartic, entertainment or consensus aspects of dispute settlement. Still others wrote about the language and etiquette of social convention or gave evolutionary typologies of law.

Based on their fieldwork, legal anthropologists advanced several theories about the general nature of legal systems during this period. Bohannan postulated that customary rules become law when they are "reinstitutionalized within the legal institution" of a society, a theory called the "double institutionalization of law" (1965). A norm which has been institutionalized and guaranteed within custom becomes law when it is additionally guaranteed by legal resources. Pospisil set out the multiplicity of legal levels, a theory which states that "every functioning group or subgroup of a society possesses . . . its own legal system." According to this thesis, each individual in a society stands within several concentric circles of different legal systems – family, church, community, workplace, state – which have distinct rules, sanctions, and procedures (1967).

Gluckman introduced the contrast between multiplex and single-interest relationships. Multiplex relationships (characterized as diffuse, multidimensional, and

normative) are more common in small face-to-face societies. Single-interest relationships (specialized, functionally specific, instrumentalist, and goal-oriented) are
common in large urban areas (1954). This dichotomy has been redefined and
reinterpreted many times within legal anthropology; for example, it has been reworked into a multiplex as mediation, single-interest as legal forum opposition.

The increasing influence of theories from Continental philosophers and the
enormous changes in global politics and the media have changed what legal anthropologists look at, how they look at it and how they theorize about it once they
have looked at it. With the publication of John Comaroff and Simon Roberts's
Rules and Processes (1981) and its clarion call for new approaches, the focus,
methodology, and theoretical approaches of legal anthropology have shifted. Legal and jurisprudential scholars are turning increasingly to legal anthropology for
methodologies and theories to supplement, clarify and sometimes replace what
are viewed as inadequate models for analysis.

Rather than studying little-known small-scale groups in Asia and Africa, several legal anthropologists have begun to look at systems of alternative or popular
legal culture in Western nations. Carol Greenhouse studied a group of southern
Baptists in the United States who specifically eschew the courts because they believe that an adequate Christian life can only be led by following the law of God
(1986). Sally Merry, through a series of studies of mediation and small claims
courts in the northeastern United States, has refined the nature of American folk
legal conceptualizations with concepts such as legal consciousness and legal discourse (1990). Barbara Yngvesson has looked at the interactions of the clerk of a
small court in western Massachusetts (1993) and David Engel has worked extensively on the narratives and myths presented by parents of the disabled in western
New York (1993).

Recent work in the area of legal language has focussed on how language is used
in disputing, in the courts and in law school classrooms, what kind of "work" it
does, how identities and categories get constructed through legal language, and
how routines, repertoires, and types of discourse determine outcome. O'Barr and
Conley have looked at how language is used in courts and in small claims forums
(1982, 1990) to identify effective speech styles, powerful and powerless speech,
rule-talk versus relationship-talk and different stereotypes of judicial authority.
The gendered basis of legal language and the use of narrative are intriguing new
aspects of these studies. The role that legal documents play within a culture, their
social production, use, and reproduction has provided new insights in legal anthropology. Messick (1986) in his work on Yemeni legal documents and other
scholars have asked questions about the social status of documents, the relationship between the oral and written, the role of documents in legal transactions and
the cultural characteristics of documents.

Legal pluralism has resurfaced with a new emphasis on combining the local,
global, and international stages of legal phenomena. Understanding the effects of
colonialist law and its ubiquitous reconfigurations of local understandings of property, work, marriage, kinship, family, causation, and time is part of this project.
Sally Falk Moore has suggested that the focus of study be "semi-autonomous social

401

fields." She defines these fields as porous borders, arranged by national and international laws, which are simultaneously locations for the production of local laws and local meanings (1978). The recent outpouring of works on indigenous claims, ethnic sovereignty and human rights are part of this interest in the combination of different pluralities. Work on the construction of legal identities, from both the insider and the outsider perspective, attempts to provide the individual viewpoint in this work.

The way in which legal anthropologists look at legal situations has changed as well. Legal anthropologists began in the mid-1980s to take a more self-reflexive approach and to question their epistemological conventions and their positivist research methodology. They have begun to shift from the case method to a focus on narratives, practices, events, and processes with less emphasis on holistic contextual background. Rather than conflict and dispute, they have begun to look at consensus. In her book *Harmony Ideology* (1990), an example of this new trend, Laura Nader found that among the Zapotec of Mexico the cultural ideal of harmony is achieved through systematic confrontation with the non-harmonious.

Paralleling the critical legal studies movement in legal academics, scholars in the field began to use Foucaultian concepts and the ideas of Raymond Williams to ask questions about the role of power in the law and the ways in which the law encodes hierarchy and domination (Comaroff and Comaroff, 1992; Messick, 1993; Lazurus-Black, 1994). Viewing law as non-neutral and embedded in asymmetrical power relations, these works study the forms of resistance which respond to such encoding and its results. Boundary creation and appropriation questions with respect to ethnicity have also been taken up as ethnic subcultures move into courts to question the ownership of certain cultural items and rights by other subcultural units. Several recent works in legal anthropology have engaged the historical dimension – the change in legal institutions, ideas, and processes through time (Starr and Collier, 1989). For example, June Starr locates the small Turkish village courts which she has studied for over several decades within the larger picture of the historical changes in regional and national politics (1992).

An interpretive and hermeneutic approach to law has been championed by Clifford Geertz (1983), Larry Rosen (1989), and others. Rather than positing law as a separate field which should be studied as a distinct entity, this approach advances a view of law as a distinctive way of "imagining the real," and focusses on discourse, translation, meaning and what law shows us about local culture, particularly the similarities between ordinary and judicial concepts. In his studies of Islamic law in Morocco, Rosen found that the discretion of the Qadi judge "lies not in the development of a body of doctrine which is consistent with . . . itself, but rather in the fit between the decisions of the Muslim judge and the cultural concepts and social relations to which they are inextricably tied" (Rosen, 1989, 18).

New theories have also developed in legal anthropology to help understand and connect the older methodologies and data with the new foci and orientations. John Comaroff and Simon Roberts (1981) began by pointing to the natural internal contradictions of the cultural logic of dispute. Actors in the legal system of the Tswana in South Africa negotiated disputes with reference to contradictory normative repertoires. Rules were being constantly negotiated, not merely manipulated, by the participants. John and Jean Comaroff have also redefined our notions of power by theorizing the hegemonic as what members of a society take for granted as true. This view of the status quo, the normal as dominant power, leads to investigations of how the status quo is reflected in cultural ideology, and articulated in its system of meaning (1992).

Merry (1990) and Conley and O'Barr (1990) have been working with a dichotomy in the legal consciousness of groups. Through observing and recording cases in several small claims courts in the United States, they found that petitioners couched their arguments in terms of either rules (understood as "true law" and "clean") or relationships (understood as "non-law" and "dirty" or "messy"). True/rule law is typically associated with high-status male professionals deciding resolvable, unambiguous cases while dirty/relationship law evokes images of low-status female mediators handling unresolvable, interpersonal ambiguous disputes. This dichotomy resonates strongly with the underlying concepts which are encoded into the legal system of the United States and provides a paradigm for further testing.

Noting that an historical view of legal relationships is always necessary, Barbara Yngvesson took a new look at the basic Gluckman bipolar model (1985). She pointed out that his model is complicated by the fact that formal, legal conflict (single-interest) may actually be useful to define informal, continuing relationships (multiplex interests). Parties recognize that the use of law in one setting may enhance non-legal solutions in others. To counterbalance theories which present legal systems as autonomous and self-referential systems, French has posited the cosmology of law as a useful concept for legal anthropology (1995b). In her work on the Tibetan Buddhist legal system, French found that the tacit assumptions and rituals that shape and motivate the Tibetan world-view – concepts of time, the nature of the mind, myths, ritual language, power, hierarchy, and the arrangement of legal space – are more important to understanding the legal system of Tibet than the institutional procedures and substantive rules.

Legal anthropology is a vital and productive approach to the analysis of legal systems. Based in the cultural context of a society and aimed at understanding legal systems at all levels through their particular historical, cultural and social circumstances, it seeks to observe and describe the local understandings of legal practice, from the perspective of the insider. With its rich history of cross-cultural data, methodology and theoretical innovation, legal anthropology stands as an important lens and critique for the social scientist and legal sociologist as well as the lawyer and legal academic.

References

Barton, R. F. 1919: *Ifugao Law*. Berkeley: University of California Press.
—— 1949: *The Kalingas, Their Institutions and Customary Law*. Chicago: University of Chicago Press.

Bohannan, P. 1957: *Justice and Judgment among the Tiv*. Oxford: Oxford University Press.
—— 1965: The differing realms of the law. In L. Nader (ed.), *The Ethnography of Law*, vol. 67, no. 6, pt 2, 33–42, Washington DC: American Anthropologist Special Publications.
Brenneis, D. and Myers, F. 1984: *Dangerous Words: language and politics in the Pacific*. New York: New York University Press.
Collier, J. 1973: *Law and Social Change in Zinacantan*. Stanford: Stanford University Press.
Conley, J. and O'Barr, W. 1990: *Rules versus Relationships: the ethnography of legal discourse*. Chicago: University of Chicago Press.
Comaroff, J. and Comaroff, J. 1992: *Ethnography and the Historical Imagination*. Boulder: Westview Press.
Comaroff, J. and Roberts, S. 1981: *Rules and Processes: the cultural logic of dispute in an African context*. Chicago: University of Chicago Press.
Engel, D. M. 1993: Origin myths: narratives of authority, resistance, disability and law. *Law and Society Review*, 27, 785.
French, R. 1995a: Tibetan legal literature: the law codes of the dGa' ldan pho brang. In R. Jackson and J. Cabezon (eds), *Tibetan Literature*, Ithaca: Snowlion Press.
—— 1995b: *The Golden Yoke: the legal cosmology of Buddhist Tibet*. Ithaca: Cornell University Press.
Geertz, C. 1983: *Local Knowledge; Further Essays in Interpretive Anthropology*. New York: Basic Books.
Gluckman, M. 1954: *The Judicial Process among the Barotse of Northern Rhodesia*. Manchester: Manchester University Press.
Gomme, G. L. 1880: *Primitive Folk Moots*.
Greenhouse, C. 1986: *Praying for Justice: faith, order and community in an American town*. Ithaca: Cornell University Press.
Gulliver, P. H. 1979: *Disputes and Negotiation: a cross-cultural perspective*. New York: Academic Press.
Gutmann, B. 1926: *Das Recht der Dschagga*. Munchen: Beck (also available in translation as *Chagga Law*, New Haven: HRAF Publishing, 1953).
Hoebel, E. A. 1954: *The Law of Primitive Man*. Cambridge Mass.: Harvard University Press.
Holleman, J. F. 1952: *Shona Customary Law*. Cape Town: Oxford University Press.
Howell, P. P. 1954: *A Manual of Nuer Law*. London: Oxford University Press.
Just, P. 1990: Dead goats and broken betrothals: liability and equity in Duo Donggo Law. *American Ethnologist*, 13, 43–61.
Lazurus-Black, M. 1994: *Legitimate Acts, Illegal Encounters: law and society in Antigua and Barbuda*. Washington DC: Smithsonian Institution Press.
Llewellyn, K. and Hoebel, E. A. 1941: *The Cheyenne Way: case and conflict in primitive jurisprudence*. Norman Okla.: University of Oklahoma Press.
Maine, Sir H. S. 1897: *Ancient Law: its connection with the early history of society and its relation to modern ideas*. London: John Murray.
Malinowski, B. 1926: *Crime and Custom in Savage Society*. London: Routledge & Kegan Paul.
Merry, S. 1990: *Getting Justice and Getting Even: legal consciousness among working-class Americans*. Chicago: University of Chicago Press.
Messick, B. 1986: The mufti, the text and the world: legal interpretation in Yemen. *Man*, 21, 102–19.
—— 1993: *The Calligraphic State: textual domination and history in a Muslim society*. Berkeley: University of California Press.
Moore, S. F. 1978: *Law as Process: an anthropological approach*. London: Routledge & Kegan Paul.

—— 1986: *Social Facts and Fabrications: "customary" law on Kilimanjaro, 1880–1980*. Cambridge: Cambridge University Press.

Morgan, L. H. 1877: *Ancient Society*. New York: H. Holt.

Nader, L. 1990: *Harmony Ideology and the Construction of Law, Justice and Control in a Zapotec Mountain Village*. Stanford: Stanford University Press.

Nader, L. and Todd, H. F. (eds) 1978: *The Disputing Process: law in ten societies*. New York: Columbia University Press.

O'Barr, W. 1982: *Linguistic Evidence: language, power and strategy in the courtroom*. New York: Academic Press.

Pospisil, L. 1958: *The Kapauku Papuans and their Law*. New Haven: Yale University Publications.

—— 1967: Legal levels and multiplicity of legal systems in human societies. *The Journal of Conflict Resolution*, 9 (1), 2–26.

—— 1971: *The Anthropology of Law*. New York: Harper & Row.

Rattray, R. S. 1929: *Ashanti Law and Constitution*. London: Oxford University Press.

Rosen, L. 1984: *Bargaining for Reality: the construction of social relations in a Muslim community*. Chicago: University of Chicago Press.

—— 1989: *The Anthropology of Justice: law as culture in Islamic society*. Cambridge: Cambridge University Press.

Schapera, I. 1938: *Handbook of Tswana Law and Custom*. London: Oxford University Press.

Smith, W. and Roberts, J. M. 1954: *Zuni Law: a field of values*. Cambridge, Mass.: Peabody Museum.

Starr, J. 1992: *Law as Metaphor: from Islamic courts to the palace of justice*. Albany, NY: State University of New York Press.

Starr, J. and Collier, J. F. 1989: *History and Power in the Study of Law: new directions in legal anthropology*. Ithaca: Cornell University Press.

Yngvesson, B. 1985: Re-examining continuing relations and the law. *Wisconsin Law Review*, 623–46.

—— 1993: *Virtuous Citizens, Disruptive Subjects: order and complaint in a New England court*. New York: Routledge.

28

The sociology of law

M. P. BAUMGARTNER

Sociology is the scientific study of social life, and the sociology of law is accordingly the scientific study of legal behavior. Its mission is to predict and explain legal variation of every kind, including variation in what is defined as illegal, how cases enter legal systems, and how cases are resolved. Differences in law are evident across societies, historical periods, and individual cases, and all are subject to sociological explanation. An act may be prohibited in one time and place but not another, for example, a person may call the police or file a lawsuit over a matter that another individual ignores, the same illegal conduct may result in a given penalty in one instance but not the next, and so on. Variation like this is evident even when all technical elements of potential cases are taken into account and all relevant formal rules applied.

In developing theories to account for legal variation, the sociology of law turns to facts about the social environment in which law functions. Dealing only with what is observable and measurable, it works to discover the social principles that govern how law actually operates in practice. Already, the field has made considerable progress toward this goal, identifying many social factors that affect legal behavior and accumulating an ever-growing body of knowledge about how they shape law. As presented in *The Behavior of Law* by Donald Black, a classic work of sociological theory, these factors include the following: social stratification, or inequality of wealth and resources; social morphology, or patterns of interpersonal connectedness; culture, or symbolic behavior; organization, or the degree to which people are mobilized for collective action; and other social control, or the nature and extent of non-legal mechanisms for defining and responding to wrongdoing (Black, 1976). Societies differ in their patterns of social stratification, morphology, and so forth, and this produces differences in their legal systems. Within particular societies, individuals and situations also differ from one another in regard to these factors – some people may be wealthier or more respected than others, for example, some relationships more intimate, some conflicts more readily handled by non-legal means of social control. These differences affect legal outcomes on a case by case basis, predicting such things as who calls the police or files lawsuits, who wins legal cases, and who is subjected to what sorts of sanctions.

The sociological theory of law

Some aspects of the link between law and its social environment are better explored, better documented, and better understood than others. Among the best studied of the factors that affect law are the social status of the parties involved in legal matters and the degree of intimacy or distance that exists between them. An examination of the relationship between these factors and law can provide a good illustration of how sociological theory accounts for legal variation that is otherwise difficult or impossible to explain. The following discussion features such an examination, concluding with an overview of the role of other social forces in the shaping of legal outcomes.

Social stratification

Social stratification, or the unequal distribution of material resources, is a powerful predictor of law, important in understanding legal variation of every kind. First, looking across all known societies of the past and present, it helps to account for the fact that some have legal systems while others do not, and that among societies with law, some have highly developed legal systems while others have considerably simpler and more rudimentary ones. Stratification and law go hand in hand: Stratified societies virtually always have legal systems, while egalitarian ones virtually never do. The more unequal the members of a society are among themselves, the greater the role law is likely to play in their affairs and the more elaborate their legal system is likely to be (see, for example, Engels, 1884; Fried, 1960; Black, 1976, ch. 2).

Social stratification also has a significant impact on the day to day handling of individual legal cases. Offenders, victims, witnesses, and legal officials all have a social status determined by their position in a hierarchy of wealth and prestige. Some may be high-status people with many possessions, others low-status people who own very little, and still others people who fall between the extremes. Research in the sociology of law has shown that at every stage of the legal process, the outcome of cases depends heavily on the status mix of all the participants involved. Offenses against high-status victims are more likely to result in legal action than those against low-status people, and they are more likely to be treated as serious and to result in severe sanctions. When the status of the victim is held constant, lower-ranking offenders are treated more harshly by the law than higher-ranking ones. The overall result is that low-status people who offend high-status people face the greatest likelihood of legal severity, followed in order by high-status people who offend other high-status people, low-status people who offend other low-status people, and high-status people who offend those beneath them on the status ladder (Black, 1976, pp. 28–9).

Empirical documentation of these patterns is abundant. In the contemporary United States, for example, studies have found that police officers relate differently to higher-status crime victims than they do to victims who are less privileged. They more often do what higher-status complainants ask of them (Black, 1980,

p. 136; Smith and Klein, 1984), write up more offenses against them as crimes (Black, 1970), and make more arrests on their behalf (Smith et al., 1984). Detectives generally devote more time and effort to the investigation of crimes with high-status victims (see, for example, Sanders, 1977, pp. 95–6), while prosecutors are likely to proceed more aggressively under these circumstances, choosing to bring more numerous and more serious charges against offenders (Myers and Hagan, 1979; Stanko, 1981–2). Finally, the same principles are evident in the behavior of judges and juries, who are more likely to convict people who offend high-status victims and who come from lower-status backgrounds, and having done so, to sentence them harshly. Thus, in the United States, where blacks as a group have lower status than whites, a recent study found that convictions in Boston courts were nearly six times more frequent in cases of interracial rape (virtually all of which involved black offenders and white victims) than in cases of intraracial rape (Holmstrom and Burgess, 1983). Other research has shown that blacks who rape whites are sentenced to longer prison terms than other rapists (LaFree, 1980). In regard to the death penalty, a particularly severe and dramatic punishment that has been the subject of much investigation, it is clearly established that blacks who kill whites run greatly elevated risks of execution; death is meted out next most often to whites who kill whites, followed by blacks who kill blacks and whites who kill blacks. This has been true historically and is still the case (see, for example, Bowers and Pierce, 1980).

Not only does the social status of the principals in legal matters affect case outcomes, but so does the social status of others who become involved, including witnesses and legal officials themselves. Thus, individuals supported in their legal efforts by witnesses of high social status have an advantage over those who cannot muster such support (Black, 1989; Baumgartner, 1992, pp. 148–52). As far as officials are concerned, evidence shows that the more elevated their rank relative to that of the people whose cases they handle, the more authoritative they are likely to be. In the contemporary United States, this can be seen in comparing the behavior of officials who are male, white, or the products of middle- or upper-class backgrounds with the behavior of their female, black, or working-class counterparts. Among police officers, for example, men have been found to arrest more often and to conciliate less often than women do (see Milton, 1972; Bloch and Anderson, 1974; Sherman, 1975). Judges raised in middle-class families or communities, those who have attended expensive law schools, those from more privileged ethnic or religious backgrounds, and those with more seniority and national-level responsibilities all tend to be more severe in their decisions from the bench, convicting more often and sentencing more harshly (see Nagel, 1962; Cook, 1973; Ulmer, 1973; Levin, 1974; Goldman, 1975; Uhlman, 1979). Similarly, higher-status jurors – those who have more education and higher occupational status, who live in affluent suburbs, and who are white – appear more prone to convict than lower-status ones (see Reed, 1965; Simon, 1967; Bernard, 1979; Hastie et al., 1983, p. 129).

Findings from the study of legal systems other than the contemporary American reveal that status is a determinant of legal processing everywhere. In general, the more stratified a society is, the more extreme the inequities in its legal decision making. Among the many settings in which social stratification is known to have shaped legal outcomes are ancient Babylonia (Harper, 1904), ancient Rome (Garnsey, 1968), traditional India (Gough, 1960), Inca Peru (Moore, 1958), Aztec Mexico (Offner, 1983), Manchu China (van der Sprenkel, 1962), colonial New England (Baumgartner, 1978), seventeenth- to nineteenth-century England (Beattie, 1986), and the Caribbean of the same period (Trotman, 1986) – to name only a few of the places for which this pattern is documented. The weight of evidence is overwhelming that social status has a consistent and powerful effect on legal systems everywhere. Knowing the status configuration of cases makes it possible to predict how those cases will be handled. Disparities in legal outcomes that make no sense in technical or doctrinal terms appear considerably more comprehensible when seen in light of the sociological relationship between law and stratification.

Relational distance

Another social factor that has a dramatic impact on the operation of legal systems is relational distance, or the degree to which people know one another and are involved in each other's lives (Black, 1976, pp. 40–8). This can range from the extremes of distance that exist between total strangers to the extremes of intimacy found among the closest of family members and friends. When people become involved in legal matters, the nature of their relationships with their adversaries and all other participants greatly affects what will happen in their cases. In general, law is more likely to play an active role in the affairs of those who are distant and is less likely to enter into matters concerning intimates.

Like social stratification, relational distance can explain legal variation both at the level of total societies and on a case-by-case basis. As far as the first of these is concerned, law is more likely to exist, and to be more developed and complex, in societies that include large numbers of strangers. By contrast, communal societies in which everyone knows everyone else are unlikely to have legal systems. Law is thus more likely to be found in societies that are more densely populated and more highly urbanized (see Hoebel, 1954, pp. 328–9; Schwartz and Miller, 1964; Stevenson, 1968). It is also likely to be more punitive and severe in these settings (Spitzer, 1975).

On a case-by-case basis, relational distance is a powerful predictor of legal outcomes. Intimacy tends to confer immunity from law at every stage of the legal process, beginning with the decision of victims whether or not to invoke law in the first place. Research in the contemporary United States has found, for example, that victims of crime who are intimate with their assailants are less likely to notify the police (see, for example, Block, 1974, pp. 560–1; Gove et al., 1985). In regard to civil matters, negligence actions are less likely between intimates than strangers (Engel, 1984), while suits over breach of contract arise less often between longstanding business partners than between those more casually connected (Macaulay, 1963).

Just as offended parties seem to find law a less appropriate remedy for conflicts involving intimates, so too do legal officials. Recent studies examining the legal response to crimes such as rape, homicide, assault, and robbery have all discovered significantly different treatment of people who victimize those close to them. Thus, in one study of rape cases, the researchers found that prior relationships between victims and rapists decreased the willingness of police, medical personnel, prosecutors, judges, and juries to define the offenses as serious and to pursue them aggressively. The effect was so strong that virtually all cases involving acquaintances dropped out of the legal arena long before actual adjudication; as a result, those who raped people they knew rarely faced a day in court to answer for their conduct (Holmstrom and Burgess, 1983). Similar findings emerged from a study of homicide cases in Houston, Texas. A variety of legal actors – including police officers, prosecutors, grand juries, trial juries, and judges – were all found to treat homicides between intimates as considerably less serious matters than ones between strangers. The cumulative effect of their responses produced striking differences in outcome for different kinds of murderers. While 64 percent of those who killed strangers were subjected to some form of legal punishment, the figure dropped to only 47 percent of those who killed acquaintances and 39 percent of those who killed relatives. The most likely outcome in cases of family homicide was for either a prosecutor or grand jury to decline to bring charges against the offender. Even if convicted, people who killed relatives still tended to fare better than other killers: They were given probation more often, sentenced to prison less often and for shorter periods of time, and, at least in the study in question, never condemned to suffer the death penalty that was handed down to 9 percent of those who killed strangers (Lundsgaarde, 1977).

Studies of other kinds of crime and of a wide variety of legal agencies and officials also show that relational distance between the parties is a crucial predictor of legal outcomes. One overview of the disposition of felony cases in New York City revealed the existence of a dual justice system, in which police, prosecutors, judges, and others distinguish between "real" and "technical" crimes primarily on the basis of the prior relationship that exists between offenders and victims. Matters seen as "real" felonies usually involve strangers and are handled aggressively; comparable victimizations between intimates are seen as "technical" felonies and are not given high priority (Vera Institute of Justice, 1981). Other studies that have documented the same pattern include ones of the police (for example, Black, 1970; 1971; 1980; Smith and Visher, 1981), prosecutors (for example, Miller, 1970; Hall, 1975, p. 318; Stanko, 1981–2, pp. 234–5), court clerks (Yngvesson, 1988), and judges (for example, Feeley, 1979, pp. 132, 161–2).

The nature of the relationship that links legal officials to the parties in a case also plays an important role in how the case is handled. If, for example, officials are tied more closely to one of the principals than the other, they are likely to favor that individual over his or her adversary. For this reason, many legal systems insist that judges and other legal actors who have close ties to one of the parties excuse themselves from participation in the case. Even so, occasions arise in which the distance between a legal official and each of the two sides to a case is unequal, and when this happens, the outcome is likely to be more favorable to the closer side. This pattern can be seen in cases in which citizens complain to the police about the behavior of fellow officers. Whether the offensive conduct occurred on or off the job, police officers under these circumstances tend to be sympathetic toward their colleagues and rarely take aggressive legal action against them (see, for example, Chevigny, 1969; Black, 1980, p. 174). The same principle explains the difficulty that people from out of town often have in pursuing legal matters against residents in small communities. One recent study of an American court in a small midwestern town indicated that an outsider suing a local defendant who was well known to the jury had virtually no chance of winning (Engel, 1984).

Even when legal officials are equidistant from both parties in a case, relational distance is still important. The more intimate officials are with both of the principals, the less likely they are to be severe toward either, preferring instead to adopt an informal and conciliatory approach. This can be seen in the behavior of judges and juries in close-knit communities, where legal officials are well acquainted with the people whose cases they handle. In these settings, third parties tend to acquit more often and to sentence less harshly than similar officials do in larger and more anonymous environments (see the evidence assembled in Horwitz, 1990).

An extensive body of evidence reveals that relational distance, like social stratification, is an important determinant of legal behavior not just in the contemporary or Western world but everywhere that law is found. Studies of traditional African societies, for example, have documented the reluctance of intimates to use courts (see, for example, Bohannan, 1957, p. 210; Gulliver, 1963, p. 204; Tanner, 1966, p. 7), and also the tendency of courts to favor informality and conciliation over severity when intimates appear before them (see Gluckman, 1967). The same patterns have appeared in a comparative survey of law and other social control in a sample of 30 societies from around the world (Cooney, 1988). Among the many specific settings for which the effects of relational distance have been documented are Japan (Kawashima, 1963), Afghanistan (Jones, 1974), Bavaria (Todd, 1978), sixteenth-century Spain (Kagan, 1981, p. 19), eighteenth-century New York (Greenberg, 1974), and nineteenth-century France (Donovan, 1981). In any legal system, the relational configuration of cases is one of the most important predictors of how cases actually get processed.

Other social factors

Social stratification and relational distance are only two of the social factors known to play a crucial role in the operation of legal systems, although they are especially well-researched and well-documented ones that provide excellent illustrations of how sociology explains legal behavior. The sociology of law has identified other variables that determine such things as which societies have law, which citizens invoke it, and who is likely to prevail in legal confrontations. It is impossible in the present context to review all of these factors in detail, but it is important to point out the significance of at least some of them. One of these additional factors is how integrated and active in social life the parties to a legal matter are, as seen in their

411

history of marriage and parenthood, employment, military service, community involvement, and so on; integration confers a legal advantage, with offenses against integrated victims treated as more serious and integrated offenders treated with less severity. Also important is how culturally conventional or unconventional the parties are in terms of their religion, appearance, aesthetic preferences, and ethnic background; conventional people are more likely to invoke law and to be successful in their legal affairs. The behavior of law is also affected by the respectability of the participants in legal matters, as reflected in their known past histories of conformity and deviance, by whether or not any of them is a formal organization, and by whether or not they have ready access to other, non-legal means of social control. Respectability and organization have effects similar to those of high status, integration, and conventionality, while the absence of other social control increases the likelihood of forceful legal intervention. (Evidence bearing on these relationships can be found in Black, 1976, where many of them were first described, as well as in Black, 1989; Horwitz, 1990, and Baumgartner, 1992.) The social characteristics of offenders affect the legal process, as do those of complainants and of any and all third parties who become involved. Every legal case in every legal system has a social structure defined by the complex of traits, identities, and relationships that exist among its participants, and this structure predicts and explains how it will be resolved.

The relevance of legal sociology

As an effort to apply the scientific method to the study of legal behavior, the sociology of law measures its achievements by the range of facts about law it uncovers and especially by its success in developing testable theories to explain those facts. Since it is restricted to a consideration of what is observable in the conduct of real people, it does not participate directly in moral discourse about how law ought to behave or how justice should be defined (see Black, 1972). The sociology of law entails the adoption of an observer's perspective (Black, 1989, pp. 19–22). An observer can maintain detachment in the face of facts of every kind and can follow those facts to whatever empirical conclusion they may lead, but no farther. In adopting an observer's outlook, the sociology of law contrasts with the jurisprudential perspective of more traditional legal scholarship. Empirical description and explanation are not the latter's primary concerns, which revolve rather around issues of evaluation and assessment – fairness, justice, equity, and effectiveness, and how to obtain these things. This perspective is devoted to the more immediate and practical question of how legal systems ought to be structured and how cases ought to be handled (Black, 1989).

The sociology of law thus represents a very different enterprise from traditional legal scholarship. It starts from different premises, uses different methods, and pursues different goals. At the same time, however, many of its findings are of great relevance to participants in the legal system. Many of its formulations challenge longstanding conceptions about law, while many of the facts it uncovers raise difficult questions for those concerned with issues of justice and fairness. The sociology of law even suggests new possibilities for manipulating legal systems deliberately in order to bring about desired results, techniques of social engineering likely to become highly controversial as well as highly effective. The consequences of legal sociology, then, are far reaching and of ever more significance as the discipline itself grows.

Conceptual relevance

As work in the sociology of law has accumulated, it has put into new perspective many of the most time-honored notions of lawyers and legal scholars. Consider, for example, the concept of discretion, used to refer to the latitude legal officials have in deciding how to handle cases. The traditional understanding of discretion is that it allows officials to decide cases "according to the dictates of their own judgment and conscience, uncontrolled by the judgment and conscience of others" (Black, 1968, p. 553). Discretion is seen to introduce a significant measure of unpredictability into legal systems, and much variation in legal processing is attributed to it. In this view, discretion is associated with idiosyncrasy and caprice – products of a human element in legal functioning that is ultimately beyond comprehension or control.

Research in the sociology of law suggests that the exercise of discretion is really something quite different, and that the traditional understanding is inaccurate and constitutes a myth about how legal systems operate (Baumgartner, 1992). It indicates that the discretionary decisions of officials are not random and capricious, but rather highly regular and patterned. While they may be largely unpredictable in terms of statutes, case law, evidentiary guidelines, and the like, they are quite predictable when analyzed sociologically. Factors such as the ones discussed above – the social status of everyone involved in a case, the nature of their personal relationships with each other, and so forth – determine how discretion is exercised. Seen in this light, discretion turns out to be something far different from the uncontrolled use of personal judgment, appearing instead as the behavior of people whose conduct is constrained by the dictates of social laws.

Another traditional understanding called into question by the sociology of law is that of discrimination. In the usual jurisprudential analysis, discrimination appears as a deviation from the rule of law, something that happens when social factors like wealth or race are allowed to contaminate the legal process (Black, 1989, pp. 21–2). Discrimination is contrasted with what should occur under more normal circumstances – the strict application of relevant rules in light of the known facts of a case. The sociology of law suggests, however, a different understanding of discrimination (Black, 1989). The weight of its accumulated research findings reveals that social influences on legal outcomes are not exceptional, but rather ubiquitous, and that the handling of cases solely in terms of technically relevant criteria is something that essentially never happens. What is more, discrimination is not limited to the effects of social class or race. Legal systems everywhere distinguish among people on the basis of a host of other social characteristics as well,

413

including their respectability, cultural conventionality, organizational member-ships, intimacy with their adversaries, and similar considerations. Discrimination thus turns out to be vastly more extensive and routine than the traditional under-standing has recognized, "an aspect of the natural behavior of law, as natural as the flying of birds or the swimming of fish" (Black, 1989, pp. 21–2).

Advances in the sociology of law also have implications for some more limited and technical legal concepts. One such concept, for example, is that of the tradi-tional "reasonable man" or "reasonable person." This hypothetical individual rep-resents the responsible citizen, whose degree of understanding, knowledge, caution, and moral sensitivity serves as a yardstick against which that of other individuals can be measured. The construct of the reasonable person plays a role in the fram-ing and resolution of a variety of legal matters, such as those dealing with allega-tions of recklessness and negligence. The reasonable person takes on a very different appearance from the traditional one, however, in the light of empirical research indicating that conceptions of reasonableness can vary considerably across differ-ent groups of people. Depending on the specifics of a case, men may define what is reasonable differently than women do, highly educated persons may define it differently than those with less education do, blacks may define it differently than whites do, and so on (see, for example, Kornstein, 1993). The reasonable person turns out to be different in different social locations, so that in heterogeneous societies like the contemporary United States there may be no single reasonable person at all. Accordingly, any legal provision that assumes the existence of a common standard of reasonableness is likely to require rethinking.

As significant as the sociology of law may be for the understanding of any number of individual legal concepts such as discretion, discrimination, and the reasonable person, it has a still broader conceptual relevance as well. This lies in the alterna-tive perspective it provides on the fundamental nature of law itself. While law is traditionally understood as an affair of rules, the sociology of law sees it as an affair of human actors responding in predictable ways to their social environment. Instead of seeing the rigorous and detached application of formal standards as the heart of legal behavior, it sees instead moral confrontation and moral struggle between adversaries whose chances of success are largely determined by their social identities. Rather than formality, logic, and consistency, it sees in law a variability fine-tuned to respond to every social feature of every case. From the vantage point of sociology, law appears not as a self-contained system of rules and procedures, but as a kind of social behavior integrally connected with every other. For those who adopt a sociological perspective, then, law looks very different from what it is commonly taken to be. Once approached sociologically, law can never seem quite the same.

Moral relevance

As a scientific enterprise, the sociology of law is not in a position to pass judgment on the facts it uncovers. Those facts, however, often possess great moral relevance for participants and critics of a legal system. This is particularly true in societies like the contemporary United States, where it is widely accepted that justice requires similar legal treatment of socially dissimilar individuals, or where, to put it another way, it is largely taken for granted that legal discrimination is always wrong. Where such values prevail, the findings of legal sociology can be very disturbing indeed.

Of course, evidence that legal systems treat people differently on the basis of their social characteristics would not present a challenge to those who find such discrimination morally acceptable. There have, in fact, been many settings in which at least some forms of legal discrimination have been seen as perfectly appropriate. One student of law in the Roman Empire has concluded, for example, that "the Romans rejected juridical equality, the equality of all citizens before the law, as easily as they rejected political equality. Cicero viewed as unequal that kind of equality which 'does not recognize grades of dignity'" (Garnsey, 1968, p. 165). Romans expected their legal system to favor the wealthy and privileged, as indeed it did. In Rome and in many other places, the written law itself explicitly called for the differential treatment of different kinds of people. The earliest known legal code, that of Hammurabi, stipulated penalties of varying severity for an assortment of offenses based on the social standing of both wrongdoer and victim (Harper, 1904). In many societies, then, legal discrimination has been practiced overtly and without apparent guilt of any kind. In these places, the sociology of law would have only limited ability to scandalize.

In most contemporary Western societies, by contrast, the realities of discrimination revealed by the sociology of law are in stark contradiction to the widespread ideological commitment to legal equality. What the sociology of law documents is that the social factors openly acknowledged to dictate legal outcomes in some societies continue to exert a profound effect even when they are officially repudiated or denied. As one sociologist has put it: "Legal sociology therefore invites modern jurisprudence to face reality: Cases are not decided by rules alone" (Black, 1989, p. 100). A powerful though unwritten moral sense guides legal decision making in modern societies, one in which different outcomes are considered appropriate for different kinds of people and different social circumstances. This folk ethic not only conflicts with the official one, but appears the stronger of the two, for it is the one that prevails in practice.

Faced with evidence of systematic social variability in modern legal behavior, people may maintain the position that all of it is morally wrong and must somehow be eliminated. Another possibility is to survey the range of variability that has been uncovered and to make distinctions as to which forms of social discrimination are least acceptable and which might, after all, be justifiable (see Black, 1989, pp. 100–1). Giving preferential treatment to wealthier people who have legal conflicts with poorer people might be considered indefensible, for example, but a moral debate on the effects of factors like intimacy or prior reputation might reach a different conclusion. It might be felt that those who offend intimates ought to be treated differently from those who offend strangers, or that special consideration should properly be given to victims who have always lived a blameless life over those who have frequently violated social conventions.

415

Whatever the outcome of these moral debates might be, it seems likely that the debates will indeed occur as findings from the sociology of law become more widely known. What to make of the social patterns research has revealed is not obvious, and there may well be disagreements as different people come to different conclusions. The existence of pervasive social discrimination in the legal system, however, is more and more obvious with every advance in the sociology of law. Coming to terms with this reality is something increasingly difficult to avoid.

Policy relevance

The sociology of law is a potentially powerful tool available to those who would like to change or control the legal system. Traditionally, most legal engineering has proceeded on an ad hoc basis, guided only by intuition and conviction, and not surprisingly, much of it has failed to achieve its ends. With legal sociology, however, comes a better understanding of the principles underlying legal behavior and thus new possibilities for effective manipulation. Whether the application of sociological knowledge is seen as a good thing in any particular instance will depend largely on whether people approve of the goals being sought, but, like it or not, there is no turning back from the new power over law that sociology makes available.

One possible application of legal sociology that has recently been discussed at some length is "sociological litigation," or the systematic use of sociological knowledge in the day-to-day practice of law (Black, 1989, ch. 2). Many decisions that lawyers have to make in handling cases could be affected by sociology, including "screening cases for professional attention; scheduling fees; choosing case participants; deciding whether to seek out-of-court settlements; preparing cases for trial; selecting judges, jurors, and venues; devising tactics during trial; and, when losses occur, deciding whether to appeal to a higher court" (Black, 1989, p. 25). The sociology of law indicates which people are most likely to win legal cases – high-status people confronting those of low status, for example, respectable people confronting known deviants, formal organizations confronting individuals, and so forth. It points out the social characteristics that make for effective and thus desirable witnesses, as well as ones that make for sympathetic and thus preferable third parties like judges and jurors. A careful analysis of the social identities of all those involved in a legal matter reveals the sociological strengths and weaknesses of a case, allowing attorneys to determine how good a risk a client is and how best to manage and present a case to maximize the likelihood of success. Lawyers may advise people with sociologically weak cases not to bother pursuing them, may request payment on an hourly rather than a contingency basis should they go ahead in such matters, or may aggressively try to negotiate outcomes in these cases rather than run the risk of a trial. In court, an attorney engaged in sociological litigation can be certain to draw attention to every advantageous fact about the client and disadvantageous one about the opponent, can advise clients on ways to improve their chances of victory by altering facts about their identity that are within their power to control (such as by finding employment, for example, or by entering a drug rehabilitation program), and can call witnesses who have been carefully screened to enhance the sociological strengths of the client's case. These and related tactics can greatly enhance a lawyer's success, making him or her more useful to clients and more imposing in the eyes of peers. Of course, not everyone may welcome legal practice of this kind. While some may be enthusiastic, others may find the thought of lawyers using sociology in this way disturbing, if not chilling. The morality of sociological litigation remains to be debated, but its feasibility is already at hand and its use hard to regulate.

The sociology of law can also be useful in designing and implementing large-scale strategies of reform. The prospects here are many, with possible applications only beginning to be suggested. Among those already discussed include some sweeping and dramatic ways to redress current imbalances in legal advantage by doing things like the following: creating organizations especially designed to champion the causes of members who have legal difficulties; systematically reducing the amount of social information available to officials about the parties to legal matters so as to remove the basis for discrimination; and reducing the role of law itself in modern societies by curtailing the availability of legal resources and encouraging people to rely on nonlegal means of social control. (All of these reforms are presented and analyzed in Black, 1989, where they are labeled "the incorporation of conflict," "the desocialization of law," and "the delegalization of society" respectively.) Any number of other applications of legal sociology are possible, not all so comprehensive in scope, and the future will undoubtedly see many proposed and implemented. Controversy is likely to surround these efforts at legal engineering, but as with sociological litigation, it will be difficult to prevent people from using knowledge at their disposal to go after the ends they desire.

Sociology provides a new way of thinking about law, understanding it, and manipulating it. The law of the future may well be different because of it, as people apply sociological insights in ways only beginning to be conceived. It is not only law, however, that determines the nature of social control in human groups. People also rely on a rich array of other mechanisms to define and sanction wrongdoing, including mediation, negotiation, violent self-help, therapy, and avoidance. Such techniques are used instead of law or alongside it to handle conflicts in families, schools, workplaces, neighborhoods, public places, the international arena, and everywhere else that people interact with each other.

The sociology of law is thus only the starting point for the wider examination of moral life in all its dimensions, and, in fact, sociological investigation into other forms of social control has already begun (see, for example, the papers collected in Black, 1984). This work has made important theoretical advances and has considerable conceptual and practical significance beyond the legal arena. In the pursuit of a general sociology of social control, however, the study of law has a special place. It has been in trying to explain and predict law that sociology has had its greatest success in establishing a framework applicable to the study of all moral life. Furthermore, among the many ways in which people respond to conduct of which they disapprove, law stands out as the most formal, self-conscious, authoritative, and ambitious means of social control ever devised.

417

References

Baumgartner, M. P. 1978: Law and social status in colonial New Haven, 1639–1665. In R. J. Simon (ed.), *Research in Law and Sociology: an annual compilation of research*, Greenwich, Conn.: JAI Press, 153–74.

—— 1992: The myth of discretion. In K. Hawkins (ed.), *The Uses of Discretion*, Oxford: Clarendon Press, 129–62.

Beattie, J. M. 1986: *Crime and the Courts in England, 1660–1800* (Princeton, NJ: Princeton University Press.

Bernard, J. L. 1979: Interaction between the race of the defendant and that of jurors in determining verdicts. *Law and Psychology Review*, 5, 103–11.

Black, D. 1970: Production of crime rates. *American Sociological Review*, 35, 733–48.

—— 1971: The social organization of arrest. *Stanford Law Review*, 23, 1,087–111.

—— 1972: The boundaries of legal sociology. *Yale Law Journal*, 81, 1,086–100.

—— 1976: *The Behavior of Law*. New York: Academic Press.

—— 1980: *The Manners and Customs of the Police*. New York: Academic Press.

—— 1989: *Sociological Justice*. New York: Oxford University Press.

Black, D. (ed.) 1984: *Toward a General Theory of Social Control*. Orlando: Academic Press, 2 vols.

Black, H. C. 1968: *Black's Law Dictionary*. St Paul, Minn.: West Publishing Company.

Bloch, P. and Anderson, D. 1974: *Policewomen on Patrol: final report*. Washington, DC: Police Foundation.

Block, R. 1974: Why notify the police: the victim's decision to notify the police of an assault. *Criminology*, 11, 555–69.

Bohannan, P. 1957: *Justice and Judgment among the Tiv*. London: Oxford University Press.

Bowers, W. J. and Pierce, G. J. 1980: Arbitrariness and discrimination under post-*Furman* capital statutes. *Crime and Delinquency*, 26, 563–635.

Chevigny, P. 1969: *Police Power: police abuses in New York City*. New York: Vintage Books.

Cook, B. B. 1973: Sentencing behavior of federal judges: draft cases – 1972. *University of Cincinnati Law Review*, 42, 597–633.

Cooney, M. 1988: The social control of homicide: a cross-cultural study. Unpublished doctoral dissertation, Harvard Law School.

Donovan, J. M. 1981: Justice unblind: the juries and the criminal classes in France, 1825–1914. *Journal of Social History*, 15, 89–107.

Engel, D. M. 1984: The oven bird's song: insiders, outsiders, and personal injuries in an American community. *Law and Society Review*, 18, 551–82.

Engels, F. [1884] 1942: *The Origin of the Family, Private Property and the State*. New York: International Publishers.

Feeley, M. M. 1979: *The Process is the Punishment: handling cases in a lower criminal court*. New York: Russell Sage Foundation.

Fried, M. H. 1960: On the evolution of social stratification and the state. In S. Diamond (ed.), *Culture in History: essays in honor of Paul Radin*, New York: Columbia University Press, 713–31.

Garnsey, P. 1968: Legal privilege in the Roman Empire. *Past and Present*, 41, 3–24.

Gluckman, M. 1967: *The Judicial Process among the Barotse of Northern Rhodesia*, Manchester: Manchester University Press, 2nd edn.

Goldman, S. 1975: Voting behavior on the United States courts of appeal revisited. *American Political Science Review*, 69, 491–506.

Gough, E. K. 1960: Caste in a Tanjore village. In E. R. Leach (ed.), *Aspects of Caste in South India, Ceylon and North-West Pakistan*, Cambridge: Cambridge University Press, 11–60.

Gove, W. R., Hughes, M., and Geerken, M. 1985: Are uniform crime reports a valid indicator of the index crimes?: an affirmative answer with minor qualifications. *Criminology*, 23, 451–501.

Greenberg, D. 1974: *Crime and Law Enforcement in the Colony of New York, 1691–1776.* Ithaca, NY: Cornell University Press.

Gulliver, P. H. 1963: *Social Control in an African Society: a study of the Arusha, agricultural Masai of northern Tanganyika.* Boston: Boston University Press.

Hall, D. 1975: Role of the victim in the prosecution and disposition of a criminal case. *Vanderbilt Law Review*, 28, 931.

Harper, R. F. (tr.) 1904: *The Code of Hammurabi, King of Babylon: about 2250 B.C.* Chicago: University of Chicago Press.

Hastie, R., Penrod, S. D., and Pennington, N. 1983: *Inside the Jury.* Cambridge: Harvard University Press.

Hoebel, E. A. 1954: *The Law of Primitive Man: a study in comparative legal dynamics.* Cambridge: Harvard University Press.

Holmstrom, L. L. and Burgess, A. W. 1983: *The Victim of Rape: institutional reactions.* New Brunswick: Transaction Books, 2nd edn.

Horwitz, A. V. 1990: *The Logic of Social Control.* New York: Plenum Press.

Jones, S. 1974: *Men of Influence in Nuristan: a study of social control and dispute settlement in Waigal Valley, Afghanistan.* New York: Seminar Press.

Kagan, R. L. 1981: *Lawsuits and Litigants in Castile, 1500–1700.* Chapel Hill, NC: University of North Carolina Press.

Kawashima, T. 1963: Dispute resolution in contemporary Japan. In A. T. von Mehren (ed.), *Law in Japan: the legal order in a changing society.* Cambridge: Harvard University Press, 41–72.

Kornstein, S. 1993: The "reasonable person": the link between cultural diversity, law, and social science. Unpublished master's paper, Department of Sociology, Rutgers University.

LaFree, G. D. 1980: The effect of social stratification by race on official reactions to rape. *American Sociological Review*, 45, 842–54.

Levin, M. A. 1974: Urban politics and judicial behavior. *Journal of Legal Studies*, 3, 339–75.

Lundsgaarde, H. P. 1977: *Murder in Space City: a cultural analysis of Houston homicide patterns.* New York: Oxford University Press.

Macaulay, S. 1963: Non-contractual relations in business: a preliminary study. *American Sociological Review*, 28, 55–67.

Miller, F. 1970: *Prosecution: the decision to charge a suspect with a crime.* Boston: Little Brown.

Milton, C. 1972: *Women in Policing.* Washington, DC: Police Foundation.

Moore, S. F. 1958: *Power and Property in Inca Peru.* New York: Columbia University Press.

Myers, M. A. and Hagan, J. 1979: Private and public trouble: prosecutors and the allocation of court resources. *Social Problems*, 26, 439–51.

Nagel, H. H. 1962: Judicial backgrounds and criminal cases. *Journal of Criminal Law, Criminology and Police Science.* 53. 333–9.

Offner, J. A. 1983: *Law and Politics in Aztec Texcoco.* Cambridge: Cambridge University Press.

Reed, J. 1965: Jury deliberation, voting and verdict trends. *Southwest Social Science Quarterly*, 45, 361–70.

Sanders, W. B. 1977: *Detective Work: a study of criminal investigations.* New York: Free Press.

Schwartz, R. D. and Miller, J. C. 1964: Legal evolution and societal complexity. *American Journal of Sociology*, 70, 159–69.

Sherman, L. J. 1975: Evaluation of policewomen on patrol in a suburban police department. *Journal of Police Science and Administration*, 3, 434–8.

419

Simon, R. J. 1967: *The Jury and the Defense of Insanity*. Boston: Little Brown.

Smith, D. A. and Klein, J. R. 1984: Police control of interpersonal disputes. *Social Problems*, 31, 468–81.

Smith, D. A. and Visher, C. A. 1981: Street-level justice: situational determinants of police arrest decisions. *Social Problems*, 29, 167–77.

Smith, D. A., Visher, C. A., and Davidson, L. A. 1984: Equity and discretionary justice: the influence of race on police arrest decisions. *Journal of Criminal Law and Criminology*, 75, 234–49.

Spitzer, S. 1975: Punishment and social organization: a study of Durkheim's theory of penal evolution. *Law and Society Review*, 9, 613–35.

Stanko, E. A. 1981–2: The impact of victim assessment on prosecutors' screening decisions: the case of the New York County district attorney's office. *Law and Society Review*, 16, 225–39.

Stevenson, R. F. 1968: *Population and Political Systems in Tropical Africa*. New York: Columbia University Press.

Tanner, R. E. S. 1966: The selective use of legal systems in East Africa. *East African Institute of Social Research Conference Papers*, pt E, no. 393.

Todd, Jr, H. F. 1978: Litigious marginals: character and disputing in a Bavarian village. In L. Nader and H. F. Todd, Jr (eds), *The Disputing Process: law in ten societies*, New York: Columbia University Press, 86–121.

Trotman, D. V. 1986: *Crime in Trinidad: conflict and control in a plantation society, 1838–1900*. Knoxville, Tenn.: University of Tennessee Press.

Uhlman, T. M. 1979: *Racial Justice: black judges and defendants in an urban trial court*. Lexington, Mass.: D. C. Heath.

Ulmer, S. S. 1973: Social background as an indicator to the votes of Supreme Court justices in criminal cases: 1947–1956 terms. *American Journal of Political Science*, 17, 622–30.

van der Sprenkel, S. 1962: *Legal Institutions in Manchu China: a sociological analysis*. New York: Humanities Press.

Vera Institute of Justice 1981: *Felony Arrests: their prosecution and disposition in New York City's courts*. New York: Longman.

Yngvesson, B. 1988: Making law at the doorway: the clerk, the court, and the construction of community in a New England town. *Law and Society Review*, 22, 409–48.

29

Law and theology

EDWARD CHASE

Law and theology is the discipline that seeks to bring the conceptual categories of theology (for example, God, creation, fall, covenant), or the insights of particular theologians (for example, Karl Barth, Dietrich Bonhoeffer), to bear on the theory and practice of law. In the form of theoretical reflection on the nature of law or its place in human affairs, law and theology bears a strong resemblance to jurisprudence, although its categories of reflection derive from biblical and theological sources, and, as noted, legal theory can itself be a focus of reflection in law and theology. The discipline can also be pursued, however, through a narrative methodology rather than as a matter of systematic analysis; in that form it has considerable resonance with the law and literature movement. Both the systematic and the narrative modes will be considered in this article, although emphasis will be placed more on the former.

Practitioners of law and theology generally use theology as the basis for critiques of law, but, in principle, the relationship is reciprocal, so that theology can learn from, as well as instruct, law, as illustrated in a recent study employing the legal category of contract to refine and deepen the biblical category of covenant (Newman, 1991). However practiced, the domain of law and theology can be as broad as that of law itself, comprehending public as well as private law, and procedures in addition to doctrines and concepts, as in the use of the Judaeo-Christian ethic of reconciliation to discuss alternative dispute resolution (McThenia and Shaffer, 1985). Among the most provocative studies in the field are those that bring theology into correlation with general or fundamental questions about law and legal practice – questions of jurisprudence, constitutional theory and ethics – and it is these studies which occupy the bulk of the present article.

Law and religion, which is covered in a separate entry in this companion (see Article 6, CONSTITUTIONAL LAW AND RELIGION), deals with the ways in which the institutions of law and religion as social and intellectual phenomena resemble and differ from each other, and interact. The interactions can be studied at the level of political theory, as in Michael Perry's important 1991 study of the proper role of religious convictions in political decision making. The interaction between government and religion as set out in the establishment and free exercise clauses of the first amendment is also one important focus of constitutional doctrine and theory. The relationship between law and religion can also be pursued in the form of phenomenological studies of the religious dimensions of law or the legal dimensions of religion, as in the seminal work of Harold Berman (1974). When theological concepts are brought to bear on any of these topics, the interaction of law and religion can also be a matter for law and theology; a recent study using H. Richard Niebuhr's theology of culture to assess the deficiencies in the Supreme Court's cases on the free exercise of religion (Carmella, 1992), and one critiquing the Court's use of the theology of Paul Tillich to determine the meaning of religion in the first amendment (McBride, 1988) are examples. The *Journal of Law and Religion*, a major resource, eschews any attempt at rigid categorization and publishes articles on both law and religion and law and theology. Articles in both fields may also be found under the heading "Religion" in the "Index to legal periodicals."

To some readers, the idea of law and theology as a discipline will be curious if not incoherent, because the central animating concept of theology – God – is deeply problematic to the thoroughly secularized modern academic mind. As Professor Linell Cady has nicely shown, however, the view that theology is irretrievably a parochial discipline rests upon a failure to distinguish dogmatic reliance on authority from contextual inquiry – the "appropriation of and engagement with the texts, symbols and experiences of a particular tradition." "To assume that theology is not a form of public inquiry because of its engagement with a particular tradition presumes a highly misleading, ahistoric sense of public . . . It falsely presumes that reason operates outside of local contexts, that it can escape from the influences of particular traditions of interpretation. It reflects . . . the Enlightenment legacy that continues to inform our outlook" (Cady, 1991, p. 114). Writers in law and theology, no less than others, are entitled to claim the benefits of this important insight of late modernity into the contextuality of all thought. Cady's formulation, however, raises some further issues that deserve discussion, by way of some concluding remarks at the end of the present survey.

Although reflection on the relationship between law and theology has a long history (for example, Aquinas, Luther), the present article is not a historical survey. It, rather, focusses on law and theology as one of several recent disciplines, such as law and literature, mentioned earlier, that have come to prominence since the 1970s as vehicles for critical and constructive reflection on law.

Legal philosophy and theology

The debate between legal positivism and natural law over the meaning of the concept of law provides much of the substance of "traditional jurisprudence" (Murphy and Coleman, 1990). Positivism contends that law consists essentially of rules, whose validity depends on proper promulgation rather than on their correspondence with morality or any other extra-legal or transcendent standard (H. L. A. Hart, 1961). Ronald Dworkin, the leading anti-positivist, argues that principles as well as rules are part of law, that these principles have moral content, and that an understanding of the proper "fit" among principles requires resort to an overarching political theory. Writers in law and theology who have focussed their attention on jurisprudence share Dworkin's rejection of the exclusivist claims of positivism, although they develop their critiques in different ways and from different perspectives.

Harold Berman's specifically jurisprudential and theological project (as distinct from his historical and philosophical interest in the interaction of law and religion, mentioned earlier) is contained in a major 1988 law review article, "Toward an integrative jurisprudence: politics, morality, history" (subsequently included as part of a 1993 collection of his essays entitled *Faith and Order*, from which all references below are taken). In keeping with the irenic impulse that undergirds all of his work in law and religion, Berman describes his "integrative jurisprudence" as an attempt to synthesize the familiar schools of legal positivism and natural law with a third classical (although far less well known) school, historical jurisprudence. As it turns out in Berman's presentation, historical jurisprudence, which has deep roots in theology, provides the principles and methods to accomplish the integration or reconciliation of the positivist and natural law philosophies, so that Berman's project can accurately be understood as the major one of reviving historical jurisprudence – which has been "almost universally disparaged and has virtually disappeared from almost all jurisprudential writings in the twentieth century" (Berman, 1993, p. 304) – for a modern audience.

In Berman's historicist view, law is more than the posited rules of a system, or the posited rules plus the principles of morality that validate those rules; instead, law is best described as an ongoing, purposive activity or enterprise (1993, p. 305).

> The essence of historical jurisprudence is not historicism but historicity, not a return to the past but a recognition that law is an ongoing historical process, developing from the past into the future . . . A genuinely historical jurisprudence . . . rests on the premise that certain long-term historical experiences of a given people lead it in certain directions; and more particularly with respect to law, that the past times through which the legal institutions of a given people have developed help to determine the standards according to which its laws should be enacted and interpreted, the goals to which its legal system strives.

As that excerpt suggests, a central tenet of Berman's historical jurisprudence is that the past is normative – it is the source of "standards" for the interpretation and promulgation of laws, and of the normative "goals" of the legal system. Berman thus argues that the legal tradition contains values that perform the normative and critical function assigned to morality in natural law approaches, but that perform it better in two ways. First, in terms of the specificity of the values located in the tradition, the historicist is "apt to be concerned not with universal moral principles but rather with those specific moral principles that correspond to the character and traditions of a given people or a given society" (1993, p. 291). Second, the moral values that are to serve as standards and goals to guide lawmaking are located at least in part within the legal tradition itself, rather than external to it, so that it is possible to claim, after the positivists, that law is not dependent on general moral principles, and still subject it to criticism.

423

Since the historicist perspective reveals *patterns* or regularities of development of legal doctrines and institutions, the legal tradition also performs the regulative function which positivism assigns to law. But Berman goes beyond positivism by refusing to view the available tradition as being constituted solely by the enactments and pronouncements of licensed state officials (it includes customs, for example), and he also finds in historical jurisprudence, although he does not develop this point in any detail, an answer to the positivist's claim that ultimate authority resides in state power. "The historicity of law in the West . . . was linked with the concept of its supremacy over the political authorities who made it. The developing body of law, whether at a given moment or in the long run, was considered to be binding on the state itself. The ruler could make law, but he could not make it arbitrarily, and until he remade it – lawfully – he was bound by it" (p. 306).

Berman's historical jurisprudence is rooted in theology in two ways. First, he notes that the very concept of an ongoing, normative and regulatory tradition is unthinkable apart from the Western belief in a providential history (1993, p. 310), the Western view of history "as destiny and as mission" (p. 306). Only in the West does the view prevail that law "has an internal logic, that [the] changes that are made in law over generations and centuries are part of a pattern of changes, that law is not merely ongoing, it has a history, it tells a story" (1993, p. 306). In short, Berman sees historicity as an essential dimension for thinking about law, and he sees historicity as essentially a religious phenomenon (Wagner, 1993, p. 1,054).

Second, in delineating the elements of his view of historicity, Berman makes the future a decisive category when he invokes Jurgen Moltmann's theology for the claim that

> our sense of history is based on hope. When we say "history" we mean something more than chronology; we mean not merely change but patterns of change, implying direction in time, which in turn implies either purpose or fate . . . It inevitably contains a prophetic element. (*1993, pp. 309–10*)

The emphasis on the prophetic future seems to be a way of countering the potential conservatism, and perhaps romanticism, of historical jurisprudence's emphasis on tradition. As helpfully elaborated by William Wagner, who considers eschatology to be the key to Berman's jurisprudence, the emphasis on the prophetic future expresses

> the need of each tradition to acknowledge its incompleteness and to abandon its claim to supremacy . . . [Berman] asserts that transcendent values can be realized in transformative patterns of action. But . . . he asserts that these values are denatured where they are not coupled with an acknowledgement of their holiness, that is, of their divine and transcendent ground. (*1993, pp. 1,056–7*)

Much of the appeal of Berman's historical jurisprudence is its rich suggestiveness, as well as its introduction of a different vocabulary into the study of legal philosophy.

Berman's emphasis on the legal past as normative implies the broader notion that law's authoritativeness is internal to the legal tradition, a view which will resonate with modern "neotraditionalists" in legal philosophy (Posner, 1990, ch. 14), who seek to restore law as an autonomous discipline, independent of disciplines such as economics or political or moral philosophy; it may be that it is just that emphasis of positivism that Berman is seeking to validate as worthy of being integrated into a useful jurisprudence. It is part of the suggestiveness of Berman's work, however, that he resists, much as does Dworkin, any easy categorization. Berman's historical jurisprudence contains a competing accent to legal autonomy in the centrality that he gives to the category of the prophetic future, which in some unspecified sense stands in judgment over the values that are only incompletely realized in the legal tradition. Berman's view that the normative values guiding law are both internal to and beyond law has theological warrant; it is at least formally parallel to the theological claim that God is both transcendent to, and immanent in, the world. Indeed, what is most provocative about Berman's integrative jurisprudence is just this reliance on the categories of a theology of history, in contrast to the much more familiar reliance among legal scholars on moral or political philosophy, to delineate a theory of law. In his study of the origins of historical jurisprudence (1994), Berman has repeated his central claims about its significance. One hopes that Berman will soon extract the specifically philosophical and theological elements of his historical jurisprudence from his historiographic interests, and state them in a systematic or at least a programmatic way.

Whereas Berman draws on a Judaeo-Christian philosophy of history and Moltmann's theology of hope in his critical and constructive efforts in jurisprudence, Frank Alexander, a promising younger lawyer-theologian, draws on the biblical doctrines of creation, covenant, and redemption to develop a different response to positivism, which deserves a brief comment. In short, Alexander's argument is this: positivism focusses exclusively on legal rules and legal systems and thus offers a narrow and unsatisfactory theory of law; to go beyond positivism and locate law in its rich context, we must consult ontology, understood as "the study of what it means to be human" (1986, p. 1,090); contemporary American legal thought is particularly weak in ontology, and hence could profit from the study of theology, which "undertakes as one of its major pursuits an inquiry into the nature of individual and collective being" (p. 1,091).

Alexander's ontology consists of the categories of individuality, community, and purpose, which are slighted in positivist analyses, but which find expression in the biblical doctrines of creation, covenant, and redemption. On the question of community, for example, positivism assumes the Hobbesian minimalist position that law is needed strictly to preserve tolerable order while individuals atomistically pursue their discrete goals. The ontological question "is whether law emerges and develops because a number of individuals happen to find themselves together, and need protection against each other, or whether law emerges and develops as an integral part of a community to foster and protect interpersonal bonds that define the community" (p. 1,098). Against positivism's assumption of the former answer,

425

the biblical accounts of creation and covenant suggest the latter view. The doctrine of creation asserts the interrelatedness rather than the isolation of individuals, and the covenant tradition

> points to the existence of responsibility for our actions and stands as a call for the greatest degree of human responsibility in all relationships. It indicates a role for human rationality in the experience of personal relationships, and places emphasis upon the exercise of individual and collective reason. (*p. 1,131*)

Alexander's theme of community and "communitarianism" (Posner, 1990, p. 414) is a recurring one in the literature of law and theology, linking it with strands of feminist jurisprudence, with constructive theorists in critical legal studies, and with the civic republicanism strand of constitutional theory.

Alexander asserts that positivism also tends to relegate consideration of purpose in the law to the penumbral case in which the application of a legal rule to particular facts is in doubt because of the "open texture" of the language of the rule, and calling on the purpose of the rule aids the interpreter in resolving the difficulty (H. L. A. Hart, 1961, pp. 121–32). In Alexander's view, however, purpose is much more pervasive; law is the handiwork of human beings, and "insofar as human nature is purposive in its very essence, legality – the whole body of law – is purposive in its essence" (p. 1,100). One who thus focusses on law as the purposive activity of essentially purposive creatures might argue "that human nature is characterized by its orientation toward transcendent purposes, which purposes clarify the nature and function of law" (p. 1,100).

Alexander's emphasis on law as purposive activity oriented ultimately to transcendent values rather than as a means of social control aligns him with Berman, although as noted, he draws on different theological resources to illuminate the theme. In terms of the emphasis which they place on purpose and value as constitutive categories for the study of law, their indebtedness to the legal philosophy of Lon Fuller is apparent, and is acknowledged by both.

Constitutional theory and theology

Preoccupation with theories of adjudication – how courts decide cases – and the importance of the United States Supreme Court in the American system of constitutional government, combine to make constitutional theory an important topic in American legal philosophy. "Constitutional theory" is itself broad, and some of the law and theology perspectives on it can only be mentioned. Constitutional interpretation is covered in a separate entry in this companion; the contribution of law and theology is to focus on the constitution as scripture and to exploit the parallels between biblical and constitutional interpretation (for example, Ronald Garet 1985). The Court's controversial abortion decision in *Roe* v. *Wade*, which is a central text in the modern debate over methods of constitutional interpretation, has been approached in different terms by writers in law and theology. Edward Gaffney (1973) uses a theological anthropology to explore deficiencies in the

Supreme Court's discussion of whether the fetus is a person. Elizabeth Mensch and Alan Freeman (1991) approach abortion as a central example of the difficulty which a pluralistic society experiences in finding a common vocabulary for conducting rational moral discourse on controversial topics, and they offer a wide-ranging survey of the contributions which Protestant and Catholic theological ethics might make to the creation of such a vocabulary.

Two somewhat more unusual contributions to constitutional theory and theology are the focus of the present section. Graham Walker's *Moral Foundations of Constitutional Thought: current problems, Augustinian prospects* (1990) assesses two "normative impasses" that have developed in modern constitutional theory, and offers Augustine's theology as a response to those impasses. The majority of modern constitutional scholars have arrived at the first impasse – they offer normative theories, which require "an authoritatively real morality" (p. 19), while simultaneously undercutting the possibility of such authoritativeness by espousing the relativity and subjectivity of all values. In more philosophical terms, the impasse for these "nihilist skeptics" is that their philosophical commitments (objective reality doesn't exist or isn't knowable) cause them to see morality simply as convention, while conventionalism undercuts the very moral objectivity presupposed by the constitutional system and texts on which they base their scholarship.

A minority of scholars reject moral skepticism in favor of "moral realism," which claims that the good "is a morally authoritative reality that transcends the relativities of culture, social power relations, and private preferences" (p. 25), and is "somehow accessible to human reason" (p. 26). These moral realist views satisfy the logical requirements of prescriptive theorizing, but the impasse for the realists is that by so powerfully asserting the reality of the moral order, they tend to collapse politics and law into morality, and to sanctify "an open-ended moral jurisprudence by errant judges" (p. 63) in which the standard of adjudication is the "judge's own best current theory of goodness" (p. 146). The sum of Walker's discussion is that conventionalism's pessimism about values makes normative constitutional theorizing incoherent, while realism's optimistic confidence in judicial insight into values endangers it.

Walker claims that Augustine's theology offers just the kind of resource that constitutional theory needs to move out of its impasses. Relying heavily on the biblical doctrines of divine creation and human fall, Augustine explicates an ontology that couples an affirmation of the goodness and moral orderliness of creation (and of the possibility of at least rudimentary human knowledge of that order) on the one hand, with a realistic assessment of humanity's fallen and vitiated condition that relativizes all human accomplishments or aspirations in history.

> [C]reated things, made out of nothing, are mutable and so capable of retracting toward nothingness. Man, whose rational nature enabled him freely and lovingly to cleave to the ground of his being, or to defect, chose the latter. Thus men fell . . . The vitiated condition of human nature manifests itself in viceful proclivities that cannot be overcome so long as man insists on aspiring to be his own point of integration. (*p. 108*)

427

The important payoff of Augustine's ontology for Walker is that it leads to a political theory of the limited role of the state that has direct implications for the current constitutional impasses. Augustine assigns "lower and safer tasks" to politics and to law than current reformist constitutional theorists (both in the realist and conventionalist camps) envision. In the Augustinian rendering, "the possibilities of inculcating virtue through law are narrow. Political rule does what good it can while the real drama [of history] proceeds on other levels" (p. 109). Politics, including law, has only the "provisional and palliative" task (p. 106) of keeping peace and order, not the higher one of "rescuing created being from its fundamental instability" or of regenerating man (p. 107). In short, Walker's reading of Augustine leads him to the paradoxical conclusion that the premises of moral realism, which are logically required by the enterprise of normative theorizing, lead to the cautionary conclusions embraced by the more conservative of the moral skeptics.

Jefferson Powell's *The Moral Tradition of American Constitutionalism: a theological interpretation* (1993) views the same terrain as Walker's *Moral Foundations*, but from a different perspective. This emphasis yields somewhat more detailed, if still subdued, conclusions. Whereas Walker draws on the categories of conventionalism and realism to identify the impasses faced by constitutional theorists, Powell analyzes the same perceived problem in terms of MacIntyre's notion of an "epistemological crisis" – the inability of a tradition of inquiry to resolve in its own terms the conflicts it generates. As an expression of Enlightenment liberalism, American constitutionalism claims "to privilege . . . the dispassionate reason of the judge over the expedient decision of the legislator or executive official" (p. 8). That central claim, however, can no longer be sustained because courts and scholars have been no more successful in articulating an authoritative and principled textual or other basis for the modern expansive judicial protection of supposedly fundamental, but unenumerated, individual rights (such as the right to an abortion) than pre-1937 courts were in justifying their expansive protection of property rights. In contrast to Walker, who concentrates exclusively and in detail on the work of constitutional theorists, Powell balances shorter but equally penetrating critiques of the roster of modern constitutional scholars with discussions of how the epistemological crisis has played out in Supreme Court jurisprudence, particularly in cases like *Lochner* v. *New York, Eisenstadt* v. *Baird*, and the abortion decision, *Roe* v. *Wade*.

While Powell's descriptive case is equally as rich as Walker's, his study is most interesting for present purposes for its theological response to American constitutionalism. Drawing on John Howard Yoder's theology, supplemented at critical points by reference to Augustine's thought, Powell draws two conclusions about a Christian response to the current crisis in constitutional theory. Yoder's negative case for democratic government is that it "makes strong self-justificatory claims about its grounding in the people as a political community" (p. 281); because democratic leaders must periodically stand for office before the people, the personnel and policies of democratic government are endlessly revisable. Powell finds that this "corrigibility" of democratic government points at least marginally in favor of Christian support for majoritarian over judicial decision making, since American constitutional rhetoric "is a language of permanence, of settled decision, of absolute political value. Matters subject to judicial decision in the name of the Constitution are, by definition, beyond ordinary revision, perhaps beyond legitimate revision altogether" (p. 289).

Yoder's positive case – "the argument that democracy may be relatively justifiable in theological terms because of its relative openness in some situations to voices of dissent" (p. 289) – provides Powell with the basis for "additional and somewhat more definite elements" for a Christian response to the current crisis in the relationship between majoritarian and judicial policy-making. Powell adduces the Supreme Court's protection of "discrete and insular minorities," as well as the "specifically political-process aspects of the Court's free expression jurisprudence," and finally, its procedural due process decisions, as "supportive in a fairly direct way of the ability of the weak, the victimized, and the outsider to make their voices heard" (p. 289), and to that extent, as "valuable in Christian terms as means of opening or keeping open the avenues of minority leverage" (p. 290). Powell recognizes that this is "a relatively austere view of American constitutionalism" (p. 292), but argues that it is the view required by Christian commitments. "There is no Christian constitutionalism; Caesar remains Caesar" (p. 292).

That quote from Powell in fact identifies what may be the central value of the Walker and Powell studies, which contrasts them with much of the other work in law and theology canvassed in this article. Both Walker and Powell have the merit of reinvigorating a longstanding negative theological emphasis on the role and limits of law that has always competed historically with more positive assessments. Both studies raise the recurring theological theme that law, while not irrelevant to a society's highest aspirations, is not – at least not clearly – the path to accomplishing them either. To borrow David Luban's distinction (and to use it for different purposes), both writers employ theological sources to explore the possibility that the best normative vision of law is one that sees it more as a technology of governance than a moral achievement.

Ethics: theology and law practice

In addressing the relationship between Christian commitments and constitutional government, Powell's study stands in the broad tradition of theological social ethics. However, since the specific provocation for his reflections, and those of Walker, is constitutional theory, it has seemed more informative to the non-specialist reader to consider their work as examples of constitutional law scholarship rather than as ethics proper. In broadest terms, the ethics discussions of lawyer-theologians focus on the existential question of authentic existence in law. Two distinctive themes emerge: that law practice is a vocation or calling, indeed, a kind of ministry; and that authentic law practice involves representation of society's poor. The work of Thomas Shaffer sounds the first theme in detail, and it is the focus of the present discussion.

The legal profession tends to locate ethics within law rather than the other way around. In his book *On Being a Christian and a Lawyer* (1981), Shaffer addresses this fundamental difference in orientation by asking whether it is possible to be both a Christian and a lawyer. His answer is a conditional yes, and he specifies four conditions.

> To the extent that one determines to conduct his practice as moral conversation, his advocacy as moral discourse, his lawyer skill as the virtue of hope, his life as an affirmation that justice is a gift not a commodity one has from the government, I think it is possible to be a Christian and a lawyer. Seen that way, the law is a calling in which "we are saying something that we do not know, that is true only when it comes true" (Buber). (*p. 32*)

In brief, Shaffer's critique is that the professional culture of the law makes justice its main aspiration, and commits itself to the adversary system as the best way to accomplish justice. That adversary orientation, in turn, is foundational. It defines the lawyer's relation to clients (as a hired gun), and to tribunals (as an advocate). It establishes the underlying dynamic of the lawyer's activity as the manipulation of state power to serve the client's interest. In this scheme of things, the chief ethical virtue of the lawyer is loyalty to the client. Shaffer is determined to state a theology of law practice and law culture that voices entirely different aspirations for dealing with clients and tribunals, and which makes a very different assessment of the state than are found in the adversary ethic.

In arguing that the Christian lawyer must conduct the counseling of clients as a moral conversation, he distinguishes the ethics of role (do what the client wants or tell the client what to do) and the ethics of isolation (respect but don't try to change the client's moral position) from the risky but potentially transformative ethics of care. The theology underlying the ethics of care takes its specific text from Corinthians (2 Corinthians 10:18), and its emphasis on relationships from Martin Buber. In Shaffer's words, "[t]he theology of the matter . . . is that my client was sent to me by God; God proposes to deal with me through my client. We are told that we have to deliver one another" (p. 37).

Shaffer pairs his view of counseling as moral conversation with a view of advocacy as moral discourse, which has a unique content, audience, and goal, all of which distinguish it from the more conventional view of advocacy as a kind of private warfare. Advocacy attempts to tell the unique story of the client, it is addressed to the conscience of the tribunal, and its goal is reconciliation – of advocate to client, advocate to tribunal, and tribunal to client. Advocacy in this understanding is both an expression of community and a contribution towards building it. Shaffer's view of counseling and advocacy as moral discourse exemplify his conception of the lawyer's vocation as ministry.

Shaffer's discussion of the dialectic of hope and skill, and their relation to state power, is one of the most interesting parts of his presentation. Hope is an imperative in Shaffer's theological ethics; the New Testament "is not about using power, but about how God provides the means to live hopefully rather than powerfully" (p. 192). A competent lawyer can live hopefully because skill is a basis for hope, just as hope is itself a skill. The essential lawyer's hope is that "analysis and knowledge will go a long way toward containing power" (p. 197), that "those who have power are bound to respect skill and knowledge in the wielding of power – skill and knowledge even among those who merely wield power, who do not have it" (p. 195). That particular legal hope is part of a broader theological affirmation that government, and hence power, is limited (p. 194), and that only goodness can justify power (p. 202). What ultimately animates Shaffer's view is the affirmation contained in the Jewish and Christian moral tradition that "meaning triumphs over power" (p. 102).

Shaffer's most provocative theological critique is that the highest value of the adversary system – its aspiration to do justice – is misplaced. The adversary system "announces that justice is the goal of professional activity and that the means to justice is zealous loyalty to the interests of one's client" (p. 163). In Shaffer's Christian ethics, this is wrong both as to ends and means, and both errors flow from a mistaken premiss. Justice is penultimate to compassion and hope as goals of the lawyer's ministry (p. 162), and the way to those goals is through faithfulness to the client rather than loyalty. In any event, the state in Shaffer's view dispenses force, not justice (p.178); justice in Shaffer's view is not a dispensation of the state secured by skillful advocacy, but a gift. "The reliance on government that justice . . . implies is always open to the collective notion that government has real power" (p. 163). The belief that government rather than the people has real power is undemocratic; in theological terms it is a kind of idolatry.

Shaffer's views of the lawyer's vocation are undoubtedly idealistic (he subtitles the book "law for the innocent"); but that is the great strength of the book. To be sure, there are places where the book provides analytical riffs (as in his distinctions between loyalty and faithfulness, and hope and optimism) on matters that deserve more sustained development. What Shaffer has provided, however, through a wide-ranging discussion of the lawyer's most essential tasks and the culture in which those tasks are carried out, is no less than an alternative paradigm for thinking about the work that lawyers do. What he has said about the most recent work of Milner Ball could also aptly be applied to his own work; although it will be passed around by scholars and teachers, "the significant passing around will be among the young people who still come to universities, in inexplicable and record numbers, saying they want to be lawyers" (Shaffer, 1994, p. 162).

Narrative method and theology

The work of Milner Ball represents something of an intellectual odyssey across much of the terrain of law and theology discussed in this article; his earlier books deal with the relationship of theology to constitutional theory (1981) and to jurisprudence (1985), and deserve reading along with the works discussed above in connection with those topics. As his thought has evolved, however, he has moved away from what he now sees as a confining concentration on theory and on the work of appellate courts to a focus on law practice, the law in action. Fittingly, he begins his latest work, *The Word and the Law*, with extensive and sharply etched biographical sketches of seven practitioners and judges. His beginning with narrative – and with these particular stories, which recount various forms of public-interest law – is not casual; as the book unfolds, one sees that the stories express his distinctive substantive and methodological commitments in theology.

The theology that Ball uses to illuminate the practices he narrates is Karl Barth's theology of the Word of God, in which *Word* is understood comprehensively as the subject matter to which the biblical texts point, the texts themselves, and the preaching that arises from those texts. The subject of text and preaching is God's self-revealing activity in the world, particularly God's decisive action in becoming human, and suffering for others, in the person of Jesus. No "special applications" – such as religious devotion – are needed to appreciate this Word and its significance; indeed, Ball's estimate of religion is negative – it tends to be a distraction and a kind of unbelief, directing the self toward solipsism rather than toward the neighbor and community. The believer's role is not to be religious, but rather "to discern, rely on, and celebrate the Word present in the common, actual life of the world" (p. 76).

For Ball, the law practices which he celebrates in his first chapter are exemplary of the Word at work in the "common, actual life" of the world. They are exemplary of the Word at work, however, because they exemplify a particular *kind* of involvement, and it is here that the distinctive substantive theme in Ball's work surfaces. All of Ball's practitioners or judges devote their professional lives to practicing or adjudicating law "for the unimportant," to use Thomas Shaffer's felicitous phrase. This is not an accidental choice of Ball's; it has a theological warrant. Quoting Barth's observation that the God of the biblical stories favored the weak and the oppressed "almost to the point of prejudice," Ball argues that "[p]overty and self-giving rather than power, wealth, and self-aggrandizement still constitute the likely sites for gathering evidence of the Word taking positive form" in the world of action (p. 152). Thus Ball's disclaimer that his book is not ethics but is instead "the kind of description that . . . precedes it" (p. 100) is true only if one understands ethics as the more inclusive kind of presentation offered by Shaffer. Much of the undoubted power of Ball's presentation is his insistence on the centrality of a theological ethic that accords the highest priority to service of the poor.

The other distinctive accent of *The Word and the Law* is its methodological emphasis on narrative and storytelling. The widespread interest in that methodology is no doubt related to the "interpretive turn" taken in recent years by a variety of disciplines, including theology and law. This is not the place to attempt an evaluation of the merits of that turn, or of narrative. It bears noting, however, that narrative in Ball's view is not only an epistemological category, it is also an ethical one; he sees it as central not only to the communication of truth, but also to what he apparently understands to be the ethics of participating in a community through dialogue. He distinguishes repeatedly between rigorous argument, which he regards as coercive, and his more invitational, performatory mode of presentation through story, and he repeats *passim* his introductory caution that *The Word and the Law* does not make "a linear argument or advance a set of propositions toward a conclusion designed to compel readers' assent by the force of its logic" (pp. 1–2).

That last assertion of Ball's implicates larger issues, and offers an opportunity for a few comments that might serve to conclude this survey of law and theology. As noted at the outset of this article, Linnell Cady has suggested that theology's dependence on particular traditions of inquiry does not disqualify it from participation in discussions of important public issues. That observation, however, leaves open the question of *how* theology addresses the broader culture to which it speaks. In theological terms, Ball's distinction between the coerciveness of linear argument and his own invitational approach echoes the distinction between a theology which is apologetic and one which is confessional (in these terms, Ball's approach is radically confessional). Apologetics in the best sense, however, is an attempt not just to state one's theological commitments, but to argue for and defend them to a secular culture in the most rigorous terms available; theological imperialism, the kind of thing that Ball rightly detests but which he generalizes to the whole mode of logical and systematic argument, is not a necessary part of it. This question of method arises in other work canvassed herein. Graham Walker pursues a version of Paul Tillich's well-known "method of correlation," in which theological categories – in Walker's case, Augustine's – supply an answer to modern philosophical predicaments. In Tillich's apologetics, however, philosophy correlates to theology by supplying the questions *and* the form taken by the answers that theology suggests (Grentz and Olsen, 1992, ch. 4). If Walker's own prescriptive case for Augustine's relevance to modern constitutional theory is less successful than his powerful descriptive account of the modern impasses, as several reviewers have indicated, it may be because of his failure to translate Augustine's theological categories into a more modern idiom, that is, to go far enough down the road that he has rightly started on. There are no doubt dangers the other way; Karl Barth vigorously disputed the validity for theology of letting philosophy set the agenda of questions. Maybe all that needs to be said is that methodological flexibility is useful, and that in addressing the predominantly secular legal academy, practitioners of law and theology might usefully lean in the direction of apologetics.

A second problem, also methodological, concerns the propriety of meshing distinct, though not necessarily incompatible, theologies. Robin Lovin's excellent study of theological ethics shows both similarities and differences between Barth's "ethics of obedience" and Bonhoeffer's ethics of "Christian realism," to name two theologians who have been particularly influential to writers in law and theology. Whether those differences matter is an issue that needs to be addressed when those theologians are invoked for the contributions they can make to the interaction of law and theology.

Those questions aside, it remains true that the important themes highlighted by the writers canvassed in this survey – for example, law's dependence on or independence from transcendent values; law as a mechanism for control or for

433

reconciliation of a polity's citizens; law practice as the manipulation of power on behalf of self-interest or as a kind of other-directed ministry; the importance of community – are central to modern jurisprudential and ethical thought, and that theology can be an important resource for illuminating them.

Bibliography

Alexander, F. S. 1986: Beyond positivism: a theological perspective. *Georgia Law Review*, 20, 1,089.

Ball, M. S. 1981: *The Promise of American Law: a theological, humanistic view of legal process*. Athens, Ga.: University of Georgia Press.

—— 1985: *Lying Down Together: law, metaphor, and theology*. Madison, Wisconsin: University of Wisconsin Press.

—— 1993: *The Word and the Law*. Chicago: University of Chicago Press.

Berman, H. J. 1974: *The Interaction of Law and Religion*. Nashville: Abingdon Press.

—— 1993: *Faith and Order: the reconciliation of law and religion*. Atlanta: Scholars Press.

—— 1994: The origins of historical jurisprudence: Coke, Selden, Hale. *Yale Law Journal*, 103, 1,651.

Cady, L. E. 1991: H. Richard Niebuhr and the task of a public theology. In R. F. Thiemann (ed.), *The Legacy of H. Richard Niebuhr*, Minneapolis: Fortress Press.

Carmella, A. C. 1992: A theological critique of free exercise jurisprudence. *George Washington Law Journal*, 60, 782.

Dworkin, R. 1986: *Law's Empire*. Cambridge: Belknap Press.

Gaffney, E. M. 1973: Law and theology: a dialogue on the abortion decisions. *The Jurist*, 33, 134.

Garet, R. R. 1985: Comparative normative hermeneutics: scripture, literature, constitution. *Southern California Law Review*, 58, 35.

Grentz, S. J. and Olsen, R. E. 1992: *20th Century Theology: God and the world in a transitional age*. Downers Grove, Ill.: InterVarsity Press.

Hart, H. L. A. 1961: *The Concept of Law*. Oxford: Clarendon Press.

Lovin, R. W. 1984: *Christian Faith and Public Choices: the social ethics of Barth, Brunner, and Bonhoeffer*. Philadelphia: Fortress Press.

Luban, D. 1993: Getting the Word. *Michigan Law Review*, 91, 1,247 (review of M. Ball, *The Word and the Law*).

McBride, J. 1988: Paul Tillich and the Supreme Court: Tillich's "ultimate concern" as a standard in judicial interpretation. *Journal of Church and State*, 30, 245.

McThenia, A. W. and Shaffer, T. L. 1985: For reconciliation. *Yale Law Journal*, 94, 1,660.

Mensch, E. and Freeman, A. 1991: The politics of virtue: animals, theology and abortion. *Georgia Law Review*, 25, 923.

Moltmann, J. 1967: *Theology of Hope: on the ground and the implications of a Christian eschatology*. New York: Harper & Row.

Murphy, J. G. and Coleman, J. E. 1990: *Philosophy of Law: an introduction to jurisprudence*. Boulder: Westview Press.

Newman, L. E. 1991: Covenant and contract: a framework for the analysis of Jewish ethics. *Journal of Law and Religion*, 9, 89.

Perry, M. J. 1991: *Love and Power: the role of religion and morality in American politics*. New York: Oxford University Press.

Posner, R. A. 1990: *The Problems of Jurisprudence*. Cambridge, Mass.: Harvard University Press.

Powell, H. J. 1993: *The Moral Tradition of American Constitutionalism: a theological interpre-tation*. Durham: Duke University Press.

Shaffer, T. L. 1981: *On Being a Christian and a Lawyer: law for the innocent*. Provo, Utah: Brigham Young University Press.

—— 1994: Book review. *Theology Today*, 51, 162 (review of M. Ball, *The Word and the Law*).

Wagner, W. J. 1993: "The just and the holy are one": the role of eschatology in Harold Berman's vision of normative jurisprudence. *Emory Law Journal*, 42, 1,045.

Walker, G. 1990: *Moral Foundations of Constitutional Thought: current problems, Augustinian prospects*. Princeton: Princeton University Press.

30

Law and morality

ROGER A. SHINER

Human beings are both particular individual persons and ineluctably social creatures. Their individual projects, interests, and lives overlap and intertwine in complex ways. These relationships need management if human life is to bring pleasure
and satisfaction to those who live it. Both the law and morality are normative
systems designed for such management. The similarities and differences between
them need careful charting if they are to complement each other, rather than
compete with each other, and human flourishing requires such complementarity.

Legal positivism as a jurisprudential theory is well known for urging the separation of law and morality. Positivism distinguishes sharply between what it is
for a norm to exist as a valid law and what it is for a norm to exist as a valid moral
standard. Even a system of iniquitous norms may count as a system of law. The
family of anti-positivistic jurisprudential theories, the classical natural law tradition being the central and most well known case, urge instead that it is the nature
of law to have some essential connection with morality. The valid substantive
norms of morality must exercise some influence over whether a candidate norm
or system of norms counts as a system of law.

Given such a disagreement, it is hardly surprising that a perennial controversy
exists within jurisprudence concerning the relation between law and morality. In
fact, so many issues within analytic jurisprudence concern the relation between
law and morality that an article about "Law and morality" runs the risk of turning
into a survey of the field of analytic jurisprudence. But the temptation must be
resisted. This article will not join the jurisprudential debate over the relation between law and morality. The relationship can be mapped extensively in pre-philosophical or commonsensical intuitive terms, terms which are compatible with all
legal theories. We shall conduct such a mapping first, and then indicate where the
jurisprudential issues have been traditionally joined and where there are opportunities for further work.

Relationships between law and morality

Let us begin with some positive relationships between law and morality. Since law
and morality are both extensively implicated in the realization of human flourishing,
it should hardly be surprising that there are such positive relationships.

436

(1) Law and morality clearly overlap: they contain norms identical in content. They both have norms relating to the avoidance of interpersonal harm and the management of limited resources, norms which prohibit causing harm to another person, and norms which regulate the distribution and holding of goods. These correspondences include not merely the inventory of actions proscribed, but also such other elements as the conditions under which the causing of harm attracts responsibility and liability and the specification of circumstances under which the causing of harm may be justified or excused. There are considerable correspondences between the circumstances under which morality acknowledges a promise to be binding or justifiably broken, and those under which the law will enforce or release a contractual obligation. Provisions in law concerning the tort of negligence mirror moral norms about the moral culpability of neglectful behavior. Norms in morality about fair procedure and distribution are mirrored in regulations concerning the operation of administrative and judicial tribunals. Or rather – for all these cases – either there is such mirroring, or the legal arrangements attract moral criticism on the assumption that such mirroring is desired.

Hart (1961, pp. 189–95) has argued that, given survival as a fundamental human goal, and given the facts of our physical vulnerability to each other, our rough equality of strength, and our limited natural resources, then norms concerning the avoidance of interpersonal harm and the distribution and possession of resources will inevitably occur in any normative system for the regulation of human behavior. *A fortiori*, both human law and human morality will contain such norms. He refers to such norms as "the minimum content of Natural Law," and, though defending legal positivism, acknowledges that there is just that much falsity to the claim that law may have any content and still be law. Law cannot but have the "minimum content," for a legal system is a normative system regulating human behavior, and any normative system regulating human behavior will have that content.

Hart clearly believes that acceptance of the doctrine of the minimum content of natural law is consistent with the defence of positivism. What it is for a norm to be a norm of morality, and what it is for a norm to be a norm of law, will still be quite different. However, quite clearly, acceptance of the doctrine of the minimum content of natural law is also consistent with the defence of anti-positivism. In fact, arguably, anti-positivism must be committed to some such doctrine. Whether Hart is right to claim that the doctrine is compatible with positivism cannot be settled here.

(2) A body of positive law, as a matter of empirical social psychology, often comes to have the content that it has because the law-maker (whether legislature or court) seeks to have the content of the law track the content of morality. Stock exchange rules against so-called "insider trading," for example, are a relatively recent phenomenon. At least part of the reason for their enactment was the gradual perception that use of inside information in the manner proscribed was a source of unfairness in an enterprise in which fairness was important. Marital rape has become criminalized because of the prior realization that norms of interpersonal

437

behavior which condoned it were mistakes from the moral point of view. Laws, of course, come into existence as a matter of empirical fact for a variety of reasons. Even in cases where the origin seems to lie in moral judgments, a more detailed examination of motive might reveal the efficient cause to be a legislator's desire to act in accord with the wishes of constituents, whether or not he or she would judge likewise. In such a case, it would be misleading to assert the change to be the result of moral judgment. All the same, the content of morality is one standard cause of the content of law through such psychological mechanisms.

Recognition of such a cause, however, is as compatible with legal positivism as with its opponents. The separation thesis concerning law and morality that positivism asserts has to do with the status of a norm as valid law, not with empirical claims about trains of thought in the minds of law-makers.

(3) Legal systems may in different ways quite explicitly leave places where the details of the legal substance need to be filled out by appeal to moral notions. (Note again that this claim is meant to be commonsensical and pre-philosophical. What jurisprudential significance it may have we shall discuss at p. 447, below, "Moral arguments in courts of law.") The best examples might be documents such as Constitutions, Charters or Bills of Rights. The full extent of the legal guarantee of freedom of expression, for instance, of a right to life, liberty, and security of the person, or to equal treatment under the law, will need to be filled out by reference to the moral concepts themselves which such provisions seek to translate into legal rights and liberties, powers, and immunities. Administrative tribunals may be called upon to act, or to judge whether others acted, "fairly," to say whether a procedure or a distribution was "fair." Here, too, it is natural to construe the term as referring to background moral notions of fairness.

History may have some role to play, though. The Canadian Charter of Rights and Freedoms came into force in 1982, and it is still true that many issues the Supreme Court is asked to decide as ultimate interpreter of the Charter are issues which have never before been litigated as constitutional issues. While the Court's rulings never wholly escape political or moral criticism, the Court has on the whole taken seriously the task of reviewing from the moral ground up what a commitment to the values contained in the Charter amounts to for adjudication. Because the Charter is too new for there to be a long institutional history of what "security of the person," or "equality," or "fundamental justice" mean in the relevant sections of the Charter, moral principle makes a strong contribution. But where there is a long institutional history, there may be both the temptation and the tendency to take references to seemingly independent moral notions as no more than disguised references to the institutional history of the interpretation of those notions. All the same, it is not possible to say that judicial activism (interpreting a Constitution broadly) or judicial restraint (interpreting a Constitution narrowly) are, as such, either good or bad from the moral point of view. If the content of constitutional law has developed in a morally attractive way, then restraint will be good, and activism bad. If the content has developed in a morally unattractive way, then activism will be good and restraint bad.

438

(4) A stronger claim yet may be made, that it is a proper task of the law to enforce morality. Let us call this claim "the enforcement thesis." How far such a claim may be justified depends considerably on exactly what the claim is taken to mean. If it is simply the denial of the thesis that it is never proper for the content of law to mirror the content of morality, then, while unquestionably true, it is not particularly interesting, since the thesis which it denies is nowhere held. Often, however, particularly in contexts such as the legal restriction of obscenity or the criminalization of homosexuality, the claim about the enforcement of morality is the claim that it is a proper task of the law to track the actual moral beliefs of the majority of citizens about some matter, whether those beliefs are sound from the moral point of view itself or not. The law is regarded as an aspect of the democratic process like any other. No inquiry is made into the objective soundness of the winning side in a referendum; that the side secured the majority of votes is sufficient. Whether the enforcement claim in this form is correct raises deep questions about the extent to which the goals and values of democracy may compatibly with those goals and values be served by non-democratic procedures. This is an issue that has been with us since the beginning of political theory in classical Greece: it will not be settled here.

Sometimes, however, the debate over the enforcement thesis takes place with different presuppositions. There was a famous exchange in the early 1960s in Britain between Hart and Lord Patrick Devlin over the public response to the publication of the Wolfenden Report which recommended decriminalizing homosexual intercourse between consenting adults. Lord Devlin (1965; much of the material was originally published earlier) took the view that the viscerally powerful reactions of the majority of ordinary people should be respected by the law, not for reasons of democratic proceduralism, but because he believed that such reactions were a sound guide to the content of morality. Thus, for the law to enforce the content of these reactions would be for the law to enforce morality. Hart in response (1963, pp. 17–24) formulated his well-known distinction between the "positive morality" and the "critical morality" of a society. The former consisted of the set of moral beliefs independent of reflection that a society held at a point in time. The latter consisted of the set of moral beliefs arrived at after checking "positive morality" for such things as coherence, accuracy of factual assumptions, and so on. Lord Devlin's version of the enforcement thesis, therefore, urged that the law should enforce "positive morality," which seemed implausible. Hart himself clearly believed that it would be a good thing from the moral point of view if the law of a society did track the content of "critical morality." But, as a positivist, his adherence to that belief could not be, and was not, any part of his theory of law. His view was, rather, an expression of his commitment to a liberal state in which individual autonomy and freedom of expression would flourish.

Lord Devlin also seems to defend, at times, the further claim that the content of morality *just is* the content of such visceral reactions. Ronald Dworkin (1978, ch. 10), while energetically rejecting Lord Devlin's view on what counts as morality and how we would know it, defended a version of his enforcement thesis. Dworkin's "Rights Thesis," that legal decisions enforce antecedently existing political and

439

moral rights, states that it is not merely a proper task of the law to enforce morality, but even that it is *the* proper task of the law so to do. Dworkin himself notes some limits on the enforcement thesis. In an essay entitled "Principle, policy, procedure" (reprinted in (1985), ch. 3) he considers whether we have a right to the best procedurally possible legal system, "best" in the sense of "best from the moral point of view, independent of questions of utility and policy." His answer is that, as long as threshold criteria of equality and procedural justice are met, then issues of institutional design and structure in the legal system may be properly decided on grounds of efficiency, utility, or policy, not on moral grounds. The argument is only about legal procedure, but it seems capable of extension to substantive issues. Once Dworkin's enforcement thesis, however, goes beyond the assertion that it is a proper task of the law to enforce morality to his stronger claim, then the thesis is no longer theory-neutral. Dworkin's enforcement thesis is part of his general repudiation of legal positivism.

(5) The possibilities of a comparison of law and morality at the level of substantive content are huge. Only a most general comment can be made here. It is not disputed that there are substantive differences. Whether or not, as the sceptics urge, "legal ethics" is an oxymoron, an official at whatever level of importance of the legal system has rights and duties flowing from their institutional role that non-officials do not have. The shape the substantive issues have arguably derived in the end from their being special cases of the general problem of how to relate public morality (the morality of public life and institutions) to private and personal morality. Nagel (1978) sets out a plausible general framework for approaching such questions.

Within morality as a whole (as in any other practical domain), a distinction can be drawn between *result-oriented* moral reasons and *action-oriented* moral reasons – between, that is, reasons which focus on the consequences flowing from an action (that it promotes the welfare of a disadvantaged group, for example), and reasons which focus on some quality of an action itself (that it fulfills a duty, or constitutes the exercise of a right, for example). Private morality tends to give greater weight to the latter kind of considerations. Actions done in the name of personal relationships, for instance, are accorded great respect even if they contribute little to, or perhaps even somewhat damage, overall societal welfare. In the public domain, however, results and consequences for overall societal welfare have greater prominence. Impartiality between persons is crucial. Consider the difference between the propriety of parents feeding their own children and no one else's in their home, and of hiring their own children and no one else's to positions in government service.

Against such a background, two ways of thinking about the substantive relations of law and morality are mistakes to be avoided. Both are mistakes about the relation of private morality to morality as a whole. One mistake is to assume that the rights and duties of an official of the legal system are always properly judged by the normative standards of private morality. They are not: the official's position in a public institution means that quite different standards may be appropriate.

Private morality is not all of morality as a whole. The other mistake is to assume that occupying the position of official in a public institution insulates the occupant from the demands of morality as a whole. It does not; the demands of public morality are part of, and in the end answerable to, morality as a whole. Legal ethics, as the inquiry into what standards of behaviour are appropriate for members of the legal profession, therefore raises issues of public morality and its place within morality as a whole.

Differences between law and morality

Positivism's thesis about the essential separation of law and morality does not materialize out of thin air. There are significant differences between law and morality as normative systems, differences which give rise to the separation thesis as a way of representing these differences at the level of theory. Fundamentally, a legal system is an institutionalized normative system; the morality of a group or society is not. Let us explain and discuss this fundamental difference in more detail.

(1) First, laws typically come into existence, are changed, or cease to exist at specific points in time, and as a result of the following of specific procedures. The example which is perhaps most familiar is the parliamentary or congressional bill − a set of provisions which become law through the act(s) of a legislative body. Norms become law in a variety of other ways too, but their existence as laws is comprehensible best by seeing the connection to the above central case. In non-democratic societies, the command of the President, or of the ruling junta, or of the monarch might be sufficient to make a norm law. In democracies with a bi-cameral legislature, and perhaps a residual formal power vested in a monarch, a specified series of acts is needed before a norm becomes law. In common law systems, acts of the judiciary may also result in law − distinguishing precedents, overruling precedents, varying form and substance of statutory interpretation. In all of these cases, whatever a person might feel about whether a given norm should or should not be part of the law, in fact it will not be part of the law unless it has met some appropriate institutional test for the existence of law. It is important to understand that the preceding sentences are not written in the spirit of arguing the case for legal positivism. They are written in the spirit of stating plain facts about the law as a contemporary social institution. As such, they neither confirm nor refute legal positivism or any other legal theory. They are the data which legal theory seeks to interpret.

Moreover, customary practice, whether of officials of the system or of citizens, may suffice in some cases to bring law into existence. In a modern developed legal system, the customary element will be a quantitatively minor part, although, since in some common law systems aspects of the society's constitution may have a purely customary basis, the customary norms may not be qualitatively minor. In this customary aspect, however, law becomes most like morality. For the formal

441

existence of norms of morality is nothing but customary. Moral norms evolve and develop, become established or vary, over time. In essence, what is meant by the morality of a society is the set of customary norms by which the members of the society regulate significant social and private behavior. Again, that sentence is offered as a pre-philosophical statement of plain fact. It should not be read as stating the philosophical thesis that moral norms are "nothing but customs" and that moral value cannot be objective: all options for the metaphysics of morals are intended to be left open. What would make the Ten Commandments, for instance, the morality of the ancient children of Israel would be that they lived their lives by such norms, not that the norms were inscribed on tablets of stone and enunciated to the people by a leader at a particular point in time. From the point of view of social anthropology, it may be possible retrospectively to date the observance of these norms from the time of that announcement, and to explain the observance of them in terms of the peoples' belief that the norms were the commands of God to them. But if the people had not subsequently regulated their lives by those norms, all the formalities in the world would not make those norms the morality of the children of Israel.

(2) The fact that a legal system is an institutionalized normative system leads to another typical difference between law and morality. The laws of a society are in an important sense *public*. Legislative enactments are written down and published in official records to which, in principle, any citizen has, and must have, access. Decisions of official tribunals are similarly made public in reports. The laws of a society have a status whereby notions of fairness within background political morality drive requirements of public announcement and accessibility, of clarity and comprehensibility, of non-retroactivity for law. The morality of a society is not expected to be public in the same way. Suppose an outsider, a visitor comes to sense that some aspect of his behavior is being negatively judged from the moral point of view by members of the society he has entered, but he has no idea why; nothing was explained to him in advance. He may feel frustration, even anger. He may make negative judgments of his own about the openness of the other group to outsiders and visitors. He cannot so obviously complain of the procedural unfairness of being so treated.

(3) Because the law is public, mechanisms for many constitutive sub-systems of the law are essentially public too. These include sub-institutions for the enforcement of law, for the determination of breaches of the law, for the settlement of disputes and the administration of activities under the law, for the imposition of sanctions for breaches of the law, for authoritative interpretation of the law, and for the use by citizens of the facilitative aspects of the law. Sanction in a public normative system for breach of public laws must be by and in public institutions. The persons sanctioned will be persons who in the nature of the case have displayed rejection of the normative force of those public norms. Morality is again fundamentally different. The above tasks in relation to moral norms are handled by the members of the society themselves as part of their ongoing social interactions.

It has been argued by H. L. A. Hart (1961, p. 84) that pressure to conform and sanction for non-conformity in the case of law is typically physical, and in the case of morality typically psychological. As a conceptual claim, this is implausible. As an empirical claim, it is, at best, a very rough-edged truth. The parent who sends the child to their room, or withdraws some privilege for a period of time for a damages has its analog in withholding of compensation or reward. The individual who secures conformity to their wishes by manipulating others' feelings is not so different from the state which secures conformity through fear of the sanction. The essential publicity of law together with the practicalities of public policy do mean that a public criminal justice system has only cruder or blunter forms of sanction available to it. Because morality is more directly interpersonal, greater opportunities for responses which respect the individual as rational being are available. Antony Duff has argued (1986) that public punishment systems can approximate far more to the model of moral discourse than they presently do. Even if he is right, the distinction between the law as a public institution and morality as (in this sense) private remains.

(4) One further difference between law and morality may be explored. Joseph Raz (1975, pp. 150–4) asserted that legal systems as a species of normative system have the characteristics of being "comprehensive," "supreme," and "open," and that, as a result, the legal system of a society is the most important normative system of that society. In one obvious intuitive sense of "supreme" and "important," this claim is implausible. Morality has to do with as many matters crucial to human flourishing as does law, if either one is compared with a normative system such as etiquette or fashion. Raz, however, does not mean to contest such an obvious claim. He intends his assertion to make certain technical points. Legal systems are "comprehensive" because they claim authority to regulate any type of behavior: "supreme" because they claim authority to regulate the setting up and application of other institutionalized normative systems: "open" because they give binding force within the system to norms which do not belong to it. (The reasons why Raz says "claim authority," rather than "have authority," have to do with Raz's commitment to legal positivism. For a discussion, see Shiner (1992, ch. 5). Those reasons are not relevant here.)

Now certainly if it indeed is of the nature of law to do such things, then law will just, so far, be different from morality. We recognize many practical matters as not issues of morality – for instance, issues of etiquette or fashion. It is not a *moral* issue whether neckties this year should be wide or narrow, or whether tables should be laid with the dessert spoon inside or outside the dessert fork. These issues can become moral issues if the appropriate background is filled in. A change of fashion which results in increased exploitation of garment manufacturers' sweatshop workers may be said to have moral significance, as may the failure to observe correct etiquette when such a failure is known to cause great offence to one's great-aunt. But in these cases the moral significance comes from the wider network of human relationships in which the matters of fashion or etiquette are embedded, not from those matters themselves. Raz's point is that there is nothing in the nature of law to prevent law-makers from subjecting any part of human life to a regime of legal regulation. If law-makers wanted to make the failure to wear a tie of the width fashion deemed correct, or the failure to set a table the way etiquette deemed correct, failures subject to legal penalty, nothing in the nature of law would prevent them from doing so.

Is this claimed difference concerning the potential scope of law as opposed to morality the kind of pre-philosophical difference we are here tracking, or can it be a difference only within the presuppositions of a given theory of law? The answer is the latter. The reason why morality can take control of an issue only by co-opting it so that it becomes a moral issue is that morality as a normative system is, in part, defined by its content. Morality is, that is, a content-dependent norma-tive system. The reason why by its own nature law could claim authority to regu-late *any* behavior and *any other* normative system could only be because law is conceived of as by nature a content-independent system. To claim that law is by nature a content-independent normative system is to assert a positivist theory of law. The formal differences (1) to (3) above between law and morality do not entail positivism, even if they make it tempting. If like some versions of anti-positivism one thinks of law as "an ordinance of reason for the common good," then a norm, or perhaps more plausibly a system of norms, which is not directed at the common good cannot be a norm of law/a legal system, whether it is directed at an end which will frustrate the common good, or whether it is directed at an end which is from the point of view of the common good indifferent. Raz's claimed differen-tiation between law and morality fails therefore as a difference of the kind sought here – a theory-neutral difference. The claimed difference (4) does entail positiv-ism. But it is not a theory-neutral proof of the superiority of positivism. It entails positivism only because the initial stating of the difference already presupposes positivism.

Law, morality and jurisprudence

Many facts, then, about the differences between law and morality as normative systems can be stated intuitively without begging jurisprudential questions. These differences are focussed around the fact that a legal system is an institutionalized normative system, and a system of morality is not. When we turn to jurispru-dence, it is obvious that legal positivism begins with such a fact about law. Legal positivism also, however, ends with that fact. "Legal positivism" is perhaps more properly thought of as the name for a family of legal theories: there are substantive differences between different forms of positivism, and the forms share resemblances more than they share one single common property. If there is one common focus to all forms of positivism, it lies, first, in the fact of the existence of a legal system as an institutionalized normative system. It lies, second, in the tacit claim that to acknowledge *that* fact about law is to acknowledge the most fundamental fact about law, that fact which makes law essentially what it is. This pre-philosophical fact about law thus becomes the content of a theory of law. It is important to represent positivism in this way, for only then can the opposition between positivism and anti-positivism be rightly understood. Sometimes anti-positivism is caricatured as though it believed law reduced to morality; as though it made the mistake of failing to see what is at the end of its nose, that a legal system is an institutionalized normative system. Anti-positivist theories, however, typically do acknowledge the existence of positive law, or (as it is sometimes called) human law. They do acknowledge all those philosophical facts about law which have been recited above, and which form the starting-blocks for legal positivism. The typical anti-positivist thesis is in some form that the concept of law, the nature of law, the nature of legal system cannot be understood without attention to the connections between law and morality as well as the separations. The previous sentence states perhaps the weakest form of anti-positivism, and many theories hold stronger views (see, for example, "Morality and legal semantics," below). Jurisprudential dispute concerns the role to be played by the relationship(s) that unquestionably do(es) exist between law and morality in the account of the concept of, or the nature of, law. To explore possible versions of positivism or anti-positivism in further detail and discuss their merits would be to go far beyond the aims of this article.

Morality and legal semantics

Sometimes the debate in jurisprudence over the relation between law and morality expresses itself in terms of semantics. The question is raised over whether a relationship to propositions of morality can ever, or does ever, form part or all of the truth-conditions for a, or for some, or many, propositions of law. To understand this debate, some distinctions must be drawn.

First, within philosophy of language itself, there is a distinction (and a lively debate) between "realist" and "anti-realist" approaches to semantics. Realist theories defend the claim that propositions are true (or false) because facts in the world make them true (or false). A realist theory of the semantics of legal propositions says that a legal proposition is true or false, if it is true or false, because some fact in the world – say, that the sovereign has commanded thus and so – makes it true or because no such fact does so and it is false. On an "anti-realist" conception, a proposition is not true or false by correspondence with facts in the world, but acceptable, unacceptable, neither acceptable nor unacceptable, or (apparently) both acceptable and unacceptable if and only if the ground rules of some relevant enterprise make it warrantedly assertible, warrantedly deniable, provide no warrant either way, or provide both warrants. As applied to propositions of law, an anti-realist says that a proposition of law is warrantedly assertible, if it is, if and only if it is, licensed by the rules of the judicial enterprise – the rules of statutory interpretation, of precedent, of enactment, of judicial custom, and so on, whether procedural or substantial.

The same kind of distinction might be made within meta-ethics concerning

445

propositions of morality. Moreover, some meta-ethical theories are "realist" because they take propositions of morality to have truth-conditions from a relation to an independent moral order (moral absolutist theories), and other theories because they take propositions of morality to have truth-conditions from a relation to social facts (relativist or subjectivist theories). If we put these distinctions together, we get a quite complex taxonomy of legal theories and how they view the relation of the truth-conditions for propositions of law to the truth-conditions for propositions of morality. The taxonomy is as follows:

1   A theory which believes that propositions of law are understood by knowing the independent facts in virtue of which they are true or false, believes the same about propositions of morality, and takes propositions of law to be true or false in virtue of an independent moral order.

2   A theory which believes that propositions of law are understood by knowing the independent facts in virtue of which they are true or false, believes that propositions of morality are understood by knowing the conditions that warrant their assertion, and takes propositions of law to be true or false in virtue of an independent moral order.

3   A theory which believes that propositions of law are understood by knowing the conditions that warrant their assertion, may believe that propositions of morality are understood either in terms of truth-conditions or in terms of conditions for warranted assertion, and takes propositions of law to be in part warrantedly assertible in virtue of rules which connect propositions of law with propositions of morality.

4   A theory which believes that propositions of law are understood by knowing the independent facts in virtue of which they are true or false, takes propositions of law to be true or false in virtue of independent social fact, and has no views (or no relevant views) on the semantics for propositions of morality.

5   A theory which believes that propositions of morality are understood by knowing the independent facts in virtue of which they are true or false, and gives to propositions of law no independent status.

6   A theory which believes that propositions of morality are understood by knowing the conditions that warrant their assertion, and gives to propositions of law no independent status.

The first two theories would both count as versions of anti-positivism, even of natural law theory. (1) is a theory which is realist about law, realist about morality, and anti-positivist about law. Among modern writers, for example, it is clear that both Michael Moore (see, for example, 1987 and numerous other writings) and David Brink (see 1989) sponsor versions of (1). They argue both that propositions of law map semantically on to propositions of morality, and that propositions of morality are to be given a realist semantics. Derek Beyleveld and Roger Brownsword, on the other hand, entertain the possibility of (2). They argue (see 1986, pp. 152–6) that natural law theory is quite compatible with moral relativism. They are thus realist about the law, allow for anti-realism about morality, and are anti-positivist about law. (3) seems to be the position defended by Dworkin (1986), a theory which is anti-realist about law, anti-realist about morality, and anti-positivist about law. (4) constitutes a strong form of positivism which traces the origin of law strictly to a social source, and regards no relation to morality as any part of what it is for law to be law. Other forms of positivism can be conceived for which social sources provide rules only for the warranted assertibility of propositions of law. By (5) and (6), I understand different possible versions of rule-sceptical or instrumentalist accounts of law, which regard law as in itself essentially indeterminate, and its content as supplied by politics, morality, or both.

The following brief comments on this taxonomy are in order (for longer discussion, see Shiner, 1992, chs 2.6, 8). First, note that from the point of view of *legal theory*, (2) gives a realist account of the propositions *of law*. It does not follow from the fact that a constructivist or anti-realist account of morality is correct (if it is), that to make the truth of propositions of law depend on a relationship to such a scheme yields an account of law which is also constructivist (see Shiner, 1992, ch. 8.3.3; Dworkin (1978) seems to miss this point). Second, positivism as much as anti-positivism may legitimately be realist or anti-realist about propositions of law. Positivism differs from anti-positivism over whether a relationship to propositions of morality plays any role in the truth- or assertibility-conditions for propositions of law. Third, positivism and anti-positivism, natural law theory paradigmatically, are on one side of a dispute about whether propositions of law can have determinate meaning (whether because they have truth-conditions or conditions for warranted assertibility). The parties on the other side are those versions of rule-scepticism, of Critical Legal Studies for example, which stress radical indeterminacy in the law, the impossibility of legal doctrine, and so forth. This common ground holds, despite the serious disagreements between the positivist and the anti-positivist supporters of determinate meaning and acceptability for propositions of law.

Moral argument in courts of law

Strong versions of legal positivism deny any room for moral argument in legal reasoning except where the court has, and exercises, discretion. A court has discretion when it is not bound by any strictly institutional or intra-legal standards. Anti-positivism by contrast urges that it is part of the obligation of a court to reason from the moral point of view whenever the goal of justice overall would be served by doing so. There seems room between these extremes for a weaker version of positivism which asserts that sometimes a court may have an obligation to use moral argument to reach a legal conclusion, and sometimes it may not. The plausibility of such a weaker positivism seems increased when the role is taken into account of constitutions, charters of rights, bills of rights and such documents in a legal system. Such documents, with their direct references to fundamental rights and freedoms, seem to invite courts directly to use moral argument. Wilfrid

447

Waluchow in (1994) defends what he calls "inclusive legal positivism." Using legal systems with constitutions as a model, his "inclusive legal positivism" allows courts to use moral argument to determine legal conclusions when directed by the legal system to do so. The resulting theory claims to be a richer positivistic theory than the stronger form which forbids legal status to be determined by moral argument only through the legitimate exercise of discretion.

It is surely plausible to construe a constitution as directing courts to use moral argument to determine legal conclusions. The issue remains of whether acknowledgment of this fact requires a desertion of stronger forms of positivism. Raz, for example (1979, p. 46), uses the analogy of a directive to decide a private international law case by reference to the law of another country. He argues that even in a constitutional case where reference must be made to fundamental moral values, morality as much as the foreign legal system remains an independent normative system. Morality is not "incorporated" into law by the clauses of a constitution. Raz therefore thinks that strong forms of positivism are not threatened. It is difficult to settle the issue, not the least because key terms like "incorporate" are being used metaphorically; there is no well-understood theory-neutral jurisprudential meaning for the term which could be appealed to.

Is "morality" a jurisprudentially neutral term?

So far we have been speaking as though the term "morality" as a foil to "law" has meaning independently of any jurisprudential dispute about the relation between law and morality. This may not necessarily be so (see Shiner (1992), chs. 13.1–3 for more detailed discussion). The point of view from which law and morality emerge as distinct normative systems by the kind of criteria discussed in "Differences between law and morality," p. 441, above, is the point of view of the outsider, the observer of social fact – "if you want to find the law, look *here*; if you want to find the morality, look *there*." Law and morality are thought of in extensional terms; they are pictured by spatial images, as occupying areas with boundaries, and as overlapping or not in complex ways. The boundaries of neither law nor morality are coincident with the boundaries of life. Such a perspective seems to force positivism, with its commitment to the limits of law, on theory. Anti-positivist views, by contrast, think of law and moral value as organically related, perhaps as ultimately interdependent. Both positive law and positive morality owe their significance to the basic values at the foundation of human life. The images here are not spatial, and the observer viewpoint is excluded. The debate within jurisprudence between positivism and its opponents is often held to revolve around competing conceptions of the relation of law to morality. If "morality" is thought of in terms of the first set of images, then it will be unsurprising that positivism has the more plausible account of how law is related to morality so understood. The challenge presented by anti-positivism may be to re-think the concept of morality as well as the concept of law.

Bibliography

Beyleveld, D. and Brownsword, R. 1986: *Law as a Moral Judgment*. London: Sweet & Maxwell.
Brink, D. O. 1989: *Moral Realism and the Foundations of Ethics*. Cambridge: Cambridge University Press.
Devlin, P. 1965: *The Enforcement of Morals*. London: Oxford University Press.
Duff, R. A. 1986: *Trials and Punishments*. Cambridge: Cambridge University Press.
Dworkin, R. [1977] 1978: *Taking Rights Seriously*. Cambridge, Mass.: Harvard University Press.
—— 1985: *A Matter of Principle*. Cambridge, Mass.: Harvard University Press.
—— 1986: *Law's Empire*. Cambridge, Mass.: Harvard University Press.
Hart, H. L. A. 1961: *The Concept of Law*. Oxford: Clarendon.
—— 1963: *Law, Liberty and Morality*. Oxford: Oxford University Press.
Moore, M. S. 1987: Metaphysics, epistemology and legal theory. *Southern California Law Review*, 60, 453–506.
Nagel, T. 1978: Ruthlessness in public life. In S. Hampshire (ed.), *Public and Private Morality*, New York: Cambridge University Press, 75–91.
Raz, J. 1975: *Practical Reasons and Norms*. London: Hutchinson.
—— 1979: *The Authority of Law*. Oxford: Clarendon.
Shiner, R. A. 1992: *Norm and Nature: the movements of legal thought*. Oxford: Clarendon.
Waluchow, W. J. 1994: *Inclusive Legal Positivism*. Oxford: Clarendon.

31

Law and literature

THOMAS MORAWETZ

The label, "law and literature," reveals little about the nature of the intellectual and academic enterprise to which it refers. Other conjunctions, marrying law to other disciplines, are saturated with intuitions about content. "Law and sociology" or "law and economics" implies an agenda that studies how lawyers use sociology or economics *or* how law can be seen as a sociological/economic phenomenon. "Law and epistemology" or "law and ethics" are labels that foreshadow an inquiry into the kinds of knowledge or the ethical concerns to which law gives rise. However disparate they are in other ways, each of these *other* conjunctions pairs law with an enterprise that can appropriately be called a "discipline," a structured enterprise self-conscious about its own methodology.

By contrast, literature is a "discipline" only in a quixotic sense. While law, as well as the social sciences, is concerned with persons collectively and with making generalizations about individuals, literature is preoccupied with individuality in special ways: its essential subject is the individual and it exercises its power through communication from one individual to another, one author and one reader at a time.

To think of literature as a discipline is to try to define its essence. But this task is perilous because the essence of a literary work often lies in its idiosyncrasy. The purpose and spirit of literature are arguably deeply anarchic. Thus, from the time of Plato on, literature has been seen as a threat not only to political order but to "disciplined" and generalized thinking of all kinds.

If the concept of literature itself is so elusive and Protean, what can one make of the marriage, or at least the engagement, of law and literature? I shall describe four ways in which law-and-literature can constitute an activity if not a discipline. Then I shall look more deeply into those activities that occupy the energies of most practitioners of law-and-literature and that are symptomatic of interdisciplinary thought about law in our time.

The varieties of law and literature

There are myriad fruitful interactions between law and literature. Each can form the basis of a provocative academic course and the subject of a worthwhile research agenda. Each way of interacting has its practitioners and proponents. At any given time, some ways of thinking about and pursuing research into law-and-literature are favored by the prevailing intellectual trends. Indeed, a particular way of conceiving and investigating the relationship of law and literature may play a central role in reflecting and advancing a cultural agenda. In the last section of this article, I shall consider why fictional as well as non-fictional narratives have recently assumed a special role in jurisprudence and how literary strategies are being used to discuss the possibilities and limits of legal understanding. Before doing so, it is necessary to explain and distinguish different ways of thinking about law-and-literature.

Law in literature

The first expectation of almost any law student and of most lawyers is that law-and-literature concerns the depiction of lawyers and legal institutions in literature. That expectation is usually not disappointed. Most courses of law-and-literature traverse a more or less familiar canon of literary works. An unabated, if relatively thin, stream of academic articles and books explicate those same works.

The terrain of law in literature has its regions. One domain consists of literary accounts of legal proceedings, in particular trials, which summon readers to reflect on the meaning and achievement of justice. *The Apology* (the trial of Socrates), *The Merchant of Venice*, *The Brothers Karamazov*, *Inherit the Wind*, *The Ox-Bow Incident*, *Judgment at Nuremberg*, and *The Caine Mutiny* are the high end of a scale that includes untold libraries of genre novels, plays, and films.

A different domain encompasses the lives and character of lawyers. Lawyers may be depicted as heroes or anti-heroes, fools or villains. More significantly, literature may explore the circumstances of becoming and being a lawyer, the psychological and moral demands and costs. Every profession, one imagines, forms and deforms human character in distinctive ways. Works of fiction offer opportunities to consider both the perennial characteristics of life in the law and the special social and economic constraints of law practice in the present and other eras.

Yet another way of understanding law in literature stresses symbolic uses of law. Law is often freighted with such obvious symbolism that it is difficult to distinguish the characteristics of law *in itself* from the uses of law as a metaphor. Thus, law represents the various ways in which persons give order and structure to lives lived in common. Law can stand for various institutions that use coercion, and it can also stand for the ways in which persons work together in institutions to realize their shared goals and values. In representing both kinds of institutions, law stands for a whole greater than the individuals that make up its parts. Law symbolizes order and rule-governance as opposed to arbitrariness and chaos, but it also symbolizes the artificiality of man-made order as against the pre-existing order of nature or of God. Authors as different as Dickens (*Bleak House*), Kafka (various parables), and Samuel Butler (*Erewhon*) appeal to law as a surrogate for the many institutions by which persons seek – for better or worse – to give life coherence.

451

Law in literature may also serve more limited didactic agendas, yielding insight for example into the treatment of minorities and women by law, into the resolution of conflicts between classes and cultures, and into the significance or absurdity of law's rituals and language.

Law as literature

Some of the most interesting ways of addressing law and literature do not take literature simply as a vehicle for telling stories, as a transparent medium for considering situations, characters, and institutions. Rather, this second set of ways of practicing law-and-literature involves self-consciousness about law and literature as a system of texts and as a vehicle for creating and conveying meaning.

In its simplest terms, to look at law as literature means to inquire into the use of literary devices and strategies in legal texts. It is also to look at the rhetorical and stylistic methods that are distinctively legal rather than literary. Such self-conscious reflection has been part of the activity of both literature and law throughout their existence.

Traditionally, such inquiries into the use of rhetoric and style have been of limited scope and ambition. For example, many critics have compared and analyzed the use of metaphor in legal texts and in literary ones. In doing so, they took for granted the existence of a stable lexicon of rhetorical devices and strategies embedded in a stable underlying view of how language functions – of how meaning is enshrined in texts and retrieved from them. In other words, they took for granted that one can look at rhetoric and style without looking at language and communication in ways that implicate controversies in epistemology and the philosophy of language. They presumed, among other things, that language is representational, that the denotative and figurative uses of language can be separated and classified, and that one can easily identify and distinguish issues of logic, syntax, and semantics.

Postmodern understandings of language have generally undermined these assumptions. Contemporary literary theorists, influenced by the critical and deconstructive methodology of such writers as Jacques Derrida and Paul deMan, treat the retrieval of meaning as problematic. Many legal theorists, in turn, have come to regard questions of hermeneutics as central to an understanding of the role of legal texts. Accordingly, literary and legal theorists have joined forces in considering whether meaning is implanted by authors or constructed by readers, how interpretive communities play their role in making communication through texts possible, and how one can determine the parameters of agreement and disagreement in text-based discourse. As a result, the work of such philosophers as Wittgenstein, Foucault, Habermas, and Gadamer has had a determinative influence on examinations of law and literature as vehicles of meaning.

In this sense the study of law as literature has become the study of legal hermeneutics, in particular the study of similarities and dissimilarities between law and literature with regard to the role of author, reader, and institutional context. Just as law-and-literature in the first sense (literature as a resource for moral lessons) maintains a strict intuitive distinction between primary works of literature and secondary works of criticism and commentary, law-and-literature in the second sense deconstructs that distinction by posing questions of meaning that are equally relevant to all texts.

Law of literature

Law-and-literature can also be reconceived as the law of literature. Because our constitutional framework privileges freedom of expression, American courts are perennially faced with defining the limits of free speech. Contemporary debates about the limits of literary and artistic expression change kaleidoscopically, assembling familiar issues in new patterns. Recent debates about obscenity as impermissible speech turn upon the definability and usefulness of such terms as "prurient interest" as criteria of obscenity and upon the existence and relevance of local standards for what is obscene.

A notable feature of current controversies is the blurring, or perhaps the disappearance, of the traditional identification of the political right with a narrowing of free speech and of the political left with a broadening of it. In much contemporary discussion, liberalism, which advocates tolerating expression that some regard as offensive, stands opposed to critical theory, which tends to argue that toleration of offensive speech tacitly maintains hegemony by the powerful over the powerless. Accordingly, feminist and critical race theorists accuse liberals of perpetuating inequality by naively (or invidiously) protecting discriminatory and hate-driven kinds of expression. These critics sometimes borrow the language of deconstruction to argue that the celebrated neutrality of liberalism masks a covert agenda and that the favored literary canon can be understood as an ideological tool for discrimination.

Literature and legal reform

Just as one can investigate the effects of legal constraints on literary expression, one can also examine the ways in which literature, especially popular literature, has influenced the course of law. In this activity, the interests and skills of the literary and the legal historian join forces.

From *Uncle Tom's Cabin* through the "muckraking" novels of Emile Zola and Upton Sinclair to the more recent writings of Toni Morrison and Nadine Gordimer, literature has often been politically inspired and has served the causes of political and legal reform. At the same time, the effects of literature on law have not always been benign. Arguably, much popular literature dehumanizes criminals, reinforces racial and ethnic stereotypes, and depicts the exigencies of international relations (war, espionage) in unrealistic ways. Such writings tend to shape popular attitudes; these attitudes in turn may affect legal approaches to the procedural rights of offenders, to the welfare and other social claims of the underclass, and to curbs on individual rights for the sake of national security.

Law-and-literature as the study of the socio-legal effects of literature is only a small tributary in the current flood of research. There seem to be several reasons for this. Representational and didactic literature, unless elevated by the passage of time (Dickens, Zola), currently tends to be disdained as popular culture, unworthy of the academic attention given to *serious* literature. Second, the broadcast media are seen, probably correctly, as having so great an influence on social beliefs and values that the effects of contemporary literature are diluted. Finally, assessing the effects of any of the media, including literature, on popular views and measuring the impact in turn of popular views on legal decisions and policies are notoriously difficult and controversial tasks.

These four ways of thinking about law-and-literature reflect respectively the treatment of literature as representation and narrative, literature as a vehicle for the investigation of epistemological and hermeneutical questions, constitutional law as it affects literature, and literary/legal history. Practitioners of each approach often claim hegemony and treat these several approaches as mutually exclusive. At present, the first two approaches compete for dominance both as areas of academic research and in law school pedagogy. I shall look more closely at these two approaches and, in the last section, I shall consider certain ways in which they complement each other in epitomizing contemporary attitudes about law.

Law and fiction

Notwithstanding the influence of both modernism and postmodernism, the overwhelming number of teachers and scholars look from law to literature with the didactic purpose of drawing moral lessons. In so doing, they use stories as they have been used since storytelling began. They implicitly reject the lesson of modernism that literary artifacts are to be taken on their own terms as special artifacts and not merely as representations of reality and therefore as objects of secondary status. They also reject the lesson of postmodernism that the meaning of a text is not stable but is constructed by the reader.

Moral lessons can be elicited from literary representations of lawyers and legal situations in two opposing ways. Law can be seen as morally positive, as an instrument of justice, and lawyers can be seen as models of rectitude and fair treatment. On the other hand, one can take a critical and even dystopian view of law and consider its destructive and subversive effects on persons and society. One can see law as deforming the personalities of its practitioners and can see lawyers as agents of power and discrimination. Countless literary works lend themselves to these uses.

Nonetheless, the message of modernism must not be lost. The didactic use of literature begs two questions, whether moral lessons exhaust the significance of such literary works and whether those lessons are fairly drawn. Modernism raises these questions in negative form: a fictional depiction of a lawyer or a legal situation, shaped as it is by the choices and acts of an author, is not simply on a par with a *real* particular lawyer or legal situation. But neither is it necessarily offered to support generalizations about lawyers or legal situations.

454

Thus, it is easier to say what a particular literary artifact is *not* than to say what it *is*. As a result, any attempt to draw moral lessons from literature must be tentative. The author of a short story or novel may be as elusive when forced into the role of moral arbiter as would be a painter or a composer. Understanding the act of creation implies respect for the special status and character of the created object.

If modernism teaches that the characters and events of fiction are not reducible or assimilable to the characters and events of life but must be examined as artifacts on their own terms, postmodernism teaches one to question whether those terms are stable enough that one can regard any particular understanding of an artifact as more correct or appropriate than any other understanding. What gives the author's understanding of her work, if it is available, priority over the (conflicting) understanding of a particular reader? What gives one reader's understanding priority over that of any other reader? What gives the interpretation offered by one subcommunity in a multicultural environment priority over that of another subcommunity? Postmodernists suggest that attempts to use literature didactically cannot ignore such questions.

In the face of this criticism, some contemporary theorists have attempted to derive a different kind of didactic use for literature in law, one that incorporates modernist and postmodernist scruples about literary stories. They draw lessons not from the content of literary stories but from the process of literary interpretation. Mindful of the dangers of using literary characters and situations as moral examples, they do not focus on particular works of literature but on the common denominator of all literature, its creative and interpretive dimensions. James Boyd White, for example, alerts his readers that "resort to the plain words [of a text] always requires *an act of creation, a making of something new*, yet the original text cannot be forgotten, for fidelity is always due it" (italics supplied) (White, 1990, p. 246). The underlying idea for law is that legal actors (lawyers, judges, scholars) tend to forget that all language use is creative, that language use is in a sense constitutive not merely of a way of regarding reality but of reality itself. The author of a judicial opinion, no less than the author of a work of literature, shapes and manipulates the terms through which social reality is constructed.

This way of using literature to draw lessons for law about creativity and responsibility, suggestive as it is, can be faulted as vague and problematic. For one thing, it is not clear why an account of the creative responsibilities of language users needs to focus on *literature* in preference to any other kind of language use. If it is said to do so because literature involves creative readings that are transparently creative, this response is both dubious and paradoxical. It is dubious to the extent that the creative role of *readers* is itself problematic; postmodernism poses it as a question, not as a given. It is paradoxical because such theorists' underlying assumption is that *all* uses of language in general, and all readers in particular – literary, legal, scientific, historical, and so on – are *equally* creative/constructive and none has priority over others.

Yet another problem with this way of treating literature didactically is that appreciating one's options (as a judge, as a legal representative, as a reader of any kind) in interpreting a text is not to be confused with being morally constrained by the text. Self-consciously creative uses of language (for example, deviations from precedent) – by judges, lawyers, readers – are as compatible with injustice and moral irresponsibility as with their opposites. Even so, the underlying idea remains important: in interpreting law or literature, these actors make interpretive choices insofar as the implications of a text for a new situation are never wholly predetermined, and these choices are characteristically ones with moral parameters.

Hermeneutics

We have considered the lure of literature as a moral resource. Even when their approach raises conceptual questions, legal scholars, teachers, and practitioners look to literature for the indicia of justice and for guidance in leading exemplary lives within the law. And even when they concede that literature is not like life and that literary stories are constructed by the reader and not the author, they persist in finding moral significance in the very process of constructive reading.

As a result, much of the lure of law-and-literature for lawyers and students disappears when intractable questions of hermeneutics seem to jeopardize any such moral yield. The import, as we have seen, of much recent scholarship in law-and-literature is that it is useful to compare law and literature as hermeneutic processes wholly apart from any consideration of moral implications.

This way of thinking about law and literature is the offspring of the union between constitutional theory and deconstructive literary criticism. Since the 1970s, constitutional theorists have waged a peculiarly quixotic campaign for legitimacy. Goaded by the accusation that constitutional interpretations merely translate political agendas into doctrine, some scholars and jurists have tried to justify one reading over others as the *correct* or *true* meaning of relevant constitutional language. For liberals, this technique has tended to devolve into appeals to an underlying moral consensus that favors one set of constitutional results over another; conservatives have tended to construe meaning as authorial intent.

In a seminal essay, H. L. A. Hart sees the search for a univocal meaning for legal, in particular constitutional, texts, as a response to the fear of political relativism. He says it embodies a "noble dream" and that it stands opposed to the "nightmare" of judicial arbitrariness. This bipolar way of posing the epistemological alternatives, whereby texts either have a univocal (correct) reading or are meaningless (that is, arbitrary in meaning), seems to rest on a naive understanding of hermeneutics. As literary and philosophical critics have long recognized, the retrieval of meaning is a complicated transaction. To understand how communication and argument are possible, how readers/speakers can understand one another, is to go beyond the polar possibilities of seeing the meaning of a text as univocal and beyond disagreement or as being wholly indeterminate.

Thus, through the influence of literary hermeneutics, constitutional theory has evolved over the last twenty years from a search for constitutional determinateness to a wide-ranging comparison of how meaning is found in literary and legal texts. This brief evolution has had two stages. In the first stage, debate has tended to focus on the transaction between author and reader, and on the question of which of the two participants determines meaning. In the second stage, the complexity of the process has tended to be more fully appreciated. On this view, to understand meaning is to understand the history of the text, the situation and expectations of the reader, and the constraints imposed by the institutions and community context within which interpretation occurs.

Because literary theory explores these factors and their roles, it serves as a model for legal hermeneutics. Just as it is possible to take seriously readings of literature – a Marxist reading of Jane Austen, a Freudian reading of Shakespeare – that could hardly have been framed by their authors, it is similarly possible to read constitutional provisions – equal protection, freedom of expression – in ways their authors could not have anticipated. But to deny that meaning is set unambiguously and clearly (by the author, by shared interpretive principles) is not to affirm that the process of finding meaning is unconstrained (the "nightmare" of judicial arbitrariness). The parameters of contemporary debate are real. Some accounts – of Austen, Shakespeare, the Constitution – cohere better than other conceivable accounts with the interests and self-understanding of persons here and now, and those possibilities constitute the spectrum available to contemporary interpreters.

Literature informs the study of legal epistemology in two ways. On the one hand, it is useful to compare the interpretive history of particular works of literature with the comparable history of particular legal texts. On the other hand, the hermeneutic investigations of literary theorists are often generalizable to legal materials. But, for many observers, the differences between legal and literary texts and processes are as important for an understanding of hermeneutics as the congruences. Legal questions, unlike literary ones, require definitive and simple answers. A panel of literary critics may resolve to disagree about the use of symbolism in *Moby Dick* or the moral implications of *Billy Budd*; a panel of judges must arrive at a decision whether X's speech is protected by the First Amendment (even though individual judges may dissent). Thus, law is institutionalized in a way that literary study is not and does not need to be. The interpretive acts of legal actors have the aim of structuring social and economic relationships and settling conflicts; the acts of literary critics have no such aims and consequences. The resources and methods of legal research and argumentation are highly formalized; decision makers are expected to respect precedent and to be mindful of the formal hierarchy of courts. Literary research and criticism, even at its most formal and formularized, has no comparable constraints.

Law-and-literature as a hermeneutical investigation explores the implications of these epistemological and social concerns. In the eyes of most scholars, this way of exploring the intersection of law and literature is a different enterprise from the didactic use of literary stories. In another sense, however, the two approaches complement each other as writers in legal theory explore the claim that both literature and law constitute converging social narratives.

Law as narrative

I have already referred to the seismic fault that runs through much of contemporary jurisprudence, the opposition between liberalism and critical legal theory. Although the lines of demarcation between jurisprudence and law-and-literature remain fairly clear, the preoccupations of the two fields have come to influence and reinforce each other in unprecedented ways.

Some of the central assumptions of liberal jurisprudence grow out of the confrontation between legal positivism and legal naturalism. Rejecting the positivist identification of law with whatever rules of order are imposed by authority (regardless of the content of such rules), liberals borrow from naturalism the idea of continuity between law and a consensus about social value, in particular a consensus about the role of government in securing and protecting private freedom, respect among persons, and personal autonomy. Accordingly, liberals presuppose that law as an ideal must be capable of transcending particular political and moral agendas and that governments must strive to use law to maintain an arena in which such diverse political and moral agendas compete. The existence of law and the work of legal actors are justified by appeal to this ideal.

Critical legal theory questions and rejects the fundamental premise of the liberal reappropriation of legal naturalism, namely that law can and must be justified as disinterested and politically neutral. There are both particular and general versions of this critique. Particular critiques examine specific legal arguments, doctrines, and results to show how the appearance of fairness and neutrality is maintained only at the cost of blindness to many aspects of the legal situation. In other words, particular critiques identify legal winners and losers to show how some political goals triumphed over other – perhaps equally defensible – alternative goals. The generalized version of such critiques is that *every* legal issue is resolved politically and that those who claim that law generally embodies a moral consensus and/or value neutrality delude themselves.

Criticisms of this kind are especially familiar in the work of feminists and critical race theorists, whose arguments have the following structure. The justifications offered by liberals are said to be both partial and defective. They are partial because the liberals' narrative about the progress of law, about successes and failures, is only one of many possible narratives. It is characteristically the story told by the powerful rather than the disempowered. They are defective because they *claim* to be the only correct narrative, the only way in which the processes and progress of law should be understood.

In this way critical theory borrows some themes familiar in law-and-literature. First of all, it echoes the didactic use of literary stories for moral purposes. One point of seeking out various potentially conflicting narratives is a moral point. The narratives – both autobiographical and fictionalized – are not ends in themselves; they are used to cast doubt on the moral claims of the "winners" (that is, of liberals) to be acting in the interests of all, to be above self-interest and partisanship. The narratives put forward the moral claims of victims and portray law as a tool

458

of victimization, characteristically of minorities and of women. Such an indictment may be made through the prism of an individual life, as in an autobiographical narrative, or less personally through the legal history of a community bound together by race or gender.

This didactic use of narrative in critical jurisprudence prompts some methodological questions. These "alternative" narratives seem to be put forward to replace and discredit the liberal story whereby law is above politics and redounds to the benefit of all, whereby the rule of law has and deserves respect, and whereby an evolving system of equal rights forwards the goal of individual autonomy. But an alternative account is possible, namely that they simply represent a subgroup of possible perspectives on law with no claim to be more or less "correct" than the "winners' " narratives.

It is unclear whether these narratives are to be seen as competing approximations of the truth or merely as stories told from differing perspectives. If one labels the problem of multiple perspectives the "*Rashomon* problem" one finds the same ambiguity in *Rashomon* itself: shall we sort out the competing perspectives to determine what *really* happened and not just to marvel at the perspectival aspects of experience? Note that many of the processes of law, in particular the rules of litigation, seem to presuppose that one way of regarding experience is true and that, for example, the job of juries is to make such factual judgments.

The proponents of critical narratives thus seem to make two tendentious claims, that we are indeed concerned with approximations of truth rather than mere stories or mere perspectives and that their narratives, the victims' narratives, are closer to truth than the narratives of others. In making the first of these claims, they remain traditional lawyers insofar as they remain committed to an ontology whereby the characteristics of events are fixed and univocally true descriptions may, in principle, be given. In making the second of these claims, they undercut law by asserting that the constructive processes of law conceal and subvert the truth about events. Such processes as drafting legislation and conducting trials remain, it is said, ongoing ways of maintaining oppression and inequality – and of denying that that is so.

To be sure, a number of writers who emphasize the importance of narratives in understanding law adopt the alternative horn of the dilemma. They argue for an extreme perspectivism whereby legal situations are best understood in terms of multiple conflicting narratives. These theorists, drawing on the work of Richard Rorty and Stanley Fish, challenge the expectation that narratives are approximations of truth and claim that a pragmatic understanding of legal events requires contextualization of both the events themselves and the narratives or reports offered about those events. It is impossible to do justice to such suggestions in a discussion of the present scope. However, one can hardly avoid the question of how one can reconcile the kind of relativism entailed by this account with the commitment to a preferred narrative that seems to be required of legal actors engaged in legal decision making.

The significance of these developments in critical jurisprudence is that critical and pragmatic legal philosophers, perhaps echoing the culture at large, have come to see literature as a metaphor for law. Confusion about literature is transmuted into confusion about law. The distinction between fiction and reality is eroded and ultimately erased.

Consider how this comes about. The confusion about literature, as indicated above, is reflected in three available, but incompatible, attitudes toward it. The traditional or naive attitude is to treat fictional stories and characters as one would treat real events and persons and draw moral lessons. The modernist attitude is to treat fictional stories and characters as special artifacts, created by an authorial intelligence, that must not be confused with reality. in part, because of the selectivity and intentionality that went into their creation. The postmodernist attitude is to treat fictional stories and characters as shaped by the perspective of the reader as well as the author and as having no fixed or immutable characteristics. Thus, the postmodernist attitude threatens to dissolve the distinctions between author and reader (by treating readers as authors), between text and commentary (by treating commentaries as primary texts), and between reality/truth and fiction (by questioning the claims of descriptions of reality to be true).

These three attitudes may be applied to law and legal events in the following ways. The use and incompatibility of the first two attitudes have long been familiar in legal philosophy. Moralism in literature corresponds to moralism in law: the traditional attitude of naturalism, seen by some as naive, is that law incorporates shared social values and is to be judged by its conformity to moral norms. The alternative attitude of legal positivists is that law is a distinctive artifact and reflects a special kind of intentionality. The critical challenge plays havoc with both of these attitudes by raising the possibility that the moral character of law may depend on the beholder (the "reader"), that the very nature of legal texts and legal institutions may depend on whether they are seen by winners or losers, and that therefore the very idea that law is the sort of thing about which one can make objective claims rather than offer endless fictions may itself be an illusion.

In this way our confusions about literature infect our attitudes to law as law is equated with legal stories and legal stories, in turn, are treated as a subcategory of literature. Whether these methodological questions for legal philosophy are cul-de-sacs or opportunities remains to be determined.

Bibliography

Fish, S. 1989: *Doing What Comes Naturally: change, rhetoric, and the practice of theory in literary and legal studies.* Durham: Duke University Press.
—— 1994: *There's No Such Thing as Free Speech . . . and It's a Good Thing, Too.* Oxford: Oxford University Press.
Gadamer, H.-G. 1976: *Philosophical Hermeneutics.* tr. D. E. Linge. Berkeley: University of California Press.
Hart, H. L. A. 1983: American jurisprudence through English eyes: the nightmare and the noble dream, *Essays in Jurisprudence and Philosophy*, Oxford: Clarendon Press.
Hoy, D. C. 1985: Interpreting the law: hermeneutical and poststructuralist perspectives. *Southern California Law Review*, 58, 135–76.

Levinson, S. and Mailloux, S. (eds) 1988: *Interpreting Law and Literature: a hermeneutic reader*. Evanston: Northwestern University Press.

Leyh, G. (ed.) 1992: *Legal Hermeneutics: history, theory, and practice*. Berkeley: University of California Press.

Mitchell, W. J. T. (ed.) 1982: *The Politics of Interpretation*. Chicago: University of Chicago Press.

Posner, R. A. 1988: *Law and Literature: a misunderstood relation*. Harvard: Harvard University Press.

Rorty, R. 1991: *Objectivity, Relativism, and Truth*. Cambridge: Cambridge University Press.

White, J. B. 1984: *When Words Lose Their Meaning*. Chicago and London: University of Chicago Press.

—— 1990: *Justice as Translation*. Chicago and London: University of Chicago Press.

Wishingrad, J. (ed.) 1992: *Legal Fictions: short stories about lawyers and the law*. Woodstock: The Overlook Press.

461

PART IV
TOPICS

32

The duty to obey the law

M. B. E. SMITH

Few issues in jurisprudence have received so much attention in recent years as whether citizens have a distinctive moral duty to obey the law. Yet the differences among the disputants might well seem slender to the unprofessional eye. No one holds that the duty is absolute: even its most passionate advocates allow that it is sometimes morally permissible to disobey the law, as when abolitionists aided runaway slaves before the American Civil War. But neither does anyone advocate open or frequent disobedience. Those who doubt the supposed duty yet hold that we very often have a strong moral reason to do what the law requires independently of its commands, for example, not to assault, cheat, or rob others. The doubters allow that we are obligated to obey whenever the law has established patterns of conduct that are dangerous to depart from, such as driving to the left in Great Britain. They believe that disobedience is permissible only when there is no independent moral reason to obey or when the weight of independent reasons favors disobedience; and they do not suppose that in reasonably just societies these conditions obtain often. Finally, those who are sceptical about the duty of obedience, nonetheless, prize the great social benefits that quite obviously can only be achieved through government; and they believe that one which is reasonably just deserves its citizens' co-operation and support. It therefore seems probable that the putative duty's advocates and disbelievers alike would virtually always agree in their judgments of particular illegal conduct – or at least that any differences between them would not flow from their disagreement about the philosophical issue.

Despite the debate's apparent lack of practical significance, many philosophers and academic lawyers yet disagree hotly about whether there is a *prima facie* duty to obey the law. I shall later conclude that their controversy is primarily metaethical rather than political, being fueled by disagreement about the very point of positing *prima facie* duties. Let us look first at some particular arguments.

The *prima facie* duty to obey – a brief history

Philosophical worries about the precise contours of the duty citizens owe to the state date back at least to Plato. But the claim that there is a *prima facie* duty to obey the law was first voiced in 1930, by the great British classicist and moral intuitionist, W. D. Ross, in *The Right and the Good*.

465

Twentieth-century intuitionism is part of an older family of meta-ethical theories that ascribe to humanity a common moral faculty. (Older siblings include the moral sentiment theories of Hutcheson or Hume and the moral rationalisms of Aquinas or Richard Price.) Ross devised the distinction between *prima facie* duty and absolute duty in the hope of solving the problem bedeviling all such theories: namely, that of setting out the principles that explain the moral faculty's deliverances about particular kinds of morally relevant factual circumstances. Ross's intuitionistic contemporaries generally agreed that Sidgwick had shown the futility of any attempt to frame exceptionless general principles of rightness or wrongness – that every promising candidate will turn out either to be inconsistent with our firm intuitions about examples or else be a disguised tautology such as "Murder is wrong" or "Justice is giving every man his due." But Ross thought it possible to frame absolute principles of what he called "prima facie" rightness or wrongness. His distinction is often explicated by the practice of promising: it is obvious to everyone that it is sometimes permissible to break promises; but it is also plausible to suppose that this is wrong "other things being equal" – by which is meant some such notion as "wrong unless justified by one's thereby fulfilling some moral consideration of equal or greater weight" (see Thomson, 1990, ch. 12, for the best intuitionistic account of the moral constraint of promises). Ross offered a list of our separate *prima facie* duties, comprising inter alia those of fidelity, gratitude, beneficence and non-maleficence. Somewhat as an afterthought, he suggested that there is also a duty to obey the law:

> Thus . . . the duty of obeying the laws of one's country arises partly (as Socrates contends in the Crito) from the duty of gratitude for the benefits one has received from it; partly from the implicit promise to obey which seems to be involved in permanent residence in a country whose laws we know we are *expected* to obey, and still more clearly involved when we ourselves invoke the protection of its laws . . . and partly (if we are fortunate in our country) from the fact that its laws are potent instruments for the general good. (Ross, 1930, p. 27ff)

Ross did not repeat these arguments in his later, longer book, *The Foundations of Ethics* (1938). His suggestion found little attention until 1955, when it was taken up by H. L. A. Hart in his seminal article, "Are there any natural rights." Hart offered a fresh argument in support of the duty of obedience, based upon his formulation of what has come to be known as the principle of fair play:

> when a number of persons conduct any joint enterprise according to rules and thus restrict their liberty, those who have submitted to these restrictions when required have a right to a similar submission from those who have benefitted by their submission. (Hart. 1955, p. 185)

John Rawls refined Hart's argument in a series of influential articles. By 1964 Ross's suggestion had become a philosophical commonplace, so much so that Rawls could confidently assert:

466

I shall assume, as requiring no argument, that there is, at least in a society such as ours, a moral obligation to obey the law, although it may, of course, be overridden in certain cases by other more stringent obligations. (*Rawls, 1964, p. 3*)

This consensus was broken in 1973, when an alternative position began to be developed by a number of philosophers, including the present author (see inter alia: Smith, 1973; Sartorious, 1975; Raz, 1979; Simmons, 1979; Woozley, 1979; Greenawalt, 1987). I shall now sketch what I take to be a broad area of agreement among those who reject the duty of obedience (but the reader is cautioned that I cannot include many necessary qualifications and subtleties). First, most of us acknowledge the existence of legitimate authority; but, unlike many political theorists, we analyze the concept of authority without reference to a duty of obedience. For instance, in my early paper on the topic, I offered a perhaps overly simple definition, which counts a government as possessing legitimate authority when it has a moral right (in the sense of "that which is morally permissible") to coerce its citizens' obedience. Kent Greenawalt has refined this definition by adding further conditions, for example, that if a government has legitimate authority its citizens are virtually always obligated not to interfere with enforcement of its commands (Greenawalt, 1987, p. 55). But he, too, finds it unnecessary to posit a *prima facie* duty of obedience to every law in order to account for governmental authority.

Second, we doubters have in various ways criticized the sundry arguments that have been offered in support of the duty to obey the law. We do not launch frontal assaults upon them; rather we attempt to show that, when their underlying principles are properly understood, it is evident that the factual situation of most citizens fails to trigger their conditions of application. Thus, we do not deny that a genuine, voluntary consent to obey every law would found a general duty to obey; rather we follow Hume in denying that most citizens of any nationality have performed acts which constitute such consent ([1777] 1948). Similarly, after analyzing the scope of the obligations of fair play, gratitude, rule and act utilitarianism, we have concluded that these principles do not reach every situation in which the law requires us to act. (The best comprehensive account of these arguments is in Greenawalt, 1987.)

Third, as a positive argument against the supposed general obligation to obey the law, we have observed that contemporary law comprises a very comprehensive scheme of social regulation, most of which, undoubtedly, is very necessary to the public weal, but which also contains (as Lord Devlin put the point) "many fussy regulations whose breach it would be pedantic to call immoral" (1965, p. 27). Contemporary landlord–tenant law is rife with examples: for example, Mass. Gen. Laws. c. 186 § 15B requires landlords who accept security deposits to keep them in interest bearing escrow accounts in Massachusetts banks. A Massachusetts landlord who for reasons of convenience places a security deposit in a Vermont bank will pay triple damages if sued by his tenant. His practice is imprudent; but would anyone say that it is morally wrong?

467

Lastly, we doubters have pointed out that the supposed general obligation to obey the law must be redundant in every normative theory that has any plausibility whatsoever. That is because every such theory must contain proscriptions against assault, reckless endangerment, fraud, breach of serious promises, and so on, whose conjunction arguably specifies each important moral interest that we are bound to respect. Hence, regardless of whether a theory provides specifically for obedience to the law, it will imply trivially that there is a *prima facie* duty to obey whenever disobedience puts an important moral interest at risk. Moreover, we contend, it is the strength of these independent moral reasons that determines the strength of the reason to obey. Our argument is broadly speaking intuitionistic, being primarily based upon our considered moral judgments about particularly described examples. We point out that no one supposes that mere illegality gives rise to moral concern: no one condemns the prudent driver who slowly and safely runs through a lengthy stop light at an empty rural intersection at two in the morning. Nor does anyone suppose that illegality worsens what is independently wrong: no one would say that the practice of husbands raping their wives has recently been made more reprehensible by having belatedly been made illegal. (Here we echo Blackstone: "Neither do divine or natural duties . . . receive any stronger sanction from being also declared to be duties by the law of the land" (1793, p. 54).) Hence, we conclude, the supposed general obligation of obedience plays no useful explanatory role in normative theory, and so there is no good reason to accept it.

Many philosophers have not been convinced by these arguments. Virtually no one seems to believe that any of the classic arguments from rule or act utilitarianism, gratitude, consent or fair play, can be refurbished so as to yield a general *prima facie* duty of obedience. (But see Klosko, 1987; and Walker, 1988). Instead, fresh arguments have been offered (Finnis, 1980; Honore, 1981; Mackie, 1981; Dworkin, 1986). What has not been noticed is that there is a meta-ethics supposed in these arguments that is vastly different from Ross's intuitionism – one so different as to raise doubt that they affix the same meaning as did he to "prima facie duty." Summed briefly, the difference is this: Most who favor the *prima facie* duty of obedience conceive of normative theory as catechistic and perhaps even as political. They believe that philosophers ought to aim at formulating a set of principles that the rest of humanity might accept and articulately employ in arriving at their considered moral judgments. However, Ross had no such ambition at all. He spoke primarily to other philosophers, and he did not expect to find catechumens there or in the public at large. Rather than preaching at humanity, he assumed that we all have a faculty that permits us to discern moral truth. He thought that the proper task of normative theory is to explain the principles that the moral faculty employs. These different meta-ethical visions yield different conclusions about whether there is a *prima facie* obligation to obey the law. Hence, what appears to be a dispute about politics is in reality a dispute about the proper end of normative theory. It is no wonder then that the disputants differ so slenderly over particular instances of illegal conduct.

Implications of catechistic meta-ethics for the duty of obedience

Apart from their common project of framing moral principles for general adoption, catechistic philosophers are a diverse meta-ethical lot. They comprise the moral realist, John Finnis, an avowed defender of Thomistic natural law theory, who attempts to delimit the obligations of humankind by speculating about which principles would best promote the common good were ordinary people to accept and to act upon them (Finnis, 1980, esp. pp. 303–8). The rule-utilitarian pre-scriptivist, Richard Hare, is also in their company (Hare, 1981). And they include the moral sceptic, John Mackie, whose argument for the obligation of obedience shall be our exemplar from the class (Mackie, 1981).

The first sentence of Mackie's book, *Ethics: Inventing Right and Wrong*, boldly proclaimed "There are no objective [moral] values" (1977, p. 15). But he, none-theless, offered arguments in normative theory, whose point he thought is to in-vent a morality that will allow humanity to flourish peacefully were it generally accepted (1977, p. 193). It need not be created wholly new: all moralities contain restrictions upon the free use of violence, theft, promise-breaking, and so on; and it is evidently necessary that the one to be recommended to society must have some such content if it is to promote human welfare. Still, we cannot suppose that existing moralities adequately serve the goal of human flourishing: for example, "some more traditional obligations traditionally attached to status, not created by contract, are dispensable; patriotism . . . may have outlived its usefulness" (1977, p. 123). Mackie's conception of normative theory requires philosophers always to determine the consequences of general belief in a large variety of alternative moral principles, and to settle upon that set whose acceptance would best make us flourish. (Once a list is complete one supposes that its adherents would then try to persuade us all to adopt their revised morality. However, Mackie does not even address how they ought to set about this.)

What then about the duty of obedience? In an article devoted to the topic, Mackie began by announcing without a shred of argument or evidence that "the domin-ant conventional morality of our present society" recognizes its existence (1981, p. 144). However, he placed no weight upon this, but focussed instead upon whether:

> If we were quite literally inventing right or wrong – constructing a system of moral ideas – might we include in it, as a basic and *underived* element, an obligation to obey the law as such? *(1981, p. 151)*

He returned an affirmative answer, on this ground:

> The norm that lays down a prima facie obligation to obey the law as such is a further, though more extensive, reciprocal norm, like those that prescribe gratitude and loyalty to friends, collective action or forbearance, and honesty about property

... The general recognition of [this] obligation ... therefore shares with these other reciprocal norms a feature that makes it more viable than the norm of rational benevolence. (*1981, pp. 153–4*)

If we accept Mackie's methodological presuppositions, it is hard to demur from his conclusion, given the obvious practical empirical truth that general obedience to law is essential to human well-being. The objections that I set out earlier against the obligation of obedience have no force against him. He is unfazed by the fact that the obligation cannot be derived from other moral principles, such as gratitude or fair play, because he contends that it follows directly from the goal of human flourishing. Neither is it a telling argument against him that the duty plays no useful explanatory role in normative theory, because he rejects the supposition that there is any moral reality for philosophers to explain. Nor will he be impressed by the suggestion that the obligation does not fit our intuitions about particular kinds of cases, because he rejects the intuitionistic meta-ethics that lies behind this style of argument. Lastly, he will not care that the duty is redundant in any colorable normative theory, because he does not aim at explanatory economy. He may respond that redundancy is even a virtue in normative theory, because it is desirable that conduct tending to promote human flourishing be morally over-determined. Since obedience to the law promotes this end, it is well that ordinary people accept more than one principle that will inspire them so to behave. Greenawalt criticizes Mackie's argument primarily on the ground that the available evidence does not show that recognition of an obligation of obedience is necessary to sustain adequate compliance with the law. (Greenawalt, 1987, pp. 179–85.) But this too seems weak: if recognition of the duty will do no harm – Greenawalt does not allege that it will – and if it may do some good by reinforcing citizens' tendencies to abide by the law, it seems that we ought to place it in our catechism of principles, even if we do not know that its recognition is essential to achieving the ameliorating aim of normative theory. Given Mackie's catechistic meta-ethics, he is clearly right to endorse a *prima facie* duty of obedience to law. Let us now consider how the duty fares from a Rossian point of view.

Implications of commonalist meta-ethics for the duty of obedience

It is often said that meta-ethics and normative ethics are wholly independent of one another. That commonplace captures one important truth: philosophers' moral sympathies do vary [independently of their meta-ethics; the entire political] spectrum can be found in philosophers of every stripe. But the claim of independence hides the more important truth that a philosopher's meta-ethics sets constraints upon the form of the principles her normative theory can recognize and upon the arguments that may be deployed in their support.

Since it is impossible to argue for all one's premises, every philosophical theory must rest in the end upon intuition – upon the theorist's unsupported bare beliefs,

470

which she hopes her readers will share. But the role that intuition plays differs greatly among meta-ethical theories. Catechistic philosophers typically suppose that an acceptable normative theory must be one satisfactory to philosophy, and so presuppose that only philosophers' intuitions (perhaps restricted to those of "logic" or "language") have authority for normative theory (cf., Hare, 1981, §§ 1.3, 1.6). Ross thought that philosophers' substantive moral intuitions are authoritative, but only because he supposed that everyone's are (Ross, 1939, pp. 1ff). Like Judith Jarvis Thomson, our most celebrated contemporary intuitionist, Ross was a meta-ethical rationalist: he believed that fundamental moral principles are necessary truths and that virtually all humanity has a faculty of reason by which it can recognize such truths in favorable circumstances. As did many great philosophers before him (for example, Aristotle, Cicero, Aquinas, Hume, Adam Smith, Kant), Ross supposed that the moral faculty is fungible. Let us call this assumption "commonalism." Let us also adopt this model of the common moral faculty: whether reason, sentiment or something else again, it is a mentalistic "black box" into which non-moral beliefs are fed as stimuli and from which moral conclusions issue. (A psychologically accurate model must posit reciprocal causal relations between non-moral and moral belief. But since normative theory concerns the conditions of passage from premisses of empirical fact to moral conclusions, the one-way model will suffice for our purposes.)

Since commonalists presume that the deliverances of the moral faculty are true and that everyone has one, they also suppose that the proper task of normative theory is to explore and explain "commonsense" morality, but is emphatically not to change it. (For example, Kant held that ordinary folk can perfectly well discover their duties without aid of philosophers, and that philosophy's only practical office is to explain the basis of ordinary practical reason in necessary truth, which may help those who understand this to be less tempted to follow specious arguments and inclinations contrary to duty. (Kant, [1785] 1964, pp. 71–3).) Hence, setting very different goals for normative theory, commonalism implies constraints upon its principles and arguments that are very different from those of catechistic meta-ethics.

First, commonalists suppose that the primary constraint upon normative theory is that it adequately explain those of our own and others' moral intuitions that are made in circumstances conducive to reliability. Roughly, these are: that we are not prey to false relevant non-moral belief (for example, about whether Sally hit John); and that we are not relevantly subject to influences likely to corrupt judgment (for example, family feeling, racial prejudice). Commonalist methodology, which relies heavily upon our intuitions about hypothetical (often fantastical) examples, produces intuitions that are maximally reliable. That is because our personal interests are then disengaged and we are immunized from non-moral error, since the facts upon which the moral faculty works are stipulated. (But we must note as a caveat that philosophers' theories sometimes badly skew their intuitions. For example, Gilbert Harman believes that morality is merely a matter of group convention, which prompted him to the spectacularly counter-intuitive claim that "it would be a misuse of language to say of hardened professional

471

criminals that it is morally wrong of them to steal from others or that they ought morally not to kill people" (1977, p. 113)).

Second, because commonalists assume that we have somehow all acquired an inchoate knowledge of a common morality, they do not suppose that normative principles are subject to learnability constraints or that they must be easily understood by the vulgar. (Those troubled about how anyone could recognize moral truth but not be able to understand a summation of its principles should reflect upon the familiar fact that few – if any – have a complete articulate understanding of the principles of English grammar but many have inchoately mastered them (cf., Smith, 1979)). And indeed, the normative theories offered by leading commonalists, such as Hume and Kant, or more lately Ross and Thomson, are exceedingly abstract and fearsomely complex. In contrast, the principles of catechistic theories are constrained by what not-too-terribly-well-educated people can be expected to apply. Catechistic principles must therefore be aphoristic, so that they can effectively be inscribed upon and kept before the minds even of the dull (cf., Hare, 1981, § 2.4). (Arguments in support of catechistic principles may, of course, be as complicated as one pleases, since they are addressed primarily to philosophers.)

Third, unlike catechists, commonalists should never argue for moral principles by appealing to supposed favorable consequences of ordinary persons accepting and acting upon them. For again, they hold that ordinary citizens' considered moral judgments are as reliable as any philosopher's and have equal authority for normative theory. Hence, commonalists (in professional moments) ought not even attempt to prescribe political principles for non-philosophers to follow. (Indeed, given the complexity of their theories, they would be naive to expect wide readership among non-philosophers.) They should instead attempt to discern what principles we would settle upon in ideal conditions of judgment: that is, if we knew all relevant non-moral facts (but philosophers should be diffident about whether their training gives them competence to speak authoritatively upon matters of empirical fact), and if we were reasoning consistently, were uninfluenced by invidious bias, and had adequate time for reflection and consultation with others engaged in the same difficult task. In consequence, commonalists must forswear arguing for a general obligation of obedience from any such premise as Mackie's, namely, that humanity would better flourish were we all schooled in a catechism containing this principle of duty. The principles of the commonalist enterprise imply that speculation about the consequences of humanity's general articulate acceptance of this (or any other moral principle) has no probative force in normative theory.

Commonalists will therefore rightly reject the catechists' principal argument for a distinctive *prima facie* duty of obedience. Nor is there any other argument toward this conclusion that their meta-ethical principles can accord any weight. To the contrary, as was noted above, the appeal to our moral intuitions shows that the existence and weight of a moral reason to obey the law is always a function of some independent moral reason which argues in this direction. And that same appeal shows also that we sometimes have no moral reason whatever to do what the law requires, as when one outstays the parking meter by five minutes at a time when there is ample available parking. Constraints of explanatory adequacy and economy, to which catechists are indifferent, ought decisively incline commonalists to exclude the duty of obedience from their normative theories.

Conclusion

It appears then that whether a normative theorist ought recognize a distinctive duty of obedience depends upon her meta-ethics: catechists should; commonalists should not. Hence, the question can receive no decisive answer except in the context of a full-blown meta-ethical theory. It is a mistake to suppose, as I once did, that it may be addressed discretely (Smith, 1973).

Nonetheless, since I believe that some version of commonalism is true and that catechistic theories are wrongheaded, I hold to my earlier doubts about the duty of obedience. I cannot here defend commonalism (but see, Smith, 1979, 1992). Still, I can offer these summary criticisms of catechistic theories as a promissory note to be paid in full on some other occasion. First, although many philosophers have thought that their professional office is to correct society's erroneous moral beliefs, virtually everyone else has ignored their schooling. It is evident upon brief reflection that anyone who sets herself this goal dooms herself to frustration. Philosophy is difficult reading, and few have either time or inclination to wade through it. Most non-philosophers who do – virtually all of them academics in other disciplines – doubt that a philosophical education confers any special store of wisdom. But if non-philosophers won't defer or even listen to us, what is the point of our trying to correct their opinions?

Second, despite the interest and subtlety of various catechists' arguments, there is scant intrinsic plausibility to the supposition that ordinary people require philosophers' aid to discover what they ought individually and collectively to do. When voiced by philosophers it seems suspiciously self-aggrandizing. But its primary implausibility lies in its making normative ethics into something wholly anomalous. The historically dominant conception of analytical philosophy is that its task is explanatory, not hortatory or prescriptive. Its "philosophy of" branches generally (for example, language, law, science, mathematics, and so on) do not undertake to tell speakers, judges, scientists, mathematicians, and the like, how they ought behave in these roles. Rather, philosophers attempt to formulate explanatory theories about what such speakers actually do and how they do it, and about the nature of the various entities with which they work (for example, meanings, laws, scientific theories, numbers, and so on). No one supposes that native speakers of English need study philosophy of language to speak it correctly, that mathematical or scientific proofs would be improved were mathematicians and scientists all proficient in the "philosophies of" their respective disciplines, or that constitutional decisions would be more just were Supreme Court Justices required to be schooled in analytical jurisprudence. Why would normative ethics break this pattern? In default of a convincing answer to this question we should reject all catechistic meta-ethics out of hand – and with them the supposed distinctive duty of obedience.

Bibliography

Blackstone, W. 1793: *Commentaries on the Laws of England*. London: Strahan & Woodfall, 12th edn.

Devlin P. 1965: *The Enforcement of Morals*. New York: Oxford University Press.

Dworkin, R. 1986: *The Realm of Rights*. Cambridge, Mass.: Harvard University Press.

Finnis, J. 1980: *Natural Law and Natural Right*. New York: Oxford University Press.

Greenawalt, K. 1987: *Conflicts of Law and Morality*. New York: Oxford University Press.

Hare, R. 1981: *Moral Thinking*. New York: Oxford University Press.

Harman, G. 1977: *The Nature of Morality*. New York: Oxford University Press.

Hart, H. 1955: Are there any natural rights. *Philosophical Review*, 64, 175–91.

Hume, D. [1777] 1948: Of the original contract, ed. H. Aiken *Hume's Moral and Political Philosophy*. Darien: Hafner, 356–72.

Honore, T. 1981: Must we obey? Necessity as a ground of obedience. *Virginia Law Review*, 67, 39–61.

Kant, I. [1785] 1964: *Groundwork of the Metaphysic of Morals*, tr. H. J. Paton, New York: Harper & Row.

Klosko, G. 1987: The principle of fairness. *Ethics*, 97, 353–62.

Mackie, J. L. 1977: *Ethics: inventing right and wrong*. Harmondsworth: Penguin.

—— 1981: Obligations to obey the law. *Virginia Law Review*, 76, 143–58.

Rawls, J. 1964: Legal obligations and the duty of fair play. In S. Hook (ed.), *Law and Philosophy*. New York: New York University Press, 3–18.

Raz, J. 1979: The obligation to obey the law. In *The Authority of Law*. New York: Oxford University Press, 233–49.

Ross, W. 1930: *The Right and the Good*. Oxford: Oxford University Press.

—— 1938: *The Foundations of Ethics*. Oxford: Oxford University Press.

Sartorius, R. 1975: *Individual Conduct and Social Norms*. Encino: Dickinsen.

Simmons, A. 1979: *Moral Principles and Political Obligations*. Princeton: Princeton University Press.

Smith. M. 1973: Is there a prima facie obligation to obey the law? *Yale Law Journal*. 82. 950–76.

—— 1979: Ethical intuitionism and naturalism: a reconciliation. *Canadian Journal of Philosophy*, 9, 609–29.

—— 1992: The best intuitionistic theory yet! A review of J. Thomson, *The Realm of Rights*. *Criminal Justice Ethics*, summer/fall, 85–97.

Thomson, J. 1990: *The Realm of Rights*. Cambridge, Mass.: Harvard University Press.

Walker, A. 1988: Political obligation and the argument from gratitude. *Philosophy and Public Affairs*, 17, 191–211.

Woozley, A. 1979: *Law and Obedience*. Chapel Hill: University of North Carolina Press.

33

Legal enforcement of morality

KENT GREENAWALT

In modern Western political and legal thought, the subject of legal enforcement of morality is narrower than the literal coverage of those terms. That is because much legal enforcement of morality is uncontroversial and rarely discussed. Disagreement arises over using the law to enforce aspects of morality that do not involve protecting others from fairly direct harms. More precisely, people raise questions about legal requirements: (1) to perform acts that benefit others; (2) to refrain from acts that cause indirect harms to others; (3) to refrain from acts that cause harm to oneself; (4) to refrain from acts that offend others; and (5) to refrain from acts that others believe are immoral. Answers to some of these questions *may* be affected by whether the relevant moral judgments are essentially religious. Subsidiary questions concern the status of taxes adopted to discourage behavior the government should not forbid outright and the status of prohibitions on others profiting from such behavior. Since a single argument for restricting behavior rarely stands alone, a conclusion on any of these general issues will not usually yield a decisive answer to whether any particular action should be left free; but a conclusion can significantly affect the overall power of the totality of appropriate arguments. For example, if someone concludes that the claimed immorality of homosexual behavior is not an appropriate basis to forbid it, this will substantially affect the overall strength of reasons in favor of prohibition.

A final subtlety concerns two perspectives from which the subject of the legal enforcement of morality can be considered. One is a matter of legislative philosophy: "Should the legislature enforce morality by law?" The second perspective is that of a court in a constitutional regime: "Should enforcement of morality count as a legitimate basis for legislation that is challenged as invalid?" One *might* think that certain reasons should really not be relied upon by legislatures but should be accepted by courts as adequate if they are relied upon. More complicated relations between these kinds of reasons might exist. A reason might be acceptable for most legislation, but not, say, for legislation that infringes on liberty of expression. Or, a reason might be acceptable as a matter of general philosophy of government, but not in a constitutional regime that includes separation of church and state.

I explain these major questions in turn, but I first address the obvious point that legal enforcement of morality is usually appropriate.

Legal enforcement of moral norms against causing harm

Any comprehensive morality includes restraints against harming other people. Murder, assault, theft, and fraud are immoral. In any society sufficiently developed to have a law distinguishable from its social morality, the law will forbid murder, assault, theft, and some forms of fraud. As H. L. A. Hart pointed out (Hart, 1961, pp. 188–95), law and social morality will constrain much of the same behavior. That does not mean, of course, that every aspect of morality that concerns preventing harm to others will be enforced by the law. Law is a crude instrument, requiring findings of uncertain facts, with rules backed by a limited arsenal of coercive sanctions. Most lies and many other immoral acts that hurt others are left unregulated by law. Nevertheless, no one doubts that, in principle, protecting others from harm is an appropriate task for legal rules. Exactly what protection should be extended is a matter of prudential judgment or some kind of balancing of morally relevant factors. These plain truths may obscure some complexities that matter when one asks if legal rules should prohibit acts on *other* grounds.

The idea of harm to someone else needs to be clarified and developed. If every unpleasant feeling or negative thought counted as a harm, an act might be prohibited because it made some people envious or disturbed them. With such an expansive notion of harm, enforcement of all aspects of morality could be swallowed up as prevention of harm to others. (However, the weight of reasons in favor of a legal rule would still be influenced if one had to focus on such harm.) Questions whether legal rules appropriately prevent harm to oneself or appropriately enforce morality *as such* would then have much less practical significance. In his nuanced and exhaustive treatment of the subject, Joel Feinberg suggests that, *for a principle of preventing harms to others*, the "harms" that count are "setbacks to interests" that are in some way wrong (Feinberg, 1984, pp. 31–104). Thus, if an actress is chosen for an important role, that does not harm a competitor who is envious and who loses the opportunity to earn $1,000,000. Exactly what count as relevant harms to others is a problem that emerges as of central importance when we move on to bases for legal regulation that are contested.

One significant point is that the prevention of harm to others includes prevention of harm that is most directly inflicted on people as a collective. Thus, the "harm principle" generates no difficulty for a law against spying on the government. What harms count as collective harms, however, is an issue to which we will need to return.

There are two related problems about harm to others that affect much of the rest of the essay. Their explication here will clarify what follows. (1) Could decisions about legal regulation be made without any moral judgment whatsoever? (2) If moral judgment is necessary in deciding what counts as relevant harm, does it follow that general enforcement of morality is appropriate? In answer to the first question, a distinction between wrongful and non-wrongful harms does involve moral judgment, such as, that suffering envy at the deserved success of others is not a relevant harm. Could this sort of judgment be avoided? We could *imagine* legal regulation being based on some assessment of negative consequences that takes account only of overall individual preferences, happiness, or ability to pay, relying on no (other) moral judgments. ("No other" is the precise characterization here because deciding that only preferences, happiness, or ability to pay should count is itself a moral judgment.) If someone conceived the grounds for legal regulation as so limited, would they seem *more* limited than the grounds for moral judgment? That depends. An "average happiness utilitarian" thinks all moral judgments should be based on actual and prospective happiness. It would be misleading to put that position as one in which legal regulation is determined without moral judgment; because one would use the same kinds of assessments to make correct moral judgments as to determine appropriate legal restrictions. Suppose, by contrast, someone thought that sound morality includes many bases for judgment, and that these are irrelevant for legal regulation. That position might be cast as one in which legal regulation could be determined without moral judgment. But it is hard to understand how that position could be defended. Why should moral distinctions that govern the evaluation of acts cease to be of direct relevance for evaluating legal rules? We are left, I believe, with the conclusion that, on any defensible understanding, principles guiding legal regulation must include moral judgments.

If moral judgment infuses determinations of harm, does it follow that legal rules appropriately enforce morality in general? No. It may be that for reasons of moral and political philosophy, harm to others (determined partly by moral judgment) should be an appropriate basis for legal regulation, whereas moral evils that do not involve harm to others should be left free of legal regulation. I now turn to some doubts about whether the law should enforce morality.

Legal requirements to perform acts that benefit others

This topic can be introduced most sharply by asking whether people should have any legal duty to rescue others. In most states of the United States and in many other countries, people do not have such a duty. A person in the park who is walking by a shallow pool in which a baby is drowning, fully aware that he can save the baby easily with no more harm to himself than wet feet, can keep on walking without criminal or civil (tort) consequence. On occasion, this legal principle has been defended on the ground that the law should not enforce morality. Whatever other grounds may exist for the legal principle, this claim is either confused or unpersuasive.

It helps initially to narrow the genuine basis of contention. People often suppose that omissions to act have a different moral status from actions. If *A* breaks *B*'s arm, *A* has done something worse morally than if *A* fails to prevent *C* or a falling limb from breaking *B*'s arm. An extreme utilitarian might deny the moral significance of any distinction between action and omission, but I shall assume it in what follows. Everyone agrees that preventing easily avoidable serious harms is

477

morally preferable to letting them occur, and most would probably acknowledge that the stronger language of moral duty is apt for the rescue situation I have posed, that is, that the passerby has a "moral duty" to rescue the baby.

If we turn to the law, we can quickly see that no universal line is drawn between action and omission. When people have a special responsibility to care for others, they cannot stand by and let them suffer avoidable injury. A parent or hired nurse who, with full awareness, let the baby drown would be guilty of murder or manslaughter. People perform a wide range of roles that include responsibilities to care for others. Further, people have general duties to act for the benefit of the public. They have a legal duty to testify, even if they would rather not; they must pay taxes, and submit to jury service. Anyone who is not an anarchist is likely to acknowledge that governments properly impose on people some positive duties to act. Thus, few doubt that the law imposes on some people some requirements to act to avoid harm and to contribute to the common welfare.

Any principled controversy appears to be over whether strangers should be legally required to assist other individuals in need. Some of the arguments against such liability are that determining the state of mind of someone who could rescue but did not is usually very difficult, that people in a position to rescue (say on a beach, or at home with their telephones as a rape happens outside) frequently believe someone else may do the job, that a free floating duty to help others in need is too vague, and that such a duty imposes inappropriately on the autonomy of citizens to pursue their own projects. From a consequentialist perspective, these problems are matters of degree. A legal duty to prevent death or severe injury to another when one is fortuitously in the position to do so at no risk and slight cost to oneself would be a very slight imposition on one's pursuit of one's own projects. (The idea of one's being fortuitously in the position to help is included so that those with special skills, mainly doctors, are not on constant call to assist strangers in need.) If the duty were limited to persons who find themselves in situations where others are not equally able to help, the complexity concerning many available potential rescuers would be avoided. If determining the state of mind of someone who fails to assist is deemed too difficult, a failure to rescue could be treated as criminal or civil negligence. Someone may reasonably conclude that a legal duty would cover so few circumstances it would not be worth imposing, that it might even detract from nobler motivations to help; but there could be no principled objection to the basic idea of such a duty.

Does a deontological perspective (based on moral rights and justice) yield a different conclusion? I have assumed that a moral duty to rescue exists. (If one assumed that rescue were only a question of what is morally preferable, not of moral duty, one still might believe that a *legal* duty was appropriate, since in some domains the law requires more than is required by independent moral duty.) Given that the law properly imposes legal duties to rescue on those with special responsibilities and also imposes general legal duties to satisfy public responsibilities, no basis exists for some absolute principle against requiring stranger rescue. People, in advance, imagining that they might be in the position of needing rescue or being able to make a rescue easily would choose to have such a legal duty (at least, if they didn't think they could rely for rescues on the moral sense of others). Such a duty is a reasonable responsibility of citizens. *Perhaps*, on balance, imposing the duty is unwise, but it involves no breach of any defensible principle that law should not enforce morality.

Requirements to refrain from acts that cause indirect harm to others

Before we examine claims that self-protection, offense, and perceptions of immorality are themselves inappropriate bases for regulation, we need to look at indirect harms to others. Many acts that do not cause direct harm may hurt people indirectly. In *On Liberty*, the most famous work on the legal enforcement of morality (and on enforcement of morality by public opinion), John Stuart Mill wrote, "the only purpose for which power can be rightfully exercised over any member of a civilized community, against his will, is to prevent harm to others" (Mill, 1975, p. 15). Mill acknowledges that when people harm themselves, this affects others through their sympathy and interests, but only when "a person is led to violate a distinct and assignable obligation to any other person or persons [is] the case taken out of the self-regarding class" (Mill, 1975, pp. 99–100). As an example, Mill says, "no person ought to be punished simply for being drunk; but a soldier or policeman should be punished for being drunk on duty" (Mill, 1975, p. 100).

May indirect harms to others, contrary to Mill, properly be a basis for legal restriction? I shall consider three kinds of instances: (1) when an action will certainly cause harm to others; (2) when a likely future consequence of action is harm to others; (3) when an action is likely to make one a burden on society. If parents with young children commit suicide, they are unable to provide further material and emotional support for them. That is certain. Criminalizing suicide may be pointless, but is the harm to young children a proper basis for preventing such parents from committing suicide, when that is possible? Whatever conceptual division between direct and indirect effects makes sense, a consequence that is certain to follow from an action is one on which society may base regulation.

Likely, but not certain, future consequences pose a more complex problem. Suppose evidence strongly indicates that if use of a particular psychedelic drug were legal, most people who began to use it would eventually become addicted and would at that stage (because of cost and physical effects of the drug) be unable to perform family obligations; further, once people used this drug extensively, their desire to consume it would be much more intense than when they had never or seldom used it. Would this typical harm "down the road" be a proper basis for forbidding *all* use of the drug or all use by parents of young children? If a high percentage of parent-users would eventually neglect their children and no one could estimate in advance who these were, forbidding all use, at least by parents of young children, would make practical sense. From a consequential perspective, it might be warranted. Any claimed consequential basis for an absolute principle against prohibitions based on such indirect effects would have to contend that

479

governments cannot be trusted to limit legal restraint to extreme situations in which expected future harm is so serious and pervasive, and restraint at the initial stage is so much more effective.

If one focussed on some non-consequential right to liberty, one *might* believe that people who are capable of controlling themselves should not be restricted because other people, even a high percentage of users, lack such control and will end up doing harm. Were the percentage of non-addicted users very slight, the cost in human misery of recognizing this claimed right would be very high; and the idea of any absolute right of this sort is unattractive. Nonetheless, the basic idea of some such claim to liberty does suggest a counter to any analysis of the problem that is simply consequentialist. The appeal of the claim to liberty seems most powerful when the high-risk activity is thought to reflect some commendable striving of the human spirit, as with extremely dangerous mountain climbing expeditions.

What of actions that are said to bear an unacceptable risk that one will become a burden on society? This is one justification offered for making automobile drivers wear seat belts and motorcyclists and bicyclists wear helmets. From a consequential point of view, the value of liberty and the pleasure of riding unconstrained might somehow be weighed against likely cost. The cost appraisal would need to be reasonably comprehensive; if cigarette smoking leads to public medical expenses, does it also save public money because smokers tend to live less long after retirement? Someone who places a great intrinsic value on liberty may claim that the public burden argument is, in principle, an insufficient basis for restriction. If society wants to protect itself, it can demand that people who engage in dangerous activities buy insurance to cover possible expenses of injury. Since that lesser restriction is available, ease of administration, on this view, cannot warrant across-the-board-prohibition.

In summary, *some* arguments for restriction based on likely indirect effects run into claims of autonomy that will seem more or less powerful depending on one's overall approach to moral and political philosophy.

Requirements to refrain from actions that hurt oneself

Is harm to the actor an appropriate reason for legal prohibition? For this question, it is widely assumed that adults voluntarily engaging in behavior together, such as sexual acts, are not distinguishable, in principle, from individuals acting by themselves. If morality bears on how we treat ourselves and the law should not interfere to prevent harms to ourselves, this respect would be one in which the law should not enforce morality. Mill put the principle in favor of non-restriction boldly. A person's "own good, either physical or moral, is not a sufficient warrant" for society exercising power over him (Mill, 1975, p. 15). In the part of conduct "which merely concerns himself, his independence is, of right, absolute" (Mill, 1975, p. 15). Were this principle of Mill's followed (and were indirect effects on others not regarded as an adequate basis to regulate), there would probably be no seat belt and helmet laws, no laws generally restricting voluntary sexual activities among adults, no laws against most presently proscribed drugs, no rules forbidding swimming at unguarded beaches, no legal restraint of suicide, and much less extensive regulation of food, medical drugs, and related matters.

Mill speaks of an absolute right, but his claimed basis for the right is consequential. He argues that given differences among individuals, what is good for most people often is not good for everyone, and that, in any event, people grow by learning through experience. Experiments in living are vital for the progress of the human race. The majority cannot be trusted to restrict wisely. When one thinks of most sexual activities, these arguments are powerful. But what of an activity like cigarette smoking? Few adults (in the United States at least) are pleased to be smokers; but most smokers find it very difficult to stop. Given the nearly universal desire for decent health, can we not confidently say that cigarette smoking is harmful to smokers (or at least unwisely reckless)? Unless one's distrust of the majority is extreme, one cannot come up with a principle as absolute as Mill's on consequentialist grounds.

Such an absolute principle is more comfortably defended on the basis that adults should have autonomy to decide how to live their lives, making even foolish choices so long as they do not harm others. The value of autonomy seems most directly opposed to restriction that is designed to protect the actor himself.

In considering the defensibility of a powerful principle against legal "paternalism" that protects people from themselves, it helps to consider voluntary choice, paternalism that serves the reflective values of the actor, and paternalism that imposes values that the actor rejects. Restriction of people for their own good is easiest to justify when voluntary choice is absent. If voluntary choice is present, restriction on behalf of values the actor accepts involves less severe restriction on autonomy than restriction on behalf of values that the actor rejects.

The problem of seat belts provides an apt introduction to these points. For most people, using seat belts in automobiles is a minor restriction; very few people are indifferent to loss of life or grave physical injury, and use of seat belts prevents those in many automobile accidents. Yet a great many people choose not to use seat belts. One *might* analyze these facts in the following way. The chance of a bad accident on any one occasion of driving is very slight. Some people are not fully aware of the value of seat belts in accidents; others find it hard to act rationally in the face of a very slight risk of injury, and they are disposed not to imagine that they will actually be in a serious accident. For complex psychological reasons, they do not act rationally in light of risks involved. A requirement that people wear seat belts might be viewed as forcing them to do what is prudent and reasonable given their own values. One might even argue that choice in ignorance or under conditions when rational assessment is difficult is not *really* voluntary. I shall not explore the problem of voluntariness further, but the more robust one conceives the conditions of voluntariness to be, the more one will accept state restrictions as countering undesirable choices that are not sufficiently voluntary.

The most serious breach of someone's autonomy involves coercion against one's own rational, reflective judgment. Practicing homosexuals believe that their life-

481

style is best for them. If they are told they must refrain because such a life is really psychologically unhealthy and abstinence is preferable, their own deep sense of how to live is disregarded. (I pass over the complicated status of coercion that successfully alters the subject's judgment about what is worthwhile.) This justification for restriction is more an insult to their status as autonomous persons than any serious justification cast in terms of harm to others.

Exactly how much paternalism a person will countenance, on reflection, depends on how strongly that person rates the value of autonomy and distrusts the judgments of the government about what is in people's self-interest. Perhaps no one has given as much careful study to these problems as Joel Feinberg; writing from a straightforwardly liberal perspective, he, like Mill, endorses an absolute principle that someone's own physical, psychological, or economic good should not be a basis for criminal prohibitions against voluntary behavior (Feinberg, 1986a, pp. 1–49). That position is substantially more libertarian than the practices of modern societies and what most people in them would endorse.

Some secondary questions about legal regulation involve civil law consequences when criminal prohibitions would be inappropriate, rules against third persons (such as pimps) profiting from consensual acts between others, and taxation designed to discourage behavior. Much could be said on each of these subjects, but I will limit myself to brief comment on the third. Mill decisively concludes that although raising money disproportionately on unhealthy activities is all right (liquor sales can be taxed at a higher rate than milk sales), it is unacceptable to tax *in order to* discourage behavior that in principle should be left free of criminal restriction. (Mill, 1975, pp. 123–4.) Put aside the fact that cigarette smoking harms nonsmokers and assume the following table for the amount of sales under various levels of cigarette taxes.

Tax rate per pack ($)	Sales (millions)	Revenue ($ millions)
(A) 0	20	0
(B) 1.00	15	15
(C) 1.50	8	12

The only reason for preferring tax (C) to tax (B) would be to discourage smoking; that choice would be barred by Mill's conclusion. That conclusion, however, is not warranted on consequentialist grounds. People who have a very strong desire to smoke will continue to do so if tax (C) is in place and the "experiment in living" of smoking will not be squelched. A *payable* tax has a quite different effect on choice than a successful prohibition. (Of course, an enforced tax of $300 per pack will be a more severe restriction than an unenforced prohibition.) If a set amount of tax is unfair to poor smokers, that problem could be met by calibrating the amount of tax to a smoker's wealth. Thus, the consequentialist reasons against outright prohibition apply with much less force to a discouraging tax that is not too high. Matters are more complex if one focusses on a smoker's intrinsic right to autonomy. One might think autonomy is breached if the state tries to manipulate behavior for the smoker's own welfare. In that event, tax (C) is not distinguishable, in principle, from a prohibition. On the other hand, the choice to smoke is still available, and the price of cigarettes is no greater than if ordinary natural (disastrous storms) or economic factors drove the price of cigarettes up. In its actual import on effective choice, the tax still differs from a successful prohibition. My claim here is that no easy step takes us from belief that the law of crimes should leave behavior free to a conclusion that taxation to discourage the behavior would be inapt.

Requirements to refrain from acts that offend others

Some acts that do not cause harm in a more restricted sense offend others who observe them or who know they take place. Often people regard the offending behavior as immoral in some sense. Is offense an appropriate basis for legal restraint or is this an aspect of morality that the law should not enforce?

Analysis is fairly simple for activities that offend unwilling witnesses (for example, sexual intercourse in public) and that may be carried on in private. The immorality here is not in the basic activity, but in failing to respect the cultural sense of what may decently be done in public, before involuntary witnesses. (A "public" performance before *willing consumers* is a different matter.) Of course, the law should not enforce the sensitivities of the most timid, and many things that social conventions treat as offensive (for example, belching loudly in a restaurant) do not rise to the level of legal regulation; but almost everyone agrees that, in principle, criminal restrictions appropriately protect people against instances of public offensiveness. This broad conclusion is qualified in certain respects by countervailing rights. Suppose what *offends* the majority are religious symbols worn openly by a minority or forms of speech (say, flag burning) by dissidents. Rights of free exercise of religion and free speech may preclude using offense as a basis to restrict religion and speech. In the United States, courts treat such laws as unconstitutional infringements on liberty.

Some acts cause offense to others who are not witnesses. Homosexual acts are striking instances; some people are disturbed to know they are occurring. Mutilation of the bodies of those who have died and cannibalism are more perplexing examples. Isolating the issue of whether offense should be a basis for restriction is not easy. Conceptually we can imagine people being offended by private acts they do not regard as immoral, but that is unusual. Typically this kind of offense accompanies belief that behavior is wrongful. In practice, asking whether a broad opinion that behavior is deeply wrongful is a justification for prohibiting the behavior is not too different from asking whether deep offense is such a justification. But the elements are, or can be, distinguishable bases for legal enforcement, and this section focuses on the offense people feel.

For the element of offense, some near absolute, or absolute, principles are plausible, which I offer without a sustained defense. First, if those offended *do not have any moral objection*, behavior should be allowed; people's liberty to live their own lives as they choose should not be restricted because some others feel mere disturbance at what they do. Second, offense at religious practices that cause no

483

secular harm cannot be a basis for restriction in a country that recognizes religious liberty. Third, offense at non-religious practices (such as homosexual acts or eating pork) because the practices violate some people's religious beliefs should not be a basis for restriction in a country that values religious freedom and does not maintain a close connection between some religion and the government. (*Perhaps* in a country that is overwhelmingly Jewish or Muslim, prohibitions on pork eating would be acceptable).

We are left with the possibility of a restriction that is based on deep offense connected to belief in wrongfulness that is not perceived as primarily a matter of religious belief. If other appropriate bases for restriction are present, deep offense may count in the balance; but could it ever be the primary basis for restricting liberty? I am very doubtful, but that doubt involves a particular view about mutilation of bodies, desecration of graves, and so on, which are sometimes presented as the strongest candidates for appropriate restriction based on offense. When those we love die, our deepest emotions do not fully divorce the body from the person we love. Abuse of the body would feel like abuse of the person. More broadly, abuse of the bodies of strangers feels like abuse of people. According to our emotions, if not our reason, mutilation is a harm to the person who lived in the body; it is also a harm to those who identify strongly with the person, and it may threaten our concern over what will happen to our own bodies. I think it is misleading to characterize as "offense" the deep sense that this behavior causes harm. Protection of human remains is proper, but it should be understood as a special example of accepting (non-rational?) sentiments of what constitutes harm to others.

Requirements to refrain from acts others believe are immoral

Can legal restriction be justified because acts are regarded as immoral, apart from harm (to others and self) and offense they may cause?

Sometimes this seems to be *the* issue about legal enforcement of morality, but conceptual clarity is not easy. Part of the difficulty is that claims that such enforcement of morality is improper dissolve into rather different kinds of arguments. Part of the difficulty is doubt that any acts really are regarded as immoral, apart from some perception of harm. On the latter point, beliefs about homosexual acts provide a helpful illustration. Almost everyone who thinks these acts are morally wrong also believes they are psychologically unhealthy for those who practice them. But someone who believes the Bible reveals that God has condemned cities whose inhabitants practice sodomy may implicitly rate the evil of the acts as much greater than the particular harm (in this life, at least) to practicing individuals. One *could* conceivably think certain individuals are condemned to a completely miserable life no matter what they do and still object to their committing immoral acts. Such a complete divorce of morality from harm may be unusual, but since moral perspectives (especially religious ones) have different dimensions, the *magnitude* of moral wrong may seem greater than any harm. Thus, it does matter whether a basic sense of moral wrongness may underlie restriction.

A claim that the law should enforce morality *as such* might assert a rationale that: (1) objective immorality should be punished; (2) that a community properly punishes what it regards as immoral, without more; (3) that a community may preserve its moral structures, without more; (4) that people have a legitimate interest in preserving structures of life familiar to them; (5) that liberty in self-regarding matters may weaken a community and dissolve bonds of other-regarding morality, to the detriment of people in general.

The last claim is plainly consequentialist. The notion is that people who perceive the law as accepting acts that they regard as abhorrent will fail to identify with other citizens, and will over time lessen their respect for the rights and interests of others. Although various passages may be interpreted differently, this seems to be the drift of Patrick Devlin's argument that legal enforcement of (private) morality is, in principle, appropriate (Devlin, 1965). It may be answered, as did H. L. A. Hart (1961), that communities could observe other regarding morality well, while respecting wide variations in private life, just as communities now respect wide variations in religious belief and practice. Neither position is illogical; the real issue is factual, and the answer could vary among communities. Given normal fears of change and the actual capacity of social communities to survive change (among religious beliefs, for example), one should regard claims of social disintegration with great skepticism, but they cannot be ruled out, in principle, as conceivable justifications behind social restrictions.

Within societies based on particular views about religious truth, punishment of objective immorality may seem perfectly appropriate, but probably that *alone* is not a sufficient justification in a liberal democracy. If one takes the position advocated by certain liberal theorists that the state should be neutral among conceptions of the good life, it will follow that the state has no business punishing objective immorality; but even if one thinks the state should not be neutral, coercion of adults in respect to behavior apart from its damaging consequences may not seem appropriate. This tentative conclusion is tested by examples like sex with animals and staged bear fights. Human sex with animals, bestiality, is almost universally criminal, and the main reason is not animal protection. One may perhaps find sufficient justification in its unhealthiness for the human participants, and perhaps the morally grounded offense felt by others. But these probably do not capture all the bases for prohibition; a sense of fundamental immorality also contributes. Similarly with bear fighting, worries that it would make human observers more cruel and aggressive may be only part of the story. These examples show that even in liberal democracies, a sense of objective immorality affects feelings about legislation. Whether acting on those feelings is fully consistent with liberal principles is debatable.

Those who are skeptical about the existence of objective morality or about the role of any government's enforcing such a morality may retreat to the idea that any community may enforce its *own* morality, independent of harm and offense. But apart from negative consequences of non-enforcement, why should existing morality be frozen in amber, if members of the community do not assume that

485

it is objectively required? (I pass over the complex intermediate possibility of an observer who does not think a particular morality is objectively required, but who is asking himself if a community is justified in enforcing moral norms that the community thinks are objectively required?)

Claims about moral structures and structures of life seek to provide an answer why the community may enforce its morality. Both claims come down to the idea that members of a community have some interest in preserving forms of life familiar to them. If the argument is not to reduce either to a bald contention that a community can enforce its morality or to an assertion that offense justifies restraint, the claim must be based on the value of continuity and psychological security in people's lives. This is a kind of consequentialist basis, although one whose power would need to be very strong if it is to override the liberty of people to choose their own ways of life. As I have already suggested in respect to offense, such a justification probably should not prevail in a liberal society to sustain a morality that is directly dependent on a religious perspective.

The relation between political philosophy and constitutional requisites was sharply at issue in *Bowers* v. *Hardwick* (1986), an American Supreme Court case reviewing the constitutionality of a ban on sodomy as it applied to homosexuals. A majority of five justices said that a public view that such actions were immoral was a sufficient basis for a prohibition, as far as the Constitution was concerned. The dissenters did not express disagreement with this conclusion in all applications, but said that this basis was inadequate when the fundamental interest of sexual intimacy was involved. Although judges are influenced by their sense of sound political and moral philosophy, any individual judge might conclude that a legislature is allowed by the Constitution to rely upon bases for prohibition that would be eschewed under the best understanding of appropriate grounds to infringe individual liberty.

If this essay has a central point, it is the need to avoid reductionist simplicities when questions are put whether, and when, the law should enforce morality.

Bibliography

Bowers v. *Hardwick* 478 U.S. 186 (1986) (US Supreme Court case upholding state law as it applied against consenting homosexual acts.)

Devlin, P. 1965: *The Enforcement of Morals*. London: Oxford University Press. (Defends state's right to forbid acts regarded as immoral even though they cause no direct harm.)

Dworkin, G. (ed.) 1994: *Morality, Harm, and the Law*. Boulder: Westview Press. (Collection of essays, about general theory and specific problems, and cases.)

Feinberg, J. 1984: *The Moral Limits of the Criminal Law: harm to others*. New York: Oxford University Press.

—— 1986a: *Harm to Self*. New York: Oxford University Press.

—— 1986b: *Offense to Others*. New York: Oxford University Press.

—— 1988: *Harmless Wrongdoing*. New York: Oxford University Press. (Very thoughtful and thorough treatment of subject.)

Grey, T. 1983: *The Legal Enforcement of Morality*. New York: Knopf. (A collection of varied materials and commentary.)

Hart, H. L. A. 1961: *The Concept of Law*. Oxford: Clarendon Press. (Develops claim the law and social morality will inevitably overlap.)

—— 1963: *Law, Liberty, and Morality*. Stanford: Stanford University Press. (Libertarian response to Devlin.)

Mill, J. S. [1859] 1975: *On Liberty*. London: Oxford University Press. (Classic arguments that only direct harm to others justifies prohibition.)

34

Indeterminacy

LAWRENCE B. SOLUM

Introduction

Does the law determine the outcome of particular legal disputes? The simple, common-sense answer to this question might be, "Yes, the laws (the statutes, cases, and so forth) fix the way that judges decide cases." A more sophisticated answer might go, "Yes and no, the laws have a big influence, but other things (politics, preferences, and so on) may also come into play." A very cynical answer to the question could be, "No, the laws have nothing to do with how cases come out. They are just window dressing that skillful lawyers and judges can manipulate to justify any decision they please." This final answer to the question is a version of the claim that law is indeterminate.

The indeterminacy debate is about the claim that the law does not constrain judicial decisions. Put differently, the claim is that all cases are hard cases and that there are no easy cases. This claim has been associated with two schools of legal theory, the critical legal studies movement and legal realism, although many scholars associated with the contemporary critical legal studies movement do not believe that a radical critique of law should involve claims about legal indeterminacy. The strongest version of the claim is the notion that any result in any legal dispute can be justified as the legally correct outcome, but the thesis can be modified or weakened in various ways.

The indeterminacy debate has been called "the key issue in legal scholarship today," (D'Amato, Pragmatic Indeterminacy, 1990, p. 148), but the debate has also been referred to as "ultimately vacuous" (Patterson, 1993, p. 278). These wildly inconsistent evaluations underscore the one thing that is clear about the indeterminacy debate. The participants in this controversy do not agree as to what it is they are arguing about. As one observer put it, "Perhaps no phrase has been more misunderstood by legal scholars than the 'indeterminacy thesis' developed by the Conference of Critical Legal Studies" (Cornell, 1988, p. 1,196). Care about what is meant by indeterminacy is especially important because advocates of the thesis charge that the thesis is badly misunderstood by its critics (Binder, 1988, p. 892; Feinman, 1990, p. 1,312; Gordon, 1984, p. 125; Millon, 1992, p. 35; Singer, 1988, p. 624; Yablon, 1987, p. 634).

What does the indeterminacy thesis mean?

Call the claim that the laws (broadly defined to include cases, regulations, statutes, constitutional provisions, and other legal materials) do not determine legal outcomes *the indeterminacy thesis*. Because there are many different versions of the indeterminacy thesis, our approach will be to identify clearly the distinct versions of the indeterminacy thesis and then to consider each version of the thesis on its own merits. As a preliminary step, we will consider the point of the indeterminacy thesis by examining its relationship to radical critiques of liberal legal theory.

The role of indeterminacy in radical critiques of law

Contemporary versions of the indeterminacy thesis are part of a radical critique of liberal legal theory. The overall thrust of the critique might be summarized by the slogan, "Law is politics." The contrasting liberal claim is expressed by the ideal of the rule of law. This ideal requires that disputes be settled by general rules that are announced in advance and applied by courts that follow fair procedures; the ideal of the rule of law forbids arbitrary decision and requires that like cases be treated alike (Rawls, 1971, pp. 235–43). The rule of law is a complex notion, but if the indeterminacy thesis is true, then legal justice will fall short of the ideal of the rule of law in at least three ways: (1) judges will rule by arbitrary decision, because radically indeterminate law cannot constrain judicial decision; (2) the laws will not be public, in the sense that the indeterminate law that is publicized could not be the real basis for judicial decision; and (3) there will be no basis for concluding that like cases are treated alike, because the very idea of legal regularity is empty if law is radically indeterminate.

As we examine a variety of formulations of the indeterminacy thesis, the relation of that thesis to radical critiques of the rule of law must be kept in mind, both as a guide to understanding what is meant by the thesis and as a measure of the adequacy of particular versions of the thesis for critical purposes.

Indeterminacy versus underdeterminacy

The next step in clarifying the indeterminacy debate is to distinguish between "indeterminacy" and "underdeterminacy" of law. Thus far, we have accepted the implicit assumption that indeterminacy and determinacy are exhaustive categories, that is, that the decision of a case is either determined by the law or it is indeterminate. This assumption is not correct. A legal dispute may be constrained by the law, but not determined by it.

Roughly, a case is underdetermined by the law if the outcome (including the formal mandate and the content of the opinion) can vary within limits that are defined by the legal materials. This approximation can be made more precise by considering the relationship between two sets of outcomes of a given case. The first set consists of all possible results – all the imaginable variations in the mandate (affirmance, reversal, remand, and so on) and in the reasoning of the opinion.

The second set consists of the outcomes that can be squared with the law – the set of legally acceptable outcomes. The distinctions between indeterminacy, underdeterminacy and determinacy of the law with respect to a given case may be marked with the following definitions:

- The law is *determinate* with respect to a given case if and only if the set of legally acceptable outcomes contains one and only one member.
- The law is *underdeterminate* with respect to a given case if and only if the set of legally acceptable outcomes is a non-identical subset of the set of all possible results.
- The law is *indeterminate* with respect to a given case if the set of legally acceptable outcomes is identical with the set of all possible results.

The notion of a "hard case" can now be explicated with reference to the idea of underdeterminacy. A case is a "hard case" if the outcome is underdetermined by the law in a manner such that the judge must choose among legally acceptable outcomes in a way that changes who will be perceived as the "winner" and who the "loser." The point is that the outcomes of a case need not be completely indeterminate in order for it to be a hard case; a case in which the results are underdetermined by the law will be "hard" if the legally acceptable variation makes the difference between loss or victory for the litigants. The distinction between indeterminacy and underdeterminacy is rarely observed in the indeterminacy debate, but it is, nonetheless, important to assessing the debate. Claims that the law is radically indeterminate are implausible, but more modest claims about underdeterminacy may both be defensible and play a role in a radical critique of liberal legal theory.

Is the law radically indeterminate?

The following discussion summarizes several moves made in the indeterminacy debate, with the aim of identifying different versions of the indeterminacy thesis. Exposition begins with the strongest or most radical version of the thesis. An objection to this version is considered, followed by a variety of defenses and modifications of the thesis.

The strong thesis or radical indeterminacy

Our investigation of the indeterminacy debate begins with the formulation of the strongest (the most ambitious) claim about the indeterminacy of law. As a preliminary formulation, we might say that *the strong indeterminacy thesis* is the claim that in every possible case, any possible outcome is legally correct. In other words, the strong indeterminacy thesis is the claim that the law is radically indeterminate.

Our preliminary and somewhat informal statement of the strong indeterminacy thesis can be made more precise by analyzing its constituent elements. A case is a legal event, in which a court or other legal body processes a legal unit (identified by pleadings or other legal events) that includes a set of facts about events and actions. The final outcome of a case is the end product of the processing of facts and law by the court. Typically, in common-law courts, the final outcome of a case includes three elements: (1) the decision (a verdict for one or more parties); (2) the order (a criminal sentence or civil relief); and (3) the opinion (a formal statement of the reasons for a decision). Reformulated in accord with this analysis, the strong thesis makes the following claim:

- *The strong indeterminacy thesis.* In any set of facts about actions and events that could be processed as a legal case, any possible outcome – consisting of a decision, order, and opinion – will be legally correct.

To falsify the strong indeterminacy thesis one needs to establish that there is at least one possible case in which at least one possible outcome is legally incorrect. This refutation would disprove the strong indeterminacy thesis only in the sense stipulated here; it would not establish that the law is always, usually, or even frequently determinate.

The argument from easy cases

One way to establish that there is at least one possible case in which at least one outcome is legally incorrect has been called "the argument from easy cases" (Schauer, 1985, p. 399). In its simplest form, the argument from easy cases points to a hypothetical case in which at least one outcome is legally incorrect. The following discussion attempts to formulate one such easy case.

Consider the following case, consisting of facts, a legal rule, and a legal event. First, postulate the following set of events and actions: I (the author) visited Point Magu State Beach in Ventura County, California, between the hours of 12:30 p.m. and 4:00 p.m. on Sunday, February 14, 1993. Second, consider the following legal rule: Section 2 of the Sherman Antitrust Act states, "Every person who shall monopolize or attempt to monopolize, or combine or conspire with any other person or persons, to monopolize any part of the trade or commerce among the several States, or with foreign nations, shall be deemed guilty of a felony" (26 Stat. 209 (1890)). Third, consider the following claim about a possible case: my visit to the beach on the date and time specified would not constitute a violation of Section 2 of the Sherman Act. In order fully to convince you of this, I would need to tell you more about what went on at the beach on that day. The details will include my looking at the ocean, speaking with friends about politics, reading a book, and so forth. Children flew kites; a friend grilled chicken and hot dogs. You might want to know whether I discussed any business dealings at the beach: I did not. But no matter how many questions you asked, no matter how hard you tried, you would not be able to make out a legally valid case that the Sherman Act was violated. If a prosecution were filed against me based only on the events specified, a verdict of guilty would be legally incorrect. This is not to deny that it is possible that things

491

would go wrong in some way. Perjury might be committed; the judge assigned to the case might be deranged. Our system of justice is hardly foolproof, but that does not entail the further conclusion that any result is legally correct.

The upshot of my example of an easy case is this: there is at least one possible case in which at least one possible outcome is legally incorrect. Therefore, the strong indeterminacy thesis (as I have defined it) is false. Notice my argument is not that the outcome of an antitrust prosecution based on the facts I describe is predictable. Rather, my claim is that one possible outcome, that is, conviction, would be legally incorrect. If the law is correctly applied and the witnesses testify truthfully, the prosecution should fail.

At this point, one might object that there is an illicit move in my argument. I have set up a hypothetical case in which I am prosecuted for violating Section 2 of the Sherman Act based on an actual trip to the beach. Is this legitimate? Could such a legal event really be called a case? Anthony D'Amato has raised similar concerns with respect to another alleged easy case:

> If a homeowner eats ice cream in the privacy of her home, it will not give rise to any legal action. But there is no dispute here! No one is claiming that the homeowner has injured anyone else by eating ice cream, and hence there is no occasion to cite a legal rule that she may have violated . . .
>
> Nonetheless, given temporary license to be gruesome, the [advocate of the indeterminacy thesis] can supply such a case: the homeowner's child is starving (and indeed starves to death) while the homeowner eats ice cream. In this case, the homeowner's action (or inaction) gives rise to a criminal case; the state will (or at least should) bring charges of criminal manslaughter. (D'Amato, 1989, p. 256)

D'Amato makes two points in his attempt to refute this example of the argument from easy cases. First, the ice-cream example is not a case, because no legal event has occurred. Second, one can add facts to the hypothetical situation so that the legal outcome would be changed.

The first charge is a fair one, although one can alter the example to add a legal event, such as the charge of manslaughter that D'Amato himself adds in the second paragraph of the quoted passage. The trip-to-the-beach example introduced above does provide such a legal event – a Sherman Act prosecution.

D'Amato might respond that the addition of the hypothetical prosecution is not sufficient to transform a simple trip to the beach into a case. Just as no prosecutor would have any reason to prosecute the innocent homeowner (the one who did not have a starving baby) for manslaughter, no one in the Antitrust Division of the Justice Department would see my expedition to Point Magu as a case under the Sherman Act. In normal circumstances, this is absolutely right. Our perception of the beach trip or the ice-cream case is filtered by our understanding of what constitutes a legally redressable wrong, and we do not see such a wrong in these easy cases.

The next question is, "What shall we make of the fact the law shapes our perception of what constitutes a case?" This fact does not show that the law is radically indeterminate. Rather, the phenomenon that D'Amato identifies is powerful evidence that the strong indeterminacy thesis, as I have defined it, is untrue. The fact that the law shapes our perception of what counts as a case is very persuasive evidence for the proposition that the law does in some way determine outcomes. At this level, the agent by which the law works to determine outcomes is not a judge; rather, it is the person responsible for deciding whether to initiate a legal proceeding. In a potential criminal case, this agent may be the prosecuting attorney. In potential small claims court actions, the agent who determines whether a case will be filed is an aggrieved citizen. The outcome which is determined is not a verdict or judgment; rather it is the decision whether to institute a formal legal proceeding. Notice, however, that the filtering which takes place at the institution stage limits the range of possible outcomes at the judgment stage.

The second point – that the hypothetical can be changed so as to change the legally correct outcome – is not responsive to the argument from easy cases. Let us stipulate for the sake of argument that it is always possible to add facts to an easy case such that the addition of the new facts will change the legally correct outcome of the case. This does not demonstrate that there are no easy cases. Quite the contrary, the fact that the advocate of the strong indeterminacy thesis needed to add facts to the easy case in order to change the legally correct outcome shows that, as originally stated, the easy case was not indeterminate. If the strong indeterminacy thesis were true, then a reasonable legal argument should be available on the facts as originally stated in the hypothetical. The additional facts should not be necessary. That facts must be added to transform an easy case into a hard one demonstrates that the law does constrain the set of legally correct outcomes.

Rule skeptic defenses of radical indeterminacy

The argument from easy cases suggests that from the point of view of lawyers and judges the law is not radically indeterminate. Thus, the defender of radical indeterminacy needs to show that this point of view, a commonsense perspective internal to the practice of law, is in some way mistaken. One such defense draws on philosophical skepticism about rules that is associated with Saul Kripke's interpretation of certain remarks by Ludwig Wittgenstein (Kripke, 1982). Our purposes do not require a summary of the voluminous debate over rule-skepticism and the proper interpretation of Wittgenstein. In the context of the indeterminacy debate in legal theory, rule skepticism is the contention that because rules (including legal rules) cannot, by themselves, determine their own application, there is no such thing as following a rule.

Legal rule skepticism is inspired by Kripke's interpretation of Wittgenstein's discussion of teaching a mathematical series, for example the series of numbers generated by the rule add two (+2). Imagine that the pupil has learned to generate the series and completes the sequence, "0, 2, 4, 6, 8 . . . " by writing "10, 12, 14, 16." Wittgenstein writes,

> Now we get the pupil to continue a series (say +2) beyond 1000 – and he writes 1000, 1004, 1008, 1012.
> We say to him: "Look what you've done!" – He doesn't understand. We say, "You

were meant to add *two*: look how you began the series!" He answers: "Yes, isn't it right. I thought that was how I was meant to do it." – Or suppose he pointed to the series and said: "But I went on in the same way." – It would now be no use to say: "But can't you see . . . ?" – and repeat the old examples and explanations. – In such a case we might say perhaps: It comes natural to this person to understand our order with our explanations as *we* should understand the order: "Add 2 up to 1000, 4 up to 2000, 6 up to 3000 and so on." (*Wittgenstein, 1958, pp. 74–5*)

Wittgenstein's example can easily be transposed into the context of a simple legal rule. We are teaching someone the meaning of the provision of the motor vehicle code which makes it an offense to not to stop at a red light. We illustrate the rule by stopping at red and going at green at First Street, Second Street, and Third Street. We turn the car over to the pupil, who successfully stops during the red at Fourth Street, Fifth Street, and Sixth Street. We drive along a bit further, and then ask the student to continue following the rule. But at Tenth Street, the student begins to go on red and stop on green. We say, "No, you had it before. Stop on red, go on green." But the student replies, "Right, that is what I am doing."

There is nothing magical about the verbal formulation of the motor vehicle code that prevents this sort of interpretation of the red light rule. There is no logical inconsistency internal to an interpretation of "It shall be an offense to drive through a red light at an intersection," that says that "driving through" means *going* until one gets to Tenth Street but means *stopping* after that. Put another way, we might say that the red light rule does contain the complete set of all its applications.

This sort of possibility illustrated by the red light rule can be conjured up with respect to the application of any legal rule in any particular case: that was not murder because the victim was wearing a red sweater on a Tuesday in June before 7:00 a.m., that was not speeding because I was on my way to my dentist, and so on. Returning now to the indeterminacy debate in legal theory, the question is whether general rule skepticism provides support for a strong version of the indeterminacy thesis.

Initially, it should be noted that the attractiveness of rule skepticism as a foundation for the indeterminacy thesis may be undercut by its wider consequences. Pushed to the limit, general rule skepticism seems to imply that there are no rules for the application of language to any situation. But the proposition that any sentence can mean anything would seem to be equivalent to the proposition that no sentence means anything or that human communication is impossible. The conclusions generated by general rule skepticism are wildly implausible.

Moreover, it is not clear that Wittgenstein's examples really lead to general rule skepticism. We can concede that the verbal formulation of a rule does not determine its own application without conceding that the rule is indeterminate. Rules are embedded in a social context. The meaning of the red light rule is the subject of a wide social agreement, and someone who adopts a deviant interpretation, like "go on red after Tenth street," will get a ticket and lose in court. Moreover, our agreement on the meaning of many legal rules is rooted in our shared forms of life and our biological nature as humans. Rule skeptics who practiced what they preach and went through red lights at random would cause accidents and hurt themselves and others. This is not to say that there could not be a human society in which the red light rule meant stop from First through Ninth streets and go after Tenth, but in our society the red light does not mean that. In sum, the rule skeptic defense of radical indeterminacy fails.

Deconstructionist defenses of radical indeterminacy

A different sort of defense of the indeterminacy thesis invokes the deconstructionist techniques associated with Jacques Derrida (Balkin, 1987; Dalton, 1985). The deconstructionist version of the indeterminacy thesis makes the ambitious claim that the indeterminacy of legal rules is the function of deep contradictions within liberal society, or of the failure of liberal society to reconcile or mediate a deep contradiction within the individual. The contradiction is phrased as being between "self" and "other" or between "individualism" and "altruism." Indeterminacy results from contradictions in the underlying principles or policies that are used to justify legal decisions (Peller, 1984, pp. 3–4; Feinman, 1983, p. 847).

In order to make out this deconstructionist defense of the indeterminacy thesis, one would have to demonstrate that the contradiction between self and other runs through the policies and principles underlying all aspects of law. Critical scholars have attempted to show that contract law contains some principles that permit selfish behavior and others that encourage altruism among the parties to a contract, but it seems unlikely that this program could be carried out for the law as a whole.

More fundamentally, the existence of tensions between legal principles that promote altruism and those that protect selfish behavior does not demonstrate that the law is radically indeterminate. Many particular legal doctrines have nothing to do with such tensions. Even in the cases in which these tensions exist, there may be legal rules that reflect a compromise or balancing of conflicting values. Tension at the level of justification does not imply indeterminacy at the level of application. In order to demonstrate that the law is radically indeterminate on the basis of such contradictions, the deconstructionist would need to convince us any outcome in any case can be defended on the basis of existing legal principles that rely on one side of the contradiction between self and other.

Epiphenomenalist defenses of radical indeterminacy

The epiphenomenalist defense grants the existence of easy cases, but denies that it is the law that explains the results. The core idea is that outcomes are predictable, but that the predictability stems from extralegal factors. Legal doctrines, statutes, case law, and so forth are all mere epiphenomena – entities without any real causal role in determining the results of legal proceedings. If the law does not determine results, what does? In line with the role of the indeterminacy thesis in radical critique, the answer is likely to be politics, class bias, or ideology. A Marxist version of the epiphenomenalist defense might identify the material base as the

495

real cause of the outcome of legal proceedings. For the epiphenomenalist, apparently easy cases are not easy because the law determines the outcome; rather, we can predict the outcome of such easy cases because we know that these outcomes are favored by the politics, biases, and ideologies of the legal establishment (Singer, 1984, pp. 20–2).

It is important to note that the epiphenomenalist defense requires that the link from the real, underlying causal factors to the results in particular cases does not go through the law. If the causal chain went through the intentional actions of judges who decided cases on the basis of doctrine, then the indeterminacy thesis would be false: law *would* determine results, although the law would itself be determined by non-legal factors.

The question then becomes precisely how the causal linkage does work, if the law is not part of the chain. The usual explanation is that judges decide the case on the basis of their political or ideological preferences first and then dress up the result with legal arguments. This may sometimes happen, but in other cases, judges believe that their decisions are constrained by the rules: judges frequently report that they felt the law required them to decide a case in a way that was contrary to their own wishes. Another possibility is that judges themselves are unaware of subconscious ideological influences on their decision making, but until the proponents of the indeterminacy thesis offer a fully developed account of the subconscious basis of judicial decisions, there is no good reason to believe that all judges who believe their decisions are constrained by law are deluded in this way.

Another approach to the basic point of the epiphenomenalist defense draws on the distinction drawn by Jules Coleman and Brian Leiter between the indeterminacy of reasons and indeterminacy of causes (Coleman and Leiter, 1993, pp. 559–60). Contemporary versions of the indeterminacy thesis tend to focus on the indeterminacy of reasons. Liberal defenders of the rule of law must admit that sometimes judges go astray and are causally influenced by their passions or corruption or political pressure. Given this admission, liberals cannot claim that the law is the only causal factor determining legal outcomes. Rather, the claim is that the law does not determinately justify a uniquely correct outcome in particular cases. This focus on indeterminacy of reason was not always the focus of indeterminacy claims. Leiter and Coleman argue that the legal realists were more concerned about causal indeterminacy than about indeterminacy of reasons (Coleman and Leiter, 1993, pp. 581–2).

Causal indeterminacy implies that something other than the law determines the results in particular cases. As Coleman and Leiter note, lawyers frequently can predict outcomes:

> Presumably they do it with some degree of informal psychological, political, and cultural knowledge constituting a "folk" social scientific theory of adjudication. The success of this folk theory, which is, after all, all largely coextensive with the talents of lawyers (i.e., their ability to advise clients what to do, when to go to trial, when to settle, etc.), may constitute success enough for the purposes of predictability and authority, regardless of the prospects of social scientific theories. Even liberalism's

harshest critics do not appear to deny the possibility of "folk" theories of judicial behavior. Thus, Crits and Feminists correlate judicial decisions with wealth, gender, race, cultural mores, and ideologies. Indeed, doing so is essential to part of their program, which is to establish the ideological bases of adjudication. (*Coleman and Leiter. 1993. p. 584*)

As Coleman and Leiter point out, "If individuals can predict what the law will require of them, then, in principle, they are on notice and have the opportunity to conform their behavior to the law's demands. Notice requires predictability, not determinacy" (Coleman and Leiter, 1993, p. 584).

It is true that some degree of predictability of legal outcomes is required by the rule of law, but it is not the case that predictability is all that is required. First, predictability does not address the problem of rule by arbitrary decision. An arbitrary judge may still be predictable if lawyers or litigants can accurately foretell what her whims will be. Second, the ability of lawyers to predict outcomes in particular cases does not satisfy the rule-of-law requirement that the rules be public. Lawyers and other specialists may be able to predict how particular judges will decide, while the public is unable to discern the true standards of conduct from the published law, for example, the Constitutions, statutes, rules, and decisions. Particular judges may be predictable, but because of random assignments, one may not be able to predict which judge will hear a particular dispute. Third, predictability does not entail that like cases will be treated alike, because outcomes may be predicted on the basis of legally irrelevant factors, such as the political orientation of judges. Treating like cases alike requires more than predictability; it requires that the basis for prediction be the legally relevant features of the cases in question. These considerations suggest that causal indeterminacy, that is, the epiphenomenalist defense, if true, would undermine liberal claims that the existing legal order substantially satisfies the ideal of the rule of law.

Is a modest version of the indeterminacy thesis defensible?

If the strong indeterminacy thesis cannot be supported, is there a more modest claim about indeterminacy that is defensible and has critical bite?

Underdeterminacy of actually litigated cases

One modest version of the indeterminacy thesis might be the following: in most (or almost all) of the cases that are actually litigated, the outcome is underdetermined by the law. This claim about indeterminacy is not refuted by the argument from hypothetical easy cases. Confirmation of the actually litigated underdeterminacy thesis would require empirical investigation, but there are some good reasons to believe that cases which actually proceed to filing, trial, or appeal will frequently be underdetermined by the law. Litigants will rarely have an incentive to settle easy cases. For example, in a civil dispute where the law gives a determinate answer to the question of who will win and what the amount of their judgment will be, the parties to litigation will usually prefer to settle, rather than incur the expenses of litigation. Uncertainty about the law is one of the factors that selects which cases will be filed, go to trial, and be appealed. This point should not be exaggerated, however: litigation may proceed for any number of reasons, including an irrational over-confidence in a hopeless case, uncertainty about facts in a case in which the law is clear, and so forth.

Even if we were to concede that there is substantial legal underdeterminacy in every litigated case, there remains an important question about the critical force of this version of the thesis: if potential litigants choose not to settle in part on the basis of underdeterminacy, does the actually litigated underdeterminacy thesis have any critical bite? In particular, will the requirements of the rule of law be met? Notice that underdeterminacy of litigated cases does not entail a violation of the requirement that the laws be public; the vast majority of potential disputes may be resolved by recourse to publicly available laws, even if there are hard cases in which litigation is required to resolve legal uncertainty.

On the other hand, it might be argued that underdeterminacy in actually litigated cases would entail that judges will make arbitrary decisions, because their decisions will not be determined by the law. In this connection, we should note the important distinction made by Ken Kress between metaphysical and epistemic indeterminacy. Is it the indeterminacy of the law itself or of our knowledge about the law that is at issue in debates about indeterminacy? Ken Kress calls the claim that the law itself is indeterminate "metaphysical indeterminacy" and the claim that it is our knowledge of the law that is indeterminate "epistemic indeterminacy" (Kress, 1990, pp. 138–9). As Kress explains the distinction:

> Metaphysical indeterminacy speaks to whether *there is* law; epistemic indeterminacy, to whether the law *can be known*. We might say that the question of abortion in a particular jurisdiction is metaphysically (or ontologically) determinate (at some particular time) if there is a right answer to the question whether a woman has a right to an abortion in that jurisdiction. It might nevertheless be epistemically indeterminate whether women have that right, because the right answer is not demonstrable, or because there is no method for determining the right answer, or because there is great controversy among lawyers or other persons about what that right answer is. (*Kress, 1990, pp. 138–9*)

We can now reconsider the thesis that the results of actually litigated cases are underdetermined by the law in light of Kress's distinction. Put in Kress's terminology, we might say that litigants make settlement decisions in part on the basis of epistemic indeterminacy, and therefore many of the actually litigated cases are likely to involve epistemic indeterminacy. But does epistemic indeterminacy mean that judicial decisions are arbitrary? Not necessarily. If judges engage in a good faith effort to determine the correct legal result, then we might say that they have not made an arbitrary decision, even though their decision cannot be demonstrated to be uniquely correct (Dworkin, 1986).

498

Important cases

Some critical scholars have advanced the claim that it is the important cases that are indeterminate (Kairys, 1982, pp. 13–17); a similar claim is that all interesting cases, including all Supreme Court cases, are indeterminate (Tushnet, 1983, p. 819). Put more precisely, the claim might be that the important issues in important cases are underdetermined by the law. If true, this claim might preserve almost all of the critical force of the strong indeterminacy thesis. Yes, there are easy cases, but those cases are unimportant.

One difficulty with the important case version of the indeterminacy thesis is its potential circularity. Our concept of what counts as an important case may have indeterminacy as a component. Part of what makes a case important is that the result is not certain or predictable; if we all knew how the case would come out, we would not be interested. Likewise, the Supreme Court may select cases in part on the basis of their legal indeterminacy.

Another possibility is to limit the indeterminacy thesis to the important cases in a particular legal culture in a particular period. The critical legal studies movement has been, in part, a critique of liberal legal theory and practice in the United States, emphasizing the period from the end of World War II to date. Thus, the indeterminacy thesis might be limited to the important decisions of the Warren, Burger, and Rehnquist courts. The thesis would be that these key decisions (for example, *Roe* v. *Wade*, the Supreme Court's abortion decision) were not determined by the text of the Constitution, the original intent of the framers, or the Court's prior decisions, but were, instead, determined by the political preferences of the Justices. In this version, the indeterminacy thesis may well be true. Moreover, this version of the indeterminacy thesis might well play a role in a critique of contemporary liberal legal theory and practices. After all, legal justification of the important Warren Court decisions has been a major item on the agenda of liberal legal theorists (Dworkin, 1986).

With respect to all of the versions of the important case indeterminacy thesis, it is important to recall the distinction between metaphysical and epistemic indeterminacy. The arguments for the indeterminacy of important cases are usually arguments about uncertainty and unpredictability. Yet, there are plausible theories of law that maintain that there can be a legally correct result even if there is disagreement about what that result might be. Some of the critical force of the important case version of the indeterminacy thesis comes from an equation of epistemic indeterminacy with arbitrary decision making, but as Ronald Dworkin has made clear, judicial decisions can be principled even if there is disagreement over the question whether they are correct (Dworkin, 1986).

Modal indeterminacy

Another way to weaken the indeterminacy thesis is to weaken its modal status. Rather than claiming the law is indeterminate, one could claim that the law *might* be indeterminate. For example, Robert Gordon contended that the point of the indeterminacy thesis was, not that the outcome of particular cases is unpredictable, but rather, is that legal regularity is not a "necessary consequence of the adoption of a given regime of rules. The rule-system could also have generated a different set of stabilizing conventions leading to exactly the opposite results and may, upon a shift in the direction of the political winds, switch to those opposing conventions at any time" (Gordon, 1984, p. 125).

The critical bite of a modally weakened indeterminacy thesis hangs on the meaning given to "necessity," and this, in turn, depends on the kinds of possibilities that are allowed to demonstrate that case results need follow from particular legal rules. If one allows logical possibilities, that is, all those possibilities that do not involve a logical contradiction, then it follows that no law is necessarily determinate. For example, Gary Peller argued, "It is possible that the age thirty-five *signified* to the Framers a certain level of maturity rather than some intrinsically significant number of years" (Peller, 1985, p. 1,174). It is possible, logically and physically, that the term "thirty-five" meant "mature" to the founders, but it did not, as a matter of historical fact, actually mean that. Therefore, it is logically and physically possible that the Supreme Court could hold that a mature 22-year-old can legally become President of the United States on the ground that for the framers "thirty-five" meant "mature." Despite this logical and physical possibility, the Supreme Court will never actually make such a decision on that ground. Indeterminacy may also be a logical possibility, but this sort of possible indeterminacy utterly lacks critical bite.

Gordon's statement of a modally weakened version of the indeterminacy thesis suggests a sense of possibility that might have critical bite. If a shift in the political winds could change the outcome of any case, then there might be an important sense in which we could say, "law is politics." But if the modally weakened indeterminacy thesis is formulated to include only realistic political possibilities, then there will still be easy cases, the outcomes of which will not shift with the political winds. There is no political movement that would make beach parties violations of the Sherman Act. Indeed, that are many actually litigated cases, from traffic violations to ordinary torts, the outcomes of which would not be affected by any shift in the political winds. The modally weakened thesis might be further restricted; for example, it might be argued that there is a subset of politically important cases which might come out differently if there were a shift in the political winds. This sort of move was discussed above in connection with the important case version of the indeterminacy thesis.

Conclusion

What conclusions should be drawn from the debate over the indeterminacy thesis? Initially, it is clear that radical critiques of liberal legal theory are strengthened to the extent that they forgo reliance on claims of radical indeterminacy. In this regard, it should be noted that some of the most interesting critical work has been done in response to the arguments made against the indeterminacy thesis. David Millon has argued that the admission that the determinacy of law depends on social context and convention highlights the problem that the legal subculture may rely on tacit assumptions that are not shared by the public as a whole, and this divergence may be problematic in a democratic society in which the law ought to be publicly available and responsive to majority will (Millon, 1992, p. 66). Duncan Kennedy's work on a critical phenomenology of judging has reformulated many of the critical points developed in association with the indeterminacy thesis but avoids implausible claims about the radical indeterminacy of law (Kennedy, 1986).

Moreover, the indeterminacy debate has sharpened our understanding of how the law does determine outcomes. The liberal defense against the indeterminacy thesis has produced distinctions between indeterminacy and underdeterminacy, between epistemic and metaphysical indeterminacy, and between indeterminacy of causes and reasons, that have clarified the claims of liberal legal theory. In addition, the indeterminacy debate has made it clear that almost no one defends a strong formalist claim that the law determines every aspect of the outcome of every case. The demise of strong formalism in turn has implications for liberal theorizing regarding the rule of law in a world in which it is acknowledged that the law underdetermines at least some part of the outcome of most (or even almost all) of the actually litigated cases. If the claim that the law is radically indeterminate turns out to be silly, it is also the case that the strong formalist claim that the outcomes of cases are completely determined by the law is just as implausible.

References

Binder, G. 1988: Beyond criticism. *University of Chicago Law Review*, 55.

Coleman, J. L. and Leiter, B. 1993: Determinacy, objectivity, and authority. *University of Pennsylvania Law Review*, 142.

D'Amato, A. 1989: Aspects of deconstruction: the "easy case" of the under-aged president. *Northwestern University Law Review*, 85.

—— 1990: Pragmatic indeterminacy. *Northwestern University Law Review*, 85.

Dworkin, R. 1986: *Law's Empire*. Cambridge, Mass.: Harvard University Press.

Feinman, J. M. 1983: Critical approaches to contract law. *UCLA Law Review*, 30.

—— 1990: The significance of contract theory. *University of Cincinnati Law Review*, 58.

Gordon, R. W. 1984: Critical legal histories. *Stanford Law Review*, 36.

Kairys, D. 1982: Legal reasoning. In D. Kairys (ed.), *The Politics of Law: a progressive critique*. New York: Pantheon Books.

Kennedy, D. 1986: Freedom and constraint in adjudication: a critical phenomenology. *Journal of Legal Education*, 36.

Kress, K. 1990: A preface to epistemological indeterminacy. *Northwestern University Law Review*, 85.

Kripke, S. 1982: *On Rules and Private Language*. Cambridge: Harvard University Press.

Millon, D. 1992: Objectivity and democracy. *New York University Law Review*, 67.

Patterson, D. 1993: Conscience and the Constitution. *Columbia Law Review*, 93.

Peller, G. 1984: Debates about theory within critical legal studies. *Lizard*, 1.

—— 1985: The metaphysics of American law. *California Law Review*, 73.

Rawls, J. 1971: *A Theory of Justice*. Cambridge: Harvard University Press.

Schauer, F. 1985: Easy cases. *Southern California Law Review*, 58.

Singer, J. W. 1988: The reliance interest in property. *Stanford Law Review*, 40.

Tushnet, M. 1983: Following the rules laid down: a critique of interpretivism and neutral principles. *Harvard Law Review*, 96.

Yablon, C. M. 1987: Law and metaphysics. *Yale Law Journal*, 96.

Further reading

Altman, A. 1990: *Critical Legal Studies: a liberal critique*. Princeton: Princeton University Press.

Edmundson, W. 1993: Transparency and indeterminacy in the liberal critique of critical legal studies. *Seton Hall Law Review*, 24.

Greenawalt, K. 1992: *Law and Objectivity*. Oxford: Oxford University Press.

Kress, K. 1989: Legal indeterminacy. *California Law Review*, 77.

Patterson, D. (ed.) 1992: *Wittgenstein and Legal Theory*. Boulder: Westview Press.

Solum, L. B. 1987: On the indeterminacy crisis: critiquing critical dogma. *University of Chicago Law Review*, 54.

Winter, S. L. 1990: Indeterminacy and incommensurability in constitutional law. *California Law Review*, 78.

35

Precedent

LARRY ALEXANDER

Introduction

The doctrine of precedent, or *stare decisis*, requires courts to follow earlier judicial decisions on matters of law. Precedent is one of several doctrines of repose – that is, doctrines for settling issues with finality. The doctrine of *res judicata* dictates that courts not allow relitigation of particular lawsuits after they have been decided. It applies only to the particular parties to a lawsuit and only with respect to the factual issues that were raised or should have been raised in that lawsuit. The doctrine of collateral estoppel prevents the relitigation in a second lawsuit of particular factual issues that were decided in the first lawsuit, even if the second lawsuit is distinct from the first, and in certain circumstances even if the parties are different. The doctrine of precedent, on the other hand, makes a court's determinations of law in one lawsuit binding on all other courts of equal or inferior rank within the first court's jurisdiction, even if the lawsuits and the parties in the subsequent cases are completely distinct from the lawsuit and the parties in the precedent case.

The constraint imposed on courts by the doctrine of precedent can be analyzed both in terms of the *scope* of the constraint and in terms of the *strength* of the constraint. The scope of precedential constraint refers to the number of possible cases that the precedent case controls. Put differently, questions of scope ask how broad or narrow are the legal issues that the precedent case has settled. The strength of precedential constraint refers to types of reasons a court must have to justify refusing to be bound by a precedent. Questions of scope are far more complex and have been dealt with far more extensively than questions of strength (Goldstein, 1987; Monaghan, 1988; Perry, 1987; Schauer, 1987). Accordingly, I shall spend the bulk of this essay discussing questions of scope, turning to questions of strength only briefly toward the conclusion.

The scope of precedential constraint

Common-law cases

Suppose we have a case that does not involve the interpretation of a constitutional provision or a statute, and there is no prior case that is, even arguably, a precedent

503

for this case, whatever that means. In other words, we have what is called a common-law case of first impression. (I shall deal with precedent in constitutional and statutory cases in the next section.)

Further suppose that in this case of first impression, the facts are A, B, and C. The court – the "precedent court" – decides in favor of plaintiff, announcing in its opinion that in all cases with fact A, plaintiff shall prevail.

A subsequent case arises with facts A and B but not C. The court in the later case – the "constrained court" – believes that defendant should prevail. It has no quarrel with the precedent court's decision in favor of the plaintiff in the precedent case; however, it does not believe that in all cases with A, plaintiff should prevail. In particular, it believes the absence of C should be decisive for the defendant. Does the doctrine of precedent mandate a decision for plaintiff in the constrained case, or is the constrained court free to decide for defendant?

The issue of the scope of precedential constraint is frequently framed in terms of the distinction between distinguishing a precedent case and overruling it. Thus, if one takes as significant the full panoply of facts in the precedent case, the precedent case is distinguishable from the constrained case and does not control it. That is so because fact C was present in the precedent case but not the constrained case, and the constrained court believes the absence of fact C is a material difference. On this view, the precedent court has settled only the legal issue of what to do when A and C are both present. On the other hand, if one takes the announced rule in the precedent case to be its significant aspect for future cases, the constraint of precedent appears much greater. The precedent court has settled what to do in all cases where A is present, a larger set of cases than those with both A and C.

In cases such as I have hypothesized, in which the precedent court reaches the correct result but announces a rule that produces incorrect results in future cases – where correct and incorrect refer to the point of view of the constrained courts – it may appear that a version of the doctrine of precedent that permits the constrained courts to reach the correct decisions – by distinguishing the precedent case or, the same thing, refining the rule announced in that case – is superior to any version of precedent that requires the constrained courts to reach incorrect results. On such a version of the doctrine of precedent, what is constraining is the precedent court's decision in light of the facts before it, not the general rule it announced. The latter, framed in specific circumstances, is likely to produce regrettable outcomes in circumstances covered by the precedent court's rule but not envisioned with the clarity that only the facts actually before the court possess. Therefore, the constrained court should be able to distinguish the precedent case by pointing to factual dissimilarities that militate in favor of a different outcome.

The problems with this approach to the scope of precedential constraint emerge more clearly in cases where the constrained court believes the precedent case is wrongly decided on its facts, and not just the source of an overbroad rule. Suppose again, for example, that the precedent case had facts A, B, and C, and the decision was for plaintiff. And suppose again that the constrained case has facts A and B, and that the constrained court believes defendant should prevail. In addition, however, the constrained court believes defendant should have prevailed in the precedent case because it believes that whenever fact *B* exists, defendant should win.

If the precedent court is only bound to decide its case as the precedent court decided its case when the facts are the same, then the constrained court always will be able to do what it thinks best regardless how the precedent case was decided. For there will always be some factual differences between the precedent case and the constrained case. Because there are always factual distinctions between cases, the view that precedent cases only constrain subsequent courts presented with the same facts is a view that denies any precedential constraint whatsoever.

If precedents are to constrain, they must do so even in cases that are factually dissimilar in some respects. Three different models, or types of models, exist for explaining or justifying precedential constraint in the literature.

The natural model of precedential constraint   According to this model, past decisions naturally generate reasons for deciding present cases the same way. These reasons can be boiled down to two: equality and reliance (Moore, 1987). Equality dictates that present litigants should be treated the way past litigants have been. And because not upsetting expectations is a value that courts should take into account, reliance by actors on the way precedent courts have decided cases is also a reason for deciding subsequent cases in a similar manner (Perry, 1987, pp. 248–50).

The natural model is so called because the model does not depend on the existence of any posited doctrine of precedent. Rather, according to the natural model, precedents naturally generate reasons in favor of similar decisions, and precedents constrain only insofar as the weight of equality and reliance require constrained courts to decide differently from how they would have decided in the absence of the precedents. According to the natural model, precedent cases are just facts about the world that, like other facts, influence what is correct in the present.

The natural model can be criticized on two grounds. First, it is doubtful that equality is ever a *moral* reason for departing from decisions that would otherwise be morally correct. (Alexander, 1989, pp. 9–13) To take a dramatic example, past genocide does not generate an equality reason – not even a weak one – for continuing genocide in the present. Nor do any less dramatic past injustices have the effect of making what would otherwise be a present unjust act no longer unjust. Moreover, the constrained court has access to only those facts about the precedent case that the precedent court thought pertinent, not all the facts that might bear on an equality claim.

Second, although protecting justified reliance is an important value, giving full effect to that value will probably require a stronger doctrine of precedential constraint than the natural model provides (Alexander, 1989, p. 16). That is so because actors, though they know that their reliance will be taken into account, will be uncertain how much weight will be given to their reliance by the constrained courts, or whether those courts will deem their reliance to have been justified. Such actors will therefore be quite uncertain regarding how the constrained courts will decide. The disvalue caused by such uncertainty and unpredictability militates in favor of a stronger precedential constraint.

505

Finally, it should be noted that there are no such things as distinguishing a precedent case or overriding a precedent case if one is operating under the natural model of precedential constraint. Because the constrained court is always supposed to reach what it believes to be the correct decision in the case before it, and is supposed to treat past judicial decisions no differently from how it treats any other facts about the world, there is nothing in a past decision to distinguish or overrule.

The rule model of precedential constraints   According to this model, precedent courts in deciding cases promulgate rules of law (Hardisty, 1979, pp. 53–5). It is these rules that constrain subsequent courts. And it is these rules on which actors may justifiably rely, and which further predictability and stability.

There are several versions of the rule model of precedent that differ according to how the rule of the precedent case is to be defined (Alexander, 1989, pp. 18–19). The rule of the precedent case might refer to some canonical formulation of a rule that appears in the opinion of the precedent case (Wasserstrom, 1961, p. 36). Thus, in the hypothetical with which I began, the constrained court must hold for the plaintiff, even though it would hold for defendant in the absence of the precedent case, because the rule of the precedent case – "if A, then hold for plaintiff" – dictates that result. Or, particularly when no canonical rule formulation appears in the opinion, the rule might refer to some premiss held by the precedent court which is inferable from the court's decision and opinion (Stone, 1985, pp. 124–9). Obviously, such a premiss cannot be too abstract – as it would be if, for example, it were "do justice" – or it will fail to provide any meaningful constraint on the constrained court and hence fail to promote the reliance values of predictability and stability. Moreover, to be consistent with the rule model, such a premiss would have to be expressible in canonical form and have to be a premiss that the precedent court wanted to control future cases. Finally, when the rule of the precedent case conflicts with the actual result reached in the case – and it is logically possible that a court that announces a canonical rule will fail to apply it correctly in the very same case – different views regarding what should be considered *the* rule of the case produce different versions of the rule model.

The rule model of precedential constraint is subject to three basic criticisms. First, as I have just pointed out, identifying the rule of the precedent case can be controversial. Even if one adopts the version of the model in which the rule is some actual canonical formulation in the court's opinion, not every case will have such a formulation. If identifying the precedent rule is difficult and controversial, however, the reliance values that the rule model of precedential constraint was supposed to promote are undermined.

Second, some might object to the rule model of precedential constraint because the model explicitly recognizes and endorses judicial legislation (Alexander, 1989, pp. 27–8). If one's view of the proper role of courts excludes their legislating, even interstitially, then the rule model of precedential constraint would be objectionable and only the natural model would be acceptable.

506

The first two criticisms of the rule model of precedential constraint are normative. The third criticism is positive, namely, that the rule model fails to account for the practice of *distinguishing* precedents (Alexander, 1989, pp. 19–25). Distinguishing a precedent case, which is directed at the scope of the constraint it imposes, is supposed to be different from *overruling* a precedent case, which is directed at the strength of its constraint. Yet the only questions of scope that a constrained court asks under the rule model are "What is the rule of the precedent case?" and "Does the constrained case fall within the terms of the rule?" There is no further question of scope that might provide a toehold for distinguishing the precedent case. For example, "distinguishing" the precedent case by narrowing its rule amounts to amending the rule, which in turn is the same as overruling the rule in part. ("Broadening" the rule is never an issue because a rule that is too narrow to cover the constrained case does not constrain it in any way.) Therefore, the rule model cannot account for what is at least supposed to be an aspect of the doctrine of precedent.

The result model of precedential constraint A third model of precedential constraint is the result model (Hardisty, 1979, pp. 53–5). According to this model, the result reached in the precedent case, rather than any rule explicitly or implicitly endorsed by the precedent court, is what binds the constrained court. Unlike the natural model, however, the result model gives the result in the precedential case more constraining scope than it "naturally" carries.

What does it mean to say the constrained court is bound by the result in the precedent case? (I shall refer to the precedent case in the singular, although the result model, by eliminating the focus on rules, makes all decided cases precedents for the constrained court; the result model is thus holistic in approach.) There will always be factual differences between any two cases, so that if the precedent court's opinion is ignored, no decision by the constrained court will logically contradict the decision of the precedent court.

The result model of precedential constraint can be formulated in two ways that are ultimately equivalent in meaning (Alexander, 1989, pp. 29–34). First, the model can be said to require the constrained court to decide in favor of the analogous party to the party who won the precedent case if the arguments in favor of that party in the constrained case are equal to or stronger than the arguments in favor of the analogous party in the precedent case, even if without the precedent, those parties should lose. This can be called the "*a fortiori* case" formulation of the result model.

Second, the model might be said to require the constrained court to decide analogously to the precedent court if in a world in which the precedent court's decision were correct, the analogous decision by the constrained court would be correct.

The equivalence of the two formulations of the result model of precedent can be seen by noting the difficulties of the "*a fortiori* case" formulation. That formulation assumes a metric by which the strength of reasons for a result can be weighed and compared. To make matters simple, let us assume the proper metric is a utilitarian one. In the precedent case, facts A, B, and C were on the plaintiff's side and facts X, Y, and Z were on the defendant's side. A, B, and C outweighed X, Y, and Z on the utilitarian metric (say, by ten utiles), but the precedent court decided (wrongly) in favor of defendant.

In the constrained case, the facts are again A, B, and C for plaintiff. The facts for defendant are W (instead of X), Y, and Z, plus N, the natural weight of the precedent case (say, its reliance value). A, B, and C still outweigh W, Y, Z, and N on the utilitarian metric, but they do so by less than they did in the precedent case (say, by five utiles). Therefore, the constrained case is a stronger (*a fortiori*) case for defendant.

The problem with this approach is that the precedential constraint it establishes is either devastatingly far reaching or else completely indeterminate (Alexander, 1989, pp. 35–7). In every case where a decision for a party would produce a loss of fewer utiles than in the precedent case, such a decision will be an *a fortiori* case under the result model of precedential constraint no matter how unrelated the two cases appear to be. Moreover, all correctly decided cases will also constrain all other cases, but in the opposite direction. Finally, if an incorrect decision is, nonetheless, an *a fortiori* case relative to the incorrectly decided precedent, then a correct decision would also be an *a fortiori* case.

For example, criminal cases upholding a privilege against self-incrimination where the threat against defendants for remaining silent is loss of employment appear to make administrative cases involving threats of criminal prosecution for failures to file incriminating reports *a fortiori* cases in favor of defendants. Yet the decisions in the latter cases were decided against those invoking the privilege. Thus, they make the criminal cases *a fortiori* cases in favor of the state.

The upshot of these examples is that we cannot use a correct metric of weight for determining what is an *a fortiori* case relative to a precedent case that was incorrectly decided (by that same metric). Either the incorrectly decided precedent case is like a misshaped piece of a jigsaw puzzle that cannot be pieced together with correctly decided precedents, or, alternatively, correct decisions will always dominate incorrect decisions on the *a fortiori* analysis, producing no precedential constraint.

The result model of precedential constraint therefore must abandon all reliance on correct principles or metrics and invoke those principles or metrics that, though actually incorrect, would justify the precedent result in a world in which those principles or metrics were correct (Alexander, 1989, pp. 37–42). In other words, on the result model of precedential constraint, precedents have what Ronald Dworkin refers to as "gravitational force" in that they generate governing principles that, although not correct principles (because they are generated by incorrect decisions), would be correct in a world in which the incorrect precedents were correct (Dworkin, 1977, pp. 110–15). (On the rule model, precedents have what Dworkin calls "enactment force.")

The result model of precedential constraint thus construed has two principal difficulties. First, there is the same access to the facts of the precedent case problem that I adverted to in the discussion of the natural model. (The result model asks questions that advert to the particular facts of the precedent and constrained cases; however, if the precedent court favors an abstract rule – such as, "if fact A, decide for plaintiff" – the constrained courts may know no more about the precedent case than that fact A was present.)

The more serious problem the result model faces, however, is whether the counterfactual question it poses – "What decision would be correct in a world in which the incorrect precedent decision were correct?" – is quite probably either incoherent or else coherent but cannot account for constraint. (It would be the latter if the answer to the question were that the constrained court should follow principles that produce correct results in all cases except the past incorrect ones.) In other words, viewed one way, the result model asks a question that cannot be answered: "What would be right in a world in which certain decisions that are wrong in our world were correct?" (Compare that question to this question: "What would 3 plus 3 equal in a world in which 2 plus 2 equals 5?") Or the model asks a question that is answerable, but in a way that negates precedential constraint: "In such a world, everything that is right in our world is right, except for the decisions in the precedent cases as particulars, which fortunately are in the past." The result model either cannot be followed or cannot constrain.

Other false starts in explaining the scope of precedential constraint

(1) *Analogy.* Sometimes the scope of precedential constraint is explained by reference to analogical reasoning. The precedent case constrains to the extent the constrained case is more closely analogous to the precedent case than to any other case.

The difficulty with constraint by analogy is that every case is analogous to every other case in some ways and disanalogous in other ways. Picking the dimension by which cases are compared requires reference to some norm beyond the facts of the case. Once we have identified that norm, however, reasoning by analogy does no work, for the norm itself identifies what the constrained court must do.

(2) *Constraint by the precedent court's reasoning.* Sometimes it is said that the constrained court is bound, not by the precedent court's rule, but by its "reasoning" (Monaghan, 1988, pp. 764–5; Summers, 1978, pp. 730–5). Now, such a statement might just refer to a version of the rule model that rejects the canonical rule formulated in the court's opinion in favor of a more abstract premiss from which the precedent court reasoned to the stated rule. (The premiss cannot be so abstract that it fails to constrain, as it would be if it were "do justice," for example.)

On the other hand, if being bound by the precedent court's reasoning refers not to some rule-like premiss, but to the precedent court's process of inference, then it runs into the same problem the result model ran into (and can be viewed as one way of describing the result model): in cases decided incorrectly, the precedent court's inferences were mistaken. And determining what one should do in a world in which fallacious reasoning is (sometimes) non-fallacious is probably impossible.

509

(3) *The skeptical view.* Legal realists were skeptical regarding whether precedents could ever constrain because they noted that there were always factual distinctions between precedent cases and constrained ones (Stone, 1985, pp. 124–9). ("In the precedent case, the defendant's horse was white, and the plaintiff's name was Joe.") Therefore, a constrained court that wished to reach a different result from that reached in the precedent case could always point to some distinguishing factual difference between the cases.

The realist's skeptical critique, however, does not apply to the three models of precedential constraint described above. It does not apply to the natural model because that model does not locate constraint in a doctrine of precedent. Rather, it merely directs the constrained court to decide as that court believes is correct, taking into account all material facts, including past decisions and the reliance they generated.

Nor does the skeptical criticism apply to the rule or result models. It does not apply to the rule model because the only factual differences that can be taken into account under that model are those factual differences that are material according to the precedent court's rule. And according to the result model, factual differences are significant only if they dictate different outcomes under the principles that the precedent cases reflect.

Conclusion   The natural model of precedential constraint in reality does not represent any sort of legal doctrine of precedent. Although it instructs courts to take account of changes in the world effected by prior judicial decisions, that fully exhausts its force. The result model of precedential constraint is undesirable because it requires the constrained court to answer an unanswerable question: "What would be a correct decision in a world in which the precedent court's incorrect decision were correct?"

Some version of the rule model of precedential constraint appears to be necessary if there is to be a coherent doctrine of precedent. Such a version would require settling what is to count as the rule of the precedent case and accepting the legislative role of the precedent court.

Postscript: the relation between the natural and rule models of precedential constraint   If, according to the natural model, one of the values that following precedent is supposed to promote is reliance; and if, according to the rule model, reliance is best promoted by requiring constrained courts to follow the rules announced in precedent cases; then one could conclude that the natural model itself requires adoption of and thus subsumes the rule model (Alexander, 1989, pp. 48–51). That view of the relationship between the two models may be correct, but it illustrates the tension inherent in all normative decision making between getting the particular case right and following rules. That tension, which almost amounts to a practical paradox, exists because the best rule to promulgate in a precedent case may be one that produces incorrect results in some particular cases. In these cases, the constrained courts must choose between deciding the particular case correctly and deciding it according to the rule, which it also believes to be correct as promulgated, that is, with no exception provided for the case at hand.

510

In cases governed by canonical texts (statutory and constitutional cases)

Many believe that constraint by precedent is problematic in cases of statutory or constitutional interpretation as opposed to common law decision making (Brilmayer, 1988; Lawson, 1994). After all, if the constrained court believes the precedent court misinterpreted the statutory or constitutional provision at issue, would it not defeat the purpose of law-making through statutes and constitutions for the constrained to follow the precedent rather than what is in its view the correct interpretation of the statutory or constitutional provision?

The answer is that although precedential constraint in statutory and constitutional cases *would* be problematic in a pure statutory/constitutional regime, our statutory/constitutional regime is an impure one, and for good reason. We have statutes and constitutions rather than merely a general injunction to "do justice" because we believe that statutes and constitutions, being more determinate than the injunction to "do justice," will actually produce more justice long-term than the general injunction, even though in some cases statutes and constitutions will depart from what justice requires. The very reason we have statutes and constitutions rather than merely the general injunction – that is, to "settle" what justice requires – also can be invoked (though not conclusively) in favor of other institutions for settling matters, including settling the meaning of the statutory and constitutional provisions themselves. Thus, we have the institution of judicial review in cases arising under the Constitution, so that the Supreme Court's interpretation of the Constitution is treated as authoritative – as if it were the Constitution – even if it is mistaken. (Schauer, 1994; Alexander, 1989, p. 57.) And from treating a judicial decision in a statutory or constitutional case as final *for that case* even if mistaken, it is but a short step to treating the interpretation the court announces as final *for all other cases*. In other words, the argument for a doctrine of precedent in statutory and constitutional cases is the same kind of indirect consequentialist argument that supports judicial finality generally and that ultimately supports the authority of statutes and constitutions themselves (Alexander, 1989, pp. 57–8; Monaghan, 1988; Schauer, 1994).

The model of precedential constraint in statutory and constitutional cases must necessarily be the rule model. What the precedent court does in statutory and constitutional cases is translate the canonical formulation at issue into the court's own, alternative formulation, which then, by virtue of the doctrine of precedent, becomes canonical for subsequent courts.

The strength of precedential constraint

In the previous section I analyzed the *scope* of precedential constraint: what does following precedent require the constrained court to do that is different from what it would do in the absence of the precedent case? In this section I shall discuss the *strength* of precedential constraint: when – for what reasons – may the constrained court disregard precedential constraint? (This question does not arise under the natural model, given that the natural model never requires the constrained court to reach a result it regards as incorrect.)

In dealing with the strength of precedential constraint, one must distinguish cases of *vertical* constraint from cases of *horizontal* constraint (Alexander, 1989, pp. 51–2, 60–1). (There is a third class of cases in which the precedent court has no authority to constrain the court in question, though the latter might be *influenced* by the precedent court's decision.)

Cases of vertical constraint are cases in which the constrained court has a status inferior to the precedent court within a particular hierarchy of courts. For example, a decision by the Supreme Court of Iowa acts as a vertical constraint in later cases before the lower courts of Iowa. In vertical constraint cases, the constraint is usually regarded as absolute. That is, once it is clear that the case falls within the scope of the precedent, there are no reasons that would justify the constrained court's departing from what the precedent requires.

Cases of horizontal constraint are cases in which the precedent court is the same court as the constrained court. For example, a decision by the Supreme Court of Iowa acts as a horizontal constraint on later cases in the Supreme Court of Iowa.

It is in horizontal constraint cases that the strength of precedential constraint is controversial. No one today argues that the strength should be absolute (that horizontal precedents should never be overruled). To overrule a precedent, it is, of course, necessary that the constrained court find that the precedent court erred. Otherwise, it would have no good reason to overrule the precedent. On the other hand, if error by the precedent court were sufficient for overruling, precedents could never constrain.

Therefore, in order for a constrained court to overrule a horizontal precedent, the precedent must be more than wrong: it must be both wrong and also mischievous to a certain degree of gravity. What that degree of gravity is, will determine the strength of precedential constraint. That strength will vary from jurisdiction to jurisdiction and from court to court. It may also vary in the same court depending upon whether the case is common law, statutory, or constitutional (Alexander, 1989, p. 59).

Finally, although the strength of precedential constraint can be a function of the weight of the reasons required for overruling, the doctrine of precedent itself is not a legal norm that has the dimension of weight. In other words, although the doctrine of precedent can operate as a rule requiring constrained courts to follow precedent unless moral or political reasons of a certain weight dictate otherwise, the doctrine of precedent does not have weight in its own right. This point is part of a broader and controversial argument against viewing any *legal* norms as having the dimension of weight (Alexander and Kress, 1995).

Bibliography

Alexander, L. 1989: Constrained by precedent. *Southern California Law Review*, 63, 1–64.

Alexander, L. and Kress, K. 1995: Against legal principles. In A. Marmor (ed.), *Law and Interpretation*. Oxford: Oxford University Press, 279–327.

Brilmayer, L. 1988: The conflict between text and precedent in constitutional adjudication. *Cornell Law Review*, 73, 418–21.

Dworkin, R. 1977: *Taking Rights Seriously*. Cambridge, Mass.: Harvard University Press.

Goldstein, L. (ed.) 1987: *Precedent in Law*. Oxford: Clarendon Press.

Hardisty, J. 1979: Reflections on stare decisis. *Indiana Law Journal*, 55, 41–69.

Lawson, G. 1994: The constitutional case against precedent. *Harvard Journal of Law & Public Policy*, 17, 23–33.

Monaghan, H. P. 1988: Stare decisis and constitutional adjudication. *Columbia Law Review*, 88, 723–73.

Moore, M. S. 1987: Precedent, induction, and ethical generalization. In L. Goldstein (ed.), *Precedent in Law*. Oxford: Clarendon Press, 183–216.

Perry, Stephen R. 1987: Judicial obligation, precedent and the common law. *Oxford Journal of Legal Studies*, 7, 215–57.

Schauer, F. 1987: Precedent. *Stanford Law Review*, 39, 571–605.

—— 1994: Precedent and the necessary externality of constitutional norms. *Harvard Journal of Law & Public Policy*, 17, 45–55.

Stone, J. 1985: *Precedent and Law*. Sydney: Butterworths.

Summers, R. S. 1978: Two types of substantive reasons: the core of a theory of common-law justification. *Cornell Law Review*, 63, 707–88.

Wasserstrom, R. A. 1961: *The Judicial Decision*. Stanford: Stanford University Press.

36

Punishment and responsibility

GEORGE P. FLETCHER

The notions of punishment and responsibility display a tight conceptual connection. Punishment reveals the point of holding someone responsible for a wrongful act; and responsibility enables us to make sense of punishment.

Both punishment and responsibility are recognized "for" something. The object of the "for" bears certain logical characteristics. Punishment consists in unpleasant consequences imposed for something that has happened in the past. It makes no sense to punish someone now for something that may or may not happen in the future. Also, punishment is typically imposed for a human action. At times in the past, governments ventured to punish animals, but that happened presumably because officials attributed to them responsibility for their actions.

What is punishment?

The answer to the question "What is punishment?" is philosophical or conceptual. We have a strong intuition that it is not apt to call shooting a dog with rabies an instance of punishment. It is a preventive measure designed to protect the health of human beings. This intuition leads us to perceive the implicit rule for saying that shooting a dog with rabies is non-punitive in nature. We can infer that punishment is always imposed "for" some past event and not for the sake of protecting people from an ongoing danger.

There are many human institutions that resemble our preventive actions toward animals. Civil commitment of the mentally ill is the primary example, but others, such as disbarment, impeachment, and deportation typically qualify as non-punitive in nature. All these actions by the government adversely affect the interests of individuals, and the latter three, like punishment, are imposed for breaches of legal obligations. That their purpose is primarily to separate the individual from an office (disbarment, impeachment) or civil status (deportation), however, implies that they are not punitive in nature. Or at least the courts have so held.

Courts are not interested, abstractly, in the question whether a governmental action is punishment. The question typically arises in efforts to decide whether a governmental action against an individual constitutes a "criminal prosecution" as that term is used in the Sixth Amendment; if it is, then the affected individual may invoke certain procedural rights, such as the right to a jury trial and the right to confront adverse witnesses. The controlling test whether proceedings are criminal in nature is whether, if the defendant is found liable, the sanction applied will be tantamount to punishment.

If a purpose to remove someone from an office renders a governmental action non-punitive, then what kind of purpose is required to make the action punitive? One might say that, unlike measures that separate individuals from offices, punishment must offer the offending individual an opportunity to reintegrate himself in the society that holds him responsible for a wrongful act. This might be true of punishment inflicted within the family: the child suffers the penalty for his or her "offense" and then returns to the good graces of the judging parents. In this sense, the punishment erases the offense.

Some theorists think that this is the way punishment works in our time. Yet there are certain obvious objections to the claim that punishment enables offenders to pay their "debts" and resume their role in society. First, it fails to account for the death penalty, which has, in fact, been the oldest form of punishment and the most common in the course of history. Further, if we look at modern recidivist statutes. particularly the popularity of statutes that impose life imprisonment for the third violent felony ("three strikes and you're out"), we have trouble finding much regard for the principle that punishment erases the offense. If punishment truly erased the offense, it would not be a factor that justified an increased penalty for a second or third offense.

We are left, then, with the question: is there a positive feature of punishment that distinguishes it from sanctions, such as disbarment and deportation, that are regarded as non-punitive in nature? One is tempted to say that punishment must inflict pain for its own sake – and not for the purpose of removing the offender from an office or other position of privilege. But speaking of punishment "for its own sake" seems to take a position on the long dispute about whether the purpose of punishment should be retribution or deterrence.

The best approach to the concept of punishment might be to avoid verbal definitions and simply point to certain paradigmatic instances of punishment – the death penalty, flogging, caning, and imprisonment (at least since the early nineteenth century). We can assume that these are punishment, if anything is. Beyond these core cases, there is endless dispute. Treble damages in antitrust actions are punitive in nature, but no one contends that the Sixth Amendment, with its abundant procedural protections, should apply to the levying of treble damages.

In addition, punishment is an expression of authority, and in this respect it differs from vengeance. The classic agents of punishment are parents, the state, and God. A private killing may be vengeance, a simple act of tit for tat, but it is not punishment in the narrow sense.

Purposes of punishment

Assuming we know what punishment is, we should turn to the long-standing dispute about the purposes of punishment. The general division is between those who favor arguments that from the standpoint of the trial are retrospective and those who favor arguments that are prospective. Retribution is said to be retrospective: it looks only to the crime not to the beneficial consequences of punishment; on this axis of time, utilitarianism is prospective; it looks to the beneficial consequences of punishment rather than to imperatives implicit in the facts. Yet there are other variations on the axis of retrospective and prospective or consequential theories. Let us distinguish among them:

1   *Purely retrospective.* The only arguments permissible are those based on events in the past, in particular the details of the crime. This argument that the punishment must fit the crime, regardless of the consequence, represents a paradigm of retributive thinking.

2   *Factually consequential.* The argument that punishment is justified by deterrence, both special (the criminal himself) and general (the rest of society), represents a factual prediction. If neither the criminal nor the rest of society is deterred, then the prediction is false. Whether punishment is justified on these grounds, therefore, requires careful observation of what happens in the aftermath of punishing. The problem, particularly in tests of the death penalty's efficacy, is distinguishing between those things that would have happened anyway from the consequences attributable to the act of punishment.

3   *Conceptually consequential.* Some of the consequences by which punishment is justified are conceptually linked to the act of punishing; the desirable consequences follow logically from the act of punishing. Nineteenth-century philosopher G. W. Hegel reasoned that punishment vindicates the right or the legal order over the wrong represented by the crime (Hegel, 1952). This act of vindication is conceptually connected to the punishment in the sense that if you believe it occurs, there are no facts that could disprove its occurrence.

4   *Utilitarianism.* This collection of theories conditions the ethical quality of an act on its factual consequences. The benefits to the society, as a whole, of punishing must outweigh its costs – to the offender, to his family, and indirectly to the rest of society. Schools of utilitarianism differ in the way they purport to measure these benefits and costs. Hedonistic utilitarianism regards happiness – pleasure and pain – as the common denominator in both. Economists believe that dollar signs can be attached to these consequences and thus toted up and compared.

These, then, are four positions of the spectrum from retrospective to prospective conceptions about the purpose of punishment. Taking one of these positions should not be confused with making an argument in favor of one of them. The arguments for prospective, instrumental theories are more easily made than arguments for retrospective theories. Most people gravitate toward the view that harming people by punishment should have a purpose; it should accomplish some good to offset the harm inflicted.

The argument for retributive theories relies often on an appeal to authority. The Bible is a favorite source. Immanuel Kant is another. Authority, of course, is not an argument. If we take a close look at Kant's arguments for retribution, we may find most of them suggestive, but wanting. Of the many arguments he deploys, at least three will be rehearsed here. Kant was so strongly opposed to utilitarian theories of punishment that he wrote:

> The principle of punishment is a categorical imperative, and woe to him who crawls through the windings of eudaemonism [utilitarianism] in order to discover something that releases the criminal from punishment. (*Kant, 1991*)

This famous passage expresses Kant's perception that utilitarianism – or cost–benefit analysis – leads invariably to breaches in the principle of equality. Some people will be exempt from punishment if their exemption serves a useful social purpose. Kant believed that there should be no exceptions either for those who serve the state on purpose, say, by submitting to medical experiments (Kant, 1991), or whose punishment does not, in fact, serve the society's welfare. The term "categorical imperative" that Kant casually invokes in this passage is not used in its ordinary sense. It means no more, it seems, than a commitment to general and universal laws, equally applied.

In his second argument in favor of non-utilitarian punishment, equally applied, Kant stresses the equality or equivalence of the crime and the punishment. Drawing on the teachings of the biblical principle of the *lex talionis*, he insists that the scales of justice as well as the concept of law require this equivalence. No other standard would, he claims, be sufficiently precise to meet the desiderata of "strict justice" under law (Kant, 1991).

The third argument elicits Kant's understanding of "retribution" as captured in the German term *Vergeltung*. The categorical imperative requires people to act on their maxims (subjective plans) only if they can be universalized and made to apply (*gelten*) as a universal law. The same it seems should be true of criminals in a negative version of the categorical imperative that Kant, trading on the association with *gelten*, calls *vergelten*. The justification of punishment, as it emerges in this argument, requires that the criminal's maxim be universalized and applied to him. If he kills, his killing should be universalized and applied to him. If he steals, his stealing should be regarded as a universal law, which would imply that all property would be subject to theft. If property is undermined, then the criminal should be treated as not having any resources as his own. If he has no resources, Kant concludes (playfully, it would seem) that he should be put into prison (Kant, 1991).

Though this argument blurs the distinction between the poor house and the prison, it should be recalled at the time of Kant's writing in 1795 that imprisonment had yet to become the common mode of punishment. Kant struggles to find a rationale for putting people behind bars rather than executing, exiling or castrating them. The latter forms of punishment he regards as fitting, respectively, for murder and treason (Kant, 1991), sex with animals (Kant, 1991, p. 1,142 [333]) and rape (Kant, 1991). The general theme in Kant's writing on punishment is that the crime should be turned back on the criminal. Sometimes this can be done by universalizing his maxim and making him suffer the consequences or by making the punishment "fit" the crime as castration fits rape. The notion of fitting punishment may bear some resemblance to the idea developed by Michel Foucault in *Discipline and Punish*, that punishment was originally thought to expiate the crime by re-enacting the horror on the body of the victim.

An alternative theory of punishment

The most intriguing of Kant's arguments for justice in punishment leads the way to an alternative view of what punishment is about. Kant imagines that a society is about to disband, but it has a problem: there are still murderers, condemned to die, languishing in prison. What should they do about them. Kant insists that the murderers should be executed "so that each has done to him what his deeds deserve and blood guilt does not cling to the people." Executing them seems to be pointless because no good could possibly follow. This is precisely Kant's point.

The notion of a society's disbanding should be treated as a thought-experiment, very much like the idea of a society's coming together in a social contract. Neither of these events ever occurred in history. but they are useful constructs for testing our intuitions about the conditions of a just social order. Further, the biblical reference to blood guilt is highly suggestive. It brings to bear an ancient rationale of punishment that lies some place between the theories I have labeled conceptually and factually consequential. The view in biblical culture, apparently, was that a manslayer acquired control over the victim's blood; the slayer had to be executed in order to release the blood, permitting it to return to God as in the case of a natural death (Daube, 1949). The failure to execute the murder meant that the rest of society, charged with this function, became responsible for preventing the release of the victim's blood.

These ideas lend themselves to a modern interpretation. The idea of gaining control over another person's blood suggests that criminal violence is typically a form of dominance. In fact, it is. Criminal conduct establishes the dominance of the criminal over the victim and, in the case of homicide, the victim's loved ones or next of kin. This is obvious in some crimes, such as rape, mugging, and burglary, where victims characteristically fear a repeat attack by the criminal. It is also true in blackmail, where the offender induces services or money in return for silence and is in a position to return at any time and demand additional payments (Fletcher, 1993). Instilling fear and this form of subservience is a mode of gaining dominance. Punishment counteracts domination by reducing the criminal to the position of the victim. When the criminal suffers as the victim suffered, equality between the two is re-established.

Thus the institution of punishment provides an opportunity to counteract the criminal's dominance over the victim. The failure to use the institution, the passively standing by when there is an opportunity to punish justly, provides the foundation for shared responsibility. This is the sense in which the "blood guilt . . . cling[s] to the people" when they refuse to punish those who deserve it. The practice of punishing crime provides an opportunity for the victim's co-citizens to express solidarity and to counteract the state of inequality induced by the crime. If they willfully refuse to invoke the traditional response to crime, they disassociate themselves from the victim. Abandoned, left alone, the victim readily feels betrayed by the system.

A primary function of punishment, then, is to express solidarity with the victim. It is a way of saying to the victim and his or her family: "You are not alone. We stand with you, against the criminal" (Fletcher, 1995).

The connection between punishment and solidarity has become apparent in the last few decades in the numerous countries that have overcome dictatorial regimes and have begun the transition to democracy. The first notable example was Argentina, which in the mid-1980s began a program of prosecuting the generals who were responsible for the mass-disappearances in the period of the military junta. The victim's families themselves – led by *las Madres* – insisted on prosecution as a means of vindicating their dignity as citizens. Since the shift of government from Presidents Alfonsin to Menem, the leaders of the junta have been pardoned (Malamud-Goti, 1991). Those connected to the victims must endure the sight of those responsible for their suffering now leading the good life as free citizens.

The transition to democracy in Eastern Europe has led to repeated demands to punish the leaders of the Communist governments that were responsible for evil deeds ranging from encouraging Soviet intervention in Budapest in 1956 and Prague in 1968 to shooting escaping East German citizens in the 1980s. Technical problems, such as the statute of limitations, prevent many of these prosecutions. Yet the Germans have been insistent about prosecuting border guards for killings at the border, and the Hungarians seem resolute about prosecuting former Communists who committed the most egregious crimes, particularly those that can be classified as "war crimes."

Responsibility

Punishment makes little sense unless those who are punished are indeed responsible for the wrongs that trigger a punitive response. The first stage of legal analysis is always to determine whether an untoward event has occurred for which someone ought to be held responsible. For purposes of criminal punishment, this negative state of affairs must constitute the violation of a statute promulgated in advance and which gives fair warning to citizens of the possibility of incurring responsibility for violating the statute. Once this negative state of a statutory violation is established, we can turn to the question whether a particular individual is responsible for having brought it about. If he or she is responsible, then in the normal case, the legal system will impose punishment for the action.

There are many synonyms used to describe this second stage of the inquiry about responsibility. The question might be put as whether the actor is "accountable" or "answerable" for the legal violation, or whether the violation is "attributable" or "imputable" to the actor. All of these terms converge on the single meaning whether it is fair to hold the actor responsible for the violation.

519

Unlawful action

We may refer to the first stage of legal violation as determining whether an "unlawful act" has occurred. The question is not so simple as whether an action violates a statutory rule. First, the violation must bear the characteristics of a human action. Only human actions can generate criminal responsibility. That one's body is the instrument of harm hardly suffices. If *B* forces *A*'s hand down on a valuable vase, thus breaking it, *A*'s hand is the immediate cause of the injury, but *A* is not personally responsible for the damage orchestrated by *B*. This is an easy case for exclusion from the field of responsibility. As soon as it looks like *A* is acting in some fashion, however, the attribution of responsibility becomes more difficult.

Criminal law seems to be the arena where the requirement of human action is most often posed. The defendant throws his child out the window, and the claim is made that because of a brain tumor operating on him, he was really acting. Or the defendant kills somebody when he is sleepwalking, and the argument is heard: no responsibility because there is no human action. The criminal law has even coined the general term "automatism" to pinpoint the question whether there is any action or agency in the bodily movements leading to the victim's harm. Yet no one quite knows what this component of "action" or "agency" is beyond the simple fact of bodily movements. It is not too helpful to require that the action be dictated by the will, for how do we know whether the will is operative without first classifying the bodily movements as human action? The way we approach this problem in practice is to assume that unless some known factor negating agency is present – brain tumors, sleepwalking, hypnosis, epilepsy – then we assume that the nominal appearance of agency signifies agency.

For action to be unlawful, it must not only be an instance of acting instead of being acted upon. It must also be unlawful in the sense of constituting the violation of a statutory norm and being unjustified. An action is not unlawful if it is justified on grounds of consent, lesser evils, or legitimate defensive force, for example, for protection of self, others, or property. These topics of justification require treatment in their own right. The important feature of these defensive claims is that they do not deny personal responsibility. On the contrary, when someone argues that his action is justified, he means to say that what he did was right and proper and that he has every reason to take responsibility for the action. The problem of responsibility is reserved, therefore, for the analysis of excusing conditions.

Responsibility and excuses

Since Aristotle, the discussion of excuses has focussed on the question of involuntary action. The assumption is that someone who brings about an unlawful state of affairs is not responsible for his action if it was involuntary. An action might be involuntary for one of two reasons, either it is subject to coercion or it is carried out in ignorance of the relevant facts. Coercion, in turn, might be either external or internal. The standard cases of external coercion are duress and personal necessity.

520

The proverbial mode of duress is the gun pointed at the head of the victim. She gets an offer that she cannot refuse. Either she opens the safe or she dies. The clearest case of coerced action, therefore, is but a short step from physical coercion, from the case of actually forcing the hand of another. Yet she can always say no and be shot. Her "will" is engaged by the act of submission to the gunman. Because she is acting rather than just being acted upon, we need an argument why we should excuse her.

There are two primary starting points for generating an explanation of excuses such as duress. One is a version of causal analysis. The roots of her action lie not in her character, in her nature as a person; rather, they derive from the threats of the gunman. Although her will is nominally expressed in opening the safe, that action says nothing, or very little, about her as a person. She does not express the personality or character of a thief in permitting the gunman to take the money. She is not complicitous in the crime. The true cause of the action is not her personality, her traits of character, but the gun pointed at her head. The argument of character, therefore, extends the causal analysis as a way of denying the responsibility of those who act under insuperable pressure.

The alternative way of thinking about excuses is to stress the involuntariness of submitting to the dictates of a gun-toting bank robber. If the action is involuntary, it is treated as the equivalent of no action at all. And in the absence of action, voluntary action, there is no basis for imposing responsibility. Yet it is not so clear what one means by "involuntary" action. The judgment of involuntariness invariably entails a comparison of the threat and the action that the allegedly coerced party must undertake in response to the threat. As the threat becomes less severe and the action becomes more harmful, the judgment of involuntariness loses its grounding. Sooner or later, we reach the point at which we conclude that the actor should have resisted the threat. If she must kill in order to avoid damage to her car, she hardly acts involuntarily. The threat of property damage is one she should resist, particularly if the only way of avoiding the threat is to kill an innocent person.

The boundary between voluntary and involuntary behavior lies some place between the extreme paradigms, the first requiring opening of the safe in order to avoid being killed, and the second, exacting the death of an innocent person in order to avoid property damage. The way the line is drawn depends on our sense of what we can fairly expect of each other under circumstances of pressure. Different cultures will draw this line at different places. Some cultures are indulgent toward those who must act under severe pressure; others are more exacting and refuse, for example, to excuse the killing of an innocent person, no matter how severe the threat of harm to the coerced party. The point to remember about excuses is that the question is always focussed on the actor's having done something wrong. Excusing is a matter of recognizing that people cannot always do the right thing. Yet a severe and puritanical culture might well demand that individuals sacrifice themselves rather than identify themselves with evil.

Apart from duress, English and American courts have been loath to recognize excuses based on external coercion. As threats made by persons excuse

521

wrong-doing, it should also be the case that coercion generated by natural circumstances would have the same impact on criminal responsibility. In the famous case of *Dudley and Stephens*, 14 QBD 285 (1885), the Queen's Bench rejected this analogy and held the circumstance of starvation on the high seas would not excuse homicide and cannibalism. Perhaps duress is more easily recognized than the personal necessity present in *Dudley and Stephens*. In the former case, there is always someone responsible for the crime, namely the threatening party; in the latter case, recognizing the excuse would imply that no one could be held accountable for the wrongful act. Yet the availability of an alternative party to hold liable should not bear, in principle, on whether those who acted under the pressure of starvation should be treated as responsible and subject to punishment.

The internal analog to external pressure is mental illness. It is common to think of mental illness as a kind of compulsion that interferes with the actor's freedom in the same way that external coercion undermines the possibility of voluntary action. Yet we need not necessarily think of insanity as a weight that bears down on the actor's freedom of choice. An alternative approach treats mental illness and insanity as conditions that go to the foundation of the actor's capacity for rational thought.

According to Aristotle, actions can be involuntary either if they are the product of coercion or if they are carried out in ignorance. The actor cannot be said to choose his action unless he knows what he is doing. The problem with the theory of ignorance and mistake is that no one ever knows everything about the circumstances and the consequences of action. What did Bernhard Goetz know when he pulled his gun and began to shoot at the four black youths on the subway? He knew the elementary facts of his situation, but he was ignorant about the important features of his situation. There was no way for him to know what would have happened had he not drawn his hidden revolver. Yet we would have to say that Goetz acted voluntarily despite his ignorance of factors that mattered to his fate.

The knowledge that people have about their actions is always a matter of degree. No one ever knows everything about the circumstances and consequences of action. Thus there is no conceptually clear standard for deciding when ignorance and mistake should negate the voluntariness of the action. As in the analysis of coercion, we arrive finally at the point at which the judgment of involuntariness merges with moral criteria of fairness. The problem always is what we can fairly expect of each other in resisting pressure and in paying attention to signals implicit in the circumstances under which we act. When we do meet the common standard we set for each other, we are at fault, we are personally to blame, and we cannot properly invoke an excuse for the wrongs we have committed.

References

Daube, D. 1949: *Studies in Biblical Law*. New York: KTav Publishing House, 122–4.
Fletcher, G. 1993: Blackmail: the paradigmatic crime. *University of Pennsylvania Law Review*, 141, 1,617.

—— 1995: *With Justice for Some: victims' rights in criminal trials*. Reading, Mass.: Addison-Wesley.

Hegel, G. F. W. 1952: *Philosophy of Right*, tr. T. M. Knox, London and New York: Oxford University Press, section 99.

Kant, I. 1991: *The Metaphysics of Morals*, tr. M. Gregor, Cambridge and New York, Cambridge University Press, [333] 141.

Malamud-Goti, J. 1991: Punishment and human dignity. *S'vara: A Journal of Philosophy and Judaism*, 2 (1), 69.

37

Loyalty

GEORGE P. FLETCHER

Loyalty and partiality

The ethic of loyalty provides a vehicle for understanding partial as opposed to impartial morality. The standard liberal moral theories – Kantianism and utilitarianism – are impartial in nature: friends are worthy of no more attention than strangers. By definition, loyalty is partial: it extends to those who are close and not to those who are distant or foreign.

The core cases are loyalty to people we know – friends, lovers, and family members. But by extension, we feel the pull of loyalty toward groups, many of whose members we do not know personally. Loyalties are tendered to corporate bodies, such as universities, companies, professions, and political parties. At higher levels of abstractions, loyalties extend to peoples, nations, and states. We also speak of loyalty to principles and to schools of thought. And those who are religious can understand their faith as an expression of loyalty to the true God.

In all these contexts, loyalty has the same basic meaning. For every loyal friend or lover, there is always a third party who could, in the fashion of the classic triangle, tempt the loyal away from the object of his or her loyalty. In a matrix of loyalty, then, there are three parties. Let us call them: A, B, and C. A can be loyal to B only if there is or could be a third party C who stands as a potential competitor to B, the focal point of loyalty. The competitor is always lurking in the wings, rejected for the time being, but always tempting, always seductive. If the competitor appears and beckons, the loyal will refuse to follow.

Loyalty to principle means, therefore, that one will not be tempted by competitive principles. Loyalty to God means that one will not be tempted by false gods.

There is some dispute about whether acts of personal loyalty are always negative – abstaining from sexual infidelity, disclosing secrets, and other acts of intimacy with third parties. Some would maintain that the lover who did no more than abstain from adultery was hardly loyal and faithful. Some positive acts also seem necessary, acts of devotion that reflect the importance of the other in one's sense of priorities. It seems that simply by losing interest one could be an unfilial child, faithless friend, or disloyal lover; being loyal in this fuller sense requires devotion as well as abstaining from betrayal.

In the case of loyalty to nations, the potential tempter is the enemy to whom, in the language of the Constitution, one would "adhere" and commit treason by giving it "aid and comfort." Some people might think that positive acts of patriotism are required to be loyal to the nation, as acts of devotion are required in personal relationships. All can agree that the minimum foundation of loyalty is captured in the definition of treason. One need not "adhere" emotionally to one's own nation, so long as one does not go over to the other side.

Let us refer to my account as the triadic theory of loyalty. It stands opposed to diadic theories that treat the subject who tenders loyalty and the object who receives it as sufficient to account for the phenomenon. So far as there is an existing literature on loyalty, it is dominated by an implicit acceptance of diadic theories. A good example is the definition offered by Josiah Royce, who treats loyalty as a species of voluntary commitment, a "willing and thoroughgoing devotion to a cause." The commitment of A, the subject, to B, the cause, purports to be sufficient to account for loyalty. Diadic theories make the mistake of overemphasizing the element of devotion in loyalty. Loyalty becomes like love; loyalty to the nation, like patriotism. The advantage of the triadic theory is that it underscores a minimal dimension of loyalty as no more than abstaining from adultery, betrayal, and treason.

It is important to distinguish between feelings of loyalty and duties of loyalty. Neither implies the other. One can feel sentimental loyalty to an institution without being under a duty to do so, and one can be under a duty of loyalty to parents or children without tendering positive feelings toward them. Loyalty becomes interesting as a moral concept only so far as it expresses a duty of loyalty.

Loyalty: unilateral and reciprocal

Expressed as a moral duty, loyalty carries feudal overtones. Loyalty is, typically, expressed from those lower to those higher in the feudal hierarchy. The serf had a duty of fealty to his lord. But the lord was under no reciprocal duty to any particular serf. His duty was to provide protection and security to those who were loyal to him. The same structure carries forward in the modern conception of the state's duties to its citizens. The state tenders protection to citizens in return for their loyalty, and the loyalty of the nation indeed facilitates defense against external enemies. The notion of loyalty of the state to its citizens lacks a conceptual grip, but it does seem possible to speak of the King's or the government's duty of loyalty (or disloyalty) to some weak and dependent segment of the body politic, such as the poor.

The most dramatic example of unilateral loyalty is God's insistence of submission and loyalty from the Jewish people. The Prophets accuse the Jews of persistently "whoring after other gods." Worshipping false gods is an act of adultery, of betrayal. But God is under no reciprocal duty of loyalty to the Jews. The theology is clear on this point. God may choose subject peoples others than the Jews, but the Jews may not have other gods. The most that subject peoples may hope for is protection against enemies and destruction, and on this point the Holocaust has generated a crisis of faith among many.

The modern ideal of loyalty in friendship and marriage rejects the feudal model in favor of the liberal principle of reciprocity. In friendship, loyalty is tendered in exchange for loyalty. Modern marriage more closely resembles the model of friendship than an anachronistic feudal conception based on the exchange of the wife's loyalty for the husband's protection.

More and more, in contemporary institutions, when we speak of loyalty we expect reciprocal loyalty. A good example is the relationship between employers and employees. Factory owners seek to induce employee loyalty to the firm. They will use the language of the "family" and the "community" to describe the workforce. In turn, however, employees expect owners to remain loyal in the face of declining profits. So far as there is a moral duty of the owners to keep a factory of declining profits in the city where it is located, the duty is expressed as one of loyalty.

Contract and history

In the modern legal culture, duties of loyalty are frequently grounded in contract. Charles Fried writes of his loyalty, as Solicitor-General, to the President who appointed him. Lawyers and physicians are under conventionally defined duties of loyalty to their clients and patients. Fiduciary duties of corporate managers can be understood as duties of loyalty, namely, to place the interests of the corporation ahead of competing interests. Contract is a source of duties of loyalty, but not the only source.

Duties to family, friends, lovers, and nations are based not on contract but on a shared history. Sometimes this duty of loyalty derives from past care and nurturing that enables a child to grow into adulthood. In many traditional cultures, the reverence for teachers takes this form. The Japanese term *sensei* or the Hebrew term *mori* are appellations that express gratitude and submission, without an expectation of reciprocal loyalty.

Recognizing duties of loyalty based on a shared history affirms identity. The soldier willing to fight for his country declares where he stands in the world of fractured nationalities. Sometimes the decision to fight derives primarily from a family identity. Robert E. Lee was, in fact, loyal to the Union and he was opposed to slavery, but he chose out of loyalty to his "kith and kin" to fight for the Confederacy. Those who organize fighting forces know that the intense personal loyalties that soldiers feel to their units often outweigh the abstract calls of patriotism.

History lays the foundation both for loyalty as an expression of identity and sets limitations on possible loyalties. However much Alexis de Tocqueville admired America, he could not suddenly declare his loyalty to that nation. Six thousand French regulars fought under General Rochambeau in the American Revolution, but this was not an act of loyalty to the emergent American republic. A Virginia farmer can put aside his plow and take up arms as an act of loyalty, but a Parisian who comes to fight in the same cause does not make the same statement about where he stands. Even if he believes firmly in his heart that the Americans should win (and not as his government, that, for political reasons, the English should lose), he fights as an outsider. The soundness of his cause influences how hard he fights, but his fighting neither expresses nor confirms his historical roots.

No one can decide, as a matter of taste, to be loyal to someone with whom the requisite historical bond is lacking. Fond as I am of French culture and cuisine, I cannot decide tomorrow that I shall be loyal to the French nation. My connection to the French remains that of a fond observer. I may continue to appreciate French culture as an outsider, but on the fringes of the culture, looking in, I am not in a position to be either loyal or disloyal to the French people.

The exact relationship between historical experience and duties of loyalty, however, remains controverted. People do change locations, jobs, and cultures and sink new roots. It is not clear how much time is required for fresh soil to resonate in new found loyalties. As Aristotle says, friends must have "eaten salt" together. But how much salt and the quality of the salt seem to be a matter of individualized taste and judgment.

Individualism and communitarianism

Understanding loyalty as historically grounded provides a window on the contemporary debate between liberal individualists and communitarians. Liberal individualists reject the principle that history is destiny, that our pasts can dictate duties for the present. For the individualist, loyalty smacks of feudalism, of a time when one's station in life determined one's duties. If history means anything, they would say, it means that we have evolved from the duties of status to duties based on contract and voluntary choice.

Of course, liberal individualists recognize that some duties arise regardless of choice. The moral theories of the eighteenth-century philosophers, Jeremy Bentham and Immanuel Kant, ground their theories of obligations in the common traits shared by all humans. Bentham claims that our common denominator is our capacity for pleasure and pain and infers that everyone has an obligation to act in a way that takes account of the pleasures and pains of everyone else. The Kantian claim that all human beings are connected by their capacity to reason and to know the moral law implies that they bear, therefore, a common humanity. Their commonalty generates a duty to respect the humanity in themselves and in others as an end in itself.

The version of the Kantian theory developed by John Rawls presupposes the capacity of the purely rational self to decide upon principles of justice that should govern society. Rawls attributes to the rational self the aim of maximizing certain basic goods such as liberty, wealth, and self-esteem. His achievement is to have generated principles of justice on the bare bones assumption that rational beings, who do not know their position in society, would seek to maximize the basic goods that everyone desires.

The communitarian critique of Rawls, particularly as developed by Michael Sandel (Sandel, 1982), argues the implausibility of a rational "unencumbered self" choosing the basic goods that motivate Rawls's principles of justice. The self must be situated in a particular society, Sandel argues, in order to explain why we have the commitments and loyalties we have. Sandel begins with an intuitive sense of our commitments and argues backwards to a self that must be "encumbered" by its historical roots.

An alternative line of reasoning begins with the rootedness of the self in a historical situation and asks what follows from our invariably localized circumstances. One argument is that our historical situations entail obligations to those who have played a "significant" part in the shaping of our personalities. The claim is that the "historical self" generates duties of loyalty toward the families, groups, and nations that enter into our self-definition. These duties may be understood as an expression of self-esteem and self-acceptance. To love myself, I must respect and cherish those aspects of myself that are bound up with others. Thus, by the mere fact of my biography, I incur obligations toward others, which I group under the general heading of loyalty.

We do not choose our historical selves in any direct and immediate sense. We are born into a particular culture, acquire a mother tongue, receive exposure to certain political and religious ideas, learn a national history – all without significant choices on our part. The responsibility for our initial sense of historical self is left to our parents, those who run our schools and the media, and the religious leaders who have an impact on us. Of course, some choice is left to us as adults to leave our native cultures and attempt to assimilate as immigrants or converts in a new world. Whether the assimilation succeeds depends, in large part, on the will and talents of the individual and the receptivity of the immigrant culture. It is obviously easier to assimilate as an immigrant to the United States than to most other national cultures. The possibility of engaging in this structural change, engendering a whole new set of loyalties, represents the limited control that we have over our historical selves.

In some areas, of course, we reach our critical decisions as adults and we can alter our commitments to friends, marital partners, religion, and profession in mid-life. The range of our freedom in making these structural changes depends, as well, on the receptivity of the culture in which we seek to act. As compared with Western countries, it is relatively difficult to restructure one's religious commitments in Iran or one's professional loyalties in Japan.

Loyalty in the legal culture

The law, particularly Anglo-American law, is loath to recognize duties that derive exclusively from birth or personal history. The notable exception is the crime of treason, which is applicable only to citizens or permanent residents of the United States. Foreigners cannot commit treason against the US. Choice or consent – some voluntary act – seems to be essential to the Anglo-American view of legal duty. Parents have duties toward their children, for they choose to bring them into the world. But children have no legal duties to their parents, not even to support them if they are incapable of earning their own livelihood. The argument is that children do not choose their parents, and therefore there is no moral basis for a duty to care for them. Yet other legal systems do recognize the duty of children to provide for elderly, impoverished parents. The new Russian Constitution, for example, carries forward the communitarian spirit of their culture by explicitly recognizing this filial duty (Russian Constitution, art. 38(3)).

True, Anglo-American law recognizes duties of loyalty when the duty rests on choice and contract. Fiduciary duty is a matter of loyalty; it is an obligation to put first the interests of the company or the individual toward whom one must act as a fiduciary. Lawyers are under duties of loyalty toward their clients. They must treat their interests as paramount and protect the secrets of the relationship. These examples of contractual loyalty differ fundamentally from, say, the duty of children to support their parents. The latter is a duty rooted not in choice and consent, but in birth and blood.

Loyalty based on the historical self may not generate duties in a liberal culture, as is now dominant in Western jurisprudence. But there is another way that the state may recognize loyalty as a relevant value in the legal culture. The state chooses to stay its hand – not to intervene – in relationships based on loyalty. A good example of this deferential attitude is exempting people in certain relationships from the duty to testify against each other. A wife may choose not to testify against a husband, and vice versa (Fletcher, 1993). Many writers advocate extending this exemption to other relationships within the family and some, even to relationships between friends (Levinson, 1984). The law permits, therefore, persons who are close to each other to choose to remain silent rather than testify and harm someone dear to them. The processes of justice suffer, of course, for the courts must thereby forego valuable evidence, but the relationships thereby protected prosper.

Another example of the proper deference to the value of loyalty is the nearly universal attitude toward inheritance. Even though strict egalitarians object to transmitting wealth from one generation to another, the practice survives everywhere. Even the Communist regimes dared not eliminate it. Leaving property to another at death is a way of expressing a bond with the recipient. Writing wills permits people to express their loyalties to some and not to others. The possibility of transmitting wealth across generations is important because it permits personal loyalties to flourish (Fletcher, 1993, pp. 87–9).

It is important to note that neither of these institutions rests explicitly on the value of loyalty. My claim is that the recognition of loyalty as a moral value is implicit in the legal practice. The mode of interpretation used resembles the arguments of economists who contend that the pursuit of efficiency is implicit in the legal practices they observe.

Two other examples of deference to loyal relationships are worth noting. Some people support surrogacy contracts on the basis of the liberal principle of contractual autonomy. The courts declare these contracts to bear children for a fee void as a violation of "public policy" (Farnsworth, 1990). A good account of this limit on contractual autonomy is that no one should be able to contract to commit an act of disloyalty to a child.

529

Similarly, the legal accommodation accorded to acts of religious faith represents a form of official deference to loyalty of believers to their God. The First Amendment provides special protection for the "free exercise of religion," which the courts long interpreted to mean that the faithful could claim an exemption from laws applicable to others. The Supreme Court reversed itself on this question and held in 1990 that neutral, non-discriminatory laws must apply to everyone, regardless of their claims of religious conscience. Congress intervened with a statute that reinstated the special exemption accorded to those who claimed that for religious reasons they could not, for example, work on the Sabbath, send their children to public school, take off their head covering indoors, or pledge allegiance to the flag. The best interpretation of this policy of deference is that the state recognizes the value of pre-existing loyalty to instruction perceived as coming from God. The state will not force people into the crisis of betraying one set of loyalties in order to remain obedient to secular law.

Though loyalty is an important value in many contexts, it cannot trump all conflicting considerations. Members of the Mafia may be guilty of criminal conspiracy even if their way of life rests heavily on an ethic of personal loyalty. Yet the value of loyalty often captures one important side of many disputes.

Loyalty and its critics

Opponents of loyalty as a moral imperative stress the dangers of partiality. In an article generally sympathetic toward loyalty and patriotism, Alasdair MacIntyre writes: "Patriotism turns out to be a permanent source of moral danger. And this claim, I take it, cannot in fact be successfully rebutted" (MacIntyre, 1984). He obviously has in mind the slippery slope toward fascism, of blind, unthinking adherence to "my country right or wrong" (This famous phrase comes from Stephen Decatur's toast in 1816: "Our country! In her intercourse with foreign nations may she always be in the right; but our country, right or wrong.") Blind adherence to any object of loyalty – whether friend, lover or nation – converts loyalty into idolatry. There is a moral danger in thinking that any concrete person or entity could become the ultimate source of right and wrong, but the moral danger is no greater in the case of patriotism than it is in friendship, erotic or filial love, or political commitment.

Loyalty and patriotism are often subject to attack because of the risk of excessive attachments. One philosopher claims that "patriotism is like racism" (Gomberg, 1990). These charges of guilt by association serve to remind us of the importance of setting limits to loyalty. Yet defining these limits poses considerable theoretical difficulty.

One technique for setting limits on particular loyalties derives from the inevitable conflict between higher and lower loyalties. The higher, more abstract values of God and country seem to have a greater moral claim on us than our more immediate attachments to family and friends. But this structure of values often gets turned around, as illustrated by General Robert E. Lee's choosing, despite his political convictions, to stand by his kith and kin in the Confederacy.

Another possible technique for setting limits is to invoke the idea of a "true" version of the person or group that gains our loyalty. In his attempt to assassinate Hitler, Colonel von Stauffenberg arguably acted in the name of the true Germany. A mother's continuing to nurture a son turned violent criminal expresses a commitment to the good man behind the corrupt surface.

In some contexts, loyalties are out of place. We expect judges and juries to decide impartially, regardless of their loyalties to people on one side of the dispute or the other. This is also true of those who judge contests based on merit. Yet there are situations, such as employment decisions, where loyalties seem in constant tension with commitments to merit. Democratic voting is also an area where everyone might be better off if everyone acted solely on the basis of their perception of merit, but where loyalties to political parties, gender, and ethnic groups invariably shape the pattern of voting.

Alas, there is no definitive theory to account for the relative sway of loyalties, on the one hand, and impartial morality, on the other. Impartial morality and loyalty remain independently binding; neither reduces to the other. Loyalty cannot be seen as a version of impartial morality any more than impartial morality can be understood as deriving from loyalty. Contrasted at the level of pure theory, the differences between the ethic of loyalty and impartial morality are manifold. The former is grounded in our relationships with others; the latter is universal in its appeal. The ethic of loyalty brings to bear an historical self; impartial morality derives from the universality of reason or of human psychology. The former is pitched to humans as they are; the latter, to the spiritual aspirations of humans as they might be. Systems that are so radically different cannot be brought together on any single common denominator.

Bibliography

Baron, M. 1984: *The Moral Status of Loyalty*.

Farnsworth, E. A. 1990: *Contracts*. Boston: Little, Brown, 323–39.

Fletcher, G. P. 1993: *Loyalty: an essay on the morality of relationships*. New York: Oxford University Press.

Gomberg, P. 1990: Patriotism is like racism. *Ethics*, 101, 144 (response to MacIntyre, 1984).

Janowitz, M. 1983: *The Reconstruction of Patriotism*. Chicago: University of Chicago Press.

Ladd, J. 1967: Loyalty. *Encyclopedia of Philosophy*, 5, 97–8.

Levinson, S. 1984: Testimonial privileges and the preference of friendship. *Duke Law Journal*, 631.

MacIntyre, A. 1984: *Is Patriotism a Virtue?* Kansas City: University of Kansas, 15.

Nathanson, S. 1989: In defense of moderate patriotism. *Ethics*, 99, 535 (response to MacIntyre, 1984).

Nation 1991: July 4 (collection of short comments about the meaning of patriotism today).

Oldenquist, A. 1982: Loyalties. *Journal of Philosophy*, 79, 173.

Pettit, P. 1988: The paradox of loyalty. *American Philosophical Quarterly*, 25, 163.
Royce, J. [1908] 1920: *The Philosophy of Loyalty*. New York: Macmillan.
Sandel, M. 1982: *Liberalism and the Limits of Justice*. Cambridge and New York: Cambridge University Press, 15.
Schar, 1973: The case for patriotism. *American Review*, 17, 59.
Wolff, R. P. 1968: Loyalty. In *The Poverty of Liberalism*, ch. 2.

38

Coherence

KEN KRESS

An idea or theory is coherent if it hangs or fits together, if its parts are mutually supportive, if it is intelligible, if it flows from or expresses a single, unified viewpoint. An idea or theory is incoherent if it is unintelligible, inconsistent, ad hoc, fragmented, disjointed, or contains thoughts that are unrelated to and do not support one another. Historical, strict, rationalist, idealist coherence theories flow from a single principle. Modern *normative* coherence theories tend to be pluralistic.

After roughly characterizing seven properties which might enhance coherence, or be thought necessary or sufficient for it, this essay will set coherence theories of law in context by briefly describing coherence theories of truth, justified belief, ethics, and justice. Coherence of theories of *law* are then analyzed by asking: (1) what besides constitutions, statutes and precedents are in the base of legal sources; and (2) how that base is to be coherently reconstructed into valid law. Areas of agreement and disagreement among coherence theories are described. Representative coherence and (non-coherence) theories of law are examined in light of the above analysis.

Attention is next focussed on the concept of coherence itself. Three candidates for necessary requirements for coherence – consistency, comprehensiveness, the right answer thesis – are acknowledged to enhance coherence despite not being, at least generally, required for it. Seven techniques for enhancing coherence by eliminating or resolving conflicts among principles and counter-principles are described. The core concepts of coherence, monism, and unity, are then examined. A taxonomy of monisms and unities is developed which employs the seven techniques to characterize degrees of coherence in normative theories. Finally, the essay turns to the issue of the normative value of coherence and rejects Dworkin's claim that a coherent legal system is morally more legitimate than its less coherent counterparts.

As a first approximation, whether a theory is coherent, and if so, to what degree, may be analyzed under seven properties. Each property may be argued to be necessary for, or sufficient for, coherence. Alternatively, it may be claimed that the more of that property a theory manifests, the more coherent that theory is.

1   *Consistency.* A theory is consistent if its principles and propositions are logically consistent. In moral or legal theory, logical consistency is a weak constraint.

A stronger constraint would find a theory consistent only if its underlying principles are consistently applied in creating rules and deciding concrete cases.

2   *Comprehensiveness.* A theory is comprehensive if it provides answers (including the answer, "the theory cannot resolve this issue,") to all questions within the scope of the theory.

3   *Completeness.* A theory is complete if it provides single right answers to all questions within its scope, with no gaps, no unresolvable issues. Each proposition of a complete theory is either true or false, with no indeterminate or other truth values.

4   *Monism.* A theory is monistic if it flows from a single principle. It is nearly monistic if it flows from a handful of principles with a unified spirit.

5   *Unity (internal relations).* A theory displays unity when its principles imply, justify, or mutually support one another.

6   *Articulateness.* A theory is articulate if its methods for deciding issues, integrating and unifying its principles, and resolving conflicts among competing principles are expressed in language and are not merely "intuitive" techniques.

7   *Justified.* A theory is "justified" if it resolves conflicts with reasons. A pluralistic, normative theory is justified if its articulated meta-principles and means for resolving conflicts among principles are normatively intelligible.

Some would urge that utilitarianism is coherent because it is monistic and flows from a single normative principle: maximize happiness. Similarly, Sir Robert Filmer's Divine Right of Kings justifies a king's authority based on ancestry. Classical Newtonian mechanics manifests coherence because it is founded in three axioms of motion expressing a unified theory. Thermodynamics is similarly founded in a handful of principles expressing a single spirit.

Suggesting examples of seriously held incoherent theories is a dangerous occupation. Its proponents are likely to accuse one of bias and of failing to appreciate the simplifying and unifying aspects of the theory. A science in crisis, as described by Kuhn, would be incoherent insofar as it requires ad hoc principles to explain anomalies. The Ptolemaic, geocentric view of the universe is arguably incoherent because it employs ad hoc, unmotivated epicycles to describe planetary motion. The Copernican heliocentric theory is more coherent because it requires fewer, more motivated, and unified principles. Newtonian mechanics just prior to the discovery of relativity theory may be another example of a science in crisis, requiring ad hoc adjustments to explain anomalies. In normative theory, nihilistic and intuitionist perspectives are less coherent than those of their more articulated, justified, and optimistic opponents.

For example, Rawls criticizes intuitionists' failure to provide articulated, ethically justified metaprinciples which weigh principles off against counterprinciples because it ends rational discourse about normative matters prematurely: "An intuitionist conception of justice is, one might say, but half a conception" (Rawls, 1971, p. 41).

Coherence theories of law and morals may be understood as an outgrowth of coherence theories of truth and justified belief, which have a longer ancestry. The coherence theory of truth can be crudely characterized as the view that a proposition is true if and only if it fits with other believed propositions. This theory sharply contrasts with the correspondence theory, which holds that a proposition is true if and only if it corresponds to the facts, where the facts are conceived as external to us, and independent of our beliefs about them (unless the proposition itself is about our beliefs). Correspondence theories of truth evoke the image of true propositions mirroring reality. The correspondence theory of truth is frequently associated with realism, the metaphysical claim that there exists an external world independent of our beliefs or social conventions. The denial of realism, anti-realism, which maintains that reality is dependent upon beliefs and conventions, entails the coherence theory of truth and may be entailed by it.

In modern theories of knowledge, coherence theories contrast with foundationalist theories. Foundationalist theories assert that certain basic beliefs – such as those reporting immediate sense impressions – are justified despite not being supported by (or inferred from) any other beliefs. Foundationalism maintains that justified beliefs consist of basic beliefs and justified inferences from basic beliefs. By contrast, coherence theories of justified beliefs maintain that a belief is justified if and only if it fits with other believed propositions. Foundationalist theories of justified belief conjure the picture of linear justification from basic beliefs; by contrast, coherence theories of truth and justified belief suggest a spider's web, a double geodesic dome, a link necklace, or a unified field. Perhaps the most illuminating metaphor for coherence is a puzzle with identically shaped pieces, say, one-inch squares, which must be arranged into a meaningful, coherent picture.

The most famous coherence methodology in modern normative theory is the technique of reflective equilibrium developed by Rawls to resolve issues about ethics and justice. Rawls's early method in *Outline of a Decision Procedure for Ethics* (1951) requires that we determine the considered judgments about concrete normative issues that would be made by individuals with average intelligence in idealized circumstances which promote integrity, impartiality, and insight. One then induces principles much like a scientist would – only the data to be explained are the morally competent actors' considered judgments, not scientific observations.

In *A Theory of Justice* (1971), Rawls substantially extends the method. Considered convictions no longer have epistemic priority over principles. We compare our considered concrete convictions – now about justice – to the abstract principles of justice chosen by rational individuals in circumstances designed to eliminate bias and self-interest to determine whether the principles and convictions fit together. There is an appropriate fit if someone following the principles would reach the convictions or, in the alternative, if the convictions could be viewed as a normatively attractive extension of the principles. If not, the method of reflective equilibrium engages in real work. Insofar as there are discrepancies between the principles and convictions, one or the other (or both) must be revised. The antifoundational aspect of the method consists in giving neither principles nor convictions *a priori* preference in the process of revision. We go back and forth revising first one and then the other until the principles imply the convictions, thereby rendering our convictions coherent and justified (Rawls, 1971, pp. 20–1).

What motivates coherence theories, especially normative coherence theories? Coherence seems desirable – or necessary – in a theory because what is coherent is intelligible and forms a rational, understandable unity rather than a patchwork quilt. Second, it appears that truth, morality, justice (and perhaps justified belief) must be coherent. In law, coherence accounts appear preferable to those legal positivist perspectives which link law to the intentions of their authoritative authors because it frees law from the dead hand of the past, promoting responsiveness to contemporaneous concerns (Raz, 1992, p. 292).

Each of these motivations for coherence is problematic. First, intelligibility does not guarantee truth, justification, or legal validity (but see Weinrib, 1988, 1995). Moreover, "coherence" as employed here is a technical philosophical term continuous with, but not identical to, its ordinary meaning (Raz, 1992, pp. 276–7). Second, as positivists and critical legal scholars urge, law may well be a patchwork quilt, the handiwork of political forces and actors proceeding at cross purposes with inconsistent ideologies. Third, while pure morality and justice must be coherent, given human fallibility, it is controversial whether practical day-to-day theories of morality, justice, and law should be coherent (Sayre-McCord, 1985, pp. 181–7). Moreover, while pure morality and justice must be coherent, surely positive law need not be. On the other hand, positive law requires techniques to eliminate strict inconsistencies. Why not limit incoherence by the same or similar methods?

Irrespective of the plausibility of other coherence theories, several considerations suggest that coherence theories of *law* have a special claim on us. The idea that law is a seamless web, that it is holistic, that precedents have a gravitational force throughout the law, that argument by analogy has an especial significance in law, and the principle that all are equal under the law, provide strong *prima facie* support for a coherence theory of law.

Coherence theories of law

Despite the apparent claim of some that a coherence theory of law is a coherence theory of truth for law (Kress, 1985, pp. 369–71; Raz, 1992, p. 283 and passim), a coherence theory of law is logically compatible with a correspondence theory of truth (Fumerton, 1994, pp. 90–1) or a deflationist theory of truth (Coleman, 1995, pp. 54–61). Theories of truth and theories of valid law are logically distinct, for all we know. For example, correspondence theories must be able to account for truths involving coherence, including claims that coherence is a (or the) determinant of legal validity. Consider the proposition that comparative negligence is valid law because it coheres better with general negligence principles than any alternative (including contributory negligence). That proposition will be true according to the correspondence theory just in case that proposition corresponds to the facts. The relevant factual questions are: first, does comparative negligence cohere better with negligence principles than contributory negligence or other alternatives and, second, assuming it does cohere better, does that mean it is valid law? If both questions are answered affirmatively, the correspondence theory will declare the proposition "comparative negligence is valid law" true by virtue of *correspondence with "facts"* about the *coherence* of comparative negligence and general negligence, and about coherence as the criterion for legal validity. No persuasive argument has yet tied theories of law in any interesting way to general theories of truth.

Characterizing theories of law and adjudication clarifies differences among versions of coherence and non-coherence theories of law. With the exception of pure coherence natural law theories which assert that law is morality and justice, and that morality and justice are constituted by coherence, all coherence theories of law contain at least one non-coherentist aspect, and some contain more than one. This non-coherentist aspect consists in what Raz calls "a base" which is to be made coherent by some reconstructive method (Raz, 1992, p. 284). Almost all agree that bases include Constitutions, statutes, and precedents. Controversy arises over: (1) the best characterization of Constitutions, statutes and precedents; (2)(a) what else the base of a possible legal system could include, (2)(b) what else the base of some particular legal system does include; and (3) what method of coherent reconstruction (a) could in possible legal systems, or (b) does in some actual jurisdiction, produce valid law as output, that is, in what the coherence relation consists. Analyzing differences between coherence theories in these three ways is often useful, but the classification will not bear intense scrutiny. The categories are not entirely distinct. For example, natural law coherence theorists may be conceived as adding morality to the base, or as employing a method of reconstruction combining moral and coherence considerations.

Disagreements will arise, for example, about the best characterization of enactments and precedents. Does the base contain only present institutional acts or also past institutional acts? If so, how far back? Is there a principle of desuetude for statutes? Does the base include hypothetical acts which courts, but not legislatures, are prepared to make? Are hypothetical acts better accounted for under the method of reconstruction? Are precedents the words in reporters? The outcomes of cases given the actual facts? The outcomes given the facts as described by the court, plus the *ratio decidendi* and justifying principle provided by the court? Are dissenting opinions part of precedents?

Controversy exists over what besides enactments and precedents is in the base. Does it include conventional or critical morality? If the base includes conventional morality, is it constituted by judges', the legal profession's, or society's moral views? If the base includes conventional or critical morality, yet there is no foolproof method for determining what morality requires, what methods may courts legitimately employ to discover moral principles?

As developed in greater detail below, theories differ over whether reconstruction aims at coherence alone, or also at moral and political values. If other values are included, how are they combined with coherence? The best combination of coherence and morality? The morally best reasonably coherent theory? The most coherent, reasonably moral theory? *The most important differences are over what coherence itself means.* Is a theory coherent if its principles imply the base of legal sources? Justify the sources? If the principles and sources form a unified theory? If the base is derivable from a single principle (monism)? If the theory provides an answer to all possible legal questions (comprehensiveness and right answer thesis?)

Non-legal coherence theories also require bases. In moral theory and the theory of justice, employment of an individual or society's moral beliefs as a base to be coherently reconstructed by reflective equilibrium, as in Rawls, appears ineffective. Unless it is reconstructed according to a justified coherence theory of truth, the reconstructed set appears as likely to reflect biases and socialization as moral truth.

Employment of a base of beliefs in coherence theories of truth and justified belief may illegitimately sneak in a realist or foundationalist element. By contrast, employment of a base of legal sources is innocuous. It serves to secure a coherence theory, or any legal theory, to authoritative sources of law (Raz, 1992, p. 291 and n. 29). Only extreme natural law perspectives might question the legitimacy of a base in law.

Raz's parsimonious positivist sources thesis (1979, ch. 3, 1985) maintains that law consists of source-based law only: constitutions, statutes, and precedents. Since legal authorities may generate an incoherent mishmash of legal sources, the sources thesis is not a coherence theory.

A positivist pure coherence theory maintains that, in addition to the base, law includes those principles and policies which cohere with – by implying – the base. Finally, anything which follows from the principles, policies, and the base is law (cf. Sartorius, 1975, p. 192). This theory parallels Rawls's early theory of reflective equilibrium (1951, described above) with the base of enactments and precedents playing the role which considered convictions play for Rawls. Like considered convictions in Rawls's early work, enactments, precedents and other sources of law have priority over abstract principles (and policies) – the principles are chosen to fit (by implying) the sources of law. The coherence in this theory is a version of unity. The underlying principles and policies imply the base and are in that way internally related to it.

Quine's under-determination thesis implies that many sets of principles and policies will imply the base. This suggests that where coherence is understood as the principles implying the base many sets of principles will be equally coherent because they each imply the base. Yet the theory supplies no method for choosing among those multiple sets of principles and policies. To minimize indeterminacy, coherence theories might be motivated to employ non-coherentist elements such as morality as a tie breaker between equally coherent theories. That is, morality could be a second element in a lexical ordering (defined below).

Other coherence theories may define law as the best combination of coherentist and other considerations. Coherence is one element among many. For example, law consists of the best combination of unity, comprehensiveness (coherentist elements) and morality (a noncoherentist element). Where coherence is one factor among many, however, theories of law may be incommensurate and indeterminate. One theory is more unified and comprehensive, another is morally preferable. Unless there is a metric which balances these values against one another, neither theory is better than the other. Nor are they equally good. In mathematical jargon, this coherence theory is only partially ordered. Dworkin chooses a yet more complex relation between coherentist and non-coherentist aspects: law is the morally most appealing of all those sets of principles and policies which explain or imply the legal base.

Burton's positivist theory (1985; 1995) takes a more expansive view of the sources of law, including within it dissenting opinions, legal scholarship, and conventional moral beliefs within the legal profession, in addition to constitutions, statutes and precedents. Law, for Burton, is the most coherent reconstruction of the legal community's beliefs and dispositions about what would lead to order and justice.

Eisenberg's positivist theory of the common law (1988) is worth exploring at greater length than can be provided here. His discussions of overruling (pp. 104–45) and of what constitutes legally acceptable evidence that a proposition has social support (pp. 16–19, 29–32, 40–2) are especially valuable contributions, and deserve more attention than they have received. Eisenberg begins with a base of sources similar to Burton's, although he looks beyond the legal profession to society at large to determine conventional moral norms and policies.

Eisenberg argues that conflicts among moral norms may be resolved by reflective equilibrium, on the basis of which norm fits better with policies, or determining which norm fits better with doctrinal propositions. The theory provides for two more important roles for coherence as a regulative ideal. First, the social propositions should imply the valid doctrinal rules. Second, the body of valid legal rules should be consistent in the sense that the principles, policies, and the like which imply those doctrinal rules must be consistently applied. Although in ideal theory doctrinal propositions would reflect social propositions perfectly, and be as close to being implied by them as is possible in normative practices, in the real world, this will not be so. Eisenberg adds an overarching non-coherentist element: doctrinal propositions will and should lag behind changes in social propositions in consequence of rule of law and other conservative principles which ground a principle of doctrinal stability, thereby slowing the evolution of doctrinal propositions toward conventional morality and policy.

The most famous and influential coherence theory of law and adjudication, Dworkin's natural law theory, is discussed below. A pure natural law theory holding that law is critical morality, political theory, or justice is coherentist to the degree – if any – that its theory of morality, political theory, or justice is coherentist, and not otherwise.

What coherence is

Beyond providing a base, coherence theories must explain how to modify the base to produce law as output. Put differently, a coherence theory must specify in more detail what it means for legal norms to cohere or fit together. Coherence theorists agree that some – but not extensive – modification of the base is permitted.

To understand coherence in law, techniques thought to promote coherence, or properties or states thought to be aspects of, explanations of, or to be necessary or sufficient for coherence, will be examined. The discussion will focus on justificatory coherence within normative theory, particularly ethics and law, although concepts more appropriate to the theory of knowledge will be discussed in passing. The primary aim throughout is to serve as background for the later taxonomy of coherence in normative theory, although much of what is said here applies more generally.

First, three possible necessary requirements for coherence – consistency, comprehensiveness, and the right answer thesis – will be described and claimed to generally enhance coherence. Still, comprehensiveness and the right answer thesis will be found not to be necessary for coherence, while consistency is necessary in ideal theory but not in practice.

Second, seven techniques aimed at reducing or resolving conflicts among principles of theories, such as pre-emption and reflective equilibrium (described above) will be examined. Characterized thinly as bare or mechanical methods for resolving conflicts, the techniques appear relevant only to consistency, comprehensiveness and the right-answer thesis dimensions of coherence. The appearance is misleading because the conflict-resolution techniques can be articulated and justified. For example, in the United States, federal law expressly or implicitly intended to cover a field pre-empts state law because: (1) the ultimate authority, the US Constitution, so provides; (2a) Congressional power to create uniform national law is essential or helpful to sound policy and moral ends, and (2b) state authority to develop law in the absence of Congressional pre-emption is also desirable. So articulated and justified, federal pre-emption of state law may be part of a coherent unity of doctrine exemplifying a unified spirit in which abstract principles of federalism imply (and are thereby internally related to) principles of pre-emption which in turn imply pre-emption rules and outcomes in concrete cases.

Finally, the core concepts of coherence – monism and unity (internal relations) – will be examined.

Consistency at a time is necessary *in theory* for normative coherence, but is not sufficient for it. By normative coherence is meant a coherence theory in a normative area where the coherence requirements do substantial justificatory work. *Consistency over time* is not necessary for a coherence theory such as Dworkin's, which permits – indeed requires – change over time. Insofar as common-law adjudication is one of the features to be explained by coherence, the theory should not demand consistency or coherence among the principles of the theory at different times, but only a coherent path of movement over time (Kress, 1985). Finally, although consistency at a time is necessary in theory, or metaphysically, for coherence, it is not necessarily required in practice. Although we aim for consistency in the long run, modest skepticism may recommend that we do better day-to-day if we retain some inconsistencies until we are able to resolve them satisfactorily, rather than force consistency via ad hoc solutions. Given the difficulty of developing consistent, coherent, and complete theories, and the value of experimentation, especially in a federal system, consistency (and coherence) are arguably less desirable and necessary *in practice* than as a regulative ideal (Sayre-McCord, 1985, pp.

181–7), despite Rawls and Dworkin's insistence that coherent explanations articulating underlying principles are required of governmental actors to minimize the prospects for bias, self-interest, and deceit, and thereby to help legitimize the use of force and coercion (for example, Dworkin 1978, pp. 162–3; but contrast, Dworkin, 1986, pp. 217–19).

Some claim that coherence requires that a theory must be *comprehensive* and cover the entirety of the relevant field, supplying an answer to each question within its scope, including, where appropriate, the answer "indeterminate." For example, a theory might hold abortion legal or moral in the first trimester, and illegal and immoral in the final trimester; but indeterminate in the middle trimester because at that stage of gestation it is indeterminate whether the fetus has a right to life. This perspective is unduly restrictive. Comprehensiveness improves coherence, but is not required for all conceptions of it.

More controversial yet is a third possible requirement of coherence, the *completeness* requirement. Called by some the "right answer thesis" and by others the "bivalence thesis," it maintains that each proposition within the scope of the theory is either true or false, with no gaps, no unanswerable questions, and no indeterminate truth values. A normative theory may be substantially coherent, even while leaving some vague, borderline or other cases unanswered. The right answer thesis is not necessary for coherence. Nonetheless, it cannot be denied that in certain circumstances, right answers will enhance coherence, while gaps will undermine it.

Shifting focus to methods for eliminating or resolving conflicts and deciding concrete cases, one coherentist method is *reflective equilibrium*, discussed above. A second coherentist technique weighs and balances norms against one another. *General equilibrium* – a third route to coherence – succeeds when things fit together even when individual elements are warring; an overall theory may make sense although its principles conflict (Dworkin, 1986, p. 183; Hobbes, 1962, pp. 105, 110, 164, 229; Sartorius, 1975).

A fourth coherentist method is *lexical ordering*. In a lexical ordering, the first principle must be completely satisfied before the second principle is considered; the second must be completely satisfied before the third is considered; and so on. In this way, Rawls asserts, a lexical ordering avoids weighing and balancing and gives earlier principles "absolute weight, so to speak, with respect to later ones." (1971, pp. 42–3, 60ff). Rawls ranks the principle of equal liberty before the difference principle distributing social and economic resources (1971, p. 61).

A fifth coherentist method is *scope*. By restricting some principles to mutually exclusive areas, concrete conflicts cannot arise. Each standard is limited to its own sphere of influence. For example, a jurisdiction might provide that the principle of equal opportunity governs official employment, while private employment is regulated by freedom of contract. Similarly, antidiscrimination principles might regulate government and public enterprises while freedom of association regulates private activities like private clubs.

Pre-emption, a sixth coherentist method, assists in avoiding conflict among standards. If occasionally, or always, when two principles conflict, one pre-empts the

541

other over all or some portion of their range, potential inconsistency and incoherence will be avoided. In the United States, federal statutes intended to cover a field pre-empt state law on the same subject, thus (in principle) avoiding conflicts.

In their arguments that law is indeterminate, incoherent, and contradictory, critical legal scholars cite the lack of explicit meta-principles to adjudicate among competing principles and counter-principles (Kennedy, 1976, pp. 1,723–4). A seventh possible way for a theory to achieve coherence is to encompass explicit *meta-principles* which resolve conflicts among principles.

The two most important aspects of coherence have been saved for last: *monism* and *internal relations*. The "single fountain" or monistic theory aims to avoid or resolve all conflicts by confining the theory to one fundamental principle from which all subprinciples follow. Utilitarianism is a well-known example of a single fountain theory.

In fact, monism does not guarantee the absence of concrete conflict. First, conjoining multiple principles into a "complex fundamental principle" will permit the conjoined principles to conflict as in any pluralistic theory, and there is no easy way to discriminate between true monistic theories and pluralistic theories in monistic dress. Even true monistic theories may yield conflicting directives under certain factual circumstances: "obey your parents" is the fundamental principle, but mother and father give inconsistent commands. Moreover, even when a monistic theory avoids conflicts, it might fail to provide right answers as a result of vagueness or a failure to be applicable under the circumstances.

Along with monism, the most important consideration in assessing coherence is the internal architecture within the theory – that is, the internal relations among the principles (and norms, rules, policies) of the theory. In its strictest version, internal relations (unity) require that each principle entail and be entailed by every other principle. Such strict versions of internal relations are implausible for most normative theory. Less strict versions of internal relations require that each principle entail or be entailed by some other principle or principles of the theory. Even less strict versions hold that each principle must justify or be justified by some other principle, explain or be explained by another principle, make probable or be made probable by another principle, or be evidence for or be supported by some other principle. These even less strict versions of internal relations may be called one-one versions, to distinguish them from the one-many or one-all versions. For example, one-all versions of internal relations require that each principle be related by some inferential, justificatory, or evidentiary relation not to a single other principle, but to all the rest as a whole. That is, the other principles, taken as a whole, entail, justify or support the principle in question.

Strong internal relations promote coherence by limiting the risk of multiple subject matter incoherence. An example of multiple subject matter incoherence is the following three sentences. Sally is smart. Two is the smallest prime number. Inflation is not a function of the money supply. These three sentences lack coherence because they are about too many different subject matters, and are not mutually supportive.

Another version of internal relations is narrative: I came. I saw. I conquered (Balkin, 1993, p. 114).

Strong versions of internal relations have been out of style for half a century. Weaker forms have survived – for instance, in Dworkin's requirement that the individual coherent principles underlying legal doctrine fit coherently with each other.

Internal relations as described above in either one–one or one–many versions do not guarantee coherence. Thus, it is possible that several subsystems of principles exist, where each member of each subsystem is related by the relevant inferential or justificatory relation to other members of that *same* subsystem, yet the different subsystems have at most weak or no relation to one another. In this way, internal architecture that relates principles one to one, or unidirectionally many to one, does not necessarily prevent multiple subject matter incoherence. Prevention of multiple subject matter incoherence is more likely if the justificatory–inferential relations among principles are reciprocal, holistic, and pervasive. The degree to which this obtains is one measure of the degree of coherence within a theory (Bonjour, 1985, pp. 97–8).

The characterization of normative coherence theories

From here on, the discussion is limited to coherence in moral, legal, and political theory, and would not necessarily apply to coherence theories of knowledge or truth. The remarks that follow are not intended to be a complete and final definition of coherence in normative theory. Coherence is much too difficult a concept for that. There is a range of conceptions of coherence, not just one. What is offered here is a first approximation of a taxonomy of conceptions of coherence.

Referring to reflective equilibrium and concluding the discussion is inadequate to account for coherence in normative theories. The analytical tools described thus far provide the means for a richer, deeper, and more comprehensive analysis.

Moreover, characterizing varying conceptions, and how they differ, will advance efforts to assess their normative virtues. Distinguishing the subconcepts of coherence permits identifying which are part of a particular conception of coherence, singly or in combination. Such identifications aid evaluation of whether a particular conception is morally legitimate, desirable, or partakes in any other normative virtue by determining whether the subconcepts it has induce those virtues.

As noted above, comprehensiveness and right answers enhance coherence but are not necessary for all forms of it. Consistency at a time is a theoretical but not a practical requirement for coherence. The core of coherence is monism and internal relations.

Three versions of monism shall be discussed. No claim is intended that other categorizations are unworthy of investigation. First, strict monism requires that the entire theory "flow from" one master principle so that each subprinciple is implicit in the master principle. "Flow from" means entailment, near entailment, or similar logical and theoretical relations. Moreover, the subprinciples must flow from the master principle together and in harmony so that they are an integrated whole. Weinrib's formalist view that private law, especially tort law, is justified and made intelligible by the principle of corrective justice is a strict monism. Corrective justice holds that those wrongfully causing harm must compensate their victims. Weinrib (1989, 1995; see Article 21, LEGAL FORMALISM) claims that the principle of corrective justice explains, integrates, and harmonizes tort law's bipolar procedure, breach, causation, and damages requirements (Kress, 1993, pp. 648–9, 659–61).

Second, there is moderate monism, wherein methods of reflective equilibrium, weighing and balancing, general equilibrium, lexical ordering, scope, pre-emption, meta-principles, and the like resolve competition and conflict among principles and counter-principles, thus achieving substantial or complete coherence and consistency. Moreover, some master principle or norm explains for each of the following subprinciples that are employed in the theory:

1   why reflective equilibrium eliminates some data and principles, keeps the rest, and adds others;
2   why principles and counter-principles are balanced as they are, why each has the weight (in context) it does (and what justifies the particular weighing mechanism employed);
3   why general equilibrium reaches stasis and makes the theory intelligible;
4   why the lexical ordering is ordered as it is;
5   why the various norms are limited in scope as they are;
6   why those norms which pre-empt others do so;
7   why the particular meta-principles employed for resolving conflict are appropriate; and so on.

In short, the master principle provides a *normatively intelligible explanation and articulation* of arithmetical and abstract methods and meta-principles for resolving conflict among principles. Such a master principle, in combination with the resolution device, serves as the monistic principle, and as a functional substitute for *strict* monism. Yet it is not strict monism, because it allows for disharmony among subprinciples and for subprinciples that do not flow from the master principle. In near monism, a small number of principles irreducible to each other perform the function of the master principle.

By subtracting some articulateness and justifiedness, the second version of monism is transmuted into a third where resolution of concrete cases is accomplished via reflective equilibrium, weighing and balancing, general equilibrium, lexical ordering, scope, pre-emption, meta-principles, and the like, but without recourse to any articulated master principle. Nevertheless, the principles, norms, and conflict resolution devices must reflect a single, unified normative vision. This conception of monism is supported by pragmatist impulses and by atheoretical interpretations of Wittgenstein. Whether these are forms of monism is debatable.

If, however, the resolution devices are interpreted as creating functional monism (plausible, perhaps, if they resolve almost all issues) and the normative vision is clear, version three may be monistic.

Ironically, the first two versions of monism are foundationalist in the respect of being built upon a master principle (except for near monism). Modern coherence theorists might reject this foundationalist imputation, claiming that the master principle is induced by the scientific method of hypothetico-deduction, that is, by determining which master principle (best?) implies the lower norms, as in Rawls's early version of reflective equilibrium, described above. A better perspective simply rejects the alleged opposition between coherence and foundationalism in *law*. Although foundationalism contrasts with coherence theories of justified belief (although even here sophisticated versions of either incorporate aspects of the other), the contrast is not universal: coherence theories of truth are generally compared to realist, correspondence theories, not foundationalist perspectives.

The concept of unity is close to monism in spirit, but it is distinguishable in form, focussing more on internal architecture among the principles of the theory. One way to look at unity is through the version of internal architecture employed. That perspective is more appropriate to theories of justified belief and will not be discussed here. Instead, a taxonomy halfway between that and the classification provided for monism will be explored.

First, unity might be provided by a single master principle that entails all the principles, and thereby relates each to the others in a normatively intelligible fashion. In weaker forms of this first version of unity, the single master principle justifies, explains, makes probable, is evidence for, or otherwise supports all the rest of the principles.

Second, the principles might be united by some form of reflective equilibrium, weighing and balancing, general equilibrium, lexical ordering, scope, pre-emption, meta-principles, or the like that is entailed (or, in weaker versions, justified, explained, made probable, or otherwise supported) by an articulated master principle.

Third, unity might be achieved by one or more of the techniques of reflective equilibrium, weighing and balancing, general equilibrium, lexical ordering, scope, pre-emption, meta-principles, or the like, without any articulated supporting master principle. In its strongest form, this unity would be a matter of entailment between the principles, each to every other. In a weaker version, each would entail or be entailed by some other. Yet weaker versions, would replace entailment with justification, or probabilistic and similar less-strict evidentiary relations. Finally, some minimal unity may be achievable by the above techniques without any evidentiary relations being created (or existing?) among the principles of the theory. The third version of unity may be understood as the second version with less articulateness.

Strong versions of monism entail some version of unity or internal relations. Theories exemplifying weak forms of version three for both monism and unity are, at best, weakly coherent.

Consistency (in theory but not practice) and at least one of monism or unity are clearly necessary for ideal coherence. It is less certain whether both monism and

545

unity are necessary for coherence. But it is clear that, with consistency, they are sufficient for it. There is no single central concept of coherence, but instead many different conceptions of it. Stronger forms of monism and unity give rise to stronger versions of coherence.

The normative value of coherence

An important question about coherence which will only be discussed briefly here is whether a legal system exemplifying coherence, or a coherent legal (or normative) theory is more morally legitimate, desirable, or better respects individual rights than one which does not. Naturally, the answer will differ for different conceptions of coherence. Dworkin's claim that legal systems manifesting the version of coherence he dubs "integrity" better legitimizes law than less coherent legal systems will be evaluated, although the arguments employed are intended to apply broadly to other coherence theories.

Dworkin's early writings maintained that a legal proposition is true if it follows from that (coherent) scheme of principles which best justifies and explains the precedents, statutes and constitution. His conception of coherence was a version of Rawls's mature method of reflective equilibrium in *A Theory of Justice*, emphasizing the requirement that the underlying principles must be consistently applied in justifying surface rules and reaching concrete judicial decisions.

Dworkin's mature theory differs slightly in a way which, as noted earlier, admits a second non-coherentist element besides the base and obscures its connection to a pure coherence theory (Kress, 1985, p. 378, n. 53). In Dworkin's later writings, a proposition is law if it follows from the morally most appealing set of principles that meet or exceed a (vague) threshold of fit with legal institutional facts (constitutions, statutes, precedents (Dworkin, 1978, pp. 340–1, 360)). In yet later writings, he allows that the threshold is not an absolute floor: one may drop beneath the threshold for urgent or exceptional moral gains (Dworkin, 1986). Raz argues – somewhat disingenuously – that Dworkin may not be a coherence theorist because in *Law's Empire* the moral elements – justice, fairness, and due process – do all the work, leaving coherence (fit) idle (Raz, 1992, pp. 315–21, esp. 317).

Dworkin supported coherence in his early work with four main abstract arguments. The first three were arguments for his rights thesis that judges do and should decide cases on the basis of principle, not policy. The rights thesis imposes a constraint of coherence on judges since Dworkin defined principles as requiring an equality – consistency in application – much stricter than that required of actions justified on policy grounds.

The rights thesis was defended by Dworkin on three main abstract grounds. First, Dworkin argues that the democratic principle that elected and politically accountable officials, and not judges, should make law has far more force against judicial decisions generated by policy than it has against those generated by principle. The second abstract political argument for the rights thesis is that it is unfair for the judge to create a new duty based upon policy and apply it retroactively because "then the losing party would be punished, not because he violated some duty he had, but rather a new duty created after the event" (Dworkin, 1978, p. 84; but see Kress, 1984). Third, Dworkin argues that the best explanation of the requirement of precedent that like cases be treated alike is that adjudication is restricted to arguments of principle because principle requires more consistency from case to case than policy does. In addition to the support provided for coherence by the argument for the rights thesis, Dworkin argues directly that the doctrine of political responsibility requires consistent, articulated rationales for government actions.

One objection to coherence theories of law, including Dworkin's, is that they are path-dependent (Kress, 1989, pp. 5–53, esp. 50–3, 20–6) and lead to morally troubling retroactive application of law. Dworkin's theory of legal reasoning is built on the proposition that litigants are entitled to the enforcement of pre-existing legal rights. One way in which Dworkin's early work expressed this major claim was by presupposing that litigants have a right to have decisions determined by settled law. In Dworkin's theory, settled law together with moral theory determines litigants' rights and litigants' rights determine the proper outcome. Thus, decisions are a function of, among other things, settled law.

Retroactivity is a consequence of legal rights being a function of settled law and upon the temporal gap between events being litigated and their eventual adjudication. Judicial decisions change the settled law. Often, if not always, the settled law will be changed between the occurrence of events being litigated and their eventual adjudication. In consequence, a litigant's rights will sometimes also be changed. If changes in the settled law change the dispositive legal right, the litigant who would have prevailed given the legal rights existing at the time of the occurrence will lose because she no longer has the right at the time of the adjudication. The opposite is true of the opposing litigant. This is retroactive application of law (Kress, 1985, 1989; Alexander and Kress, 1995, pp. 296–301).

Hurley (1990), following a suggestion of Dworkin's, objects that legal rights do not change in coherence theories when judges decide cases correctly, but only when judges make mistakes. This is a problematic conception of precedent. What could justify a doctrine of precedent which provides a reason to follow (and a right to equal treatment of) mistaken and unjust decisions, but no reason to follow correct, just ones? (Alexander and Kress, 1995, p. 300).

Raz (1985, 1992) claims that coherence theories are unable to satisfactorily account for the authority of law, and the proper role of legal sources within the law. Although Raz views the criticism as a structural, evaluative but not moral criticism, it could also be read as a moral critique (cf. Perry, 1995). Raz claims that, in general, legal authorities are legitimate to the extent that they aid individuals in doing the right thing, that is, in acting in accord with the reasons that apply to them (normal justification thesis). This requires that legal authorities promulgate norms on the basis of the reasons and circumstances which apply to individuals (dependence thesis). Where legal authorities are better than individuals at figuring out what the applicable reasons require of individuals, individuals following the authoritative acts of legal authorities will act correctly more frequently

547

than if they follow their own lights. But this means that once an alleged legal authority has been shown to be legitimate (generally by the normal justification thesis), then its authority is respected only if individuals to whom its decisions apply act on the basis of the authority's reasons and standards, and not on the basis of the reasons which applied to the individuals prior to the authority's utterance: authoritative utterances pre-empt dependent reasons (pre-emption thesis).

But coherence theories, including Dworkin's, are inconsistent with this conception of the authority of law. First, the most coherent account of the legal sources may be entirely original, thereby severing all connections with the reasons and norms uttered by legal authorities. Dworkin's conception cannot account for the mediating role of authority.

Moreover, it denies the pre-emption thesis. On Dworkin's theory, citizens deciding how to act must determine the morally best reconstruction of the authoritative sources of law. But this means that the identification of law depends upon the very considerations which applied to the individual before the authoritative act and which law is supposed to settle. In summary, "Coherence accounts take the base [of legal sources] because it is too absurd to disregard it; then they strive to ignore it and to explain the law in a way which transcends the inherent limitations of the workings of human institutions, and by transcending them they misunderstand them" (Raz, 1992, p. 297).

An urgent question about the moral value of coherence is whether it promotes the moral legitimacy of legal systems exemplifying it. By coherence, which he now calls "integrity," Dworkin means at least:

1(a)   the principles underlying official government acts must be individually coherent and intelligible;
1(b)   the individual principles must be consistently applied, with applicable principles receiving similar weight in relevantly similar situations;
2(a)   the principles, as a whole, must be consistently applied, with like situations being treated alike;
2(b)   the principles as a whole must fit together into a single and comprehensive vision of justice.

Moreover, the justification for each of (1)–(2) is the same: "consistency in principle . . . requires that the various standards governing the state's use of coercion against its citizens be consistent in the sense that they express a single and comprehensive vision of justice" (Dworkin, 1986, pp. 134, 88, 116–17, 166; Alexander and Kress, 1995, p. 311). The justification for coherence generally and of the specific conception of it embodied in (1)–(2) is importantly connected to the nearly universally accepted internal point of view that law is a matter of practical reason, intended to provide guides to conduct for its subjects, and grounds for criticism of violations of its commands. While an external observer might be able to understand a foreign legal system as a patchwork quilt of conflicting norms resulting from the respective fortunes of opposed ideologies, someone adopting an extreme internal point of view cannot do so. She regards legal norms as valid and as guides to her behavior and judgment. Yet she cannot accept the norms as her own unless she can regard the norms as "valid and justified, and [she] cannot regard them as justified unless they form a coherent body" (Raz, 1992, p. 293; Dworkin, 1986, p. 189).

Dworkin gives several arguments explaining how the form of coherence exemplified in the theory he calls "law as integrity" legitimizes law as integrity. The argument that he develops at greatest length, and on which he relies most heavily, is the argument from community. To understand this argument, we must recall that for Dworkin, integrity involves discerning principles that underlie and justify governmental acts (such as legislation and judicial decisions) and following those principles in making future governmental decisions (such as decisions in hard cases at law). Dworkin claims that "[A] political society that accepts integrity as a political virtue becomes a special form of community, special in a way that promotes its moral authority to assume and deploy a monopoly of coercive force" (1986, p. 188).

Dworkin's argument for this proposition is difficult to decipher; what follows is a reconstruction. Dworkin begins with the claim that the major traditional grounds for political legitimacy and political obligation (consent, tacit consent, fair play, duty to uphold just institutions) do not succeed in bestowing legitimate authority on governments to coerce and use force; nor do they generate moral obligations on citizens to obey the law. An interpretive reconstruction of the argument from fair play, however, is sufficient. Dworkin's new interpretive version of the argument from fair play reconstrues political obligation as a form of associative obligation – that is, the obligations arising within groups or communities such as families, law faculties, and clubs. For Dworkin, a bare political community, such as the United States, is a true community giving rise to true associative obligations only if the obligations arising from the community have four characteristics, of which two are relevant here:

1   each must be thought of as flowing from an underlying and pervasive concern for the other members; and
2   each must be predicated not only on concern for the other members, but on equal and reciprocal concern.

Of particular concern here is the first requirement that particular obligations must be thought of as flowing from a deep, underlying, and pervasive concern for other members of the community, because Dworkin argues that a community that accepts integrity as political ideal is better able to meet this requirement than a community that does not. This first requirement tracks Dworkin's early criticism of legal positivism that besides rules the law includes those principles which underlie and justify the rules (1978, pp. 14–45).

Dworkin claims that citizens' political obligations clearly include those obligations laid down in explicit rules of law. To satisfy the first requirement, however, citizens' obligations cannot be thought of as exhausted by the explicit rules. Citizens must think of themselves as having whatever obligations and rights can be shown to flow from the values of equal concern that underlie the explicit rules.

Citizens can infer such inexplicit obligations and rights from the values underlying the explicit only if the explicit rules are coherent. If the explicit rules are incoherent, the only principles and values that can be said to be underlying them will be similarly incoherent, or even contradictory. This incoherent or contradictory foundation would frustrate citizens' attempts to successfully infer, and engage in dialogue about, what their inexplicit obligations and rights are. If individual principles are incoherent or unintelligible, citizens will not be able to apply them. If the individual principles are not consistently applied, but receive different weights in similar situations, their weight in novel but similar situations will be indeterminate. If the principles as a whole are not consistently applied but principles and counter-principles with the same pattern of relative weights sometimes are decided in favor of the principles and sometimes in favor of the counter-principles, new situations with the identical pattern of opposing norms will be unpredictable and indeterminate. If the principles do not fit together into a single and comprehensive vision of justice, then they contain all, or part, of contradictory visions which cannot be reconciled, or they are incomplete or incoherent. Once again dialogue and decision making will be hindered or prevented altogether. Thus, the political system can be legitimate only if its explicit rules and the underlying principles are coherent.

There are many ready avenues of attack of this reconstruction of Dworkin's text. For example, the duty to uphold just institutions, in addition to the argument from fair play, may legitimize government. But let us ignore these issues.

For Dworkin, an act's manifesting integrity does not insure its justice and legitimize it. The relationship is more complicated than that. Rather, a governmental act justified by justice, charity, efficiency, or other grounds, is permitted and legitimate only if that act can be shown to flow from, or cohere with, other actions taken in the name of the community in the past (Dworkin, 1986, p. 93; Alexander and Kress, 1995, pp. 312–14). But this constraint of coherence is unattractive if it prevents a government which has so far limited itself to promoting the welfare of its citizens from broadening its horizons to doing justice, or offering its services as an international mediator, or engaging in charity, unless it can engage in intellectual contortions demonstrating that these new roles cohere with prior governmental acts.

More importantly, it is not true that when a new initiative or incoherent act is taken, this disrupts the ability of citizens to engage in dialogue about, or judges to make inferences about, what the law now is, thereby undermining law's legitimacy. For example, suppose that until now a jurisdiction has operated on a color blind antidiscrimination principle. Proponents of affirmative action now convince the legislature to vote, or a court to hold, that affirmative action for some historically discriminated against group is required. The defender of integrity will allege that the law has now become incoherent in a way that diminishes the ability of citizens and officials to coherently work out the law's implications. But the defender of affirmative action may respond that the new affirmative action law brings along with its own set of underlying principles, on the basis of which dialogue and inference about the law's commands should proceed. There is no loss in the ability to engage in dialogue; rather, the principles justifying affirmative action have now replaced the principles of color blindness in making authoritative determinations. The Dworkinian conception of coherence does not legitimate law better than following the demands of morality and justice. (For a fuller development of the argument, see Alexander and Kress, 1995, pp. 308–26.)

Bibliography

Alexander, L. and Kress, K. 1995: Against legal principles. In A. Marmor (ed.), *Law and Interpretation*, Oxford: Clarendon Press, 279–327.

Balkin, J. 1993: Understanding legal understanding: the legal subject and the problem of legal coherence. *Yale Law Journal*, 103, 105–76.

Bonjour, L. 1985: *The Structure of Empirical Knowledge*. Cambridge: Harvard University Press.

Burton, S. 1985: *An Introduction to Law and Legal Reasoning*. Boston: Little, Brown and Co.

—— 1995: *An Introduction to Law and Legal Reasoning*. Boston: Little, Brown and Co., 2nd edn.

Coleman, J. 1982: Negative and positive positivism. *The Journal of Legal Studies*, 11, 139–64.

—— 1995: Truth and objectivity in law. *Legal Theory*, 1, 33–68.

Dworkin, R. 1978: *Taking Rights Seriously*. Cambridge: Harvard University Press.

—— 1985: *A Matter of Principle*. Cambridge: Harvard University Press.

—— 1986: *Law's Empire*. Cambridge: Harvard University Press.

Eisenberg, M. A. 1988: *The Nature of the Common Law*. Cambridge: Harvard University Press.

Fumerton, R. 1994: The incoherence of coherence theories. *Journal of Philosophical Research*, 19, 89–102.

Hobbes, T. [1651] 1962: *Leviathan*, ed. M. Oakeshott, New York: Collier.

Hurley, S. 1990: Coherence, hypothetical cases, and precedent. *Oxford Journal of Legal Studies*, 10, 221–51.

Kennedy, D. 1976: Form and substance in private law adjudication. *Harvard Law Review*, 89, 1,685–778.

Kress, K. 1984: Legal reasoning and coherence theories: Dworkin's rights thesis, retroactivity, and the linear order of decisions. *California Law Review*, 72, 369–402.

—— 1993: Coherence and formalism. *Harvard Journal of Law and Public Policy*, 16, 639–82.

Perry, S. 1995: Interpretation and legal theory. In A. Marmor (ed.), *Law and Interpretation*, Oxford: Clarendon Press, 97–135.

Rawls, J. 1957: Outline of a decision procedure for ethics. *Philosophical Review*, 66, 177–97.

—— 1971: *A Theory of Justice*. Cambridge: Harvard University Press.

Raz, J. 1979: *The Authority of Law*. Oxford: Clarendon Press.

—— 1985: Authority, law and morality. *The Monist*, 68, 295–324.

—— 1992: The relevance of coherence. *Boston University Law Review*, 72, 273–321.

Sartorius, R. 1975: *Individual Conduct and Social Norms: a utilitarian account of social union and the rule of law*. Encino, Ca. Dickinson.

Sayre-McCord, G. 1985: Coherence and models for moral theorizing. *Pacific Philosophical Quarterly*, 66, 170–90.

Walker, R. 1989: *The Coherence Theory of Truth: realism, anti-realism, idealism*. London: Routledge.

Weinrib, E. 1988: Legal formalism: on the immanent rationality of law. *Yale Law Journal*, 97, 949–1,016.

—— 1995: *The Idea of Private Law*. Cambridge: Harvard University Press.

39

The welfare state

SANFORD LEVINSON

What are the proper functions of the state? One answer is the facilitation of decisions made by autonomous individuals, coupled with prevention of the use of force or fraud by insufficiently socialized individuals and provision of a "common defense" against foreign enemies. This answer underlay the classical–liberal, nineteenth-century theory of the "night-watchman state," limited to enforcing private contracts, providing protection against those who violated basic legal norms, and defending the society from hostile incursions. Contemporary theorists of the minimal state would presumably include within the state's proper ambit the provision of certain "public goods," a special set of goods – the usual examples are national defense or the building of dams to prevent flooding – whose enjoyment cannot be limited only to those specific individuals who wish to purchase them. Instead, precisely because there is no effective way to prevent non-purchasers from enjoying what they did not pay for, they become "free riders." As a consequence, most economists would argue, there is underinvestment in the goods in question because of the reluctance of investors to subsidize the free riders. The answer to this problem is to force potential free riders to pay their "fair share" through compulsory taxation. For most economists, though, the category of true "public goods" is relatively restricted, and the state's domain can remain quite limited. Moreover, the taxation and subsequent spending on public goods is in no way redistributive, since by definition the potential "free riders" are compensated for their taxes by the supply of what is stipulated to be a valuable good.

Such views about the minimal role of the state are historically linked with the intellectual development of free-market economics and the economic rise of capitalism. As Gilbert (1983, pp. 4–5) has written, "Capitalism encourages competition and risk-taking behavior," with victory going to those who are the beneficiaries of both their talents and the sheer luck of market vagaries. In turn, however, "misfortune and failure can lead to harsh consequences," for "[t]here are few market mechanisms to mitigate the consequences of accident, illness, ageing, and vicissitudes of industrial society."

As a matter of empirical fact, *no* state has ever adopted a completely minimalist role, however strong its advocacy by such proponents of *laissez-faire* as Herbert Spencer. Whatever the power of that vision, reflected today in the thought of economists like Milton Friedman or the philosopher Robert Nozick (not to mention political leaders like former Prime Minister Margaret Thatcher in Britain and Speaker of the United States House of Representatives Newt Gingrich), it has obviously not occupied the field unchallenged. Indeed, almost all Western states, especially in the twentieth century, have adopted some version of a "welfare" rather than a "night-watchman" state.

One must recognize, though, that even most devotees of the "welfare state" have only limited notions of the citizen's "welfare" that is a proper concern of the state. Should the state be concerned with the religious salvation of its members? A tenet of the political liberalism identified with John Locke and his later American followers like Thomas Jefferson was that getting right with God was the responsibility of each individual, with the state having no role to play. Few contemporary adherents of a "welfare state" have been critical of this absolutely central aspect of political liberalism, even though proponents of a more traditional tutelary state might well argue that *nothing* could provide greater welfare to the citizenry than the state's firm guidance of the recalcitrant in the paths of eternal life or, at least, the avoidance of sin. Similarly, an Aristotelian might argue that the state should be concerned with the *virtue* of its members and act consciously so as to mold in them a sufficiently virtuous character. Although contemporary debates about the role of the state in, say, regulating pornography or sexual conduct or inculcating in the young the precepts of virtuous living are usually not couched as debates about the reach of the "welfare state," they could well merit that description under a broad conception of that term.

Most critics of the minimal state, however, especially those persons identified with the political left, have accepted the liberal notion of state neutrality in regard to basic questions about what counts as a life well lived. Critics have therefore focussed on other questions, especially those involving the *distributive justice* of the allocation of economic resources found within a given society and the state's role, if any, in rectifying ostensible maldistributions.

Although any inquiry into the demands of "distributive justice" necessarily has many dimensions, two, in particular, have tended to frame much of the debate, especially since the publication of John Rawls's extremely influential *A Theory of Justice* (1971). One involves the *equality* of distribution and implicitly criticizes, or at least asks for justification, of any deviation from equal distribution of resources. Another, quite different, approach accepts with relative equanimity inequality of resources; it asks, however, if even those with the least resources are assured some set of basic goods, such as food, clothing, or shelter, and a reasonable opportunity to try to achieve their own conceptions of the good life.

A pure egalitarian might be upset that the millionaire has a yacht while the ordinary citizen has, at most, a motorboat, or that only the millionaire would be able to achieve a vision of life that included a great deal of foreign travel. Someone focussing more on the satisfaction of "minimum needs" or "minimum just wants," however, might find that unproblematic, though concerned about those who lack all access to *any* kind of transportation or those who seem unable to realize even the most modest of their visions of a good life. In fact, most theorists of the welfare state are in the second camp, emphasizing the dire economic straits of those who lose out in the unfettered competition of the liberal market and end up with so few resources that they cannot afford to pay the market price for even "basic" needs. Or, what is much the same thing, these theorists have rejected the justice of a state that allows forcing persons who need such resources to have to accept the most onerous of labor conditions, including child labor, 70-hour work weeks, subjection to constant risk of dangerous accidents, and the like, as an alternative to starvation or other similar privation. These critics therefore resist the vision of a minimalist state that is indifferent to the fate of the poorest among it.

Although some critics of the minimal state rejected capitalism itself and embraced some variety of socialism, more moderate – and certainly, in the United States, more numerous – critics accepted the basic desirability of capitalism and free markets as ways of generating incentives and efficiently allocating scarce resources; at the same time, though, they wanted to limit the costs of failure in such a society. They therefore endorsed the provision of a "safety net" that assures even those at the bottom of the class structure with a tolerable set of resources.

Historian Asa Briggs (1961, p. 228) describes the welfare state as one "in which organized power is deliberately used (through politics and administration) in an effort to modify the play of market forces in at least three directions": (1) guaranteeing members of the social order "a minimum income irrespective of the market value of their property"; (2) in effect, insuring everyone against the particular kinds of insecurities linked with "social contingencies" such as sickness, old age, and unemployment; and (3) "ensuring that all citizens without distinction of status or class are offered the best standards available in relation to a certain agreed range of social services." All of these present difficult problems of definition, not to mention that some generate considerably more controversy than do others.

The first two categories, for example, can easily coexist with the acceptance of considerable inequality of resources and the linked ability of those with more property to purchase better goods and services than those with less. The last category, though, seems to be considerably more egalitarian in its thrust insofar as it would require that even those with minimal or no resources receive "the best" of at least some set of social services; this entails that even the millionaire, for all of his freedom to purchase yachts while the rest of us are limited to motorboats (or worst), would be unable to use his market power to purchase better supplies of at least some goods. Michael Walzer (1983) is perhaps the best known political theorist to have sketched out such a position. Markets, according to Walzer, are completely appropriate structures to allocate some goods, but are, concomitantly, almost completely inappropriate in regard to others. Should, for example, a millionaire be allowed greater access to life-saving treatment than a pauper, even if we gladly allow greater access to exotic vacation spots? Walzer believes not, even as he accepts the justice of the latter.

What might explain the adoption of a "welfare state"? One answer is ruthlessly pragmatic, emphasizing the "buying off" of those at the bottom end of the income ladder lest they become sufficiently discontented to engage in crime or even rebellion (see, for example, Posner, 1986, p. 439). At a more theoretical level – given that one response to the pragmatic argument is simply to adopt more severe mechanisms of punishment – one's support of a welfare case seems to depend in significant measure on one's propensity to attribute responsibility to individuals for their fate. If everyone's bundle of resources, at the end of the day, is a function of his or her own uncoerced and informed decisions, then it is hard indeed to figure out why those who choose to behave in foreseeably counter-productive ways, as by refusing to learn certain job skills, should be entitled to state-mandated redistribution of resources from their more successful fellow citizens. The parable of the ant and the grasshopper comes quickly to mind. Particularly charitable persons might. of course, choose to contribute for the relief of those who are downtrodden by virtue of their own bad decisions, but this is obviously different from state compulsion.

To the extent, however, that the distribution of resources is less attributable to personal choices – that is, even persons with excellent character diligently doing "the best they can" seem unable to prosper at all, because their carefully honed job skills become irrelevant owing to market vicissitudes – then it seems at best heartless and at worst manifestly unjust to turn away from their plight and leave them to the vagaries of private charity (especially if private charity does not, in fact, suffice to alleviate the plight of all with "just claims" to aid). Surely the easiest way to make this point is by reference to young children; no one argues that 3-year-olds are responsible for their own conditions of privation. There might, obviously, be great contention about exactly what ought to be done. On the one hand, one might support direct income grants to the parents to purchase goods for the child; on the other, if one attributes responsibility for the inadequate conditions to the parents themselves, one might want more active intervention in the parental setting or even support placing the child in a state-run institution. All alternatives, though, concede that the state cannot properly remain indifferent to the welfare of the child. Similar analyses might be offered in regard to others deemed "child-like" by the society, including, for example, the severely mentally retarded.

Far more controversial, obviously, are "normally functioning" adults. Are they properly viewed as responsible for their own circumstances in life or, on the contrary, as more hapless (and sometimes helpless) victims of fate? There can be little doubt that the rise of the welfare state was linked with the adoption of more general theories of society that found agency more in impersonal structures and less in the particular individuals living within them. If economists, generally speaking, with their predilection for images of "rational actors" making best use of their bundle of resources in order to maximize their individual (and incommensurable) utilities, provide the ideological underpinning for the free-market and minimal state, then sociologists, generally speaking, with their own images of "the individual" as simply a product of surrounding socio-economic structures, provide similar underpinning for the interventionist state and its attempts to check the consequences of leaving these social structures unregulated.

Indeed, a number of important thinkers associated with American legal realism – and very much influenced by sociological critiques of liberal individualism – witheringly criticized the very image of "unregulated" or "natural" structures. They emphasized, for example, that the very notions of private property were the product of distinctive social formations that enjoyed the coercive power of the state to enforce certain conceptions of property. Other conceptions would have resulted in distinctively different patterns of allocation. The millionaire, being the beneficiary of state regulatory largesse rather than the possessor of truly "private" property – the realist critique savaged the general distinction between public and private – could not really complain if the state changed its mind and decided to redirect its largesse elsewhere, even at the cost of reducing the millionaire's set of legal entitlements.

Although the most dramatic instances of the modern welfare state often involve direct transfer of income from taxpaying "haves" to "havenots," it is important to realize that earlier instantiations of the welfare state were more likely to be limited to self-conscious *regulation* of the market place in the interest of those who would otherwise remain unacceptably deprived of necessary resources. Examples of such regulation include minimum-wage and maximum-hours laws, safety regulations, protection of labor unions, and the like. Economists could argue cogently that almost all such regulation, if carefully analyzed, involved income transfers, even if they did not take the direct form of receipt of checks or goods from the state. Instead, for example, increases in minimum wages would generally be passed along to the purchasers in the form of increased prices for goods and services, though some of the increase was paid for in diminished profits by the employers. Indeed, some costs were even borne by those marginal workers who lost their jobs entirely because of the inability of the employer to continue employing them at the higher rate. Economists, especially, delighted in pointing out that this last group was scarcely helped by minimum wage laws and that their dire circumstances might even be worse than before. The fact, though, that such redistributions were not reflected in governmental tax bills or spending budgets offered a certain kind of political insulation absent once the welfare state had to be financed through taxation and acknowledged government expenditures in regard to direct governmental expenditures.

In the American context, almost all jurisprudential questions mutate into debates about the meaning of the United States Constitution, and this is certainly true in regard to the welfare state. The first question that was raised, historically, was whether the Constitution even allowed a welfare state, with its provision of what Gilbert has described as "a sort of communal safety net for the casualties of a market economy." The United States Supreme Court, in a remarkable decision (*Coppage* v. *Kansas*, 1915), suggested that the Constitution was basically inhospitable to any attempts to redistribute resources. "[W]herever the right of private property exists," said Justice Pitney for the majority, "there must and will be inequalities of fortune . . . [I]t is self-evident that unless all things are held in common, some persons must have more property than others." Pitney referred to "the nature of things" as making it "impossible to uphold . . . the right of private property without at the same time recognizing as legitimate those inequalities of fortune that are the necessary result of the exercise" of the ability to work one's will on the world that having more property than others brings one. *Coppage* did not involve direct redistribution of income. Direct redistribution was present, though,

557

in an act of the Ohio legislature offering modest sums to "worthy blind" persons. The Ohio Supreme Court (*Lucas* v. *State of Ohio*, 1906) did not hesitate to strike it down:

> If a bounty may be conferred upon individuals of one class, then it may be upon individuals of another class, and if upon two, then upon all. And if upon those who have physical infirmities, then why not upon other classes who for various reasons may be unable to support themselves? And if these things may be done, why may not all property be distributed by the state?

This quasi-syllogistic, "slippery slope," style of reasoning was obviously thought to be unanswerable. The prospect of the state's redistributing "all property" from haves to politically favored groups of havenots was sufficiently frightening to counsel precluding even the most modest redistributions.

To be precise, decisions suggested that redistributive regulation, taxation, and spending would be tolerable if and only if politically unaccountable courts were themselves persuaded that the legislation was truly in the public interest and not simply a "naked preference" for the political friends of the legislative majorities. Though courts in fact sometimes upheld measures, they often did not. Legislative decision making took place in the shadow of potential judicial invalidation.

The New Deal revolution of 1937 brought this era to an end, and the state was given immense discretion in regard to decisions to regulate, tax, or spend. Judicial oversight of the "public purposes" underlying these decisions was reduced to what courts themselves described as "minimal" scrutiny leaving legislatures basically free to redistribute as they wished. By the late 1960s, scholarly debate had shifted from whether the welfare state was permitted to whether it might even be *required*. Thus Harvard law professor Frank Michelman, acknowledging Rawls's influence on his own thought, suggested in a widely noted, aptly named, article, "On protecting the poor through the Fourteenth Amendment" (1969), that the Constitution was best read as guaranteeing provision by the state to all citizens of some set of "minimum just wants" should they not be able to attain these goods through their own efforts.

Although the Supreme Court then dominated by a liberal majority led by Justice William Brennan seemed open to views like Michelman's, any such hopes – or fears – were dashed in the early 1970s. Four new justices appointed by Richard Nixon joined other moderates already on the Court in rejecting Brennan's expansive views and adopting instead a considerably more cautious notion of constitutional meaning. By 1990 it was crystal clear that the Supreme Court did not read the Constitution as requiring the state to alleviate any particular suffering, however dreadful, that it could not be viewed as causing. This obviously raises important problems summarized as the "act–omission" problem: Are overt acts causing some harm X truly distinguishable from an omission to act in a situation where the omission will foreseeably tolerate the occurrence of X? Few questions are thornier philosophically, and the answers to few philosophical questions are so fraught with implications for one's very notion of the reach of the state. In any event, the Supreme Court has adopted a quite restrictive notion of causation and, therefore, a quite latitudinarian approach to state indifference to those without resources.

Even if the Court rejected arguments that a redistributive welfare state was constitutionally required, this did not in any way mean that the growth of the welfare state came to an end. A host of new programs continued to be passed by Congress and state legislatures. The point, though, was that passage of these programs involved the exercise of relatively unfettered political choice rather than submission to constitutional duty. Even in the 1990s and its atmosphere of worldwide political ferment in regard to issues surrounding the welfare state, few persons seriously suggest eliminating it entirely. Important constitutional– jurisprudential questions therefore remain, even if one concedes that the state, as a theoretical matter, need not have embarked on those programs it has, in fact, chosen to initiate.

As already suggested, especially important is the precise definition of what is meant by the welfare state. Politically, the term tends to be applied only to redistributions from haves to havenots, even though it is clear that many other redistributions, including many from havenots to haves, also take place in any complex society. If one defines "welfare," for example, as the provision to selected persons of certain important goods below their market price, then a perfect example of the welfare state would be a state law or medical school whose tuitions recapture from students only a modest fraction of the true cost of the goods and services provided them. Similarly, massive redistributions from New Jerseyites and Texans to Californians or Iowans who are the victims of earthquakes or floods can easily be viewed as examples of the modern welfare state in its "insurance" function, and often no effort is made to ensure that benefits go only to those who are without other funds (including the ability to have purchased private insurance against the readily predictable calamities of nature). Such expenditures, often directed at middle- or even upper-class constituencies, rarely draw the attention directed at those expenditures involving the poor. The same is true of what some theorists call "corporate welfare," the use of tax funds in effect to subsidize business enterprise.

What are some other key issues? One involves a classic question of "the rule of law": to what extent should welfare entitlements be clearly set out, as against being subject to a variety of discretionary decisions by administrators within welfare bureaucracies? To the extent that administrators need conform only with relatively vague "standards," rather than clear rules, the recipients of welfare benefits may become dependent not only on the grants themselves, a much discussed topic in the 1980s and 1990s, but also on the bureaucrats whose acquiescence is necessary to receive a grant. Hayek (1944) condemned this aspect of the welfare state as "the road to serfdom."

Linked with this debate about "rules" versus "standards" is one about how closely bureaucratic decision makers should be monitored by courts. This issue was debated in the United States in the 1970s particularly in regard to the right of welfare recipients to receive hearings *before* their welfare benefits were cut or terminated

559

for alleged infraction of one or another rule linked with these benefits. Generally speaking, courts have ended up accepting as constitutionally sufficient legitimacy of *post*-termination hearings, even though this entails that at least some individuals will be wrongfully deprived for some period of time – until the hearing can be held and the wrongful termination invalidated – of what, by definition, are necessities of life, because of bureaucratic error. The alternative, though, is tolerating other individuals wrongfully continuing to receive benefits that they are not by law entitled to. Especially if one assumes a relatively fixed overall budget for any given welfare program, there may be direct trade-offs between what is spent on achieving maximally fair procedures and how much is in fact distributed to the beneficiaries of the program. Would, for example, recipients rather receive $100 and a post-termination hearing or $95 and the possibility of a pre-termination hearing? It is doubtful that either jurisprudential or constitutional reflection suggests a determinate answer to the question that would make it improper to allow the legislature to do whatever it thinks best.

Knotty issues surround what in the United States take the form of "equal protection" challenges to particular coverage of any given program. Consider, for example, a health-benefits program. The first question likely to arise is who should (or, as a constitutional matter, *must*) be covered. Certainly the most common classification is that of income. Is it fair to limit coverage only to persons with less than $X income, given the obvious arbitrariness involved in saying that $X + $1 is substantially different from $X alone? This may take on even greater poignancy once one realizes that even $X + $n may fall well short of a "subsistence" income. Other classifications likely to be imposed involve residence or citizenship. Can the state legitimately limit its succor only to those who are part of its own social or political community? Both in the United States and Europe, part of the great debate about the future of the welfare state involves determining whether the state must be as generous to resident aliens, guest workers, and political refugees as to its own citizens.

Even if everyone agreed *who* should be covered, intense controversies would still remain about the *scope* of coverage. A committed egalitarian would presumably give the poor whatever medical care is available to the millionaire. Others might be less generous, limiting coverage to the most common, or most dangerous, illnesses, or pay for treatment only up to a certain amount. Might expensive heart transplants be limited only to those persons with sufficient resources to purchase them on the open market (or, more to the point, purchase insurance plans that would cover transplants)? Medical care presents only the most (melo)dramatic examples of the problems of classification attached to any redistributive welfare program.

A final question of great import concerns the *conditions* that can be placed by the state on the receipt of welfare benefits. Can, for example, health benefits be made contingent on recipients' willingness to stop smoking or grants to parents made contingent on their willingness to engage in certain disciplinary practices *vis-à-vis* their children? All other citizens would remain free to smoke or treat their children as they wish (subject to general laws against child abuse). No topic of theory or legal practice is more tangled than that of "unconstitutional conditions," which attempts to set out the limits of the state's putting strings on those whom it benefits.

Almost all political systems in economically advanced countries throughout the world are embroiled in controversy about the maintenance of their own versions of the welfare state. To escape these controversies entirely requires either that the invisible hand of market capitalism, including the role of private charity, works to assure that everyone in the society, in fact, procures enough to meet basic needs or that society becomes so completely indifferent to the fate of losers that it accepts without question the presence of dying or starving persons in the streets for whom the state takes no responsibility at all. Otherwise, we must continue to wrestle about how to combine the advantages of a capitalist economy with due concern for those whom capitalism leaves without basic resources.

Bibliography

Briggs, A. 1961: The welfare state in historical perspective. In 2 Europaisches Archiv fur Soziologie, 21–258.

Coppage v. *Kansas*, 236 U.S. 1 (1915).

Gilbert, N. 1983: *Capitalism and the Welfare State*. New Haven: Yale University Press.

Goodin, R. 1988: *Reasons for Welfare: the political theory of the welfare state*. Princeton: Princeton University Press.

Gutmann, A. 1988: *Democracy and the Welfare State*. Princeton: Princeton University Press.

Hayek, F. A. von 1944: *The Road to Serfdom*. Chicago: University of Chicago Press.

Lucas County v. *State of Ohio*, 75 Ohio St. 131 (1906).

Mead, L. M. 1992: *The New Politics of Poverty: the nonworking poor in America*. New York: Basic Books.

Michelman, F. 1969: On protecting the poor through the Fourteenth Amendment. *Harvard Law Review*, 83, 7.

Pierson, C. 1991: *Beyond the Welfare State*. University Park, Pa.: Pennsylvania University Press.

Posner, R. 1986: *Economic Analysis of Law*. Boston: Little, Brown & Co., 3rd edn.

Rawls, J. 1971: *A Theory of Justice*. Cambridge: Harvard University Press.

Walzer, M. 1983: *Spheres of Justice*. New York: Basic Books.

Wolfe, A. 1989: *Whose Keeper? Social science and moral obligation*. Berkeley: University of California Press.

Legal scholarship

EDWARD L. RUBIN

The contours of legal scholarship

Most academic disciplines suffer from some uncertainty about their boundaries, but legal scholarship, like several others, experiences basic problems with its core identity. The difficulty arises from the diffuse nature of both its topic and its methodology. The legal system is deeply intertwined with the history, politics, and sociology of any given era, while its theoretical analysis merges with more general issues of philosophy. Thus, scholars working in other disciplines will often deal with the law at length, and those aspiring to comprehensive treatments of society or moral systems are compelled to do so. Of course, both the social sciences and the humanities also overlap among themselves, but most are distinguished by fairly well-defined methodologies. Legal scholarship, in contrast, continually debates its methodology, with different groups of scholars advancing such divergent claims that there often seems to be no common ground. There is thus a serious question whether legal scholarship constitutes a discipline at all, or whether it is simply the body of work produced by university professors who teach in programs that prepare their students for careers in law.

In fact, legal scholarship possesses both a distinctive subject matter and a distinctive methodology, although these are more frequently assumed than invoked by scholars working in the field. The subject matter can be summarized as an internal, as opposed to an external view of law. Historians, political scientists, and sociologists treat the law as one component of a social institution, to be studied for the ideas it embodies and the effects it produces. Legal scholars approach law as a set of significant normative statements that are intended to comprise a meaningful system. As such, its provisions should be described in detail and evaluated according to their moral or social value. This is a question of purpose, not of methodology, and does not imply anything about the use of other disciplines; it simply means that any methodologies or disciplines that are deployed will be devoted to an inquiry into the internal structure and meaning of the legal system. Similarly, it is a question of focus, not commitment or belief; several recent movements in legal scholarship, most notably critical legal studies, deconstruction and postmodernism challenge the meaningfulness of the legal system. But they remain within the field because this challenge is their central theme, and is leveled at other legal scholars who maintain the opposite position. As a contrasting example, judicial opinion studies, now coming back into vogue as a result of positive political theory, begin from the premise that the legal system has no inherent meaning, that it is a set of beliefs or strategies without any internal relation. Consequently, these studies are generally recognized as political science about law, not legal scholarship.

Since legal scholars, as opposed to historians of law, tend to write about their own legal system, they often adopt an internal perspective without arguing for their choice or even indicating conscious awareness of it. This might suggest that their approach embodies nothing more than intellectual naivety. But as Alfred Schutz (1962, pp. 3–66) and others have suggested, an internal perspective allows the observer to actively participate in the social system, or more precisely, in the social practice being studied. It thus provides a separate mode of understanding that cannot be duplicated by external observation. The social scientist who views institutions from outside obtains insights into their causes and effects, but only inadequately understands the meaning that the institution possesses for its members. Because such meanings are components of a comprehensive lifeworld, as complex as that of an observer's, they cannot be fully understood unless the observer participates on the same terms as the members (Dworkin, 1986, pp. 13–15; Post, 1992).

The point can be illustrated by considering scholarship about a legal system other than our own. A historian of ancient China might discuss the differences between the Confucian and the legalist schools or the social effects of Confucian ascendancy in some detail. All this would remain securely within the realm of historical scholarship. The legal scholar's approach would be to analyze how someone could effectively pursue a lawsuit in ancient China, or why particular legal doctrines were ineffective ways of achieving either contingent social goals or general moral principles. Such scholarship is relatively rare in the West, precisely because we are external with respect to ancient China, but immersed within our own society. Consequently, we are less motivated to understand ancient Chinese law at such high levels of detail, or to engage in normative debates about its desirability.

To define the ambit of legal scholarship in this fashion places several significant sub-disciplines, such as legal history, legal sociology, and legal anthropology outside its bounds. Epistemologically, this is probably the correct result, since these sub-disciplines tend to derive their methodology from the non-legal component of the diad. A more sociological approach would regard these sub-disciplines as occupying an intermediate position, since that is the way that legal historians or legal sociologists and anthropologists regard themselves and are regarded by their colleagues. There is little clarification to be gained by choosing between these alternatives. The important point is that the internal perspective on law identifies the central subject matter of legal scholarship, the area of inquiry that comprises its unique preserve. Interdisciplinary efforts can then be located in a variety of ways without affecting the basic understanding of the field.

Having identified the subject matter of legal scholarship, it is now possible to catalogue its methodologies. In essence, there are three, most characteristically associated with treatises, analytic or argumentative writing and jurisprudence. This may seem to be a rather polyglot list; in fact, its elements are the commonly recognized forms of a systematic division of legal scholarship among descriptive work, prescriptive work, meta-description and meta-prescription.

The categories of description and prescription are defined by Hume's familiar distinction between "is" and "ought." Strong claims about the significance of this distinction have gone out of fashion with the decline of legal positivism. Many philosophers no longer find the is–ought dichotomy particularly meaningful and almost all now recognize it is not the golden key to understanding. But it remains a working principle for organizing research and analysis in a variety of fields, including public policy, political science, and sociology, as well as law. Some writers, like Habermas, assert that descriptive (or objectivating) and prescriptive (or norm-conformative) statements represent different modes of social action, each with their own characteristic validity claims (Habermas, 1981). But even if one does not want to go that far, the distinction still holds as part of the sociology of knowledge, and thus serves to categorize the scholarship of many academic fields.

Descriptive scholarship

Descriptive scholarship in law, most commonly associated with the treatise, involves an internal account of the legal rules that govern a particular subject matter. The individual subjects are defined by the legal system itself, being used on a daily basis of judges, attorneys, legislators, administrators, and other active participants. They include common-law subjects such as contract as well as more specialized, legislatively created ones such as environmental law. Within each subject, the description may be either comprehensive or particularized. Comprehensive treatments are book-length, almost by necessity, and are generally characterized as treatises. More particularized treatments can be book-length as well, given the ever-increasing complexity of the legal system, and while they might more logically be called monographs, the term treatise applies to them as well. In addition, there are many descriptions of specific doctrines, or sub-areas that are presented in article-length treatments.

The internal quality of these descriptions is displayed most notably in their doctrinal focus. They present the field as a coherent body of rules whose inter-relationships are sufficiently precise to resolve a range of pragmatic issues. The treatise writer's task is to organize the rules in a systematic structure, identify the areas where one rule seems to contradict the other, and define the boundaries between them. The reader of a treatise, whether from inside or outside the society whose law is described, will learn how that society carries out activities and resolves disputes in a specific area.

Most of the descriptive work in legal scholarship is not purely descriptive, but contains at least a sprinkling of prescriptive or normative statements. Such statements can be based on the author's particular views, but the most common ones reflect a general preference for the coherence of law. The treatise or article writer, having identified an area where the meaning of a rule is unclear, or where two rules conflict, will recommend that the uncertainty be resolved. The proposed resolution will generally be one that renders the law more coherent, either by resolving an internal uncertainty or by making an outmoded or idiosyncratic legal rule conform to the principles that inform the field as a whole. Wide-ranging legal reform efforts, including the codification of commercial law and the American Law Institute's Restatements of the Law, have been spawned by this approach.

Quite often, the treatise-writer's preference for coherence reflects a genuine political or normative position. But this preference also appears to be generated by the methodology of descriptive scholarship; since an internal description only makes sense if the system of rules possesses coherence, a scholar working in this mode will naturally tend to favor changes in the law that increase that coherence. To say that these scholars are trying to ensure the continued vitality of their own enterprise ascribes to them both an overly cynical instrumentalism about the purpose of a legal treatise and an unrealistic naivety about its potential influence on legal actors. More likely, because the treatise writer's enterprise is premised on the law's coherence, the recommendation that this coherence be increased does not strike the author as a normative position at all, but simply an application of the law's inherent logic.

Descriptive work was once the dominant form of ordinary legal scholarship, and the comprehensive treatise was regarded as the apogee of scholarly attainment. Its appeal derived from the prevailing theories of law, originally natural law, later legal formalism. If the law was an embodiment of necessary moral principles or of socially embedded formal ones, then an accurate, well-organized description would not only provide the information necessary for ordinary transactions, but also elucidate those underlying principles (Simpson, 1981). There is nothing naive about this approach; in fact, it remains the methodology of physical science, where description is our means of perceiving what we call the laws of nature.

In legal scholarship, descriptive work declined during the twentieth century because a new approach to law developed. Since the legal realist movement, most scholars have been convinced that law is a social instrumentality, a collection of strategies and compromises that have developed over time in response to changing circumstances. It possesses meaning, and generally forms a system, but it is a system whose components are derived from social policy, not from either a universal moral order or the collective wisdom of the ages. This policy-oriented approach suggests that the level of coherence in any given area of law is too low to support the treatise writer's instinctive commitment to that norm. More importantly, it means that description can no longer unlock the legal system's animating principles; it merely provides necessary information to those who act within that system.

Despite its decline, however, descriptive work remains an important element in legal scholarship. Prevailing views about the contours and structure of entire legal subjects, as well as insights into the analysis of specific legal issues, are regularly

565

derived from scholarship of this nature. Comparative law is frequently descriptive, since it derives much of its value from the accurate presentation of contrasting legal rules. At its best, descriptive work can illuminate the structure of an entire subject or clarify a previously disorganized subject with genuinely transformative effect.

Prescriptive scholarship

The second major form of ordinary legal scholarship is prescription; its purpose is not to describe existing law, but to frame recommendations for the law's improvement. In order to be comprehensible, such scholarship must be explicit about the features that descriptive scholarship usually leaves unspecified – the intended audience and the normative basis of the recommendation. All scholarship must have an audience, of course, but descriptive scholarship can simply be addressed to "anyone who is interested." Similarly, all scholarship has some normative basis, but the norms underlying descriptive scholarship, such as the value of knowledge, are sufficiently general that they are only of concern from a philosophical perspective. Prescriptive scholarship, in contrast, is addressed to a particular audience and frames recommendations based upon specific, often controversial norms.

Since legal scholarship in general is characterized by its internal approach to law, prescriptive legal scholarship is addressed to those who generally adopt such a perspective, that is, those who think and act within the legal system. One obvious audience, albeit somewhat circular in its effect, consists of other legal scholars; prescriptions for this audience would typically involve criticisms of existing scholarship or recommendations for future work. A second audience is the judiciary. Judges are expected to follow legal doctrine, they view themselves to be doing so, and generally couch their decisions in doctrinal terms. Consequently, prescriptions addressed to judges generally focus on doctrinal law: how to follow or distinguish precedents, how to interpret statutes, how to incorporate social policy considerations. The classic format is to present the decision in a recent case and then offer a critique that is structured as a prescription for reaching a better decision or writing a better opinion to support the decision that was reached. This technique is often extended to entire lines of decisions, while the recommended basis for decision ranges widely across different disciplines and non-doctrinal arguments. But the essence of this scholarship continues to be a recommendation to a judicial decision maker.

Still another audience to whom prescriptive scholarship can be addressed are legislators and administrators. Some administrators function like judges, in the sense that they interpret a pre-existing source of law – most typically a statute, but sometimes a regulation or judicial decision. Scholarship addressed to them tends to resemble scholarship addressed to the judiciary, although the broader discretion that such administrators are afforded tends to emphasize social policy at the expense of doctrine. Other administrators, and all legislators, are primarily lawmakers. When addressing them, the scholar critiques an existing law or proposes a new one. Since legislation is not expected to conform to prior law, the prescriptions are generally not based on doctrinal arguments but on considerations of social policy or public morality. Scholarship of this sort is most distinctive when it concludes with proposed statutory language, but much other scholarship falls within this category. At its boundaries, of course, it merges into scholarship addressed to law-interpreters as inevitably as the underlying legal actions overlap.

Finally, internal prescriptions about law can be addressed to practicing attorneys, that is, attorneys representing clients. This body of scholarship, generally known as professional responsibility or legal ethics, concerns the lawyer's obligation to restrain herself from engaging in certain behaviors despite the fact that those behaviors are legally permissible. The question, of course, has institutional ramifications, involving bar associations, court rules and eligibility for public appointments, but the central concern is to prescribe ethical, or non-legal modes of conduct. Other prescriptions that can be addressed to lawyers are generally regarded as "skills" issues. Prescriptive discussions of substantive law that are directed toward practicing attorneys – ranging from "contract drafting in the European community" to "defending the drunk driver" – fall within this category. There is a great deal written in this mode, but it is rarely regarded as true legal scholarship.

Prescription not only implies an audience, but also depends upon an identifiable normative position. While description can rely upon the ambient and unspoken norms of the prevailing legal or academic culture, one cannot frame recommendations for legal actors without some sense of the purpose that the recommendation is intended to achieve. In some cases, legal scholars base their prescriptions on the same desire for legal coherence that contributes a prescriptive element to otherwise descriptive treatises; the argument is that the judge should have decided a case differently because the alternative decision would be more consistent with existing law. More often, however, the scholar argues that a different decision would be more consonant with social policy. There has been a notable dispersion of the normative systems that animate prescriptive scholarship in recent years. Divergent political views, which, except for Marxism, were relatively rare, have now become quite prevalent in the academy. Much contemporary scholarship, including critical legal studies, feminist legal theory, deconstruction, postmodernism and critical race theory now derives from normative positions lying well outside of mainstream politics. The result, not surprisingly, has been an increasing self-awareness among scholars of their normative commitments, and an explicit debate about the character and consequences of various positions.

Some analyses of discourse distinguish interpretive statements from descriptive or prescriptive ones, with interpretation being viewed as the effort to discern the meaning of the subject matter. In legal scholarship, such efforts are associated with the law and literature movement. The difficulty this movement has encountered is that law itself is often an interpretive enterprise; thus, descriptive and prescriptive treatments of a judicial decision necessarily incorporate the interpretive element that is intrinsic to the judge's methodology. As a result, law and literature has generally contributed a sensibility to legal scholarship, rather than a distinctive category of analysis.

567

One of the most striking developments in modern legal scholarship is the predominance of the prescriptive, policy-oriented voice. The modal law review article is now distinctly prescriptive, and the prescriptive monograph has replaced the treatise at the acme of the academic hierarchy. This development is a natural consequence of our changing theories about law. Law is now viewed largely as an instrument of social policy, rather than as a system of inherently and logically connected rules. From this perspective, voluminous descriptions, leavened with some scattered recommendations based upon an unexamined norm, are far less nourishing than they originally seemed. Instead, legal scholars have become engaged in the social policy debate, recommending changes in the law to produce the social results they deem desirable (Cotterrell, 1992).

Given this new, social policy orientation, however, it is equally striking that legal scholarship continues to be centered on judicial decision makers, just as it was when the descriptive voice predominated. The shift to policy-oriented scholarship has not been accompanied by a shift in audience to the leading policy-makers of the modern state, namely the legislative and the executive. Even the new methodologies of law and economics or critical legal studies have tended to focus on the efficiency and incoherence, respectively, of judicial decisions. One reason for this may be traditionalism; addressing judges preserves the continuity of current legal scholarship with the scholarship of the common-law era, when judges were the dominant legal decision makers. A deeper reason is that prescriptions advanced by academics seem to make sense only when addressed to a rational decision maker, that is, a decision maker who will listen to reasoned argument. Our age-old belief is that judges are decision makers of that sort; the notion that legislators and administrators are similarly rational would seem risible in any era.

Several consequences have flowed from prescriptive scholarship's continued tendency to address itself to the judiciary. The first is that a great deal of legal scholarship continues to analyze legal issues in the same terms that judges do, deploying the same sorts of legal arguments and invoking social policy considerations to the same extent. This phenomenon, which may be called the unity of discourse between scholars and judges (Rubin, 1988), has the virtue of preserving a relatively consistent legal culture. Its disadvantage is that the analysis of statutes, regulations, and administrative implementation mechanisms has been underemphasized. In addition, the unity of discourse between scholars and judges precludes extensive incorporation of social science into legal scholarship and limits interdisciplinary efforts to the modicum of social science research that the judicial process is capable of absorbing (Friedman, 1986).

While prescriptive scholarship suffers from some serious limitations, one must recognize that it is neither as idiosyncratic or as artificial as a naive distinction between description and prescription might suggest. To begin with, there is a substantial amount of descriptive material in most full-length prescriptive articles and in almost all prescriptive monographs. In order to critique a legal action or propose a new one, it is generally necessary to describe the existing state of the law. Thus, judges, administrators, scholars and students regularly consult prescriptive books and articles in the same way that they consult legal treatises.

Moreover, given that the legal system is a dynamic institution, prescriptive analysis will often be more informative than pure description; it is tomorrow's persuasive argument that both lawyers and decision makers may want to know. To be sure, the author of a particular piece may possess idiosyncratic norms that preclude the adoption of his position, but in the process of advancing that position he is likely to canvass other arguments based on more generally accepted norms.

This leads to a more general point about the purpose of prescriptive scholarship. Since this scholarship is addressed to a particular type of decision maker, there is a tendency to assume that its purpose is to persuade, and that the failure to do so – which is the usual result – indicates the futility of the entire enterprise. But, as stated above, the internal perspective of legal scholarship allows the scholar to achieve a mode of understanding that is only possible through participation, and prescriptive scholarship is part of that participatory process. Its premiss is that engagement in the field's normative debates reveals the meaning of the subject matter. External descriptions, and even internal descriptions that stand apart from the normative debate, cannot duplicate the understanding which prescriptive scholarship achieves by addressing recommendations to legal decision makers. This amphibious quality of prescriptive scholarship, as both a recommendation and an elucidation, may seem paradoxical, but the law itself is a normative construct and thus presents a particularly strong case for the idea that normative engagement can serve as a mode of understanding.

The link between normative discourse and understanding helps to explain the status of skills-oriented writing in the academy. This writing is as prescriptive as any other – it tells practicing lawyers how to act effectively – but since it is narrowly strategic, the general view is that it does not contribute to our understanding of law's position in society, or of society in general. It is understanding, not direct influence on legal actors, that constitutes the primary purpose of prescriptive scholarship.

Jurisprudence

Jurisprudence is generally recognized as a separate category of legal scholarship, but the nature of its separate identity is far from clear. It is sometimes described as the philosophy of law; this is probably correct, and would be useful if we only knew the precise meaning of the term "philosophy." Jurisprudence is also described as the theory of law, but since everyone aspires to be theoretical these days, relying on this definition quickly leads to the notion that there is a jurisprudence of contracts, a jurisprudence of consideration, and finally a jurisprudence of the pre-existing duty rule, at which point one has made complete hash of the word.

While there is undoubtedly something "philosophical" about jurisprudence, it is distinguished from philosophy by being part of legal scholarship. This means that jurisprudence, like legal scholarship in general, adopts an internal approach to the legal system. It discusses the general structure or the underlying morality of the legal system from the perspective of that system and aspires to capture the meaning

569

that the legal system possesses for its participants. Thus, Hume is a philosopher, not a jurisprude, because he is concerned with the nature of society and the state; law appears in Hume's work as one component of these larger structures and is viewed from the perspective of the state in general. Kelsen, in contrast, is a jurisprude. While his approach is consistent with Hume's, he focusses on the legal system itself and he derives his insights from the examination of that system rather than a general analysis of the state.

If jurisprudence is distinguished from philosophy by its internal approach to law, it is distinguished from ordinary descriptive and prescriptive legal scholarship by its meta-descriptive character. This somewhat formidable prefix is simply intended to indicate that jurisprudential writing rises above or cuts across the ordinary categories into which law is divided by the active participants in the field. Practicing lawyers, judges, legislators, and administrators make use of standard categories such as contract, torts, and crimes; a work of ordinary legal scholarship defines its scope of concern by reference to these same categories. The fact that a work compares the rules that prevail in several categories, or analyzes the inevitable overlaps between them, would not alter this characterization. Thus an article suggesting that tort concepts should be used to measure damages in contract cases, or that the boundary between contracts and corporations is being effaced by modern business practices, does not thereby become a work of jurisprudence. This term, as it is commonly used, refers to discussions of the law that do not depend upon these standard categorizations to define their ambit or their mission.

Some jurisprudential writing is immediately recognizable by its generality. H. L. A. Hart's *Concept of Law* (1961), for example, discusses the legal system in its totality, rarely making reference to the categories of law that are used for everyday purposes by the participants in the system. But Hart and Honoré's *Causation in the Law* (1985) is also recognized as a work of jurisprudence, although it is quite specific and makes constant reference to standard categories. It would be difficult to describe this book as more "general" than a criminal law treatise. While Hart and Honoré also discuss tort and contract, they ignore many topics, such as sentencing, the exclusionary rule, and the indictment process, that would be included in the treatise. What renders *Causation in the Law* a work of jurisprudence is that it cuts across the standard categories, defining its own frame of reference rather than operating within existing ones.

The widely held belief that the interdisciplinary character of a work renders it jurisprudential (Stone, 1964, p. 16) no longer seems to reflect common usage, if indeed it ever did. With the decline of the formalist faith in law as an autonomous discipline possessing its own internal logic, and the increasing social policy orientation of both law and legal scholarship, much ordinary legal scholarship is heavily interdisciplinary. It is common these days, on opening any law journal, to find a corporate law article that employs economic analysis, an administrative law article that relies on political science or a civil rights article that invokes sociological research. Thus, a more accurate statement would be that the interdisciplinary character of a work is a separate, independent variable from its jurisprudential character. Of course, many works that are recognized as jurisprudence are also highly interdisciplinary, and there remain numerous works of ordinary scholarship that do not venture beyond legal doctrine. But the other combinations exist as well. The corporations article that employs economic analysis is still regarded as ordinary scholarship, not jurisprudence; conversely, Fuller's *Morality of Law* (1969) contains relatively few references to non-legal philosophy for a work of its generality, but its jurisprudential character is clear.

There are, however, several fields that lie athwart the boundary between ordinary scholarship and jurisprudence. The most notable is probably constitutional law. This is a category used by practicing lawyers and other legal actors, but even relatively specific issues in the field tend to implicate basic questions about the nature of the individual or the state, and general discussions have a distinctly jurisprudential cast. Is Alexander Bickel's *The Least Dangerous Branch* (1962) a work of constitutional law, jurisprudence, or both? Linguistic clarity may favor the former choice, but, in truth, the value of categorization is quickly exhausted at this point. Indeed, extensive overlap between ordinary scholarship and jurisprudence is hardly surprising, since there are no organizational or sociological structures to police the boundary between the two. Both types of scholars are found on precisely the same faculties, with precisely the same training; in fact, they are often precisely the same people since many academics who begin their careers as specialists aspire to end them as jurisprudes.

Jurisprudence, like ordinary legal scholarship, can be either descriptive or prescriptive. The *Concept of Law* describes existing legal systems, while Finnis's *Natural Law and Natural Rights* (1980) or Roberto Unger's *False Necessity* (1987) offer recommendations for reordering the legal system. The distinction between the two approaches is less apparent in jurisprudence than it is in ordinary scholarship, since it does not appear to divide the field into works that are stylistically distinct. One reason may be that the distinction is itself a major issue in jurisprudential literature. Thus, descriptive works regularly argue against the meaningfulness of jurisprudential prescription, although not against the social policy prescriptions of ordinary scholarship. Prescriptive jurisprudence, on the other hand, often criticizes descriptive work for its positivistic focus.

While this debate tends to efface the categorization among jurisprudential works, it emphasizes the distinction between jurisprudence and philosophy. Because jurisprudence is legal scholarship, with an internal approach to law, its practitioners are concerned with the character of law itself – whether it is inherently normative or merely a means of implementing externally established choices. This debate is not particularly relevant to non-legal philosophers, who would be prepared to consider either characterization, and then judge the result by whatever conceptual or ethical system they employ.

References

Bickel, A. 1962: *The Least Dangerous Branch*. Indianapolis: Bobbs-Merrill Co.
Cotterrell, R. 1992: Law's community: legal theory and the image of legality. *Journal of Law and Society*, 19, 405–22.

Dworkin, R. 1986: *Law's Empire*. Cambridge, Mass. and London: Belknap Press.

Finnis, J. 1980: *Natural Law and Natural Rights*. Oxford: Clarendon Press.

Friedman, L. 1986: The law and society movement. *Stanford Law Review*, 38, 763–80.

Fuller, L. 1969: *The Morality of Law*. New Haven: Yale University Press, rev. edn.

Habermas, J. [1981] 1986: tr. J. Habermas, *The Theory of Communicative Action*. Boston: Beacon Press.

Hart, H. L. A. 1961: *The Concept of Law*. Oxford: Clarendon Press.

Hart, H. L. A. and Honoré, A. 1985: *Causation in the Law*. Oxford: Clarendon Press, 2nd edn.

Post, R. 1992: Legal scholarship and the practice of law. *University of Colorado Law Review*, 63, 615–25.

Rubin, E. 1988: The practice and discourse of legal scholarship. *Michigan Law Review*, 86, 1,835–1,905.

Schutz, A. 1962–6: *Collected Papers*. The Hague: M. Nijhoff.

Simpson, A. W. B. 1981: The rise and fall of the legal treatise: legal principles and the forms of legal literature. *University of Chicago Law Review*, 48, 632–79.

Stone 1964: *Legal Systems and Lawyers' Reasoning*. Stanford: Stanford University Press.

Unger, R. 1987: *False Necessity*. New York: Cambridge University Press.

Further reading

Useful symposia on legal scholarship may be found in *Journal of Legal Education*, 33 (1983), 403; *Michigan Law Review*, 89 (1991), 707; *Texas Law Review*, 69 (1991), 1,595; *Stanford Law Review*, 45 (1993), 1,525; *University of Colorado Law Review*, 63 (1992), 521; *Yale Law Review*, 90 (1981), 955.

41

Authority of law

VINCENT A. WELLMAN

In political philosophy and philosophy of law, the idea of authority presents a set of issues regarding the justification of government and the corresponding obligations of citizens, especially the obligation of citizens to obey the law. Law, it is said, claims authority (Green, 1990, p. 1; Raz, 1979, p. v). What is meant by this assertion is two things. Legal systems, to begin with, issue directives which aim to control the behavior of their subjects and, moreover, seek to secure compliance with those directives by sanctions and other forms of suasion. But, systems of law do more than just wield power. As they seek to control their subjects' behavior they claim that their control is justified or in some other way legitimate. Law assumes that its directives are binding and that, as Raz (1979, p. v) has phrased it, its subjects owe obedience and even allegiance to the system which governs them.

The forms and limits of authority

The idea of authority finds currency in a wide variety of contexts. Those who are expert in a field are said to be authorities about issues within their area of expertise. This context of authority is often described as *theoretical* authority, or authority about what to believe. Theoretical authority may be distinguished from *practical* authority, authority about what to do. In some contexts, both forms of authority are at work. Parents are standardly acknowledged to have authority over their children, and military commanders are held to have authority over their subordinates. The authority in such hierarchical relationships may be both theoretical and also practical. A parent will both instruct her children about the nature of the world and also lay down directives for their behavior.

Law's authority too takes various forms. Even legal positivists like H. L. A. Hart regard law as the source of duties on the part of those governed by each particular legal system (Hart, 1961, passim). Law is also held necessary to control the actions of individuals, lest our lives be reduced to strife and uncertainty. Sometimes the authority of law is at issue in the requirement that some questions be decided, one way or another, and some norms be established, without regard to the merit of competing alternatives. Without commonly observed norms of automobile driving, for example, traffic of any density would be impossible, and so traffic laws must be promulgated and enforced. In this context, it is less important which particular rules are chosen than that some rules be laid down and enforced. In other contexts, however, we may properly evaluate the particular rules which are made law. Laws segregating people according to racial or sexual characteristics cannot be accepted with the same easy lack of concern as can the laws which tell us to drive on the right, or the left side of the road.

Authority may also be differentiated along other lines as well. There are those who hold themselves out as authorities, though we may doubt their warrant. A self-promoting diet guru or wildly optimistic exponent of cold fusion may claim expertise, but from that bald claim of authority it, of course, does not follow that the claimant is properly so recognized. Similarly, one country may conquer another and set itself up to rule its new subjects, but the mere claim of authority to govern, even when backed by sufficient force, may not yield genuine authority. And, there are those who exercise *de facto* authority, who play a salient role in the lives of others because their influence and control is accepted as authoritative. But, we may withhold from these as well the appellation of legitimacy, and the idea of *legitimate* authority – as opposed to mere claims of authority or even *de facto* authority – raises interesting and subtle questions about law.

The justification of authority

The example of traffic laws shows that law's authority is clearly not just theoretical. Instead, most recent discussions have focussed on law's practical authority, (for example, Raz, 1986; Greenawalt, 1987; Green, 1988) and that focus raises questions about the justification of practical authority, and law's claims to such justification.

Someone who has practical authority (whether *de facto* or legitimate) exercises a measure of control over the activities of others. Systems of law lay down rules governing the others' behavior and back those rules with some force or sanction, and legal authority therefore clearly involves some notions of power. But authority is more than power. A kidnapper may exercise control over my child, but does not have authority over her. Uncontrolled gangs may dominate a town or even a country, but may, nonetheless, lack authority over the affected citizens. The idea of authority implies in addition some normative characteristics.

Consider first the case of theoretical authority. To say that Farnsworth is an authority on contract law is to credit Farnsworth with superior knowledge or understanding of his field. Further, Farnsworth's authority implies certain conclusions about what we should believe. Claims of theoretical authority sustain inferences along the following lines.

> X is an authority with regards to D, some domain of discourse.
> X says that p is true, and p is within D.
> Therefore, you should believe p.

At bottom, what is claimed about a theoretical authority is that her utterances are reliable within her area of expertise. If X really is an authority, what she says about her area is significantly more likely to be true. Therefore, your beliefs about D will more likely be true if you believe as does X. Thus, the issue presented by this inference is epistemic, and the justification for X's authority is derived from the likely truth of her claims.

But, the matter is different for practical authority. Consider the following inference, adapted from Raz (1986, p. 29).

X has authority.
X has decreed that you are to do A, some act.
Therefore, you ought to do A.

This inference offers the authoritative utterance as a reason for acting as the authority decrees. What justification can be offered for following the authority's dictates? One justification, that would parallel the claim for theoretical authority, would cite the authority's wisdom. Your actions, on this claim, will more likely be satisfactory if you act as the authority indicates.

A set of deep philosophical problems lurks behind this conception of practical authority. What kind of reason is the authoritative utterance, and how does it figure in our practical reasoning? Ordinarily in practical reasoning, we decide what to do after weighing the balance of reasons that are operative for us. And, if others seek to influence our reasoning, they will usually advance reasons which are relevant to our deliberations: they may point to facts about the world which will show us that our ends can be better served by some different plan of action, or they may seek to show us that our ends are different from what we had thought them to be. Law's claims of authority have two important characteristics which diverge from this standard picture of practical reasoning. First, the authoritative utterances are advanced as *content-independent* reasons (Hart, 1982, ch. 10). Second, those authoritative utterances are advanced as *pre-emptive* (Raz, 1986, pp. 42, 57–62) or *exclusionary* (Green, 1988, pp. 36–40) reasons. Raz (1986, p. 35) explains content-independence in this way:

> A reason is content-independent if there is no direct connection between the reason and the action for which it is a reason. The reason is in the apparently "extraneous" fact that someone in authority has said so, and within certain limits his saying so would be a reason for any number of actions, including (in typical cases) for contradictory ones. A certain authority may command me to leave the room or to stay in it. Either way, its command will be a reason.

There are other types of content-independent reasons for acting. Threats are one, and promises are another (Raz, 1986, pp. 35–7; Green, 1988, pp. 40–1). If I have promised to meet with a student at a particular time, the fact that I have committed myself operates as a reason for me to act in that way, independent of my desire (or unwillingness) to meet with that student. These kinds of speech-acts create reasons for one, or both, of the parties involved because of some aspect of their relationship, not because the speaker has advanced reasons which connect directly with the action at issue. Authority operates along similar lines. No facts are adduced for our practical deliberations, except that the authority has decreed that we are to act in some way, and none of our ends are invoked, except that we should obey the authority.

Law's claims of authority also differ from other reasons by virtue of their claim to preclude some of the agent's other reasons. A legal norm is advanced as demanding our obedience, without regard to whatever reasons we may have for acting to the contrary. Indeed, law is standardly understood to serve us, at least in part, by virtue of the fact that it replaces the self-interested calculations of individuals with other norms of behavior, thereby allowing us to live together in society. Therefore, law's decrees, if they are to function as authoritative, must, in some way, supplant the individual citizen's deliberation about how to act.

Some have described this facet of practical authority as involving a "surrender of judgment" whereby the agent takes the authority's "will instead of his own as a guide to action and so to take it in place of any deliberation or reasoning of his own" (Hart, 1982, p. 253). This metaphor is fraught with peril, and sometimes authority has been rejected altogether as illegitimate because its claim to replace the will or reason of its subjects is held incompatible with the autonomy or the reason of the individual (Wolff, 1970, passim). This idea has been framed in terms of "paradoxes of authority" (Raz, 1978, pp. 3–5). If you act as the authority directs because its directives converge on the result of your independent deliberations, then you are not really *obeying* the authority; conversely, if you are truly obedient, then you act as the authority decrees, even though it diverges from your own independent deliberations.

One response to this line of reasoning would be to conclude that law lacks genuine authority and can be said at most to have *de facto* authority. A more satisfying response has been advanced by Raz (1986) and also by Green (1988), involving the nature of practical reasoning. These responses are substantially the same, but Green's discussion, relying on Raz's (1975, pp. 37ff) distinction between *first-* and *second-order* reasons, is the more straightforward.

Practical reasoning involves ordinary reasons for acting – beliefs, desires, needs and interests – and in simple deliberations we balance these factors against other factors of the same sort. Call these factors first-order reasons for acting. In addition to these sorts of reasons, we also respond to other, second-order reasons, which are weighed for and against our acting on various first-order reasons. Consider, for example, a professor and a student who are sexually attracted to one another. Notwithstanding the attraction, the professor may decide to avoid involvement with the student because he regards faculty–student relationships as inappropriate. The professor's attraction to the student would be, on this distinction, a first-order reason for acting, but his actions would result instead from his second-order reasons about the propriety of acting, in those circumstances, on such first-order reasons. The conflict between the second-order and the first-order reasons is not resolved because the former outweighs the latter . . . Rather, [the second-order reason] excludes action taken on the first-order balance of reasons alone and is thus an *exclusionary* reason. Such reasons exclude those they defeat by kind, not weight. (*Green, 1988, p. 38, footnote omitted, emphasis in the original*)

Practical authority, in general, and legal authority, more particularly, can be understood as offering second-order, exclusionary reasons for acting in the way decreed by authority. Suppose the professor's college has promulgated a rule against student–faculty liaisons, or suppose that the professor's dean has recognized the smoldering passions and has directed him to avoid involvement. Those directives, if authoritative, would function by excluding certain considerations – his sexual attraction to the student, or perhaps his belief that the student too desires an affair – from the professor's practical deliberations. So, too, for the law. Its directives, if authoritative, would function by excluding certain first-order reasons from the deliberations of those subject to the legal system; the citizens would act because the law directs it, even though their own individual interests might lead them to break the law.

This answer defuses the "paradoxes" of authority. Second-order exclusionary reasons are, on this answer, a standard part of practical reasoning, and are particularly common to reasoning with regard to systems of law. Appeal to such exclusionary reasons can be found in various forms of reasoning by reference to rules, or by reference to precedent. Moreover, while exclusionary reasons preclude appeal in a particular deliberation to first-order reasons, it is still cogent to question the satisfactoriness of such second-order reasons. One might, for example, challenge the coherence of one second-order reason with other such reasons, or argue that decisions according to such exclusionary reasons too often result in decisions that are ill advised. So, the use of second-order reasons is incompatible with neither reason nor autonomy.

Raz's picture of practical reasoning highlights the problem of authority's justification. Authoritative utterances are understood, on this picture, as reasons which exclude other of the agent's reasons for acting. Accepting some person or institution as authoritative means that we accept their reasons as excluding some of our own first-order reasons. Why should we regard the putative authority's decrees as authoritative? What could justify the claim of authority, understood along these lines?

Raz (1986) argues for the following picture of the justification of authority, which he calls *the normal justification thesis.*

the normal way to establish that a person has authority over another person involves showing that the alleged subject is likely better to comply with reasons which apply to him (other than the alleged authoritative directives) if he accepts the directives of the alleged authority as authoritatively binding and tries to follow them, rather than by trying to follow the reasons which apply to him directly. (*Raz, 1986, p. 53*)

This thesis parallels the justification for theoretical authority that was offered earlier: following the authority's directives will more likely lead you to do what it is that you really want to do than if you try to reason it out for yourself.

The parallel with theoretical authority is instructive in other ways as well. Any practical authority's claim of justification must be limited, as are any theoretical authority's claim of reliability, to distinct domains over which the claim could be supported. But applying this notion of justification leads quickly to the conclusion that law lacks the authority that it claims for itself. Law claims authority generally. It demands that all its subjects obey all its directives, not just those which are likely to be wise. Law's claim of authority will therefore outrun any reasonably persuasive claim of its justification. To begin with, only just governments, with well-reasoned legal systems, could claim that obeying the norms of law will more likely lead its citizens to act in ways that will fulfill their practical deliberations than they would achieve by reasoning for themselves about how to act. And, even if the government is just and the legal system well reasoned, it is implausible that the system's decrees will, in fact, satisfy the criteria of normal justification for *each* citizen in *every* arena that is regulated by law. This line of reasoning, in sum, denies law's claims of authority.

Why authority?

The negative conclusions just reached stand in contrast to a line of inquiry that connects authority with an obligation to obey. Among the reasons for thinking about law's authority, the most pressing reasons have arisen out of debates about the existence of a general obligation to obey the law.

Traditional arguments that we are generally obligated to obey the law have clustered into two families. One family of arguments maintains that we have such an obligation because we have, in some meaningful sense, promised to obey our community's laws. Some versions of this argument emphasize a social contract between the citizen and the state, and others use some notion of an implied agreement. Whatever the particulars, these arguments share a common feature: the moral obligation to obey the law is an application of a more general moral obligation to fulfill our promises. The other family of arguments derives an obligation to obey from the fact that one receives benefits from one's state or community. On some versions, the purported benefits are the security and comfort we enjoy because our lives are governed by the law-making and law-enforcing apparatus of the state. Other versions emphasize the advantages of being part of a community – living among other persons, making it possible to be sociable and involved, rather than isolated atomistic individuals. For this family of arguments, the fact that we have received and retained the benefits of our society generates an obligation to obey the law: either we are obligated to repay the society for the benefits we have received or we are obligated to bear our share of the burdens of sustaining community life.

Both the promise-based and the benefit-based arguments can be seen to depend on some version of the following hypothetical.

If X performs an action A in circumstances $C1$, $C2$, $C3$, . . . , Cn then X has an obligation to obey the law.

The promise-based arguments depend on X's promising to obey the law, which promise is expressly or impliedly made in those types of circumstances that make us obligated to live up to our promises. If such facts obtain, then X is obligated to obey the law. Benefit-based arguments, on the other hand, depend on X's voluntarily receiving benefits in those circumstances which give rise to an obligation either of restitution or else of burden-sharing.

However, this schema highlights the now-standardly recognized inadequacies of both families of argument. Such arguments are advanced to show that there is a general moral obligation to obey the law, and they could fulfill that ambition only if, for every X, X has, in fact, performed the appropriate act in the required circumstances. But, it is implausible that such would be true for every agent. For example, not everyone has, in fact, promised to obey the law, and some of those who have so promised have done so in circumstances that defeat the obligation, like those of fraud or duress. It is, of course, possible to expand the ways in which the required action or the required circumstances are specified, so that those conditions are true of more agents. Thus, it could be asserted that citizens have impliedly promised to obey their government's laws because they have continued to reside within its jurisdiction; continued residence is thus treated as tantamount to promising to obey the applicable laws. The more the specifications are relaxed, however, the less compelling it is that acting in that fashion in those circumstances gives rise to an obligation to obey the laws. Suppose the citizens continue to reside, but on a daily basis explicitly disaffirm their commitment to obey their government's laws. They cannot easily be said to have promised to obey, and hence would seem to be beyond any promise-based obligation to obey.

The authority of law, however, might seem to finesse this problem of generality. In asking about law's authority, we ask about the attributes of the state or its legal system, rather than the characteristics of the governed, and one attribute of authority is held to be a correlative obligation to obey. "Part of what 'authority' means is that those subject to it are obligated to obey" (Pitkin, 1966, p. 40). If authority implies an obligation to obey, then a general obligation of fidelity to law can be established, without reference to the particular circumstances of each agent, by demonstrating law's authority. Sometimes this idea is expressed in terms of the language of rights. "Authority is the right to command, and correlatively, the right to be obeyed" (Wolff, 1970, p. 4). Or, "authority is a regular right to be obeyed in a domain of decisions" (Anscombe, 1978, p. 3).

Kent Greenawalt has argued cogently that authority does not, by itself, imply an obligation to obey. The idea of legitimate political authority, Greenawalt (1987, pp. 50–1) contends, is associated with at least seven components:

1. Persons with political authority are justified in issuing certain kinds of directives to those they govern.
2. They are justified in using force to induce compliance with these directives.
3. Other persons in the society are not warranted in issuing the kinds of directives appropriate for political authority, and they also lack the right to employ coercive force on behalf of their wishes.
4. The governed should pay attention to the directives of the persons with authority.
5. The governed should not interfere with the exercise of force by those with authority.
6. The governed should co-operate with enforcement efforts.
7. The governed should obey the directives of those with authority.

By itself, he maintains, the idea of political authority implies only the first few of these characteristics: the justification of those with authority to act in certain ways (numbers 1 and 2), and perhaps a corresponding lack of justification on the part of others to act in similar or competing ways (number 3). Other claims, especially those about a citizen's duty to cooperate or to obey (numbers 6 and 7), can be derived only with the addition of further premises, most plausibly those about "the importance of government and the requirements of effective government and . . . the implication of those premises for individual duties" (Greenawalt, 1987, p. 56).

A similar conclusion has been reached by Ladenson (1980, pp. 139–41) using the language of rights. He argues that a government has a "justification right" to issue certain kinds of directives, and to use force to try to secure compliance with those directives. But, a justification right is not a claim right; where the latter would imply a corresponding duty to obey on the part of the governed, a state's justification right carries no such implication. Instead, the state's justification right provides only a rebuttal to the claim that it is doing something morally wrong in attempting to govern.

The claims of Greenawalt and Ladenson can be generalized beyond the question of an obligation to obey authority. Ascribing authority to a state implies its justification to act in certain ways. The legal system has *de facto* authority insofar as those subject to it accept its claims of justification. But that leaves open the question: what justification really obtains for the legal system's claims of authority? Greenawalt's argument implies that different justification must be provided for different aspects of the legal system's claims of authority.

The justification for the state or the legal system acting as political authority, by issuing directives and seeking to enforce them, will plausibly take the familiar Hobbesian form. Some such directives are necessary, lest social life degenerate into chaos, and some enforcement of the directives will be necessary, so long as the subjects are likely to act on the strength of their own desires.

The justification for taking the legal system's decrees as exclusionary reasons will therefore derive from the value of precluding the members of a community from deciding what to do entirely on the strength of their own first-order deliberations. Understood in this way, the justification reveals an important exception.

Suppose a country conquers its neighbor, and proceeds to install its own legal system in the place of the previously existing and legitimate regime. Does the Hobbesian argument compel the conclusion that the usurper has genuine authority? After all, it might be observed, the usurper is now fulfilling the role of political authority by issuing, and enforcing, directives that seek to preclude the members of the now-conquered society from deciding through their own individual deliberations, how to act. The short resolution of this difficulty is to recall the source of the Hobbesian justification for the state: without the state, life would be disastrous. But that justification does not hold for the usurper, for, without the usurper the previous regime would still be in power and its directives would suffice to govern. (Although the usurper's legal system would lack authority as a whole, some of its directives may legitimately claim authority to the extent that they duplicate the prior regime's directives on the same issues.)

In sum, law's decrees are authoritative to the extent that their status as exclusionary reasons can be justified. By itself, this justification does not imply a general obligation to obey those directives; in particular, the citizenry is free, on this argument, to disobey in ways and to an extent that does not challenge the efficacy of the regime. A second point follows as well. Law's authority is sometimes held to be exclusive (Greenawalt, 1987, p. 56, number 3 above) or monopolistic (Ladenson, 1980, p. 138). However, it can be seen that the justification for the authority of a legal system does not preclude a comparable justification for other authority within the same society, nor does it preclude the use of force by other authority to enforce compliance with its directive. Law's authority, in other words, does not by itself require law's monopoly. This idea should be obvious enough to those familiar with the history, in various legal systems, of joint secular and religious authority and jurisdiction. Both secular and ecclesiastical courts can promulgate and enforce norms, and each can have legitimate authority. By extension, other institutions in a given society can also exercise political authority as well. To be sure, each authority will be less effective to the extent that the limits of each authority's proper sphere are not clearly drawn, or where there is some conflict between the different attempts to govern. But, the idea of authority does not inherently require that the power to make or enforce directives be reserved exclusively to a single set of political authorities.

Conclusion

The results reached here are essentially negative. Law claims authority, but such claims must be viewed with substantial skepticism. At most, law's authority can be understood as a justification for the legal system to act in certain characteristic ways, by issuing directives and seeking to enforce them. But a legal system's claim on the obedience or allegiance of its subjects stands ever in need of justification, depending on the character and reach of its directives and the nature of its enforcement.

Bibliography

Anscombe, E. G. 1978: On the authority of the state. *Ratio*, 20, 1.

Flathman, R. E. 1972: *Political Obligation*.

Green, L. 1988: *The Authority of the State*. Oxford: Clarendon Press.

Greenawalt, R. K. 1987: *Conflicts of Law and Morality*. New York: Oxford University Press.

Hart, H. L. A. 1961: *The Concept of Law*. Oxford: Clarendon Press.

—— 1982: *Essays on Bentham*. Oxford: Clarendon Press.

Ladenson, 1980: In defense of a Hobbesian conception of law. *Philosophy and Public Affairs*, 9 (winter), 134.

Pitkin, H. 1966: Obligation and consent – II. *American Political Science Review*, 60, 39.

Raz, J. 1975: *Practical Reason and Norms*. London: Hutchinson.

—— 1979: *The Authority of Law: essays on law and morality*. Oxford: Clarendon Press.

—— 1986: *The Morality of Freedom*. Oxford: Clarendon Press.

Wolff, R. P. 1970: *In Defense of Anarchism*. New York: Harper & Row.

42

Analogical reasoning

JEFFERSON WHITE

Analogy and the principle of justice

Traditional understanding takes similarity recognition to be a central factor in legal reasoning and legal judgment: "The finding of similarity and difference is the key step in the legal process" (Levi, 1949, p. 2). Part of the reason for this is a requirement imposed by the principle of justice itself: "The rule of law . . . implies the precept that similar cases be treated similarly. Men could not regulate their actions . . . if this precept were not followed" (Rawls, 1971, p. 53).

The likeness in question for lawyers and judges is likeness with respect to applicability of a legal rule or principle exemplified in a precedent. A precedent derives its legal status from the fact that it was decided on the basis of legal rules and standards, and it is these to which courts appeal for justification of their decisions. Adjudication is thus a matter of applying prescribed legal rules and standards, but as everyone knows, such application can be problematic. One of the primary difficulties was stated long ago by Plato:

> Law can never issue an injunction binding on all which really embodies what is best for each; it cannot prescribe with perfect accuracy what is good and right for each member of the community at any one time . . . The variety of man's activities and the inevitable unsettlement attending all human experience make it impossible for any art whatsoever to issue unqualified rules holding good on all questions at all times. (Statesman, p. 1,063)

This understanding is reflected in a standard fixture of Anglo-American jurisprudence, namely, the doctrine of dictum.

> Where case law is considered, and there is no statute, [a judge] is not bound by the statement of the rule of law made by the prior judge even in the controlling case. The statement is mere dictum, and this means that the judge in the present case may find irrelevant the existence or absence of facts which prior judges thought important . . . It is not alone that he could not see the law through the eyes of another, for he could at least try to do so. It is rather that the doctrine of dictum forces him to make his own decision . . . Thus it cannot be said that the legal process is the application of known rules to diverse facts. (Levi, 1949, pp. 2–3)

The reason is that: (1) known rules are applied by judges on a case-by-case basis; and (2) the *meaning* of rules is given only in legal precedents.

If reasoning which satisfies the principle of formal justice must pass a similarity test relative to legal precedents, then it is not merely the case that reasoning from analogy is *sometimes* involved in legal judgment. It must *always* be involved, whether explicitly or by implication, because: (1) justice requires that like cases be treated alike; and (2) no two cases are identical. Both this supposition of general-rule limitation and the principle of formal justice contribute to the central role accorded analogical reasoning in traditional jurisprudence.

The logical form of analogical inference

The form of legal reasoning from analogy can be stated schematically as follows: (1) cases $a, b, c \ldots$ and the case at bar share the properties $p, q, r \ldots$; (2) cases a, b, c share the property of having been decided in favor of X; therefore, (3) the case at bar (or some issue in the case at bar) should be decided in favor of X. The general form of an inference of this type is discussed in elementary logic texts under the rubric "induction by analogy," a variety of inductive reasoning pervasive in everyday thought. In most instances of induction by analogy the conclusion drawn is a prediction of some sort – for example, the conclusion that a future event will resemble past events in some way. Thus if: (1) Mary, Joe, Tom, and Sue have all enjoyed many meals at Pat's, their favorite restaurant; and (2) Mary, Joe, and Tom have enjoyed the new entry in Pat's menu, they might reasonably infer that Sue will enjoy the new entry if she orders it tonight.

Conclusions drawn by inference from analogy in law are, for the most part, neither causal nor predictive in this way. In legal argument from analogy the similarities referred to in the premises support a normative, not a causal, inference, that is, an inference about correct legal outcome. This difference between induction by analogy in everyday reasoning and in law is a difference worth noting, and we shall explore some of its significance in what follows, but the difference should not obscure the fact that analogical reasoning, as a distinctive type of inductive inference, is pervasive both in legal and extra-legal processes of thought.

Limitations of analogical reasoning

While pervasive in law, the effects of analogical reasoning on legal decision making are limited. At least two reasons for this deserve comment. The first has to do with the nature of similarity judgments upon which analogical reasoning is based. Nelson Goodman has observed (1972, p. 444) that any assertion that "A is similar to B" is essentially incomplete. Just as we need to supplement the assertion that something "is to the left of" by specifying what it is to the left of, so, in order to be clear about a similarity claim, we must individuate the properties to which the similarity claim refers. But here we encounter a problem. Any two objects are

584

alike in an infinite number of respects. This chair and this computer are alike, for example, in weighing less than a hundred pounds, in being located in a university office, in being employed in an example, and so on indefinitely. Absent some restriction on what counts as a *relevant* property, the required individuation is impossible. The problem is that while relevance and importance of similarities must be restricted *in some way*, there is no *single correct way* to make the necessary restriction. Individuation of similarities, in other words, depends upon an *intrinsically relative* judgment. Goodman notes (p. 445), for example, that a passenger at an airport check-in station may recognize three pieces of luggage, A, B and C as similar – say, in design, color, and ownership. To a pilot observing the same pieces, only A and C may be recognized as similar – with respect to weight, for example, they may be too heavy for safety's sake. Accurate understanding of similarity judgment must include recognition of the fact that which pieces of luggage are more alike than others depends on who makes the judgment and why.

The implications for law are obvious. Just as persons at a baggage-train often fail for good reason to agree in their judgments of similarity because of different interests and/or points of view, so lawyers and judges fail for good reason to agree in their judgments of similarity among cases. The trial stage of a legal proceeding is designed to explore *alternative* theories of a case and the schemes of analogy connected with them.

This presents a problem for legal theory, namely, how to think about *choice* between plausible, but inconsistent, precedents. One temptation is to suggest that one line of precedents is more similar to the undecided case (X) because it shares more similarities with X than another. But this is no solution to the problem of choice.

> If there are just three things in the universe, then any two of them belong together in exactly two classes and have exactly two properties in common: the property of belonging to the class consisting of the two things, and the property of belonging to the class consisting of all three things. If the universe is larger, the number of shared properties will be larger but will still be the same for every two elements ... If the universe is infinite, all these figures become infinite and equal. (*Goodman, 1972, p. 443*)

Counting similarities is no solution to the problem of choice, because in order to count we must know what and what not to count. There is no normatively independent way of counting similarities and thus no value-neutral way of deciding which of two conflicting lines of precedent is the correct line to employ in justifying decision in a case.

A second limitation of analogical reasoning adds support for the idea that normative theory must be the center-piece of any adequate account of legal reasoning, including reasoning from analogy. In deciding a case at bar one normally argues from similarity among precedents to a conclusion about only some *part or parts* of a case, that is, about specific, identifiable legal issues within a case. Before a final decision is made, the similarities which bear upon various specific issues

585

within a case must be *collectively* assessed in order for a determination of overall fit between precedent cases and the case at hand to be made. While this type of reasoning may incorporate *conclusions* drawn by analogy, the reasoning process at work does not have the structure described above as the basic form of analogical inference. This is evident when we recognize: (1) that inference from analogy may count toward a defendant on one issue and toward a plaintiff in another; and (2) that analogies may differ in strength of their support for a conclusion from one issue to another. Such variations in analogical support must somehow be summed over in a court's decision for one party rather than another. The "summing over" process involves, among other things, assignment of "weight" or "significance" to established analogies. Analogies, in other words, must be evaluated, and in the process they inevitably become embedded in a wider web of legal reasoning which must include non-analogical, normative elements.

Challenges to traditional theory

Recognition of the evaluative element in analogical reasoning has led most contemporary legal theorists to deny traditional claims about the centrality of analogy per se in the process of legal reasoning. The fact that analogical reasoning in law is not simply the problem of identifying similarities between cases, but the problem of identifying, or individuating, legally *significant* similarities is a starting point for most discussions of the subject. Evaluation of significance and relevance requires appeal to legal rules and principles, and contemporary accounts of legal reasoning focus primary attention on normative theory, that is, on the nature of legal norms and standards and on the way in which these are established.

The role accorded precedents and examples within normative legal theory varies widely. Some authors minimize their importance:

> In a normative context, justificatory reasoning can proceed only from standards, and "reasoning by example," as such, is virtually impossible. Reason cannot be used to justify a normative conclusion on the basis of an example without first drawing a maxim or rule from the example, or, what is the same thing, without first concluding the example "stands for" a maxim or rule. (*Eisenberg, 1988, p. 86*)

Most, however, understand reasoning from precedent and example as a significant, but preliminary or condition-setting, phase of legal interpretation.

An example is Ronald Dworkin. His approach to normative theory is to construe the legal community as directed toward philosophical ideals, whether explicitly expressed or only implicit in legal judgment. He compares a judge deciding what the law is on some issue with members of some associative community – for example, a family, a friendship, or a fraternal order – deciding what the associative relationship requires in a situation which is unprecedented, that is, where rules have not been established that prescribe exactly what one should do. The member of an associative community to which he compares a judge most closely is a writer of chain novels (1986, p. 28). He imagines that such a writer is given a novel, part (or parts) of which have been written by others. The challenge is to continue the novel by making out of what one is given the best possible continuation of the novel. In doing this Dworkin says that the writer operates under two constraints. First, there is the *dimension of fit*. How one continues the story must be consistent with the bulk of the material supplied by the other authors. Second, there is an *aesthetic constraint*. How the writer proceeds depends on how he or she can make the work in progress best, all things considered.

As applied to law, the "dimension of fit" incorporates traditional concern with precedent. Any justifiable interpretation of a case "must not expose more than a low threshold number of decisions, particularly recent decisions, as mistakes" (Dworkin, 1978, p. 340). Choice between interpretations, each of which can pass a "threshold of fit" test, depends on another dimension of interpretation – moral theory. This corresponds to what he called the "aesthetic constraint" which operates in the work of a chain novelist. For Dworkin, which interpretation of a given case best advances legal practice involves inevitable appeal to political morality because every legal decision asserts the rights of one party over another. In doing so it provides sanction for use of society's collective force against someone's rights. Such a decision must be justified in some way, and for Dworkin the only means of providing such justification is appeal to some principle such as fairness, justice or due process.

> General theories of law . . . for all their abstraction, are constructive interpretations: they try to show legal practice as a whole in its best light . . . So no firm line divides jurisprudence from adjudication or any other aspect of legal practice . . . Any judge's opinion is itself a piece of legal philosophy, even when the philosophy is hidden and the visible argument is dominated by citation and lists of facts. Jurisprudence is the general part of adjudication, silent prologue to any decision in law. (*Dworkin, 1986, p. 90*)

Dworkin's notion that normative theory in law is inherently philosophical presents its own set of problems, of course. Some object to his claim (1986, pp. 248–50) that a judge employs his or her own convictions not because they are personal convictions, but because they are believed to be convictions the best morality would require. Melvin Eisenberg, for example, regards the distinction between "personal" and "philosophical" justification as of no theoretical significance since "Almost everyone thinks his own moral convictions are the convictions that the best morality would require, and thinks the method by which he arrives at his convictions is the best method of arriving at moral convictions" (Eisenberg, 1988, p. 194).

Others find practical problems with any philosophical understanding of normative theory. Steven Burton, for example, acknowledges that adjudication raises many "difficult, if not unanswerable, philosophical questions," but in his view, these are "of little value to practicing lawyers and judges" (1985, p. 110). His alternative to an explicitly philosophical account of normative theory in law adapts some ideas of Lon Fuller who claimed (1946) that the key to legal interpretation is discovery of the purposes of law as applied to an undecided case. In his view, legal rules and standards are expressions of social aims and goals. Understanding these requires legal-specific, not philosophical, analysis, and the normative theory which should control the outcome of an undecided case will be the product of inquiry into the point and purpose of applicable legal rules and standards. Only such inquiry can produce knowledge of what the law should be trying to accomplish in the case.

A number of problems arise in connection with this conception of adjudication. It is often very difficult, for example, to give a clear answer to the question, "What *is* the point or purpose of a legal rule?" We have seen that agreement about the meaning of legal rules is far from extensive within the legal community – at least as applied to "hard" cases. Agreement in belief about the purposive underpinning of legal rules is even less extensive, and this raises a critical question for Fuller's general approach to normative theory in law: "What if we can't determine the normative theory, that is, the social point or purpose, underlying a legal rule?" What is the legal effect of this circumstance on application of the rule? Do (or should) doubts about purposive theory weaken a legal rule or standard?

Mention of such questions is important here only to indicate that particular difficulties attach to a "socially purposive" conception of normative theory just as they do to a "philosophical" conception such as we find in Dworkin. It is important to recognize, however, that both these conceptions operate with roughly the same understanding of the limitations of analogical reasoning in law, namely, whether or not a factual similarity between an undecided case and a precedent case is legally significant depends on generalized, or at least generalizable, normative interpretation. For Dworkin, the norms are supplied by a judge's theory of political morality; for Fuller, they are supplied by a theory of the social point or purpose of relevant legal rules.

Analogical reasoning and normative legal theory

From even a cursory comparison with traditional theory it seems clear that recent accounts of legal reasoning are surely correct in their recognition of the limitation of similarity judgment and analogy in determining legal outcomes. Insofar as Edward Levi's well-known book on the subject fails to take these into account, it is incomplete. It is not clear, however, how much recent accounts contribute to a precise understanding of legal reasoning. So far as the analysis of the nature of analogical claims is concerned, progress is evident, as we have seen. But once this is acknowledged, signs of progress are difficult to make out. Richard Posner observes about the normative theoretical approach to adjudication, "When you think of all those . . . theories jostling one another . . . you see the range of choice that the approach legitimizes and, as a result, the instability of . . . doctrine that it portends" (1992, p. 445). One is reminded here of Plato's comment, cited earlier:

"the variety of man's activities and the unsettlement of human experience make it impossible for any art to issue unqualified rules holding good for all questions at all times." Substitute "normative theory" for "rules" in Plato's remark and you have a fair assessment of recent normative accounts of legal reasoning.

Normative theory aside, it is hard to ignore a stubborn fact: among practicing lawyers the idea persists "that general [legal] terms without examples are largely empty of meaning" (Gardner 1987, p. 37). Even a normative theorist of legal reasoning like Posner seems grudgingly to accept some role for analogy in legal thought, though he is not sure how to describe it. He claims (1990, pp. 86–98) that analogical *reasoning*, as distinct from similarity judgment, does not amount to much. But he admits that "cases accepted within a theory provide testing instances for its further application" (1992, p. 436). This lends support to the more or less standard "staging ground" view of precedent and analogy in legal reasoning and decision making, the view we find in Dworkin's "threshold of fit" criterion for the theory of an undecided case.

The underlying problems evident in discussions of similarity judgment and analogical reasoning in law stem from the fact that at present we do not understand how these processes work – whether in law or in other kinds of knowledge acquisition. In particular, we do not understand how similarity recognition interacts with normative legal judgment in case-by-case adjudication. Until more progress is made in scientific and philosophical understanding of these cognitive functions and their interaction it is likely that some purely conditional or stage-setting conception, like Dworkin's "threshold" metaphor, will control accounts of analogical reasoning in law. Absent a more exact conception of how, apart from mere counting, similarity recognition enters into the formation of normative legal judgment, analogy-making and reasoning from analogy are certain to play second fiddle to generalized normative theory of some sort, so far as our understanding of legal reasoning is concerned. This is for good reason, but doubt may linger about whether the second-fiddle view is entirely correct. Reasons for such doubt are explained at the beginning of this article.

Bibliography

Burton, S. J. 1985: *An Introduction to Law and Legal Reasoning*. Boston: Little, Brown and Co.
Dworkin, R. 1978: *Taking Rights Seriously*. Cambridge: Harvard University Press.
—— 1986: *Law's Empire*. Cambridge: Harvard University Press.
Eisenberg, M. A. 1988: *The Nature of the Common Law*. Cambridge: Harvard University Press.
Fuller, L. L. 1946: Reason and fiat in case law. *Harvard Law Review*, 59, 376–438.
Gardner, A. von der L. 1987: *An Artificial Intelligence Approach to Legal Reasoning*. Cambridge, Mass.: MIT Press.
Goodman, N. 1972: *Problems and Projects*. New York: Bobbs-Merrill Co.
Levi, E. H. 1949: *An Introduction to Legal Reasoning*. Chicago: University of Chicago Press.

Posner, R. A. 1990: *The Problems of Jurisprudence*. Cambridge, Mass.: Harvard University Press.

—— 1992: Legal reasoning from the top down and from the bottom up. *Chicago Law Review*, 59.

Plato 1961: *Statesman*, tr. J. B. Skemp, *Collected Dialogues of Plato*, ed. E. Hamilton and H. Cairns. New York: Bollingen Foundation.

Rawls, J. 1971: *A Theory of Justice*. Cambridge: Harvard University Press.

Index

access, control of 146;
exclusive 146; limitations
on 146; protection from
unwanted 146;
restricted 146, 147, 148;
to information 146–9
accountability 53, 54
Ackerman, B. A. 119, 137
act utilitarianism 468
acts/omissions 27, 85–8,
477–8, 558
action/s 84–5; immoral
484–6; (in)voluntary
521–2; legal
requirements 477–9;
refraining from 479–86;
that hurt oneself 480–3;
that offend others
483–4; unlawful 520
activist policy
implementation 193
adjudication 242, 250,
296–7, 298, 587–8;
descriptive theory of
269–75; idiosyncrasy
wing 271–2; normative
theory of 276–8;
sociological wing 272–5;
truth-finding in 173–4,
181–2
Adler, Z. 180
adversarial process 180–1,
283–4
advocacy 430
affirmative action 159,
160, 550–1
agency 74, 75, 337–8
Aleinkoff, T. A. 206
Alexander, F. 425–6
Alexander, L. 82–3, 505,
506–7, 508, 510, 511,

512; and Kress, K. 512,
547, 548, 550, 551
Alexy, R. 352
Allen, A. L. 146, 150,
308
Allen, R. J. 180
alternative care 63, 65
Altman, I. 146
Amar, A. 137
analogical reasoning,
challenges to 586–8;
limitations of 584–6;
logical form 584; and
normative legal theory
588–9; and principle of
justice 583–4
Andre, J. 152
annulment theory 77
Anscombe, E. G. 579
anthropology 397–9; and
bipolar method 403; and
correct model of law
399; and customary
rules 400; and dispute
402–3; and groups 403;
and imagining the real
402; and insider/outsider
perspective 399–400;
and language 400, 401;
and legal pluralism
401–2; and multiplex/
single-interest
relationships 400–1; and
nature/definition of law
400; and role of power
in law 402
anti-nomian thesis 174,
175, 176, 177, 179
anti-positivism 437, 445,
447, 448; see also legal
positivism; positivism

anti-realism 445, 446–7;
see also legal realism;
realism
antihumanist theory 367,
372
Aquinas, T. 42, 43,
225–7, 228, 229, 231,
232–7, 341, 422,
466, 471
Arendt, H. 145
argument, evolutive 383;
historical 382–3; linear
433; rigorous 432–3;
textual 380–2
Aristotle 11, 26, 43, 157,
226, 335, 336, 338,
471, 522, 527
Arminjon, P. et al. 191
at-fault pool 75
Atiyah, P. 25, 29–32
Augustine, St 226, 427–8,
433
Austin, J. L. 226, 231,
241, 242, 244–6, 262,
263
authority 193, 242,
246–9, 259, 516–17,
547–8, 573; co-ordinate
193, 254–5; de facto
574, 576; forms and
limits of 573–4;
hierarchical 193; and
incorporationism 255–9;
and internal point of
view 244–6, 253;
justification of 574–8;
and legality 243–4;
legitimate 467, 574;
paradoxes of 576–7;
practical 575–7, 578;
Raz's theory of 253–5;

reasons for 578–81; and
sanctions 244–6, 253;
theoretical 574–5, 578
Ayres, I. and Tally, E. 326

Baba Metzia 115
Babeuf manifestos 163,
168
Baker, C. E. 284, 286–7
Balkin, J. M. 137, 281,
368, 369, 370, 372,
543
Ball, M. S. 431–2
Barnett, R. E. 32, 40–3, 55
Barth, K. 421, 432, 433
Barton, R. F. 398
base-superstructure thesis
358–9
basic goods 228–30
Baumgartner, M. P. 408,
409, 412, 413
Baxter, W. 213
Beale, J. 209, 211, 276
Beattie, J. M. 409
behaviorism 268
Beirne, P. and Sharlet, R.
360
Bell Jr, D. A. 285
Benedict, R. 397
beneficial reliance 51
Benn, S. I. 151
Benson, P. E. 27, 44, 47,
55, 71, 73–4
Bentham, J. 11, 96, 172,
173–4, 241
Berger, M. 148
Berger, R. 137
Berman, H. 113, 422,
423–5
Berman, J. 172
Bernard, J. L. 408
Beyleveld, D. 239; and
Brownsword, R. 446
Bickel, A. M. 129, 133,
136, 137, 300, 571
bilateral litigational
procedure 73
Binder, J. 348, 349, 351
Black, D. 406, 407, 408,
410, 411, 412–14, 415,
416, 417
Black, H. C. 131, 136, 413
Black Jr, C. I. 132, 136
blackmail paradox 90–2
Blackstone, Sir W. 225,
226, 468

Blaustein, A. P. and Flanz,
H. F. 140
Bloch, P. and Anderson, D.
408
Block, R. 409
Bloustein, E. 151
Boas, F. 397
Bobbitt, P. 381
Bohannan, P. 411
Bok, S. 146
Bonhoeffer, D. 421
Bonjour, L. 543
Boone, C. K. 146, 151
Bork, R. H. 136–7
Bowers, W. J. and Pierce,
G. J. 408
Boyd, J. 455
Brandeis, L. 133, 142, 145
breach of contract 25–9,
26, 38–40
Brennan, W. 137, 558
Brest, P. 205; and
Levinson, S. 137
Briggs, A. 555
Brilmayer, L. 215, 218,
511
Brink, D. 446
Brownsword, R. 239
Buber, M. 430
Buchanan, J. 17
Bülow, O. 348
Burger, W. 204
Burton, S. J. 539, 587
"but-for" test 60, 67, 73
Butler, S. 451

Cadi justice 277
Cady, L. E. 422, 433
Cain, M. and Hunt, A. 356,
358
Calabresi, G. 59, 61, 65,
68, 69, 123, 206, 320;
and Bobbitt, P. 128,
137; and Melamed, A. D.
320
Calvin, J. 114, 123
Calvo clauses 99, 106
Canaris, 351
capitalism 285, 287, 289,
553, 561
Cardozo, B. N. 201, 203,
340
Carmella, A. C. 422
Caroline rules 101
Carroll Towing case 312,
313–30

Carter, S. L. 119
causation 60, 67–8, 73,
83–4, 85, 359
choice 229, 529, 585, 587
choice of laws, and after-
acquired domicile 214;
and choice of decision
217; classical 209,
210–13, 218–19; and
individual forums 210;
and instantaneity 212,
213–14; and interests
215, 217, 218, 219; and
legal pluralism 219;
modernist 209–10,
213–17; and nation-
states 210; outcome-
neutrality 215, 217; and
practical standards 212;
and retreat from rules
213; substance-
independence of 212,
214–15, 218; and
territorialism 211, 214,
218; and vestedness
210–11, 213, 215,
216–17, 218
chose-in-action 4
Cicero, Marcus Tullius
223–5, 228, 231, 415,
471
civil rights 285, 286
Civil Rights Act (1866)
203
class, interests 355–6;
relations 363–4
class of legal reasons
265–9
Coase, R. 16, 59–61, 64,
288, 319
Coase Theorem 16, 60
coercion 481–2, 520–2
Cohen, F. 261, 262, 263,
267, 272, 274, 275,
278
Cohen, H. 350
Cohen, L. J. 172, 178
Cohen, M. 280
coherence 335, 336, 337,
340, 565, 567; base
theory of 537–8;
characterization of
normative theories of
543–6; as complete 541;
as comprehensive 541,
543; as consistent

540–1; constraint on 550; of convictions 535; core concepts of 542–3; and correspondence theory 536–7; defined 539–43; and general equilibrium 541; as inconsistent 548; and indeterminacy 538; and internal relations 542–3; of knowledge 535; and lexical ordering 541; and meta-principles 542; and monism 542, 543–6; motivations for 536; and negligence 536; non-legal 538; normative value of 546–51; as one element among many 538–9; as path-dependent 547; as pluralistic 533; and positivism 538, 539; and pre-emption 541–2; and reflective equilibrium 535, 541, 543; requirements for 533–4, 540; scope of 541; techniques of 540–1; of truth 178–9, 534–5, 536
Coleman, J. L. 49, 60, 61, 66, 68, 69, 72, 73, 75, 77, 78, 243, 251, 252, 257, 258, 536; and Leiter, B. 496–7
Colker, R. 152
Collins, H. 361
Comaroff, J. 401; and Comaroff, J. 402, 403; and Roberts, S. 402
commonalism 471–2, 473
communitarianism 527–8
community 425–6, 434
commutative justice 43, 44–5
comparative law 184; basic principle of 189–90; and difference theory 193–7; and families of legal systems 190–2; and functionalism 187–90; and ideal types 192–3; and universalism 185–7
comparative research 184

compensation 75, 334; dilemma 49
complicity 88–90
Comte, A. 397
conceptual analysis 241–2, 262–4
conflict 253, 363, 390, 399, 410; of laws 209
conflict resolution 193, 387
Conley, J. and O'Barr, W. 401, 403
consent-based theory 41–3, 468
consequentialism 481, 485
Constantinesco, L.-J. 184
constitutional interpretation, and academic commentary 136–7; and doctrine 134–5; and ethos 135; and history 128–30; official 126–8; and prudence 132–4; and structure 131–2; and text 130–1
constitutional law 571; and equality 156–70; and privacy 139–53; and religion 113–24
constitutional theory; and hermeneutics 456–8; and theology 426–9
constructivism 235–6, 347, 348
contract 24–5, 54–5, 363, 529, 570; Aristotelian approach 43–5; autonomous 25, 33–43; and benefit/detrimental reliance 29–32, 36; classical view of 29–30; and consent 41–3; decisions in 299–300; distributive analysis approach 45–8; economic approach 48–54; and expectation of damages 25–9, 39; and loyalty 526; and promise 37–40; promise-based theory 37–40; reliance-based theory 29–32; teleological theories of 43–54; transfer theory of 42; valid 238

contributory negligence 63, 316
convergent behaviour 247–8, 252, 259
Cook, B. B. 408
Cook, W. W. 209, 214, 216–17, 261, 269, 280
Cooke, J. 141–2
Cooley, C. 145
core interests 57–8, 73, 74
Cornell, D. 307, 369, 371, 372, 488
correspondence of truth 179
Cotterrell, R. 568
counselling 430
Cover, R. 115, 219
Craswell, R. 42
criminal law 10, 410; and actions 84–5; acts/omissions 85–8; and causation 83–4, 85; and complicity 88–90; General Part of 83–90; and principle of maintaining high standards of propriety 176; and principle of protecting the innocent 176; and punishment 80; purpose of 80; and retributivism 80–3; and self-incrimination 173, 177; special part 90–5
criminal malice 238
criteria of legality 262
critical, morality 246; race theory 168, 567
critical legal studies 280, 357, 458, 567; as analytic jurisprudence 280–1; and instrumental reformism 284–6; and instrumentalism 282–4; and normativism 205–6; and revolutionary instrumentalism 286–9; as social theory 281–9; see also legal scholarship
Croley, S. and Hanson, J. 322, 323
Cross, Sir R. 174
cryptotypes 195
Currie, B. 209–10, 214, 216, 217–18
customary practice 441–2

Dalton, C. 368, 370
Damaska, M. 176, 193
D'Amato, A. 488, 492
Dane, P. 210, 216
Darwin, C. 186
Daube, D. 518
David, R. 194; and
    Brierley, J. 191, 194;
    et al. 187
Davis, A. 303
de Sloovere, F. 202
Decatur, S. 530
DeCew, J. 149
decisions 175, 201, 267,
    272–3, 283, 285, 297,
    299, 547, 553, 569,
    584; in contract
    299–300; first-order/
    second-order 217, 219;
    majoritarian 284;
    segregation 299, 300
deconstruction 367, 567;
    as adaptable 373; as
    antihumanist 372; and
    conceptual oppositions
    368–9; and critical legal
    studies 369–71, 372–3;
    and feminism 371; and
    iterability 369; and
    privileging 367–8; and
    social justice 371–2; of
    texts 368–9
del Vecchio, G. 186
Derrida, J. 282, 367, 369,
    371, 452
Descartes, R. 376
descriptive, scholarship
    564–6; theory 274
determination thesis 359
deterrence theory 61–8,
    321, 326, 327, 334
Devlin, P. 439, 467, 485
Dickens, C. 451
Dickerson, R. 203
Diderot, D. 157
difference theory 165–6,
    193–7
dirty/relationship law 403
discretion 413, 414
discrimination 159,
    413–14, 415; intentional
    159; reverse 159
distributive justice 16, 18,
    19, 26, 46–7, 59, 71–2,
    336–7, 339, 554;
    localized 75

Dixon, R. 146
doctrine of dictum 583
Donovan, J. M. 411
Douzinas, C. et al. 370
Drobnig, U. 192
due care 63, 78
due process 238
Duff, R. A. 81, 443
Duns Scotus 42
Durkheim, E. 26, 397
duties 573
duty of care 38
duty to obey 465, 473;
    history of 465–8; and
    implications of catechistic
    meta-ethics for 469–70;
    and implications of
    commonalist meta-ethics
    for 470–3
Duxbury, N. 291, 292, 296
Dworkin, R. 116, 128,
    167–8, 184. 206,
    234–7, 242, 249–51,
    252, 255–6, 297, 300,
    312, 352, 380, 422,
    425, 439, 440, 447,
    468, 498, 499, 508,
    539, 541, 546, 547–51,
    563, 586, 587, 588,
    589

Easterbrook, F. H. 204,
    205; and Fischel, D. 311
economic analysis 284,
    311–13; and activity
    levels 314, 321–2, 323,
    327; and administrative
    costs 59, 322; *Carroll
    Towing* model 313–19; of
    contract 48–54; costs
    and benefits 315, 517;
    and deterrence effects
    321, 326, 327; and
    efficiency 315–16,
    325–8; and Hand
    Formula 323–4; and
    legal knowledge 323;
    and limitations of law
    328–30; normative
    mode 311; positive
    mode 311–12; and
    risk-neutrality 314,
    322–3; and simultaneity
    324–5; and transaction
    costs 60, 61, 314,
    319–21, 326

efficiency 16, 288–9,
    311–12, 315–16,
    325–8; analysis of
    328–30
Ehrlich, E. 348
Eisenberg, M. A. 539, 586,
    587
Ellickson, R. 323, 329
Ely, J. H. 137, 150, 218,
    300
empiricism 376
Engel, D. M. 401, 409, 411
Engels, F. 358, 397, 407
Enlightenment 157–8
enterprise liability 69–70
entitlement theory 72
epistemology 264
Epstein, R. 66, 76
equal rights 156, 158,
    162, 170; and freedom
    162–3
equality 47. 71, 156, 415,
    438; absolute 156;
    according to Dworkin
    167–8; according to
    Rawls 164–6; complex
    169; and constitutional
    law 158–61; and the
    Enlightenment 157–8;
    and inequalities 170; and
    liberty 161–2, 165–6;
    of opportunity 156;
    proportional 156; of
    protection 158–9, 161,
    163; radical critique/
    dilemma 162–4; of
    resources 167–8;
    unmodified 168–9; as a
    value 169–70
Eskridge Jr, W. N. 204,
    206, 382–3; and
    Frickey, P. P. 206
Esser, J. 349, 351
Estrich, S. 308
ethical autonomy 167–8
ethics 429–31; challenge
    model 167
ethnography 397–8
evidence 172; and
    Benthamite legacy
    173–4; discovery of 179;
    evaluation of 179–80;
    future directions of
    179–82; and "new"
    scholarship 177–9; and
    rationalist approach to

173–5, 178; regulation of 174–7, 179; and regulation of proof 174–7; and risk of error 175, 176; and risk of prejudice 180; and role of parties/adjudicators at trial 180–1; rules of 172, 175–6; testing 178
expected accident losses 61–2

fair play 466, 468
Fallon, R. 137
false conflicts 214, 216
family theory 190–2; benefits of 191; contribution of 192; limitations of 191–2
Farber, D. 206
Farnsworth, E. A. 529
The Federalist 141
Feeley, M. M. 410
Feinberg, J. 148, 149, 151, 476, 481
Feinman, J. M. 488, 495
Feller, A. H. et al. 202
feminism 169, 170
feminist jurisprudence 567; defined 302–3, 305–6; as distinctive 307–8; value of 308–9
Fichte, J. G. 344–5
fiduciary duty 529
Filmer, Sir R. 534
Finkelstein, M. O. and Fairley, W. B. 178
Finnis, J. 225, 228–30, 237, 468, 469, 571
First Occupancy Theory 20
Fish, S. 459
Fisher, W. W. et al. 261, 278
fit 422, 587, 589; adequate 235, 236
Flaherty, D. H. 141
Fletcher, G. P. 75, 78, 518, 519, 529
formalism 67, 283, 332; attack on 275–6; as internal to law 340–1; nature of 333–5; project of 332–3
Foucault, M. 282, 402, 452, 518

foundationalism 376, 387–90; epistemological 376
Frank, J. 261, 262, 263, 267, 268, 270, 271–2, 274, 275–6, 277–8, 292
Frankenberg, G. 193, 194–5
Frankfurter, F. 129, 202; and Hart, H. M. 296
Franklin, M. A. 333
fraud on the law 94–5
free; labor 287, 288, 289; law movement 348; riders 553
freedom 7, 162–3, 168, 388; of association 299
Freeman, A. 284, 285
French Civil Code 197
Fried, C. 30, 32, 35, 37–40
Fried, M. H. 407
Friedman, L. 568
Friedman, M. 15, 553
Frug, G. 368, 370
Frug, M. J. 303
Fuchs, E. 348
Fuller, L. L. 201, 202, 231–4, 237, 297, 571, 588; and Perdue Jr, W. W. 25–9, 55
Fumerton, R. 536
functionalism 187–90

Gadamer, H.-G. 452
Gaffney, E. M. 426
Galligan, D. 174
Gardner, A. von der L. 589
Garet, R. 426
Garnsey, P. 409, 415
Garrett, R. 146
Garrison, L. and Hurst, W. 202
Gavison, R. 146, 148–9
Geertz, C. 402
Gerber, 348
Gescheider, G. A. 81
Gewirth, A. 239
Gilbert, N. 553, 557
Gilles, S. 65. 323
Gilmore, G. 115
Gluckman, M. 403; and Bohannan, P. 399–400
Goetz, C. J. and Scott, R. E. 50–2, 53–4

Goldman, A. 265
Goldman, S. 408
Goldschmidt, J. 348–9
Goldschmidt, L. 274
Goldstein, L. 503
Gomme, G. L. 397
good faith 277
Goodman, N. 584, 585
Goodrich, P. 370
Gordley, J. 24, 42, 43–5
Gordon, R. W. 282–3, 370, 488, 499–500
Gough, E. K. 409
Gove, W. R. et al. 409
Gramsci, A. 361
gratitude 466, 468
Gray, J. C. 201
Green, L. 573, 575, 576–7
Green, T. H. 14
Greenawalt, K. 467, 469, 574, 579, 580, 581
Greenberg, D. 411
Greenhousse, C. 401
Gregory of Rimini 227
Grentz, S. J. and Olsen, R. E. 433
Grey, T. C. 3, 137
Griffin, S. 137
Grisez, G. 228
Gross, R. A. 147
Grotius, H. 11, 40, 42, 185, 227, 228
Gulliver, P. H. 411
Gutmann, A. 303
Gutmann, B. 398
Gutteridge, H. 184

Habermas, J. 145, 352, 452, 564
Hale, R. 278, 280
Hall, D. 410
Hamilton, A. 141
Hand Formula 65, 66, 78, 313, 320, 322, 325–7; application of 323–4; criticism of 324–5; economic model of 313–19
Hand, L. 61, 62, 63, 64, 65, 136, 312–13, 318, 321, 324–5
Hardin, G. 11
Hardisty, J. 506, 507
Hare, R. 469, 471, 472
harm 35, 36, 57, 59–60, 62, 67, 152, 336, 475,

476–7, 480–6; defined
476; indirect 479–80;
intentional 65–6
Harman, G. 471
Harper, R. F. 409
Hart, H. L. A. 136, 203,
230, 231, 241, 243,
244–6, 248, 250, 252,
257, 261, 262, 263,
264, 270, 292, 422,
426, 437, 439, 443,
456, 466, 476, 485,
570, 573, 575, 576
Hart Jr, H. M. and Sacks,
A. M. 203, 204, 205,
297–8
Hastie, R. et al. 408
Hayek, F. A. 13, 559
Heck, P. 348
Hegel, G. W. F. 11, 14, 42,
47, 338, 341, 344,
345–6, 347, 351, 516
Heidelberg School 350
Henkin, L. 149
Herder, J. G. 186
Historical School 186,
347–8
Hobbes, T. 11, 42, 157,
227, 541
Hoebel, E. A. 399, 409
Höffe, O. 352
Hohfeld Jr, O. W. 280
Holleman, J. F. 398
Holmes Jr, J. 262, 263,
267, 277
Holmes, O. W. 76, 159,
201, 231
Holmstrom, L. L. and
Burgess, A. W. 408,
410
Honoré, T. 75, 468, 570
Horwitz, A. V. 411, 412
Horwitz, M. J. 282, 291
Howe, M. DeW. 120
Howell, P. P. 399
Hume, D. 5, 11, 17–18,
157, 376, 466, 471,
472
Hunt, A. 361, 363
Hurley, S. 547
Hurst, J. W. 203
Hutcheson Jr, J. 270, 271,
272, 466
Hutchinson, A. 357; and
Morgan, D. 205
Hyland, R. 189, 193, 195

ideal community 206
ideal types 3, 192–3;
charismatic legal
revelation 192; empirical
law 192; imposition of
law 192; systematic
elaboration of law 192
idealism 343–6
identification 257
ideology, as law 361
incorporationism,
arguments against 257;
and authority 255–9;
and legality 251–3
indeterminacy 265, 281,
283, 291, 488, 500–1;
in actually litigated cases
497–8; causal 267–9,
496–7; deconstructionist
defenses of 495; defined
489–90; easy cases of
491–3; epiphenomenalist
defenses of 495–7; and
important cases 499;
local 267; modal
499–500; modest
version of 497–500;
problem of 300; as
radical 490–7; rational
265–7; role of 489; rule
skeptic defenses of
493–5; strong 490–1,
493, 501; and
underdeterminacy
489–90
individuals/individualism
3, 425, 527, 556
initial distribution 15–16,
19
injurer/s 64–5, 67, 74, 76
Inness, J. 146, 150
institutionalism 273
instrumentalism 281–2;
critique of 282–4; and
reformism 284–6;
revolutionary 286–9
integrity 236, 548,
549–51
intellectual/non-intellectual
property 4, 5
intention 78
interests 283–4, 286; and
choice of law 215, 217,
218, 219; class 355–6;
and contacts 215, 217;
protected 57

internalization theory
59–61
International Institute for
the Unification of Private
Law (UNIDROIT) 187
international law 96; and
construction of treaties
101–2; and continuity
104–5; customary
109–10; and general
principles 110; and
global areas 99–100;
and human rights
106–7; and integrity
105; and judicial
decisions 111; and
jurisdiction 97–8; and
movement of persons 99;
and nationality 98–9;
and operation of
intergovernmental
organizations 102; and
personality 104; and
recognition 103; sources
of 107–11; and
sovereignty 103; and
state 102; and state
liability 105–6; subject
matter of 96–107; and
territory 97; and treaties
108–9; and use of force
100–1
interpretation 202–3, 235,
442; formal theories of
204–5
intrinsic goods 228
intuition 468, 471
is/ought distinction 564

Jackson, J. D. 179
Jackson, Justice 132
Jaggar, A. 303
Jarvis Thomson, J. 87
Jessop, R. 362
Jhering, R. von 188, 347,
348
joint care 63, 65
Jones, H. W. 202
Jones, S. 411
judge/s 242, 261, 267,
269–70, 271–5, 566,
568
judicial discretion 249,
250–1
jurisprudence 300,
569–71; defined 304;

descriptive 304; future 424–5; historical 423–5; internal approach 570; mechanical 200, 201; methodology of 241–2, 262–5; as neutral 302, 303; normative 304; subject-matter of 241–2; traditional 302–3, 422

justice 26, 165, 166, 206, 233; corrective 26, 59, 72–8, 335–7, 338

justification 4, 5, 268; and damages 28–9; formalism as theory of 332–3; general aims 11–15; ground of 337–9; Humean approach 17–18; Lockean approach 19–22; need for 8–10; particular distributive arguments 15–16; personal 587; philosophical 587, 588; Rousseaunian approach 18–19; structures of 335–7; theories of 11–22

Kafka, F. 451
Kagan, R. L. 411
Kahn-Freund, O. 196
Kairys, D. 499
Kaiser Wilhelm Institute (Berlin) 187
Kaldor-Hicks criterion 48, 49
Kant, I. 18, 40, 42, 47, 338, 339, 341, 343–4, 350, 471, 472, 516–17
Kantorowicz, U. 348
Kaplow, L. 323
Katz, A. 283
Katz, L. 93, 94
Kawashima, T. 411
Kelman, M. 284
Kelsen, H. 231, 241, 349–50
Kennedy, D. 281, 282, 283, 284, 542
Kent, J. 185
Kitch, E. W. 292
Klare, K. E. 284, 285
Klosko, G. 468

Knapp, V. 191
knowledge 262, 378–9
Kohler, J. 186
Konvitz, M. 145
Kornblith, H. 264, 265
Kornstein, S. 414
Kramer, L. 218
Kress, K. 67, 498, 536, 540, 546, 547
Kripke, S. 493
Kroeber, A. 397
Kronman, A. T. 43, 45–8, 52, 274, 275, 276, 295
Kuhn, T. 534

Ladenson, 580, 581
Ladeur, K.-H. 352
LaFree, G. D. 408
Lambert, E. 186
Landes, W. M. and Posner, R. A. 62, 66, 67, 311, 325
Langdell, C. 276
language 376, 377, 379, 400, 401, 473; and morality 445–7
Larenz, K. 351
Lasswell, H. D. and McDougall, M. S. 293–5
Latin, H. 323
law, actors in 195; aggregate effects of 364; as arena of struggle 364; autonomy of 115–16; breaches of 442; concept of 262; culture of 195; and deference 120, 121; defined 231–2; and dialogue/conversation 206; eclecticism/specific intent 200–2; and economic relations 363; enforcement of 442; and Establishment Clause 116–19, 120; extension of system 195; facilitative aspects of 442; failure of 181; and free-exercise clause 118–19, 120, 121; gaps in 235; as ideology 361; immanent intelligibility of 339–41; imposition of 442; integrity of 116; as it is 237; lack of realism in 329; legitimacy of 203;

limitations of 328–30; nature of 197; and neutrality 119; penetration of 195; in practice 429–31; processes of 195, 295–6, 296–8; as public 442; role of 114–15; and separation 120, 121; structures of 195; unification of 187, 196; (un)just 225–7

law-state connection 361–3

Lawson, G. 511
lawyer-client privilege 173
Lazarus-Black, M. 402
Lee, R. E. 526
Leff, A. A. 292
Leflar, R. 215
legal formants 195
legal positivism 241, 304, 422–3, 425–6, 436–7, 440, 458; Austin vs Hart 244–6; and authority of law 246–9; defined 444–5; inclusive 448; incorporationism and authority 255–9; incorporationism and legality 251–3; and judicial discretion 249–51; legality and authority 243–4; method and subject-matter 241–2; and morality 436–48; and Raz's theory of authority 253–5; see also anti-positivism; positivism
legal realism 242, 261, 304; and adjudication 269–75, 276–8; and attack on formalism 275–6; jurisprudential methodology 262–5; and legal indeterminacy 265–9; and public/private distinction 278–9; see also anti-realism; post-realism; realism
legal scholarship 562; descriptive 564–6; jurisprudence 569–71; methodologies of 564;

prescriptive 566–9;
subject-matter of 562–3;
see also critical legal
studies
legislator/s 242
legitimacy 390
Legrand, P. 194, 196
Leiter, B. 265
Lempert, R. 178
Levi, E. H. 583, 588
Levin, M. A. 408
Levinas, E. 372
Levinson, S. 137, 529
liability rule 57, 76, 320;
and activity-level effect
321; and level of care
315, 321, 324–5, 327
liberal theory 38, 165–6,
280–1
liberty principle 14–15,
45–7, 76, 161–2,
165–6, 480
Lindgren, J. 91
Lipkin, R. J. 385
literature 450; fiction
454–6; and
hermeneutics 456–8;
law and 450–1; law as
452–3; law in 451–2;
law of 453; and legal
reform 453–4; narrative
458–60
Littleton, C. 308
Llewellyn, K. 201, 261,
262, 266, 267, 269,
270, 271, 272, 273–5,
276, 278, 399
local law theory 216
Locke, J. 11, 12, 13,
19–22, 157, 227, 554
loss spreading theory
68–71, 74–6
Lovin, R. W. 433
loyalty, and
communitarianism
527–8; and contract
526; critics of 530–1;
feelings/duties of 525;
and history 526–8; and
individualism 527; in
legal culture 528–30;
and partiality 524–5,
530–1; triadic theory of
525; unilateral/reciprocal
525–6
Luban, D. 429

Luhmann, N. 349, 352–3
Lundsgaarde, H. P. 410
Luther, M. 422
Lyons, D. 243

Macaulay, S. 409
McBride, J. 422
McConnell, M. 119, 121
MacCormick, D. N. 174,
175
MacCrimmon, C. 180
MacIntyre, A. 428, 530
Mackie, J. L. 468, 469–70,
472
MacKinnon, C. 152, 303,
306, 307–8
McThenia, A. W. and
Shaffer, T. L. 421
Maine, Sir H. S. 158,
185–6
Malamud-Goti, J. 519
Malinowski, B. 398, 399
Maltz, E. M. 206
Man, P. de 371, 452
Mansfield, Lord 185
Marburg School 350
Maritain, J. 228
market economies 12–13
Marmor, A. 250
Marshall, J. 131
Marshall, W. P. 117
Marx, K. 11, 163–4,
287–8, 346, 358, 360,
397; and Engels, F. 358,
359
Marxist theory 303,
355–65, 364–5, 377;
alternative approach to
358–60; and capitalism
363; and class relations
363–4; and desire 287;
object of 355–6; outline
of 356–8; and the state
361–2
Mead, M. 397
meanings 200, 201
Meese, E. 137
Mensch, E. and Freeman,
A. 427
Merkl, A. J. 348, 349
Merry, S. 401, 403
Merryman, J. 195
Messick, B. 401, 402
meta-ethics, catechistic
469–70, 473;
commonalist 470–3

Michelman, F. 312, 558
Mill, J. S. 11, 144–5, 149,
151, 479–81, 482
Miller, F. 410
Millon, D. 488, 500–1
Milton, C. 408
minimal state 554–5, 556
Minow, M. 206, 303, 307,
308
misfeasance 27, 47
moderate monism, and
lexical ordering 544; and
master principle 544,
545; and meta-principles
544; and norms 544;
and reflective equilibrium
544, 545; and scope
544; and weighing and
balancing 544
modernism 375–7, 454,
455, 460; *see also*
postmodernism
Moltmann, J. 424, 425
Monaghan, H. P. 503, 509,
511
monism 542, 543–6;
consistency in 545–6;
moderate 544–5;
resolution of concrete
cases 544; strict 543–4;
strong 545
Montesquieu, C.-L. 185,
196
Moore, B. 151
Moore, M. 238, 446
Moore, M. S. 505
Moore, S. F. 401–2
Moore, U. 261, 264, 268,
269, 271, 272, 273; and
Callahan, C. 264; and
Hope, T. 269; and
Sussman, G. 270
moral, hazard 70;
principles 252, 255–7;
realism 427; rights 357;
skepticism 427
morality 229, 231, 233,
238, 243–4, 246, 262,
436; in courts of law
438, 447–8; differences
between law and 441–4;
and duty to obey
465–73; and
enforcement thesis
439–40; and
jurisprudence 444–5;

legal enforcement of 475–86; and legal semantics 445–7; in literature 454–5, 457; as neutral term 448; objective 485; positive/ critical 439; private 440–1; relationship between law and 436–41; result-oriented/ action-oriented 440; structures of 486

Morgan, L. H. 174, 397

Muller, 201

Munzer, S. 14

Murphy, J. G. and Coleman, J. L. 422

Murphy, N. and McLendon, J. 376

Myers, M. A. and Hagan, J. 408

Nader, L. 402

Nagel, H. H. 408

Nagel, T. 440

natural law 200, 201, 304, 305, 349, 351, 422, 458; Aquinas on 225–7; Cicero on 223–5; Dworkin on 234–7; in early modern Europe 227; Finnis on 228–30; Fuller on 231–4; general considerations on 237; modern 230–9; perspective on 227–8; traditional 223–30

natural rights 227, 283, 338–9

naturalism 264, 274

Nazi jurisprudence 350–1

negative positivism 251

negligence 58, 62–3, 76, 78, 312–13, 316, 327, 340, 388

NESS test 73

Nesson, C. 177

Newman, L. E. 421

Nicolson, D. 178

Niebuhr, R. N. 422

night-watchman state 553, 554

no liability rule 316, 328

nonprofits 122–3

normal justification thesis 254, 577–8

normative ethics 470, 473

normative theory 262, 265, 337–8, 387–9, 585, 587, 588–9; as comprehensive 443; and critical scholarship 205–6; examples and precedent 586; and obedience 468, 469–70, 471; as open 443; as supreme 443

norms 243, 244, 385–6, 390, 400, 437–8, 441–2, 576; as minimum content of Natural Law 437

Nozick, R. 11, 13, 19, 21, 91, 553

nuisance 57

Nutting, C. B. 202

Oakeshott, M. 341

obligation/s 27, 30–2, 230, 231, 549–50, 573, 578; and coercion 40; and duty to obey 388, 390–1, 465–73; voluntary 33–7

O'Brien, D. 141, 146

Offner, J. A. 409

Oliphant, H. 261, 272, 276

Olsen, F. 152, 307

omissions see acts/ omissions

Otis, J. 146–7

outcome-responsibility 75–7

ownership 3; and liberty of use 7–8; and power of transfer 8, 9; and right to exclude 8

Parent, W. A. 148

Pareto principle 12, 46, 47, 48, 49, 53

Parfitt, D. 85

Parker, R. 284

Pashukanis, E. 360

paternalism 481–2

patriarchy 306–7, 308

Patterson, D. M. 206, 488

Peirce, C. S. 386–7

Peller, G. 205, 282, 368, 370, 495, 500

Pennington, N. and Hastie, R. 178

Pennock, J. R. 146, 151

Perry, M. J. 421

Perry, S. R. 60, 73, 74, 76, 77, 78, 263, 503, 505, 547

Pigou, A. C. 59

Pitkin, H. 579

Pitney, Justice 557

plain meaning 200, 201

Plato 11, 223–4, 226, 465, 583, 588–9

pluralism 219, 387, 388, 389, 401–2

policy science 293–5

Polinsky, A. M. 53, 315, 325

positivism 200–2, 225, 231, 232, 234, 283, 311–12, 315, 349, 549; as new legal process 206–7; revival of 204–5; see also anti-positivism; legal positivism

Posner, R. A. 62, 63, 66, 151, 204, 206, 311, 312, 322, 324, 325, 326, 329, 381–2, 425, 426, 555, 588, 589

Pospisil, L. 400

Post, R. 137, 151, 563

post-realism 291, 292; and legal process 295–6; and policy science 293–5; see also realism

postmodernism 352–3, 375, 384, 452, 455, 460, 567; defined 377–80; and law 380–3; see also modernism

poststructuralism 367

Poulantzas, N. 361, 362

Pound, R. 188, 200, 201

Powell, H. J. 130, 137, 428, 429

praesumptio similitudinis 189–90, 196

pragmatism 207, 379, 555; and actually-in-use norms 386, 387, 389, 392–3; defined 385–7; foundationalist vs non-foundationalist 387–90; and legitimacy 390–2; and truth 386

pre-emption thesis 548
precedent 266, 268, 503–12, 547, 585, 586
precedential constraint, by analogy 509; by canonical texts 511; by court's reasoning 509; and common-law cases 503–5; natural model of 505–6, 510; result model of 507–9; rule model of 506–7, 510; scope of 503–11; skeptical view of 510; strength of 511–12; vertical/horizontal 512
predictive theory 262–3; failure of 263; and judicial mistake 263
prescriptive scholarship 566–9
Price, R. 466
Priest, G. L. 59, 69, 70, 311
prima facie duties 465–8, 472; beneficence 466; fidelity 466; gratitude 466: non-maleficence 466
principles 52, 206–7, 232–3, 234, 297; absolute 481–2; affirmation of 298–300
privacy 139–40; and access 146; decisional 148–9; informational 146–9; meaning and definition 145–50; physical 149; reasonable expectation of 147; right to 139, 141–4, 145; theoretical accounts of 144–50; in the US 141–4; value of 150–3; and world constitutions 140–1
private property 3, 5, 6–7, 556–7; and justification 8–10; justificatory theories of 11–22; and ownership 7–8; rules of 10
probability theory 178
promising 579; benefit/detrimental reliance 51–2, 53–4; and

contract 30–2, 37–40; general convention of 37–40; and intention 33, 36; and tort 32, 33; and trust 38–40; as voluntary obligation 33–7
promissory obligation 30–2, 33–5, 38–9
property 363; collective 6, 7, 12; common 5–6, 11, 12; objects of 4–5; and ownership 7–8; rights 280; rule 320; types of 57
Prosser, W. 139, 209
public choice theories 217
public goods 553
public/private distinction 144, 278–9, 557
Puchta, G. F. 347
Pufendorf, S. 11, 185, 227, 231
punishment 80–3, 443, 514, 556; alternative theory of 518–19; and control/dominance over victim 518; defined 514–15; purposes of 515–18; puzzle 92–4; retrospective/prospective 516–18
Purcell Jr, E. A. 291
pure theory of law 349
purposive approach 202–3, 298, 425, 426

quietism 276–8
Quine, W. V. O. 264, 378–9, 380, 536

Rable, E. 187
race discrimination 159, 160
Rachels, J. 151
Radbruch, G. 350, 351
radical proceduralism 348–9
Radin, M. J. 201, 202, 206, 261, 266, 270, 274, 277, 303
Rashomon problem 459
rationalism 173–5, 178
Rattray, R. S. 398
Rawls, J. 11, 19, 72, 119, 184–6, 352, 466–7,

489, 527, 534, 535, 538, 541, 554, 583
Raz, J. 32, 33–7, 243, 250, 251, 253, 255–6, 443–4, 448, 467, 536, 537, 546, 547, 548, 549, 573, 574, 575, 576, 577
realism 201, 282, 445–6, 556; core claim of 269–71; impact of 291–2; *see also* anti-realism; legal realism; post-realism
reason/s 253–5, 361; practical 338, 576–7
reasonable man 414
Redish, M. H. 206
Reed, J. 408
reflective equilibrium 544, 545, 546
regret 49, 53
Rehnquist, W. H. 129, 132
relational, approach 356–8; distance 409–12
relative autonomy 359
relevance 412–13; conceptual 413–14; moral 414–16; policy 416–17
reliance, and contract 29–32; and tort 32, 33
religion, and corporate forms of churches 122; definitions of 122; and Establishment Clause 116–19, 120; and exemptions 117–18, 121; and free-exercise clause 118–19, 120, 121; and law 113–24; neutrality towards 158; and religious individuals 122–3; and traditions 114; *see also* theology
responsibility 27, 53, 75, 76–7, 167–8, 363, 519, 547; and excuses 520–2; and unlawful action 520
retribution 516–18
Rheinstein, M. 188, 192
Rhode, D. 303
Richards, D. A. J. 119, 151

rights 3, 216, 357, 363, 580; individual 7–8; procedural 174, 193
Rights Thesis 439–40, 546
risk 70, 152, 340, 388
risk-aversion 68, 166, 314
Rivers, W. H. R. 397
Roberts, S. 401
Rorty, R. 379–80, 386–7, 459
Rosen, L. 402
Ross, W. D. 465, 466, 468, 471, 472
Rousseau, J.-J. 11, 18–19, 157
Rubenfeld, J. 149, 151
Rubin, E. 568
rule-skepticism 213, 270, 292, 493–5
rules 160–1, 197, 201, 202, 235, 400, 423, 445, 468, 559, 570, 588; of competence 180; content of 246; exclusionary 180; and material facts 175; model of 249; over/under inclusiveness 161; primary and secondary 245, 249; of proof 172, 175–6, 179; of recognition 247, 248, 250, 251–2, 256–8; social 245–6, 247

Sacco, R. 195, 196
Sacks, A. M. 203
Sandel, M. J. 118, 527
Sander, F. 349
Sapir, E. 397
Sargent, L. 308
Sartorius, R. 250, 467, 536, 541
satisfaction 113
Sauser-Hall, G. 191
Savigny, C. F. von 186, 347
Sayre-McCord, G. 536
Scalia, A. 117, 204
Schapera, I. 399
Schatzki, T. 378
Schauer, F. 491, 503, 511
Schavell, S. 325
Schlafly, P. 308
Schlag, P. 368, 369, 372–3

Schlegel, J. H. 280, 291
Schlegelberger, F. 192
Schlesinger, R. 190
Schmitt, C. 350, 351
Schneider, C. 151
Schneider, E. 152–3
Schnitzer, A. 191
Schoeman, F. 146, 150, 151
Schum, D. 178
Schutz, A. 563
Schwartz, R. D. and Miller, J. C. 409
Schwartz, T. 85
Seigel, M. 178, 181
self-evidence 229
Seligman, C. G. 397
Sellin, T. and Wolfgang, M. 81
Sen, A. 329, 330
separability thesis 242, 249, 251
sex discrimination 159, 160
Shaffer, T. L. 429–31
Shavell, S. 62, 63, 64, 65, 67, 68, 321, 322
Sherman, L. J. 408
Shiner, R. A. 443, 447, 448
Sidgwick, H. 54, 466
Simmons, A. 467
Simon, R. J. 408
Simon, W. H. 283, 284, 285
Simpson, A. W. B. 332, 565
Sinclair, U. 453
Singer, J. W. 205, 280, 390–2, 488, 496
skepticism 376
Smith, A. 11, 157, 471
Smith, D. A.; et al. 408; and Klein, J. R. 408
Smith, M. 467, 472, 473
Smith, P. 302, 303
Smith, W. and Roberts, J. 399
social contract 165–6
Social Darwinism 299
social status 407–9
socialism 360; scientific 163–4; utopian 163
society 376, 377
sociology, and cultural conventions 412; defined

406; and integration/ activity in social life 411–12; and law 416–17; relational distance 409–12; relevance of 412–17; and social stratification 407–9; theories of 406–7
Soloveitchik, J. B. 114
Soper, E. P. 243
Sophocles 224
source thesis 255–8
sovereign/ty 103, 244–5, 248, 283
Spanish natural law school 43
Spencer, H. 553
spheres of justice 168–9
Spitzer, S. 409
Stammler, R. 350
standards 559
Stanko, E. A. 408, 410
Starr, J. and Collier, J. F. 402
state 102, 388, 431; and law 361–3; liability of 105–6; proper functions of 553–4
statutes, interpretation of 200–8, 266, 268; legal process era (1938–69) 202–3; positivist era (1890s–1930s) 200–2; post-legal process (1969–present) 204–7
Steinfeld, R. 288
Stephen, J. F. 145
Stevens, R. 293
Stevenson, R. F. 409
Stoll, H. 348
Stone, J. 506, 510, 570
strict liability 10, 58, 59, 64–5, 76, 316
structuralism 367
Suarez, F. 227
Sugarman, S. D. 66, 72
Summers, R. S. 509
Sumner, C. 361
Sunders, 408
Sunstein, C. R. 150, 206, 278, 329
Sutherland, J. 200

Taft, W. H. 130
taking care 61–2

Taney, R. 130
Tanner, R. E. S. 411
Taub, N. and Williams, W. 307
tax 122
Teubner, G. 352
Thayer, J. B. 174, 179
theology 421; apologetic/confessional 433; and constitutional theory 426–9; and law 421–6; and narrative method 431–4; in practice 429–31; use of 421; see also religion
things 4
Thomson, J. J. 151, 466, 471, 472
threshold of fit 587, 589
Tillers, P. 178
Tillich, P. 422, 433
Todd Jr, H. F. 411
tort 32, 33, 57–9, 123, 325, 333–4, 337, 570; abolition of 334–5; bilateral nature of 72; and corrective justice 72–8; and damages 57, 70; and deterrence 61–8; and distributive justice 71–2; and economic analysis 59–71, 311; formalist theory of 67; and internalization 59–61; and loss spreading 68–71; and right to privacy 139
Tourtoulon, 26
"tragedy of the commons" argument 11
transcendental conditions 350
Trebilcock, M. J. 48, 49
Tribe, H. L. 137, 178
Trotman, D. V. 409
true conflicts 216, 217
true/rule law 403
trust 38–40
truth 178–9, 181–2, 247, 380, 386, 391–2, 446, 534–5, 536
Tunc, A. 191

Tushnet, M. 137
Twerski, A. 214
Twining, W. L. 173, 174, 292

Uhlman, T. M. 408
Ulmer, S. S. 408
underdeterminacy 489–90, 497–8
unfreedom 14
Unger, R. M. 205, 287, 291, 341, 368, 371
unilateral acquisition 20–1
unity 545
universal cognitive competence 172
universalism 185–7
unprovided-for case 217–18
utilitarianism 173–4, 517; and property 11–13

validation 257–8
value 320; and equality 169–70; judgements 233
Van den Haag, E. 146
van der Sprenkel, S. 409
Vera Institute of Justice 410
victim/s 64–5, 67, 74, 76
virtue 14

Wacks, R. 146
Wagner, W. J. 424
Waite, Chief Justice 117
Waldron, J. 3, 14
Walker, A. 468
Walker, G. 427–8, 429, 433
Waluchow, W. J. 243, 448
Walzer, M. 169, 555
Warren, E. 298
Warren, S. 142, 145
Wasserstrom, R. A. 506
Watson, A. 197
Weber, M. 192, 397
Webster, D. 101
Wechsler, H. 136, 298–9, 300
Weinreb, L. 238
Weinrib, E. J. 67, 68, 69, 74, 332, 335, 340, 536, 544

welfare, corporate 559
welfare economics 59, 189; maximization 49, 50, 54
welfare state 553–61; adoption of 555–6; conditions of 560–1; and the Constitution 557–9; and decision-making 559–60; defined 559; described 555; and equal protection 560; permitted or required 558; and redistributive regulation 557–8, 559; rules and standards 559; scope of 560
welfare system 285–6
Wells, C. 387, 388–9, 392
West, C. 385
West, R. 307
Westin, A. 145
White, J. B. 455
Wigmore, J. H. 174, 178, 191
Williams, G. 178
Williams, J. C. 307
Williams, R. 359, 402
Willke, H. 352
Windelband, 350
Wittgenstein, L. 377, 380, 452, 493–4, 544
Wolfenden Report 439
Wolff, R. P. 576, 579
Wollstonecraft, M. 303
Woozley, A. 467
Wright, R. W. 67, 68, 73, 387–8, 389, 390, 392
Wroth, L. K. and Hiller, B. Z. 147

Yablon, C. M. 488
Yngvesson, B. 401, 403, 410
Yntema, H. 261
Yoder, J. H. 428–9

Zola, E. 453
Zollmann, C. 122
Zuckerman, A. A. S. 175, 176
Zweigert, K.; and Kotz, H. 188, 189–90, 191, 192; and Puttfarken, H.-J. 184